Venture Capital and Tax Incentives: A Comparative Study of Canada and the United States

CANADIAN

TAX PAPER

NO. 108

Venture Capital and Tax Incentives: A Comparative Study of Canada and the United States

Daniel Sandler

CANADIAN TAX FOUNDATION

L'ASSOCIATION CANADIENNE

D'ÉTUDES FISCALES

338.43
S 217 v

ML

Library and Archives of Canada Cataloguing in Publication

Sandler, Daniel
    Venture capital and tax incentives : a comparative study of Canada and the United States / by Daniel Sandler.

(Canadian tax papers, ISSN 0008-512X ; no. 108)
Includes bibliographical references and index.
ISBN 0-88808-194-4

    1. Venture capital—Government policy—Canada.   2. Venture capital—Government policy—United States.   3. Technological innovations—Government policy—Canada.   4. Technological innovations—Government policy—United States.   5. Tax incentives—Canada.   6. Tax incentives—United States.   7. Small business—Finance—Government policy—Canada.   8. Small business—Finance—Government policy—United States.   I. Canadian Tax Foundation.   II. Title.   III. Series.

HG4751.S36 2004   338.4'3'000971   C2004-902812-X

Printed in Canada.

For Jennet

Contents

List of Abbreviations xiii
Preface xvii

1 **A Role for Government in Venture Capital Formation?** 1
A Blueprint for Silicon Valley 1
The Venture Capital Marketplace 4
Informal Venture Capital: Of Love and Angels 5
Formal Venture Capital 6
Exiting the Venture Capital Investment 10
The Role of Government in the Venture Capital Marketplace:
Responding to Market Failures 13
Market Failures Affecting Investment in Small Businesses 13
Rapid-Growth SME Geography 16
Government Venture Capital Programs 18
Structure of This Book 21
Notes 24

2 **The Venture Capital Industries in North America** 35
Informal Venture Capital 35
Formal Venture Capital 38
United States 43
US Pension Fund Venture Capital Investment 47
Canada 55
Canadian Pension Fund Venture Capital Investment 57
Canadian Individual Retirement Savings Venture Capital
Investment 61
Venture Capital and the Tech Boom and Bust: Where to from Here? . . . 62
Notes 64

3 **Venture Capital and Capital Gains Taxation** 75
Preferential Tax Treatment of Capital Gains 76
United States 77
Characterization of Gain on Disposition of Venture Capital
Investment 86
Canada 87
Characterization of Gain on Disposition of Venture Capital
Investment 94
Evaluation of the Preferential Tax Treatment of Capital Gains 96
Preferential Treatment of Gains from Small Business Securities 100
United States 100
Canada 102

Evaluation of the Preferential Treatment of Gains from Dispositions
of Small Business Securities 103
Angel Capital Rollover 105
United States 106
Canada 107
Evaluation of the Angel Capital Rollover 109
Preferential Treatment of Capital Losses from Small Business Securities 112
United States 112
Canada 114
Evaluation of the Preferential Treatment of Capital Losses from
Small Business Securities 115
Notes 119

4 Employee Stock Options: "Sweat Equity" Venture Capital 153
Accounting for Employee Stock Options: Increasing the Bottom Line 154
The Current Accounting Standards 154
Proposed Reforms to the Accounting Treatment of Employee
Stock Options 156
Taxation of Employee Stock Options 159
The Benchmark Tax Treatment 159
The Tax Treatment of Employee Stock Options in the United States ... 164
Non-Statutory Stock Options 164
Statutory Stock Options 169
The Tax Treatment of Employee Stock Options in Canada 179
Five Key Differences and One Observation Concerning the Tax
Treatment of Employee Stock Options in the United States
and Canada 183
Evaluating the Favourable Tax Treatment of Employee Stock Options 187
Increasing Productivity 188
Allowing Small Companies To Attract and Retain Employees 189
Stemming the Brain Drain 190
Notes 194

5 Tax Credits for Direct Investment in Small Businesses 215
Salient Features of Direct Investment Tax Credit Programs 215
Evaluation of Direct Investment Tax Credit Programs 216
Eligible Investors 216
Restrictions on Relationship Between Eligible Investor and Eligible
Business 217
Nature of Investment 219
Nature of Incentive 219
Eligible Businesses 221
Eligible Uses of Capital 222
Cost-Benefit Analyses of Direct Investment Tax Credit Programs 222

Appendix 5A: Summary of Angel Capital Tax Credit Programs,
  All Provinces and Four Select States 225
    Governing Legislation 225
    Eligible Investors 225
    Nature of Investment 226
    Nature of Incentive 226
    Maximum Tax Credit/Maximum Investment 227
    Eligible Businesses 228
    Use of Proceeds 230
    Application for Registration 231
    Restrictions on Relationship Between Eligible Investor and
      Eligible Business 232
    Holding Period 233
    Limit on Amount Raised by Each Eligible Business for Which a
      Tax Credit Is Available 233
    Government Expenditure Limits 233
    Sunset 234
  Notes 235

6 **Tax Incentives for Investment in Venture Capital Funds** 241
   Taxation of Limited Partnership Venture Capital Funds: A Primer 243
     Characterization of Gains on Disposition of Portfolio Company Shares ... 244
       United States 244
       Canada 244
     Distribution of Partnership Property to Partners 252
       United States 252
       Canada 253
   Historical Evolution of the LSVCC and CAPCO Programs 254
     LSVCCs 255
     CAPCOs 260
   Salient Features of VCF Tax Credit Programs 266
   Evaluation of VCF Tax Credit Programs 267
     Organizational Form of VCF 267
     Eligible Investors and Nature of Investment 268
     Minimum/Maximum Capitalization 271
     Nature of Incentive 273
     Government Expenditure Limits and Government Profit Share 274
     Eligible Investments of the VCF 275
     Timing Issues Affecting VCFs 277
     Cost-Benefit Analyses of VCF Tax Credit Programs 279
       Cost-Benefit Analyses of LSVCC Programs 281
       Cost-Benefit Analyses of CAPCO Programs 288
   Using Tax Credits To Guarantee Investment in VCFs 292
   Conclusion 294

CONTENTS

Appendix 6A: Summary of Provincial Venture Capital Fund Tax
  Credit Programs 296
    Governing Legislation 296
    Number of VCFs Permitted 296
    Organizational Form of VCF 296
    Minimum/Maximum Capitalization 297
    Eligible Investors 297
    Nature of Investment in VCF 297
    Nature of Incentive 298
    Holding Period 299
    Government Expenditure Limits 300
    Eligible Investments 300
    Pacing Requirements 301
    Consequences of Failure To Meet Investment Requirements 302
Appendix 6B: Summary of Selected State Venture Capital Fund Tax
  Credit Programs 303
    Governing Legislation 303
    Number of VCFs Permitted 303
    Organizational Form of VCF 304
    Minimum/Maximum Capitalization 305
    Eligible Investors 306
    Nature of Investment in VCF 306
    Nature of Incentive 306
    Holding Period 308
    Government Expenditure Limits 308
    Eligible Investments 309
    Pacing Requirements 311
    Consequences of Failure To Meet Investment Requirements 312
Appendix 6C: Summary of Federal and Provincial LSVCC Programs 313
    Governing Legislation 313
    Number of LSVCCs Permitted 314
    Sponsoring Organization 314
    Organizational Form of LSVCC 315
    Board of Directors of LSVCC 315
    Minimum/Maximum Capitalization 315
    Eligible Investors 316
    Nature of Incentive 316
    Holding Period 317
    Government Expenditure Limits 317
    Eligible Investments 317
    Pacing Requirements 319
    Consequences of Failure To Meet Investment Requirements 320
Appendix 6D: Summary of State CAPCO Programs 321
    Governing Legislation 321
    Organizational Form of CAPCO 321

Minimum/Maximum Capitalization 323
Eligible Investors 323
Nature of Investment in CAPCO 323
Nature of Incentive 324
Maximum Investment/Benefit for Any One Certified Investor 325
State Share in Distribution 326
Government Expenditure Limits 327
Eligible Investments 327
Pacing Requirements 331
Requirements for Voluntary Decertification or for Distributions
Other Than Qualified Distributions 332
Consequences of Failure To Meet Investment Requirements 332
Notes 334

7 Venture Capital Investment from Retirement Funds 361
Individual and Employer-Sponsored Retirement Funds: An Overview
of Applicable Pension and Tax Legislation 363
United States 364
Application of the Internal Revenue Code to Retirement Funds 365
Pension Legislation 370
Canada 371
Application of the Income Tax Act to Retirement Funds 372
Pension Legislation 375
Venture Capital Investment Using Individual and Employer-Sponsored
Retirement Funds 376
Informal Venture Capital Investment by Individual Retirement Funds ... 378
United States 378
Canada 378
Accessing Individual Retirement Funds To Make Informal Venture
Capital Investments 380
United States 380
Canada 382
Accessing Employer-Sponsored Retirement Funds To Make Informal
Venture Capital Investments 385
United States 385
Canada 386
Individual Retirement Fund Investment in VCFs 387
United States 387
Canada 387
Employer-Sponsored Retirement Fund Investment in VCFs 388
United States 389
Canada 396
Evaluation of Venture Capital Investment by Individual and
Employer-Sponsored Retirement Funds 402
Evaluating the Use of Retirement Funds for Informal Venture
Capital Investment 402

Evaluating the Use of Retirement Funds for Formal Venture
    Capital Investment 406
Venture Capital Investment by Government-Administered Pension Plans ... 416
    US Social Security 416
    Canada Pension Plan: Leading by Example 417
Notes 422

8   Selected Non-Tax Government Venture Capital Programs 453
Primary Federal Small Business Development Agencies 455
    US Small Business Administration 455
    Business Development Bank of Canada 458
The Sputnik Crisis, Military R & D, and Venture Capital Funds 462
    DARPA and Innovative Research 463
    The SBIC Program and the Evolution of US Private Venture
        Capital Funds 464
    Government Leveraging Versus Tax Credits 469
Innovation in the Venture Capital Industry: Angel Capital Networks
    and Incubators 472
    Angel Capital Networks 472
    Business Incubators 475
Notes 477

9   The Way Forward 489
Informal Venture Capital and "Sweat Equity" 489
    Preferential Tax Treatment of Capital Gains 490
    Preferential Treatment of Gains from Small Business Securities 491
    Angel Capital Rollover 491
    Preferential Treatment of Capital Losses from Small
        Business Securities 492
    Employee Stock Options: "Sweat Equity" Venture Capital 493
    Tax Credits for Direct Investment in SMEs 494
    Accessing Retirement Savings for Informal Venture
        Capital Investment 495
Pension Funds and the Formal Venture Capital Industry 496
Notes 499

Selected Bibliography 501
Index 511

List of Abbreviations

ABIL	allowable business investment loss	CPP	Canada Pension Plan
AMT	alternative minimum tax	CPPIB	Canada Pension Plan Investment Board
AMTI	alternative minimum taxable income	CRA	Canada Revenue Agency
ARD	American Research and Development Corp.	CSBIF	community small business investment fund
ARPA	Advanced Research Projects Agency	CVCA	Canadian Venture Capital Association
BDC	Business Development Bank of Canada	DARPA	Defense Advanced Research Projects Agency
CanSBIC	small business investment corporation (Canada)	DPSP	deferred profit-sharing plan
CAPCO	certified capital company	EBC	eligible business corporation
CASE	Counseling Assistance for Small Enterprises	EOLSVCC	employee ownership labour-sponsored venture capital corporation
CCIP	Canada Community Investment Plan	ERISA	Employee Retirement Income Security Act of 1974
CCPC	Canadian-controlled private corporation	ESBC	eligible small business corporation
CDC	Canadian Development Corporation	ESPP	employee stock purchase plan
CED	Canadian Enterprise Development Corporation Limited	FAME	Finance Authority of Maine
CEDC	community economic development corporation	FASB	Financial Accounting Standards Board
CEDIF	community economic development investment fund	FBBIB	Florida Black Business Investment Board
CFC	capital formation company	FBDB	Federal Business Development Bank
CICA	Canadian Institute of Chartered Accountants	FICA	Federal Insurance Contributions Act
CLMPC	Canadian Labour Market and Productivity Centre	FSTQ	Fonds de solidarité des travailleurs du Québec
CODA	cash or deferred arrangement	FTQ	Fédération du travailleurs du Québec
COIN	Canada Opportunities Investment Network; Computerized Ontario Investment Network	HOOPP	Hospitals of Ontario Pension Plan
		IASB	International Accounting Standards Board

IBA	Investment Bankers Association of America	OMERS	Ontario Municipal Employees Retirement System
ICIB	Iowa Capital Investment Board	OSC	Ontario Securities Commission
ICIC	Iowa Capital Investment Corporation	OSRD	Office of Scientific Research and Development
IDB	Industrial Development Bank	PA	pension adjustment
IPO	initial public offering	PBA	Pension Benefits Act (Ontario)
IRA	individual retirement account; individual retirement annuity	PBSA	Pension Benefits Standards Act (Canada)
IRC	Internal Revenue Code	PIAC	Pension Investment Association of Canada
IRR	internal rate of return		
IRS	Internal Revenue Service	PRIM	Pension Reserves Investment Management Board
ISO	incentive stock option		
ITA	Income Tax Act		
IWTA	Income War Tax Act	PRIT	Pension Reserves Investment Trust Fund
KBI	knowledge-based industry		
LBO	leveraged buyout	PVCF	private venture capital fund
LLC	limited liability company	QBIC	Quebec business investment company
LLP	limited liability partnership		
LSIF	labour-sponsored investment fund	QLP	qualified limited partnership
LSVCC	labour-sponsored venture capital corporation	QORSBV	qualified Oklahoma rural small business venture
MER	management-expense ratio	QOSBV	qualified Oklahoma small business venture
MIT	Massachusetts Institute of Technology	QPP	Quebec Pension Plan
MVCF	Michigan Venture Capital Fund	QRSBCC	qualified rural small business capital company
NAFTA	North American free trade agreement	QSBC	qualified small business corporation
NASVF	National Association of Seed and Venture Funds	QSBCC	qualified small business capital company
NMVCC	New Markets Venture Capital Company	QSBS	qualified small business stock
NSO	non-statutory stock option	QSO	qualified stock option
NVCA	National Venture Capital Association	R & D	research and development
		RCA	retirement compensation arrangement
NYSE	New York Stock Exchange		
OCIB	Oklahoma Capital Investment Board	ROIF	research-oriented investment fund
OECD	Organisation for Economic Co-operation and Development	RPP	registered pension plan
		RRIF	registered retirement income fund

RRSP	registered retirement savings plan	SIMPLE	savings incentive match plans for employees
RSO	restricted stock option	SME	small or medium-sized enterprise
SBA	Small Business Administration	SRI	Stanford Research Institute
SBB	small business bond	SSBIC	specialized small business investment company
SBDB	small business development bond	STTR	small business technology transfer
SBDC	Small Business Development Center (US); small business development corporation (Ontario)	TSX	Toronto Stock Exchange
		UBIT	unrelated business income tax
SBIA	Small Business Investment Act	UBTI	unrelated business taxable income
SBIC	small business investment company	VCC	venture capital company (US); venture capital corporation (Canada)
SBILP	small business investment limited partnership	VCF	venture capital fund
SBIR	small business innovative research	VCN	Venture Capital Network
		VCOC	venture capital operating company
SBIT	small business investment trust	VEIC	venture enterprise investment company
SCORE	Service Corps of Retired Executives	VIC	venture investment corporation
SEC	Securities and Exchange Commission	WOF	Working Opportunity Fund
SEP	simplified employee pension	WVEDA	West Virginia Economic Development Authority
SFAS	Statement of Financial Accounting Standards	WVVCC	West Virginia venture capital company
SFC	specialized financing corporation		

Preface

During the sabbatical year that my family and I spent in Berkeley in 1999-2000, the NASDAQ climbed to an all-time high, reaching 5,048.62 on March 10, 2000. Venture capital firms clustered along Sand Hill Road in Menlo Park and the high-tech firms throughout Silicon Valley that they financed were buzzing with activity. The high-tech industry was hot and the supply of venture capital to promising (and not-so-promising) startups seemed limitless. US venture capital firms raised over US$105 billion in 2000, almost 70 percent more than the amount raised in the previous year and over 10 times the amount raised five years earlier. The Canadian venture capital industry was also robust. Although it did not enjoy the exponential growth of the US venture capital market in the latter half of the 1990s, it raised Cdn$3.8 billion in 2000, over 85 percent more than in the previous year and over four times more capital than that raised 1995. The appetite of the public equity markets, particularly the NASDAQ, for initial public offerings (IPOs) of tech stocks seemed insatiable.

That was then. The NASDAQ reversed direction in the second half of 2000, shortly before we left Berkeley. It shed half of its value by the end of 2000 and continued its more or less steady decline to October 2002, dropping to levels not previously seen since 1996. Since then, the NASDAQ has recovered to some extent, although it is still valued well below half of its 2000 peak. The rapid decline in the NASDAQ was mirrored by an equally rapid decline in IPOs. Given that IPOs are the most profitable exit mechanism for venture capitalists, it is not surprising that the venture capital industries in both the United States and Canada have suffered since 2000. In 2002, the US venture capital industry raised less capital than it did in 1994. New capital commitments recovered somewhat in 2003, when US$10.8 billion was raised, an increase of more than US$3 billion from 2002, but still less than the amount raised in 1996. The Canadian venture capital industry has not suffered as steep a decline. Capital levels grew from 2000 to 2001, but began falling in 2002, when 15 percent less capital was raised than in 2000. Commitments continued to decline in 2003, down 39 percent from 2002, to the same levels as in 1999. The Canadian venture capital industry has yet to reverse the downward trend.

My interest in government incentives for venture capital dates back to 1997, when I began studying Canada's labour-sponsored venture capital corporations (LSVCCs) with Duncan Osborne, then a third-year law student at the University of Western Ontario. (Our study was subsequently published in the *Canadian Tax Journal* in 1998.) The Canadian venture capital industry is frequently contrasted with the US industry, which is often touted as a capitalist success story. Private venture capital firms make up over 80 percent of the US venture capital industry, with subsidiaries or affiliates of financial institutions and industrial corporations making up most of the rest. In contrast, Canada's venture capital industry relies significantly on government handouts. LSVCCs, which would not exist without the federal and provincial tax credits provided to their investors, control over 35 percent of all capital under management and, together with government funds, control almost half of all capital under management in Canada. However, this superficial contrast between the Canadian and US industries masks significant similarities. It is true, for example, that government incentives have played and continue to play a significant role in the Canadian industry, but also true that government incentives have been instrumental in the development of the US industry. Government incentives remain important to the success—indeed, in some places, to the existence—of a venture capital industry in parts of the United States outside a few geographic pockets of activity. In addition, the "informal" venture capital industries in both countries—the largely unseen investments by business founders, family, and friends (often referred to as "love capital"), as well as investments by employees and business "angels"—benefit from significant and substantially similar tax incentives.

This book explores, compares, and critiques tax incentives targeting venture capital formation in Canada and the United States, at both the federal and the provincial and state levels. The features of the various incentive programs examined in this book are based on the laws in force in August 2003, as well as, in some cases, more recent provisions. In its study of these programs, this book focuses less on their technical detail—those elements subject to frequent adjustment—than on their broad, structural principles in order to determine what government policies can best address the market failures that adversely affect the capital needs of small and medium-sized enterprises (SMEs).

This book was five years in the making. Some parts of the book, including substantial portions of chapter 4 and parts of chapter 6 (dealing with LSVCCs), were published in the *Canadian Tax Journal* in 1998, 2001, and 2003. When I began my research for the book, in mid-1999, the US and Canadian venture capital industries were climbing toward all-time highs. As I review the page proofs for the book, in the spring of 2004, the outlook is much less clear. A consideration of government incentives for venture capital formation is particularly timely now, when the industries in both countries have retreated sharply, in terms of capital commitments and capital investments, from the peaks reached at the start of this century. It is an opportune time to evaluate past government policies and practices in order to determine the most appropriate way forward, to ensure a thriving venture capital marketplace.

Many people assisted me over the course of this project. Mary Macdonald and Kirk Falconer of Macdonald & Associates Limited (Toronto and Ottawa) and Anthony Romenello of Thomson Financial Venture Economics (New York) provided me with statistical data on the Canadian and US venture capital industries. They shared many resources with me on numerous occasions, and took the time to discuss aspects of the formal venture capital industries in each country and many of my ideas regarding the role that governments can play in venture capital formation.

My research and writing tend to be comparative. In previous books I have contrasted various aspects of tax systems in countries around the world, and out of necessity I have relied on the assistance of individuals in other countries to provide information or review my technical descriptions of tax regimes in which I profess no expertise (and written in languages I do not understand). I had hoped that the comparative work for this project would be simpler, limited as it was to Canada and the United States. However, as the importance of subnational government incentives for venture capital formation in both countries became clear to me, it was obvious that this comparative work would far exceed any that I have previously undertaken. All of Canada's 10 provinces (plus one territory) have, had, or have considered tax incentive programs for venture capital formation. The same is true of most US states. I limited my US research to a relatively small number of states (15) that illustrated the variety of tax incentive programs in use. Researching the tax incentive programs in over 25 jurisdictions (including incentives offered at the federal level in both countries) was a monumental task, especially given the paucity of comparative studies in this area in both countries. I am grateful to the many individuals in various federal, provincial, and state ministries and agencies who took the time to speak with me and provide me with information and materials about their programs. Particular thanks go to Charlie Spies, a director of the National Association of Seed and Venture Funds and former CEO of the Finance Authority of Maine; Lori Schenewerk, formerly of the Missouri Department of Economic Development; Dave Fontalbert, formerly of the West Virginia Economic Development Authority; Robert Heard, founder of Edge Development Capital Inc., which manages the Oklahoma Capital Investment Board; James Zen, Department of Finance, Canada; Charles Cazabon, vice-president, venture capital, Business Development Bank of Canada; David Baleshta, British Columbia Ministry of Small Business and Economic Development; Alex Killoch, Ontario Ministry of Finance; and Kevin Redden, Nova Scotia Department of Finance.

Over the past four years, I benefited from the efforts of a number of student research assistants: Jason Moyse; Ian Keay; Michelle Campbell; and especially Michael Gemmiti, whose dedication and good humour over the 16-month period from May 2002 to August 2003 assisted me greatly in the final push to complete the manuscript. I am also grateful to Marianne Welch, the reference librarian at the John and Dotsa Bitove Family Law Library, who was very helpful in tracking down a number of obscure references; Pat Nelligan, a librarian at the Richard Ivey School of Business Library, who helped me with a variety of business databases; and Vincent Gray, data resources librarian at the Faculty of Social Science's Data Resources Library, who assisted me with a number of statistical databases.

My sabbatical year at the University of California (UC), Berkeley was funded in part by a Fulbright fellowship, granted by the Foundation for Educational Exchange Between Canada and the United States of America. In addition to this financial support, the Fulbright fellowship enabled me to make a number of useful contacts in Silicon Valley, many of which were arranged by the Canadian

Consulate Trade Office, San Francisco | Silicon Valley. I am grateful to Andrew Thompson, public affairs officer; Norman Lomow, former consul and senior trade commissioner; John Roxburgh, former consul and trade commissioner (all in the San Francisco office); and Handol Kim, former consul and trade commissioner (in the San Jose office) for their assistance with and interest in my project. These individuals introduced me to a number of people directly involved in the venture capital industry in Silicon Valley. I learned much from my interviews with Charles Chi, a general partner at Greylock in San Mateo, CA; Robert Halperin, a successful angel capitalist in Atherton, CA; Robert Antoniades, former executive director of CIBC Capital Partners, Menlo Park, CA; and Kathleen Borie, formerly of PricewaterhouseCoopers, San Jose, CA. All of these individuals were generous with their time and provided interesting insights into the operation of the venture capital industry.

I have had the opportunity to present some of my work in progress at various forums, including informal talks at the International Bureau for Fiscal Documentation in Amsterdam in 1999; UC Berkeley and the Canadian Consulate Trade Office in San Francisco in 2000; and the University of Western Ontario in 2001. I also delivered a talk on my project at the Institute for Fiscal Studies Tenth Residential Conference in Oxford, England in 2001. My research benefited from the comments of the participants in all of these forums. I also benefited from informal discussions with a number of other individuals who have an interest in venture capital formation, whether as entrepreneurs, venture capitalists, fund managers, government policy makers, or academics, including Don Allen, Alan Auerbach, Kul Bhatia, Donna Bridgeman, Michel Carreau, Roger Cox, Doug Cumming, Denise Deganais, Jean-Yves Duthel, Mike Heimricks, Stacey Hurst, Michael Kaufmann, Josh Lerner, Jeff MacIntosh, Jamie Meyer, Jim McNulty, Charles Ransom, Richard Rowley, Gordon Sharwood, and Bob Siskind.

Jack McNulty, the Roger J. Traynor professor of law at UC Berkeley, kindly supported my application to be a visiting scholar at UC Berkeley and helped make our stay a memorable one. I enjoy his company every time our paths cross in various corners of the globe. I am also grateful to the faculty and staff at UC Berkeley for accommodating me as a visiting scholar for the year, particularly Eloise Schmidt, the coordinator of the visiting scholar program, and the reference librarians at the UC Berkeley Law Library.

Jack McNulty was one of the few people who read the entire manuscript for this book. Neil Brooks at Osgoode Hall School of Law and Tim Edgar, my colleague at Western Law, were the other two. The comments of all three readers greatly assisted me in improving the structure of the book and focusing my arguments. I would also like to thank Eva Krasa and Yvette Morelli, who provided comments on selected portions of the manuscript.

I am grateful to Western Law for giving me much of the time needed to complete this work. The faculty not only allowed me the sabbatical year to start the project, it also let me juggle my teaching loads (with Tim's help) in order to create uninterrupted blocks of time in which to complete the project. Tim has been a great colleague and friend to me at Western. His interest in my scholarship and willingness to discuss ideas at any time is very much appreciated. Amy Jacob, an administrative assistant at Western Law, assisted me with computer glitches, including the conversion of various figures from one software program to another.

I am deeply grateful to the Canadian Tax Foundation, not only for its financial support of this study, but also for the resources that it devoted to its publication. The support and patience of Robin MacKnight, the Foundation's former director, Stephen Richardson, its current director, and Laurel Amalia, the Foundation's editor-in-chief, have been much appreciated. Michael Gaughan's reference editing, Jim Lyons's copy-editing, and Paula Pike's indexing were exemplary. Carol Mohammed, the librarian at the Canadian Tax Foundation, provided valuable assistance in tracking down certain publications for me. It has been a pleasure to work with the staff of the Canadian Tax Foundation.

Finally, and always, I thank my wife, Jennet, and our two children, Jacob and Naomi, for their continued support, encouragement, and love. Without their good humour and tolerance of my long absences and distracted presence at numerous times in the past five years, this book would not have been possible.

Daniel Sandler
London, Ontario
April 2004

1

A Role for Government in Venture Capital Formation?*

A Blueprint for Silicon Valley

Canada, like many countries around the world, looks with envy upon the success of companies and the venture capitalists who back them, concentrated in a relatively small geographic area in the Santa Clara Valley around Palo Alto, California. Many jurisdictions both inside and outside the United States believe that venture capital built Silicon Valley and that by fostering a venture capital program in their jurisdiction they can create their own success story. The amount of venture capital raised and invested in California, primarily in Silicon Valley, is staggering on any scale: at the peak, in 2000, over $44.7 billion was committed to venture capital funds and almost $44 billion was invested in venture-backed businesses located in the state, and most of those funds and businesses were located in Silicon Valley.[1] The amount of venture capital raised and invested in California represented over 40 percent of the $105.8 billion of venture capital raised and $106.3 billion invested in all of the United States in 2000. In contrast, in the same year, less than $3.8 billion in venture capital was raised and $5.8 billion invested in all of Canada.[2] While the size of the Canadian economy is approximately 10 percent that of the US economy, the amount of venture capital raised and invested in Canada in 2000 was only 3.6 percent and 5.4 percent (2.4 percent and 3.7 percent, taking currency exchange rates into account) of the venture capital raised and invested in the United States.

But it was not just money, and not just private sector money, that originally built and now sustains Silicon Valley as the region with the highest concentration of high-tech companies in the world. Government defence contracts, both during and after the Second World War, and the presence of strong research universities, particularly Stanford University and the University of California at Berkeley, both of which have developed and fostered strong ties with the surrounding entrepreneurial community and encourage both faculty and students to entrepreneurial ends, have been critical to the success of Silicon Valley.

Today's economy is a knowledge-based economy. Technological innovation—from the steam engine that drove the Industrial Revolution to trains, cars, and airplanes; to the harnessing and delivery of electricity; to the advancement

---

* Unless otherwise stated, US monetary amounts are in US dollars and Canadian monetary amounts are in Canadian dollars.

of computers and communication systems; to biotechnology and the genome—
rather than the efficient allocation of resources in a free market, has been and
continues to be the most important determinant of economic growth. Although
technological innovation occurs primarily in large corporations (those with more
than 500 employees) due to their economies of scale (large volume production),
scope (different products based on the same technology that use the same distri-
butional networks), and speed of production,[3] a significant amount of innovation
is generated by small companies, particularly in the high-tech sector.

This book examines the role of government expenditure programs, particularly tax expenditure programs, used by federal, provincial, and state governments
in Canada and the United States to enhance the supply of venture capital. Venture
capitalism may be described as the high-risk investment of equity or near-equity
(for example, debt convertible into equity) in a business with limited tangible assets
that has the potential to grow significantly. Natural resource exploration industries are historically good examples of high-risk, potentially high-reward industries
(consider the origin of the phrase "strike it rich"). Today, the term "venture capital"
usually brings to mind high-tech industries—industries that rely significantly
on human or intellectual capital—which seek to create and develop commercial
uses of new technologies. Some of the best-known high-tech companies today—
Hewlett-Packard, Intel, Apple, Microsoft, and Netscape, to name a few—were
all at one time venture-backed companies.

It is the potential of venture-backed businesses to grow significantly that
distinguishes these businesses from the vast majority of small and medium-sized
enterprises (SMEs).[4] SMEs are often touted, particularly by their own lobby
groups, as the keys to growth in the Canadian and US economies. The numbers
are certainly impressive; for example, SMEs account for over 99.7 percent of all
employers, employ over half of all employees, are responsible for over half of the
research and development in both Canada and the United States,[5] and account for
most of the job growth in the past few decades.[6] Facts like these give the impression that SMEs should be viewed as a collective deserving of government support.

However, the term SME covers a broad range of businesses. One important
distinction must be drawn at the outset of this discourse: between small businesses that plan to grow rapidly and other small businesses that provide a
livelihood to a relatively small and stable (in terms of number) group of people.[7]
"Rapid-growth" or "high-growth" SMEs, sometimes referred to as "high-potential"
firms or "gazelles," intend to expand quickly, generally in order to capture a
large market share by exploiting new technology, and require significant capital to
achieve their objectives. The vast majority of small businesses (over 90 percent),
sometimes referred to as lifestyle businesses, are generally not businesses that
venture capitalists consider for investment because there is little likelihood of
growth and it is significantly more difficult to exit the investment. Moreover,
from a government policy perspective, lifestyle businesses are not so much job
creators as job churners, and the jobs they churn are generally not "good" ones,
but low-paying jobs with few benefits, little security, and few prospects for
advancement.[8] Good jobs are created not by small businesses per se, but by small

businesses that grow big. Rapid-growth SMEs represent only 4 to 8 percent of all small businesses in the United States, yet since 1979 they have accounted for 70 to 75 percent of net new jobs, and one-fifth of the rapid-growth SMEs accounted for almost one-half of all jobs generated by autonomous new firms.[9] As Robert Heilbroner and Lester Thurow put it:

> In the last two decades the assertion has often been made that most of the jobs in America are being created by small businesses and that, as a result, such business should be seen as the engines of national economic success. By implication, nothing else is necessary or important. Such assertions are neither factually correct nor economically true.
>
> What creates jobs are not small businesses as such but small businesses that grow large (Wal-Mart, Hewlett Packard, Microsoft). . . . At any time, the bigger the firm, the more likely it is to be a comparatively desirable employer. Perhaps more important, large firms are the source of most of the nation's private research and development. If big firms were privatized, much of the steady advance in technology and research would disappear.[10]

The focus of this book, then, is on that small number of SMEs that have aspirations to grow big, and on government incentives, particularly tax incentives, that are intended to enhance the supply of venture capital to these firms. These SMEs, which are concentrated in the high-technology sector, require capital infusions to develop ideas and create marketable products. They often start with little but the intellectual capital of their founders and have a long time horizon before profits—indeed, before sales—may be realized. They are generally considered too high-risk for bank loans, the traditional source of financing for small businesses. For these companies, venture capital may be the only source of capital available.

The creation of pools of venture capital, in and of itself, is not the goal of government venture capital programs. Rather, their ultimate goal is to foster innovation and economic growth through the creation and development of high-growth SMEs. As a result, many government venture capital programs target SMEs specifically in the high-tech sector. This targeting is influenced by the natural selection that currently occurs in the private venture capital industry and perhaps by a desire to replicate the success of Silicon Valley. Venture capital programs that are designed to assist SMEs in the high-tech sector have been delivered predominantly through tax incentives. However, most of the variables that influence the growth of SMEs and venture capital activity lie outside the tax system. These variables include direct government investment in infrastructure, research and development, and higher education; government regulation that protects innovative development, such as patent laws; a government-regulated financial system that facilitates both venture capital funds and a small-capitalization equity market; and, efficient bankruptcy laws that protect the creditors of such businesses if they fail. In other words, government expenditure and government regulation are essential for technological innovation.[11] Although this book focuses on tax incentives for venture capital formation, they are only a small piece of the much larger puzzle of government fiscal and regulatory policy in this area.

The Venture Capital Marketplace

Like the more formal stock markets in North America, the venture capital marketplace involves three principal players: the person in need of capital (the entrepreneur), the person with capital to invest (the high-risk investor), and the person who puts the two together (the venture capitalist). In the early stages of a firm's development, the three principal players may be rolled into one player (the self-financing entrepreneur) or two (the high-risk investor and the entrepreneur). It is important to have an understanding of this marketplace, what makes it different from the formal stock market and what motivates its participants,[12] in order to discern whether the marketplace is operating efficiently and, if it is not, to determine whether the government can play a role in correcting or compensating for these deficiencies.

In the context of this study, the venture capital marketplace is best examined along the timeline of a business, from the entrepreneur's decision to start a business through its various stages of financing. This book focuses on the sources of venture capital available as a business evolves.

The supply channels of venture capital may be roughly divided between informal venture capital and formal venture capital. While there is no bright line dividing the two in terms of, say, deal size or characteristics of the investor, informal venture capital typically refers to direct investment in an SME by individuals. Informal venture capital comprises "love capital" and "angel capital."[13] Love capital is provided by the founder of a business and his or her family and friends. Love capital is often the primary source of capital for firms in the early stages of development. Angel capital is provided by high-net-worth individuals unrelated to the business founder who invest equity capital in entrepreneurial ventures (ventures that define themselves by their growth potential).

The formal venture capital industry consists primarily of venture capital funds managed by professional venture capital firms. Unlike investors of informal venture capital, most high-risk investors of formal venture capital do not invest directly in SMEs, but rather in professionally managed venture capital funds that invest in SMEs. Venture capital firms are firms whose sole business is investigating, investing in, and monitoring entrepreneurial ventures. Most of the expertise in the venture capital industry is in venture capital firms. Firms (or individual fund managers) may be specialists in certain industries, certain geographic regions, and/or certain stages of venture capital investment. A venture capital firm commonly acts as the promoter and general partner or manager of venture capital funds. Investors in these funds can include both taxable investors, such as corporations and high-net-worth individuals or family trusts, and non-taxable entities, such as pension funds and university endowment funds. Unlike the venture capital firm and unlike investors of informal venture capital, the investors in formal venture capital funds are passive investors. Venture capital funds are commonly organized as limited partnerships (or some other flowthrough vehicle) so that capital from both taxable and non-taxable investors can be commingled without imposing an additional level of tax on non-taxable investors.

Informal Venture Capital: Of Love and Angels

At the outset, it is necessary to focus on the entrepreneur and related individuals because the earliest stages of a business's development are generally funded by the entrepreneur himself or herself and perhaps by family and friends. This initial stage is often referred to as the *seed stage*, when the entrepreneur takes an idea, does some preliminary market research, and develops a business plan. The primary investors at the seed stage (founders, family, and friends) are sometimes referred to as the "three Fs," and their investment is referred to as "love capital."

The sources of capital available to seed-stage investors are varied: personal savings, which may include funds in retirement savings accounts, home equity, lines of credit, and credit cards. Sweat equity (investment in the form of labour or services rather than cash) may also be considered a form of seed capital investment. Government policy that focuses on investment at this stage must consider not only the sources of capital available but also the factors that motivate an individual to pursue an entrepreneurial endeavour, including factors that influence a person's decision to leave employment. For example, the manner in which gains or losses realized on a founder's sweat equity in the business are taxed may influence the decision of the would-be entrepreneur to leave employment. The ease with which an individual can access capital in a personal or employer-sponsored retirement savings plan may also be an important consideration in this decision (and, indeed, in the decision whether the individual participates in a retirement savings plan in the first place). Access to retirement savings may also affect the extent to which family and friends can invest in the enterprise.

In the next stage of a business's development, the *startup stage*, financing may be required to take a product prototype to the level of product development and test marketing (sometimes referred to as beta testing). Businesses in the startup stage have not begun to sell products commercially, but will have undertaken market studies, assembled key management, and developed a business plan. Love capital remains an important source of capital at this stage.

In the startup stage (and even in the seed stage), financing beyond the means of the three Fs may be crucial, and external sources of capital must be sought. Capital may come from suppliers or potential customers of the business through the development of strategic alliances. Another important source of capital at this stage is the business "angel."[14] Relatively little is known about business angels owing to their invisibility, but a vast amount of literature attests to their importance as a significant source of capital for small businesses, not only in Canada and the United States, but also in most developed countries.[15] Some of the world's best-known companies—Bell Telephone, Ford, Apple, Hewlett-Packard, and Body Shop—received their start from angel investors.

In considering the appropriate policy instruments that affect angel capital investors, it is important to understand the motivations of both the entrepreneur and the investor. The primary motivation of the entrepreneur seeking capital is obvious: money. However, a number of other factors should influence the entrepreneur's decision of whom to approach for capital and on what terms. This assumes that the entrepreneur is aware of all of the possible sources of angel capital, but that is simply not the case. Angel capitalists do not advertise and there is no general registry that lists them. This initial informational threshold is particularly daunting in the informal venture capital industry and leads to significant market inefficiencies. Assuming that the entrepreneur can surmount this information barrier and identify a source of capital, he or she should consider what an angel investor can offer in addition to financing. Many angel investors are entrepreneurs themselves who can provide experience as well as money to a growing firm. Angels also may have valuable contacts with other sources of capital, including other angels and institutional venture capitalists. For the entrepreneur, it is important that the receipt of capital from an angel investor in return for an equity interest in the business does not impair his or her ability to get access to further capital.

In contrast to non-angels (that is, potential investors), angels have already decided that venture capital is an appropriate investment, are prepared to devote some of their investment portfolio to venture capital, and are willing to invest in the early stages of a company's development.[16] A number of factors influence an angel's decision to invest. As it is for the entrepreneur, awareness of investment opportunities is a threshold issue for the angel. Most angels rely on personal or business contacts as the primary sources of information about investment opportunities.

Because the vast majority of love and angel capitalists are taxable individuals, it is not surprising that governments in both Canada and the United States have focused on tax measures affecting individuals as a means of addressing the financing difficulties faced by SMEs. In fact, tax measures have been the typical means of government intervention (and expenditure) in the area of informal venture capital. For example, if a significant number of angels are repeat investors, then targeted incentives that leave them with more money to reinvest may be an appropriate fiscal tool. Both a lower rate of capital gains tax and a rollover or deferral provision for reinvestment would accomplish this goal. The more difficult issue is whether there are any fiscal incentives that would encourage potential investors to become business angels.

A third important source of informal venture capital in the early stages of a company's development are employees. Similar to the founders of a business, employees often accept less compensation in exchange for either an equity interest in the business or options to acquire an equity interest. The manner in which employee stock options are taxed and how they are reported for accounting purposes may affect their use by startup companies and their ability to attract key employees. Whether employee stock options should be treated differently from other forms of non-cash compensation is an important policy consideration for governments seeking to assist SMEs in the early stages of development.

Formal Venture Capital

As a business grows and its capital needs increase beyond the means of love and angel investors, its owners may turn to venture capital firms for financing because the business is still too risky for bank lending and cannot yet offer its shares to the public. The formal venture capital industry is relatively young compared with the informal venture capital industry; it dates back to 1946 in the United States and to the mid-1950s in Canada. In the short history of the formal venture capital industry, there have been numerous success stories (and a great many more failures). Digital Equipment Corporation, Apple, Federal Express, Compaq, Sun Microsystems, Intel, and Microsoft were all backed by formal venture capital funds and are all now household names.

Unlike informal venture capital, formal venture capital involves three distinct players in the venture capital marketplace: the entrepreneur, the investor, and an intermediary, the institutional venture capitalist. Thus, unlike love and angel investors, who put their own money at risk, institutional venture capitalists primarily invest other people's money. In this respect, the formal venture capital industry shares certain features with public equity markets. However, institutional venture capitalists play a much more active role in the businesses in which they invest than do investors or investment brokers in the public equity markets. Aside from the level of scrutiny prior to the initial investment and in each subsequent financing round, venture capitalists typically demand representation on the board of directors of the business—even control of the board despite the absence of voting control of the company—and take a proactive role in overseeing the managers of the business. They often assist the business in attracting key personnel, particularly on the management side. They may also be involved in marketing, financing, and product development. The significant time commitment both before and during investment has several consequences. Institutional venture capitalists invest in only a small number of businesses, the investments tend to be large, and the size of deals has increased significantly in recent years because of the relatively few venture capital firms managing increasingly sizable venture capital funds. The time commitment also accounts for the geographic proximity of portfolio businesses, not only to the angel capitalists who finance them, but also to the venture capital fund managers that provide formal venture capital.

Both informal and formal venture capitalists tend to co-invest in portfolio companies (referred to as syndicated deals). In an informal syndicated deal, there is typically a lead investor who is more knowledgeable than other investors about the particular business, industry, technology, product, or market. Informal investment tends to be highly concentrated in certain geographic regions primarily because syndicated deals often involve friends and associates. Formal venture capital is also typically invested in syndicated deals with a lead venture capital firm or fund, and deals will also be geographically close to the lead investor, although syndication does allow for greater geographic dispersion of venture capital.[17]

There are various stages of financing that may attract formal venture capital. Relatively little formal venture capital is invested at the seed stage, where most money is supplied by love and angel capitalists. The informal and formal venture capital markets are complementary but relatively distinct. Formal venture capitalists generally do not become involved before *first-stage financing*, which refers to capital required to start commercial production and sales. *Second-stage financing* is usually the initial expansion capital provided once sales have commenced but before a company is profitable or profitable enough to finance further growth internally or from traditional capital sources such as banks or the public stock market. *Third-stage financing* generally refers to financing for major growth opportunities, such as expanded production facilities or significant marketing expenditures. *Later-stage financing* refers to financing provided to businesses that have achieved a relatively stable growth rate after the expansion stage. Companies at this stage generally have positive cash flows.

Until the 1980s, venture capital referred to "classic" venture capital: the provision of new equity to create and build new firms. Classic venture capital has a long time horizon—7 to 10 years or more—because investment is made before a corporation becomes profitable, often before it has even commenced sales. Beginning in the late 1980s, large elements of the formal venture capital industry shifted their focus to later-stage financing, which is more akin to merchant banking, with an increased focus on mezzanine financing, leveraged buyout financing, and bridge financing. *Mezzanine financing* refers to financing that takes the form of subordinated debt (financing that is below senior debt but superior to straight equity financing). Mezzanine financing often has an equity element, such as warrants permitting the investor to acquire common shares of the company. Mezzanine financing may be used to fund a particular stage of a business's development (such as third stage or later stage). *Leveraged buyout financing* (LBO financing) refers to financing that is provided to a management group to acquire a product line or particular business at any stage of development. LBO financing often involves companies that are closely held or family-owned with entrepreneurial management acquiring a significant equity interest. LBO financing is generally provided through debt with very little equity. *Bridge financing* refers to the financing needed when a company intends to make an initial public offering (IPO) of its shares, generally within six months to a year preceding the IPO. Bridge financing is often structured so that it is repaid out of the proceeds of the IPO.

As the private equity markets have matured in the United States and Canada, venture capital firms have become more specialized. Market watchers tend to separate the private equity market into three distinct market segments: venture capital, mezzanine capital, and LBO capital. Venture capital refers to early-stage financing of young companies primarily in innovative sectors of the economy. Mezzanine capital and LBO capital refer to capital provided for mezzanine financing and LBO financing, as described above. Private equity statistics in the United States and Canada have evolved as the private equity market has matured.[18] In the United States, LBO financing and mezzanine financing have been reported separately since 1979. In Canada, where the private equity market is not as mature as in the United States, the separate reporting of venture capital as distinct from LBO financing and mezzanine financing is much more recent. Statistics on LBO financing and mezzanine financing in Canada are not available in the public domain to the same extent as venture capital statistics.

The organizational structure favoured for private venture capital funds in both the Canadian and US formal venture capital industries is the limited partnership,[19] because of the nature of the investors (both taxable and non-taxable entities) and the management style (active management by the general partner of the fund in choosing and monitoring investments, with passive investors providing the bulk of the capital). In both countries, a limited partnership is a flowthrough vehicle: the tax consequences to investors (the limited partners) are determined by their own tax circumstances. A limited partnership permits both taxable and non-taxable entities to participate in the venture capital fund without penalizing the non-taxable entities. The general partner of the fund is usually a venture capital firm or individuals working for that firm.[20] The general partner typically contributes 1 percent of the capital of the fund; the passive investors contribute the other 99 percent. There are two elements to the compensation of the general partner: a management fee and a profit participation element (commonly referred to as a "carried interest"). The management fee is usually specified as a percentage of committed capital (that is, capital that investors have committed to invest over the life of the fund net of returns of capital to the investors), a percentage of the value of the fund's assets, or a combination or modification of these elements.[21] The profit element or carried interest can vary significantly, although a common figure is 20 percent, paid out as investment returns are realized and after the return of the limited partners' invested capital (or perhaps invested capital plus a premium).[22] The limited partnership is subject to a fixed term—typically 10 years, although extensions are possible—during which time the proceeds from exited investments must be distributed to investors. The mandatory distribution and fixed term make the success of a fund easy to compute and alleviate agency costs resulting from the control enjoyed by the general partner. A general partner's track record in previous funds is its primary advertising tool for attracting investors to new funds. Given the relatively small size and geographic concentration of the venture capital community, the reputation that a general partner builds through its fund's performance is extremely important.

Large institutional investors, particularly in the United States, may be invested in numerous venture capital, buyout, and mezzanine funds. Smaller investors may not have the expertise or resources to evaluate the various venture capital funds available or to diversify their private equity investments. Accordingly, smaller investors may invest through either a "gatekeeper" or a "fund of funds." A gatekeeper pools capital from several clients and invests the proceeds as a limited partner in one or several venture capital funds. A fund of funds is a venture capital fund that invests in other venture capital funds. Gatekeepers and funds of funds have become more common in the United States.

Also typically included in the formal venture capital industry are banks and other financial institutions that make both direct and indirect (through venture capital funds) venture capital investments, generally through affiliates or subsidiaries incorporated specifically for private equity investment.[23] Non-financial corporations may also create a directly controlled venture capital fund or subsidiary to invest in private equity. These corporate venture funds typically make "strategic" venture investments in suppliers or customers.[24] In addition, large institutional investors, such as pension plans and universities, sometimes internally manage all or a portion of their private equity portfolio, making direct investments in SMEs. It is difficult to place these investors on one side or the other of the informal-formal divide.

Exiting the Venture Capital Investment

Exit strategies—the ways in which venture investments are liquidated—are particularly important to angel investors and venture capitalists because most of their investments are equity investments that do not pay dividends. The return on a venture capital investment is generally deferred until the investment is liquidated, and is equal to the exit (sale) price less the entry (purchase) price. Accordingly, the ability to profitably exit a venture investment is an important criterion in the decision whether to invest in a particular business and, if so, on what terms.[25] The ability to exit thus has a significant impact on the entire venture capital process, affecting both the ability to raise capital and the types of investments that are made.

There are a variety of methods by which venture capitalists, both informal and formal, can realize their investment.[26] The most profitable exit mechanism, and certainly the most visible and glamorous, is an IPO. Although an IPO will provide further external capital to the business, the primary motivation for an IPO of a venture-backed firm is to provide share liquidity and, therefore, an exit for venture capitalists. Venture capitalists (as well as founders) are generally considered insiders when the business is taken public, so the disposition of their shares on the public exchange will be subject to certain trade restrictions. Although an IPO is a relatively rare exit strategy for venture capitalists, the IPO market affects the overall health of the venture capital marketplace.

The most common profitable exit strategy is the sale of shares to a third party, perhaps in the context of a corporate merger. Typically, the third party acquires all of the shares of the company (or perhaps all of its assets) in exchange for cash or shares of the acquiring company. Other exit strategies include a buyback, in which the entrepreneur or the company repurchases the shares held by the venture capitalist; a secondary sale, in which only the shares of the venture capitalist are sold to a third party; and the writeoff of the investment. A writeoff may involve the complete failure of the company, or simply the venture capitalist's decision to treat the investment as non-viable (although the venture capitalist continues to hold the shares).

The market for IPOs was particularly healthy in the latter half of the 1990s and into 2000 (see table 1.1). In fact, the market's appetite for high-tech companies was so voracious that many were taken public well before they were profitable. In a semi-biographical account of Jim Clark, the founder of Netscape, Michael Lewis asserts that the Netscape IPO in 1995 represented a paradigm shift for the IPO market:

In the frenzy that followed [the Netscape IPO], a lot of the old rules of capitalism were suspended. For instance, it had long been the rule of thumb with the Silicon Valley venture capitalists that they didn't peddle a new technology company to the investing public until it had had at least four consecutive profitable quarters. Netscape had nothing to show investors but massive losses. But its fabulous stock market success created a precedent. No longer did you need to show profits; you needed to show rapid growth. Having a past actually counted against a company, for a past was a record and a record was a sign of a company's limitations. . . . You had to show that you were the company not of the present but of the future. The most appealing companies became those in a state of pure possibility.[27]

Business analysts began touting new methodologies for valuing companies based on a gross sales multiple because the "old" earnings multiple did not reflect the realities of the new economy. In this euphoria, venture capitalists themselves seemed to have forgotten that venture capital is "patient capital." In the 1950s, the 1960s, and even into the 1980s, patient capital meant investments of 7 to 10 years before exiting; in the late 1990s, 3 to 5 years or less seemed closer to the norm, particularly for companies involved in the development and exploitation of new technologies.[28] Lewis's suggestion that the old rules of capitalism were "suspended"—as opposed to discarded—proved to be prophetic, with the market meltdown beginning in the latter half of 2000.

Table 1.1 provides IPO statistics for the three major US stock indices and the Toronto Stock Exchange and TSX Venture Exchange for the period 1993 through 2002, and figure 1.1 shows the NASDAQ Composite index from 1990 through 2002. Figure 1.1 illustrates the exuberance of the markets in the latter half of the 1990s, particularly in the last two years of the decade, and the downward spiral that started in the latter half of 2000. The rout of the public equity markets beginning in 2000 and the consequent collapse of the market's appetite for IPOs, particularly of high-tech stocks, has had a profound impact on the venture capital industries in the United States and Canada from exit to entrance. The amount of new money invested in venture capital, particularly in the United States, declined considerably in 2001 and 2002 (see figures 2.1 and 2.2 in chapter 2).

In Canada through the 1990s, the pool of venture capital was disproportionately smaller than that in the United States, although the Canadian industry was not as preoccupied with the "dotcom craze" as the US industry was and has not been as hard hit in the downward spiral. That said, capital markets in Canada and the Canadian venture capital industry take their cues from the United States and have likewise suffered significant setbacks beginning in the latter half of 2000. The pace of IPOs in both countries is down considerably, as is the amount of new capital flowing into venture capital funds. While today's lack of euphoria in the public equity markets does not bode well for the venture capital industry in either country, it will likely force both countries' industries to return to the fundamentals of venture capital investment, particularly patience. The next few years will also be a crucial time, particularly in Canada, for the government to

Table 1.1 Common Share IPOs on NASDAQ, NYSE, Amex, TSX, and TSX Venture, 1993-2002

Year	NASDAQ Number of offerings	NASDAQ Value (US$ millions)	NYSE Number of offerings	NYSE Value (US$ millions)	Amex Number of offerings	Amex Value (US$ millions)	TSX Number of offerings	TSX Value (Cdn$ millions)	TSX Venture Number of offerings	TSX Venture Value (Cdn$ millions)
1993	393	14,771.7	202	40,088.5	44	1,707.0	40	886.18	23	37.85
1994	322	10,000.8	133	21,075.4	15	428.0	33	1,197.45	48	22.00
1995	343	15,298.8	65	13,503.7	9	328.2	26	2,333.70	66	22.62
1996	561	26,117.0	100	20,728.0	20	615.5	46	1,467.78	73	139.37
1997	375	19,777.8	122	24,599.4	21	996.4	37	2,070.13	128	68.38
1998	205	11,884.8	91	30,540.2	16	278.0	29	1,442.85	104	42.24
1999	422	35,503.8	55	26,543.0	23	914.4	23	2,978.01	97	44.32
2000	317	31,063.4	30	24,114.8	5	61.4	30	3,774.48	112	78.20
2001	52	7,353.7	42	30,584.2	18	1,614.5	13	756.00	91	43.55
2002	41	3,792.5	71	33,272.9	46	4,959.0	9	637.15	50	23.80

Sources: US markets: Securities Data Company, *Global New Issues* [online]; Canadian markets: FinancialPost.infomart.ca, *New Issues* [online].

Figure 1.1   NASDAQ Composite Close, 1990-2002

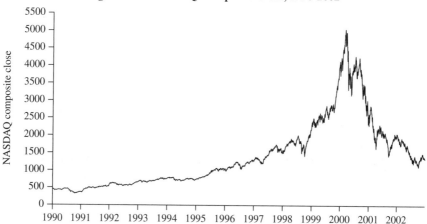

adjust its venture capital policies in order to foster a healthy industry that will have long-term sustainability without the need for significant government subsidies.

The Role of Government in the Venture Capital Marketplace: Responding to Market Failures

Market Failures Affecting Investment in Small Businesses

Government intervention in the marketplace is generally justified where it corrects or compensates for market failures, barriers that create biases causing allocative inefficiencies in the marketplace. In the context of venture capital, there are two market failures that warrant government intervention. First, the financial market itself may not be functioning efficiently, thus creating an "equity gap" for small businesses. This gap is limited to equity investment because the inability of small businesses to attract debt financing on terms comparable to those received by large corporations is not usually considered a market failure.[29] Second, small businesses generate positive externalities or spillover effects that benefit the economy as a whole but are not captured by the parties to the immediate transaction.

The efficient allocation of capital in the financial market is dependent on full knowledge of the risks and returns associated with all available investments. However, there are two issues in the context of financing rapid-growth SMEs that make "full knowledge" almost impossible to acquire. First, the long time horizon associated with investment in rapid-growth SMEs, particularly in new technology sectors, makes it virtually impossible to determine the risks and expected returns associated with investment. Second, information asymmetries can affect both the decision to make investments and the monitoring of investments once they are made. "Information asymmetries" are the differences in knowledge of an entrepreneur (or a company's managers) seeking investment on the one hand and external investors on the other. Information asymmetries are particularly pronounced for SMEs, in part because of the lack of disclosure requirements imposed on small businesses.

Pre-investment information asymmetries (commonly referred to as adverse selection) restrict the amount that external investors are willing to invest and increase the rate of return that they demand. Adverse selection is particularly pronounced for informal venture capital when entrepreneurs cannot identify sources of capital and angel capitalists cannot identify potential investments. Although it is fairly easy to identify formal sources of venture capital in both Canada and the United States—for example, the Web sites for the US National Venture Capital Association (NVCA) and the Canadian Venture Capital Association (CVCA) include lists of their members—it is much more difficult to identify sources of angel capital. This inefficiency is illustrated by the fact that small businesses complain that there is an insufficient amount of angel capital at the same time that business angels indicate that they have significant amounts of uncommitted funds available to invest but cannot find suitable investments.[30]

Post-investment information asymmetries (commonly referred to as moral hazard) reflect the agency conflict between investors and entrepreneurs or business managers.[31] For example, entrepreneurs or managers have an incentive to engage in wasteful expenditures (such as lavish offices and first-class travel) because they personally benefit disproportionately from such expenditures but do not bear their entire cost. Similarly, they may be more inclined to take undesirable risks with other people's money.[32] Moral hazard generally stems from the inability of the external investor to effectively monitor the behaviour of the entrepreneur or business manager. To compensate for moral hazard, external investors generally demand a higher rate of return than that expected from funds that a business generates internally (that is, retained earnings).

In public equity markets, public disclosure requirements as well as financial intermediaries play an important role in alleviating adverse selection and moral hazard.[33] Venture capital firms are specialized financial intermediaries that serve a similar role for private equity investments. Adverse selection is reduced in two respects. First, from the entrepreneur's perspective, venture capital firms are relatively easy to identify and contact. From the investor's perspective (the passive investors who invest in venture capital funds), venture capital firms closely scrutinize business plans of prospective firms before making investment decisions. Few businesses that submit proposals receive financing. A variety of methods are used to alleviate moral hazard. For example, venture capital firms generally provide capital to their investee firms in stages or rounds so that the firms must return frequently to justify further funding. The vast majority of funding is provided through convertible preferred stock (generally convertible to common stock on a one-for-one basis). Convertible preferred stock is used for a variety of reasons. One reason is to give the venture capital fund enhanced "control" rights. The preferred shareholders may be entitled to enhanced voting rights on certain issues; most important, the preferred shareholders typically have the right to appoint a designated number of directors to the board—

generally, more directors than the cash flow rights that the stock represents. In this manner, the venture capital fund can closely monitor its investment.[34] Staged financing reduces both moral hazard and adverse selection information asymmetries.[35] Staged financing reduces moral hazard because it creates a substantial performance incentive: the original fund can penalize the entrepreneur for failing to meet established investment goals by refusing to provide additional financing or by offering financing only on terms unfavourable to the entrepreneur. Because the venture capital firms that provided financing on the initial round typically have a right of first refusal on subsequent rounds, the entrepreneur is unlikely to attract investment for a subsequent round on better terms than those offered by the original firms.[36] Staged financing also reduces adverse selection because an entrepreneur's willingness to accept staged financing (and the scrutiny that it entails) signals the entrepreneur's confidence that he or she possesses the skills necessary for the project and that the business plan projections, which are used to evaluate the investment and to establish the goals for follow-on financing, are credible.[37]

Apart from market failures inherent in the venture capital marketplace, distortions that divert capital from small businesses may be introduced by the government itself. As Neil Brooks notes,

> since aggregate savings in the economy are limited, any measure that is successful in directing savings into a certain area will result in a lower level of financing available for other uses. Thus, for example, the exemption of principal residences from the capital gains tax [in Canada] undoubtedly results in a considerable amount of capital being diverted from small business investment to residential housing.[38]

Similarly, tax incentives for investment in individual and employer-sponsored retirement funds divert savings that might otherwise be invested in small businesses. Funds held in retirement accounts have historically been subject to more conservative investment guidelines, effectively precluding them from investing in small businesses. Tax and pension legislation affecting venture capital investment by retirement funds are considered in chapter 7. Just as the tax system may create biases against small business investment, it is often used to counteract these biases by providing stimulants for such investment.

The second market failure justifying government incentives for venture capital investment are the positive externalities associated with financing SMEs that are not necessarily captured in a free marketplace. Positive externalities are particularly prevalent in the context of research and development leading to innovation. As Robert Kuttner suggests,

> [b]ecause investments in innovation are risky and because they often benefit competitors, market forces tend to underinvest in innovation. Indeed, the more "perfect" the competition, the less money is left over to invest in innovations that have broadly diffused benefits but that may not pay off to the investor for decades, if ever.[39]

Simply put, "knowledge is not like other factors of production":[40]

> Research and development—knowledge itself—is the economy's most fa-
> mous positive externality. In a perfect market economy, a firm that develops
> a new process, a company that invests heroically in workers' skills, will not
> capture the full social return on the investment, since some of the knowl-
> edge will be imitated by competitors and broadly diffused. Hence, private
> businesses notoriously underinvest in both human capital and research.
> Studies have shown that the social return from research-and-development
> investments exceeds the private return by 35 to 60 percent.[41]

Hence a government's interest in and support for rapid-growth SMEs:
these small businesses tend to be concentrated in the high-tech sector that fuels
innovation. Peter Eisinger stated in 1988 that

> [t]he declining importance of economies of scale in the less capital-intensive
> industries dependent on advanced technology, the growing tendency to
> contract out the manufacture of component parts to independent suppliers,
> and the need for more flexible production and management systems to
> respond to the competitive challenges of rapid production innovation all
> suggested not only a role but also the necessity of a strong small business
> sector and a public policy matrix to support it.[42]

In developing this public policy matrix,

> [the finding that the increased US national venture capital pool led to
> increased good quality business propositions] suggests that a good deal of
> entrepreneurial activity was lying dormant for lack of capital. . . .
>   But the finding that the availability of venture capital in itself elicits
> attractive business proposals suggests that there probably exists virgin ter-
> ritories in the nation's midsection where entrepreneurial impulses merely
> await the appearance of potential investors in order to blossom. Because
> private venture capital firms have not yet come to the interior in significant
> numbers, some states have themselves assumed the role of venture capitalist.[43]

Rapid-Growth SME Geography

The ability to address market failures that limit venture capital investment has
certain geographic limitations. Because venture capital investments are costly
to locate and monitor, they are generally made in close geographic proximity to
the investor (that is, the angel capitalist or the venture capital fund manager),
and investors tend to locate in areas with a high density of rapid-growth SMEs
or the potential for rapid-growth SMEs. As a result, the equity gap affecting
investment in rapid-growth SMEs is more pronounced in "the nation's midsection" and outside of large metropolitan areas.

The concentration of rapid-growth SMEs in urban centres is no accident.
By its nature, the high-tech industry is localized and predominantly urbanized.
It does not happen at a national or state/provincial level, although government

policies at these levels can influence its development. Locational decision making in the high-tech sector happens at the regional or municipal level and is most affected by factors at that level: the availability of specialized labour markets, knowledge spillovers from competing firms, and the presence of critical suppliers and perhaps customers.[44] It has also been suggested that other local factors, such as cultural diversity and creativity, influence the location of high-tech firms.[45] Given the concentration of the high-tech industry in urban centres, municipalities have an important role to play, and federal and provincial or state governments must include municipalities as active partners in the formulation of appropriate policies.[46] It also explains why high-tech development does not generally occur in rural areas. Government expenditure programs that encourage rural high-tech development may be inappropriate.[47] Similarly, national and even provincial or state level programs that target the high-tech sector may suffer from political pressures to be geographically representational, despite the propensity of high-tech firms to self-select larger urban areas.[48]

There is an uneven geographical distribution of formal venture capital in both Canada and the United States, including among larger urban centres. Silicon Valley, for example, has been the leading recipient of venture capital based on region in the United States in every year from 1980 to 2002, accounting for at least 25 percent of investment and in many years over 33 percent of investment; in every year except two, the New England states have been the second-largest recipients.[49] Similarly, the bulk of venture capital investment in Canada occurs in Ontario and Quebec and is concentrated among a few urban areas, such as the National Capital Region, Toronto, the tricity area of Kitchener-Waterloo-Cambridge, and Montreal. Eisinger's rationale for supporting regional incentives for venture capital within the United States is perhaps equally apropos for supporting government venture capital incentive programs across Canada—with the caveat that such programs will, by necessity, benefit urban rather than rural areas. Over the past two decades, Canada has been in a position comparable to the US "midsection" referred to by Eisenger. It has had to compete with a much more mature and highly geographically concentrated venture capital industry in the United States (or, more specifically, along the east and west coasts of the United States). More problematical in terms of Canada's economy, the innovative small businesses of today—the focus of venture capitalists, both private and public—are engaged much more extensively in the high-tech sector. Employees in this sector are highly educated and highly mobile, and their businesses, being dependent more on human capital than on infrastructure, particularly at the early stages of development, are equally mobile. Regional competition remains problematic, not necessarily because there is a fixed pool of SMEs created each year,[50] but because there is a relatively fixed number of highly educated individuals who develop and nurture businesses in the high-tech sector.

Canada's proximity to the United States, the openness of the border between the two countries, particularly for individuals involved in the high-tech sector, and the fact that the countries share a common language[51] have made competitiveness with the United States a key criterion in the evaluation of the Canadian tax system; indeed, competitiveness is often viewed as a sufficient rationale to justify government incentives for promoting knowledge-based businesses. Many of the recent amendments to the Income Tax Act targeting venture capital investors and employees of high-tech firms are premised on the belief that, in the absence of an aggressively competitive tax system in Canada, both venture capital and individuals involved in the high-tech sector (entrepreneurs and employees generally) will take wing south. Thus, it should not come as a surprise in reviewing the various tax incentive programs for venture capital investment discussed throughout this book that Canada has almost always sought to match or better US incentives.

Government incentives may be justified especially for earlier-stage financing, where the information asymmetries are high, the positive externalities are potentially great, and the formal sources of venture capital (private venture capital firms), like the firms in which they invest, do not capture the full social return from their investments. Given the upfront costs of assessing business proposals and the ongoing costs of monitoring proposals—that is, information asymmetries—private venture capital firms have tended to reject small deals because they are simply not worth the costs associated with their assessment and monitoring. Furthermore, as the size of private venture capital funds has increased (particularly in the United States), the size of the average investment per round of financing and, perhaps more important, the size of the average first-round investment have increased significantly, thus increasing the size of the equity gap at the earliest stages of development. Table 1.2 shows the size of first-round financing by industry group and overall in the US formal venture capital industry over the period 1980 to 2002. Similar trends have been observed in the Canadian venture capital industry. As a result, government venture capital policy and programs often focus on angel financing generally as well as on seed and startup financing, because financing at these stages has the chance to generate the greatest social returns through job creation and product innovation.

Finally, politics has an important influence on government policy in all areas, including venture capital investment. In the United States, for example, there is a general antipathy toward direct government investment in private enterprises—part of a general dislike of government interference in the marketplace. Government investment in private enterprise is often viewed as the antithesis of the US free enterprise system. Thus, government involvement in venture capital formation often takes the form of indirect incentives. Direct incentives, when provided at all, usually take the form of loans or debt or equity guarantees rather than equity investment by the government. This inherent mistrust of government ownership of equity investment in the corporate world has had a profound impact on the shape of government incentives for venture capital formation in the United States.

Government Venture Capital Programs

This study focuses on government programs, particularly tax incentive programs, that target the supply side of venture capital. There are other programs that

Table 1.2　US Venture Capital Average First-Round Investment, 1980-2002 (US$ millions)

Industry sector	1980	1985	1990	1995	1996	1997	1998	1999	2000	2001	2002
Communications	0.7	1.9	4.0	5.0	3.8	4.0	5.7	9.6	12.6	7.6	5.9
Computer software	0.9	1.2	2.1	2.5	2.7	3.1	3.5	4.7	6.8	5.9	4.2
Retailing and media	0.6	2.2	3.3	4.8	4.6	3.8	4.0	6.1	7.7	4.4	5.1
Computer hardware and services	1.1	1.6	2.7	3.0	3.9	3.5	3.7	7.3	8.2	5.7	6.8
Biotechnology	1.1	1.2	1.0	2.7	3.6	4.2	3.2	5.2	7.8	8.0	6.9
Health-care-related	1.2	1.2	2.2	5.0	3.4	3.7	3.5	4.3	7.0	4.2	5.8
Semiconductors and electronics	1.1	1.6	2.5	2.9	4.4	4.0	3.5	6.3	9.3	7.0	6.6
Industrial/energy	1.4	1.5	2.0	5.4	3.6	4.0	3.9	10.2	9.1	6.2	7.3
Business/financial	0.6	2.7	4.3	4.4	6.4	5.0	4.2	6.6	8.6	6.6	5.4
Overall	1.1	1.7	2.5	4.0	3.8	3.7	4.0	6.6	8.7	6.3	5.7

Source: Thomson Venture Economics, *2003 National Venture Capital Association Yearbook* (Arlington, VA and Newark, NJ: National Venture Capital Association and Thomson Venture Economics, 2003), figures 4.02, 4.11, 4.20, 4.29, 4.38, 4.47, 4.56, 4.65, and 4.74 for industry sectors; overall figures are extrapolated from figures 3.13 and 3.15.

target SMEs generally and, in some cases, are justified on bases similar to those supporting government venture capital programs (that is, market failures). These other programs, however, such as a lower corporate tax rate applicable to SMEs[52] or tax credits or accelerated writeoffs for certain types of capital expenditure,[53] tend to assist established, profitable SMEs and are not specifically geared toward SMEs in the startup phase or those seeking new capital.[54] For corporations that have not yet begun to generate profits or indeed sales—the corporations that are the focus of this study—these incentives are of limited use.

The government venture capital programs discussed in this book are concerned primarily with classic venture capital: patient capital invested in companies at the early stages of development. The book proceeds on the assumption that there exist market failures affecting the funding of rapid-growth SMEs and that government intervention is justified to correct or compensate for these market failures. The book seeks to address two issues: what shape should the policy instrument take and what level of government should be responsible for it?

There are a variety of programs that a government could use either to correct or to compensate for the market failures that have created an equity gap for SMEs. For example, it is generally acknowledged that information on informal venture capital funding and investment opportunities is not readily available, which therefore increases moral hazard. In fact, some commentators suggest that there is no shortage of informal venture capital; rather, a more efficient flow of information is required. Governments may sponsor or assist in the creation of networks designed to match businesses in need of capital with potential investors (commonly referred to as angel capital networks), or they may sponsor or provide assistance to venture capital fairs where entrepreneurs make presentations to prospective investors. Such programs are considered in chapter 8.

Most government venture capital programs are second-best solutions: they compensate for market failures by increasing the supply of venture capital, rather than correct failures by reducing information asymmetries. In providing these incentives, the government is effectively underwriting some (or all, depending on the incentive) of the risks associated with venture capital investment—in many cases, well beyond the risks stemming from information asymmetries.

The government itself may become a supplier of venture capital by subscribing for debt or equity capital of SMEs or by investing in venture capital pools that are managed by the government or by private firms. Governments may provide low-interest loans or grants to leverage private sector investment in venture capital pools. Government programs may seek to increase private sector venture capital investment in various ways. For example, tax credits may be provided to investors in SMEs or venture capital funds, but limited to particular taxpayers, such as individuals or insurance companies, or to investment in specific categories of SMEs, such as high-tech companies. Tax incentives may be provided to enhance venture investment in other ways, such as preferential tax rates applicable to gains or increased utility of losses from dispositions of investments in SMEs. Government regulation of banks, insurance companies, and pension funds—institutions that control large pools of capital—also has a direct impact on the supply side of venture capital. Similarly, securities regulation, particularly exemptions from prospectus requirements and regulations affecting IPOs, also affects venture capital investment.

This study examines various government incentive programs targeting the supply side of venture capital. Its primary focus is on the use of tax incentives to promote venture capital investment, although other programs are also examined. Programs that rely on tax incentives—commonly referred to as tax expenditure programs—should be treated and evaluated in the same manner as direct expenditure programs, using the following criteria:

- What is the program's objective?
- Is the program appropriately targeted?
- Are there any unintended distortions?
- Does a cost-benefit analysis show positive results?
- Are the compliance costs reasonable?
- Is a tax expenditure the most effective delivery mechanism?

These questions should be considered when the elements of various government venture capital programs are reviewed in the following chapters.

Structure of This Book

Evaluation of the various government venture capital incentive programs used in Canada and the United States requires some knowledge of the venture capital industries, both informal and formal, in the two countries. Chapter 2 provides a brief account of the evolution of the venture capital industries in the two countries, highlighting specific government programs that have shaped the industries.

The remaining chapters examine various government incentive programs currently used in Canada and the United States. Chapter 3 considers the taxation of capital gains. Government incentive programs, particularly those targeting the informal venture capital industry, have tended to focus on the taxation of gains (and losses) realized by investors as a means of increasing the supply of venture capital in order to compensate for perceived market failures. At the national level in both countries, recent government policy has focused on a general preference for all capital gains (although the United States has limited its preference to capital gains realized by individuals) as a means of promoting high-risk investment, despite the fact that more targeted incentives can be, and are, used in both countries. More targeted incentives include the preferential tax treatment of capital gains from small business investments, deferral of tax when proceeds of sale of a small business investment (or perhaps other investments) are reinvested in other small businesses, and an expanded use of losses from small business investments. In these respects, the tax regimes in the two countries have many similarities, with Canada often imitating measures previously adopted in the United States. The fundamental issue today is whether a general preference for capital gains taxation better responds to the market failures affecting investment in SMEs or whether this preference may further undermine investment.

Chapter 4 examines the tax treatment of employee stock options. While stock options have historically been the prerogative of senior executives, they are now a significant element of compensation for virtually all employees of high-growth companies. Their use has been encouraged both by their accounting treatment (under which employers need not recognize them as an expense in most cases) and by their tax treatment (under which employees are not taxed until the options are exercised or the underlying securities are sold, and the benefits realized are taxed more preferentially than other employment income). Employee stock options have been touted as an important source of "sweat equity" to high-growth SMEs, particularly in their earliest stages of development, when cash flow is a significant issue.

Chapter 5 considers a specific incentive targeting angel capital investment that is used by provincial and state governments in Canada and the United States: the provision of tax credits to investors in small businesses. In contrast to the incentives considered in chapter 3, which are essentially back-end incentives, tax credits are provided at the front end, irrespective of the eventual success or failure of the investment.

Tax incentives for investment in venture capital funds are considered in chapter 6. In Canada, labour-sponsored venture capital corporations (LSVCCs) are the largest source of formal venture capital, accounting for more than 35 percent of all capital under management. LSVCCs would not exist at all without the generous tax incentives provided at both the federal and provincial levels. In the United States, there are no federal tax incentives for investment in venture capital funds, although a number of states offer various types of incentives for investors. An increasingly popular program involves the provision of premium tax credits to insurance companies that invest in certified capital companies (CAPCOs). Like LSVCCs, CAPCOs would not exist without the generous state tax incentives provided to insurance company investors. The LSVCC and CAPCO programs are highlighted in chapter 6 in a review of various venture capital fund programs offered at the provincial and state levels.

Both individual retirement funds and employer-sponsored pension funds benefit from tax preferences in Canada and the United States and have become significant sources of capital in both countries. As noted previously, tax incentives for investment in retirement savings can distort the financial market and divert funds that might otherwise be invested in small businesses. Historically, retirement funds were restricted to conservative investments, primarily due to a narrow interpretation of the fiduciary obligations imposed on plan managers in the case of employer-sponsored pension funds, and under applicable tax legislation in the case of both individual retirement plans and employer-sponsored funds. Given the vast amount of capital in retirement funds, it comes as no surprise that the venture capital industry has lobbied for the liberalization of investment restrictions imposed on such plans in order to permit venture capital investments. Chapter 7 reviews the tax legislation and, where applicable, pension fund legislation governing employer-sponsored and individual retirement funds. The chapter also considers the extent to which the plan beneficiary can access such funds—through withdrawals, as a loan, or as a loan guarantee—to make venture capital investments outside the funds. The chapter concludes with a review of recent reforms to Canada's government-sponsored retirement system, the Canada Pension Plan, which have made the plan one of the largest private equity investors in all of Canada.

Chapter 8 examines a selection of non-tax programs used in Canada and the United States to promote venture investment. In particular, the chapter considers the two federal institutions that have been created to provide or facilitate investment in SMEs—the US Small Business Administration (SBA) and the Business Development Bank of Canada. The primary programs administered by the SBA are loan guarantee programs and the small business investment company (SBIC) program. The SBA also administers a number of research and development (R & D) programs. Two in particular are considered: the small business innovative research (SBIR) program and the small business technology transfer (STTR) program. Under both programs, US government agencies that spend more than a specified amount on R & D must use a portion of their budgets to finance R & D undertaken by SMEs. In this way, public expenditure on innovation is married to the financing needs of SMEs. The SBIC program is considered separately because of its historic importance in the development of the US formal venture capital industry and its continuing importance as a venture capital investment vehicle for banks. The SBIC program was established in 1958 in the wake of the *Sputnik* crisis. Another program instituted at the same time, the Advanced Research Projects Agency (ARPA),[55] is also considered to highlight the importance of US military spending on innovation; the Department of Defense has one of the largest R & D budgets in the United States. Military technological innovation has substantial commercial spinoffs, fuelling an enormous amount of innovation in the private sector. One of ARPA's best-known creations is the Internet, which began in the 1960s-1970s with the development of ARPANet and its associated TCP/IP network architecture. Chapter 8 concludes by considering two innovative programs that target the market failures underlying the equity gap faced by small businesses. Angel capital networks have been designed to match entrepreneurs requiring venture capital with sources of seed capital financing, in an effort to reduce the costs of small business investment. Incubator programs provide SMEs with services rather than capital, thus reducing the problems of moral hazard.

Chapter 9 concludes the study by highlighting a few key reforms that governments, particularly those in Canada, should consider making to their tax incentive programs targeting informal and formal venture capital investment. In theory, there should be coordination among the tax and non-tax incentive programs offered by various levels of government in Canada and the United States. In fact, there is surprisingly little, if any. One of the minor goals of this book is to provide a comprehensive examination of the various government programs, particularly tax programs, used in Canada and the United States, so that greater coordination within, and perhaps between, the countries can result.

Notes

1   Thomson Venture Economics, *2003 National Venture Capital Association Year-book* (Arlington, VA and Newark, NJ. National Venture Capital Association and Thomson Venture Economics, 2003), 23, figure 2.06, and 31, figure 3.11. Statistics are not provided for the amount of capital raised by venture capitalists located in Silicon Valley. However, of the almost $44 billion invested in California compa-nies, $34.9 billion or almost 80 percent was invested in Silicon Valley companies (ibid., at 30, figure 3.08).

2   Statistics prepared by Macdonald & Associates Limited for the Canada Venture Capital Association, available on the CVCA Web site at http://www.cvca.ca/. The disbursement statistics for Canada included approximately $1.5 billion from for-eign investment groups (primarily US venture capital funds).

3   Robert Kuttner, *Everything for Sale: The Virtues and Limits of Markets* (New York: Knopf, 1997), 202-3.

4   SMEs are generally defined, for Canadian purposes, as businesses with fewer than 500 employees and less than $50 million in assets. In the United States, a more detailed evaluation of SME status is undertaken on an industry-by-industry basis. For example, the US Small Business Administration (SBA) publishes a table of size standards of for-profit organizations that are eligible for US federal government programs. The current table, effective July 7, 2003, can be found at the SBA's Web site at http://www.sba.gov/size/. Size standards are usually based on either the number of employees or average annual receipts. The SBA's Office of Advocacy generally classifies a small business as one with fewer than 500 employees.

5   In Canada, statistics on SMEs are maintained by the Small Business and Special Surveys Division of Statistics Canada. A significant amount of this information is available from the Statistics Canada Web site at http://www.statcan.ca/. In the United States, the SBA produces statistics on SMEs primarily from data collected by the US Census Bureau. A significant amount of statistical information on US SMEs is available from the SBA Web site at http://www.sba.gov/.

The following table sets out the number of firms of various sizes and the number of employees employed by those firms in Canada in 1999 (source: Statis-tics Canada, *Employment Dynamics*, catalogue no. 61-F0020XCB, 1983-1999):

Size of firm (number of employees)	Number of firms	Percentage of firms that size or smaller	Number of employees (thousands)	Percentage of employees in firms that size or smaller
Fewer than 5	734,069	75.13	1,063.4	8.30
5-19	172,446	92.78	1,676.3	21.38
20-49	44,591	97.34	1,343.9	31.87
50-99	13,995	98.78	961.3	39.38
100-499	9,606	99.76	1,855.1	53.86
500+	2,315	100.00	5,911.6	100.00

These figures include public sector employees. It is difficult to eliminate those employees from the data because many of the categories used by Statistics Canada may include both private and public sector employees (for example, education services and health-care services). However, if the most obvious public sector employees (public administration) are removed, the importance of SMEs in the private sector increases significantly. The vast majority of government service employees (almost 700,000 in total at the beginning of 2000) are in the 500+ category. If employees in this category are removed, SMEs employed 55.7 percent of all employees, while SMEs with fewer than 50 employees employed 33.1 percent of all employees. Furthermore, the statistics do not include self-employed individuals, of whom there were about 2.46 million in 1999.

A comparable table for US SMEs in 1999 indicates the following (source: US Small Business Administration, Office of Advocacy, based on data provided by the United States Department of Commerce, Bureau of the Census, Statistics of US Businesses):

Size of firm (number of employees)	Number of firms	Percentage of firms that size or smaller	Number of employees (thousands)	Percentage of employees in firms that size or smaller
Fewer than 5	3,389,161	60.44	5,606.3	5.10
5-19	1,618,647	89.30	14,782.0	18.42
20-49	381,722	96.11	11,471.2	28.78
50-99	120,126	98.25	8,232.0	36.21
100-499	81,347	99.71	15,637.6	50.30
500+	16,740	100.00	54,976.6	100.00

6   For example, firms with fewer than 50 employees accounted for almost 60 percent of all net job creation in Canada in the 1980s and 1990s: Jim Stanford, *Paper Boom: Why Real Prosperity Requires a New Approach to Canada's Economy* (Ottawa: Canadian Centre for Policy Alternatives and Lorimer, 1999), 128. In the United States, small businesses accounted for over 75 percent of net new jobs in the period 1990 to 1995: US Small Business Administration, Office of Advocacy, "The Annual Report on Small Business and Competition," included in *The State of Small Business: A Report of the President* (Washington, DC: US Government Printing Office, 1999), 50.

7   Some commentators insert a third type of firm between rapid-growth SMEs and the smaller, stable firms. Like the rapid-growth firms, these "middle-market" firms have growth prospects, but they are not expected to grow as quickly as rapid-growth firms. See, for example, Mark Van Osnabrugge and Robert J. Robinson, *Angel Investing: Matching Start-Up Funds with Start-Up Companies—The Guide for Entrepreneurs, Individual Investors, and Venture Capitalists* (San Francisco: Jossey-Bass, 2000), 20-21.

8   Stanford, supra note 6, at 126.

9   Van Osnabrugge and Robinson, supra note 7, at 22.

10   Robert Heilbroner and Lester Thurow, *Economics Explained: Everything You Need To Know About How the Economy Works and Where It's Going*, rev. ed. (New York: Touchstone, 1998), 171.

11   In responding to the suggestion that the success of the United States rests on its history as a "laissez-faire nation," Kuttner, supra note 3, at 219, comments: "[I]t is very hard to believe that the United States in the year 2000 would be a more prosperous nation if the nineteenth-century federal and state governments had never promoted the development of railways and canals, if we had never set up

state universities, agricultural and mechanical colleges, and agricultural extension, if there had been no government program to accelerate development of radio, civil aviation, semiconductors, pharmaceuticals, and basic research in the sciences, and had the immense technical stimulus of World War II and the Cold War never happened."

12   It may be crass, but it is not untrue, to suggest that all three principal players are motivated by the same self-interested end—profit. It has also been suggested, however, that some investors and entrepreneurs are motivated by more altruistic ends, such as the betterment of society through technological advances (developed by the entrepreneur and financed by the investor) or urban renewal. See, for example, Elna B. Tymes and O.J. Krasner, "Informal Risk Capital in California," in Karl H. Vesper, ed., *Frontiers of Entrepreneurial Research*, Proceedings of the 1983 Conference on Entrepreneurial Research (Wellesley, MA: Babson College, 1984), 347-68. This and other studies are considered briefly in Patrizia E. Dal Cin, "Canadian Informal Investors: Towards a Framework for Policy Initiatives" (MMS thesis, Carleton University, School of Business, 1993), 18-19.

13   I apologize at the outset to those readers who have a more romantic notion of "love" or a more spiritual notion of "angels." These terms are common parlance in the world of venture capital and I use them throughout this text, even though they may offend some readers' sense of decorum. As one reviewer of an earlier draft of this book commented: "By and large, these investors are motivated not by a spirit of generosity or other characteristics we normally associate with angels, but by unadulterated greed. Even worse, to talk about 'love' capital is a gross misappropriation of the word love. We love one another. I will even accept that some people love their pets. But 'love' capital? Give me a break!"

14   The term "angel" was originally used in reference to wealthy individuals who backed Broadway productions in the early 1900s.

15   See, for example, Organisation for Economic Co-operation and Development, *Venture Capital and Innovation* (Paris: OECD, 1996). In the United States, the pioneer work on angel investors was undertaken by Professor William E. Wetzel Jr., beginning in the early 1980s. In 1983, Professor Wetzel founded the Center for Venture Research at the Whittemore School of Business and Economics, University of New Hampshire. Since then, a significant body of literature on angel capital has built up across the United States. Some of the earlier literature on angel capital investment in the United States is canvassed in William E. Wetzel Jr., "The Informal Venture Capital Market: Aspects of Scale and Market Efficiency" (1987) vol. 2, no. 4 *Journal of Business Venturing* 299-313.

In Canada, pioneer work in this area was undertaken by Professor Allan L. Riding and others at Carleton University. Probably the most comprehensive study of angel investors in Canada was undertaken in 1993 by Professor Riding and others in a report submitted to the federal Department of Industry, Science and Technology and to the Ontario Ministry of Economic Development and Trade: A. Riding, P. Dal Cin, L. Duxbury, G. Haines, and R. Safrata, *Informal Investors in Canada: The Identification of Salient Characteristics: A Report Submitted to the Federal Department of Industry, Science, and Technology Canada and to the Ministry of Economic Development and Trade of the Province of Ontario* (Ottawa: Department of Industry, Science and Technology, 1993). Some of the earlier literature in Canada and the United States is canvassed in Dal Cin, supra note 12.

16 In a random survey of angels and potential investors (that is, non-angels who have the financial wherewithal to make venture capital investments but either have no desire to make or, though willing, have never made such an investment), Freear, Sohl, and Wetzel found that 49 percent of angels as compared with 3 percent of potential investors would consider allocating 15 percent or more of their portfolios to venture capital deals. If the deals are reduced to 10 percent or more of the portfolios, these percentages increase to 75 percent and 29 percent, respectively. Angels are willing to commit more money to particular deals than potential investors, although both have a liking for smaller deals. More seasoned angel investors—those with a history of venture capital investing—exhibit "a slightly greater willingness to commit a larger amount to financing ventures." John Freear, Jeffrey E. Sohl, and William E. Wetzel Jr., "Angels and Non-Angels: Are There Differences?" (1994) vol. 9, no. 2 *Journal of Business Venturing* 109-23, at 113.

17 See William D. Bygrave and Jeffry A. Timmons, *Venture Capital at the Crossroads* (Boston: Harvard Business School Press, 1992), 185-206.

18 For US statistics, see *2003 National Venture Capital Association Yearbook*, supra note 1, at 22, figure 2.03. In Canada, Macdonald & Associates Limited has prepared comprehensive annual statistics on the formal venture capital industry since 1995. It maintains separate statistics for mezzanine capital and LBO capital but does not publish these statistics with its comprehensive venture capital statistics. Recent though not comprehensive statistical data about the Canadian mezzanine and LBO capital markets are provided in a report prepared by Macdonald & Associates Limited, "Canada's Private Equity Market in 2002," May 2003, available from the Macdonald & Associates Web site at http://www.canadavc.com/.

19 Other flowthrough entities may be used, such as a limited liability partnership (LLP) in Canada and the United States or a limited liability company (LLC) in the United States. For Canadian federal tax purposes, an LLP is treated as a partnership while an LLC is treated as a corporation. Thus, an LLC would not typically be used in Canada for a venture capital fund. For US federal tax purposes, both LLCs and LLPs are treated as partnerships unless the LLC or LLP elects to be treated as a corporation. For more detail, see chapter 6, at note 5 and accompanying text.

20 It is common in Canada for a limited partnership to act as the general partner of the fund, with the general partner of the top-tier partnership being the venture capital firm (or a corporate entity controlled by the venture capital firm) and the limited partners being the individuals of the venture capital firm responsible for the particular venture capital fund. This structure is typically used in order to better secure capital gains treatment for the carried interest obtained by the fund managers. The characterization of the income generated by the carried interest, as well as the income of limited partners of the venture capital fund, is considered further in chapter 6, under the heading "Taxation of Limited Partnership Venture Capital Funds: A Primer."

The limited partnership agreements governing private venture capital funds vary, although there are many common elements. See, generally, Paul A. Gompers and Josh Lerner, *The Venture Capital Cycle* (Cambridge, MA: MIT Press, 1999), 29-55.

21 Management fees based on committed capital have come under close scrutiny in the United States recently as the capital actually called from limited partners and invested in portfolio companies has declined significantly. Since 1998, US private

venture capital funds have had an average fund size of over $100 million, with some funds exceeding $1 billion. The fund size is determined by the amount of capital committed to the fund, and management fees are owed on the capital committed even before the funds are drawn down for investment. General partners have been under pressure to reduce the size of their funds to better reflect the capital that has been invested or is likely to be invested in the near future. See, for example, Nicholas Johnston, "Venture-Capital Fund Fees Seem Steep Now to Investors," *Washington Post*, January 18, 2002. See also Jesse Reyes, "Dry Powder Dilemma: A Critical Look at the Issue That Is Top of Mind for Both GPs and LPs," *Venture Capital Journal*, May 1, 2002, 32-35.

22   For a general discussion of the compensation of general partners and the factors that affect such compensation, see Gompers and Lerner, supra note 20, at 57-94. The limited partnership agreement will typically include some form of "clawback" provision to avoid problems where profitable investments (that is, investments that not only return to the investors their original capital but also provide the general partner with a return through its carried interest) are realized prior to unprofitable investments. The clawback, which may delay the general partner's carried interest or provide some form of holdback, is designed to ensure that the carried interest is calculated when the fund's actual performance is known.

23   As discussed in chapter 8, at notes 1 and 2 and accompanying text, separate entities were typically used in Canada and the United States because of the rules governing financial institutions.

24   Such funds are also used as a method of retaining key employees who may otherwise leave their employment to pursue developing ideas on their own.

25   While the exit strategy is important to both angels and venture capitalists, the latter give much more consideration to possible exit routes than informal venture investors: see Van Osnabrugge and Robinson, supra note 7, at 199-200.

26   See, generally, Jeffrey G. MacIntosh, "Venture Capital Exits in Canada and the United States," in Paul J.N. Halpern, ed., *Financing Growth in Canada* (Calgary: University of Calgary Press, 1997), 279-356.

27   Michael Lewis, *The New New Thing: A Silicon Valley Story* (New York: Norton, 2000), 85.

28   The *2003 National Venture Capital Association Yearbook*, supra note 1, provides statistics on the average and median age of companies at IPO for the period 1998-2002, grouped by industry sector (see ibid., at 75, figure 6.07). In 1999 and 2000, there were 244 and 208 venture-backed IPOs, respectively (ibid., at 75, figure 6.06); in 2001 and 2002, there were only 35 and 22, respectively. Contrast these figures with the total number of IPOs in those years in table 1.1. In 1999, the median age of companies in all of the nine industry sectors except one (biotechnology) was 70 months or less, whereas in 2000, the median age of companies in all industry sectors was 91 months or less. The median age was under 60 months in four sectors in both years. In 2001, the median age of companies in six of the eight sectors in which there were IPOs was 73 months or less, and under 60 months in five sectors. In 2002, there were IPOs in seven sectors, with the median age in four sectors being 62 months or less.

29   Neil Brooks, "Taxation of Closely-Held Corporations: The Partnership Option and the Lower Rate of Tax" (1986) vol. 3, no. 4 *Australian Tax Forum* 381-509, at 483.

30   Van Osnabrugge and Robinson, supra note 7, at 46-47.

31   The conflict was described by Adam Smith:

> The directors of such companies, however, being the managers
> rather of other people's money than of their own, it cannot well be
> expected that they should watch over it with the same anxious vigi-
> lance with which the partners in a private copartnery frequently
> watch over their own. Like the stewards of a rich man, they are apt
> to consider attention to small matters as not for their master's hon-
> our, and very easily give themselves a dispensation from having it.
> Negligence and profusion, therefore, must always prevail, more or
> less, in the management of the affairs of such a company.

Adam Smith, *An Inquiry into the Nature and Causes of the Wealth of Nations*,
vol. 2 (London: Methuen, 1930), 233 (book V, chapter 1, part III, article I). See
also Michael C. Jensen and W.H. Meckling, "Theory of the Firm: Managerial
Behavior, Agency Costs and Ownership Structure" (1976) vol. 3, no. 4 *Journal of
Financial Economics* 305-60.

32   Jensen and Meckling, supra note 31, suggest that risk levels increase when a firm
raises debt while wasteful expenditure increases when a firm raises equity. Increased (and undesirable) risk levels can also stem from employee stock options:
see Calvin H. Johnson, "Stock Compensation: The Most Expensive Way To Pay
Future Cash" (1999) vol. 52, no. 2 *SMU Law Review* 423-54, at 442.

33   The spectacular failure of companies such as Enron and WorldCom, however,
illustrate deficiencies even in the public equity markets.

34   See, for example, Ronald J. Gilson and David M. Schizer, "Understanding Venture Capital Structure: A Tax Explanation for Convertible Preferred Stock"
(2003) vol. 116, no. 3 *Harvard Law Review* 875-916, particularly at 875-76 and
references in footnotes 2-5.

35   Ronald J. Gilson, "Engineering a Venture Capital Market: Lessons from the
American Experience" (2003) vol. 55, no. 4 *Stanford Law Review* 1067-1103, at
1078-81.

36   As Gilson states (ibid., at 1080), "the potential investor knows that it will be
allowed to make the investment only if the existing investors, who have better
information about the project, believe that the investment is unattractive."

37   According to Gilson (ibid., at 1081), "[b]y accepting a contractual structure that
imposes significant penalties if the entrepreneur fails to meet specified milestones based on the business plan's projections—the venture fund's option to
abandon then becomes exercisable—the entrepreneur makes those projections
credible." See also Gompers and Lerner, supra note 20, at 139-69.

38   Brooks, supra note 29, at 484.

39   Kuttner, supra note 3, at 27.

40   Ibid., at 199.

41   Ibid., at 200.

42   Peter K. Eisinger, *The Rise of the Entrepreneurial State: State and Local Development Policy in the United States* (Madison, WI: University of Wisconsin Press,
1988), 241.

43   Ibid., at 247-48.

44　See, generally, AnnaLee Saxenian, *Regional Advantage: Culture and Competition in Silicon Valley and Route 128* (Cambridge, MA: Harvard University Press, 1994).

45　See Meric S. Gertler, Richard Florida, Gary Gates, and Tara Vinodrai, "Competing on Creativity: Placing Ontario's Cities in North American Context," a report prepared for the Ontario Ministry of Enterprise, Opportunity and Innovation and the Institute for Competitiveness and Prosperity, November 2002 (available from the Web site of the Institute for Competitiveness and Prosperity at http://www.competeprosper.ca/institute/). This study applies a similar analysis to that undertaken by Florida (one of the study's co-authors) in the US context: Richard Florida, *The Rise of the Creative Class: And How It's Transforming Work, Leisure, Community and Everyday Life* (New York: Basic Books, 2002).

　　　　Gertler et al.'s study compares four quantitative indicators for city regions: a "talent index," defined as the proportion of the population over 18 with a bachelor's degree or higher; a "bohemian index," defined as the concentration of employees in artistic and creative populations in the city region; the "mosaic index," defined as the proportion of the region's population that is foreign-born; and the "tech-pole index," which is intended to be a proxy for the region's high-technology industrial output (in the study, this index measures the concentration of high-technology employment in the city region). The rationale for the talent and tech-pole indices is self-evident. The "new growth theory" developed by Paul Romer in the mid-1980s (Paul M. Romer, "Increasing Returns and Long-Run Growth" (1986) vol. 94, no. 5 *Journal of Political Economy* 1002-37) and further explored by Robert Lucas in the late 1980s (Robert E. Lucas Jr., "On the Mechanics of Economic Development" (1988) vol. 22, no. 1 *Journal of Monetary Economics* 1-42) postulates that wealth is derived from intellectual capital—the human capacity to be innovative—and that areas with higher levels of human capital grow more rapidly and more dynamically over time.

　　　　In his study of US cities, Florida postulated that the presence of creative capital generally underlies innovation and that creative people are attracted to urban regions that promote diversity. Florida used a number of measures for diversity, including a "gay index" and a "melting pot index." He found that the most influential variable affecting the presence of creativity was a city's "gay index," which measures the prevalence of gay males in the local population (according to Florida, the gay index is a measure of a city's openness to and support of other groups). Gertler et al. used the bohemian index because Statistics Canada did not collect data on same-sex couples prior to 2001 (and the 2001 census data were not yet available), and the mosaic index, Canada's counterpart of Florida's melting pot index, as a measure of a city region's acceptance of diversity.

　　　　In the Gertler et al. report, city (or urban) regions are defined as urban areas with a population of at least 100,000, of which there are 25 in Canada (including 10 in Ontario, the focus of the study) and 284 in the United States. Looking first at Canadian cities only, Gertler et al. found strong, statistically significant, positive correlations between talent and creativity (R^2 value of 0.65) and between technology and creativity (R^2 value of 0.74). Somewhat surprisingly, there was a weaker (although still positive) correlation between talent and technology. The relationships between the mosaic index and both talent and technology were positive but relatively weak (R^2 values of 0.14 and 0.36, respectively). When the same comparisons were applied to US cities, the same positive correlations were found but the strength of the relationships between the various indices declined considerably. For example, the strongest correlation observed in Canada, between the tech-pole index and the bohemian index, had an R^2 value of 0.74, whereas the R^2 value in the corresponding US comparison was only 0.39. A stronger US correlation was found between the talent index and the bohemian index (R^2 value of 0.61, the highest in the US comparisons); the strength of the correlation was comparable in Canada (R^2 value of 0.65).

The results of the Gertler et al. study tend to undermine Florida's theory that a city's propensity for innovation (measured using either the talent or the technology index) is strongly related to the "openness" of the city (measured using the mosaic index in the Gertler et al. study and by the gay index used in Florida's study). As noted above, the R^2 values in the comparisons between the mosaic index and the talent or technology index were relatively weak among Canadian cities; the R^2 values were significantly weaker among US cities (R^2 values of 0.01 and 0.06, respectively).

46   Industry Canada's Canada Community Investment Plan (see chapter 8, at note 137 and accompanying text) is a good example of federal-municipal partnering in this area. Similar plans at the federal and provincial/state levels should be encouraged. In this respect, it is arguable that Canadian cities should have more control over their sources of income, similar to the control enjoyed by US cities: see *National Post*, December 10, 2002.

47   See, for example, Oklahoma's Rural Venture Capital Formation Incentives program, summarized in appendix 6B.

48   For example, according to Josh Lerner, "a substantial body of work on political institutions documents that even in programs that disproportionately benefit particular regions . . . some federal funds are spread across a wide number of states to insure congressional support." See Josh Lerner, "The Government as Venture Capitalist: The Long-Run Impact of the SBIR Program" (1999) vol. 72, no. 3 *Journal of Business* 285-318, at 293, note 3. Lerner's study of the small business innovative research (SBIR) program (discussed in chapter 8, at notes 61-62 and accompanying text) suggests that it suffers from the same political pressures.

49   *2003 National Venture Capital Association Yearbook*, supra note 1, at 30, figure 3.08.

50   The fixed-pool assumption is based on the theory that the number of new SMEs created in any given year is fixed, at least at the national level, by economic and market conditions. Therefore, competition among subnational governments through the use of incentives to attract SMEs leads to a collective loss to the nation as a whole. If the economic theorists who support the fixed-pool assumption are correct, then regional government policy—that is, policy at the state or provincial level or, indeed, policy at a national level where borders are relatively open—is ultimately a "race to the bottom" or "beggar thy neighbour" policy. Governments compete to attract SMEs that would have started up in some location (country/state or province/municipality) in any event. One jurisdiction's success necessarily comes at the price of another's loss. This conclusion holds true, however, only if the investment (for which the governments are competing) would have occurred somewhere else in the absence of the incentive.

51   This third similarity is perhaps an important distinction between the North American economy and the European Union where, despite the openness of borders between countries, the diversity of languages (English, French, German, Spanish,

Portuguese, Italian, Dutch, and Swedish, to name a few) raises barriers that likely reduce the movement of individuals.

52   For example, in Canada, a lower corporate tax rate is applicable at both the federal and provincial level for profits of certain small businesses, up to a threshold. Under section 123 of the Income Tax Act, RSC 1985, c. 1 (5th Supp.), as amended, a Canadian-controlled private corporation (CCPC) is entitled to a tax credit of 16 percent on its first $250,000 (for 2004, increasing to $300,000 in 2005) of income from an active business carried on in Canada (reducing the effective federal tax rate to 13.1 percent). All associated corporations must share the deduction. In addition, where the associated group's taxable capital exceeds $10 million, the small business deduction begins to be phased out and disappears completely for taxable capital of $15 million or more. Most provinces offer a corresponding reduction (although the income thresholds may vary), subject in some provinces to a clawback above specified income levels. For a critical evaluation of a reduced corporate tax rate as a tax subsidy for small business, see Brooks, supra note 29, at 471-509.

53   Canada also provides investment tax credits (ITCs) in section 127 of the Income Tax Act and a deduction for expenditures on scientific research and experimental development (SR & ED) in section 37. The ITC and SR & ED provisions are designed to stimulate new capital expenditure in Canada on certain buildings, equipment, and machinery and to carry out research and development. These incentives are not specific to SMEs and tend to favour large, capital-intensive firms. However, qualifying smaller SMEs are entitled to a refundable ITC in certain cases: see section 127.1 of the Income Tax Act. The credit is refundable to smaller CCPCs whose income does not exceed the business limit determined for the small business deduction. A refundable tax credit can obviously benefit corporations that are not profitable and is, in effect, similar to a government subsidy of particular types of activity. Evidently, refundable ITCs have been critical to the cash flow of small software firms.

54   One Canadian tax incentive that targeted the ability of SMEs to raise conventional financing was the small business development bond (SBDB), governed by section 15.1 of the Income Tax Act. There have been provisions in the Act designed to assist corporations in financial difficulty since 1935, when the income bond provisions were introduced. Under these provisions, interest on an income bond was treated as a dividend for tax purposes, and therefore the provisions permitted "after-tax financing": the financing cost to the issuer of the bond (that is, interest) is not deductible as a dividend, and the recipient of the interest is not taxed because intercorporate dividends are not subject to tax. Under the original income bond provisions, the only precondition for dividend treatment was that the debtor company had to make a profit before interest was payable. In 1978, when the preferred share rules were introduced, the income bond provisions were limited to debtor corporations in financial difficulty (see the definition of "income bond" in subsection 248(1)).

       The SBDB provisions, applicable to corporate borrowers, were introduced in 1980 as a temporary measure to provide some relief against the high cost of borrowing when a corporation was refinancing in a time of financial difficulty or business expansion. The original definition of a qualifying debt obligation included, in addition to a loan made to a corporation in financial difficulty, a loan the proceeds of which were used to make specified expenditures or to acquire specified property. Similar to the income bond provisions, the SBDB provisions allowed financial institutions to provide after-tax financing to qualified small business corporations. The incentive was originally intended to apply to SBDBs issued before the end of 1981. In the November 1981 budget, it was announced that the incentive would be extended for a further year (until the end of 1982) and expanded to include qualifying debt issued to individuals and partnerships (the small business bond [SBB] provisions in section 15.2). When the legislation implementing the 1981 budget measures was introduced (SC 1980-81-82-83, c. 140, sections 8 and 9), however, the definition of qualifying debt obligation in subsection 15.1(3) was amended to eliminate the use of SBDBs for expansion purposes for SBDBs issued after February 1, 1982; the SBB provisions were similarly limited from the outset (November 12, 1981) to businesses in financial difficulty. In effect, the SBDB and SBB provisions were limited to SMEs in financial difficulty and no longer provided an incentive for business expansion.

The SBDB and SBB provisions were further extended to the end of 1985 and again until the end of 1987. After a four-year hiatus, the provisions were reintroduced in the 1992 budget for SBDBs and SBBs issued after February 25, 1992 and before 1993 (again, applicable only to SMEs in financial difficulty). The December 2, 1992 economic statement extended the provisions for two further years, to the end of 1994. The provisions have not been extended since then and have not been reintroduced. Because the maximum period for which a qualified SBDB or SBB could be issued was five years, the incentive effectively disappeared at the end of 1999. For a tax expenditure analysis of the SBDB (and distressed preferred share) provisions, see Tim Edgar, "Distressed Preferred Shares and Small Business Development Bonds: A Tax Expenditure Analysis" (1994) vol. 42, no. 3 *Canadian Tax Journal* 659-708.

55   Later renamed the Defense Advanced Research Projects Agency (DARPA).

2

The Venture Capital Industries
in North America*

Informal Venture Capital

Because the informal venture capital industry is largely invisible, relatively little is known about it. We do know, however, that it is both older and, in terms of the amount of capital invested, larger than the formal venture capital industry. According to a 1996 study by the Organisation for Economic Co-operation and Development (OECD), there was 8 to 10 times more angel capital than formal venture capital available in the United States.[1] The OECD study did not have comparable figures for Canada, although estimates from around the same time period indicated that the pool of Canadian informal venture capital was two to four times bigger than the formal venture capital pool.[2] Both studies predated the explosive growth of the formal venture capital industry, particularly in the United States, in the late 1990s; even so, recent studies indicate that the informal venture capital industry remains larger—in many countries significantly larger—than the formal venture capital industry. According to a 2002 study, informal venture capital represented 61 percent of all venture capital in Canada and approximately 70 percent of all venture capital in the United States.[3] With the sharp decline in capital raised by venture capital funds since 2000, the relative importance of the informal venture capital industry in terms of the amount of capital supplied will certainly increase.

Of greater significance than the amount of money invested is the number of companies financed by informal venture capitalists compared with the number financed by institutional venture capital. Business angels generally invest less money and at earlier stages than formal venture capital investors, and so they finance significantly more companies than are financed by formal venture capital. Business angels are also more geographically dispersed than institutional venture capitalists, which is important because most venture capitalists, especially informal venture capitalists, tend to invest in close geographic proximity to their homes.

As investors at earlier stages in business development and in smaller amounts, informal venture capitalists are complementary to the formal venture capital industry.[4] In the United States, for example, studies suggest that in any

---

* Unless otherwise stated, US monetary amounts are in US dollars and Canadian monetary amounts are in Canadian dollars.

one year, angel investors may invest between $10 billion and $20 billion in over 30,000 ventures, with the average investment in a venture being well under $1,000,000. In contrast, in the early 1990s, the formal venture capital industry invested about $2 billion each year in only 2,000 companies, two-thirds of which were companies in which formal venture capitalists had previously invested (referred to as follow-on financing).[5] More recent data about the formal venture capital industry suggest a similar trend of increasing deal sizes, with a significant portion of the amount invested in follow-on financing.[6] With the increasing size of investments by formal venture capital funds, concerns have been raised about a widening equity gap for smaller investments, especially at the seed and startup stages. A growing equity gap will have an adverse impact on economic growth and is therefore of real concern to governments. For example, of the 500 fastest-growing companies in the United States in 2002 (measured by revenue growth over five years), 41 percent started business with $10,000 or less and 14 percent started with less than $1,000, while 22 percent started with more than $100,000 and only 2 percent received seed capital from formal venture capitalists.[7] It is not surprising that a number of recent government programs in both Canada and the United States have targeted business angels.

Business angels are not a homogeneous group. They range from the once-in-a-lifetime investor to the professional angel who is continually evaluating and monitoring investment opportunities. The consensus emerging from studies that have examined the personal characteristics of business angels is that the "typical" investor is male, middle-aged (45-50 years old) with a high annual income and high net worth, well educated, and with previous business and entrepreneurial experience.[8] As one study points out, however,

> [o]ne consequence of this consensus is the tendency of recent research to assume, implicitly, that the traits of individual venture investors (business angels) are as tightly clustered around the norm as are the traits of venture capital funds. They are not. In terms of their competence to find, evaluate, price, structure, monitor, add value and exit venture deals, individual venture investors range from the successful, cashed-out entrepreneurs on the one hand to individuals with little or no experience with venture investing on the other. At the same time, little is known about the characteristics of high net worth individuals who never ventured where angels dare to tread or about these non-angels' propensity to join the choir, so to speak.[9]

Given the importance of angel investors to the financing of rapid-growth businesses, especially in their earliest stages of development, it is important to examine the factors that influence angel capital investment, particularly the factors that influence the decision to invest and the amount of the investment. Most studies have focused on the distinction between angels and non-angels; little attention has been paid to the distinction between potential angels and non-potential angels. In the context of government policy, this latter distinction is much more important than the former. Freear, Sohl, and Wetzel[10] addressed this issue and also sought to determine what "enticements" might attract potential angels to become real angels. Although their sample size is extremely small in this respect,[11] their findings are worth considering. They sought to determine which of six enticements would increase a potential investor's willingness to invest: help in finding investments; help in evaluating the merits and risks of investment opportunities; help in pricing and structuring; help in monitoring the performance of the investment; participating with other investors; and a reduction in capital gains tax. In all cases, the contrast between interested and non-interested potential investors was marked. For example, the vast majority of non-interested potential investors (a low of 85 percent with regard to reduced capital gains tax and a high of 95 percent with regard to three of the other five enticements) indicated that the enticements would have "little or no effect" on their decision to invest. In contrast, a majority of interested potential investors (a low of 56 percent with regard to help in evaluating investments and a high of 78 percent with regard to help in monitoring performance) indicated that each of the enticements would have "moderate to strong effect."[12] Of the interested investors, 61 percent indicated that a reduction in capital gains tax would have a moderate to strong effect on their decision to invest. While capital gains taxation is thus a factor (it was one of six suggested by the survey), it was not among the most important to interested investors. Furthermore, the study did not ask respondents whether other tax measures (for example, an increased ability to utilize capital losses or an angel capital tax credit) might have a greater effect on their decision to invest.

In a study of the impact of the lifetime capital gains exemption on Canadian angel capital investment,[13] Patrizia Dal Cin found that the differences between non-angels and angel capitalists who were not influenced by the capital gains exemption (referred to in her study as investor group 2) "are so significant that suggestions made [by investor group 2] to increasing new venture investing may not have any relevance to non-investors."[14] She found that there was significantly greater homogeneity between the two groups of angel investors (those influenced by the capital gains exemption, referred to as investor group 1, and those not) than between investor group 2 and non-investors. Angels were more likely to be self-employed than non-angels and had more business experience. Angels also tended to have higher incomes, higher personal assets, and higher net worth. Her results are consistent in this respect with the results of other studies in Canada and the United States. Dal Cin concluded that non-angels do not invest because they do not have the necessary knowledge to evaluate proposals and advise entrepreneurs and because they cannot afford risky investment practices. Dal Cin also asked respondents to list other tax incentives that would influence their decision to invest or to invest more,[15] and took the responses given by all angels (those who would be influenced by the capital gains exemption and those who would not) as indicators of what might increase investment by existing angels. She concluded, however, that such incentives would not influence non-angels to become angels.

Numerous suggestions for incentives were given by the respondents in Dal Cin's study.[16] Interestingly, the ones most frequently made related to corporate taxes and included tax holidays for new businesses, reduced rates for small businesses, and accelerated depreciation for small business assets. The implication is that such incentives would increase the likelihood of success of venture investments. Of course, corporate tax incentives, other than some form of refundable tax credits, are of benefit only to profitable businesses. A limited term tax holiday would not benefit a business that did not become profitable during that term. Similarly, reduced small business rates and accelerated depreciation rates may be of limited use during the early years of a business, when venture capital is needed most. The fact that the responses focused on corporate tax measures suggests that the angels responding to Dal Cin's survey invested predominantly in lifestyle businesses, which are projected to be profitable from startup, in contrast to rapid-growth small and medium-sized enterprises (SMEs), particularly in the high-tech sector.

Unfortunately, Dal Cin's study did not examine whether non-tax factors had greater influence than tax incentives in the decision whether to invest. At this point, it is worth emphasizing that both the Dal Cin study and the study by Freear, Sohl, and Wetzel suggest that government incentives will not make angel investors out of non-angels. At best, tax incentives may compensate for market failures, which are particularly pronounced in the informal venture capital marketplace, by increasing the amount of venture capital that existing angels are willing to invest (or reinvest). Accordingly, tax incentives should target repeat investors.

Formal Venture Capital

Much more is known and has been written about formal venture capital than informal venture capital in both Canada and the United States. The formal venture capital industry is highly organized—primarily through the National Venture Capital Association (NVCA) in the United States and the Canadian Venture Capital Association (CVCA)—and represents a formidable lobby group in each country. The formal venture capital industry is closely monitored in both countries and statistics as to its financial health are released on a quarterly basis, with news stories appearing almost daily.

Detailed statistics on the US formal venture capital industry have been prepared since 1979, while Canadian statistics have been maintained since 1995.[17] Figure 2.1 shows the amount of new formal venture capital raised in the US venture capital industry since 1979. Figure 2.2 shows the amount of new formal venture capital raised in Canada since 1995. The US statistics are limited primarily to venture capital firms investing through limited partnerships with fixed commitment levels and limited lives; the statistics do not include "evergreen funds" (funds that benefit from a continuous infusion of capital from a parent organization) or true captive corporate industrial investment groups without fixed commitment levels. As such, figure 2.1 underreports new capital commitments to formal venture capital in the United States compared with Canada.[18] Figure 2.3 contrasts the formal venture capital industries in the two countries by the amount of capital under management.

**Figure 2.1   US Formal Venture Capital Industry
Annual Capital Commitments, 1979-2002**

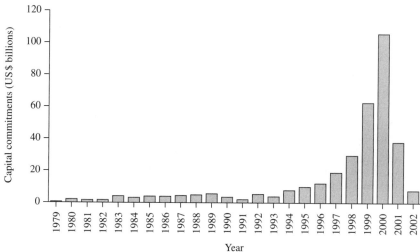

Source: Thomson Venture Economics, *2003 National Venture Capital Association Yearbook* (Arlington, VA and Newark, NJ: National Venture Capital Association and Thomson Venture Economics, 2003), 21, figure 2.03.

**Figure 2.2   Canadian Formal Venture Capital Industry
Annual Capital Commitments, 1995-2002**

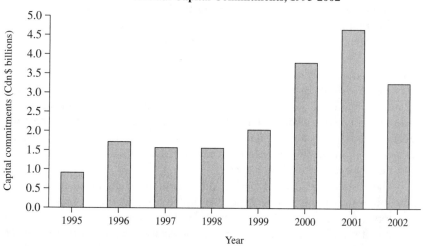

Source: Macdonald & Associates Limited (unpublished).

Figure 2.3   Venture Capital Under Management, 1995-2002

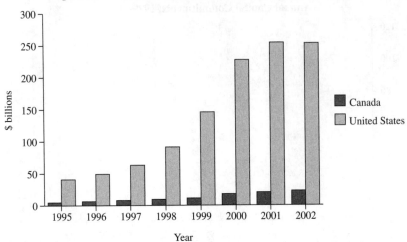

Note: US monetary amounts are in US dollars and Canadian monetary amounts are in Canadian dollars.

Sources: Canada: Macdonald & Associates Limited; United States: Thomson Venture Economics.

Underlying these statistics are fundamental differences, apart from size, in the venture capital industry in the two countries. These differences are best illustrated by comparing the types of funds that make up the industries in the two countries (figure 2.4) and the investors in these funds (figures 2.5 and 2.6). As can be seen in figure 2.4, government funds and labour-sponsored venture capital corporations (LSVCCs) make up over 45 percent of the Canadian formal venture capital industry with private funds making up less than 25 percent, whereas in the United States private funds make up 83 percent of the industry, with the remainder being predominantly funds that are subsidiaries or affiliates of financial institutions or industrial corporations. LSVCCs, the largest source of venture capital in Canada, are solely the product of federal and provincial government tax incentives. The US statistics do not adequately reflect the impact that federal and state venture capital programs have on the formal venture capital industry,[19] although the amount of capital involved is insignificant compared with the aggregate size of the industry.

The distinction in the types of funds that make up the formal venture capital industry in the two countries has a direct impact on the makeup of the investors of the funds in the two countries. In Canada, individuals make up over half of all formal venture capital investors compared to approximately 10 percent in the United States; in both cases the measure is the amount of capital contributed as opposed to the number of individuals involved. Underlying this distinction is

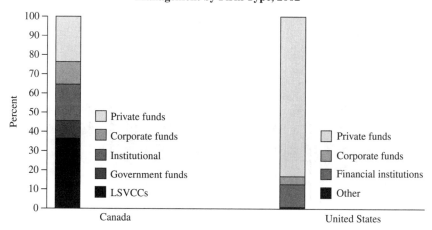

Figure 2.4   Venture Capital Under Management by Firm Type, 2002

Sources: Canada: Macdonald & Associates Limited; United States: Thomson Venture Economics.

a further disparity. Most individual investors in the United States are high-net-worth individuals, whereas individual investors in Canada cover the economic spectrum, with a sizable percentage in the lower and middle income brackets. Canadian individual investors in the formal venture capital industry have invested almost exclusively in LSVCCs,[20] for which there is no income or wealth threshold.

The other significant distinction in investors, obvious from figures 2.5 and 2.6, is the relative importance of pension fund investment in the two countries. Pension funds are the largest single source of formal venture capital in the United States, making up over 30 percent of the venture capital raised each year since 1979, and contributing as much as 60 percent in some years. In contrast, pension funds in Canada have generally contributed less than 10 percent of new venture capital. Although pension fund investment in venture capital has increased in Canada since 2000, these figures mask the extremely limited number of pension funds actually making such investments, and in particular the significant investments by the two government-administered pension funds, the Canada Pension Plan and Quebec Pension Plan.

These important distinctions between the venture capital industries in the two countries are the product of the manner in which each industry has evolved. In both countries, the formal venture capital industry is a phenomenon of the period following the Second World War. This relatively brief history highlights the importance in both countries of government expenditure and regulation in its development. Even in the United States, the modern venture capital industry can hardly be described as a creation of a laissez-faire economy. In fact, the distinction in the makeup of the investors in formal venture capital and the nature of

**Figure 2.5   US Formal Venture Capital Industry
Capital Commitment by Investor Type, 1995-2002**

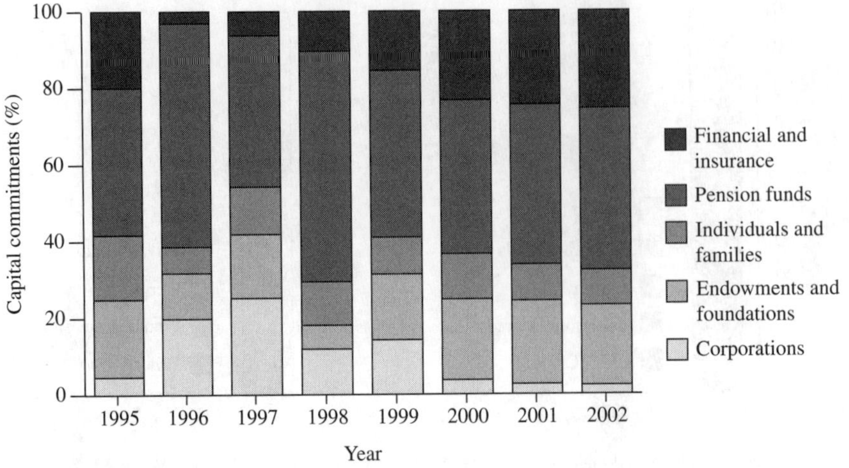

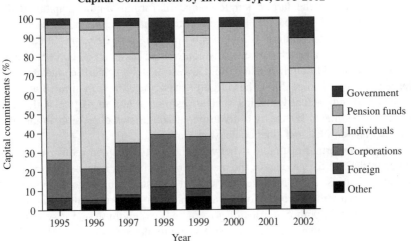

Source: Based on Thomson Venture Economics, *2003 National Venture Capital Association Yearbook* (Arlington, VA and Newark, NJ: National Venture Capital Association and Thomson Venture Economics, 2003), 22, figure 2.04.

**Figure 2.6   Canadian Formal Venture Capital Industry
Capital Commitment by Investor Type, 1995-2002**

Source: Macdonald & Associates Limited (unpublished).

the venture capital funds that make up that industry in the two countries is primarily the product of government expenditure and regulation.

United States[21]

If US history is anything to go by, there is nothing like a war or the threat of one to accelerate research and development (R & D), innovation, increased entrepreneurship, and venture investing. The Second World War had a profound effect on the development of technological industries in the United States. The need for technological innovation to enhance military strategy in a mechanized war created a science and technology boom that was funded largely through federal government research contracts and other forms of government financing. With the Cold War following almost immediately on the heels of the Second World War, government spending on R & D, especially military R & D, remained high, and this spending became an important source of innovation that had a knock-on effect for small companies, particularly in the high-tech sector:

> In a society loath to sanction direct government involvement in the economy, World War II and the Cold War allowed hundreds of billions to flow to research and development. The Pentagon also functioned as an agency of technical diffusion. The system of having a few prime contractors and two tiers of subcontractors required big companies to share advanced process-technology with small ones. Quite unintentionally, this worked as a kind of technological extension system. . . . Indeed, during the postwar boom the two main institutions counteracting the short-term horizons dictated by the structure of American financial markets were the Pentagon, with its very long planning horizons and deep pockets, and the several technically dynamic industries that were regulated cartels.[22]

Universities played a key role in both wartime research and the subsequent growth of small high-tech companies. The Massachusetts Institute of Technology (MIT) and Stanford University, in particular, played instrumental roles in the development of two of the most prolific centres of high-tech startups in the United States, Route 128 around Boston, Massachusetts and Silicon Valley, around Palo Alto in the Santa Clara Valley, California.

MIT was established in 1861 as a technical university and from the beginning encouraged strong ties to private enterprise.[23] MIT was at the centre of the developing radio industry in the first decades of the 20th century. During the Second World War, MIT performed more military research than any other US university, primarily because of the efforts of Vannevar Bush, an electrical engineering professor at MIT.[24] MIT labs received about one-third of the $330 million in contracts awarded by the Office of Scientific Research and Development (OSRD), the first federal agency dedicated to R & D, during the 1940s and 1950s.[25]

Silicon Valley is also a story of Second World War research think tanks and university-spawned entrepreneurs. Fred Terman, known as the godfather of Silicon Valley, had a profound influence on its development. Terman did his doctorate at MIT under Vannevar Bush. After graduating with his PhD in 1924, Terman became a professor of Stanford's radio engineering department (as electronics was then called). Terman inspired two of his students, William Hewlett and David Packard, to start an electronics company to exploit a variable frequency oscillator that was the basis of Hewlett's thesis in Terman's 1938 graduate seminar. Terman loaned them $538 to start producing the oscillator and helped them arrange their first loan, $1,000 from a Palo Alto Bank.[26] The business they created, Hewlett-Packard, was the original cornerstone of Silicon Valley.

During the Second World War, decentralization was an important goal in defence contracting. Decentralization increased military security, eased shipping, and used pockets of unemployed or underemployed workers. From 1940 to 1944, 3.5 million people net moved between states, including 1.5 million to California. About 90 percent of the investment capital raised in the American West during the war was federal government money.[27] Many government offices opened in San Francisco during the war, and by the end of the war, only Washington, DC had more. In the Santa Clara Valley, south of San Francisco, new manufacturing ventures formed around a nucleus of Second World War contractors, including Hewlett-Packard. Stanford did not benefit from military research nearly to the same extent as MIT did during the Second World War. One reason for this may have been that Terman left his faculty position at Stanford in the early 1940s to become the director of Harvard's Radio Research Laboratory. He returned to Stanford in 1946 as dean of engineering and, in many respects, led the development of a high-tech community surrounding Stanford's campus.[28] Stanford University built institutions that would support the growth of technology firms in three primary ways. First, it established the Stanford Research Institute (SRI) in 1946, a comprehensive research organization that developed sites for technology businesses on university land.[29] Stanford also developed intellectual property policies that encouraged faculty to develop commercial applications for their research. Second, it created an honours cooperative program, in which engineers at local firms could enrol in graduate courses directly or through a special televised instructional network.[30] Third, Stanford created the Stanford Industrial Park, one of the first university-owned industrial parks in the world.[31]

Wartime technological advances and pent-up consumer demand set the stage for entrepreneurship and venture investing after the war. The commercial exploitation of wartime technology spawned the high-tech industries along route 128 around Boston, later dubbed "America's technological highway," and around Palo Alto, California, later dubbed "Silicon Valley." Many looked to investment bankers to lead the way in developing a venture capital industry through public markets. As early as 1941, at the annual convention of the Investment Bankers Association of America (IBA), Sumner Slichter, a Harvard economist, proposed a publicly traded venture capital investment trust[32] to finance "promising new or young concerns." The "stock-in-trade" of this trust would be the "ability to investigate the prospects of new concerns." The trust would sell its investments in 5 to 10 years and reinvest the funds in other ventures.[33] In

1945, the IBA's small business committee proposed a venture financing system in which the Federal Reserve would lend to and supervise companies that would invest in new and small businesses—a system much like that created under the Small Business Investment Act (SBIA) of 1958. Congress did not implement the 1945 proposals. Increasingly, analysts suggested that venture capital was something that needed to function outside the public securities markets.

American Research and Development Corp. (ARD), generally hailed as the first non-family venture capital investment company, was founded in Boston on June 6, 1946 by a group of New England businessmen, academics, and university administrators.[34] ARD intended to supply capital to startup firms seeking to exploit military technology for commercial purposes. Among its listed objectives was "to help build the economy." At the time, ARD was unique in its approach to venture investing, particularly its intention to create a venture capital pool from institutions as well as individuals—without government assistance—and to use specialized knowledge to manage it. ARD looked primarily to two groups as potential shareholders: life insurance companies and investment trusts. Under the Investment Company Act of 1940, which governed ARD's public stock offering, there were strict limitations on the ability to attract institutional investors. However, the Securities and Exchange Commission (SEC) issued a ruling that allowed any institutional investor to buy up to 9.9 percent of ARD's stock. Final approval was contingent on ARD's receiving at least $3 million in subscriptions, including at least $1.5 million from institutions, for a proposed $5 million offering.[35]

ARD's approach to venture capital was "classic" in that it invested only in equity, for the long term, and was prepared to live with losers and negative cash flows in the short term.[36] The organizers assured investors that it would not invest in a business unless evaluation showed that its process or product "is commercially practicable and embraces prospects of ultimate profit."[37] In addition, ARD's officers were often involved in the management of their portfolio companies. ARD saw itself as a vehicle through which venture investment could be made safer, through diversification and the provision of expert management. Even so, ARD's success came primarily from a single investment. Just under $70,000 invested in Digital Equipment Corporation (DEC) in 1957 gave ARD a 77 percent ownership interest in the firm.[38] DEC's success by 1960 allowed ARD to raise further funding, this time underwritten by Lehman Brothers, of $8 million based on $74.10 per share (compared with the original issue price of $25 per share). By 1971, ARD's investment in DEC was worth $355 million and a year later ARD was sold to Textron, Inc., a large conglomerate, for the equivalent of $813 per original share. From 1946 until its sale, ARD achieved a 14.7 percent compounded rate of return; without DEC, the return would have been only 7.4 percent.

Despite the brief postwar wave of interest in venture investing, the industry waned considerably and, by 1957, the future of venture financing seemed problematic. Bills to create publicly sponsored venture capital organizations had been introduced in Congress since the 1930s, but they had always been too controversial to pass. The bill that came closest to passing was the IBA's plan (backed by the Economic Development Committee) in 1945 for the Federal

Reserve to charter and subscribe for stock in "capital banks" for small business investment; private investors would also contribute capital and expertise. However, public initiative did not seem necessary once a few private venture capital firms organized following the lead of ARD and a boom rather than the anticipated recession developed.

By mid-1957, facing complaints about industry concentration (primarily from traditional small businesses such as bakeries and glass manufacturers), Congress began new hearings to study the financing problems faced by small businesses.[39] The idea that small business needed a countervailing power to protect it in an economy increasingly dominated by giant corporations emerged in the hearings. Many still opposed a government institution to finance small business. However, the successful launch by the Soviet Union of *Sputnik I* on October 4, 1957 quieted opponents of "national investment companies" (as the organizations were called during the hearings) and galvanized supporters. In addition, members of the financial community pushed for solutions to the venture capital shortfall (which was caused in part by *Sputnik*'s signalling of increased demand for innovative new ventures).

When the Federal Reserve rejected proposals that it oversee a small business program, Senate committee members told it to study the problem and report back. The Federal Reserve's report in 1958[40] focused on venture financing as the key problem. According to the report, limited capital available to many small service ventures was probably justified, since many ventures lacked the growth potential required to attract sophisticated venture capital; their independence and small size provided no benefit other than autonomy for their owners. Technology ventures, on the other hand, had great difficulty attracting capital at the startup stage. The report suggested that investors at the startup stage (primarily individuals rather than venture capital organizations) often pulled out of technology ventures before they realized their potential. Promising technology ventures with capital requirements too small to interest financiers might be "of considerable importance in terms of economic growth and technological dynamics."[41]

The Federal Reserve report and the endorsement of a national program to stimulate venture capital investment were certainly influenced by the *Sputnik* crisis and the public anxiety that followed. After *Sputnik*, government policy makers were more willing to accept a centralized program and were concerned that regional programs that had then been developing[42] might work against national economic interests because of interregional competition.

The Small Business Investment Act of 1958[43] established a new division of the federal Small Business Administration[44] to license, regulate, and channel federal funds to small business investment companies (SBICs). Congress appropriated a $250 million revolving fund to start the SBIC program. The intention of the legislation was to

> stimulate and supplement the flow of private equity capital and long-term loan funds which small-business concerns need for the sound financing of

their business operations and for their growth, expansion, and modernization, and which are not available in adequate supply: *Provided, however,*
That this policy shall be carried out in such manner as to insure the maximum participation of private financing sources.[45]

The House report introducing the SBIA emphasized that there would be "no direct
Federal investment in any small-business concern under this program."[46]

Despite its many shortcomings, the SBIC program was a catalyst in the
development of a thriving private sector venture capital industry. It acted as a
breeding ground for venture capitalists who went on to establish private independent funds. It also allowed banks to enter the venture capital industry, where
they were previously prohibited from investing.[47] From the late 1960s onward,
private venture capital funds became the dominant investors in venture capital
in the United States.

Other government regulation is often cited in the evolution of the private
sector venture capital industry. In particular, changes to pension regulation in 1979
and 1980 as well as the reduction in long-term capital gains tax rates in 1978
are credited for the significant increase in the pool of private venture capital in
the 1980s and 1990s.[48] By 1980, there were 87 active venture capital firms (that
is, that had raised funds within the previous eight years), controlling 124 funds
with \$3.0 billion in capital under management.[49] Over the next 20 years, these
figures grew to 840 active firms controlling 1,679 funds with \$227.2 billion
under management. In 2002, there were 892 active firms controlling 1,798 funds
with \$253.2 billion under management (in all three respects, a slight decline
from the previous year). Table 2.1 shows the growth of the private venture capital
industry over this 22-year period. In addition to the number of firms, number of
funds, and amount of capital under management, table 2.1 shows the estimated
number of industry principals and the capital under management per principal.
This last figure has a direct bearing on the number of companies in which a
venture capital fund is willing to invest and the stage of investment that the fund
will consider. Because principals can monitor only a relatively small number of
investee firms, the significant increase in the amount of capital under management per principal has pushed investment to larger amounts at later stages (and
more investment committed to follow-on financing rather than first-round financing). As a result, companies at the earliest stages of development looking
for smaller amounts of capital have to find alternative sources of financing.

US Pension Fund Venture Capital Investment

Since 1979, pension funds have been the single largest source of capital for
private venture capital funds in the United States. Table 2.2 shows the monetary
commitment to US private venture capital funds by limited partner type for the
years 1979-2002. Table 2.3 shows the percentage committed by each partner type.
As can be seen from the tables, pension funds have contributed at least 30 percent
of total capital in every year and in some years contributed close to 60 percent.

Table 2.1   Growth of US Venture Capital Industry, 1980-2002

Year	Total capital under management (US$ billions)	Venture capital firms	Venture capital funds	Average fund size (US$ millions)	Estimated number of industry principals	Capital under management per principal (US$ millions)
1980	3.0	87	124	24.2	1,131	2.7
1985	17.4	289	542	32.1	2,977	5.8
1990	31.6	386	749	42.2	3,937	8.0
1995	40.9	422	709	57.7	4,262	9.6
1996	49.3	464	772	63.9	4,640	10.6
1997	63.2	540	901	70.1	5,346	11.8
1998	91.4	612	1,074	85.1	5,998	15.2
1999	145.9	734	1,371	106.4	7,120	20.5
2000	227.2	840	1,679	135.3	8,148	27.9
2001	254.3	894	1,811	140.4	8,582	29.6
2002	253.2	892	1,798	140.8	8,474	29.9

Source: Thomson Venture Economics, *2003 National Venture Capital Association Yearbook* (Arlington, VA and Newark, NJ: National Venture Capital Association and Thomson Venture Economics, 2003), 18, figure 1.04.

In mid-2000, private trusteed pension funds controlled approximately $4.8 trillion in assets, with public sector pension funds adding another $2.2 trillion.[50] Wilshire Associates Incorporated publishes an annual report on the financial condition of all state-sponsored defined benefit retirement systems. Its 2002 report covers 93 state retirement systems sponsored by the 50 states and the District of Columbia.[51] The report indicates that state pension portfolios have, on average, allocated 64 percent of assets to equities, including private equity and real estate, and 36 percent to fixed income.[52] Unfortunately, there is no breakdown of private equity between venture capital and other private equity. As an asset allocation, private equity ranged from zero percent, for 41 of the 93 plans,[53] to a high of 15.5 percent, with an average allocation of 3.9 percent. The 2002 Wilshire report sets out the expected return and risk associated with each asset class. Not surprisingly, private equity has the highest expected return and the highest associated risk.[54]

Although, according to the 2002 Wilshire report, 44 percent of state pension plans make no venture capital investments, other state plans are among the largest venture capital investors in the country. In addition to the NVCA yearbook, Thomson Venture Economics also publishes a more detailed analysis of private equity limited partnerships and their limited partners than that given in the yearbook. Its 2001 scorecard lists 36 government pension plans as "major" limited partners, although many more government pension plans make venture capital investments. The market value of the venture capital investments of the 36 major plans ranges from $36 million to $2.024 billion based on their fiscal 2000 statements.[55] Of the 36 government pension plans listed, 32 were state pension plans.[56]

Table 2.2 US Formal Venture Capital Industry Capital Commitment by Limited Partner Type, 1979-2002 (US $ billions)

Limited partner type	1979	1980	1981	1982	1983	1984	1985	1986	1987	1988	1989	1990
Corporations	0.11	0.44	0.31	0.27	0.63	0.55	0.62	0.45	0.56	0.65	1.30	0.26
Endowments and foundations . . .	0.06	0.32	0.21	0.13	0.37	0.21	0.38	0.27	0.49	0.69	0.79	0.50
Individuals and families	0.16	0.35	0.41	0.39	1.05	0.58	0.69	0.53	0.62	0.48	0.38	0.44
Financial and insurance	0.03	0.30	0.27	0.27	0.57	0.49	0.58	0.44	0.76	0.51	0.83	0.35
Pension funds	0.21	0.68	0.41	0.64	1.50	1.32	1.72	2.20	2.00	2.58	2.30	1.98
Total	0.56	2.09	1.60	1.69	4.14	3.15	3.98	3.90	4.44	4.89	5.60	3.53

Limited partner type	1991	1992	1993	1994	1995	1996	1997	1998	1999	2000	2001	2002
Corporations	0.10	0.20	0.32	0.73	0.46	2.42	4.81	3.52	8.91	3.91	0.99	0.18
Endowments and foundations . . .	0.57	1.14	0.46	1.72	2.02	1.45	3.16	1.87	10.80	22.32	8.27	1.60
Individuals and families	0.28	0.65	0.28	0.95	1.67	0.83	2.37	3.36	6.03	12.48	3.57	0.70
Financial and insurance	0.12	0.94	0.45	0.76	1.99	0.37	1.19	3.07	9.73	24.65	9.29	1.95
Pension funds	1.00	2.46	2.38	3.67	3.83	7.10	7.51	17.85	27.30	42.43	15.82	3.24
Total	2.06	5.38	3.90	7.83	9.97	12.16	19.04	29.68	62.77	105.80	37.94	7.67

Note: Columns may not add up due to rounding.

Source: Thomson Venture Economics, 2003 National Venture Capital Association Yearbook (Arlington, VA and Newark, NJ: National Venture Capital Association and Thomson Venture Economics, 2003), 22, figure 2.04.

Table 2.3   US Formal Venture Capital Industry Capital Commitment by Limited Partner Type, 1979-2002 (percent)

Limited partner type	1979	1980	1981	1982	1983	1984	1985	1986	1987	1988	1989	1990
Corporations	19.01	21.22	19.41	16.17	15.29	17.38	15.46	11.52	12.69	13.18	23.27	7.27
Endowments and foundations	11.52	15.05	13.03	7.58	9.02	6.60	9.63	6.91	11.14	14.04	4.04	14.12
Individuals and families	28.07	16.83	25.61	23.09	25.48	18.36	17.43	13.57	13.93	9.74	6.83	12.55
Financial and insurance	4.72	14.40	16.78	15.96	13.87	15.57	14.47	11.41	17.16	10.51	4.81	9.95
Pension funds	36.84	32.27	25.50	37.70	36.30	41.97	43.09	56.51	45.02	52.72	41.15	56.15

Limited partner type	1991	1992	1993	1994	1995	1996	1997	1998	1999	2000	2001	2002
Corporations	4.74	3.63	8.25	9.30	4.63	19.87	25.24	11.87	14.20	3.70	2.60	2.30
Endowments and foundations	27.52	21.24	11.89	21.93	20.28	11.90	16.61	6.31	17.20	21.10	21.80	20.90
Individuals and families	13.55	12.10	7.28	12.13	16.76	6.84	12.46	11.32	9.60	11.80	9.40	9.10
Financial and insurance	5.99	17.40	11.65	9.70	19.99	3.06	6.23	10.36	15.50	23.30	24.50	25.50
Pension funds	48.32	45.75	60.92	46.88	38.41	58.36	39.46	60.14	43.50	40.10	41.70	42.20

Note: Columns may not total 100 percent due to rounding.

Source: Same as table 2.2.

According to the 2002 Wilshire report, there were 17 state retirement systems from 11 states[57] with private equity investments forming more than 10 percent of their asset allocation in their most recent reports (primarily 2001). Table 2.4 lists the 11 state retirement systems (or the state funds' manager, where the various public sector funds are centrally managed), indicating their private equity asset allocation from the Wilshire report together with various data from the funds' 1998 and 2000 fiscal periods based on statistics prepared by Thomson Venture Economics.

In table 2.4, the "private equity" allocation from Wilshire and the "alternative assets" allocation from Thomson Venture Economics both refer to the same asset class: private equity. Thomson Venture Economics divides private equity into two subclasses: venture capital and buyout/other.[58] The fair market value of only venture capital investments is listed in the table; the fair market value of buyout/other private equity investments for each state retirement system in 1998 or 2000 can be obtained simply by subtracting the venture capital figure from the total alternative asset figure for the particular year (likewise, the percentage of private equity composed of buyout/other can be obtained by subtracting the percentage for venture capital from 100). A few observations from the table are worth mentioning. First, a number of state pension fund systems increased their private equity allocation significantly between 1998 and 2000, and for some that trend continued into 2001. In three states—Connecticut, Louisiana, and Pennsylvania—the allocation to private equity tripled over the first two years. Second, the amount of private equity allocated to venture capital varies significantly across the 11 states, ranging from a low of 1.9 percent to a high of 75.5 percent. The discrepancies stem from historical choices made by the state pension funds regarding the type of private equity in which to invest. In particular, it is difficult for a pension fund to invest in the more reputable venture capital funds if the pension fund does not have a history of making venture capital investments. That may account for the low allocations to venture capital by Oregon State Treasury and Louisiana Teachers' Retirement System. Third, the table does not divide the pension funds' private equity investments between those made directly (that is, capital invested directly in SMEs) and those made indirectly (that is, capital invested in private equity funds). Of the state pension funds listed in table 2.4, only four are listed by Thomson Venture Economics among those including direct investments in their private equity portfolio in 2000. In all four cases, the amount invested directly is insignificant compared with the amount invested in private equity funds.[59] These figures should be contrasted with those for Canadian public sector pension funds, in table 2.5 below.

In addition to the significant amount of public sector pension fund investment in venture capital, many US private sector pension plans have invested in venture capital. The Thomson Venture Economics 2001 statistics list 25 private sector corporate pension plans among major venture capital limited partners. The market value of their venture capital investments, at the end of their 2000 fiscal periods, ranged from $29 million to $2.082 billion, and had an aggregate value of $13.861 billion.[60] Five corporate pension funds were also listed among investors that made direct investments in SMEs.[61]

Table 2.4   US Public Sector Pension Fund Venture Capital Investments, 1998 and 2000[a]

Pension fund or pension fund manager	Private equity allocation (%)[b]	Aggregate assets (US$ millions)	Alternative assets (based on Thomson Venture Economics data) (US$ millions)	(%)	Market value of venture capital investments (US$ millions)	Portion of alternative assets comprising venture capital (%)
Michigan State Treasury (Michigan PERS)	15.5					
1998		42,000	3,751	8.9	743	19.8
2000		52,627	8,189	14.6	1,314	16.0
State of Connecticut Retirement Trust Funds	12.7					
1998		18,000	719	4.0	268	37.3
2000		21,900	2,565	11.7	979	38.2
Louisiana Teachers' Retirement System	12.6					
1998		12,000	364	3.0	6	1.6
2000		13,770	1,621	11.8	149	9.2
Virginia Retirement System	12.0					
1998		32,000	1,729	5.4	692	40.0
2000		41,000	3,935	9.6	1,909	48.5
Washington State Investment Board	11.7[c]					
1998		35,000	3,226	9.2	193	6.0
2000		46,552	5,534	11.9	1,666	30.1

(Table 2.4 is concluded on the next page.)

Table 2.4   Concluded

Pension fund or pension fund manager	Private equity allocation (%)[b]	Aggregate assets (US$ millions)	Alternative assets (based on Thomson Venture Economics data)		Market value of venture capital investments (US$ millions)	Portion of alternative assets comprising venture capital (%)
			(US$ millions)	(%)		
Oregon State Treasury	11.6					
1998		30,000	4,493	15.0	100	2.2
2000		41,000	5,447	13.3	106	1.9
Colorado Public Employees' Retirement Association	11.2[c]					
1998		25,000	2,349	9.4	423	18.0
2000		30,900	3,460	11.2	877	25.3
Delaware Public Employees' Retirement System	10.4					
1998		4,500	315	7.0	151	47.9
2000		5,595	650	11.6	491	75.5
Pennsylvania State Employees' Retirement System	10.0					
1998		22,000	739	3.4	328	44.3
2000		27,877	2,885	10.3	1,171	40.6

[a] Funds included with alternative asset allocation exceeding 10 percent based on Wilshire 2002 Report. [b] For 2001 unless otherwise noted. [c] For 2000.

Sources: The private equity allocation is from Wilshire Associates Incorporated, "2002 Wilshire Report on State Retirement Systems: Funding Levels and Asset Allocation," August 12, 2002, available from Wilshire's Web site at http://www.wilshire.com/. The remaining data are from Thomson Financial Venture Economics, *LP Roundup: Venture Capital 1999* (New York: Thomson Financial/Securities Data Publishing, 1999); and Thomson Financial Venture Economics, *2001 Investment Benchmark Reports: LP Analytics* (New York: Thomson Financial/Securities Data Publishing, 2001).

Viewed in isolation, the US venture capital statistics suggest a thriving venture capital industry, fuelled primarily by pension funds and other non-taxable entities, including endowments and foundations. As table 2.3 indicates, since 1985, non-taxable entities have contributed more than half—and in many years significantly more than half—of all new capital to venture capital funds every year. However, many US pension plans are invested to capacity in private equity (including venture capital) and, as a result of the recent downturn in the public equity markets, are overinvested in venture capital.[62] Pension plans may therefore be reducing their commitments to venture capital funds.[63]

In closing this overview of the US formal venture capital industry, it is worth emphasizing the importance of government expenditure and regulation both past and present. The perception that the US venture capital industry can function without government expenditure is wrong. First, the US venture capital industry remains largely confined to specific geographic regions: Silicon Valley, Route 128, and various other pockets of activity, including New York, Seattle, and Houston. Although venture capital funds do invest outside their local region, primarily through syndicated investments, most formal venture capital investment is localized.[64] As a result, beginning in the mid-1980s and continuing into the present, numerous states in the United States, particularly in the "nation's midsection,"[65] have developed a variety of venture capital programs, many of them funded through tax incentives, to stimulate venture capital investment and the development of technology-based businesses within the state. Although these programs are small in comparison to the aggregate size of US venture capital funds, collectively they have cost the states hundreds of millions of dollars in forgone taxes. For some states, there would be no formal venture capital industry at all were it not for these tax incentive programs. That said, it is at least questionable whether these programs can be considered "successful." The various state venture capital tax incentive programs are considered in chapter 5 (tax credits for direct investment in small businesses) and chapter 6 (tax credits for investment in venture capital funds). In addition to these tax incentive programs, a number of states have authorized the use of public sector pension fund assets to enhance venture capital investment within the state. A few examples of state pension fund initiatives are considered in chapter 7.

Second, the perception that the US venture capital industry can function without government expenditure ignores the continued importance of government involvement, in terms of industry regulation as well as direct expenditure or direct subsidies, in certain key industries, particularly in the high-tech sector. Government regulation and spending in key industry sectors has often been and continues to be justified in the interests of national security. Defence spending by the Pentagon as well as research partnerships directly targeting businesses in the high-tech sector, spawned in response to the *Sputnik* crisis in 1957 and developed throughout the Cold War, continue to be an important form of government financial support of rapid-growth SMEs and research universities. Although government defence spending waned during the 1990s, it has been renewed since September 11, 2001. A selection of non-tax government programs are considered in chapter 8.

Canada[66]

Canada's formal venture capital industry is generally considered to have had its start in 1952 with the establishment of Charterhouse Canada Limited, a subsidiary of UK-based Charterhouse Group Limited. It was the only corporation formally involved exclusively in venture capital until 1962, when Canadian Enterprise Development Corporation Limited (CED) began operations.[67] CED was modelled on the success of ARD in the United States. In the late 1960s and early 1970s, a number of other venture capital firms were established.[68] These early venture capitalists had similar characteristics. Generally, they did not syndicate investments (a practice that was common by then in the United States). They took minority positions in portfolio companies, ranging from 20 percent to 49 percent, had long time horizons with no returns anticipated for at least 5 years and sometimes as long as 10 years, placed little emphasis on liquidity, and were essentially passive as investors.[69]

As a result of liquidity problems in the early to mid-1970s,[70] few new players entered the venture capital arena. A number of firms stopped making new investments and eventually liquidated their portfolios. The remaining firms gradually changed their investment philosophies, particularly regarding the level of involvement in portfolio firms. A new emphasis on management capabilities led to other changes in the venture capital industry, including the demand for larger ownership interests in portfolio firms and increasing specialization among staff at venture capital firms.

A number of federal government studies released in the 1970s pointed to the need for more venture capital, and in some cases criticized income tax and other legislation for discouraging investment in venture capital.[71] A 1973 report on foreign direct investment in Canada concluded that Canadian capital markets "show evidence of weaknesses and gaps in respect of risk taking and entrepreneurship."[72] These gaps and weaknesses included venture capital for new and small firms and expansion capital for SMEs. The report suggested that the problem was not necessarily a lack of capital but matching investors with businesses in need of capital. The report also suggested that "[t]he shortage of entrepreneurship in the financial industry frustrates the kind of industrial inter-mediation—the drawing together of financing and all the many other components to bring a new enterprise into being—which could permit a larger proportion of major projects to be undertaken in Canada by Canadians."[73]

Government investment was an important catalyst for venture investment in the 1970s. In 1971, the federal government became active in the venture capital market when the Canadian Development Corporation (CDC) was established through a special act of Parliament. CDC invested $10 million through its wholly owned subsidiary, CDC Ventures Inc., for equity interests in three private venture capital companies, Venturetek International Limited (Toronto),[74] Innocan Investments Ltd. (Montreal),[75] and Ventures West Capital Ltd. (Vancouver).[76] Unlike the more traditional venture capitalists in Canada, these firms preferred majority control and were prepared to be actively involved in the management of their portfolio companies. In short, they behaved like US private venture capital firms.

Federal funds for venture capital were also made available through the Federal Business Development Bank (FBDB), which replaced the Industrial Development Bank (IDB) in 1974. The IDB was established in 1944 to help wartime manufacturers convert their facilities to commercial uses. The IDB had been a lender of last resort, providing chattel mortgages to SMEs. Although the FBDB was likewise to be a lender of last resort, it was also supposed to take greater risks and was explicitly permitted to provide equity financing to SMEs. The FBDB's successor, the Business Development Bank of Canada (BDC), which is discussed further in chapter 8, remains an important source of venture capital in Canada. In particular, it is no longer considered a lender of last resort; when the BDC succeeded the FBDB in 1995, the bank's mandate was expanded considerably to promote venture capital investment in order to demonstrate to commercial banks that investment in new economy businesses could be commercially successful.

In May 1978, the federal government proposed a scheme for venture enterprise investment companies (VEICs), based on the SBIC program initiated in the United States 20 years earlier. The scheme would provide limited tax incentives to shareholders and key employees of VEICs as well as government loan guarantees to leverage private equity raised by VEICs. Although the scheme was never introduced, several provinces introduced venture capital corporation (VCC) schemes, based loosely on the SBIC regime in the United States, beginning in the mid-1970s. The VCC schemes used various incentives, including tax credits, grants, and low-interest government loans to promote private sector investment in VCCs. VCC schemes began in 1976 with Quebec's SODEQ legislation.[77] Over the next 10 years, the other provinces introduced their own VCC schemes to enhance the supply of venture capital for SMEs,[78] although many of the provincial schemes have since been cancelled or replaced, typically by LSVCC schemes, discussed below. The current VCC schemes are considered in chapter 6.[79]

The early 1980s saw a resurgence of private venture capital and the formation of the first Canadian venture capital limited partnerships. Limited partnerships were already the predominant venture capital investment vehicle in the United States, largely because they permitted the commingling of funds from taxable and tax-exempt entities without penalizing the tax-exempt investors. It is also easier to evaluate the performance of venture capital limited partnerships because they tend to have a limited life. The primary directory of venture capital funds in Canada listed 535 funds in September 1985, of which 75 were financed exclusively by the private sector and 460 had government sponsorship or support of some form.[80]

Canadian Pension Fund Venture Capital Investment

Until the mid-1980s, federal tax legislation was considered a major impediment to the development of the Canadian venture capital industry. Pension investment was stifled by the foreign property rules in the Income Tax Act, which treated investment in a partnership (for example, a venture capital limited partnership) as a foreign property and which limited foreign property investment to 10 percent of a pension fund's capital. Pension regulatory legislation also had an adverse impact on pension venture capital investment. In addition, in the early 1980s, Revenue Canada (the predecessor of the Canada Revenue Agency) threatened to reassess a number of venture capital companies on the basis that the gains realized on the disposition of their portfolio companies were business income rather than capital gains. Evidently, this practice had "a major disquieting effect" on the industry.[81]

The 1985 federal budget introduced a number measures to stimulate venture capital investment by registered pension plans and other retirement plans, including:

- the extension of "qualified investments" for tax-favoured personal retirement funds (registered retirement savings plans [RRSPs]) to private corporations engaged in active business and to prescribed VCCs;
- small business investment corporation (CanSBIC) provisions;
- small business investment limited partnership (SBILP) provisions;
- small business investment trust (SBIT) provisions; and
- the three-to-one leveraging of "small business investments" for the purpose of the foreign property tax penalty applicable to various retirement savings plans.

All of these measures, together with the qualified limited partnership (QLP) provisions also introduced in 1985, are considered in chapter 7, because they target investment from retirement savings, particularly employer-sponsored pension funds. Coincident with these amendments and in order to further promote venture capital investment by pension funds, the federal government introduced amendments to the federal pension legislation that were similar to the changes introduced in the United States six years earlier.

These amendments were initially successful in increasing pension fund venture capital investment, but this success was relatively short-lived. Figure 2.7 compares venture capital investment by pension funds in Canada and the United States from 1985 to 2002. As shown in the figure, Canadian pension fund commitments increased significantly in 1986 and 1987, reaching almost 10 percent of US commitments, ignoring currency exchange rates (although the US figures do not include mezzanine and buyout funds, and at the time the Canadian figures did not adequately distinguish between venture capital funds and mezzanine and buyout funds).[82] In both countries, venture capital investment

Figure 2.7   Canadian and US Pension Fund Investment
in Venture Capital, 1985-2002

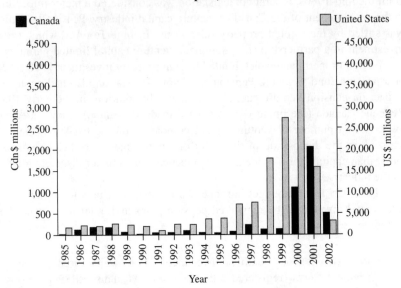

Sources: Canada: Macdonald & Associates Limited (unpublished); United States: Thomson Venture Economics, *2003 National Venture Capital Association Yearbook* (Arlington, VA and Newark, NJ: National Venture Capital Association and Thomson Venture Economics, 2003), 22, figure 2.04.

by pension funds declined in 1989 through 1991 during the recession. However, US pension fund commitments rebounded in 1992 and grew considerably through the remainder of the 1990s, while most Canadian pension funds that fled venture capital investments in 1989 and 1990 never returned.

In 1997, when the level of Canadian pension fund investment finally returned to the level of a decade earlier, it was only 3.1 percent of US pension investment (ignoring currency exchange rates). That dropped to 0.7 percent in 1998 and 0.5 percent in 1999. In 2000, when there was a resurgence of pension investment in Canada, it was still less than 3 percent of US pension fund investment (again, ignoring currency exchange rates).[83] In addition, while numerous Canadian pension funds invested in the 1980s, the recent resurgence (if one can call it that) involves only a handful of funds. In 2001, Canadian pension fund venture capital investment jumped to almost 13 percent of US pension fund venture capital investment,[84] although over 92 percent of the Canadian investment came from a single investment of $1.9 billion by the Caisse de dépôt et placement du Québec ("the Caisse") in its technology venture capital subsidiary, CDP Capital-Technology Ventures (formerly, CDP Sofinov). In 2002, Canadian pension fund investment increased to 15.7 percent of US pension fund investment[85]—or, perhaps more accurately, US pension fund investment declined to 15.7 percent of Canadian pension fund investment—although a significant portion of Canadian pension fund investment came from the federal government-administered retirement fund, the Canada Pension Plan (CPP).

Both the Caisse and the CPP were established in 1965 when the federal government set up a national government-administered pension plan to supplement old age security. All of the provinces except Quebec joined the national plan. Quebec created the Quebec Pension Plan (QPP) and established the Caisse to manage the funds in the QPP. The Caisse has grown to become by far the most significant venture capital investor in Canada (until 2002) and, in fact, the largest venture capital investor in North America, with venture capital investments worth more than double those of the next largest investor. Unlike the CPP, the Caisse's statutory investment mandate has always included a social investment policy component: investment that benefits the economic development of Quebec.[86] It has been in furtherance of this mandate that the Caisse has made substantial investment in Quebec SMEs. However, the Caisse has been the subject of intense criticism in recent years for putting this economic development mandate ahead of the interests of its investors. Particular criticism has been levied at its underwriting of high-cost takeovers to prevent the loss of Quebec ownership of businesses; its significant investment in Quebec SMEs, especially in the retail and fashion trade and in telecommunications companies; and the significant cost overruns that it incurred in building its new head-office premises in Montreal. In late 2002, following the appointment of a new chief executive officer, the Caisse underwent sweeping changes that will significantly reduce its future commitment to venture capital investments.

As the Caisse's importance as a venture capital investor has been waning, the CPP has become one of the largest single investors in private equity in Canada. From its creation in 1965 until 1999, the only investments permitted by the CPP were provincial government (other than Quebec) bonds—the bargain made by the federal government to attract provincial government support for the national retirement scheme. In response to concerns raised in the mid-1990s that the CPP would run out of money within 20 years due primarily to the aging population in Canada, significant reforms to the plan were introduced. In addition to raising contribution rates, the government expanded the CPP's permitted investments in order to increase the return that the assets generated. The Canada Pension Plan Investment Board (CPPIB) was established in 1997 to invest excess contributions to the CPP and the proceeds from maturing provincial government bonds. Under legislation passed in 2003, the management of all CPP assets will be transferred to the CPPIB over a three-year period. The CPPIB made its first private equity investments in 2001 and since then has committed hundreds of millions of dollars to venture capital funds in Canada and the United States. The role of government-sponsored pension fund investment in Canada's venture capital industry, including investment by the Caisse and the CPP, is discussed in chapter 7.

The Thomson Venture Economics 2001 scorecard lists five Canadian pension funds that at the time had made significant private equity investments. Table 2.5 is similar to and should be contrasted with table 2.4 for US state pension funds.

Table 2.5 Canadian Public Sector Pension Fund Venture Capital Investments, 1998 and 2000

Pension fund	Aggregate assets (US$ millions)	Alternative assets (US$ millions)	Alternative assets (%)	Market value of venture capital investments (US$ millions)	Portion of alternative assets comprising venture capital (%)	Portion of alternative assets directly invested (%)
Caisse de dépôt et placement du Québec						
1998	46,000	4,598	10.0	2,286	49.7	76.1
2000	84,700	9,000	10.6	4,154	46.2	84.1
Ontario Teachers' Pension Plan Board						
1998	40,000	1,747	4.4	47	2.7	40.1
2000	50,000	2,691	5.4	138	5.1	55.3
Ontario Municipal Employees Retirement System						
1998	21,600	540	2.5	0	0	75.9
2000	25,000	778	3.1	69	8.9	68.3
Province of British Columbia Pension Funds						
1998	35,000	500	1.4	175	35.0	—
2000	45,000	703	1.6	289	41.1	—
Hospitals of Ontario Pension Plan						
1998	9,800	297	3.0	76	25.6	4.4
2000	13,000	514	4.0	141	27.4	5.4

Sources: Thomson Financial Venture Economics, *LP Roundup: Venture Capital 1999* (New York: Thomson Financial/Securities Data Publishing, 1999); and Thomson Financial Venture Economics, *2001 Investment Benchmark Reports: LP Analytics* (New York: Thomson Financial/Securities Data Publishing, 2001).

In addition to the relatively few Canadian pension funds that have invested in venture capital, table 2.5 illustrates a broad range of investment management styles and alternative asset allocations for Canadian pension funds. For example, the Caisse has invested almost half of its private equity in venture capital and manages over 80 percent of its private equity portfolio. The Ontario Teachers' Pension Plan Board and the Ontario Municipal Employees Retirement System (OMERS), on the other hand, are invested primarily in LBO and mezzanine funds and manage over half of their private equity portfolios. BC Pension Funds and the Hospitals of Ontario Pension Plan (HOOPP) have significant venture capital investments, although less than half of their respective private equity portfolios, and both funds use external asset managers almost exclusively.

With a few important exceptions, employer-sponsored pension plans have not played a significant role in the Canadian venture capital industry since 1990, and have never played the role that many commentators believe that they should.[87] The reasons why and possible means to increase their participation in venture capital investment are explored in chapter 7.

Canadian Individual Retirement Savings Venture Capital Investment

Instead of pension funds, individual investors from across the economic spectrum have become the largest investors in formal venture capital funds in Canada. The reasons can be traced back to the same 1985 federal budget that sought to increase pension fund investment in Canada. The 1985 budget introduced a matching federal tax credit for individuals who invested in a provincial LSVCC. At the time of the budget, there was in fact only one provincial LSVCC, the Fonds de solidarité des travailleurs du Québec (FSTQ), although the federal government expected, indeed "encouraged other provinces to come along with their regimes to encourage labour-sponsored venture capital funds."[88] Over the next 10 years, a number of provinces did so. Some provinces established their own legislative requirements for LSVCCs;[89] others extended a provincial credit to certain federally registered LSVCCs (introduced in the 1988 federal budget).[90] Even though a number of provincial governments had enacted various types of VCC programs in the late 1970s and early 1980s, it was the LSVCC program that attracted federal government support. The federal LSVCC tax credit and the various provincial LSVCC programs introduced to take advantage of the matching federal tax credit have proven to be the catalyst that created the largest source of venture capital in Canada. It created a pool of capital so large that by the end of the 1996 RRSP season, LSVCCs had raised sufficient capital to satisfy venture capital needs for more than three years.[91] Today, there are almost 50 LSVCCs operating across Canada, although the vast majority are in Ontario, managing over $8 billion in capital.

Table 2.6 compares the amount of new capital raised by LSVCCs and the amount of capital managed by LSVCCs with total new venture capital and total capital under management in the Canadian formal venture capital industry from

**Table 2.6   Importance of LSVCCs in the Canadian
Formal Venture Capital Industry**

Year	Total VC raised (Cdn $ millions)	VC raised by LSVCCs (Cdn $ millions)	VC raised by LSVCCs (%)	Total VC under management (Cdn $ millions)	VC managed by LSVCCs (Cdn $ millions)	VC managed by LSVCCs (%)
1995	908	591	65	4,850	1,794	37
1996	1,720	1,221	71	6,444	3,061	48
1997	1,573	628	40	8,014	3,821	48
1998	552	1,564	35	9,435	4,368	46
1999	2,044	975	48	11,244	5,161	46
2000	3,787	1,386	37	17,740	6,295	36
2001	4,662	1,760	38	20,239	8,386	41
2002	3,248	1,754	54	22,469	8,199	36

VC   Venture capital

Source: Macdonald & Associates Limited (unpublished).

1995 through 2002. These figures reflect the continuing importance of LSVCCs to the Canadian venture capital industry as a whole.

Although the relative importance of LSVCCs has declined somewhat since 1999, a few points should be borne in mind. First, the amount raised by private independent funds in 2000 was substantial: $1,616 million, almost four times the amount raised in the previous year of $412 million. The amount raised by private independent funds declined to $483 million in 2001, although it rebounded to $1,126 million in 2002 (when the amount raised by US private equity funds declined significantly). Second, of the $4,662 million total venture capital raised in 2001, $1,900 million represented a single investment by the Caisse in its technology venture capital subsidiary. If this single investment were excluded, LSVCC investment represented 64 percent of total venture capital raised in 2001. Third, the CPP became a significant venture capital investor in 2002, investing over $293 million in Canadian venture capital funds (and even more in US venture capital funds). Excluding the CPP investment, LSVCCs accounted for almost 60 percent of new venture capital raised in 2002. Finally, despite the fact that LSVCCs have raised over 53 percent of all new venture capital since 1995, the proportion of the total capital managed by LSVCCs has declined by almost 0.5 percent, suggesting that they have not performed as well as other venture capital funds. LSVCCs now account for approximately 36.5 percent of venture capital under management in Canada. The LSVCC regime, including its evolution, is considered in detail in chapter 6.

Venture Capital and the Tech Boom and Bust: Where to from Here?

Before leaving the history of the venture capital industry in Canada and the United States, it is worth highlighting the different growth patterns of the industries in the past five years as contrasted in figures 2.1 and 2.2. Venture capital investment grew significantly in both countries from 1998 to 2000, although the increase in the United States was phenomenal in comparison to that in Canada or, indeed, by any measure. Annual investment in US venture capital funds grew fivefold between 1997 and 2000. In contrast, annual investment in Canadian venture capital funds only doubled over the same period. From 2000 to 2002, however, investment in US venture capital funds shrank significantly (the amount of capital raised in 2002 was less than 10 percent of the total raised in 2000), while in Canada new venture capital investment increased in 2001 before retreating in 2002; even so, 2002 was the third-best year for new venture capital commitments in Canada (after 2001 and 2000), and was less than 15 percent off the amount raised in 2000 (and 30 percent off the amount raised in 2001). The retraction in the US venture capital industry may simply reflect the fact that the phenomenal growth in size of US formal venture capital funds was not matched by increased investment over the same years, leaving a significant overhang of uninvested capital in 2001 and 2002. As of the end of 2001, Thomson Venture Economics estimated that US private equity funds had over $220 billion of uninvested capital, of which venture capital funds accounted for over $100 billion.[92] With this much uninvested capital and the reduced pace of investing in small businesses by venture capital funds, there has been little need for venture capital fund managers to raise new capital since 2000. With venture capital funds investing only $21.2 billion in 2002, there remains a significant overhang of uninvested capital in US venture capital funds. In contrast, there is significantly less overhang of uninvested capital in Canadian venture capital funds. The concern is whether the retraction in the US venture capital industry reflects more innate problems in the industry—for example, an increased conservatism on the part of investors, making fundraising a problem even when the overhang is eliminated.

The Canadian venture capital industry currently relies significantly on government incentives, and it may well be that the Canadian venture capital industry must rely more on government incentives than the US venture capital industry viewed as a whole. Given Canada's close geographic proximity to the United States and the relative ease of movement of capital and persons across the border, particularly individuals involved in the high-tech sector, the problems facing Canada in developing both entrepreneurship and a venture capital industry to support it are akin to the problems faced by many US states outside the pockets of activity concentrated around regions such as Silicon Valley and Route 128. It may be more appropriate to compare Canada's reliance on government initiatives—particularly tax expenditures—to sustain its formal venture capital industry with similar reliance by states in the US midsection than to contrast Canada to the United States as a whole.

With this history of the venture capital industry and its current state of affairs as background, we can now turn to specific government incentives, particularly tax incentives, that support venture capital investment in the two countries.

Notes

1   Adam Solomon, "Venture Capital in the United States," in Organisation for Economic Co-operation and Development, *Venture Capital and Innovation* (Paris: OECD, 1996), 94-98, at 94.

2   Allan L. Riding, *Financing Entrepreneurial Firms: Legal and Regulatory Issues*, research paper prepared for the Task Force on the Future of the Canadian Financial Services Sector (Ottawa: Department of Finance, 1998), 13.

3   Paul D. Reynolds, William D. Bygrave, Erkko Autio, Larry W. Cox, and Michael Hay, *Global Entrepreneurship Monitor: 2002 Executive Report* (Wellesley, MA: Babson College, November 2002) (herein referred to as "the 2002 GEM Monitor"). The report is available from the Global Entrepreneurship Monitor Web site at http://www.gemconsortium.org/. Figure 10 of the 2002 GEM Monitor (at 34) shows (estimated) informal venture capital and "classic" venture capital (that is, formal venture capital) as a percentage of gross domestic product (GDP) in 2001 in the 24 countries surveyed for the 2002 report. In only one country (Israel), formal venture capital exceeded informal venture capital. In the remaining countries, informal venture capital ranged from a low of 61 percent (Canada) to a high of 99.7 percent (China) of all venture capital investment.

4   John Freear and William E. Wetzel Jr., "Who Bankrolls High-Tech Entrepreneurs?" (1990) vol. 5, no. 2 *Journal of Business Venturing* 77-89. Freear and Wetzel collected data from 284 technology-based firms founded in New England between 1975 and 1986 (representing 27 percent of such firms founded in New England over this period). Of these firms, 62 percent raised capital from outside investors. Private individuals were the most common source of equity capital in terms of the number of rounds of financing provided to the various firms, although they accounted for only 11 percent of the total capital raised. However, private individuals were the largest source of seed capital (accounting for 48 percent of seed capital funds and 76 percent of all rounds of seed financing). In addition, individuals accounted for 84 percent of rounds of financing involving less than $250,000 and 58 percent of rounds involving between $250,000 and $500,000. In rounds involving more than $500,000, the role of private individuals declined rapidly.

5   A 1996 OECD study suggested that the number of companies financed by angels was 20 to 40 times greater than that financed by the institutional venture capital industry in the United States: *Venture Capital and Innovation*, supra note 1, at 8.

6   See Thomson Venture Economics, *2003 National Venture Capital Association Yearbook* (Arlington, VA and Newark, NJ: National Venture Capital Association and Thomson Venture Economics, 2003), 39-68.

7   Ilan Mochari, "The Numbers Game," *Inc. Magazine*, October 15, 2002 and Susan Greco, "A Little Goes a Long Way," *Inc. Magazine*, October 15, 2002; both articles are available from the *Inc. Magazine* Web site at http://www.inc.com/magazine/.

8   The characteristics of angels are similar in Canada and the United States: see Richard T. Harrison and Colin M. Mason, "Informal Venture Capital," in Richard T. Harrison and Colin M. Mason, eds., *Informal Venture Capital: Evaluating the Impact of Business Introduction Services* (London: Prentice Hall, 1996), 3-26, at 12 and 13, tables 1.4 and 1.5. A number of US studies examining the characteristics of angel investors are cited in John Freear, Jeffrey E. Sohl, and William E. Wetzel Jr.,

"Angels and Non-Angels: Are There Differences?" (1994) vol. 9, no. 2 *Journal of Business Venturing* 109-23, at 111.

9   Freear, Sohl, and Wetzel, supra note 8, at 111.

10 Ibid.

11 Of the 184 responses that they received to their survey (from 3,700 questionnaires sent), only 38 were identified as potential investors. Of those, 18 were classified as interested potential investors while 20 were considered non-interested.

12 Freear, Sohl, and Wetzel, supra note 8, at 117, table 5.

13 Patrizia E. Dal Cin, "Canadian Informal Investors: Towards a Framework for Policy Initiatives" (MMS thesis, Carleton University, School of Business, 1993). Dal Cin's thesis developed and analyzed questionnaires sent to informal investors across Canada. Her response rate of 42.3 percent is significant compared with that for other empirical studies of angel investors, although the sample size is relatively small (responses were received from 279 angel investors, 95 non-angel investors, 23 entrepreneurs, and 14 professional venture capitalists).

14 Ibid., at 74.

15 Question 33(b) of her questionnaire stated: "The Federal Government has provided an exemption from income taxes on the first $100,000 of capital gains income." It then asked whether this exemption influenced the decision to invest and whether greater investment would be undertaken if the exemption were increased. Question 33(c) then asked respondents to suggest tax incentives that they would like to see enacted. It is unclear why in question 33(b) she used the $100,000 exemption (then still in existence) rather than the $500,000 exemption for dispositions of qualified small business corporation shares (see chapter 3, under the heading "Preferential Treatment of Gains from Small Business Securities").

16 Investor group 2 offered significantly more suggestions (151) than investor group 1 (69).

17 In the United States, statistics are prepared for the NVCA by Thomson Venture Economics and are published in an annual yearbook. Some statistics are available on the NVCA Web site at http://www.nvca.com/. In Canada, Macdonald & Associates Limited prepares statistics for the CVCA. Some statistics are available on the CVCA Web site at http://www.cvca.ca/ and the Macdonald & Associates Limited Web site at http://www.canadavc.com/. Macdonald & Associates has data predating 1995, although they are not nearly as comprehensive.

18 The venture capital statistics in Canada and the United States have also evolved as the private equity industry has evolved. While Macdonald & Associates Limited has maintained separate statistics for mezzanine capital and leveraged buyout (LBO) capital as distinct from venture capital, the distinction was not as clear in the mid-1990s when the Canadian industry was less mature. That is not to say that the earlier statistics overstate the size of the formal venture capital industry; rather, the venture capital funds themselves have evolved over time as they did in the United States and now tend to specialize in one of three primary segments—venture capital, mezzanine capital, and LBO capital—of the private equity market. See chapter 1, at note 18 and accompanying text.

19 For example, small business investment companies (SBICs), some of which benefit from federal government guaranteed leveraging (see chapter 8, under the heading

"The SBIC Program and the Evolution of US Private Venture Capital Funds"), are included in the private fund statistics, assuming that they are not evergreen funds. The amount of capital of SBICs guaranteed by the federal Small Business Administration would not be reflected in the sources of venture capital. Similarly, if a state government program provides tax credits to investors in private venture capital funds, the funds would be included in the private fund figure (assuming that the funds are tracked by Thomson Venture Economics). The only funds benefiting from state tax credits that could be independently tracked because of their unique characteristics are certified capital companies (CAPCOs) (see chapter 6), although they are not yet tracked by Thomson Venture Economics. The Oklahoma fund of funds (see chapter 6, under the heading "Using Tax Credits To Guarantee Investment in VCFs") invests in private venture capital funds and would appear as an investor in private funds, not as a separate government-managed fund. However, the amount of capital that it and other state governments directly invest in private funds is so insignificant that state governments are not included in the sources of venture capital in figure 2.5.

20   The following table shows the amount of capital invested by individuals in LSVCCs each year compared with the aggregate amount invested by individuals in formal venture capital funds:

Year	Amount of capital invested by individuals (Cdn $ millions)	Amount of capital invested in LSVCCs (Cdn $ millions)	Proportion of individual formal venture capital investments in LSVCCs (%)
1995	594	591	99.5
1996	1244	1221	98.2
1997	730	628	86.0
1998	625	552	88.3
1999	1076	975	90.6
2000	1,822	1,386	76.0
2001	1,797	1,760	97.9
2002	1,814	1,754	96.7

Source: Macdonald & Associates Limited (unpublished).

21   See, generally, Martha Louise Reiner, "The Transformation of Venture Capital: A History of Venture Capital Organizations in the United States" (PhD thesis, UC Berkeley, 1989).

22   Robert Kuttner, *Everything for Sale: The Virtues and Limits of Markets* (New York: Knopf, 1997), 216.

23   Evidently, the first chair of the engineering department expected young professors to earn twice their salaries from consulting: AnnaLee Saxenian, *Regional Advantage: Culture and Competition in Silicon Valley and Route 128* (Cambridge, MA: Harvard University Press, 1994), 13, note 2.

24   Bush helped start the American Appliance Company, later Raytheon Manufacturing Company. The firm originally designed refrigerators but changed its name to Raytheon in 1925 after acquiring the rights to a new kind of vacuum tube that would allow radios to run on household current rather than on bulky batteries.

25   Saxenian, supra note 23, at 14. Government military contracts benefited other universities in New England, including Harvard and Tufts, as well as local industry.

26   Everett M. Rogers and Judith K. Larsen, *Silicon Valley Fever: Growth of a High-Technology Culture* (New York: Basic Books, 1984), 35.

27   Reiner, supra note 21, at 201, citing Gerald D. Nash, *The American West Transformed: The Impact of the Second World War* (Bloomington, IN: Indiana University Press, 1985), 24. See also Gerald D. Nash, "Stages of California's Economic Growth, 1870-1970: An Introduction," in George H. Knoles, ed., *Essays and Assays: California History Reappraised* (San Francisco: California Historical Society, 1973), 39-53.

28   Terman considered cooperation, or the pooling of knowhow, to be fundamental to the development of a technology-based industry. In his prophetic words, "[A community of technical scholars] is composed of industries using highly sophisticated technologies, together with a strong university that is sensitive to the creative activities of the surrounding industry. This pattern appears to be the wave of the future" (quoted in Saxenian supra note 23, at 22). Terman promoted venture investment in electronics businesses because they were changing so rapidly and were so diverse that there could not be a monopoly. In addition, individuals could invest in highly profitable companies with very little startup capital. He believed in local financing for local ventures. He also acted as a responsible intermediary between entrepreneurs (engineers) and financiers in the San Francisco Bay area. Finally, Terman used the contacts he developed in Washington while at Harvard to attract federal contracts for both university labs and local firms.

29   SRI was designed to pursue "science for practical purposes [which] might not be fully compatible internally with the traditional roles of the university": Saxenian, supra note 23, at 23, citing Michael I. Luger and Harvey A. Goldstein, *Technology in the Garden: Research Parks in Regional Economic Development* (Chapel Hill, NC: University of North Carolina Press, 1991), 124.

30   By 1961, 32 companies were involved in the program, with approximately 400 employees pursuing advanced degrees in science and engineering on a part-time basis: Saxenian, supra note 23, at 23.

31   According to Saxenian, ibid., the park was established as a source of income for a "land-rich but cash-poor" university. Leland Stanford, when he bequested his 8,100 acre farm to the university, forbid the sale of any of the land. In 1955, the park covered 220 acres; by 1961 it had grown to 652 acres and was home to 25 companies with 11,000 employees combined. Leases were granted only to technology companies that might benefit the university. Park companies frequently hired Stanford faculty as consultants and graduates as employees.

32   One year earlier, the Investment Company Act of 1940, Pub. L. no. 76-76, enacted on August 22, 1940, established guidelines for investment trusts. In part, this legislation was intended to counteract the previous abuse of investment companies, which were sharply criticized after the 1929 stock market crash. Congress passed the Investment Company Act of 1940 to prevent questionable practices such as excessive fees, unloading slow-moving securities, and fuelling speculation. Investment companies were left some investment freedom when Congress accepted arguments that they could perform the socially desirable goal of using some of their capital to finance ventures.

33   Sumner H. Slichter, "The Outlook for Private Enterprise in America," in *Proceedings of the Thirtieth Annual Convention of the Investment Bankers Association of America*, November 30-December 5, 1941 (Chicago: Investment Bankers Association of America, 1942), 76-95.

34   ARD is mentioned in every history of the US venture capital industry. More
     detailed accounts of its origins and history can be found in William D. Bygrave
     and Jeffry A. Timmons, *Venture Capital at the Crossroads* (Boston: Harvard Busi-
     ness School Press, 1992) and in Reiner, supra note 21.

35   According to Bygrave and Timmons, the officers of ARD and two investment
     bankers attempted to raise the initial $5 million on a best-efforts basis by selling
     200,000 shares at $25 per share. By October 1946, the Dow Jones had fallen to
     165, and only 139,930 shares of the offering had been sold, netting approxi-
     mately $3.5 million ($500,000 more than the targeted minimum for ARD). Of this,
     $1.8 million came from institutional investors. By the end of 1947, insurance
     companies (including John Hancock Mutual Life Insurance Company), investment
     companies (including Massachusetts Investors Trust), and universities (including
     MIT, the University of Pennsylvania, and the University of Rochester) owned
     49.6 percent of ARD and the ARD directors and officers owned 45 percent. The
     three universities bought a total of 9,000 shares in order to provide a "means for
     their faculties to engage in outside activities which would be of direct financial
     benefit to the universities": *Boston Sunday Globe*, December 28, 1946, cited in
     Bygrave and Timmons, supra note 34, at 18. However, MIT stopped its financial
     support of ARD in 1955, citing the investment in startup companies as too risky.
     According to Saxenian, supra note 23, at 15, this "calculated distancing from the
     region's new technology enterprises would typify MIT's relationship to Route
     128. In spite of the university's commitment to commercially relevant research, it
     kept firms at arm's length."

36   Investment decisions were reviewed by a board of technical advisers, the mem-
     bers of which held prestigious university posts and had experience with industry
     and government. Brigadier General Georges Doriot, professor of industrial man-
     agement at Harvard's business school, headed the advisory board and became
     president of ARD soon after it went public. The other advisory board members
     were associated with MIT.

37   Reiner, supra note 21, at 177, quoting from Securities and Exchange Commis-
     sion, "In the Matter of American Research and Development, Investment Com-
     pany Act of 1940," *Release* no. 934, at 1. ARD's registration statement warned
     investors that its investment policy would be to supply capital to companies
     mainly engaged in the "development of new enterprises, processes and new prod-
     ucts, or in the development of existing processes and products." Its focus shifted
     to advanced technologies after a number of failures in manufacturing processes.
     Among the ventures that failed were a venture to catch tuna in the Fiji Islands
     and pack it in Samoa, a frozen apple juice venture, and a frozen shrimp proces-
     sor. Early high-tech investments included High Voltage Engineering Co. and
     Tracerlab, both formed by MIT alumni.

38   According to Bygrave and Timmons, supra note 34, little is known of how this
     particular investment came about. According to them (ibid., at 20):

          One version of the story suggests that General Doriot was not at all
          enthusiastic about making even a small investment in four MIT
          graduates, all in their twenties, with an idea about computing. But
          Bill Congleton, a young associate and former student, was very
          excited about the venture's prospects. According to industry lore,
          the general thought that DEC presented an opportunity for

Congleton to learn some important lessons about the difficulties of
picking winners. The early failure of a small investment would be
instructive for his associate.

39 Arguments that high taxes had dried up venture capital appeared often in the
small business financing hearings.

40 United States, Federal Reserve System, *Financing Small Business: Report to the
Committees on Banking and Currency and the Select Committees on Small Business*, 85th Cong., 2d sess. (Washington, DC: US Government Printing Office, 1958).

41 Ibid., at 526-27.

42 Regional small business development programs started in New England's depressed economy and spread quickly by the late 1950s. Maine formed the first
state development credit corporation in 1949, New Hampshire in 1951, and the
remaining four New England states in 1953. By 1957, New York, North Carolina,
Michigan, Wisconsin, South Dakota, Arkansas, and Georgia had also introduced
programs, and many local development corporations had been formed.

43 Pub. L. no. 85-699, enacted on August 21, 1958; 72 Stat. 689 (herein referred to
as "SBIA").

44 See chapter 8, under the heading "US Small Business Administration."

45 SBIA section 102.

46 HR rep. no. 85-2060, 85th Cong., 2d sess., June 30, 1958, reproduced in [1958]
United States Code: Congressional and Administrative News 3678, at 3679.

47 The SBIC program is considered in more detail in chapter 8.

48 Bygrave and Timmons, supra note 34, at 23-25. The venture capital statistics in
table 2.2 suggest that the reduction in the capital gains tax rate may have had an
impact on individual investors, whose investment in venture capital limited partnerships more than doubled between 1979 and 1980. However, there is little
correlation between subsequent amendments to the long-term capital gains tax
rate and individual venture capital investment (through the formal venture capital
industry). Whether or not capital gains tax rates affect venture capital investment
by individuals is considered further in chapter 3, under the heading "Evaluation
of the Preferential Tax Treatment of Capital Gains."

49 The US venture capital statistics are taken from *2003 National Venture Capital
Association Yearbook*, supra note 6. Thomson Venture Economics tracks US private
venture capital funds. It does not track "evergreen funds" (funds with infinite
lives) or true captive corporate industrial investment groups without fixed commitment levels; thus, these statistics understate the true size of the US formal venture capital industry.

50 Private sector statistics are prepared by the Employee Benefit Research Institute
and are available from the EBRI Web site at http://www.ebri.org/. Statistics on
public sector pension plans are prepared by the US Census Bureau and are available from the bureau's Web site at http://www.census.gov/govs/www/retire.html.

51 Wilshire Associates Incorporated, "2002 Wilshire Report on State Retirement
Systems: Funding Levels and Asset Allocation," August 12, 2002, available from the
Wilshire Web site at http://www.wilshire.com/. The report is based on the most
recent financial and actuarial data reports of the plans. The valuation dates
ranged from June 30, 1999 to December 31, 2001. Forty-five percent of the

reports were on or after June 30, 2001, 41 percent were between June 30, 2000 and June 30, 2001, and 14 percent preceded June 30, 2000.

52   Appendix G to the report (ibid., at 25-27) provides a percentage breakdown of asset allocation of all state retirement systems. The asset classes listed are US equity, non-US equity, US fixed income, non-US fixed income, real estate, private equity, and other. Appendix G also indicates the expected return and risk of each retirement system (based on asset allocation).

53   There appear to be some errors in appendix G, so the number of state pension funds without any private equity investment may be overstated. For example, both the Massachusetts public employees' retirement system and the Massachusetts teachers pension plan show no private equity investment. However, the Pension Reserves Investment Management Board (see chapter 7, at notes 195-198 and accompanying text), which manages both of these funds, has significant private equity investments.

54   Exhibit 6 of the report (supra note 51, at 9) is a table showing Wilshire's long-term return and risk assumptions for the major asset classes. The table below shows exhibit 6 together with the average asset allocation to each of the asset classes taken from appendix G:

| | Average asset allocation (%) | Asset class assumptions | |
| | | Expected return (%) | Risk (%) |
Asset class			
US equity	43.8	8.00	17.0
International equity ..	12.5	8.00	20.0
Private equity	3.9	11.00	32.0
Real estate	3.4	6.75	14.0
US bonds	34.6	5.25	7.0
International bonds ..	1.6	5.00	13.0
Cash	0.1	3.25	3.0

Note that in appendix G, the asset classes "US bonds," "international bonds," and "cash" are not used. The comparable asset classes are "US fixed income," "non-US fixed income," and "other," and the average asset allocations for those three classes are shown in this table.

55   Thomson Financial Venture Economics, 2001 Investment Benchmark Reports: LP Analytics 2001 (New York: Thomson Financial/Securities Data Publishing, 2001), 4.

56   The remaining four were San Francisco City & Country Retirement System, Los Angeles County Employees Retirement Association, University of California Retirement Plan, and Denver Public Schools Retirement System.

57   The Wilshire report, supra note 51, lists each retirement system separately, although in some states the various public sector retirement systems are centrally managed.

58   See chapter 1, at note 18 and accompanying text.

59   The four government pension fund systems that included direct investments in their private equity portfolio in 2000 were as follows (the number in parentheses is the percentage of private equity invested directly): Michigan State Treasury (6.2 percent); Virginia Retirement System (3.2 percent); Connecticut State Treasurer (1.4 percent); and Minnesota State Board of Investment (1.8 percent). US

pension funds tend to be passive venture capital investors, investing primarily as limited partners in venture capital funds rather than directly in SMEs. One exception is the Retirement Systems of Alabama, which has directly invested its entire $512 million private equity portfolio (the vast majority of which has been LBO or mezzanine capital investments). Alabama did not make the list of the top 36 US government pension funds with venture capital fund investments. Of the remaining government pension funds that are listed as having made direct private equity investments, only two have direct investments exceeding 10 percent of their private equity portfolios: University of California Retirement Plan (11.2 percent) and Detroit General/Policy & Fire Retirement Systems (40.8 percent).

60   In comparison, the 1999 statistics listed 24 corporate pension funds with aggregate venture capital investments of $5.742 billion. The top five corporate pension funds, all with venture capital investments valued at over $1 billion, were Verizon, Lucent Technologies Inc., AT&T Investment Management Corp., SBC Communications Inc. (including Ameritech), and General Motors Corporation.

61   The five funds were General Motors Investment Management Corporation; Arthur D. Little, Inc. Employees' MDT Retirement Plan; Delphi Automotive Systems Corporation; Sears, Roebuck and Co. (Sears Pension Plan); and CBS Corporation (Viacom).

62   Telephone discussion with Anthony Romenello, Venture Economics, Newark, NJ, July 12, 2002. Venture capital is one of the alternative asset classes of a pension plan, which generally comprise a relatively small percentage of a plan's overall portfolio. Public company equity shares form a much larger portion of plan assets. For example, according to the 2002 Wilshire report on state retirement systems, the average asset allocation to private equity was 3.9 percent compared with 43.8 percent in US equity and 12.5 percent in non-US equity (supra note 51, appendix G, at 27). Consider a pension fund that under its investment terms can allocate a maximum of 10 percent of its assets to venture capital. Suppose that the maximum allocation had been made in mid-2000 (at the peak of the stock market indices in North America), at which time the fund had also allocated 40 percent of its assets to US public equities. A 30 percent decline in the value of the US equities, assuming no decline in the value of the remainder of the pension assets, would increase the venture capital investment to 11.4 percent of the portfolio, or higher than the maximum allocation for that asset type. While the value of venture capital investments has also been affected by the declining stock markets, the valuation of venture capital investments is relatively conservative and changes in value often lag changes to the public equity markets.

63   As shown in table 2.2, pension fund investment in venture capital funds dropped from a high of $42.43 billion in 2000 to $15.82 billion in 2001 and $3.24 billion in 2002. In the second quarter of 2002, US venture capital funds returned more capital to investors than new capital raised: see Owen Thomas and Stacy Lawrence, "The VC Boomerang," *Business 2.0*, October 2002, 41.

64   *2003 National Venture Capital Association Yearbook*, supra note 6, at 34-35, figure 3.19, lists the sources and targets of venture capital investment by state in 2002. Although California-based venture capital firms (the largest source of venture capital) invested in 36 different states in 2002, 73 percent of their investment was in-state. On the other hand, venture capital firms based in New York (the second-largest source of venture capital in 2002) invested in 34 states and only 6

percent was invested in-state, although almost 40 percent was invested in states along the eastern seaboard and 38 percent was invested in California.

65   See chapter 1, at note 43 and accompanying text.

66   Information on the early history of the Canadian venture capital industry (pre-1985) was obtained primarily from two sources: George Fells, "Venture Capital in Canada—A Ten-Year Review" (1984) vol. 49, no. 1 *Business Quarterly* 70-77; and Rod B. McNaughton, "Venture Capital in Canada," in Milford B. Green, ed., *Venture Capital: International Comparisons* (London: Routledge, 1991), 183-201.

67   In 1978, CED had 27 institutional shareholders, including life insurance companies, banks, and other institutions in Canada and elsewhere: Peter McQuillan and Howard Taylor, *Sources of Venture Capital in Canada*, rev. ed., prepared for the Department of Industry, Trade and Commerce (Ottawa: Supply and Services, 1978), 38.

68   Peter McQuillan and Howard Taylor, *Sources of Venture Capital: A Canadian Guide* (Ottawa: Department of Industry, Trade and Commerce, 1973), provided profiles of 50 venture capital organizations across Canada (primarily in Ontario and Quebec with a few in British Columbia and Alberta). The 1978 revised edition, supra note 67, had profiles of 46 organizations. The 1973 edition included a quantitative study of the sources of venture capital in Canada (at 129-47) by P.L. Crane and J.V. Poapst. They identified 845 possible suppliers of venture capital (including individuals, venture capital organizations, venture funds, venture managers, banks, and pension funds). They received responses from 639 investors, of whom 317 indicated an interest in making venture capital investments.

69   Fells, supra note 66, at 70. In McQuillan and Taylor, supra note 68, at 86, the operational approach of Charterhouse Canada Limited was described in part as follows:

> Charterhouse anticipates turning over an investment from five to seven years after acquisition. The company invests in all stages of corporate growth. It will not finance a situation where technical research has not been completed. The company requires one seat on the board of directors. Because Charterhouse does not provide on-going management, the applicant should have a complete management team. It is not Charterhouse policy to seek voting control. Charterhouse will acquire a minority interest in the common share capital. A part of each investment is likely to be in the form of preferred shares, notes or debentures redeemable on an agreed plan over a number of years.

70   It became difficult for venture capitalists to liquidate their investments due to the downturn in the stock market (which significantly reduced the number of initial public offerings) as well as the introduction of the Foreign Investment Review Act, SC 1973-74, c. 46, which effectively eliminated the sale of portfolio companies to foreign purchasers.

71   See J. Michael Lavery, "A Review of Developments in the Venture Capital Field," in *Report of Proceedings of the Thirty-First Tax Conference*, 1979 Conference Report (Toronto: Canadian Tax Foundation, 1980), 508-23.

72   Canada, *Foreign Direct Investment in Canada* (Ottawa: Information Canada, 1972) (the Gray report), 92.

73 Ibid., at 93.

74 Venturetek had about 50 shareholders, including CDC, Excelsior Life Insurance Company, National Life Assurance Company of Canada, Manufacturers Life Insurance Company, and Canada Permanent Trust Company. CDC paid $4.5 million for a 35 percent interest in Venturetek.

75 Innocan was formed by Kauser, Lowenstein & Meade Ltd., a privately held venture banking and merchant banking intermediary. CDC acquired a 40 percent interest in Innocan for about $4 million.

76 CDC paid slightly more than $2 million (of the $4 million initial capitalization) for a majority interest in Ventures West Capital Ltd. Other major shareholders included the Bank of British Columbia, the Bank of Tokyo, the Guaranty Trust Company, Mitsui and Co. (Canada) Ltd., and Mitsubishi Canada Ltd.

77 An Act Respecting Corporations for the Development of Québec Business Firms, SQ 1976, c. 33. SODEQ was the acronym for sociétés de développement des enterprises québécoises.

78 The various provincial incentives in effect in 1986 are discussed in Peter E. McQuillan, "An Analysis of Venture Capital Incentives," in *Income Tax Considerations in Corporate Financing*, 1986 Corporate Management Tax Conference (Toronto: Canadian Tax Foundation, 1986), 169-253. See also Lawrence Teltscher, "Small Business Financing," in *Income Tax and Goods and Services Tax Considerations in Corporate Financing*, 1992 Corporate Management Tax Conference (Toronto: Canadian Tax Foundation, 1993), 6:1-67, at 6:50-64.

79 In the late 1970s, a few provinces incorporated large Crown-type corporations, similar to the FBDB or CDC, to make direct or indirect venture capital investments in SMEs. Crown-type corporations included Saskatchewan Economic Development Corporation (Saskatchewan), Société de développement industriel (Quebec), Provincial Holdings Limited (New Brunswick), Industrial Enterprises Incorporated (Prince Edward Island), Industrial Estate Limited (Nova Scotia), and Idea Corporation (Ontario). Apart from the FBDB itself, a consideration of these types of entities is beyond the scope of this study.

80 M.J. Kostuch, "Venture Capital Financing Builds Successful Companies" (1986) vol. 50, no. 4 *Business Quarterly* 22-30, at 23.

81 Fells, supra note 66, at 72-73. The concern that gains of venture capitalists would be taxed as income rather than as capital gains was raised earlier in a study commissioned by the Ministry of State for Science and Technology: Robert H. Grasley, *The Availability of Risk Capital for Technological Innovation and Invention in Canada* (Ottawa: Information Canada, 1975) (the Grasley report), 12, which suggested that if this position were upheld, it could reduce the returns of venture capital companies so severely that "the venture capital industry in Canada might disappear completely."

82 At the time, Canadian venture capital funds did not specialize (or at least did not hold themselves out as specializing) in different sectors of the private equity market. The NVCA yearbooks have separated investment in mezzanine and buyout and other private equity funds from investment in venture capital funds since 1979. The *2003 National Venture Capital Association Yearbook* breaks down venture capital funds, mezzanine and buyout funds, and other private equity funds by investor type since 1999; in each year, pension funds contributed in excess of 50 percent

of the capital raised by these mezzanine and buyout funds: supra note 6, at 22, table 2.05.

83   If the exchange rate is taken into account, the 3 percent figure drops to 1.74 percent.

84   If the exchange rate is taken into account, the 13 percent figure drops to 8.16 percent.

85   If the exchange rate is taken into account, the 15.7 percent figure drops to 9.98 percent.

86   An Act Respecting the Caisse de dépôt et placement du Québec, RSQ, c. C-2, section 36.2 provides that the investment strategy of the Caisse must be in keeping with the practices of major North American pension funds, but that it must "also take into account the financing needs of the public sector and economic development of Québec."

87   See Mary Macdonald and John Perry, *Pension Funds and Venture Capital: The Critical Links Between Savings, Investment, Technology, and Jobs* (Ottawa: Science Council of Canada, 1985). See also Kirk Falconer, *Prudence, Patience and Jobs: Pension Investment in a Changing Canadian Economy—Technical Report* (Ottawa: Canadian Labour Market and Productivity Centre, 1999). The lack of pension fund investment in Canada was also commented on by Paul Martin, then minister of finance, in a speech to members of the CVCA and the Toronto Stock Exchange in May 2002: Ottawa, Department of Finance, *Release* no. 2002-040, May 21, 2002.

88   Canada, *Minutes of Proceedings and Evidence of the Standing Committee on Finance*, 35th Parl., 3d sess., issue no. 22, November 20, 1991, 22:29.

89   The following provinces established their own schemes (year established in parentheses): Quebec (1983); Saskatchewan (1986); British Columbia (1989); Manitoba (1991-92); Ontario (1992); Nova Scotia (1993); and New Brunswick (1994). Newfoundland announced its intention to introduce an LSVCC program in its 2001 budget and again in its 2003 budget. The Northwest Territories established its own territorial scheme in 1998.

90   In 1993, New Brunswick extended a provincial credit to prescribed federally registered LSVCCs (five have been prescribed, although only three are prescribed for 2004). In addition to its own regime (under which no LSVCC has yet been established), Nova Scotia also extends a provincial credit to prescribed federally registered LSVCCs (currently, seven are prescribed). Prince Edward Island introduced a provincial LSVCC tax credit for prescribed federally registered LSVCCs in 1992, but eliminated the credit in the province's 1997 budget, with effect from April 9, 1997.

91   Canada, Department of Finance, 1996 Budget, Budget Plan, annex 5, "Tax Measures: Supplementary Information and Notice of Ways and Means Motions," March 6, 1996, 144.

92   Thomson Venture Economics, *National Venture Capital Association 2002 Yearbook* (Arlington, VA and Newark, NJ: National Venture Capital Association and Thomson Venture Economics, 2002), 25. See also chapter 1, at note 21.

3

Venture Capital and Capital Gains Taxation*

Few issues in taxation have been the topic of as much debate and rhetoric, both political and academic, as the impact of capital gains taxation on risk investment. Both Canada and the United States provide a general tax preference for capital gains as well as specific tax preferences for gains and losses from small business securities. This chapter examines four elements of capital gains taxation and its impact on venture capital investment:

- the general tax preference for capital gains;
- the preferential tax treatment of gains on dispositions of small business securities;
- a deferral of tax or "rollover" where proceeds from the sale of shares of an eligible small business are reinvested in shares of other eligible small businesses (commonly referred to as an angel capital rollover); and
- the preferential treatment of capital losses from small business securities.

Canadian tax policy in this area has largely followed the lead of the United States and has adopted the same rhetoric. In the 2000 economic statement, the minister of finance published statistics indicating that, as a result of the reduction in the capital gains inclusion rate from two-thirds (to which it was reduced from three-quarters in the February 2000 budget) to one-half, the effective tax rate on capital gains in Canada was lower than that in the United States. With the 2003 reduction of the long-term capital gains tax rate in the United States from 20 percent to 15 percent, it will be interesting to see whether Canada will again reduce its capital gains inclusion rate to remain competitive. The race for the bottom appears to be on.

On the income side, the impact of the tax preferences is similar in both countries for angel capital investors, most of whom are individuals. For corporations, there are significant differences in the two countries. Canada's general tax preference for capital gains as well as the preferential tax treatment of capital losses from small business securities apply to all taxable entities, including

---

* Unless otherwise stated, US monetary amounts are in US dollars and Canadian monetary amounts are in Canadian dollars.

corporations and trusts. However, the manner in which the capital gains preference is delivered (a lower tax rate in the United States versus a lower inclusion
rate in Canada) affects the treatment of capital losses from small business
securities. The preferential treatment of gains from dispositions of small business securities and the angel capital rollover are limited to individuals in both
countries.

In my view, there is no justification for the general preferential tax treatment
of capital gains in either country because the general preference undermines the
more targeted preferences employed in both countries. While a targeted tax
preference for gains from small business securities is preferable to the general
capital gains tax preference, the angel capital rollover serves a similar purpose,
is better targeted, and comes at a lower cost to the government. Furthermore,
greater relief for losses from small business securities will likely have a greater
impact on venture capital investment than either a general capital gains tax preference or a more targeted capital gains preference for small business securities.
For Canada, the reduction in the tax preference for losses from small business
securities (as a result of the reduction in the capital gains inclusion rate from
three-quarters to one-half in 2000) may prove counterproductive. There is scope
for substantial amendments to the capital gains rules in Canada (and the United
States) to better target venture capital investment, especially informal investment.
In particular, I would recommend expanding the angel capital rollover and increasing the loss relief available for small business securities, although restricting the
types of business that qualify for loss relief to better target rapid-growth small
and medium-sized enterprises (SMEs).

Preferential Tax Treatment of Capital Gains

Both Canada and the United States have a general tax preference for capital
gains. In both countries, capital gains and losses are generally recognized on a
realization basis (rather than an accrual basis). In the United States, long-term
capital gains (gains on dispositions of capital property held for more than one
year) of individuals are currently taxed at a preferential tax rate of less than
one-half of the highest marginal tax rate.[1] In general, capital losses may be
deducted only against long-term capital gains, although US individuals may
deduct excess capital losses from ordinary income up to a maximum of $3,000.
In addition, US individuals may deduct certain losses from ordinary income, up to
a maximum annual amount, from the disposition of small business securities. For
US corporations, there is currently no preferential tax treatment of capital gains.
In Canada, one-half of each capital gain (referred to as a taxable capital gain) is
included in income for any taxpayer, while one-half of each capital loss (referred
to as an allowable capital loss) is deductible. In general, allowable capital losses
can be deducted only from taxable capital gains, although special provision is
made for certain capital losses from dispositions of small business securities. In
both countries, excess capital losses can be carried over to other years (for example, in Canada, losses can be carried back three years and forward indefinitely)

and deducted from capital gains in those years (and in the United States, from ordinary income of individuals up to a maximum of $3,000).

In both countries, the preferential tax treatment of capital gains has been justified in recent years primarily on the ground that it promotes risk taking, and specifically that it promotes investment in small businesses, particularly those exploiting new technologies. As a tax expenditure, however, a general preferential tax rate is a very blunt instrument for promoting venture capital investment. The preference primarily affects, indeed promotes, secondary market transactions of publicly traded securities as well as investment in other assets that give rise to capital gains, such as real estate. By enhancing the benefit of such investments, a general capital gains tax preference can detract from the very investment it is intended to promote. In addition, more targeted incentives employed in the two countries to attract venture capital investment—especially the preferential tax rate applicable to small business securities in both countries, and in Canada the preferential treatment of losses from small business securities—have been undermined by the general capital gains tax policy pursued by both governments. For example, in the United States, the tax differential between the targeted tax preference for qualified small business stock (QSBS) and the general capital gains tax preference is now virtually non-existent, though it was sizable when the QSBS provisions were introduced in 1993. Similarly, in Canada, the $500,000 capital gains exemption applicable to qualified small business corporation (QSBC) shares is less significant now that only one-half of capital gains are subject to tax, as compared with the previous three-quarters. More problematic in Canada, though, is the reduced benefit under the allowable business investment loss (ABIL) rules, because now only one-half of business investment losses are deductible from ordinary income, rather than the previous three-quarters.

I do not advocate a general capital gains tax preference. It cannot be justified as part of a normative income tax or as a tax expenditure. Under a normative tax system, capital gains should be subject to the same rate of tax as other income from property and should be taxed on an accrual basis. Taxing capital gains on a realization basis is a departure from the normative system and, in and of itself, provides a tax preference. There is no justification for compounding this preference by taxing realized capital gains at a lower tax rate. Certainly, it cannot be justified as a means of promoting venture capital investment in the two countries. While I would recommend that both Canada and the United States abolish the general capital gains tax preference entirely, it is unlikely that either country will soon eliminate the preference, and it would be political suicide for the Canadian federal government to abolish it unilaterally.

United States

Capital gains of individuals have been subject to preferential taxation since 1921, except for a brief period between 1986 and 1990. Capital gains of corporations have been subject to preferential taxation intermittently, although today corporate capital gains are subject to the same tax rates as ordinary corporate income (and corporate capital losses can be offset only against capital gains). In most cases, capital gains are recognized on a realization basis. The general preferential tax treatment of capital gains in the United States today is confined to long-term capital gains of individuals. The following is a brief history of the evolution of capital gains taxation in the United States as it concerns the taxation of venture capital (that is, primarily equity capital of corporations).[2] It deals exclusively with legislation that was enacted; there were and continue to be numerous changes proposed to capital gains legislation that never became law during the period from 1913 to the present.[3]

Capital gains have been subject to tax since the United States introduced income tax legislation in 1913, though there was no specific reference to capital gains in the legislation until 1921. Under the Revenue Act of 1913,[4] net income was defined to include "gains or profits and income derived from any source whatever, including" a number of specific inclusions. The US Supreme Court concluded that capital gains were included in "income derived from any source whatever."[5] Losses, unless specifically associated with a taxpayer's trade or business, were not deductible.

The Revenue Act of 1921[6] introduced the concepts of "capital gain" and "capital loss" and taxed capital gains of individuals (and other non-corporate taxpayers) in a preferential manner, by setting a maximum tax rate on capital gains of 12½ percent, compared with a top marginal tax rate of 58 percent.[7] "Capital gain" and "capital loss" were defined as a gain or loss, respectively, from the sale or exchange of a capital asset. A capital asset was defined as property acquired and held by the taxpayer for profit or investment for more than two years (whether or not connected with a trade or business), excluding stock in trade of the taxpayer or other property of a kind that would properly be included in the inventory of the taxpayer if on hand at year-end. According to the House Ways and Means Committee and the Senate Finance Committee, a capital gains tax preference was urgently required because the sale of capital assets, such as farms and mineral properties, was "seriously retarded" and "[i]n order to permit such transactions to go forward without fear of a prohibitive tax," a reduced tax rate was necessary.[8]

The 1921 Act permitted the full deduction of capital losses (from transactions entered into for profit) against ordinary income.[9] This asymmetric treatment of losses led to substantial revenue loss to the government. Accordingly, the Revenue Act of 1924[10] limited the deductibility of capital losses to 12½ percent of the amount of such losses, although the losses remained deductible against ordinary income.[11] The Revenue Act of 1932[12] limited the deduction of losses on stocks and bonds that were not capital assets (that is, were owned for two years or less) only to the extent of gains from the sale of the same types of assets.[13] Losses that exceeded gains in a given year could be carried forward to the next year and used to offset gains from the sales of stocks and bonds in that year. However, this limited loss carryforward was repealed, before it became effective, by the National Industrial Recovery Act in 1933.[14]

The Revenue Act of 1934[15] replaced the maximum capital gains tax rate with a stepped inclusion that declined the longer the capital asset was held before disposition.[16] The 1934 Act also limited the deduction of capital losses (determined under the same scale for individuals) against only capital gains, except that any excess could be deducted against up to $2,000 of ordinary income (for both individuals and corporations).[17] The $2,000 deduction was intended as "a concession to the small taxpayer with infrequent capital transactions."[18] In conjunction with the limitation on the deductibility of losses, the 1934 Act amended the definition of capital asset to exclude property held for sale to customers in the ordinary course of business. The primary exclusion from the definition of capital asset—which, following the 1934 amendment, read "stock in trade of the taxpayer or other property of a kind which would properly be included in the inventory of the taxpayer if on hand at year end, or property held by the taxpayer primarily for sale to customers in the ordinary course of his trade or business"—remains in the Internal Revenue Code to this day. The rationale for the amendment was to make it impossible for a stock speculator trading on his or her own account to contend that losses arising from the sale of stock were not subject to the capital loss limitation rules introduced in the 1934 Act.[19] By the same token, the gains derived by a successful stock speculator would be treated as capital gains and subject to preferential treatment, provided that the securities were held for the requisite holding period.

Thus, the US tax legislation of capital gains contains three key features that have been in place since its earliest years and stand in a sharp contrast to the general rules applicable to capital gains in Canada. First, the US preferential treatment is available only to individuals. Second, the US tax legislation includes a minimum holding-period requirement for capital gains to benefit from preferential treatment. Third, the exclusion of inventory from the definition of "capital asset" has been construed narrowly both in the legislation and by the courts in the context of corporate securities since the earliest years of taxation in the United States. The holding-period requirement and the amount of the preference for capital gains have been amended on numerous occasions, as the remaining history demonstrates. The exclusion for inventory is discussed at the end of this history.

The Revenue Act of 1938[20] enshrined the former holding-period requirement for preferential capital gains treatment in the concepts of "short-term" capital gain or loss and "long-term" capital gain or loss,[21] concepts that remain in the Code today. For individuals, both a percentage inclusion and alternative flat-rate tax applied. The amount of the capital gain or loss taken into account in determining income decreased the longer the asset was held: for capital assets held not more than 18 months (that is, short-term assets), 100 percent of the gain or loss was taken into account; for capital assets held more than 18 months but not more than two years, 66⅔ percent of the gain or loss was taken into account; for capital assets held more than two years, 50 percent of the gain or loss was taken into account. An alternative flat-rate tax of 30 percent applied to the included portion of long-term capital gains, if this tax gave rise to less tax than otherwise would be payable.[22] In the case of a net long-term capital loss, a maximum credit of 30 percent was allowed against the tax payable on other income. No carryover of unused long-term capital losses was permitted. A net short-term capital loss could not be deducted against other income, but it could be carried forward one year and deducted against short-term capital gains in that year.[23] The amount of the carried-over net short-term capital loss could not exceed the taxpayer's net income in the year the loss arose.[24] For corporations, the distinction between long-term and short-term capital gains and losses was practically irrelevant, because long-term capital gains did not benefit from any preferential tax treatment. Capital losses (whether long or short-term) were deductible against capital gains and against up to $2,000 of the corporation's other income.

The Revenue Act of 1939[25] introduced a number of amendments affecting the treatment of corporate capital losses. First, long-term capital losses became fully deductible against ordinary income and were not limited to $2,000 of such income (except in the case of personal holding companies).[26] Short-term capital losses were deductible against short-term capital gains, and any excess (that is, a net short-term capital loss) could be carried forward one year as a short-term capital loss.

The holding period that distinguished between short- and long-term capital gains or losses was reduced from 18 months to 6 months in the Revenue Act of 1942.[27] For individuals, the amount of a capital gain or loss included in the determination of income was either 100 percent (for capital property held not more than 6 months) or 50 percent (for capital property held more than 6 months).[28] The alternative flat-rate tax on a net long-term capital gain was increased from 30 percent to 50 percent, thus increasing the maximum effective tax rate on long-term capital gains to 25 percent. Net short-term and net long-term capital losses were deductible against up to $1,000 of ordinary income, and unused capital losses (whether long- or short-term) could be carried forward (as short-term capital losses) for five years.[29] For corporations, an alternative flat-rate tax of 25 percent on net long-term capital gains was introduced;[30] capital losses were deductible only to the extent of capital gains, and excess capital losses could be carried forward for five years, in the same manner as applicable for individuals.

The Revenue Act of 1951[31] amended the computation of the included portion of long-term capital gains for individuals. Previously, short-term capital losses were deducted from the recognized portion (50 percent) of long-term capital gains; in effect, each $1 of short-term capital loss offset $2 of long-term capital gain. Under the 1951 Act, net short-term capital losses were deducted from net long-term capital gains and then 50 percent of the difference was excluded from income.[32] The basic structure described to this point was retained in the Internal Revenue Code of 1954.[33]

The Revenue Act of 1964[34] extended the carryforward for excess capital losses of non-corporate taxpayers from five years to indefinitely.[35] However, the Act distinguished between excess short-term capital losses and excess long-term capital losses for carryforward purposes.[36] Previously, both types of excess losses were treated as short-term capital losses in the subsequent year; under the 1964 Act, the former were treated as short-term capital losses in the subsequent year while the latter were treated as long-term capital losses in the subsequent year. The amount of ordinary income offset by capital losses (whether long- or short-term) in the loss year (up to a maximum of $1,000) was treated as a short-term capital gain in the loss year. The effect of this characterization was to reduce first the amount of the excess short-term capital loss and then the amount of the excess long-term capital loss (up to $1,000 in the aggregate) that could be carried forward. The carried-over loss (whether short- or long-term) could also be applied to reduce ordinary income in the subsequent year (up to $1,000) if there were insufficient capital gains in the subsequent year to absorb the carried-forward losses.

The Tax Reform Act of 1969[37] increased the alternative flat-rate tax for both corporate and non-corporate taxpayers.[38] The 1969 Act amended the tax treatment of capital losses in a few respects. For corporations, a three-year carry-back of capital losses was added; the carried-over capital losses had to be used in the earliest year possible (and applied to the maximum extent possible), except that a carried-back capital loss could not be used to create a net operating loss in a carryback year.[39] For individuals, only 50 percent of long-term capital losses could be used to offset ordinary income (up to $1,000 of ordinary income) and the amount of a net long-term capital loss that could be carried forward was reduced by $2 for every dollar of loss used to reduce ordinary income.[40]

Three other amendments made by the 1969 Act also had an impact on the taxation of capital gains and losses of individuals. First, the 1969 Act introduced a limitation on the deduction of interest expense to investment income plus long-term capital gains plus $25,000 plus one-half of the interest expense in excess of that amount, with any non-deductible amount carried forward.[41] Second, the 1969 Act introduced a minimum "add-on" tax, under which an individual taxpayer would add to the tax otherwise payable a 10 percent tax on the amount by which the taxpayer's "tax preferences" less a $30,000 exclusion exceeded the taxpayer's regular tax otherwise determined (excluding certain credits).[42] Third, the 1969 Act capped the tax rate on personal service income at 50 percent (rather than the regular marginal tax rates that went to 70 percent); however, the amount of personal service income eligible for this preference was reduced dollar for dollar by tax preferences, including the excluded portion of capital gains income. Taking into account the minimum add-on tax and the "poisoning" of the maximum tax on personal service income, the effective rate of tax on long-term capital gains could approach approximately 45 percent (when fully implemented in 1972).

The six-month holding period that distinguished between short- and long-term capital gains and losses remained in effect from 1942 through 1976. The Tax Reform Act of 1976[43] increased the holding period to nine months for 1977 and to one year for 1978 and subsequent years.[44] The 1976 Act also increased the amount of capital losses that could be offset by non-corporate taxpayers against ordinary income to $2,000 for 1977 and to $3,000 for 1978 and subsequent years.[45] The 1976 Act also made two significant changes to the minimum add-on tax: the rate was increased from 10 percent to 15 percent; and the exclusion was lowered to the greater of $10,000 and one-half of the taxpayer's regular tax liability. As a result of these changes, the highest effective tax rate on long-term capital gains increased to 49.125 percent. A final amendment made by the 1976 Act, although one that ultimately never came into effect, was the elimination of the basis step up on death. Previously, the basis of property passing from a decedent to a beneficiary was stepped up to its fair market value on the date of death.[46] This step-up, combined with the fact that there was no capital gains tax on death,[47] significantly exacerbated the "lock-in" effect of capital gains taxation, particularly for elderly taxpayers.[48] The amendment in the 1976 Act,[49] under which the basis of capital property to the decedent was carried over to the beneficiary, would have reduced this lock-in effect to some extent. This provision was to become effective for property transferred after December 31, 1976.[50]

The Revenue Act of 1978[51] had a significant impact on the taxation of long-term capital gains of individuals. The amendments introduced by this Act are often credited as *the* key reasons for the rapid expansion of the venture capital industry in the early 1980s. The 1978 Act made three key changes to the tax treatment of long-term capital gains:

- it increased the exclusion for long-term capital gains from 50 percent to 60 percent;
- it removed the excluded portion of long-term capital gains from the list of tax preferences subject to the minimum add-on tax; and
- the excluded gain no longer reduced the amount of personal service income benefiting from the alternative maximum tax rate of 50 percent applicable to such income.

These three changes reduced the highest effective rate of tax on long-term capital gains from 49.125 percent to 28 percent. It also repealed the alternative maximum capital gains tax rate (of 25 percent) applicable to an individual's first $50,000 of long-term capital gains. The 1978 Act reduced the alternative maximum tax applicable to corporate capital gains from 30 percent to 28 percent.[52] The rationale given for the reduction of capital gains tax rates is illuminating:

> [T]he combined level of the present taxes applicable to capital gains has contributed both to a slower rate of economic growth than that which otherwise might have been anticipated, and also to some taxpayers realizing fewer potential gains than they would have realized if the tax rates had been lower. *In addition, the committee believes that the present level of capital gains taxes has contributed to the shortage of investment funds needed for small business and for capital formation purposes generally.*[53]

The 1978 Act also introduced an alternative minimum tax (AMT).[54] The rates of AMT ranged from 10 percent for alternative minimum taxable income (AMTI) in excess of $20,000 to 25 percent for AMTI in excess of $100,000. AMT was payable if it exceeded a taxpayer's regular tax (ordinary tax plus minimum add-on tax) otherwise determined. Essentially, AMTI was defined as a taxpayer's gross income otherwise determined plus tax preferences and minus permitted deductions. The excluded portion of an individual's long-term capital gains was an item of tax preference. However, the AMT did not increase the maximum possible effective rate for long-term capital gains.

The Economic Recovery Tax Act of 1981[55] reduced the highest marginal individual income tax rate from 70 percent to 50 percent, thus reducing the highest effective capital gains tax rate (for individual taxpayers) from 28 percent to 20 percent. The 1981 Act also reduced the highest rate of AMT to 20 percent (for AMTI in excess of $60,000). The Tax Equity and Fiscal Responsibility Act of 1982[56] eliminated the minimum add-on tax for individuals. The Deficit Reduction Act of 1984[57] reduced the holding period for long-term capital gains to six months for property acquired between June 23, 1984 and December 31, 1987. For 1988 and subsequent years, the holding period was to remain one year.

The Tax Reform Act of 1986[58] introduced significant tax reform in the United States, similar to that introduced in Canada in 1987. Under the 1986 Act, income tax rates were significantly reduced[59] and the tax base was broadened.[60] With respect to capital gains taxation, the 1986 Act repealed the individual long-term capital gains deduction (the exclusion from income of 60 percent of long-term capital gains); as a result, long-term capital gains were included in ordinary income but subject to a maximum rate of 28 percent, equal to the highest individual marginal tax rate applicable under the 1986 Act.[61] Individual capital losses continued to be deductible in full against capital gains and against up to $3,000 of ordinary income. The 1986 Act also set the maximum rate for corporate long-term capital gains at 34 percent, equal to the highest corporate marginal tax rate under the Act. The 1986 Act retained the existing statutory structure for capital gains (for example, the distinction between long- and short-term capital gains) to facilitate the reinstatement of a capital gains tax preference if there was a future tax rate increase.

The Omnibus Budget Reconciliation Act of 1990 (also referred to as the Revenue Reconciliation Act of 1990)[62] raised the top individual rate to 31 percent and the Omnibus Budget Reconciliation Act of 1993 (also referred to as the Revenue Reconciliation Act of 1993)[63] raised the top tax rate to 39.6 percent. Neither act raised the maximum individual capital gains tax rate.

Thus, following 1993, there was a significant tax preference generally attached to long-term capital gains. The 1993 Act also amended the investment interest deduction. According to the House committee,

> it is inappropriate for a taxpayer who recognizes long term capital gain [sic] taxable at favorable rate [sic] to use that gain to deduct otherwise non-deductible investment interest against ordinary income. Because the bill increases the rate differential between ordinary income and the net capital gains rate, the possibility for such inappropriate rate arbitrage is increased. The committee believes that the opportunities for this type of rate conversion should be reduced.[64]

The 1993 Act therefore allowed taxpayers to elect to treat net long-term capital gains as investment income in order to offset investment interest, but electing such treatment would make the gains ineligible for the 28 percent maximum capital gains tax rate in section 1(h).[65]

The Taxpayer Relief Act of 1997,[66] as its name implies, included a number of tax-relieving provisions. As a result of the increases in the individual marginal tax rates in 1993, the long-term capital gains tax rate was more than 10 percentage points lower than the top marginal rate. Under the 1997 Act, the maximum tax rate applicable to long-term capital gains was reduced to 20 percent (for individual taxpayers in the 15 percent tax bracket, the rate was reduced to 10 percent) for assets held longer than 18 months. These maximum tax rates were applicable both for the regular tax and for AMT. For assets held between one year and 18 months, the 28 percent rate remained applicable. In addition, for assets held longer than five years (for holding periods beginning after December 31, 2000), the maximum rate of capital gains tax was reduced to 18 percent (for taxpayers in the 15 percent tax bracket, the rate was reduced to 8 percent).[67]

It is worth quoting extensively from the rationale for the reduced rates provided by the House Ways and Means Committee (as adopted in the report of the Budget Committee) at the time of the 1997 proposals to amend the Code:

> The Committee believes it is important that tax policy be conducive to economic growth. Economic growth cannot occur without saving, investment, and the willingness of individuals to take risks and exploit new market opportunities. The greater the pool of savings, the greater the monies available for business investment in equipment and research. It is through such investment in equipment and new products and services that the United States economy can increase output and productivity. It is through increases in productivity that workers can earn higher real wages. Hence, greater saving is necessary for all Americans to benefit through a higher standard of living.
>
> The net personal saving rate in the United States has averaged less than 5 percent of gross domestic product (GDP) for the past 15 years. The Committee believes such saving is inadequate to finance the investment that is needed to equip the country's businesses with the equipment and research dollars necessary to create the higher productivity that results in higher real wages for working Americans. A reduction in the taxation of capital gains increases the rate of return on household saving. Testimony by many economists before the Committee generally concluded that increasing the after-tax return to saving should increase the saving rate of American households.
>
> American technological leadership has been enhanced by the willingness of individuals to take the risk of pursuing new businesses exploiting new technologies. Risk taking is stifled if the taxation of any resulting gain is high and the ability to claim losses is limited. The Committee believes it is important to encourage risk taking and believes a reduction in the taxation of capital gains will have that effect.
>
> Reduction in the taxation of capital gains also should improve the efficiency of the capital markets. The taxation of capital gains upon realization encourages investors who have accrued past gains to keep their monies "locked in" to such investments even when better investment opportunities present themselves. All economists that testified before the Committee

agreed that reducing the rate of taxation of capital gains would encourage investors to unlock many of these gains. This unlocking will permit more monies to flow to new, highly valued uses in the economy. When monies flow freely, the efficiency of the capital market is improved.

The unlocking effect also has the short-term and long-term effect of increasing revenues to the Federal Government. The current revenue estimating methods employed by the Congress account for this long-term behavioral response. Nevertheless, current Congressional estimates project that revenue losses to the Federal Government will arise from the reduction in the tax rate on capital gains. The Committee observes, however, that the conservative approach embodied in such estimates does not attempt to account for the potential for increased growth in GDP that can result from increased saving and risk taking. Many macroeconomists have concluded that reductions in the taxation of capital gains may increase GDP and wage growth sufficiently that future tax revenues from the taxation of wages and business profits will offset the losses forecast from the sale of capital assets. The potential for future growth and its benefits both for all United States citizens and for future Federal revenues were important considerations for the Committee.

The Committee rejects the narrow view that reductions in the taxation of capital gains benefit primarily higher-income Americans. Taking the longer view, the Committee sees a reduction in the taxation of capital gains as providing potential benefits to all individuals. Most importantly, the Committee stresses that economic growth benefits all Americans. Increased investment leads to greater productivity and leads to higher wages. Traditional attempts to measure the benefit or burden of a tax change do not account for this critical outcome.[68]

It is difficult to find a clearer acceptance of "trickle-down economics" as justification for tax reductions.

The IRS Restructuring and Reform Act of 1998[69] eliminated the 18-month holding period introduced in the 1997 Act, effective January 1, 1998.[70] As a result, the 20 percent long-term capital gains tax rate applied to assets held longer than one year, and the reduced rate of 18 percent applied to assets held longer than five years. Proposals introduced in 1999 to reduce the long-term capital gains tax rate to 18 percent (8 percent for taxpayers in the lowest tax bracket) and to eliminate the five-year holding period were ultimately vetoed by President Clinton.[71]

The Economic Growth and Tax Relief Reconciliation Act of 2001[72] reduced general income tax rates over the period 2001-2006, although the reductions are subject to a general sunset provision pursuant to which the reductions will expire on December 31, 2010 absent any further congressional action, at which time the rate bands revert to the five in effect in 2000.[73]

The Jobs and Growth Tax Relief Reconciliation Act of 2003[74] included extensive tax cuts, in an attempt to boost a flagging US economy. The long-term capital gains tax rate was reduced to 15 percent (5 percent for taxpayers in the 10 and 15 percent tax brackets), thus eliminating the need for the five-year holding period. In addition, the legislation accelerated the general income tax rate reductions introduced in 2001 so that they became fully effective in 2003 rather than 2006. As a result, the long-term capital gains tax rate is now less than one-half of the top marginal tax rate of 35 percent. Although the US federal rate of 15 percent is nearly equal to the effective Canadian federal tax rate on capital gains (14.5 percent), state capital gains tax rates are significantly lower than provincial capital gains tax rates (in many states, the rate is zero), so the effective US long-term capital gains tax rate is now significantly lower than the effective Canadian capital gains tax rate.

Characterization of Gain on Disposition
of Venture Capital Investment

Before leaving the US treatment of capital gains and losses, it is important to highlight the clear distinction that US tax law draws among "dealers," "traders," and "investors" for the purpose of the capital gains provisions affecting dispositions of securities. Under US tax law, an individual's gain arising from the disposition of securities is a capital gain unless the individual is a "dealer in securities." The distinction between dealers and others stems from the primary exclusion from the definition of "capital asset" in section 1221(a)(1) of the Code, which has remained unchanged since 1934. For a taxpayer in the business of trading securities, including commodity futures, the courts have consistently concluded that such securities are capital assets unless the securities are sold to customers.[75] It is worth repeating the rationale for the rule introduced in 1934: to ensure that stock speculators were also subject to the limited loss relief for capital losses.[76] Whether a taxpayer has customers or not distinguishes a dealer from a trader or investor. The Ninth Circuit Court of Appeals in *US v. Wood*[77] adopted these distinctions expressed by the Tax Court in *Kemon*:[78]

> A dealer is a person who purchases the securities or commodities with the expectation of realizing a profit
>
> > not because of a rise in value . . . but merely because they have or hope to find a market of buyers who will purchase from them at a price in excess of their cost. This excess or mark-up represents remuneration for their labors as a middle man bringing together buyer and seller. . . .
>
> Dealers have customers for the purposes of section 1221. . . .
> Traders, on the other hand, are sellers of securities or commodities who "depend upon such circumstances as a rise in value or an advantageous purchase to enable them to sell at a price in excess of cost." A trader performs no merchandising functions nor any other service which warrants compensation by a price mark-up of the securities he or she sells.

Regulations under the Code adopted a similar distinction between dealers and others as early as 1918.[79] A trader, like a dealer, may be engaged in a trade or business if the trading is frequent and substantial. Even so, a trader's gains and losses are on capital account unless the trading is with customers (that is, unless the trader is a dealer). Thus, a person trading securities on his or her own account will be subject to capital gains treatment regardless of the volume or frequency of the transactions or the nature of the securities traded. Whether the trader benefits from a preferential tax rate on the capital gains realized depends solely on the length of time that the asset was held.

For a dealer, gains are not considered capital gains unless "the security was, before the close of the day on which it was acquired . . . clearly identified in the dealer's records as a security held for investment" and was not held by the dealer primarily for sale to customers in the ordinary course of the dealer's business.[80] Furthermore, a dealer in securities must generally apply a mark-to-market basis of accounting for tax purposes.

In short, the United States applies a legislative bright line to the tax preference accorded to capital gains. The distinction between capital gains and ordinary income is a straightforward determination. If the taxpayer is a dealer, any gains realized or accrued are on income account. If the taxpayer is a trader or investor, any gains realized are on capital account. However, only long-term capital gains (that is, gains realized on the disposition of capital assets held longer than one year) realized by individuals benefit from preferential treatment.

This treatment is especially favourable to venture capital investments, which are generally held much longer than one year. Angel investors, unless they are dealers in securities as that term is narrowly construed, can be assured of capital gains treatment on the disposition of their venture capital investments. Even full-time venture capitalists—individuals who devote all of their time and attention to investments in SMEs—would not be considered dealers in securities, provided that they are trading on their own account. Furthermore, even if an individual invests indirectly in venture capital by becoming a limited partner in a US venture capital limited partnership, the individual's share of any gains realized by the fund will be treated as capital gains, provided that the fund is investing in securities for its own account.[81] Similarly, the carried interest of the general partner in a venture capital limited partnership would be taxed as a capital gain.

Canada

Although Canada introduced an income tax in 1917, capital gains were not subject to tax until 1972. The definition of income in the first income tax legislation in Canada included the catchall phrase "and also the annual net profit or gain from any other source,"[82] similar to the wording of the 1913 US income tax legislation.[83] In contrast to the approach taken by US courts, however, Canadian courts consistently excluded capital gains from income, relying on UK jurisprudence despite the fact that the UK income tax legislation differed significantly from Canadian legislation. As Harvey Perry suggested in 1961:

> For our income tax we borrowed our statute law substantially from the
> United States and our jurisprudence from England. The definition of income

contained in the Income War Tax Act enacted in 1917 has an unmistakable resemblance to United States income tax statutes and bears no resemblance whatever to the English Act. Yet the interpretation given it has followed with few exceptions the decisions of the English courts.[84]

The *Report of the Royal Commission on Taxation* in 1966[85] advocated the taxation of capital gains in full as ordinary income. It is readily apparent from the report that the Carter commission had considered the potential impact of its proposed reforms on venture capital (or risk capital generally). The report acknowledged that "[t]axing property gains would undoubtedly change the relative attractiveness of different kinds of investments,"[86] but that the role of the commission was to design a more efficient tax structure and not a system to increase investment and saving by Canadians. Furthermore, the commission was of the view that the investment decisions should be determined by the operation of the markets and not by government planning,[87] and that a number of other proposed measures would offset or remove any bias against risk taking in any event. These other measures included the more liberal treatment of capital losses,[88] the reduction of the tax burden on income from shares through integration, and accelerated depreciation rates for new and small businesses.[89] The dissenting members of the commission, Emile Beauvais and Donald Grant, agreed that capital gains should be subject to tax, but recommended that they be taxed at a preferential rate in order to promote risk taking.

In the commission's main background paper dealing with the taxation of capital gains, Geoffrey Conway reviewed the various arguments surrounding the impact of a capital gains tax on risk taking.[90] In Conway's view, the influence of tax considerations on investment decisions remained an open question. He cited a Harvard University study[91] that concluded that although taxes may cause some investors to become more conservative in their investment decisions, taxes may stimulate others to assume greater risks in an attempt to achieve more after-tax income. According to the Harvard study,

> the tax structure [in the United States], as of 1949, cut substantially into the investment capacity of the upper income and wealth classes—the strategic source of venture capital for investment in business—and, on balance, it also decreased the willingness of these investors in the aggregate to make equity-type investments. . . . [I]nvestors who were induced by taxes to shift to less risky investment positions appear to have over balanced the opposite reaction of appreciation-minded investors. The latter group, however, may have been so stimulated by the tax structure to seek out investments offering unusually large capital gains potentialities, such as promising new ventures, as actually to increase the flow of capital to such situations. However . . . it is clear that the combined impact of these effects fell far short of drying up the supply of equity capital which private investors were willing and able to make available to business.[92]

Conway also suggested that "the effect of taxation on capital gains . . . would appear to be nominal in comparison to the many other factors" that affect an individual's investment decisions, such as the investor's personal circumstances, expectations of inflation, and general business conditions.[93]

Perhaps most telling, Conway contrasted the taxation of capital gains and the pervasiveness of venture capital in Canada and the United States. Despite the (preferential) taxation of capital gains in the United States and the exemption of capital gains from tax in Canada, Canadians had overall smaller equity holdings than Americans. He concluded that "the extra tax incentives available to Canadian individuals on equity investments do not, in general, appear to have been capitalized"[94] and that there is "no qualitative support for the contention that Canadian tax incentives have improved the Canadian record."[95]

Following its submission to the House of Commons, the Carter report was discussed extensively, although the minister of finance made no move to implement the proposals. The introduction of a tax on capital gains was condemned by some members of the House on the ground that it would stifle risk investment in a country considered to be still in the first stages of its economic development.[96]

The Carter report was also the subject of much debate at the 1967 national conference of the Canadian Tax Foundation. A number of speakers commented on the impact of the proposed capital gains tax on venture capital and risk investing. From academe, Dan Throop Smith of Harvard University suggested that the proposals would have a "lock-in" effect on investors. Because the capital gains tax is a voluntary tax, it acts as a capital levy on the transfer from one investment to another.[97] Carl S. Shoup of Columbia University, who concentrated primarily on the economic effects of changes to the corporate income tax system, suggested that the proposals included competing forces: while the proposed tax would decrease the profit from the favourable outcome of a venture, both the allowance for capital losses and the reduction of the combined corporate-personal tax rate on corporate profits distributed to shareholders would increase the expected profit. Although any prediction would be hazardous, Shoup tentatively conjectured that the proposed system overall would reduce the degree of risk per venture. As for its impact on venture investing, Shoup commented:

> If, as seems likely, corporate investors prefer less risk to more risk given the same expected profit, the new system would then channel a larger proportion of corporate capital into ventures that tax provisions aside are more risky, than would occur under the existing system.[98]

John F. Chant of Queen's University believed that further research was required in order to evaluate the likely effects of the proposed changes to capital gains taxation.[99]

The practitioners' perspective was provided by P.N. Thorsteinsson:

> I think the business innovator in our society is motivated by the prospect of the pot of gold at the end of the rainbow, and by that prospect alone. The Commission's proposal will remove—or tend to remove—the incentive, and compensate for that by also removing—or tending to remove—the disincentive tax penalty in respect of losses. The result, to my mind, is

that the economic man will tend to just stand there. The real concern I have is that the *Report* does not seem to see the difference between the provision of a genuinely attractive incentive, and the removal of a disincentive. The *Report* seems to equate the two, and in my view the world of economic theory is the only place in which that equation holds good.[100]

In its 1969 white paper,[101] the government responded to the Carter report with its proposals for income tax reform. It adopted, in general, the Carter commission's recommendation to make realized capital gains fully taxable and realized capital losses fully deductible. Full income and deduction would apply to dispositions of shares of private corporations. However, shares of widely held Canadian corporations would be dealt with differently. First, taxpayers (other than widely held Canadian corporations) would include only one-half of the gain and deduct only one-half of the loss on the disposition of such shares; in addition, taxpayers would be required to revalue those shares every five years and take into account one-half of the resulting gain or loss.[102]

The white paper proposals were the subject of extensive public hearings and reports of both the House of Commons Standing Committee on Finance, Trade and Economic Affairs[103] and the Senate Standing Committee on Banking, Trade and Commerce.[104] The capital gains tax proposals were largely condemned by private industry in these hearings. Ultimately, both the House committee and the Senate committee rejected the full inclusion of capital gains in income. The House committee acknowledged that the full inclusion of capital gains had administrative and equity advantages and that the full deductibility of capital losses (and proposed income-averaging provisions) would likely counter the adverse effects of inclusion on savings, investment, and economic growth. However, the committee rejected a distinct treatment for shares of widely held companies. Given the desire to treat all capital gains in the same manner (subject to a few exceptions) and on the basis of repeated representations from the private sector and provincial governments that capital gains should be subject to preferential treatment, the House committee concluded, as a general rule, that only one-half of realized capital gains should be taxed. Correspondingly, only one-half of capital losses should be allowed as a deduction and only against capital gains, except that excess losses of up to $1,000 per year could be deducted against other income. Although the committee did not address the impact of a capital gains tax on risk investing, new ventures, or entrepreneurship in its report, it was a topic discussed frequently in the submissions to and arguments heard by the committee.

The Senate committee acknowledged that "[s]haring the tax burdens equitably is an excellent principle";[105] however, it thought the principle must be weighed in the context of other principles that must guide the committee's decisions, especially Canada's economic growth and competition for foreign risk capital. The committee commented that

in almost every western country, and more particularly in the United States, the taxing systems have acknowledged the desirability of applying different tax procedures with respect to ordinary income and capital gains, and your Committee sees no reason why Canada should deliberately exclude itself from the international investing community by the procedures contemplated by the White Paper.[106]

The Senate committee proposed a distinction between short-term capital gains (on capital assets held less than one year) and long-term capital gains (on capital assets held one year or more): short-term capital gains and losses would be treated as ordinary income; net long-term capital gains (the excess of long-term capital gains over long-term capital losses) would be taxed at the lower of 25 percent and one-half of the taxpayer's marginal tax rate, and any excess long-term capital losses could be carried back three years and forward eight.

The ultimate result of the Carter report, the white paper, and the hearings and reports on the white paper was Bill C-259, the 1971 tax reform legislation. It provided that one-half of capital gains would be included in income and one-half of capital losses would be deductible against taxable capital gains and (for taxpayers other than corporations) against up to $1,000 of other income.[107] The tax reform bill was first mentioned in the budget speech of June 18, 1971. It was formally introduced in the House June 30, 1971, received second reading September 13, 1971, and third reading December 10, 1971. There were 6 days of debate on the budget and another 50 days of debate on the bill before a closure motion was invoked. Most of the capital gains debate focused on the impact on family farms and the removal of estate and succession taxes. Surprisingly little debate concerned its potential impact on risk capital. The bill received first and second reading by the Senate on December 17, 1971 and third reading and approval on December 21, 1971, and received royal assent on December 23, 1971.[108]

From 1972 to 1987, few substantive changes were made to the general tax treatment of capital gains and losses. In the 1977 budget, the minister of finance introduced a number of measures designed to encourage investment in small businesses. Among these was the doubling of the amount of net capital losses that an individual could deduct against other income, from $1,000 to $2,000.[109] This amendment was the subject of some debate in the House when Bill C-11, the bill introducing the budget measures, was introduced for second reading on November 24, 1977. According to the minister of finance, Jean Chrétien, the amendment was intended to "give [people] more incentive to invest risk money so that they could be somewhat compensated for the losses incurred. . . . It is a good incentive for people to take some risk in order to develop the Canadian economy."[110] This proposal followed on the heels of a similar reform in the United States in the previous year.[111] In response to the question why the loss offset was limited to $2,000 (as opposed to being fully deductible), the minister of finance responded:

We have, of course, received a number of representations on this. These representations have suggested that there should be no limit on the deductibility of capital losses. This will not only be costly in terms of revenue, but will permit the reduction of taxes by many taxpayers with a significant investment portfolio, those we call the rich. . . .

If we were to allow tax deductions every year for losses incurred, I am sure that a great many rich people in this country would use this system to hide a lot of revenue and avoid paying taxes, , , . This $2,000 exemption is providing an incentive to take risks but if somebody has taken such risks incurring great losses, it is because he took too many risks and he must therefore pay the consequences. That is why other revenues should not be tax exempt.[112]

The 1977 budget also introduced a limited capital gains exemption. Each year, in determining taxable income, an individual could deduct up to $1,000 of taxable capital gains (at the time, one-half of the capital gain) from dispositions of "Canadian securities" (shares or debt of Canadian corporations), as well as Canadian-source interest and dividends from Canadian corporations—in effect, a limited investment income exemption.[113] With the introduction of the lifetime capital gains exemption in 1985, capital gains were removed from the annual exemption.[114] The remaining exemption was removed in the 1987 tax reform package.[115]

In 1980, the Department of Finance released a discussion paper reviewing the role of capital gains tax in Canada's tax system.[116] Although the paper prompted some parliamentary debate, it did not lead to any substantive changes to the tax treatment of capital gains.[117] In the 1981 budget, the government attempted some tax reform, aimed at broadening the tax base and reducing tax rates.[118] Many of the measures were never introduced because of the adverse reaction from the business community. In June 1982, the minister of finance, Allan MacEachen, released a consultation paper proposing various reforms to remove some of the distorting effects of inflation.[119] One of these proposals was the introduction of an annual accrual of capital gains on certain assets, the cost of which was indexed annually for inflation. This proposal was incorporated in the indexed security investment plan provisions introduced in 1983.[120] The provisions were short-lived; they were removed with the introduction of the $500,000 lifetime capital gains exemption in the 1985 budget (discussed in more detail below, under the heading "Preferential Treatment of Gains from Small Business Securities"). With the introduction of the capital gains exemption,[121] the provision allowing individuals to deduct up to $2,000 of capital losses annually from other sources of income was removed[122] as was the annual $1,000 investment income deduction as it applied to taxable capital gains.[123]

The 1985 budget also introduced an alternative minimum tax for many of the same reasons as it was introduced in the United States in 1978. According to Michael Wilson, the minister of finance:

The greatest source of concern is the ability of some high-income individuals to take advantage of existing tax incentives to shelter virtually all of their income. There is no question that such tax planning is legitimate, and that the incentives serve valid objectives. Canadians nevertheless feel frustrated when some high-income individuals pay little or no tax. I share this frustration.[124]

An individual must pay AMT if the amount of AMT exceeds the individual's regular tax liability. If AMT does exceed regular tax, the excess may be carried forward seven years and recovered to the extent that the regular tax liability exceeds the AMT liability in a future year. AMT is based on an individual's "adjusted taxable income," which is taxable income subject to a number of adjustments that are designed to remove various tax preferences. The amount on which AMT is charged is the individual's adjusted taxable income less a basic exemption of $40,000. The rate of AMT is the lowest personal income tax rate (currently 16 percent). In determining an individual's adjusted taxable income, the full amount (rather than one-half) of capital gains and capital losses has been taken into account (until 2000), although capital losses remain deductible only against capital gains.[125]

In June 1987, the minister of finance released a tax reform white paper,[126] considered by many to be the second most significant tax reform undertaken in Canada (after the 1971 tax reform). Like the 1986 tax reform in the United States, the 1987 tax reform in Canada comprised a significant reduction in overall personal tax rates as well as a broadening of the tax base.[127] The inclusion rate for capital gains was increased from one-half to three-quarters, with a phase-in over two years (during which the inclusion rate was two-thirds). Unlike the 1971 tax reform, there was no grandfathering of the one-half inclusion rate for gains accrued prior to the introduction of the new inclusion rates. In addition to the overall increase in capital gains tax rates, the lifetime capital gains exemption was reduced. For assets other than qualified farm property and QSBC shares, the lifetime capital gains exemption was frozen at $100,000 (the limit applicable for 1987). The limit applicable to QSBC shares was increased to $500,000 starting in 1988 (rather than being subject to the original five-year phase-in established in 1985) to match the exemption available for qualified farm property. This targeted capital gains exemption is considered separately below.

The $100,000 lifetime exemption was further eroded in 1992, when it was eliminated for dispositions of certain real property.[128] In 1994, the $100,000 exemption was eliminated altogether,[129] although the $500,000 exemption for qualified farm property and QSBC shares remains. None of the more limited relief measures for capital gains and losses[130] that were repealed in 1985 when the broad-based exemption was introduced have been reinstated.

As in the United States, the base-broadening measures introduced in 1987 were relatively short-lived, at least in the case of capital gains. The February 2000 federal budget reduced the capital gains inclusion rate from three-quarters to two-thirds and the October 2000 economic statement further reduced it to one-half (that is, back to the original inclusion rate that applied from 1971 to 1987). It is interesting to compare the rationale given for the reduction in the capital gains tax in the February 2000 budget with those given for the reductions in the US rate in 1978 and in 1997:[131]

The high-technology sector and other fast-growing industries are particularly important to Canada's future economic growth. Our tax system must
be conducive to innovation, and must ensure that businesses have access to
the capital they need in an economy that is becoming increasingly competitive and knowledge-based. An examination of the taxation of capital
gains in Canada suggests that this objective would be better achieved with
a reduction in the inclusion rate of capital gains from the current three-
quarters to two-thirds.[132]

In his October 2000 economic statement, the minister of finance announced
that "as part of our approach to encouraging entrepreneurship and the creation
of new jobs . . . we will go further"[133] and reduce the capital gains inclusion rate
to one-half. The supplementary documentation produced by the Department of
Finance attributes the further reduction to competition with the United States.
According to these documents, as a result of the reduction, "the top federal-
provincial tax rate on capital gains in Canada will be . . . lower than the typical
combined federal-state top tax rate on capital gains in the U.S."[134] The documents
further state that "the rates for Canada apply to all capital gains, regardless of
the type of asset or the length of time the asset is held, contrary to what is the
case in the U.S."[135]

With the 2003 reduction of the US tax rate on long-term capital gains to 15
percent, the United States has retaken the lead (so to speak) in lowering taxes on
capital gains. Political pressure appears to be mounting for Canada to follow suit.[136]

Characterization of Gain on Disposition
of Venture Capital Investment

The suggestion in the October 2000 economic statement that Canadian risk
takers will benefit from capital gains treatment "regardless of the type of asset
or the length of time the asset is held" is not necessarily true. Unlike the United
States, Canada does not distinguish between traders and dealers in securities;
for both, gains are taxed on income rather than capital account. Furthermore, a
gain realized in "an adventure or concern in the nature of trade" is also generally treated on income account.[137]

Subsection 39(4) of the Act provides a mechanism whereby a taxpayer can
elect to treat all dispositions of Canadian securities[138] on capital account. However, certain taxpayers, including a "trader or dealer in securities," are not
permitted to make this election.[139] Unlike the situation in the United States, the
phrase "trader or dealer in securities" is not defined in the Act or regulations.
The administrative position of the Canada Revenue Agency (CRA) on the
meaning of trader or dealer was originally quite narrow:

> For the purposes of subsection 39(5) the Department interprets the term
> "trader or dealer in securities" to mean a taxpayer who participates in the
> promotion or underwriting of a particular issue of shares, bonds or other
> securities or a taxpayer who holds himself out to the public as a dealer in
> shares, bonds or other securities. The term is not considered to include an

officer or employee of a firm or corporation that is engaged in the promotion or underwriting of issues of shares, bonds or other securities nor an officer or employee of a taxpayer who holds himself out to the public as a dealer in shares, bonds or other securities, unless that officer or employee transacts in securities as a result of the promoting or underwriting activities of this employer. Any person who, as a result of special knowledge of a particular corporation not available to the public, utilizes that knowledge to realize a quick gain is considered by the Department to be a "trader or dealer in securities" for those particular securities. Any corporation whose prime business activity is trading in shares or debt obligations is also considered to be a "trader or dealer" in securities, but this does not include a corporation whose prime business is the holding of securities and which sells such investments from time to time.[140]

This interpretation was similar to the meaning of "dealer" in the United States. It did not include an individual who actively trades securities for his or her own account unless the person had and relied upon insider knowledge.

However, the CRA broadened its administrative position following the Federal Court of Appeal decision in *The Queen v. Vancouver Art Metal Works Limited*.[141] There, the court concluded that the words "trader or dealer" must be given their plain and ordinary meaning, which encompasses any person "when his dealings amount to carrying on a business and can no longer be characterized as investor's transactions or mere adventures or concerns in the nature of trade."[142] This decision significantly reduces the utility of an election under subsection 39(4).

Thus, in Canada, unlike in the United States, traders in securities are treated on income rather than capital account. Whether or not a person is trading in securities (on income account) or investing in securities (generally on capital account)[143] will depend on a number of factors. As the Federal Court of Appeal suggested in *Vancouver Art Metal Products*,

> a taxpayer who makes it a profession or a business of buying and selling securities is a trader or a dealer in securities within the meaning of paragraph 39(5)(a) of the Act. As Cattanach, J. stated in *Palmer v. R.*, "it is a badge of trade that a person who habitually does acts capable of producing profits is engaged in a trade or business." It is, however, a question of fact to determine whether one's activities amount to carrying on a trade or business. Each case will stand on its own set of facts. Obviously, factors such as the frequency of the transactions, the duration of the holdings (whether, for instance, it is for a quick profit or a long term investment), the intention to acquire for resale at a profit, the nature and quantity of the securities held or made the subject matter of the transaction, the time spent on the activity, are all relevant and helpful factors in determining whether one has embarked upon a trading or dealing business.[144]

On the basis of this reasoning, a strong argument can be made that most venture capital investors are in the business of acquiring and selling shares of portfolio companies. In general, angel capitalists acquire shares in the expectation of selling them at a substantial profit.[145] Even if the shares are common shares that carry a discretionary dividend entitlement, it is unlikely that dividends will be paid (at least while they are owned by the angel capitalist). In addition, angel capitalists commonly take an active role in the businesses in which they invest and may be considered insiders. These factors are all hallmarks of someone involved in a trade (or, at the very least, an adventure or concern in the nature of trade). For passive investors in venture capital limited partnerships as well as the general partners, the partnership's gains should similarly be taxed on income account.[146] If a taxpayer disposes of shares of a portfolio company in an isolated transaction, any gain on the disposition may be protected by an election under subsection 39(4). If, however, the taxpayer is considered a trader in securities—and it is arguable that venture capitalists who devote their full time and attention to investments and actively participate in the management of portfolio companies are traders—any gain on the sale of securities would be on income account in Canada, regardless of whether a subsection 39(4) election is made.[147] In contrast, similar taxpayers trading in securities in the United States would be subject to capital gains treatment (although preferential rates apply only to individuals who realize long-term capital gains).

Evaluation of the Preferential Tax Treatment of Capital Gains

In recent amendments to the general tax treatment of capital gains, both Canada and the United States have justified an increased tax preference on the basis that it encourages risk taking. This rationale, however, is difficult to substantiate. In fact, it is arguable that reducing the general capital gains tax rate diminishes or even eliminates the incentive for investing in high-risk small businesses. It is not my intention to review the entire debate over the preferential tax treatment of capital gains: it is a topic that is much broader than the scope of this study, and has been considered in detail by many others.[148]

At the outset, I reiterate my view that both Canada and the United States should repeal the tax preference generally accorded to capital gains. I acknowledge, however, that the likelihood of either country doing so is virtually non-existent and Canada certainly would not act unilaterally in this respect. So long as there are tax preferences that require a distinction to be made between capital gains and ordinary income,[149] the income tax legislation should clearly distinguish between dispositions of venture capital investments that give rise to capital gains and those that do not. Under the US Internal Revenue Code, the distinction is clear. Under the Canadian Income Tax Act, the distinction is not. While the problems of characterizing gains from the disposition of venture capital investments may exist more in theory than in practice in Canada (as a result of the CRA's apparent assessing policy), any uncertainty may have a chilling effect on angel capitalists as well as on certain formal venture capital investors. For these reasons (and that it would reduce the amount of case law significantly), the Income Tax Act should distinguish between traders and dealers in the same manner as in the United States, at least with respect to securities transactions. Deleting the concept of an "adventure or concern in the nature of trade" from the definition of "business" would be helpful, but it is not a complete solution. The Act could be amended to eliminate the trading of securities (or perhaps any property) from the definition of business unless the trading is with customers. Alternatively, if less satisfactorily, the exclusions from the subsection 39(4) election for Canadian securities should be amended to remove the reference to traders. If the government considers that some securities trading (as opposed to dealing) should be taxed on income rather than capital account, it should adopt a statutory bright line for preferential tax treatment, such as the holding-period test applicable in the United States distinguishing between short- and long-term capital gains.

Turning to the more substantive issue—whether a general tax preference for all capital gains promotes venture capital investments—a number of reasons have been advanced for the preferential tax treatment of capital gains, few of which are even remotely connected with the issue of venture capital formation. The three leading reasons are to correct for inflation, to remove the "lock-in" effect, and to increase investment in new technologies. The first reason addresses a general concern and is not particularly relevant to venture capital formation.[150] The second is only indirectly relevant, in that it speaks to the general issue of freeing up capital. In the context of venture capital, the lock-in effect has been addressed, to some extent, by certain rollovers permitted in the United States and Canada;[151] these provisions are considered below under the heading "Angel Capital Rollover." The third reason is the most directly relevant and is explored in greater detail here.

The latest rounds of capital gains tax cuts in Canada and the United States were justified as a means of increasing investment in new technologies (that is, venture capital). A lower rate of capital gains tax arguably encourages risk taking generally, because the proportion of the return paid in the form of price appreciation increases as the riskiness of the investment increases. Given that venture capital is one of the riskiest forms of investment, it would benefit the most from a capital gains tax preference. However, the economic evidence supporting this rationale is at best mixed.

In its 1985 report to US Congress on the impact of the 1978 capital gains tax reductions, the Office of the Secretary of the Treasury suggested:

> Apart from a presumably small increase in overall saving, a reduction in capital gains taxes may be expected to encourage investment in emerging firms and industries for two reasons. First, there may be an increase in the supply of funds to these industries to the extent that lower capital gains taxes cause investors to reallocate funds from other investments. Second, there may be an increase in the number of people willing to leave stable jobs to undertake entrepreneurial activities, thereby creating an increased demand for funding of these activities.[152]

The 1985 report acknowledged that "favorable tax treatment of capital gains is not necessarily an efficient way of targeting tax incentives to emerging and

high technology industries, although it does help entrepreneurial activity generally."[153] The report cited the "spectacular" increase in capital committed to
venture capital firms following the 1978 tax reductions. Proponents of a capital
gains tax preference suggest that changes in aggregate venture capital investment in the United States provide evidence of the impact of capital gains
taxation—specifically, that venture capital investment declined after the 1969
hike in capital gains tax rates and increased after the 1978 and 1981 tax rate
cuts. However, proponents of reduced rates ignore the effect of numerous other
factors that influence venture capital investment, including technological
changes in particular industries (such as the development of fibre optic cables),
macroeconomic factors (such as stock market activity, especially the rate of
initial public offerings, inflation, and interest rate movements), and other policy
changes (such as the changes to Employee Retirement Income Security Act of
1974 [ERISA][154] in 1979). Thus, for example, the "spectacular" increase in
formal venture capital investment following 1978 was due primarily to increased
investment by pension funds, as a result of the changes to ERISA, as well as other
entities not affected by preferential capital gains tax rates.[155]

While those who cite changes in the amount of venture capital investment
in support of reduced capital gains tax rates can easily be criticized for failing
to consider the makeup of the formal venture capital industry, their critics can
equally be faulted for failing to consider, or at least underestimating the importance of, the informal venture capital industry, which consists almost exclusively
of individual investors. James Poterba, for example, relies on statistics from the
formal venture capital industry over the period 1977-1988 to challenge the view
that changes in capital gains tax rates affect the supply of venture capital funds.[156]
Although Poterba acknowledges that most informal venture capital investors
are subject to capital gains tax liability, he indicates that the precise magnitude
of the informal market is unclear.[157] Bharat Anand developed an econometric
model to test the effect of capital gains taxes on venture capital investors in the
United States.[158] His modelling contrasted changes in investment behaviour by
individuals (the investors most affected by changes in capital gains tax rates)
with the behaviour of other investors (for example, non-taxable entities and
corporations) and found that capital gains tax rates do affect individual investment. However, he found that general decreases in income tax rates, which
indirectly reduce capital gains tax rates, hurt individual investment in venture
capital. He concluded that "a decrease in the capital gains rate is *not sufficient*
to stimulate venture capital investments. What matters clearly is a cut in tax rates
specific to VC investments, relative to taxes on other types of capital income."[159]

It has also been suggested that a reduced capital gains tax rate—more
specifically, an increased differential between the employment income tax rate
and the capital gains tax rate[160]—can lead to an increase in entrepreneurial
activity.[161] That is, individuals may be encouraged to leave jobs to form new
enterprises in order to convert ordinary employment income into deferred and
preferentially taxed capital gains. This action will result in an increased demand
for venture capital. Poterba suggests that this link between capital gains tax

rates and venture capital "seems more plausible than one focused on the supply of venture funds."[162] Although this argument has some intuitive appeal, I am not aware of any empirical studies or econometric modelling that has attempted to support it. Moreover, individuals who make the change from employee to entrepreneur-shareholder benefit from the deferral of income under a realization-based capital gains tax; it is unclear why they should also benefit from a capital gains tax preference.

At the very least, it is difficult to deny that an across-the-board reduction of capital gains tax is a very blunt instrument for encouraging investment in new technology firms. In fact, it can discourage investment in new firms. Given the relative difficulty of exiting from venture capital investments, a general capital gains tax preference is likely to increase investment in capital property for which there is a larger secondary market, including public equities and real estate.[163] Furthermore, a general preference increases the attractiveness of retained earnings to all firms and therefore reduces dividend payout rates,[164] which in turn reduces the supply of capital for new business ventures, which typically have little if any retained earnings.[165]

At best, it might be argued that a general capital gains tax preference is a signal of the government's approval of risk taking. As Michael Livingston notes, "the [US Internal Revenue] Code is an important means of communicating cultural values between the nation and its citizens":[166]

> Cultural factors affect tax policy regarding risk in at least three ways. First, the celebration of risk means that policymakers will interpret economic evidence so as to emphasize the link between risk taking and the public good. . . .
>
> Second, cultural factors help to determine which risks the Code should compensate. There is a tendency to favor activities that convey an image of individual daring and self reliance, even if this image at times diverges from reality. Of particular appeal are activities, such as farming and the extractive industries, that are associated (however vaguely) with the taming of the frontier and that are subject to physical as well as ordinary economic (that is, market) risks. High technology industries (the scientific "frontier") have a similar appeal. . . .
>
> Finally, cultural risks encourage industry advocates to emphasize risk even when other factors (energy independence or technological superiority) are the underlying reasons for the subsidy. With the relative decline of national security arguments in the post-Cold War era, a renewed emphasis on risk can be expected.[167]

Livingston notes that in such signalling—or in advocating for such signalling—there is a tendency to exaggerate the benefits of risk taking and the risks involved and also to exaggerate the taxpayer's inability to control such risks. In the end, he concludes that

> culture may be the strongest argument against risk incentives. Americans admire risk taking because it is tied to individualism and daring, to the image of our frontier past. Yet, government intervention inevitably undermines

that individualist spirit. While encouraging risky activities in the short run, tax incentives foster a sense of dependency that eventually makes real risk less likely. . . . The true spirit of risk taking must come from within, and the returns achieved will be measured by the risks we are willing to bear.[168]

Given the strong arguments against an across-the-board capital gains tax preference as a means of enhancing investment in high-technology firms, it is unclear why the Canadian and US governments have pursued this approach rather than more targeted incentives.[169] Granted, both countries do have more targeted incentives, but a general capital gains tax preference has undermined their efficacy.

Preferential Treatment of Gains from Small Business Securities

In addition to a general tax preference for capital gains, both Canada and the United States have a tax preference for gains realized on dispositions of small business securities. These preferences, introduced in the United States in 1993 and in Canada in 1985, were intended to increase equity investment in SMEs. In many respects, however, these targeted incentives have been weakened considerably by changes in both countries' tax treatment of capital gains. In the United States, the preference was effectively eliminated in 1997, when the general capital gains tax rate was reduced without any corresponding relief for small business securities. In Canada, the preference still has some significance, although it lost some of its lustre when the general capital gains inclusion rate was reduced from three-quarters to one-half in 2000. Even if a substantial differential existed between these incentives and a general capital gains tax preference, it is questionable whether the more targeted preference would have the desired effect of increasing investment in the "right" SMEs—that is, innovative SMEs that will generate new (and good) jobs in the two countries—rather than all SMEs, the vast majority of which have little or no bearing on economic growth or prosperity.

United States

The Omnibus Budget Reconciliation Act of 1993 introduced a targeted incentive for individuals to invest in venture capital: 50 percent of the capital gain from a disposition of QSBS held for more than five years would be excluded from income.[170] According to the House committee:

> targeted relief for investors who risk their funds in new ventures, small businesses, and specialized small business investment companies, will encourage investments in these enterprises. This should encourage the flow of capital to small businesses, many of which have difficulty attracting equity financing.[171]

The Senate amendment to the House bill deleted this provision. However, the provision was adopted in the conference report, subject to certain amendments, and incorporated into the 1993 Act. The following is a summary of the requirements that must be met in order to benefit from the 50 percent exclusion[172] in Code section 1202:

1) To qualify as QSBS, the stock must have been acquired by the taxpayer at the original issuance (directly or through an underwriter) in exchange for cash or other property (other than stock) or as compensation for services rendered to the issuing corporation (other than services as an underwriter of the stock).[173] There are certain anti-avoidance rules (dealing with redemptions or other purchases of shares by the corporation) to ensure that the stock is newly issued.[174]

2) The corporation must be a qualified small business as of the date of issuance.[175] A qualified small business is a subchapter C corporation, the aggregate gross assets of which (based on cost) did not exceed $50 million at any time before the stock issuance or immediately after the stock issuance (taking into account the proceeds of the issue). As an anti-avoidance measure, all corporations that are members of the same parent-subsidiary controlled group are treated as one corporation.[176]

3) The corporation must meet an active business test during substantially all of the period of ownership. There are two conditions to this test: at least 80 percent (by value) of the assets must be used in the active conduct of one or more "qualified trades or businesses," and the corporation must remain an "eligible corporation."[177] A qualified trade or business is any trade or business other than certain excluded activities.[178] An eligible corporation is a domestic corporation, subject to certain limited exclusions.[179] Certain lookthrough rules apply for subsidiaries.[180] In addition, a corporation does not qualify if more than 10 percent of the total value of its assets consists of real property not used in the active conduct of a qualified business.[181]

4) The 50 percent exclusion is subject to a de maximis limitation, although an extremely generous one. The exempt gain on the disposition of QSBS of a corporation is limited to the greater of $10 million of gain from dispositions of stock of that corporation (essentially, a per-issuer lifetime limitation) and 10 times the aggregate adjusted bases of the disposed stock.

The non-exempt portion of the capital gain is subject to tax at 28 percent, the maximum rate applicable to capital gains under section 1(h) of the Code. In essence, the effective rate of tax on capital gains from dispositions of QSBS is 14 percent, ignoring AMT.

The QSBS exemption has been largely undermined by the reduction in the long-term capital gains tax rates since 1997, because the general reduction has not been accompanied by changes to the QSBS rules.[182] As a result of the 1997 amendments, for taxpayers subject to AMT, the effective AMT tax rate on QSBS gains was virtually identical to the general maximum long-term capital gains tax rate of 20 percent (which rate also applies for AMT purposes),[183] Under the IRS Restructuring and Reform Act of 1998,[184] the AMT preference for the excluded portion of the gain was reduced from 42 percent to 28 percent for QSBS the holding period for which begins after December 31, 2000, which reintroduced a slight preference for QSBS investments over other long-term capital investments.[185] With the reduction of the long-term capital gains tax rate to 15 percent in 2003, however, the preference for QSBS investments has essentially been eliminated. In the absence of AMT, the effective rate of tax for QSBS gains is only 1 percent below the long-term capital gains tax rate; if, however, the gain is subject to AMT, the preference over long-term capital gains is only 2/100 of 1 percent.[186]

Thus, as a result of reductions in the long-term capital gains tax rate beginning in 1997, and particularly the reduction in the long-term capital gains tax rate to 15 percent in 2003, the QSBS incentive has been completely enfeebled.

Canada

The 1985 budget introduced a broadly-based $500,000 lifetime capital gains exemption. The exemption was intended to help improve conditions for productive economic growth by encouraging the movement of savings into capital investment. According to the budget documents, the exemption was

> a major initiative to encourage risk-taking and investment in small and large businesses. . . . This change will support equity investment and broaden participation by individuals in equity markets. In addition, it will improve the balance sheets and financial health of Canadian companies. It will provide a tax environment that is more conducive to high technology companies raising capital. It will encourage individual Canadians to start new businesses and will help small businesses grow.[187]

The exemption was intended to encourage such investment by "rewarding success rather than subsidizing effort."[188] For dispositions of qualified farm property, the entire $500,000 exemption applied immediately. For all other capital gains, the $500,000 exemption was to be phased in over five years.[189]

Despite the suggestion that the lifetime capital gains exemption was designed to improve the health of the Canadian economy, and specifically to enhance investment in Canadian technology companies and new Canadian businesses, there were no limits on the type or location of capital property the gains from which were eligible for the exemption. It applied equally to shares of public or private Canadian or foreign corporations as well as to real estate (that is capital property) wherever located, whether Canadian rental properties or Florida condominiums.

The preference has become more targeted since 1987, although its efficacy remains questionable. When the general lifetime capital gains exemption was frozen in the 1987 tax reform at $100,000 (that is, the limit on the exemption then applicable), an enhanced $500,000 exemption remained available for gains realized by an individual on dispositions of qualified farm property and QSBC shares.

The exemption for QSBC shares has many similarities to the QSBS regime in the United States. To qualify for the enhanced capital gains exemption, shares must meet both a holding-period test and an asset test. In general, QSBC shares must have been owned by the individual (or a related person) for at least two years before their disposition.[190] The asset test has two components:[191]

1) on the date of disposition, the shares must be shares of a small business corporation, defined in subsection 248(1) as a corporation "all or substantially all"[192] of the assets of which are used in an active business carried on primarily in Canada; and

2) during the requisite holding period (generally, two years), more than 50 percent of the assets of the corporation must have been used principally in an active business carried on primarily in Canada.[193]

There are, however, three significant differences between the Canadian and US tax preferences for small business securities. First, the US preference applies only to shares originally issued from the corporation's treasury, while the Canadian exemption applies to QSBC shares however acquired. Second, although both regimes have a de maximis limitation, the US limit is much more generous than the Canadian limit. Third, the US preference excludes corporations engaged in certain types of businesses and imposes a size restriction on qualifying businesses; the Canadian preference applies to any qualified corporation engaged in any type of business and imposes no size limitations.

As in the United States, the benefit of the QSBC share exemption may be reduced by the application of AMT,[194] although the potential impact in Canada is much less significant than in the United States because an individual has always been entitled to claim the benefit of the QSBC share exemption for AMT purposes.[195]

Evaluation of the Preferential Treatment of Gains from Dispositions of Small Business Securities

As a tax expenditure, the small business capital gains exemption is more targeted than a general lifetime capital gains exemption. From the investor's perspective, Canada's $500,000 capital gains exemption for QSBC shares compares favourably with the reduced capital gains tax rate applicable to QSBS in the United States, if provincial and state capital gains taxes are ignored. Even though the exemption in Canada is small compared with the $10 million limit for QSBS in the United States, the effective federal tax rate on a gain in excess of $500,000 is 14.5 percent in Canada, which is close to the preferential 14 percent rate applicable to QSBS and the 15 percent long-term capital gains tax rate generally applicable in the United States since 2003. However, the Canadian tax preference for

QSBC share gains over $500,000 is significantly less than the US preference when one factors in state and provincial taxes.[196] If the gain is subject to AMT, the effective AMT rate in Canada (4.8 percent for gains up to $500,000 and 12,8 percent on the excess[197]) is substantially lower than the effective AMT rate in the United States applicable to QSBS (14.98 percent),[198] ignoring provincial AMT where applicable.

Although the Canadian QSBC share capital gains exemption compares favourably with the tax treatment of QSBS in the United States, at least at the federal level, the more relevant issue is whether the preferential treatment achieves the stated goal of promoting innovation through increased venture capital investment. Certainly, as a tax expenditure, it is better targeted than a general tax preference for capital gains.[199] However, while it may come closer to the target of promoting venture capital investment, it remains wide of the mark.

In Canada, the capital gains exemption applies to secondary market acquisitions of QSBC shares, which do not increase the amount of capital available to small businesses. This problem could easily be rectified by adding a condition, similar to that in the United States, that the exemption applies only to shares acquired at original issuance.[200] More important, though, in both countries the incentive is available to investors in many types of SMEs that should not benefit from favourable treatment. The US QSBS provisions include a "black list" of ineligible businesses that is similar to black lists used in many state angel capital tax credit and venture capital fund regimes.[201] In Canada, no effort is made to limit the types of businesses that benefit from the regime; there is not even a size limitation. However, even the US regime applies to many types of businesses that are not innovative (high-growth) SMEs. Since lifestyle businesses constitute more than 90 percent of all SMEs in both countries, it is likely that the bulk of the tax expenditure benefits shareholders of businesses that are not innovative and is enjoyed predominantly by lifestyle small-business owners, who are not motivated by a capital gains tax preference in any event. In sum, the expenditure does not adequately target the market failure it is intended to correct.

US tax and economic literature has not focused on the QSBS preference, likely because the preference was all but extinguished in 1997. In Canada, a 1994 special symposium on the lifetime capital gains exemption concluded that the exemption was "not an effective means of encouraging investment and risk-taking."[202] In a more detailed consideration of the effect of the lifetime capital gains exemption on risk taking in the same symposium, Vijay Jog examined aggregate data sources from Statistics Canada and longitudinal data derived from individual tax return data from the CRA. He suggested that there may be some link between the introduction of the capital gains exemption and risk taking, although he acknowledged that "proof of such causality may be a difficult, if not an impossible, task."[203] In addition to the problems with the study admitted by Jog, his rather tenuous conclusion is undermined by the fact that he did not determine the extent to which the increase in net capital gains realized on shares since 1985 was from "deemed" capital gains rather than actual capital gains. Since the 1987 budget in which the general capital gains exemption was reduced to $100,000, small-business owners have often "triggered" a capital gain on QSBC shares, perhaps in the context of an estate freeze, without disposing of the shares in an arm's-length sale. These triggered or deemed gains are often the subject of an election under subsection 85(1) (a source of data that may not have been available to Jog) whereby the gains are limited to the capital gains exemption available to the shareholder. Although these deemed gains would have been reported and included in the aggregate and micro statistics examined by Jog, they are hardly indicative of increased risk taking.

In an empirical study of the impact of the lifetime capital gains exemption on angel capital investment in Canada,[204] Patrizia Dal Cin found that 31.4 percent—less than one-third—of angel investors indicated that the lifetime capital gains exemption influenced their decision to undertake informal investing. She further concluded that angel investors, whether or not they were influenced by the capital gains exemption, were so different from non-angels that any tax incentives designed to promote angel investment might increase investment by current angels but would not encourage non-angels to invest. US angel investor studies have reached similar conclusions on the impact of tax incentives on angel and non-angel investors.[205] If this is the case, there are certainly more focused and less costly incentives to promote increased angel capital investment than a preferential tax rate on gains from all small business securities, particularly one as unfocused as that in Canada.

Angel Capital Rollover

In Canada, the 2000 federal budget introduced limited rollover relief to individuals who dispose of eligible small business securities and reinvest the proceeds in other eligible small businesses. This relief is modelled on similar relief that was introduced in the US Code three years earlier. In its original form, the Canadian provision was much more limited and more complicated in its application than its US counterpart. However, as a result of amendments introduced in the 2003 federal budget, the Canadian provision is now substantially similar to that in the United States.

From a fiscal policy perspective, this measure is more effective than the previous two for a variety of reasons. First, it is less expensive in that it provides a deferral rather than an outright tax saving for venture capital investment. Second, it is limited to the reinvestment of proceeds from successful investment in SMEs; thus, it rewards those individuals who (hopefully more through skill than luck) made good investment decisions and are therefore better able to address the information asymmetries affecting investment in SMEs. Repeat angels employ the knowledge learned from previous investments in making investment decisions, thus reducing the information asymmetries in subsequent investments. In addition, many angel investors are successful entrepreneurs who have cashed out and have decided to invest in (and provide guidance to) other business startup companies rather than start their own new ventures. Finally, the rollover acknowledges the fact that angel investors tend to be repeat investors who do not require incentives to make the first investment but can benefit from having more capital available to make repeat investments. It is therefore more appropriately targeted than the previous two measures.

United States

The first angel capital rollover was introduced in the Omnibus Budget Reconciliation Act of 1993, which added an elective rollover for individuals and C corporations that dispose of publicly traded securities and invest the proceeds in common stock of or a partnership interest in a specialized small business investment company (SSBIC) within 60 days of the date of sale.[206] The provision is limited, in the case of individuals, to $50,000 of gain per annum and a $500,000 lifetime exemption and, in the case of corporations, to $250,000 per annum and a $1,000,000 cumulative exemption. An SSBIC is a partnership or corporation licensed by the Small Business Administration under section 301(d) of the Small Business Investment Act of 1958 (as in effect on May 13, 1993) that invests in small business concerns in such a way as to facilitate ownership by "persons whose participation in the free enterprise system is hampered by social or economic disadvantages."[207] The SSBIC regime was repealed in 1996,[208] although the repeal did not revoke any SSBIC licences issued before the date of repeal. However, as a result of the repeal, the tax incentive provided in section 1044 of the Code is now of limited use.

Section 1045, which was introduced in the Taxpayer Relief Act of 1997,[209] provides a deferral to non-corporate taxpayers who sell QSBS[210] and reinvest the proceeds within 60 days in other QSBS.[211] In its original form, the provision applied only to a sale of directly held QSBS by the non-corporate taxpayer. However, the IRS Restructuring and Reform Act of 1998[212] extended the rollover to non-corporate taxpayers who are partners in a partnership or shareholders of an S corporation that disposes of QSBS. To benefit from the rollover, the partner or shareholder must have owned its interest in the partnership or S corporation at all times that the partnership or S corporation held the QSBS.[213]

To qualify for rollover treatment, the gain must meet the following requirements:

1) In order to qualify as QSBS, the stock (both that disposed of and that acquired within 60 days) must have been acquired by the taxpayer at the original issuance (directly or through an underwriter) in exchange for cash or other property (other than stock) or as compensation for services rendered to the issuing corporation (other than services as an underwriter of the stock).[214] There are certain anti-avoidance rules (dealing with redemptions or other purchases of shares by the corporation) to ensure that the stock is newly issued.[215]

2) In order for its stock to qualify as QSBS, both the corporation whose stock is disposed of and the corporation whose stock is acquired must be a qualified small business as of the date of issuance of the stock.[216]

A qualified small business is a subchapter C corporation, the aggregate gross assets of which did not exceed $50 million at any time before the stock issuance or immediately after the stock issuance (taking into account the proceeds of the issue).[217] The amount of aggregate gross assets is equal to cash plus the aggregate adjusted bases of other property.[218] As an anti-avoidance measure, all corporations that are members of the same parent-subsidiary controlled group are treated as one corporation.[219]

3) In order for the stock disposed of to qualify as QSBS and in order for the acquisition of the replacement stock to qualify for the rollover, the respective corporations must meet an active business test—for the stock disposed of, during "substantially all" of the period of ownership,[220] and for the replacement stock, during the first six months of ownership.[221] There are two conditions that must be satisfied under the active business test: at least 80 percent (by value) of the assets must be used in the active conduct of one or more "qualified trades or businesses";[222] and the corporation must remain an "eligible corporation" throughout the relevant period.[223] A qualified trade or business is any trade or business other than certain excluded activities.[224] An eligible corporation is a domestic corporation, subject to certain limited exclusions.[225] A corporation is not considered to meet the active business test for any period during which more than 10 percent of the value of its assets net of liabilities consists of stock or securities of other corporations that are not subsidiaries.[226] In addition, a corporation does not meet the test for any period during which more than 10 percent of the total value of its assets consist of real property not used in the active conduct of a qualified business.[227]

Before turning to equivalent Canadian provision, there are a few elements of section 1045 of the Code that are worth emphasizing, particularly when considering the Canadian provision. First, QSBS need not be common shares. Second, there are no monetary limits on the cost of the shares disposed of or on the amount that can be reinvested in a qualified small business. Third, the provision applies to any non-corporate taxpayer (including a trust). Finally, although the rollover does not apply to a gain that is treated as ordinary income,[228] the circumstances in which a gain would be characterized as ordinary income are much narrower in the United States than in Canada.[229]

Canada

In the February 27, 2000 budget, the minister of finance announced a limited rollover for individuals who dispose of a qualified investment (referred to under section 44.1 as an eligible small business corporation [ESBC] share) and reinvest the proceeds in other qualified investments within a certain period of time. The original proposals were broadened in the October 18, 2000 economic statement and budget update and again in the 2003 federal budget.[230] The salient features of the Canadian provision are:

1) Relief is limited to individuals (other than trusts). However, individuals are permitted to own ESBC shares indirectly through an "eligible pooling arrangement."[231]
2) ESBC shares are common shares issued from treasury to the investor.[232]
3) The corporation must be, at the time the shares are issued, an eligible small business corporation, which is defined as a Canadian-controlled private corporation (CCPC) all or substantially all of the assets of which (measured by value) are used in an active business, other than certain specified businesses,[233] carried on primarily in Canada, or are shares or debt of other related ESBCs.[234]
4) Immediately before and after the shares are issued to the individual, the total carrying value of the assets of the corporation and related corporations must not exceed $50 million.[235]
5) The ESBC share disposed of must have been held at least 185 days prior to its disposition.[236]
6) Throughout the period of ownership, the share must be a common share of an active business corporation,[237] which is defined as a taxable Canadian corporation all or substantially all of the assets of which (measured by value) are used in an active business, other than certain specified businesses,[238] or are shares of other related active business corporations.[239] The business must be carried on primarily in Canada for at least 730 days during the period that the individual owns the shares, or throughout the period that the individual owns the shares if less than 730 days.[240]
7) The proceeds of disposition must be reinvested in other ESBC shares at any time in the year of disposition or within 120 days of the end of the year.[241]

An eighth requirement—the most problematic aspect of the provision in its original form—was the $2 million monetary limit applicable to both the cost of the original shares and the cost of replacement shares of a related corporate group. These de maximis rules were eliminated in the 2003 federal budget.[242] Apart from being the primary cause of most of the complexity in the provision and the timing problems that they raised, it was unclear what purpose the de maximis limits served from a fiscal policy perspective. Suppose that an individual sold ESBC shares for $10 million, and assume that the shares had an aggregate cost of less than $2 million (the first de maximis limit). To take full advantage of the rollover, the individual would have been required to invest a maximum of $2 million each in a minimum of five other eligible small business corporations within 120 days of the sale (although this time period was extended in the 2003 budget, as indicated above). There are a number of reasons why the individual could not, and perhaps had no desire to, do so. First, the time period in which to find replacement investments is relatively short (although at least twice as long as the period in the United States, provided that the shares are disposed of before November 2 in the year of disposition).[243] Given the significant amount of due diligence that is generally undertaken before a venture investment is made, the individual may not be able to find five acceptable businesses. Furthermore, the individual may not be interested in making investments in five businesses given the time commitment that each investment may involve on an ongoing basis.[244] There are no similar monetary limitations in the United States.

The primary purpose of the provision is to promote investment in small businesses. According to the 2000 budget plan, when the rollover was introduced,

> [p]romoting innovation and growth also means ensuring that businesses have access to the risk capital they need to expand and prosper. This is particularly true for high-technology businesses, which are becoming increasingly important for innovation and economic growth. While the venture capital market has expanded considerably in recent years, start-up firms continue to have difficulty accessing risk capital because venture capitalists often focus more on established businesses. One factor that limits access to capital for small businesses is the fact that investors disposing of existing business investments to reinvest in other businesses must pay tax on the capital gains realized on the previous investment. This reduces the amount of money available for investment in new ventures.[245]

To benefit from the rollover, the individual must invest (and reinvest) in a qualifying small business that is worth no more than $50 million. It is unclear why an additional $2 million limit per group of related businesses was ever imposed. In the example above, there is no reason why the individual should not be entitled to reinvest the entire $10 million in one eligible small business in order to get the full benefit of the deferral, as is now the case. The $2 million limit essentially required an individual to diversify his or her proceeds among a number of otherwise qualifying small businesses (in this example, at least five) in order to get the maximum relief available. Perhaps this additional requirement was the government's paternalistic approach to portfolio diversification. However, individual venture capitalists are aware of the investment risks associated with this type of investment, and investment decisions should be left to the individual's business judgment and risk profile. Alternatively, the $2 million threshold may simply have been a cost-saving measure, a means of limiting the relief that was available. However, the $2 million threshold was not a lifetime or annual limitation; it was a per group of related businesses limitation. This aspect of the rollover was properly removed in 2003.

Evaluation of the Angel Capital Rollover

Considering the stated rationale for the angel capital rollover, both in Canada and the United States, some limitations common to both countries should be reconsidered. First, in both countries, corporations cannot benefit from the deferral. Given the fact that a certain amount of seed financing of small businesses is provided by corporations, it is unclear why they were excluded from the application of the provision. In the United States, the preferential tax treatment of capital gains is limited to individuals, which may have naturally led to a similar limitation for the angel capital rollover. For US corporations making venture capital investments, though, a rollover would provide a greater incentive to reinvest proceeds in other small businesses, since the gain would otherwise be subject to tax at the general corporate tax rate. In Canada, the preferential tax treatment of capital gains (that is, the one-half inclusion rate) applies to all taxpayers. It is therefore unclear why the angel rollover was limited to individuals. Perhaps Canada copied the US limitation without further consideration or perhaps it copied the same limitation applicable to the lifetime $500,000 capital gains exemption for QSBC shares. If the latter is the case, the limitation is unjustified. The $500,000 capital gains exemption is a lifetime exemption; given the relative ease with which individuals could multiply the exemption if it were extended to corporations (in the absence of complex anti-avoidance rules), it makes some sense to limit it to individuals. However, the same lifetime limitation does not apply to the angel rollover. Prior to 2003, there were obvious avoidance problems with extending the rollover relief to corporations because the $2 million limits could easily be circumvented without the introduction of exceedingly complex anti-avoidance rules. With the removal of the $2 million limits, the provision can be, and should be, extended to corporations.

Similarly, it may be argued that the deferral should extend to capital gains arising from dispositions of any capital property, provided that the proceeds are reinvested in qualified small business shares. This extension is similar to, though broader than, the rollover available for investments in SSBICs in section 1044 of the US Code. For example, if an individual disposes of publicly traded shares acquired in a secondary market transaction and reinvests the proceeds in an eligible small business corporation, is there any reason the individual should not benefit from deferral? If the provision is meant to attract investment from *potential* angels—that is, individuals who have not already made angel investments—these individuals will likely have to dispose of existing non-qualifying capital assets in order to raise the money necessary for investment. It is unlikely that either the Canadian or the US provision, available only if the first angel capital investment is successful and the proceeds are reinvested in a relatively short period of time, would prompt that first angel capital investment by someone who is not an angel. In effect, the provision as drafted in both countries is limited to repeat angels. Extending the rollover to dispositions of any capital property where the proceeds are reinvested in qualifying small businesses may make potential angels into angels at a significantly lower fiscal cost than that associated with a wholesale reduction in the capital gains tax rate.

The suggestion that the angel capital rollover relieves the "lock-in" effect of capital gains taxation is largely inaccurate. In general, non-tax considerations motivate angel investors to sell their investments, such as an initial public offering of shares or the successful sale of all of the shares of the investee firm (a sale over which an angel often has little control). Although income taxes arising on a successful investment are an important consideration, the imposition of taxes is unlikely to make an angel investor reconsider exiting (assuming that the angel is not forced to exit as a result of, say, a piggyback clause in a shareholders' agreement). The rollover is better viewed as an incentive for angel investors to reinvest proceeds in other qualifying small businesses than as a motivation to sell the original investment. If, however, the rollover were extended to dispositions of any capital property—or perhaps any corporate shares, whether public or private—where the proceeds are reinvested in qualified small businesses, the measure could relieve the lock-in effect more productively than reducing the effective rate of tax on capital gains generally.

Canada's angel capital rollover suffers from further specific problems that should be addressed. Although much of the complexity and poor drafting in section 44.1 were removed by the 2003 federal budget, there remain two key problems with the provision from a policy perspective. The first stems from the uncertainty in characterizing the gains realized by venture capitalists, including angel capitalists. Only capital gains can be deferred under section 44.1. An individual who is a trader or dealer in securities and whose gains from venture investments are on income account cannot use the provision. Experienced venture capitalists—the true business angels, who devote their full time and attention to venture investments—may be considered "traders" in securities as that term is currently interpreted for Canadian tax purposes. In effect, the very people who were meant to benefit from the provision may be prevented from doing so. This problem could be easily rectified by amending the provision so that it applies to "gains" from a qualifying disposition rather than "capital gains,"[246] although the better remedy is to provide a clearer distinction between capital gains and ordinary income in the context of venture capital investment, as discussed above.[247]

The second problem with section 44.1 is that the provision is limited to common shares issued from treasury. It does not apply, for example, to preference shares acquired from treasury even if the shares are, by their terms, convertible into common shares. If the preference shares are in fact converted into common shares prior to their sale, the common shares can qualify as ESBC shares provided that the corporation is an ESBC at the time of the conversion and the carrying value of its assets immediately before and after the conversion does not exceed $50 million. These results also apply to debt that is converted to common shares. It is common practice in the formal venture capital industry for venture capitalists to acquire convertible preference shares (and sometimes convertible debt) in their financing rounds. If an individual participates in such a financing round (for example, through an eligible pooling arrangement, as contemplated in section 44.1) or if an angel seeks to mimic this practice in an earlier financing round, the preference shares or debt acquired will not qualify for rollover treatment unless the shares or debt are subsequently converted into common shares and the common shares so acquired qualify as ESBC shares at the time of conversion. Often, preference shares acquired by venture capitalists automatically convert to common shares immediately following the corporation's initial public offering (IPO). However, common shares acquired in these circumstances cannot qualify because the corporation is no longer an ESBC following the IPO. Similarly, if preference shares are converted to common shares following subsequent rounds of financing that increase the value of the corporation's assets to more than $50 million, the common shares will not qualify. Finally, if an individual entrepreneur has undertaken an estate freeze in favour of family members (or a family trust) by exchanging his or her common shares of a closely held corporation for fixed-value preference shares, the disposition of those preference shares cannot qualify for the rollover. It is unclear why the provisions should be limited to common shares. The US rules do not have a similar limitation and this limitation should be removed in Canada.

Preferential Treatment of Capital Losses from Small Business Securities

Both the United States and Canada provide greater relief for capital losses derived from small business securities than for other capital losses. This greater loss relief is justified as a means of increasing investment in SMEs. In general, capital losses are deductible only against capital gains, with any excess carried over to other years. The United States provides greater relief than Canada, allowing the deduction of up to $3,000 of excess capital losses (whether long- or short-term) from other sources of income in the current year or a carryover year. As discussed above, Canada had a similar rule (limiting the deduction from other sources of income to $2,000), although this provision was eliminated when the lifetime capital gains exemption was introduced in 1985. Although the general lifetime capital gains exemption was reduced in 1987 and eliminated completely in 1994, no deduction of excess capital losses from other sources of income has been reintroduced.

Canada's allowable business investment loss provisions are applicable to all taxpayers regardless of the size of their investment, the size of the corporation in which they invest, or the nature of business carried on by the corporation, provided that the corporation is a small business corporation. The ABIL provisions are broader than the loss relief available for "section 1244 stock" in the United States, which is limited to the first $50,000 of loss realized by an individual ($100,000 if the taxpayer is married and files a joint return) and to only $1 million of stock issued by a corporation.[248] However, Canada's ABIL relief is limited to one-half of the actual business loss that a taxpayer suffers, whereas the US relief applies to the entire loss (subject to the monetary limits). Despite the US limitations, most love capital and angel capital investors are individuals and are unlikely to have made investments exceeding the $50,000 (or $100,000) limit. Thus, in most cases in which a love or angel capitalist suffers a loss, the relief in the United States is greater than that in Canada.

United States

Early in the history of capital gains taxation in the United States, capital losses could be deducted from all sources of income. Even when preferential tax rates for capital gains were introduced in 1921, the full amount of capital losses remained deductible from all sources of income. In 1924, the amount of capital losses deductible was reduced to an amount corresponding to the preferential inclusion rate for capital gains, but the losses remained deductible from all sources of income. However, in 1938, with the introduction of the distinction between long- and short-term capital gains, all capital losses were sequestered (and divided between long- and short-term) and were deductible only against capital gains. As a concession to smaller taxpayers with infrequent gains and losses, up to $1,000 (later increased to $2,000 and then to $3,000) of capital losses could be deducted against any source of income.

Tax measures targeting investment in small businesses were introduced in the Code in 1958, the same year that the small business investment company (SBIC) program was introduced. An SBIC is a corporation operating under the Small Business Investment Act of 1958. The Technical Amendments Act of 1958,[249] introduced later in the year at the same time as the Small Business Tax Revision Act of 1958[250] (considered below), added sections 1242 and 1243 to the 1954 Code to provide loss relief to investors in SBICs and to SBICs themselves. Under section 1242, the loss of a taxpayer (whether individual or corporate) on the disposition of stock of an SBIC is treated as an ordinary loss rather than a capital loss. Under section 1243, the loss realized by an SBIC on the disposition of stock received pursuant to the conversion of convertible debentures is treated as an ordinary loss rather than a capital loss. The SBIC program is considered in more detail in chapter 8.

It should not be surprising that the first relief measure targeting angel capital investment was not the preferential treatment of capital gains from dispositions of small business securities but rather enhanced relief for losses. The Small Business Tax Revision Act of 1958 introduced section 1244 to the 1954 Code. This provision permitted individuals to deduct from ordinary income up to $25,000 of capital losses ($50,000 for a husband and wife filing a joint return, even if the loss was incurred by only one spouse) from a "sale or exchange"[251] of common stock of a small business corporation that met certain conditions ("section 1244 stock").[252] The 1978 Act increased the amount of capital losses from section 1244 stock that could be offset against ordinary income to $50,000 ($100,000 for a married person filing a joint return).[253] It also increased the maximum amount of section 1244 stock that a small business corporation could issue, from $500,000 to $1,000,000. The Deficit Reduction Act of 1984 extended the definition of section 1244 stock to all stock of small business corporations.[254] However, neither the amount of loss that benefits from this preferential treatment nor the aggregate amount of stock that a small business corporation can issue as section 1244 stock has increased since 1978.

Section 1244 stock is defined as stock of a domestic corporation that meets three conditions:[255]

1) The corporation must have been a small business corporation at the time the stock was issued. A corporation is a small business corporation if the aggregate amount of money and other property received by

the corporation for stock, as a contribution to capital, and as paid-in surplus, does not exceed $1,000,000[256] (taking into account the stock issued at the particular time).

2) The stock must be issued for money or other property (other than stock and securities).

3) During the corporation's five most recent taxable years ending before the date on which the loss on the stock was sustained, the corporation must have derived more than 50 percent of its aggregate gross receipts from sources other than royalties, rents, dividends, interest, annuities, and sales or exchanges of stocks or securities.[257]

Canada

When capital gains taxation was introduced in Canada in 1971, capital losses could be deducted only against capital gains. Originally, up to $1,000 of allowable capital losses (that is, $2,000 of capital losses) could be deducted from other sources of income. This deduction was increased to $2,000 in 1977 (following a similar increase in the United States in 1976). When the lifetime capital gains exemption was introduced in 1985, however, this general preference for capital losses was eliminated. It was not reintroduced when the $500,000 lifetime capital gains exemption was limited to qualified farm property and QSBC shares in 1987, or when the $100,000 lifetime capital gains exemption was eliminated in 1994.

An exception to the general loss limitation for ABILs was added to the Income Tax Act in 1978. A taxpayer's ABIL from a disposition of property is one-half of the taxpayer's business investment loss from the disposition. Business investment loss is defined in paragraph 39(1)(c) as the loss arising under subsection 50(1) or on an arm's-length disposition of shares or debt of a small business corporation.[258] Unlike in the United States, there are no size restrictions imposed on a small business corporation or on the loss realized by an investor in the corporation in order for a taxpayer to claim an ABIL.

Subsection 50(1) permits a taxpayer to elect at the end of a taxation year, in certain circumstances, to be taxed as if it disposed of a small business corporation share or a debt for nil proceeds and reacquired the share or debt for nil cost. In the case of debt, the taxpayer must establish that the debt is a bad debt. In the case of shares of a corporation, one of three conditions must be met. The first two conditions are relatively straightforward and easy to apply: the corporation must either become bankrupt during the year or become subject to a winding-up order under the Winding-up Act in the year. The third condition, the most likely to arise but the most difficult to substantiate, requires that all of the following four conditions be met at the end of the year: the corporation is insolvent; neither the corporation nor a corporation controlled by it is carrying on business; the fair market value of the share is nil; and it is reasonable to expect that the corporation will be dissolved or wound up and will not commence to carry on business.[259] Subsection 50(1) effectively permits a taxpayer to recognize a business investment loss even though he or she has not actually disposed of the particular shares or debt. For venture capital investments, this provision is particularly important given the general illiquidity of shares of private corporations.

A small business corporation is defined in subsection 248(1) as a CCPC all or substantially all of whose assets are used principally in an active business carried on primarily in Canada. It also includes, for the purposes of the ABIL rules, a corporation that was a small business corporation at any time in the preceding 12 months. The extension is intended to permit taxpayers to claim a business investment loss on the disposition (including a disposition under subsection 50(1)) of shares or debt of a small business corporation where it ceases to carry on an active business because it has become bankrupt or is being wound up prior to the disposition. In the case of debt, the 12-month period is effectively extended to an indefinite period if the debt is disposed of after the corporation becomes bankrupt or is wound up under the Winding-up Act, provided that the corporation was a small business corporation at the time it last became bankrupt or the winding-up order was made.[260] This indefinite extension of the time period is not applicable to shares of a small business corporation.

Evaluation of the Preferential Treatment of Capital Losses from Small Business Securities

It is often argued that increased, or perhaps full, loss offset is more likely to increase risk taking than a capital gains tax preference, even a targeted tax preference such as the capital gains exemption for QSBC shares. Limiting the deduction of capital losses to capital gains is generally justified on other grounds, particularly the fact that realization—the timing of taxation—is wholly within the taxpayer's control. There are, however, other means of dealing with this "cherry-picking" problem short of introducing full accrual taxation of capital gains. For example, a realized loss could be deductible only to the extent that it exceeds accrued gains on capital assets owned by the taxpayer (or perhaps accrued gains on capital assets of the same class as those generating the loss).[261]

The extent to which loss limitations create a bias against risk taking is also questionable. For diversifiable risk, it is arguable that loss limitations pose no concern. Consider a sufficiently large venture capital fund (or well-diversified angel investor). The fund makes a large number of investments in companies in various industries; it does not know which investments will do well, but it does know that those that do well will generate more than enough revenue to compensate for the investments that do poorly or fail completely. An incentive such as a reduced capital gains tax rate provides the fund with a windfall when it has not taken any meaningful risk.[262] However, the same is not necessarily true of love capitalists or many angel capitalists, whose venture investments are so few that they cannot meaningfully diversify their risk. Further, an unlimited carryforward of unused capital losses is of little or no benefit if the investor is unlikely to realize gains in the near future.

For love or angel capitalists, more relaxed loss limitation provisions are a more direct and effective way to increase venture capital investment than a capital gains tax preference. As Noël Cunningham and Deborah Schenk note, a capital gains tax preference is "a very poor second-best solution"[263] to full loss relief. Consider the following example.[264] An individual, Ms. X, has a choice of two investments. The first is a risk-free investment with an annual rate of return of 10 percent. The second is a risky investment, in which there is a 40 percent chance that Ms. X's investment will triple in one year and a 60 percent chance that the investment will fail completely within one year. The expected rate of return on the second investment is therefore 20 percent.[265] All individuals are risk-adverse to some extent and would therefore limit the amount invested in the second investment despite the fact that the expected return is double that of the riskless investment. Suppose that in the absence of tax, Ms. X is unwilling to invest more than $1,000 in the second investment (that is, Ms. X will not risk losing more than $1,000). Suppose now that a 40 percent proportionate tax is introduced with full loss offset. This tax would reduce the after-tax rate of return on the first investment to 6 percent and on the second investment to 12 percent. Although the relative attractiveness of the two investments remains the same, Ms. X should be willing to invest more money in the second investment because the government has in effect assumed 40 percent of the risk.[266] If, however, the utility of losses is restricted and Ms. X has no other capital investments, she would not invest in the second investment at all.[267] If losses remain restricted but a capital gains tax preference is introduced—for example, 50 percent of the gain is excluded from tax, as is the case of the US QSBS exemption—the expected return on the second investment is 4 percent,[268] still less than the after-tax return on the riskless investment.

Although both Canada and the United States restrict a taxpayer's ability to deduct capital losses, both provide exceptions for losses from small business securities. Neither country imposes restrictions on the nature of the business carried on by the small business in this context. There are, however, important distinctions between the two countries' relieving provisions, stemming primarily from the nature of the capital gains tax preference in each country. In terms of loss relief, in Canada *any* taxpayer can deduct ABILs from all sources of income and there is no limit on the amount that may be claimed. However, mirroring the inclusion rate for capital gains, an ABIL is limited to one-half of the qualifying capital loss. In the United States, in contrast, only individuals can deduct up to $50,000 (or $100,000 for a married individual filing a joint return) of losses from section 1244 stock from ordinary income. There are other, more minor distinctions between the two countries. In Canada, ABILs are limited to shares (or debt) of small business corporations. Unlike in the United States, there is no size limitation on the corporation; it need only be Canadian-controlled and private. When the taxpayer disposes of the share (or within the previous 12 months), however, at least 90 percent of the corporation's income must have been derived from an active business carried on primarily in Canada. In the United States, more than 50 percent of the corporation's income must have been derived from business (not limited to any geographic source) in the previous five taxation years.

Business literature suggests that the typical angel investor is male, middle-aged, and well-educated with a high annual income and net worth. Consider a married individual in a 40 percent tax bracket who makes a single venture capital investment of $50,000. Assume that the investment is lost completely and that the individual earns sufficient income to fully use the benefit of the loss. If the individual is resident in Canada, the after-tax loss is $40,000;[269] in the United States, the after-tax loss is only $30,000.[270] For a married individual with no capital gains income, the after-tax loss in Canada is greater than the after-tax loss in the United States for qualifying investments up to $200,000 (ignoring currency exchange rates),[271] even though the US individual's loss relief under section 1244 of the Code is limited to the first $100,000 of loss. For qualifying investments in excess of $200,000, Canada's ABIL provisions provide greater relief than section 1244 of the Code. If, however, the individual has capital gains income in addition to the qualifying capital loss, the size of the qualifying investment that a US individual is more willing to make relative to a Canadian individual should increase.[272] Given the fact that most love capital investments and many angel capital investments are less than $200,000, Canadian individual investors are at a disadvantage compared with their American counterparts.

The changes made by Canada in 2000, which reduced the capital gains inclusion rate from 75 percent to 50 percent and likewise reduced the amount of a business investment loss deductible as an ABIL, may in fact have the opposite result to that intended and reduce love and angel venture capital investment. The concern is that the reduced benefit for ABILs will have a more deleterious effect than the increased preference attached to gains.

It is not necessary that the deductible portion of capital losses—at least, the deductible portion of certain capital losses, such as business investment losses—mirror the included portion of capital gains. In my view, the ABIL provisions should be revised to allow the full deduction of business investment losses (as that term is defined in paragraph 39(1)(c)), subject to four modifications. First, a taxpayer's deductible loss should be limited to a maximum amount, for each small business corporation (or related group) in which the taxpayer invests, sufficient to account for most love and angel investments (for example, $100,000). Second, in order to avoid cherry-picking losses, the taxpayer should be required to recognize for tax purposes, in the year of the ABIL, accrued but unrealized gains up to the amount of the ABIL on any other capital assets owned by the taxpayer. This provision would increase the cost to the taxpayer of such other capital assets by the amount of the loss (to an amount not exceeding their respective fair market values), so that only the loss on the small business investment that exceeds all accrued gains of the taxpayer would be deductible. Third, a size restriction should be imposed on the small business corporation when the shares or debt giving rise to the ABIL were originally issued. This size restriction should be consistent with that applicable to other tax incentives targeting small businesses, such as the angel capital rollover. Fourth, in order to distinguish investment in innovative SMEs from investment in other SMEs—assuming that it is desirable to more narrowly target the tax preference in this manner—the ABIL rules could be limited to corporations carrying on certain types of business (a white list of qualified businesses) or denied for corporations carrying on other types of business (a black list of disqualified businesses). Given the variety of business ventures that might be considered innovative, and especially given the rapid changes in the business sector, a black list would probably be preferable to a white list. A black list is common in other forms of tax expenditures promoting venture capital investment and would not be out of place here. For example, common forms of lifestyle businesses—personal services businesses, restaurants, real estate development, etc.—could be excluded from the tax preference. These limitations would partially fund the increased expenditure that this recommendation would likely entail because they would restrict the scope of the existing ABIL rules. For additional funding, I would recommend that Canada abolish the $500,000 capital gains exemption for QSBC shares. I would also recommend the introduction of passive loss rules (or interest expense limitation rules) similar to those in US Code section 163(d), although this proposal is far more contentious and well beyond the scope of this study.[273]

Notes

1   In 2003, the long-term capital gains tax rate was reduced from 20 percent to 15 percent and the top marginal income tax rate was reduced from 38.6 percent to 35 percent. Both reductions are subject to a sunset clause: unless the reductions are reauthorized, they will be rolled back, at the end of 2008 in the case of the capital gains rate reduction and at the end of 2010 in the case of the income tax rate. Jobs and Growth Tax Relief Reconciliation Act of 2003, Pub. L. no. 108-27, enacted on May 28, 2003; 117 Stat. 752, section 301(a)(2) (reduced long-term capital gains tax rate), and section 105 (reduced income tax rates). The sunset clauses are sections 303 and 107, respectively.

2   This summary does not deal with the taxation of capital gains from property used in a trade or business and subject to depreciation (for example, plant and machinery), personal-use property, or real property. For a detailed history of the tax treatment of capital gains from 1913 to 1950, see United States, Treasury Department, Tax Advisory Staff, *Federal Income Tax Treatment of Capital Gains and Losses* (Washington, DC: Treasury Department, 1951).

3   An understanding of the legislative process in the United States might be useful. The process for tax legislation usually begins with hearings before the Committee on Ways and Means of the House of Representatives. The US constitution requires that all revenue legislation originate in the House of Representatives, but tax legislation sometimes originates in the Senate as an amendment to a revenue bill, which is then reviewed by the House and by conference committee. At the ways and means hearings, Treasury proposals are introduced. Representatives of various public and private organizations can also present their views. Eventually, a tax bill and committee report are sent to the House of Representatives. The tax bill is debated and may be passed, in some form, by the House. Then, hearings similar to those of the ways and means committee are conducted by the Senate Committee on Finance. Eventually, the House bill, as amended by the Senate committee, is brought to the Senate together with the report of the Senate committee. The bill, as amended, is debated in the Senate and may be passed, in some form, by the Senate. If passed, the bill with Senate amendments is referred to the conference committee of the House and Senate, which resolves differences between the House and Senate bills. The actions of the conference committee are reported in a conference report, which is then usually approved by the House and the Senate. The final legislation, as approved, is sent to the president for his approval or veto. If the president vetoes the legislation, both the House and the Senate must approve it by a two-thirds majority for it to pass into law.

4   Pub. L. no. 63-16, enacted on October 3, 1913; 38 Stat. 114, section II.B.

5   *Merchants' L and T Co. v. Smietanka*, 255 US 509 (1921).

6   Pub. L. no. 67-98, enacted on November 23, 1921; 42 Stat. 227 (herein referred to as "the 1921 Act").

7   Section 206(b) of the 1921 Act. Taxpayers had to elect that their capital net gain (the excess of capital gains over capital losses) be taxed at the preferential rate. However, the total tax owed by the taxpayer could not be less than 12½ percent of the taxpayer's total net income. Under the 1921 Act, the normal tax rate was 8 percent (4 percent on the first $4,000 of net income), and the surtax ranged from 1 percent to 65 percent (for income over $1,000,000). For 1922, surtaxes ranged from 1 percent

to 50 percent (for income over $200,000). As a maximum rate, the capital gains provision benefited taxpayers only if their effective tax rate exceeded 12½ percent. For this reason, the provision was criticized as being inequitable.

8   IIR rep. no. 350, part 1, 67th Cong., 1st sess. (1921), 10-11; S rep. no. 275, part I, 67th Cong., 1st sess. (1921), 12, quoted in Louis Eisenstein, *The Ideologies of Taxation* (New York: Ronald Press, 1961), 96.

9   Section 214(a)(5) of the 1921 Act. Under this provision, losses were fully deductible provided that the transaction was entered into for profit and that, if it had been profitable, the profits would have been taxable.

10 Pub. L. no. 68-176, enacted on June 2, 1924; 43 Stat. 253 (herein referred to as "the 1924 Act").

11 Section 208(c) of the 1924 Act.

12 Pub. L. no. 72-154, enacted on June 6, 1932; 47 Stat. 173 (herein referred to as "the 1932 Act").

13 Section 23(r) of the 1932 Act. This provision was introduced because of the concern that "as a result of the collapse of security prices, capital losses were used on a large scale to wipe out tax liability on ordinary income." (US Treasury Department, supra note 2, at 30-31). Congress originally proposed to limit losses on all transactions involving stocks and bonds; however, the Senate Finance Committee limited the provision to short-term losses and its view prevailed in the conference committee.

14 Pub. L. no. 73-67, enacted on June 16, 1933; 48 Stat. 195, section 218(b).

15 Pub. L. no. 73-216, enacted on May 10, 1934; 48 Stat. 680 (herein referred to as "the 1934 Act").

16 Section 117(a) of the 1934 Act. The holding period and inclusion rates established in the 1934 Act were as follows:

Holding period (years)	Amount of gain included (percent)
< 1	100
1-2	80
2-5	60
5-10	40
> 10	30

17 Section 117(d) of the 1934 Act.

18 US Treasury Department, supra note 2, at 31.

19 H conf. rep. no. 1385, 73d Cong., 2d sess. (April 30, 1934), 22. The treatment of capital losses is considered below, under the heading "Preferential Treatment of Capital Losses from Small Business Securities."

20 Pub. L. no. 75-554, enacted on May 28, 1938; 52 Stat. 447 (herein referred to as "the 1938 Act"). The Internal Revenue Code of 1939, Pub. L. no. 76-1, enacted on February 10, 1939; 53 Stat. 1 (herein referred to as "the 1939 Code") largely adopted the section numbering used in the 1938 Act. The various statutes passed between 1939 and 1954 (when the Internal Revenue Code of 1954 was adopted) amended the 1939 Code.

21   A short-term capital gain or loss was a gain or loss from the sale or exchange of a capital asset held not more than 18 months, if and to the extent that it was included in income, and a long-term capital gain or loss was a gain or loss from the sale or exchange of a capital asset held more than 18 months, if and to the extent it was included in income. A taxpayer's net long-term capital gain (loss) was the amount by which long-term capital gains (losses) exceeded long-term capital losses (gains). A taxpayer's net short-term capital gain (loss) was similarly defined.

22   Section 117(c) of the 1938 Act. Under the 1938 Act, the normal income tax rate was 4 percent (section 11). The surtax rate ranged from 4 percent (for taxable income from $4,000 to $6,000) to 75 percent (for taxable income over $5 million). Under the alternative flat-rate tax, long-term capital gains were subject to an effective rate of 20 percent (30 percent of 66⅔ percent) for property held between 18 months and two years, and 15 percent (30 percent of 50 percent) for property held longer than two years.

23   Section 177(e) of the 1938 Act.

24   The rationale for this limitation was that the net income reflected the extent to which the taxpayer was deprived of the use of the net short-term capital loss in reducing tax liability in the year the loss arose.

25   Pub. L. no. 76-155, title II, enacted on June 29, 1939; 53 Stat. 863 (herein referred to as "the 1939 Act").

26   Section 212(a) of the 1939 Act, amending section 117(d) of the 1939 Code. Although this amendment applied to both corporations and individuals, the latter were still effectively restricted in the use of long-term capital losses by the 30 percent maximum tax credit for such losses introduced in the 1938 Act.

27   Pub. L. no. 77-753, enacted on October 21, 1942; 56 Stat. 798 (herein referred to as "the 1942 Act"), section 150(a)(1), amending certain definitions in section 117(a) of the 1939 Code.

28   Section 150(c) of the 1942 Act, amending section 117(b) of the 1939 Code.

29   Ibid. Under section 117(e) of the 1939 Code, as amended by section 150(c) of the 1942 Act, a net capital loss in any year was treated as a short-term capital loss in each of the five succeeding years. Carried-over losses had to be deducted as early as possible. If there were insufficient capital gains in the carryover year, carried-over losses could be deducted from ordinary income in the same manner as capital losses arising in the carryover year.

30   Since corporations did not benefit from the 50 percent inclusion rate for long-term capital gains, the effective rate was equal to the alternative flat rate applicable to individuals.

31   Pub. L. no. 82-183, enacted on October 20, 1951; 65 Stat. 452 (herein referred to as "the 1951 Act").

32   Section 322(a)(2) of the 1951 Act, amending section 117(b) of the 1939 Code.

33   Pub. L. no. 83-591, enacted on August 16, 1954; 68A Stat. 3 (herein referred to as "the 1954 Code). The 1954 Code adopted the section numbering that is found in the current 1986 Code. The "normal tax" and "surtax" for individual taxpayers were replaced with progressive rate bands in section 1, ranging from 20 percent (for

taxable incomes up to $2,000) to 91 percent (for taxable incomes over $200,000). The normal corporate tax rate, in section 11, was 25 percent for taxation years beginning after March 31, 1955 (for taxation years beginning before April 1, 1955, the normal rate was 30 percent), with a 22 percent surtax for taxable income in excess of $25,000. The alternative tax rates applicable to capital gains were set out in section 1201 (25 percent for both corporations and other taxpayers), and the 50 percent exclusion of long-term capital gains (specifically, the amount by which net long-term capital gains exceeded net short-term capital losses) for non-corporate taxpayers was in section 1202. Section 1211(b) permitted non-corporate taxpayers to deduct excess capital losses (whether short- or long-term) from up to $1,000 of ordinary income. Corporate taxpayers could deduct capital losses against only capital gains (section 1211(a)). Section 1212 set out the five-year carryforward for any taxpayer's "net capital loss"—that is, the amount by which the taxpayer's net long-term (short-term) capital loss exceeds the taxpayer's net short-term (long-term) capital gain. The main definition sections applicable to capital gains were sections 1221 ("capital asset") and 1222 (other definitions).

34   Pub. L. no. 88-272, enacted on February 26, 1964; 78 Stat. 19 (herein referred to as "the 1964 Act"). The 1964 Act also significantly reduced the marginal tax rates for individual and corporate taxpayers. For individuals, the marginal rates were reduced from the range of 20 percent (for taxable income up to $2,000) to 91 percent (for taxable income over $200,000; taxable income between $100,000 and $150,000 was subject to an 89 percent rate, while taxable income between $150,000 and $200,000 was subject to a 90 percent rate) to the range of 14 percent (for taxable income up to $500) to 70 percent (for taxable income over $100,000). According to the House committee, the "principal purpose of [the legislation] is to lower rates so that the free enterprise system can itself generate the higher rate of growth which our economy requires" (HR rep. no. 88-749, 88th Cong., 2d sess. (1963), 1; [1964] *United States Code: Congressional and Administrative News* (herein referred to as "USCCAN") 1313, at 1313). According to the Senate committee, the lower rates would "stimulate higher investments and increase consumer purchases" (S rep. no. 88-830, 88th Cong., 2d sess. (1964), 6; [1964] USCCAN 1673, at 1678).

35   Section 230 of the 1964 Act, amending section 1212 of the 1954 Code. The House originally approved a bill that also included a reduction of 60 percent of the gain from the sale of long-term capital assets held more than two years (for capital assets held more than six months and not more than two years, the reduction remained 50 percent) and also a reduction in the alternative capital gains tax rate from 25 percent to 21 percent. The justification given by the House committee for these further changes was

> [the] committee's desire to "unlock" capital investments where the investor is willing to undertake new and riskier investments needed by the economy but finds it unprofitable because of the substantial tax liability he incurs at the time of the sale of his present holdings. It is estimated that this unlocking effect will stimulate the realization of capital gains to such an extent that in the first year revenues from this source will increase by $450 million even though a smaller percentage of all capital gains is taken into account for tax purposes. This larger turnover of capital assets should result in

> increased investments *and will be particularly helpful in tapping new sources of risk capital* [emphasis added].

(HR rep. no. 88-749, supra note 34, at 96; 1405.) The Senate bill deleted all of the capital gains provisions from the House bill. A number of reasons were given. First, the secretary of the Treasury, in his testimony before the Senate committee, recommended the deletion of the more beneficial treatment of long-term capital gains (both the enhanced deduction and the reduced alternative rate). Second, the Senate committee was concerned about the added complexity generated by the House proposals. Finally, the Senate committee

> was also concerned about the capital gains provision of the House bill because the benefit of this provision would have been largely concentrated in the very highest income brackets. . . . Those with incomes of $100,000 or over, although representing only 0.04 of 1 percent of all taxpayers, nevertheless receive 24 percent of all capital gains.
>
> The effect of reducing the capital gains inclusion fraction, or alternative rate, because of this concentration of these gains in the higher income classes would, of necessity, have meant that most of this relief would have gone to those with the highest income levels.

(S rep. no. 88-830, supra note 34, at 161; 1836.) Under the conference agreement, only the indefinite capital loss carryover was retained.

36   Neither "excess short-term" nor "excess long-term" capital losses were defined terms in the 1954 Code (or currently). They represent the results of the equations in section 1212(b)(1) of the Code. The former refers to the amount by which net short-term capital losses exceed net long-term capital gains in the loss year. The latter refers to the amount by which net long-term capital losses exceed net short-term capital gains in the loss year.

37   Pub. L. no. 91-172, enacted on December 30, 1969; 83 Stat. 487 (herein referred to as "the 1969 Act"). The House intended the 1969 Act to close a number of loopholes that benefited high-income individuals almost exclusively. Primary among these were the deduction of donations to private charitable foundations, the full deduction of interest expense regardless of the amount of investment income, and the one-half inclusion of long-term capital gains. The House bill's measures dealing with private charitable foundations were largely adopted. The treatment of interest expense under the 1969 Act is discussed in note 41 and accompanying text, infra.

38   For corporations, the alternative capital gains tax rate was increased from 25 percent to 30 percent (28 percent for taxation years beginning in 1970). For non-corporate taxpayers, the alternative maximum capital gains tax rate of 25 percent was limited to the first $50,000 of long-term capital gains; the alternative rate was otherwise increased to 29½ percent for 1970, 32½ percent for 1971, and 35 percent thereafter. In effect, after the first $50,000, the included portion of long-term capital gains (that is, 50 percent of such gains) was taxed at regular marginal rates. With the highest marginal rate of 70 percent, the effective rate on long-term capital gains was increased from 25 percent to 35 percent, phased in over a three-year period.

39   Section 512 of the 1969 Act, amending section 1212(a) of the 1954 Code.

40   Section 513 of the 1969 Act, amending sections 1211(b) and 1212(b) of the 1954 Code. The effect of this change can be illustrated with the following example.

Suppose that a non-corporate taxpayer in year 1 had $50,000 of ordinary income (for example, income from employment), a net long-term capital loss of $2,500, and a net short-term capital loss of $100. Under section 1211(b)(1), as amended, the amount of ordinary income that could be offset was the least of (A) $50,000, (B) $1,000 (the maximum amount), and (C) $100 + $1,250 (the amount of the net short-term capital loss plus one-half of the amount of the net long-term capital loss). In effect, to get the full benefit of the $1,000 deduction, the taxpayer had to use the $100 short-term capital loss and $1,800 of the net long-term capital loss. Under section 1212(b)(2), for the purpose of determining the amount of the net short-term and net long-term capital loss that could be carried forward under section 1212(b)(1), the $1,000 deducted under section 1211(b)(1) was treated as a short-term capital gain in year 1. Under section 1212(b)(2)(A), the taxpayer had a notional net short-term capital gain of $900 ($1,000 − $100) and therefore had no short-term capital loss carried forward under section 1212(b)(1)(A) (since the entire actual net short-term capital loss was used up against ordinary income in year 1). Under section 1212(b)(2)(B), for the purpose of determining the amount of the net long-term capital loss carried forward, the taxpayer was considered to have a notional short-term capital gain equal to the amount deducted under section 1211(b)(1) plus the difference between the amount deducted under section 1211(b)(1) and the taxpayer's actual net short-term capital loss: in the example, $1,000 + ($1,000 − $100), or $1,900. Therefore, the amount of the net long-term capital loss that could be carried forward was $700, determined as follows: $2,500 (the amount of the taxpayer's net long-term capital loss) − ($1,900 − $100) (the amount of the taxpayer's short-term capital gain, as redetermined under section 1212(b)(2)(B), minus the taxpayer's short-term capital loss). In effect, since the taxpayer used up $1,800 of the net long-term capital loss in year 1 against ordinary income, only $700 remained to be carried over to year 2.

41   Section 163(d) of the 1954 Code. The House bill proposed to limit the interest expense deduction to investment income (which included long-term capital gains) plus $25,000. The Senate deleted the provision altogether, preserving full deduction. The provision as introduced was agreed to in the conference agreement. According to the House report:

> The itemized deduction presently allowed individuals for interest, makes it possible for taxpayers to voluntarily incur substantial interest expenses on funds borrowed to acquire or carry investment assets. Where the interest expense exceeds the taxpayer's investment income, it, in effect, is used to insulate other income from taxation. For example, a taxpayer may borrow substantial amounts to purchase stock which have growth potential but which return small dividends currently. Despite the fact that the receipt of the income from the investment may be postponed (and may be capital gains), the taxpayer will receive a current deduction for the interest expense even though it is substantially in excess of the income from the investment.

(HR rep. no. 91-413 (part I), 91st Cong., 1st sess. (1969); [1969] USCCAN 1645, at 1718.) The House report noted that interest on funds borrowed in connection with a trade or business would not be affected by the limitation.

42   Section 301 of the 1969 Act, adding sections 56-58 to the 1956 Code. "Tax preferences" were defined in section 57. They included, among other things,

excess investment interest (the amount by which the taxpayer's investment interest expense (supra note 41) exceeded the taxpayer's net investment income) and, for individuals, one-half of the amount by which long-term capital gains exceeded short-term capital losses (that is, the excluded portion of long-term capital gains). The House bill would have limited the amount of tax preferences that a taxpayer could deduct to 50 percent of the taxpayer's total income. The Senate amendments to the House bill replaced this provision with a minimum additional tax of 5 percent of the taxpayer's tax preferences in excess of $30,000. The conference report generally followed the Senate amendments to this provision. For a taxpayer in the highest bracket (70 percent), the extra tax from the minimum tax was 1.97625 percent in 1970, 1.75 percent in 1971, and 1.5 percent in 1972-1975.

43 Pub. L. no. 94-455, enacted on October 4, 1976; 90 Stat. 1520 (herein referred to as "the 1976 Act"). The House bill included three primary changes: an increase in the holding period to one year (in three stages); an increase in the amount of ordinary income that could be offset with capital losses to $4,000 (in three stages); and a three-year loss carryback for capital losses for individuals. The House committee described the rationale for these three changes as follows:

1) the longer holding period provided "a more equitable definition and will encourage capital to flow away from speculation and into longer-term investment" (HR rep. no. 94-658, 94th Cong., 2d sess. (1975), 12; [1976] USCCAN 2897, at 2907);

2) the increase in the amount of ordinary income that could be offset was "not only fair but also should encourage individuals to make equity investments" (ibid.); and

3) the three-year loss carryback addressed "an inequity in existing law and discourage[d] 'tax-loss' selling of securities at the end of the year" (ibid.).

The Senate proposed the removal of the capital gains provision from the bill. According to the Senate Finance Committee, the taxation of capital gains and losses required a complete re-examination and the specific changes proposed should have been addressed in the context of this review (S rep. no. 94-938 (part I), 94th Cong., 2d sess. (1976), 443; [1976] USCCAN 3439, at 3870). The conference report adopted the amendments as finally enacted, discussed below.

The 1976 Act also had a significant impact on the deductibility of interest expenses. As noted above (supra note 41), the 1969 Act restricted the deductibility of interest expenses that exceeded investment income to one-half of the excess. Under the House bill, the deduction for non-business interest (interest other than that connected with a taxpayer's trade or business), including both "personal interest" and "investment interest," was limited to $12,000 plus the amount of the taxpayer's net investment income plus the taxpayer's long-term capital gains (for these purposes, 100 percent of the taxpayer's long-term capital gains were taken into account). Any investment interest disallowed as a deduction as a result of this limitation could be carried forward indefinitely. The Senate amendment proposed to remove (prospectively) the 1969 limitation on interest deductibility, but made excess investment interest (to the extent that it exceeded net investment income, but not capital gains) a tax preference for minimum add-on tax purposes. Under the conference agreement, and as adopted in the 1976 Act (section 511(a), amending section 163(d) of the 1954 Code), interest on investment indebtedness was limited to $10,000 per year plus the taxpayer's net investment income. Investment income was defined as gross income from interest, dividends, rent, and royalties plus net short-term capital gains. Investment interest could not be deducted against long-term capital gains. The 1976 Act also added section 163(d)(7) to the Code, which permitted the deduction of an additional $15,000 of interest expense paid in connection with indebtedness used to acquire an interest in a corporation or partnership where the taxpayer, the taxpayer's spouse, and the taxpayer's children owned at least 50 percent of the stock or capital interest in the corporation or partnership. Any disallowed investment interest expense could be carried over indefinitely. The conference agreement contained no limitations on the deductibility of personal interest.

44   Section 1402 of the 1976 Act, amending certain definitions in section 1222 of the 1954 Code.

45   Section 1401 of the 1976 Act, amending section 1211(b)(1) of the 1954 Code.

46   Section 1014 of the 1954 Code.

47   The United States has levied a federal estate tax continuously since 1916, although estate (or inheritance) taxes were used as early as 1862. Gift taxes were introduced in 1924, repealed in 1926, and reintroduced in 1932. The estate tax and gift tax were combined in a single statute as part of the 1976 Act and form part of the Internal Revenue Code. See infra note 151 concerning the elimination of estate (but not gift) tax.

48   See infra note 151.

49   Section 2005 of the 1976 Act. Section 2005 included a "fresh-start" provision, under which the basis of property acquired from a decedent was stepped up, for the purpose of determining gains but not losses, to the property's fair market value on December 31, 1976.

50   However, section 702(c)(1)(A) of the Revenue Act of 1978 postponed the implementation of the carryover basis rules enacted in the 1976 Act. Under the 1978 Act, the carryover basis rules would apply to property transferred after December 31, 1979. The Crude Oil Windfall Profit Tax Act of 1980 (Pub. L. no. 96-223, enacted on April 2, 1980; 94 Stat. 229, section 401) repealed the carryover basis provisions and provided that the previous step-up provisions in the 1954 Code applied as if the changes introduced in 1976 and amended in 1978 had never been enacted.

51   Pub. L. no. 95-600, enacted on November 6, 1978; 92 Stat. 2763 (herein referred to as "the 1978 Act"). According to the House committee, the 1978 Act was "designed to stimulate consumer and investment spending, compensate for the automatic individual income tax increases which result from inflation, and improve the fairness of the tax system" (HR rep. no. 95-1445, 95th Cong., 2d sess. (1978), 1; [1978] USCCAN 7046, at 7046). Among other things, the House bill proposed to add a once-in-a-lifetime election to exclude from tax the first $100,000 from the sale of a principal residence; delete capital gains from the list of preferences subject to the minimum add-on tax; add a new alternative minimum tax on capital gains; repeal the preferential 25 percent alternative tax on the first $25,000 of long-term capital gains; and exclude from capital gains tax the effects of inflation (that is, introduce indexing).

52   Section 403 of the 1978 Act, amending section 1201(a) of the 1954 Code.

53 HR rep. no. 95-1445, supra note 51, at 119; 7148 (emphasis added). The Senate Finance Committee cited similar reasons for changing the capital gains tax provisions (S rep. no. 95-1263, 95th Cong., 2d sess. (1978), 191; [1978] USCCAN 6761, at 6955). However, the Senate bill proposed to increase from 50 percent to 70 percent the amount of net long-term capital gains that were excluded from an individual's taxable income. The Senate bill made no changes to the alternative minimum tax (except to classify the 70 percent excluded gain as a tax preference rather than the previous 50 percent excluded gain). The Senate bill also proposed to reduce from 30 percent to 28 percent the alternative rate applicable to corporate capital gains. The Senate bill did not include any provision for indexing. The conference report (H conf. rep. no. 95-1800, 95th Cong., 2d sess. (1978); [1978] USCCAN 7198) reflected the changes that were enacted in the 1978 Act.

54 Section 421 of the 1978 Act, adding section 55 to the 1954 Code.

55 Pub. L. no. 97-34, enacted on August 13, 1981; 95 Stat. 172.

56 Pub. L. no. 97-248, enacted on September 3, 1982; 96 Stat. 324.

57 Pub. L. no. 98-369, enacted on July 18, 1984; 98 Stat. 494.

58 Pub. L. no. 99-514, enacted on October 22, 1986; 100 Stat. 2085 (herein referred to as "the 1986 Act"). Under section 2 of the 1986 Act, the 1954 Code was redesignated as the Internal Revenue Code of 1986. References in this chapter to "the Code" are to the Internal Revenue Code of 1986, as amended.

59 Under the House bill (HR 3838), four tax brackets were proposed (ranging from 15 percent to 38 percent). The rates at that time ranged from 12 percent to 50 percent (applicable to individuals and married persons filing joint returns with taxable incomes above $81,800 and $161,400, respectively). Under the Senate amendments, two brackets were proposed (15 percent and 27 percent). Under the conference report, and as incorporated in the 1986 Act, there were two tax brackets, 15 percent (for taxable income up to and including $17,850 in the case of unmarried individuals and $29,750 for married individuals filing a joint return), and 28 percent thereafter. The reduced rates became fully effective on January 1, 1988.

The 1986 Act also reduced corporate tax rates. The 1986 Act included three tax brackets for corporations (15 percent for taxable income up to and including $50,000; 25 percent for taxable income between $50,000 and $75,000; and 34 percent for taxable income in excess of $75,000). The 1986 Act also phased out the effect of the lower rates (15 percent and 25 percent) for corporations with taxable income in excess of $100,000. Previously, the top corporate marginal tax rate was 46 percent (for income above $100,000), while the preferential effect of lower rates was not phased out until taxable income exceeded $1,000,000.

60 With respect to base broadening, the 1986 Act also amended the interest expense deduction. Section 511(a) of the 1986 Act amended Code section 163(d) to limit the deduction of investment interest to net investment income (defined in Code section 163(d)(4)). Investment income included the gross income from property held for investment and any net gain attributable to the disposition of property held for investment. Both long-term and short-term capital gains were included in investment income (since, under the 1986 Act, no preferential tax rate applied to long-term capital gains). The 1986 Act eliminated the additional $10,000 deduction for investment interest (supra note 43) and removed the additional $15,000 deduction for interest on debt used to acquire an interest in a family business (ibid.).

The 1986 Act also introduced passive loss rules that were designed to limit a taxpayer's ability to deduct losses from tax shelter investments against other sources of income: Code section 469. In general, Code section 469 denies a taxpayer's ability to deduct a passive activity loss, defined as an activity that involves the conduct of a trade or business in which the taxpayer does not materially participate. As in the case of interest disallowed under Code section 163, losses denied under Code section 469 can be carried forward and deducted against future gains from activities governed by the provision. Code sections 163 and 469 are mutually exclusive provisions.

61   Section 302 of the 1986 Act, introducing section 1(j) to the Code. In effect, section 1(j) provided that the maximum rate on individual long-term capital gains would not be increased in a subsequent public law in which the top individual marginal tax rate was increased unless the subsequent law specifically increased the capital gains tax rate as well.

The House bill originally proposed that the individual long-term capital gains deduction be reduced from 60 percent to 42 percent of net long-term capital gains. The rationale given by the House committee was that reduced rates

> may contribute to the efficient allocation of capital by minimizing the possible "lock-in" effect of higher regular rates, and may also serve as an incentive to investment.
>
> The committee believes it is desirable to retain a reduced rate for net capital gains of individuals. In the context of the general reduction of regular individual tax rates under the bill, however, the committee does not believe that it is necessary to retain the same degree of differentiation between regular rates and capital gains rates as is afforded under present law.

(HR rep. no. 99-426, 99th Cong., 1st sess. (1985), 196; 1986-3 CB (vol. 2) 1, at 196.) In contrast, the Senate committee believed that the reduced individual tax rates on other forms of capital income eliminated the need for a reduced rate of capital gains tax. The Senate committee indicated, however, that the top rate on individual capital gains should not exceed the rates set forth in the bill (27 percent under the Senate amendment) and therefore should not be increased in the future if the highest individual marginal tax rate was increased (S rep. no. 99-313, 99th Cong., 2d sess. (1986), 169; 1986-3 CB (vol. 3) 1, at 169). The conference agreement adopted the Senate amendment (subject to the conforming change reflecting the higher individual marginal tax rate of 28 percent).

62   Pub. L. no. 101-508, enacted on November 5, 1990; 104 Stat. 1388. Under this act, the individual marginal income tax rates were set at 15 percent (for taxable income up to $19,450 for unmarried individuals or $32,450 for married individuals filing joint returns), 28 percent for taxable income between $19,450 and $47,050 or $32,450 and $78,400, respectively), and 31 percent (for taxable income exceeding $47,050 or $78,400, respectively). The act also redesignated section 1(j) (which set the maximum individual long-term capital gains tax rate at 28 percent) as section 1(h).

63   Pub. L. no. 103-66, enacted on August 10, 1993; 107 Stat. 312 (herein referred to as "the 1993 Act"). Under this act, the individual marginal income tax rates were set at 15 percent (for taxable income up to $22,100 for unmarried individuals or $36,900 for married individuals filing joint returns), 28 percent (for taxable income

between $22,100 and $53,500 or $36,900 and $89,150, respectively), 31 percent (for taxable income between $53,500 and $115,000 or $89,150 and $140,000, respectively), 36 percent (for taxable income between $115,000 and $250,000 or $140,000 and $250,000, respectively), and 39.6 percent (for taxable income exceeding $250,000, in both cases).

64 HR rep. no. 103-111, 103d Cong., 1st sess. (1993), 642; [1993] USCCAN 378, at 873.

65 Section 13206(d)(1) of the 1993 Act, amending section 163(d)(4) of the Code and adding what is now section 1(h)(3) of the Code.

66 Pub. L. no. 105-34, enacted on August 5, 1997; 111 Stat. 788 (herein referred to as "the 1997 Act").

67 The House bill did not include the new 18-month holding period or the five-year holding period. Both of these amendments to the House bill arose from the conference report. The House bill did include an inflation adjustment (indexing) to the adjusted basis of certain assets held more than three years for the purposes of determining gain (but not loss) on a sale or other disposition of such assets by a taxpayer other than a C corporation. Assets eligible for the inflation adjustment included common (but not preferred) stock of C corporations and tangible property that was a capital asset or a property used in a trade or business. A personal residence was not eligible for indexing. This provision was not included in the Senate amendment or the conference agreement. The Senate amendments to the House bill were more targeted in their approach, concentrating on amendments to the preferential treatment of capital gains arising from qualified small business stock: infra note 182.

68 HR rep. no. 105-148, 105th Cong., 1st sess. (1997), 340-41; [1997] USCCAN 678, at 734-35.

69 Pub. L. no. 105-206, enacted on July 22, 1998; 112 Stat. 685, section 6005(f)(2). This Act (as its name implies) focuses primarily on restructuring the Internal Revenue Service (IRS). However, a number of last-minute tax amendments were added to the House bill in order to garner House support.

70 Section 5001(a)(2) of the IRS Restructuring and Reform Act of 1998.

71 Proposals to reduce the long-term capital gains tax rate were included in the Taxpayer Refund and Relief Act of 1999, HR 2488, 106th Cong., 1st sess. The House bill was originally called the Financial Freedom Act of 1999. The conference report, dated August 4, 1999, was agreed to by both the House of Representatives (in a 221-206 vote, roll call no. 379, August 5, 1999) and the Senate (in a 50-49 vote, roll call no. 261, August 5, 1999) and presented to the president on September 15, 1999. The 10 percent and 20 percent rates were to be reduced to 8 percent and 18 percent, respectively; as a result, the five-year holding period would have been removed. In addition, the 1999 Act would have provided for the indexation of capital gains arising from the disposition of capital assets held longer than one year. However, President Clinton vetoed the act on September 23, 1999 (H doc. 106-130, 106th Cong., 1st sess. (1999)).

72 Pub. L. no. 107-16, enacted on June 7, 2001; 115 Stat. 38.

73 The Economic Growth and Tax Relief Reconciliation Act of 2001 also created a new 10 percent tax bracket, carved out of the existing 15 percent bracket. It too will disappear in 2010 absent further amendment. The reductions over the period

2001-2006 applied to the 28, 31, 36, and 39.6 percent brackets. The top bracket was to be reduced to 39.1 percent for 2001, 38.6 percent for 2002 and 2003, 37.6 percent for 2004 and 2005, and 35 percent for 2006-2010. The 36 percent bracket was to be reduced to 33 percent in 2006, the 31 percent bracket to 28 percent, and the 28 percent bracket to 25 percent.

74 Supra note 1.

75 See, for example, *Marrin v. CIR*, 147 F. 3d 147 (2d Cir. 1998).

76 See supra note 19 and accompanying text.

77 943 F. 2d 1048, at 1051-52 (9th Cir. 1991).

78 16 TC 1026, at 1032-33 (1951).

79 Treas. reg. section 1.471-5 provides in part: "a dealer in securities is a merchant of securities, whether an individual, partnership, or corporation, with an established place of business, regularly engaged in the purchase of securities and their resale to customers; that is, one who as a merchant buys securities and sells them to customers with a view to the gains and profits that may be derived therefrom. If such business is simply a branch of the activities carried on by such person, the securities inventoried as provided in this section may include only those held for purposes of resale and not for investment. Taxpayers who buy and sell or hold securities for investment or speculation, irrespective of whether such buying or selling constitutes the carrying on of a trade or business, and officers of corporations and members of partnerships who in their individual capacities buy and sell securities, are not dealers in securities." This regulation was adopted from TD 2649, January 30, 1918.

80 Code section 1236(a). The regulations under this provision adopt the definition of "dealer" in the regulations under Code section 471.

81 Treas. reg. section 1.471-5, supra note 79. *Kemon*, supra note 78, concerned the taxation of partners of a trading partnership. Because the partnership was found to be trading for its own account, the partnership's (and hence each partner's) gains were considered to be on capital account.

82 Income War Tax Act, 1917, SC 1917, c. 28, section 3(1).

83 Supra note 4 and accompanying text.

84 J. Harvey Perry, *Taxation in Canada*, 3d ed. (Toronto: University of Toronto Press, 1961), 45. See also Geoffrey R. Conway and John G. Smith, *The Law Concerning Capital Gains*, Studies of the Royal Commission on Taxation no. 19b (Ottawa: Queen's Printer, February 1967). Capital gains were not subject to tax in the United Kingdom until 1965. Obviously, the distinction between a capital gain and ordinary income occupied much of the courts' time in Canada and the United Kingdom prior to the explicit introduction of capital gains taxation.

85 Canada, *Report of the Royal Commission on Taxation* (Ottawa: Queen's Printer, 1966) (the Carter commission).

86 Ibid., vol. 3, at 341.

87 Ibid., vol. 6, at 86.

88 In particular, the commission proposed that the full amount of capital losses be deductible from all sources of income (and not just capital gains), and that any unused losses could be carried back two years and forward six years. The

commission also proposed that taxpayers be permitted (but not obliged) to revalue various assets (including shares in private companies) in certain circumstances in order to allow them to claim unrealized losses or accrue unrealized gains. The commission did not set out any procedure for valuing private company shares; rather, it suggested that the valuation be left to negotiations between the private company and the tax authorities. The commission anticipated that there would be difficulties involved but had no solutions to offer: "It might become necessary, because of difficulties of supporting a revaluation of a private share, to introduce regulations permitting the use of stated valuation procedures. In any event, we hope that the tax authorities would establish procedures to be followed in a manner that would minimize uncertainty for the taxpayers concerned." Ibid., vol. 3, at 367.

89 These conclusions were supported in one of the background papers for the commission: Thomas A. Wilson and N. Harvey Lithwick, *The Sources of Economic Growth: An Empirical Analysis of the Canadian Experience*, Studies of the Royal Commission on Taxation no. 24 (Ottawa: Queen's Printer, 1968).

90 Geoffrey R. Conway, *The Taxation of Capital Gains*, Studies of the Royal Commission on Taxation no. 19 (Ottawa: Queen's Printer, February 1967).

91 J. Keith Butters, Lawrence E. Thompson, and Lynn L. Bolinger, *Effects of Taxation: Investments by Individuals* (Boston: Harvard University, Graduate School of Business Administration, Division of Research, 1953).

92 Ibid., at 50-51.

93 Conway, supra note 90, at 289.

94 Ibid., at 303.

95 Ibid., at 304.

96 See, for example, the comments by Mr. Fernand E. Leblanc in Canada, House of Commons, *Debates*, October 11, 1967, 3007-8.

97 Dan Throop Smith, "Rates, Allowances and Averaging," in *Report of Proceedings of the Nineteenth Tax Conference*, April 1967 Conference Report (Toronto: Canadian Tax Foundation, 1967), 24-32, at 28.

98 Carl S. Shoup, "Economic Implications," ibid., 70-77, at 74.

99 John F. Chant, "Fiscal Policy for Stability and Growth," ibid., 151-56.

100 P.N. Thorsteinsson, "Capital Gains," ibid., 357-61, at 359.

101 E.J. Benson, *Proposals for Tax Reform* (Ottawa: Queen's Printer, 1969) (herein referred to as "the white paper").

102 According to the white paper, the rationale for limiting the tax on widely held shares to one-half of the gain was to "put Canadians in approximately the same tax position regarding capital gains and losses on these shares as most of the non-residents who invest in Canada [specifically, US individuals and corporations and British individuals and corporations]" (ibid., at paragraph 3.34). The rationale for revaluing widely held shares every five years was to reduce the "lock-in" effect that might otherwise result. The revaluation rules would not apply until five years after capital gains became taxable. Thereafter, individuals would revalue shares in each year in which they attained an age divisible by five; corporations would revalue every five years, likely on each anniversary of incorporation divisible by five (ibid., at paragraph 3.38).

103   Canada, House of Commons, *Eighteenth Report of the Standing Committee on Finance, Trade and Economic Affairs Respecting the White Paper on Tax Reform* (Ottawa: Queen's Printer, 1970).

104   Canada, Standing Senate Committee on Banking, Trade and Commerce, *Report on the White Paper Proposals for Tax Reform* (Ottawa: Queen's Printer, 1970).

105   Ibid., at 2.

106   Ibid., at 22.

107   The legislation excluded from taxation altogether capital gains relating to any increases in the value of property before 1972. For property acquired before 1972 and disposed of after 1972, the cost of the property for capital gains purposes is its fair market value on December 31, 1971. A set of transitional rules, referred to as the Income Tax Application Rules (ITARs), deal with various aspects of the introduction of capital gains taxation.

Under the 1971 tax reform, there were 13 rate bands, ranging from 17 percent (for taxable income up to $500) to 47 percent (for taxable income over $60,000).

108   Income Tax Act, SC 1971-72-73, c. 63. Unless otherwise stated, statutory references in this section of the chapter are to this version of the Income Tax Act, as amended, or to the Income Tax Act, RSC 1985, c. 1 (5th Supp.), as amended (as applicable).

Unlike the US provisions, the Canadian capital gains tax provisions include a deemed disposition of capital property and certain other property at fair market value on death (other than property transferred to a spouse or spouse trust, in which case the deemed disposition at fair market value is deferred until the spouse's death). According to the minister of finance, the deemed disposition on death was adopted instead of the white paper proposal requiring periodic revaluation of public company shares: Canada, House of Commons, *Debates*, June 18, 1971, 6897. The federal government announced at the same time the discontinuance of federal estate and gift taxes effective January 1, 1972: SC 1971-72-73, c. 63, part II, section 2.

109   The deduction was found in paragraph 3(e). The increase from $1,000 to $2,000 was made by SC 1977-78, c. 1, section 1. Other measures included the reintroduction of preferential tax treatment of certain employee stock options, specifically those granted by a Canadian-controlled private corporation to arm's-length employees (discussed in chapter 4). The top marginal tax rate was reduced from 47 percent to 43 percent, applicable to taxable income above $60,000.

110   Canada, House of Commons, *Debates*, November 25, 1977, 1255.

111   A report by a class of Professor Neil Brooks at Osgoode Hall Law School commented (as read into the House *Debates*, ibid., at 1260):

> Even though it may appear arbitrary, the figure $2,000 was not chosen at random. In increasing the amount permitted for capital loss offset, the Liberal government has followed the lead of the United States once more, having previously borrowed the "$1,000 rule" from the *IRS Code*. The Tax Reform Bill of 1976 provides for the increase of the capital loss offset figure to $2,000 in 1977 and $3,000 in 1978 and in subsequent years. Based on the government's past method of choosing its figure for capital loss offset and its failure to conduct a cost-benefit analysis as to the merits of the

proposal, it is surprising that the proposed changes do not advocate the institution of a "$3,000 rule" in 1978.

112 Ibid., at 1270.

113 Former section 110.1 was introduced in 1974, and allowed an individual to deduct from taxable income up to $1,000 of Canadian-source interest and dividends from Canadian corporations. Capital gains from dispositions of Canadian securities were added in 1977: SC 1977-78, c. 1, section 52(1), adding subparagraph 110.1(1)(b)(iii). Subparagraphs 110.1(1)(b)(iii.1) and (iii.2) (which added certain lookthrough rules for capital gains earned through other entities) were added by SC 1980-81-82-83, c. 140, section 58(1), applicable to 1979 and subsequent years.

114 Subparagraphs 110.1(1)(b)(iii), (iii.1), and (iii.2) were repealed by SC 1986, c. 6, section 56(1), applicable to 1985 and subsequent years.

115 SC 1988, c. 55, section 78, applicable with respect to the computation of taxable income for 1988 and subsequent years.

116 Canada, Department of Finance, *A Review of the Taxation of Capital Gains in Canada: An Examination of the Canadian Experience and of Issues Involved in Proposals for Change* (Ottawa: Department of Finance, November 1980).

117 On the effect of capital gains taxation on risk taking, the paper suggested that it was "not obvious that the taxation of capital gains necessarily reduces the propensity to take risks" (ibid., at 32) and further (ibid., at 33):

> Another implication of the imprecise nature of phenomena such as riskiness, innovation, and entrepreneurship is that it is extremely difficult to design tax measures that promote businesses with these characteristics. A broad-based reduction of tax on capital gains would apply to gains earned in a variety of companies which do not possess the attributes that the measure is trying to support. It would thus be inefficient and potentially costly. However, attempting to single out gains on shares in certain businesses for special treatment, in order to improve the target-effectiveness of the measure, would involve detailed rules and bureaucratic discretion, and would lead to increased complexity and uncertainty in the application of tax law, both of which could easily vitiate the effectiveness of the measure.

118 Canada, Department of Finance, 1981 Budget, November 12, 1981.

119 Canada, Department of Finance, *Inflation and the Taxation of Personal Investment Income: A Paper for Consultation* (Ottawa: Department of Finance, June 1982).

120 Former subsections 47.1(1) to (26) of the Act.

121 The lifetime capital gains exemption was found in subsection 110.6(3), added by SC 1986, c. 6, section 58.

122 SC 1986, c. 6, section 1.

123 Supra note 114.

124 Canada, Department of Finance, 1985 Budget, Budget Speech, May 23, 1985, 14.

125 In 2000, when the capital gains inclusion rate was reduced from three-quarters to one-half, the capital gains tax preference for AMT purposes was amended so that only four-fifths of capital gains and losses are included in adjusted taxable income.

126   Canada, Department of Finance, *The White Paper: Tax Reform 1987* (Ottawa: Department of Finance, June 18, 1987).

127   The measures were included in SC 1988, c. 55. In addition to the amendments to the capital gains provisions discussed herein, the 1987 budget reduced the number of tax brackets to three, with a top marginal tax rate of 29 percent on taxable income in excess of $55,000 (indexed thereafter for inflation in excess of 3 percent). The top bracket had previously been 34 percent (reduced from 43 percent in 1982) on taxable income in excess of $24,000. In addition, a number of deductions and exemptions were converted into tax credits.

128   SC 1993, c. 24, section 47(1), amending the definition of "cumulative gains limit" and adding the definition of "non-qualifying real property" in subsection 110.6(1). Non-qualifying real property was property other than qualified farm property and real property used in an active business.

129   Individuals were permitted to file with their 1994 tax return an election to recognize gains accruing to February 22, 1994 on capital property owned by the individual.

130   The provision allowing individuals to deduct up to $2,000 of capital losses annually from other sources of income and the annual $1,000 investment income deduction (at least as it applied to taxable capital gains).

131   Supra notes 53 and 68 and accompanying text.

132   Canada, Department of Finance, 2000 Budget, Budget Plan, February 28, 2000, 94. The supplementary documentation also suggests a more benign rationale, to ensure "that capital gains are taxed at about the same rate as dividends received from taxable Canadian corporations" (ibid., at 225).

133   Canada, Department of Finance, Economic Statement and Budget Update 2000, October 18, 2000, 13.

134   Ibid., at 101.

135   Ibid., at 151.

136   See, for example, "Soft Economies Spark Cuts," *Globe and Mail*, June 26, 2003, B1.

137   "Business" is defined in subsection 248(1) to include (except in limited circumstances) "an adventure or concern in the nature of trade." A significant body of case law and literature concerns the distinction among a capital gain, business income, and income from an adventure or concern in the nature of trade. Most of the case law concerns the distinction between a capital gain and income from an adventure in the nature of trade. The distinction between an adventure and a business is relevant only in limited circumstances. For an overview of this area, see Peter W. Hogg, Joanne E. Magee, and Jinyan Li, *Principles of Canadian Income Tax Law*, 4th ed. (Toronto: Carswell, 2002), 337-54. See also Grace Chow, "Old Wine in New Bottles: Adventure in the Nature of Trade," in *Report of Proceedings of the Forty-Eighth Tax Conference*, 1996 Conference Report, vol. 1 (Toronto: Canadian Tax Foundation, 1997), 26:1-22.

138   A "Canadian security" is defined in subsection 39(6) as a security that is a share of a corporation resident in Canada, a unit of a mutual fund trust, or various debt obligations issued by a person resident in Canada. Regulation 6200 lists a number of prescribed securities that are excluded from the definition of Canadian security.

139   Subsection 39(5) of the Act.

140   *Interpretation Bulletin* IT-479R, "Transactions in Securities," February 29, 1984, paragraph 5.

141   93 DTC 5116 (FCA), application for leave to appeal dismissed without reasons, [1993] SCCA no. 181. The decision dealt with a question of law submitted by the parties for determination. The question was whether the words "trader or dealer in securities" was limited to a registered or licensed dealer or a person who in the ordinary course of business buys and sells securities on behalf of other persons, or whether the words are broad enough to include anyone other than a person engaged in an adventure or concern in the nature of trade. As indicated, the court concluded that the words are broad enough to include the latter. On the actual determination of whether the taxpayer involved in the case was entitled to make the election under subsection 39(4), in further proceedings the Federal Court Trial Division concluded that it was (2001 DTC 5337), accepting the taxpayer's submissions that its activities were adventures in the nature of trade.

142   Ibid., at 5120 (FCA).

143   Unless the transaction constitutes an adventure or concern in the nature of trade and is not covered by an election under subsection 39(4).

144   Supra note 141, at 5119 (FCA). But see note 147, infra, where the Federal Court Trial Division in *Kane* suggested that these badges of trade are found in both a business and an adventure and, therefore, the distinction between the two must lie elsewhere.

145   The argument is equally applicable to any property that does not produce income independent of a sale, particularly commodities or commodity futures. In fact, the argument is more compelling for these assets; common shares at least have the potential to produce dividends, whereas commodities cannot generate any income independent of their sale. Despite this, gains generated from the sale of gold bullion and commodity futures have been considered to be on capital account: see, for example, *The Queen v. G. Stirling*, [1985] 1 CTC 275 (FCA) and *W.W. Hastings v. MNR*, [1988] 2 CTC 2001 (TCC). In both cases, the taxpayer's characterization of the gains as capital gains was not challenged; rather, the deduction of related expenses (for example, interest and safety deposit box fees) was denied under subsection 9(3). Expenses incurred to generate capital gains are deductible only as specifically provided in the determination of the taxpayer's gain in section 40. The CRA sanctions capital gains treatment for commodity futures transactions by speculators provided that the treatment is applied consistently: *Interpretation Bulletin* IT-346R, "Commodity Futures and Certain Commodities," November 20, 1978, paragraph 7. A "speculator" in this context is any person who takes one or more futures positions or acquires a commodity other than in certain circumstances in which income treatment is specifically required. Income treatment is required in three situations: when a taxpayer acquires commodities or futures positions in commodities connected with its business operations (for example, a distiller taking a futures position in grains); when a taxpayer has special (insider) information about the commodity which it uses to its benefit (for example, a senior officer in a sugar refinery who acquires sugar futures); and when the primary or only business activity of a corporate taxpayer is trading in commodities or commodity futures. The corporate taxpayer is probably included because corporations are generally considered to be carrying on business. It is arguable, however, that the same characterization should be accorded when a partnership is engaged primarily in commodity futures.

146   For venture capital limited partnerships, the argument for income (as opposed to capital gains) treatment is perhaps stronger, because the general partner is usually a venture capital firm whose sole business is venture capital financing. See chapter 6, under the heading "Taxation of Limited Partnership Venture Capital Funds: A Primer."

147   Consider, for example, the first case to apply the principles set out in *Vancouver Art Metal Works*, supra note 141. *Kane v. The Queen*, 94 DTC 6671 (FCTD) concerned a chartered accountant who was also a shareholder, director, and president of a publicly traded junior mining company. The taxpayer traded extensively in the shares of this company in 1979-1981. In 1978, the taxpayer filed an election under subsection 39(4). The minister successfully challenged the election with respect to the shares of the junior mining company (his transactions in other publicly traded shares were not challenged) on the basis that the taxpayer was a trader or dealer in these shares. According to the court (ibid., at 6674):

> It is recognized by all that paragraph 39(5)(a) was at least intended to prevent persons who are registered or licensed traders or dealers in securities from converting their income arising from that trade into capital gains. In the normal course, however, licensed dealers trade for the account of their clients and, in that context, paragraph 39(5)(a) is of no relevance to them. It is only of relevance to them when, from time to time, they choose to trade on their own account. In that context, it seems clear that the legislator did not intend individuals who, by their trade, have professional knowledge of the market in which they deal to benefit from the election.
>
> I believe that in determining the availability of the election [under subsection 39(4)] to one who trades in securities without being licensed or registered, the focus should be the same, namely, does the author of the transactions in question possess a particular or special knowledge of the market in which he trades? To the extent that he does, he distinguishes himself from the common risk takers who "play the market" regularly or sporadically based on commonly available investment advice and information. That it seems is the guiding line which must delineate the scope of the election contemplated by section 39(4) of the Act and the limitation embodied in paragraph 39(5)(a).

If it is special knowledge of the market that distinguishes the trader from the mere investor, professional venture capitalists, who often participate in the management of the corporations in which they invest and who have insider knowledge of the corporations, likewise should be considered traders whose gains are on income account and should not be able to make an election under subsection 39(4).

148   A summary of the various arguments can be found in Walter J. Blum, "A Handy Summary of the Capital Gains Arguments" (1957) vol. 35, no. 4 *Taxes: The Tax Magazine* 247-66. Although written in 1957, Blum's discussion remains largely relevant today. For a more recent study that includes a discussion of the recent economics literature on the issue, see Leonard E. Burman, *The Labyrinth of Capital Gains Tax Policy: A Guide for the Perplexed* (Washington, DC: Brookings Institution, 1999). See also Rick Krever and Neil Brooks, *A Capital Gains Tax for New Zealand* (Wellington, NZ: Victoria University Press for the Institute of

Policy Studies, 1990), 77-86, particularly 82-86. For a more colourful discussion of the preferential tax treatment of capital gains, see Eisenstein, supra note 8, at 93-105.

149   In fact, the distinction is applicable to all four tax expenditures affecting capital gains considered in this chapter—the general preferential tax treatment of capital gains, the specific preference for capital gains from small business securities, the angel capital rollover, and the preferential treatment of capital losses resulting from small business securities—and is crucial to the first three.

150   On its face, the first argument is simple and deceptively persuasive: the general premise of this argument is that a significant portion of any capital gain reflects inflation and, if inflation were taken into account, some nominal capital gains may in fact be "real" capital losses. Therefore, the cost of capital assets should be indexed for inflation (which is or has been done in some countries, such as the United Kingdom and Australia). Preferential tax treatment (either preferential tax rates or the exclusion of a portion of capital gain) is an alternative and simpler (but much poorer) proxy for compensating for the effects of inflation. There are a number of responses to this argument. In an ideal world, assuming that capital income is subject to tax, capital gains should (like other capital income) be taxed on an accrual basis. Inflation affects the real return on all capital income, including interest and dividends. Therefore, since other forms of capital income are taxed on their nominal (pre-inflation) return, so too should capital gains. Since the taxation of capital gains is deferred until realization, the impact of inflation is, in fact, less severe on capital gains than on other forms of capital income: see Burman, supra note 148, at 48, figure 4-1, and accompanying text, at 45-48. The indexation of capital gains compounds the favourable treatment of capital gains over other forms of capital income. Furthermore, and perhaps counterintuitively, inflation has a greater impact on the effective (post-inflation) tax rate for assets held for a shorter period than for a longer period. Its greatest effect is therefore on capital income that is taxed currently (interest and dividends). The longer a capital asset is held, the greater is the beneficial impact of deferral on the effective tax rate (see Burman, ibid., at 48-51). As Auerbach states:

> contrary to the argument one often hears, a correction for inflation is more important for assets held for relatively short periods of time than for those held for extended periods. Put another way, the reduction in capital gains tax rates needed to offset the impact of inflation declines with the length of the holding period. This is a fact, not a hypothesis.

(Alan J. Auerbach, "The Effects of Reducing the Capital Gains Tax" (1989) vol. 43, no. 8a *Tax Notes* 1009-12, at 1010.)

151   The "lock-in" effect is essentially a byproduct of the fact that capital gains are taxed on a realization basis. As such, and given taxpayers' general inclination to avoid taxes, taxpayers may be loath to dispose of assets that have appreciated in value, at least when no subsequent decline in value is foreseen. The lock-in effect is compounded in the United States, at least for elderly individuals, in that there is no capital gains tax at death *and* there is a step-up in basis for assets transferred on death. The United States does levy an estate tax. However, it is impossible to sustain an argument that a preferential capital gains tax rate (or, indeed, the step-up) is a reasonable counterbalance to an estate tax. In any event, under the Economic Growth and Tax Relief Reconciliation Act of 2001, supra note 72, title V

(the Estate, Gift, and Generation-Skipping Transfer Tax Provisions), the estate tax, gift tax, and generation-skipping transfer tax rates have been reduced over the period 2002-2009, and in 2010 the estate tax and generation-skipping transfer tax will be repealed and the gift tax rate will be equal to the top individual tax rate at that time. The act also replaced the basis step-up on death with a rollover of the cost base of property transferred on death. The amendments made by the act are subject to a sunset clause at the end of 2010, at which time the law in effect at the time the act was introduced will be reinstated unless the amendments are extended by subsequent legislation. Although the elimination of the step-up on death reduces the lock-in effect, a more appropriate measure to remove this element of the lock-in effect would be to impose capital gains tax at death, as is done in Canada.

Some advocates of reducing the tax on capital gains suggest that a reduction in the lock-in effect would generate more tax revenue rather than less, because more people would sell capital assets. However, the economic impact of a reduction in capital gains tax rates is far from clear. Although there is some evidence to suggest that the short-term impact may be increased tax revenue, the long-term impact is likely to be substantial revenue loss: Alan J. Auerbach, "Capital Gains Taxation and Tax Reform" (1989) vol. 42, no. 3 *National Tax Journal* 391-401.

The impact of the lock-in effect may be stated in another way. Capital gains are not taxed until they are realized. This deferral means that capital gains are taxed more favourably than other forms of income, particularly other forms of investment income. However, because the tax is deferred, taxpayers are inclined to defer as long as possible the realization of a gain. In order to induce people to realize gains earlier—on the premise that earlier realization (or, more precisely, realization that is holding-period-neutral) leads to a more efficient allocation of resources—a further incentive must be provided to counterbalance the deferral incentive already in existence. (The notion that two wrongs somehow make a right comes to mind.) In other words, incentive must be added to incentive in order to induce taxpayers to realize their gains. It seems simpler to remove the incentive that deferral offers or, more precisely, to remove the disincentive to realize gains when it is prudent to do so in the absence of tax considerations.

There are certainly other ways to remove or reduce the lock-in effect. The ideal solution, in theory, is to tax capital gains on an accrual basis. For some capital assets whose values are easily determined at any given time, such as publicly traded securities, a mark-to-market system could be used. Obviously, accrual taxation would be more costly to administer (for both taxpayers and the tax authorities) for other assets, such as real property or shares of private corporations. Alternatively, tax could be deferred until realization, but the impact of deferral should be eliminated (or at least reduced) in some manner at that time (that is, retrospectively). Such retrospective taxation was first proposed by William Vickery in 1939 (William Vickery, "Averaging of Income for Income Tax Purposes" (1939) vol. 47, no. 3 *The Journal of Political Economy* 379-97) and further developed by Alan Auerbach in 1991 (Alan J. Auerbach, "Retrospective Capital Gains Taxation" (1991) vol. 81, no. 1 *The American Economic Review* 167-78).

152   United States, Department of the Treasury, Office of Tax Analysis, *Report to Congress on the Capital Gains Tax Reductions of 1978* (Washington, DC: US Government Printing Office, 1985), 133.

153 Ibid., at 134.

154 Pub. L. no. 93-406, enacted on September 2, 1974; 88 Stat. 829, 959 (1974). ERISA is considered in more detail in chapter 7.

155 Although investment by individuals in venture capital funds did increase in the decade following 1978, the increase was far outweighed by increased investment by non-taxable entities and corporations, neither of which benefited from the capital gains tax preference. For example, James Poterba indicates that individual investment increased from $112.7 million in 1978 to $504 million in 1987 (measured in 1987 dollars). Pension investment increased from $52.8 million to $1,638 million over the same period. Similarly, insurance company investment increased from $56.3 million to $630 million; foreign investment increased from $59.9 million to $546 million; corporate investment increased from $35.2 million to $462 million; and non-profit institutional investment increased from $31.7 million to $420 million. In relative terms, the percentage of total commitments provided by insurance companies, foreign investors, corporations, and non-profit institutions remained relatively constant over this period. Investment by individuals actually decreased from 32 percent to 12 percent of total venture capital fund commitments, while pension investment increased from 15 percent to 39 percent. See James M. Poterba, "Venture Capital and Capital Gains Taxation," in Lawrence H. Summers, ed., *Tax Policy and the Economy*, vol. 3 (Cambridge, MA: MIT Press, 1989), 47-67, at 54, table 4.

156 Poterba, ibid. See also James M. Poterba, "Capital Gains Tax Policy Toward Entrepreneurship" (1989) vol. 42, no. 3 *National Tax Journal* 375-89.

157 However, the implication of his article is that private individuals accounted for a relatively small amount of total venture capital. He cites a 1988 Freear and Wetzel study (an earlier study using the same data as John Freear and William E. Wetzel Jr., "Who Bankrolls High-Tech Entrepreneurs?" (1990) vol. 5, no. 2 *Journal of Business Venturing* 77-89) for the proposition that 21 percent of equity was provided to their sample firms as compared with 79 percent provided by venture capital funds. These figures ignore the number of firms launched without outside investors (38 percent), which were presumably financed by love capital (or debt financing). More important, for those firms that did rely on venture capital, the figure is based on aggregate investment and ignores the significance of individual investment at earlier financing stages and in smaller financing rounds: that is, their impact on the number of small businesses financed.

158 Bharat Narendra Anand, "Survivors, Angels, and Taxes: Essays in the Economics of Entrepreneurship" (PhD thesis, Princeton University, 1994).

159 Ibid., at 110 (emphasis in original).

160 Thus, increasing income tax rates applicable to employment income should have the same effect as reducing the rate applicable to capital gains: Roger H. Gordon, "Can High Personal Tax Rates Encourage Entrepreneurial Activity?" (1998) vol. 45, no. 1 *International Monetary Fund Staff Papers* 49-80. Gordon suggests that this differential acts as an incentive for high-income employees to convert their income into corporate-level retained earnings taxed at a lower rate and to defer and recharacterize the personal-level income as capital gains from the disposition of equity. Gordon acknowledges that this form of income shifting has liquidity constraints, making it attractive only for those with substantial liquid assets from

other sources. Gordon also postulates (ibid., at 71) that the likelihood of the entrepreneur obtaining outside funding "is higher the tax rate *t* faced by venture capitalists, and the lower their capital gains tax rate, *g*. . . . [However], [t]he fixed costs *C* of judging an entrepreneurial project are undoubtedly much higher than the equivalent costs for a copycat or tax shelter project, so that copycat and tax shelter projects should find it much easier to get outside financing. The effects of tax changes through the availability of outside financing are therefore likely to have less effect on entrepreneurial entrants than on these other types of new firms."

161 Department of the Treasury, Office of Tax Analysis, supra note 152; and Poterba, supra note 155. See also George R. Zodrow, "Economic Analyses of Capital Gains Taxation: Realizations, Revenues, Efficiency and Equity" (1993) vol. 48, no. 3 *Tax Law Review* 419-527, at 479-81.

162 Poterba, supra note 155, at 63.

163 Kevin McGee suggests that a reduced rate of capital gains tax is, in most cases, more beneficial to mature firms than to new firms, and in many cases results in a reduction in new firm investment: M. Kevin McGee, "Capital Gains Taxation and New Firm Investment" (1998) vol. 51, no. 4 *National Tax Journal* 653-73. Similarly, Michael Haliassos and Andrew Lyon suggest that reduced capital gains tax rates will, in many cases, reduce stockholding relative to other capital assets: Michael Haliassos and Andrew B. Lyon, "Progressivity of Capital Gains Taxation with Optimal Portfolio Selection," in Joel Slemrod, ed., *Tax Progressivity and Income Inequality* (Cambridge, UK: Cambridge University Press, 1994), 275-308.

164 This is especially true in the United States, which employs a classical tax system in which no attempt has been made to integrate corporate and shareholder-level tax. Some may view the US capital gains tax preference as a poor proxy for integration. An element of integration was introduced by the Jobs and Growth Tax Relief Reconciliation Act of 2003, supra note 1 (section 302), which removed dividends from ordinary income tax rates and made them subject to the same 15 percent rate applicable to long-term capital gains; for taxpayers in the 10 percent and 15 percent tax brackets, the dividend tax rate is 5 percent. The legislation fell short of President Bush's original proposal to eliminate tax on corporate dividends altogether.

165 Auerbach, "Capital Gains Taxation and Tax Reform," supra note 151, at 397.

166 Michael Livingston, "Risky Business: Economics, Culture and the Taxation of High-Risk Activities" (1993) vol. 48, no. 2 *Tax Law Review* 163-232, at 184.

167 Ibid., at 185-86 (notes omitted).

168 Ibid., at 231-32.

169 Canada may have felt compelled to follow the US lead in this respect, because of the mobility of labour, particularly in the high-tech sector, as well as the mobility of venture capital: see Jack M. Mintz and Thomas A. Wilson, *Capitalizing on Cuts to Capital Gains Taxes*, C.D. Howe Institute Commentary no. 137 (Toronto: C.D. Howe Institute, February 2000). The effects of international competitiveness on the mobility of labour across the Canada-US border are discussed in chapter 4.

170 Supra note 63, section 13113, adding section 1202 to the Code.

171 HR rep. no. 103-111, 103d Cong., 1st sess. (1993), 600; [1993] USCCAN 378, at 831.

172   The Community Renewal Tax Relief Act of 2000 introduced a 60 percent (rather than 50 percent) exclusion for gains from the sale or exchange of qualified stock of empowerment zone businesses held more than five years. See Code section 1202(a)(2), introduced in Pub. L. no. 106-554, appendix G, enacted on December 21, 2000; 114 Stat. 2763A-587. This measure was added at the same time as the New Markets Venture Capital Company program and serves a similar purpose. See the discussion of the new markets venture capital program in chapter 8, at note 10. A number of additional tax expenditures targeting specific geographic areas were added in the Community Renewal Tax Relief Act of 2000 for investment in "renewal communities." See Code sections 1400E to 1400J. These tax expenditures include the exclusion from gross income of a capital gain from the sale or exchange of a qualified community asset held more than five years. A discussion of these geographically targeted relief provisions is beyond the scope of this study.

173   Code section 1202(c)(1)(B).

174   Code section 1202(c)(3).

175   Code section 1202(c)(1)(A).

176   Code section 1202(d)(3). A parent-subsidiary controlled group is defined in Code section 1202(d)(3)(B) by reference to Code section 1562(a)(1). Essentially, any group of corporations connected through one or more chains through stock ownership (stock representing more than 50 percent of the votes or value) with a common parent are in the same group. For example, if P Co owns 51 percent of the voting shares of A Co, which in turn owns 51 percent of the voting shares of B Co, then P Co, A Co, and B Co are all members of the same parent-subsidiary controlled group. For these purposes, stock does not include non-voting stock that is limited and preferred as to dividends.

177   Code section 1202(e)(1). Code section 1202(e)(2) provides special rules for startup and research and development expenses. Essentially, if a corporation engages in such activities in connection with a qualified trade or business, the assets used in the activities qualify as being used in an active trade or business.

178   Code section 1202(e)(3). The excluded activities are:

> (A) any trade or business involving the performance of services in fields of health, law, engineering, architecture, accounting, actuarial science, performing arts, consulting, athletics, financial services, brokerage services, or any trade or business where the principal asset of such trade or business is the reputation or skill of 1 or more of its employees,
>
> (B) any banking, insurance, financing, leasing, investing, or similar business,
>
> (C) any farming business (including the business of raising or harvesting trees),
>
> (D) any business involving the production or extraction of [natural resources], and
>
> (E) any business of operating a hotel, motel, restaurant, or similar business.

179   Code section 1202(e)(4). Excluded corporations are domestic international sales corporations, corporations that benefit from the Puerto Rico and possession tax credit, regulated investment companies, real estate investment trusts (REITs),

real estate mortgage investment conduits and cooperatives, and financial asset securitization investment trusts (FASITs).

180   Code section 1202(e)(5). In effect, the stock of a subsidiary is disregarded and the parent corporation is deemed to own a rateable amount of the subsidiary's assets and conduct a rateable share of the subsidiary's activities. A subsidiary is defined as a corporation in which the parent owns more than 50 percent of the voting shares or more than 50 percent in value of all outstanding stock (Code section 1202(e)(5)(C)). If, however, more than 10 percent of a corporation's assets are portfolio securities, the lookthrough rules do not apply (and the portfolio securities would not, themselves, qualify as assets used in an active business). Under Code section 1202(e)(6), portfolio securities do not include assets held as part of reasonably required working capital needs or held for investment and are reasonably expected to be used within two years for a qualified purpose (including research and experimentation, use in a qualified trade or business, or increases in working capital needs of a qualified trade or business). However, for corporations in existence for at least two years, no more than 50 percent of the assets can be considered qualified on this basis alone.

181   Code section 1202(e)(7). For this purpose, the ownership of, dealing in, or renting of real property is not considered active conduct of a qualified trade or business.

182   Under the Senate amendments to the 1997 House bill that reduced the long-term capital gains tax rate from 28 percent to 20 percent (S rep. no. 105-33, 105th Cong., 1st sess. (1997), 34-35), the 50 percent exclusion for gains from dispositions of QSBS was extended to corporations and the minimum tax preference (under which one-half of the excluded gain was treated as a tax preference for AMT purposes) was repealed. For individuals, the Senate bill effectively reduced the maximum tax rate applicable to the disposition of QSBS shares to 10 percent (by extending the maximum 20 percent capital gains tax rate to the half of the QSBS gain that was included in income). The Senate amendment proposed a number of changes to the definition of a small business corporation (both the asset test and the active business test): it increased the size of an eligible corporation from gross assets of $50 million to gross assets of $100 million; it provided that certain working capital must be expended within five years (rather than two years) in order to be treated as used in the active conduct of a trade or business; and it removed the limit on the percentage of the corporation's assets that could be working capital. The Senate amendment further repealed the limitation on the amount of gain a taxpayer can exclude with respect to the stock of any corporation. The Senate amendment also allowed a taxpayer to roll over the gain from the sale or exchange of QSBS where the taxpayer uses the proceeds to purchase other small business stock within 60 days of the sale of the original stock. If the taxpayer sold the replacement stock, any gain attributable to the original stock would be treated as a gain from the sale or exchange of QSBS, and any remaining gain would be so treated after the replacement stock is held at least five years. In addition, any gain that otherwise would be recognized from the sale of the replacement stock can be rolled over to other small business stock purchased within 60 days.

Most of the Senate amendments were excluded from the conference agreement. However, the tax preference for AMT purposes was reduced from one-half to 42 percent of the excluded gain and the QSBS rollover was adopted, as discussed below, under the heading "Angel Capital Rollover."

183 For gains from QSBS shares, the tax preference was equal to 42 percent of the excluded gain (Code section 57(a)(7)). Therefore, assuming that a taxpayer realized a significant gain from QSBS shares, the effective regular rate of tax on the gain would have been 14 percent. However, the effective AMT rate would have been 0.28[0.5 + 0.42(0.5)] or 19.88 percent. This calculation assumes that the taxpayer had other taxable income greater than the aggregate of the exemption amount (then $33,750 for unmarried individuals and $45,000 for married couples filing joint returns) and the amount of alternative minimum taxable income that was subject to the lower 26 percent rate ($175,600 for both unmarried individuals and married couples filing joint returns).

184 Supra note 69, section 6005(f)(2).

185 Section 6005(d)(3) of the IRS Restructuring and Reform Act of 1998, applicable as if it were included in the 1997 Act. This change reduced the effective AMT rate on QSBS to 17.92 percent (for holding periods beginning after December 31, 2000).

186 Section 301(b)(3) of the Jobs and Growth Tax Relief Reconciliation Act of 2003, supra note 1, reduced the tax preference for QSBS gains for AMT purposes from 28 percent to 7 percent of the gain for dispositions on or after May 6, 2003. As a result of this reduction, the effective AMT rate on QSBS gains is 14.98 percent.

187 Canada, Department of Finance, 1985 Budget, Budget Papers, May 23, 1985, 3.

188 Supra note 124, at 22.

189 The lifetime capital gains exemption was found in subsection 110.6(3), added by SC 1986, c. 6, section 58. For property other than qualified farm property, the exemption (as originally introduced) had a cumulative limit of $20,000 of net capital gains in 1985, increasing to $50,000 in 1986, $100,000 in 1987, $200,000 in 1988, $300,000 in 1989, and $500,000 in 1990.

190 Paragraph (b) of the definition of "qualified small business corporation share" in subsection 110.6(1). Technically, the exemption is not available if the shares are held by anyone other than the individual or a related person in the previous 24 months. Special rules apply for various share-for-share exchanges. Newly issued shares are deemed to have been owned by an unrelated person prior to their issuance unless the shares were issued in exchange for other shares or for a transfer to the corporation of all or substantially all of the assets used in an active business carried on by the transferor: paragraph 110.6(14)(f). Under section 54.2, the shares received as consideration in the latter transfer are deemed to be capital property. Accordingly, an individual can transfer the assets of a proprietorship or partnership to a corporation on a tax-deferred basis (under section 85) and sell the shares immediately following the transfer in order to benefit from the capital gains exemption.

191 Paragraphs (a) and (c), respectively, of the definition of "qualified small business corporation share" in subsection 110.6(1).

192 The CRA has interpreted the phrase "all or substantially all" to mean 90 percent or more of whatever is being measured (in this case, the value of the assets of the corporation based on their fair market value). However, courts have held that the test is not necessarily that stringent: see, for example, *Wood v. MNR*, 87 DTC 312 (TCC); and *Eberle v. The Queen*, 2001 DTC 158 (TCC).

193 Special rules apply where shares of a holding company are sold.

194	AMT was introduced in Canada in the 1985 budget (effective commencing in 1986), and is set out in division E.1 of the Income Tax Act. Since its introduction, the AMT rate has been applicable to the lowest tax bracket (17 percent up to and including 2000 and 16 percent thereafter). The AMT rate applies to an individual's adjusted taxable income, as determined in section 127.52, less the individual's basic exemption ($40,000, unchanged since the introduction of AMT). Adjusted taxable income is the taxpayer's taxable income increased by a number of tax preferences, including, among others, the exempt portion (or a fraction thereof) of capital gains (other than the portion of a capital gain exempt as a result of the $500,000 capital gains exemption).

195	Subparagraph 127.52(1)(h)(i). From 1986 (when AMT first applied) to 1999, the full amount of an individual's capital gains was included in the determination of adjusted taxable income for AMT purposes. For 2000 and following years, four-fifths of the individual's capital gains (and capital losses) are included in adjusted taxable income for AMT purposes: paragraph 127.52(1)(d). When AMT was introduced, only one-half of an individual's capital gain was included in income, while the entire gain was included in income for AMT purposes. When the capital gains inclusion rate was reduced from three-quarters to one-half (in the February 2000 budget and October 2000 economic statement), no explanation was given for including only four-fifths of the capital gain and capital loss for AMT purposes.

196	Provincial income tax rates are, on the whole, significantly higher than US state income tax rates; in addition, a number of US states exclude capital gains from state taxation.

197	For AMT purposes, four-fifths of a capital gain is included in adjusted taxable income, but one-half of the gain from QSBC shares, up to a maximum of $250,000, remains deductible. Four-fifths less one-half leaves 30 percent of the gain subject to AMT. Therefore, the effective AMT rate on a $500,000 gain that benefits from the QSBC share exemption is 4.8 percent (compared with nil in the absence of AMT), assuming that the taxpayer has sufficient other income to offset the basic exemption for AMT and the basic minimum tax credit for AMT. For gains in excess of $500,000, the federal AMT rate is 12.8 percent ($4/5 \times 16$ percent).

198	In the United States, the general long-term capital gains tax rate (20 percent) is not considered a tax preference for AMT purposes.

199	In its original form, however, the Canadian lifetime capital gains exemption could hardly be described as targeted despite its stated goals of increasing investment in "high-technology companies" and encouraging entrepreneurs to start new businesses.

200	Supported by anti-avoidance rules to prevent its circumvention.

201	See chapter 5, under the heading "Evaluation of Direct Investment Tax Credit Programs: Eligible Businesses," and chapter 6, under the heading "Evaluation of VCF Tax Credit Programs: Eligible Investments of the VCF."

202	Jack M. Mintz and Stephen R. Richardson, "The Lifetime Capital Gains Exemption: An Evaluation" (1995) vol. 21, supplement Canadian Public Policy S1-12, at S11.

203	Vijay M. Jog, "The Lifetime Capital Gains Exemption: Corporate Financing, Risk-Taking and Allocation Efficiency" (1995) vol. 21, supplement Canadian Public Policy S116-35, at S133.

204   Patrizia E. Dal Cin, "Canadian Informal Investors: Towards a Framework for Policy Initiatives" (MMS thesis, Carleton University, School of Business, 1993).

205   See, for example, John Freear, Jeffrey E. Sohl, and William E. Wetzel Jr., "Angels and Non-Angels: Are There Differences?" (1994) vol. 9, no. 2 *Journal of Business Venturing* 109-23, discussed in chapter 2, at notes 8-12 and accompanying text.

206   Supra note 63, section 13114, adding section 1044 to the Code.

207   Section 301(d) of the Small Business Investment Act of 1958, Pub. L. no. 85-699, enacted on August 21, 1958; 72 Stat. 689, as amended.

208   Small Business Programs Improvement Act of 1996, Pub. L. no. 104-208, division D, title II, section 208(b)(3)(A), enacted on September 30, 1996; 110 Stat. 3009-724, repealing section 301(d) of the Small Business Investment Act of 1958.

209   Supra note 66, section 313(a). The provision applies to sales after August 5, 1997.

210   Code section 1045(b)(1) adopts the definition of "qualified small business stock" in Code section 1202(c) for the purposes of Code section 1045.

211   The QSBS provisions are discussed in notes 170-186 and accompanying text, supra.

212   Supra note 69, section 6005(f)(2).

213   Code section 1045 was amended to add Code section 1045(b)(5), which provides that the "rules similar to the rules in [Code sections 1202(f) through (k)]" (the lookthrough rules for the QSBS exemption) apply for the purposes of Code section 1045 (section 6005(f)(2) of the IRS Restructuring and Reform Act of 1998).

214   Code section 1202(c)(1)(B).

215   Code section 1202(c)(3).

216   Code section 1202(c)(1)(A).

217   Code section 1202(d)(1).

218   Code section 1202(d)(2).

219   Code section 1202(d)(3). See also note 176, supra.

220   Code section 1202(c)(2)(A).

221   Code section 1045(b)(4)(B).

222   Code section 1202(e)(1)(A). A number of special rules apply in determining whether the 80 percent test is met. See supra notes 177, 180, and 181 and accompanying text.

223   Code section 1202(e)(1)(B).

224   Code section 1202(e)(3). The excluded activities are listed in note 178, supra.

225   Code section 1202(e)(4), supra note 179.

226   Code section 1202(e)(5)(B).

227   Code section 1202(e)(7). For this purpose, the ownership of, dealing in, or renting of real property is not considered active conduct of a qualified trade or business.

228   Code section 1045(a).

229   Discussed above, in the context of the general tax treatment of capital gains and losses.

230   In particular, the original budget proposal limited the rollover to ESBC shares with an aggregate cost not exceeding $500,000 that are reinvested in shares of other ESBCs with a cost not exceeding $500,000 per ESBC. The October 2000

economic statement increased the cost in each case to $2 million and the 2003 budget eliminated this de maximis rule. The de maximis rule added significant complexity to the provisions and was not necessary as a targeting measure.

231   Described in the budget documents, supra note 132, at 234, as "a special-purpose partnership that is treated for the purpose of these rules as a joint venture— effectively allowing the investment vehicle to act as the investment agent for a number of investors, and to pool investments for those investors, while treating each investor as having his or her own share portfolio within the vehicle." "Eligible pooling arrangement" is defined in subsection 44.1(1); under subsection 44.1(3), a transaction undertaken by an eligible pooling arrangement is deemed to be a transaction of the individual.

232   Subsection 44.1(1) definition of "eligible small business corporation share."

233   Infra note 238.

234   Subsection 44.1(1) definition of "eligible small business corporation."

235   Under the original budget proposals, the total carrying value of the assets of the corporation and related corporations could not exceed $2.5 million immediately before the investment was made, and did not exceed $10 million immediately after the investment. Both amounts were increased to $50 million in the October 2000 economic statement.

236   Paragraph (c) of the definition of "qualifying disposition" in subsection 44.1(1). There are special rules in subsections 44.1(4) and (5) applicable to an individual who acquires shares on a rollover basis from a related individual, under which the transferee will be considered for the purpose of section 44.1 to have acquired the shares at the time and under the same circumstances that they were acquired by the transferor. The special rules can apply in only three situations: the acquisition of shares as a result of the death of a spouse or common law partner; the acquisition of a share of a family farm corporation as a result of the death of a parent; and the acquisition of shares on the breakdown of a marriage or common law partnership. Similar rules apply to shares acquired on a rollover basis pursuant to certain corporate reorganizations, including a rollover under subsection 85(1), a share exchange under section 85.1, and an amalgamation under section 87: see subsections 44.1(6) and (7). Deficiencies in the scope of subsections 44.1(6) and (7) were corrected in draft legislation released on December 20, 2002, which adds to these provisions references to sections 51 (convertible property) and 86 (share exchanges in the context of a reorganization of capital): see now Canada, Department of Finance, *Legislative Proposals and Draft Regulations Relating to Income Tax* (Ottawa: Department of Finance, February 2004).

237   Paragraph (b) of the definition of "qualifying disposition" in subsection 44.1(1).

238   The exclusion of certain types of businesses was introduced in the October 2000 economic statement, supra note 133. Subsection 44.1(10) provides that the following corporations cannot be eligible small business corporations or active business corporations: a professional corporation (defined in subsection 248(1) as a corporation that carries on the professional practice of an accountant, dentist, lawyer, medical doctor, veterinarian, or chiropractor); a specified financial institution; a corporation whose principal business is leasing, renting, or developing for sale real property; and a corporation more than 50 percent of the fair market value of the property of which (net of debts incurred to acquire the property) is attributable

to real property. Although the technical detail of the rollover provision is beyond the scope of this study, it is interesting to compare the list of excluded corporations in Canada and the United States. For example, farming is an excluded activity in the United States but not in Canada. The list of professional businesses in the United States is longer and includes a business engaged in engineering, performing arts, or athletics and "any trade or business where the principal asset is the reputation or skill of one or more employees." Finally, the real estate exclusion is much broader in Canada than in the United States. In Canada, if a corporation uses all of its assets in a qualifying active business but happens to own its business premises, and the value of those premises exceeds the value of the remaining assets of the business (including goodwill), the corporation will not qualify as an eligible active business corporation.

239 Subsection 44.1(8), although poorly worded, is intended to allow the corporation to have non-active business assets (for example, excess cash from a share or debt issuance or from a sale of property or from an accumulation of retained earnings) and still qualify as an active business corporation, provided that the non-active assets are used to acquire property to be used to earn income from an active business within 36 months. This provision is comparable to Code section 1202(e)(6), discussed supra note 180.

240 Subsection 44.1(9). The October 2000 economic statement, supra note 133, introduced the 730-day rule (described as 24 months in the economic statement) as an "additional restriction." In fact, it is a relieving provision. Although no draft legislation accompanied the original proposal in the February 2000 budget, supra note 132, the budget documents suggested that a corporation, to qualify as an active business corporation, must carry on the active business primarily in Canada *throughout* the period of ownership. This limitation, if included in the legislation, would have excluded shares of a corporation that starts in Canada but after a period of time expands its operations, including facilities, into the United States. This scenario is common particularly in the high-tech sector, where US venture capital firms have typically required, as a condition of providing capital, that at least part of the business operations be located in the United States. For many Canadian high-tech businesses, US venture capital fund investment is preferable to Canadian venture capital fund investment because the former is believed to be able to achieve a more favourable and higher-priced exit, either through an initial public offering or a strategic sale.

241 Subsection 44.1(1) definition of "replacement share." Prior to the 2003 budget amendments, the replacement shares must have been acquired within 60 days after the end of the year, but no later than 120 days after the qualifying disposition. The former limitation would apply to any share sale on or after November 2. The individual must also designate the share as a replacement share in the tax return for the year of disposition.

242 SC 2003, c. 15, sections 70(1) to (5).

243 Supra note 241. In the United States, the taxpayer must acquire replacement shares within 60 days of the qualifying disposition in all cases.

244 Section 44.1 seems to assume that venture capitalists are passive investors, whereas they generally take an active role in the businesses in which they invest.

245 Supra note 132, at 95.

246   Technically, the determination of a taxpayer's gain (or loss) in section 40 applies
      to dispositions of *any* property, including inventory and other property that is not
      capital property. Under subsection 39(1), however, a taxpayer's capital gain (or
      capital loss) excludes the amount of the gain (or loss) otherwise included in
      income of the taxpayer. Thus, the capital gain on a disposition of inventory would
      be nil because the entire amount of the gain is otherwise included in income.

247   Supra note 149 and accompanying text.

248   Unlike the preferential treatment of gains from QSBS and the angel capital
      rollover, the preferential treatment of losses from small business securities is not
      restricted to certain types of small businesses.

249   Pub. L. no. 85-866, title I, enacted on September 2, 1958; 72 Stat. 1606 (herein
      referred to as "the TAA 1958").

250   Pub. L. no. 85-866, title II, enacted on September 2, 1958; 72 Stat. 1606 (herein
      referred to as "the SBTRA 1958").

251   Code section 165(g)(1) provides as a general rule that "[i]f any security which is
      a capital asset becomes worthless during the taxable year, the loss resulting
      therefrom shall, for purposes of this subtitle, be treated as a loss from the sale or
      exchange, on the last day of the taxable year, of a capital asset." Accordingly, if
      Code section 1244 stock becomes worthless in a taxable year, the loss arising
      therefrom (that is, the cost of the stock less nil proceeds) is recognized at the end
      of the taxable year: Treas. reg. section 1.1244-1(a)(1). For an example of the
      application of this rule to Code section 1244 stock, see *Maze v. US*, 98-2 USTC
      85,480 (Dist. Ct.). This provision is substantially similar to subsection 50(1) of
      Canada's Income Tax Act (infra notes 258-259 and accompanying text), except
      that the US provision is not an elective provision.

252   Section 202(b) of the SBTRA 1958, adding section 1244 to the 1954 Code. The
      conditions currently applicable are discussed in notes 255-257 and accompanying
      text, infra.

253   Section 345(b) of the 1978 Act, amending section 1244(b) of the 1954 Code.

254   Pub. L. no. 98-369, enacted on July 18, 1984; 98 Stat. 847, section 481(a),
      applicable to stock issued after July 18, 1984. According to the House committee,
      HR rep. no. 98-432, part II, 98th Cong., 2d sess. (1984), 1581; [1984] USCCAN
      697, at 1208, "The committee believes that to encourage new venture capital, an
      ordinary loss deduction should be available on preferred stock, as well as com-
      mon stock, of small business corporations."

255   Code section 1244(c)(1).

256   This amount was increased from $500,000 in 1978. Where the corporation has
      received consideration in excess of $1,000,000 for stock, then in the year in
      which this limit is exceeded, the corporation must designate which shares are
      section 1244 stock. See further Treas. reg. section 1.1244(c)-2.

257   A number of specific rules apply for this purpose. First, if a corporation has been
      in existence for less than five taxable years, all of the taxable years before the loss
      are reviewed; if the corporation has been in existence for less than one taxable
      year, the entire period before the loss is reviewed. Second, if, during the period in
      issue, the corporation's total deductions exceed its gross income, the condition
      does not apply.

258   If the taxpayer is a corporation that disposes of a debt, the corporation must have dealt at arm's length with the small business corporation. For others, the relationship between the taxpayer and the small business corporation is irrelevant.

259   Satisfying the fourth condition can be difficult in practice: see, for example, *Turner v. The Queen*, 2000 DTC 6442 (FCA); rev'g. 99 DTC 13 (TCC); and *Jacques St-Onge Inc. v. The Queen*, 2003 DTC 153 (TCC).

260   Clauses 39(1)(c)(iv)(B) and (C), respectively. If the taxpayer disposes of a debt, subparagraph 40(1)(g)(ii) may deem the loss to be nil if the taxpayer did not acquire the debt for the purpose of gaining or producing income. For example, if no interest is charged on the loan or if the debt arose from the taxpayer's obligations under a guarantee provided for no or inadequate consideration, the CRA may take the position that the debt was not acquired for the purpose of gaining or producing income. However, the CRA's administrative position is somewhat more generous in the case of debts disposed of by a shareholder of the corporation. In *Interpretation Bulletin* IT-239R2, "Deductibility of Capital Losses from Guaranteeing Loans for Inadequate Consideration and from Loaning Funds at Less Than a Reasonable Rate of Interest in Non-Arm's Length Circumstances," February 9, 1981, the CRA states (at paragraph 6):

> Where a taxpayer has loaned money at less than a reasonable rate of interest to a Canadian corporation of which he is a shareholder, or to its Canadian subsidiary, or has guaranteed the debts of such a corporation for inadequate consideration, any subsequent loss arising to him from the inability of the corporation to discharge its obligations to him, or from having to honour the guarantee, may be a deductible capital loss to him despite the absence of a reasonable rate of interest or adequate consideration. Generally it is the Department's practice to allow a loss on such a loan or guarantee and not treat it as being nil by virtue of subparagraph 40(2)(g)(ii) if the following conditions are satisfied:
>
> (a) the corporation to whom the loan was made or whose debts were guaranteed used the borrowed funds in order to produce income from business or property, or used the borrowed funds to lend money at less than a reasonable rate of interest to its Canadian subsidiary in turn to be used to produce income from business or property,
>
> (b) the corporation has made every effort to borrow the necessary funds through the usual commercial money markets but cannot obtain financing without the guarantee of the shareholder at interest rates at which the shareholder could borrow,
>
> (c) the corporation has ceased permanently to carry on its business, and
>
> (d) the loan from the shareholder to the corporation at less than a reasonable rate of interest (or at no interest) does not result in any undue tax advantage to either the shareholder or the corporation.

The CRA has applied this administrative position rather restrictively. For example, if the taxpayer is related to a shareholder of the corporation but is not a shareholder himself or herself, the loss arising on the debt is generally denied: see, for example, CRA document no. 74144, September 1, 1989. The courts have supported this position: see, for example, *Ellis v. MNR*, 88 DTC 1070 (TCC).

261   Krever and Brooks, supra note 148, at 120-22.

262   Timing can have an important impact on this argument. If, as is generally the
      case, poor investments appear soon after initial investment while successful in-
      vestments take a longer period of time to mature (the "J-curve" phenomenon),
      then even a diversified venture capital fund is adversely affected in that the
      economic value of an earlier-realized loss declines over time before it can be
      used. However, the economic loss arising from the deferred use of the capital
      loss could be compensated by imputing interest on the loss until it can be used.

263   Noël B. Cunningham and Deborah H. Schenk, "The Case for a Capital Gains
      Preference" (1993) vol. 48, no. 3 *Tax Law Review* 319-80, at 343.

264   Similar examples are provided in Cunningham and Schenk, ibid., at 341-42, and
      Livingston, supra note 166, at 169.

265   (200 percent [gain] × 40 percent) − (100 percent [loss] × 60 percent) = 20 percent.

266   In theory, Ms. X should be willing to increase her investment to $1,666.67,
      because the after-tax value of a loss of that size is $666.67, which reduces the
      amount at risk (after tax) to $1,000. This example assumes that Ms. X has
      sufficient income from other sources to make full use of the loss.

267   If Ms. X invested $1,000 in the second investment, there is a 40 percent chance
      of an after-tax profit of $1,200 ($2,000 net gain less $800 tax) and a 60 percent
      chance of an after-tax loss of $1,000 (assuming that Ms. X has no capital gains).
      Ms. X's expected return on the investment is therefore a loss of $120 (0.4 ×
      $1,200 − 0.6 × $1,000), or −12 percent.

268   If Ms. X invested $1,000 in the second investment, there is a 40 percent chance
      of an after-tax profit of $1,600 ($2,000 net gain less $400 tax, since half of the
      gain is excluded) and a 60 percent chance of an after-tax loss of $1,000 (assum-
      ing that Ms. X has no capital gains). Ms. X's expected return on the investment is
      therefore $40 (0.4 × $1,600 − 0.6 × $1,000), or 4 percent.

269   The after-tax benefit of the loss relief is $10,000 ($25,000 ABIL × 40 percent tax
      rate).

270   The after-tax benefit of the loss under Code section 1244 is $20,000 ($50,000
      loss × 40 percent tax rate).

271   This figure ignores the fact that in the United States, $3,000 of the loss in excess
      of $100,000 is also deductible from ordinary income under Code section 1211.
      Before the capital gains inclusion rate in Canada was reduced from three-quarters
      to one-half, the US capital loss tax relief exceeded that in Canada for investments
      up to $133,333. For investments in excess of this amount, assuming that the
      individual had no capital gains income, Canadian angels were better off than US
      angels in the same tax bracket.

272   Consider two married individuals, both in a 40 percent tax bracket, one in
      Canada and the other in the United States, each of whom realizes a loss from
      qualified small business securities of $300,000. Each individual also realizes
      capital gains (in the United States, long-term capital gains) of $150,000 in the
      aggregate from sales of publicly traded securities. Suppose further that each
      individual has income from other sources of $200,000. In the United States, the
      taxpayer's ordinary income subject to tax would be $100,000 and the taxpayer
      would have a net long-term capital loss of $50,000 (which could be carried

forward), since loss on the section 1244 stock in excess of $100,000 remains a long-term capital loss. Thus, the total tax payable in the United States is $40,000. (In fact, the individual can deduct $3,000 of the long-term loss from ordinary income under section 1211, thus reducing income to $97,000 and tax payable to $38,800.) In Canada, in contrast, the taxpayer's income is $125,000 ($200,000 + ½($150,000) − ½($300,000)), all of which is subject to the 40 percent rate. Thus, the total tax in Canada is $50,000 (with no capital loss that can be carried forward). If the US individual realizes long-term capital gains in excess of the loss that does not qualify under section 1244, the preference in the United States increases. Consider the same example, except that the individuals realize long-term capital gains of $250,000, again from publicly traded securities. The US individual would report ordinary income of $100,000 plus a net long-term capital gain of $50,000. The total tax payable (ignoring AMT) would be $47,500, assuming that the long-term capital gain is subject to a preferential rate of 15 percent. In Canada, the taxpayer's income would be $175,000 ($200,000 + ½($250,000) − ½($300,000)), giving rise to total tax payable of $70,000.

273   Following a series of Supreme Court of Canada judgments adverse to the government, including *The Queen v. Singleton*, [2002] 1 CTC 121 (SCC); *Ludco v. The Queen*, [2002] 1 CTC 95 (SCC); *Stewart v. The Queen*, [2002] 3 CTC 439 (SCC); and *The Queen v. Walls*, [2003] 3 CTC 421 (SCC), the minister of finance announced in the 2003 budget that the department would review the interest expense rules and introduce legislative amendments: Canada, Department of Finance, 2003 Budget, Budget Plan, February 18, 2003, 342. On October 31, 2003, the minister of finance released draft legislation that establishes a statutory "reasonable expectation of profit" (REOP) test. Proposed subsection 3.1(1) will deny a taxpayer's loss for a taxation year from a business or property unless "it is reasonable to expect that the taxpayer will realize a cumulative profit from that business or property" over the entire period that the taxpayer can "reasonably be expected" to carry on the business or hold the property. Subsection 3.1(2) specifically excludes capital gains and capital losses from the determination of cumulative profit for this purpose. For a critique of the proposals, see Daniel Sandler, "REOP Resurrected—This Year's Hallowe'en Trick," *Tax Topics* no. 1653 (Toronto: CCH Canadian, November 13, 2003), 1-3.

4

Employee Stock Options: "Sweat Equity" Venture Capital*

Until recently, employee stock options were the preserve of senior executives of large companies. With the rapid growth of the high-tech sector, however, stock-based compensation has become an increasingly important component of employee compensation for all employees, not just senior executives. Employees of startup companies often accept lower salaries in exchange for stock options as part of their overall compensation package. In many cases, stock options are the key form of (anticipated) remuneration used to attract employees to startups. In 1997, it was suggested that "Silicon Valley wouldn't be what it is today without stock options—nor, arguably, would the U.S. stock market be quite as supercharged or the economy be buzzing along as smoothly."[1] While the US stock market is no longer "supercharged" and the economy is not exactly "buzzing along," stock options remain an important form of compensation in new economy businesses and a significant part of executive compensation in all business sectors. The increased use of employee stock options has been encouraged by—indeed, may be due to—favourable accounting and tax treatment. It is important to understand the accounting treatment of employee stock options to appreciate their popularity and to consider the recent proposals for reform of their accounting treatment, which may diminish their popularity significantly. In considering their tax treatment, this chapter does not examine the technical details of the employee stock option provisions in the Income Tax Act or the Internal Revenue Code, such as the treatment of options in the event of corporate reorganizations, employee emigration or immigration, and other such niceties. These issues have been dealt with in depth elsewhere[2] and are not germane to this discussion.

The acceptance by employees of stock option compensation rather than monetary compensation for their human capital may be construed as a venture investment by the employees (hence the term "sweat equity"), similar to a direct investment of monetary capital by an angel capitalist in exchange for an equity interest in the employer.[3] Both Canada and the United States offer generous tax incentives for employee stock options—option benefits are not taxed until the options are exercised at the earliest or, in many cases, until the underlying securities are sold, at which time the benefits are often taxed at capital gains tax

---

* Unless otherwise stated, US monetary amounts are in US dollars and Canadian monetary amounts are in Canadian dollars.

rates. Contrary to popular belief, the tax treatment of stock options in Canada is significantly more generous than that in the United States. In my view, however, the generosity of the treatment in both countries is wholly inappropriate. Stock options should be taxed no differently from other non-cash compensation. The full value of the options should be included in the employee's income when the options are (unconditionally) received, and that value should be deducted by the employer as an expense at that time.

This chapter begins with an examination of the accounting treatment of employee stock options, including recent proposals for reform. The favourable accounting treatment of employee stock options—the fact that they do not generally need to be expensed for financial accounting purposes—likely explains the prevalence of their use,[4] particularly by high-tech companies. The chapter then examines the tax treatment of stock options, first by considering an appropriate benchmark treatment and then by reviewing the actual tax treatment in the United States and Canada. The chapter concludes with an evaluation of the preferential tax treatment of employee stock options.

Accounting for Employee Stock Options: Increasing the Bottom Line

The Current Accounting Standards

Unlike monetary compensation, employee stock options are not generally deducted as an expense for accounting purposes or tax purposes. Historically, the accounting profession has taken a simplistic approach to valuing stock options for financial statement purposes. For options that are not related to performance,[5] an enterprise can claim an expense on the date the option is granted equal to the intrinsic value of the option (the difference between the exercise price under the option and the share price at that time). In other words, the enterprise need not report any expense unless the option is "in the money" at the time of grant.

This approach, introduced in the United States in 1972 in Accounting Principles Board *Opinion* no. 25 (APB 25),[6] predated the pioneer work on option pricing of Fisher Black and Myron Scholes published in the following year.[7] The Black-Scholes model recognizes that the value of an option generally depends on five factors:

1) the option exercise price,
2) the current value of the underlying security,
3) the riskless rate of interest,
4) the time to expiration, and
5) the volatility of the stock price.

In essence, the Black-Scholes model recognizes three determinants in valuing a stock option: the intrinsic value of the option (the first two factors), the time value of money (the next two factors),[8] and the share's volatility. Even ignoring a share's volatility, it is readily apparent that the approach of APB 25 significantly undervalues employee stock options because it ignores the time value of money. Consider the following simple example. An employee, A, receives vested options to acquire 10,000 shares of X Co at the price of $1 per share, equal to the value of each share on the grant date. The options may be exercised at any time over the next 10 years. Since the exercise price is equal to the value of the shares on the grant date, the employer does not recognize any expense on account of the options under APB 25. Even if one ignores the volatility of the shares, however, the options must have some current value because of the time value of money. This value is commonly referred to as the minimum value of the stock option. If one assumes that the riskless rate of return is 5 percent and that there is no volatility in stock price, the stock options have a minimum value on the grant date of $3,860.87.[9] This amount reflects the present value of deferring payment of $10,000 (to acquire something worth $10,000) for 10 years (or, from the employer's perspective, it represents the carrying cost to the corporation of setting aside $10,000 worth of shares for 10 years).

If the volatility of the stock is factored in, the value of an option on the grant date can only increase. The more volatile a stock is, the greater the value of the option is, because the greater will be the potential value of the stock at the end of the option period. Although a highly volatile stock also has a high probability of declining in value, the value of the option can never be less than zero because the option holder will simply choose not to exercise the option. Since the value of the option on its expiry date is the value of the stock on that date less the exercise price of the option, the more volatile the stock price is, the more likely it is that the stock's value on the exercise date will exceed the exercise price by a substantial amount, if it exceeds it at all.

As this example illustrates, if employee stock options were valued using even their minimum value (that is, ignoring volatility) rather than their intrinsic value, they would have a significant impact on a corporation's bottom line. Assuming that the options are exercised, they will definitely have a significant impact on the corporation's earnings per share, diluting the position of other shareholders. Financial accounting standards—which are designed to provide readers of financial statements (for example, existing or potential shareholders and creditors) with an accurate (and conservative) account of a corporation's profits—ought to recognize this impact. For the past 30 years, however, corporations have not been required to account for anything other than the intrinsic value of stock options in their income statement. By failing to account for employee stock options, financial statements overstate the corporation's earnings. With the substantial increase in the use of stock options, particularly for corporations in the high-tech sector, the overstatement has increased significantly, and has led to criticisms that financial statements do not present an accurate picture of a corporation's profitability.

After 30 years of inaction, and largely in response to the "tech bust" and various accounting scandals in recent years, the accounting profession in Canada, the United States, and elsewhere has recognized that a corporate employer should recognize, as an expense, the value of employee stock options when they are granted, determined in accordance with an appropriate option-pricing model. In fact, the US Financial Accounting Standards Board (FASB) proposed such treatment in 1993, when it issued an exposure draft[10] recommending that enterprises recognize an amount of compensation expense on account of employee stock options determined using a modified Black-Scholes model. The proposal was strongly criticized, however, and in December 1994 the FASB voted to require the *disclosure* of option values (that is, in the notes to financial statements) but to make the recognition of such expense in the corporate income statement voluntary. When the FASB issued its *Statement of Financial Accounting Standards* (SFAS) no. 123, "Accounting for Stock-Based Compensation," in 1995—the standard currently in effect in the United States—it acknowledged that this decision was primarily political.[11] Thus, although SFAS no. 123 mandates disclosure of the value of stock options, this disclosure can be buried in the notes to a corporation's financial statements, so the impact on the corporation's profitability is not readily apparent to readers.

In an effort to create international consensus in the accounting treatment of employee stock options (and other stock-based compensation), the International Accounting Standards Board (IASB) released an exposure draft International Financial Reporting Standard on November 7, 2002.[12] One month later, the Accounting Standards Board of the Canadian Institute of Chartered Accountants (CICA) issued an exposure draft proposing amendments to section 3870 of the *CICA Handbook* that would make the reporting of stock-based compensation mandatory in all circumstances.[13] If adopted, the changes would apply to financial periods beginning on or after January 1, 2004. In a news release issued on March 12, 2003, the FASB announced its plans to review the treatment of stock-based compensation "with a view to issuing an Exposure Draft later this year that could become effective in 2004."[14]

It has thus taken the accounting profession 30 years to reach the point where it appears ready to adopt rules that mandate the reporting of employee stock options as an expense whose value is based on an appropriate option-pricing model. In considering the appropriate tax treatment of employee stock options, the draft IFRS and proposed amendments to section 3870 of the *CICA Handbook* warrant further examination.

Proposed Reforms to the Accounting Treatment of Employee Stock Options

The draft IFRS and section 3870 are similar in many ways. Both require that an enterprise determine the "fair value" of employee stock options on the date the options are granted and amortize that amount as an expense over the vesting period of the options; if the options vest immediately, the expense is recognized on the grant date. Both the IASB and the CICA require that the fair value be estimated using an option-pricing model (such as the Black-Scholes model) that takes into account the following factors:

1) the exercise price,
2) the current market price of the share,
3) the term of the option,[15]
4) the risk-free interest rate for the life of the option,
5) expected volatility of the share price, and
6) expected dividends.[16]

In addition to these six factors, both the IASB and the CICA recognize that employee stock options include features not present in traded options. For example, both organizations require that the expected life of options rather than their term be used in determining the fair value of the options. The expected life is used because an employee is generally unable to transfer vested options. The fact that employee stock options are non-transferable and cannot be pledged as security for a loan generally means that an employee has no way of diversifying the risk associated with the options. Thus, an employee cannot make the same exercise decision as an unconstrained option holder, for whom exercise at expiration is generally optimal. Empirical evidence of employee stock option exercises indicates that early exercise of options is pervasive, although the exact time of exercise varies significantly from firm to firm and from employee to employee.[17] As a result of the difficulties in estimating the expected life of stock options for employees (whether individually or on average for the particular corporation), section 3870 notes, "in the absence of reliable evidence on a stock option's expected life, its contractual life is to be used."[18]

There are important differences in the approaches of the IASB and the CICA. In particular, the existence of vesting conditions has an impact on the manner in which the fair value of options is determined on the grant date and the manner in which forfeited options are accounted for (if at all). These differences stem from differing theories underlying the reporting requirement for employee stock options. According to the CICA:

> The objective of the measurement process is to estimate the fair value, based on the stock price at the grant date, of stock options ... to which employees become entitled when they have rendered the requisite service and satisfied any other conditions necessary to earn the right to benefit from the instruments.[19]

Thus, the CICA takes an expense-based approach to the reporting of stock options. The objective of section 3870 is to report the cost to the employer of the benefit provided to employees. The IASB takes the opposite approach, focusing on the benefit to the employer of the services provided:

> In an equity-settled share-based payment transaction, the accounting objective is to recognise the goods or services received as consideration for the entity's equity instruments, measured at the fair value of those goods or services when received. For transactions in which the entity receives employee services, it is often difficult to measure directly the fair value of

the services received. In this case, the [IASB] concluded that the fair value
of the equity instruments granted should be used as a surrogate measure of
the fair value of the services received.[20]

Under section 3870 of the *CICA Handbook*, the risk of forfeiture (that is,
from failing to satisfy the vesting conditions) is not taken into account in determining an option's value because the total amount of compensation recognized
by the enterprise is based only on the options that eventually vest. Although the
value of the option is not discounted, an enterprise may, in determining the expense
to be recognized over the vesting period, estimate the number of options that
are expected to vest and, at the end of the vesting period, make any necessary
adjustments to reflect the compensation cost for the number of options that
actually vest.[21] The draft IFRS, in contrast, requires that vesting restrictions be a
factor incorporated into the option-pricing model. This distinction reflects the
differing objectives of the CICA and the IASB for the financial accounting of
employee stock options: the rationale underlying section 3870 is to determine
the expense associated with the options (and therefore only vested options are
taken into account), whereas the rationale underlying the draft IFRS is to determine the value of the employment services provided to the enterprise (which
value is provided whether or not the options vest). As discussed further below,
this distinction is irrelevant in the proposed tax treatment, under which the
employment expense is not computed or recognized until the vesting date (at
the earliest).

Similarly, the draft IFRS and section 3870 of the *CICA Handbook* differ in
the manner in which forfeited options are dealt with. Under the IASB's approach, the
objective of which is to measure the value of goods or services received, any
amount recognized for received services is not reversed in the event that the
options are forfeited. Under the CICA approach, the objective of which is to
measure the value of the compensation provided to employees, any amounts
recognized on account of employee services received during the vesting period
(that is, expenses deducted on account of these services) will be subsequently
reversed if the stock options are forfeited. Again, this difference is irrelevant
under the proposed tax treatment.

One other important difference between the draft IFRS and section 3870
concerns the determination of the fair value of options granted by private corporations. The IASB recognizes that two of the factors in an option-pricing model,
current price (or value) of the underlying shares and expected volatility, are
particularly difficult to measure for private corporations. Nevertheless, it concludes that an option-pricing model that employs these factors must be used by
all entities.[22] The CICA, in contrast, permits an enterprise whose shares are not
publicly traded and which has not filed a prospectus for a proposed share issuance to exclude volatility in determining an option's value. In effect, the CICA
permits private corporations to report only the minimum value of employee
stock options.

The CICA's concession to private corporations is perhaps understandable
for financial accounting purposes, where the disclosure is intended for those who

will rely on financial statements of the corporation (that is, existing and prospective shareholders and creditors). Private corporations generally have relatively few shareholders, all of whom should be aware of employee stock option plans and are better positioned (at least in comparison to shareholders of a public corporation) to assess the impact of those options on corporate profits and share value. Creditors or potential creditors of the corporation are, at best, ambivalent about a corporation's use of stock options; in fact, they would prefer that the corporation compensate its employees with stock or stock options because such compensation does not reduce the assets of the corporation available to creditors in the event of default. As Calvin Johnson indicates, however, creditors should be concerned about the accounting treatment of options (particularly the current "no-cost" treatment) because the profits of the corporation, which reflect the corporation's current and future ability to carry its debt, are otherwise overstated.[23]

In considering the appropriate tax treatment of employee stock options, the impact of volatility for private corporations should not be ignored, assuming that the options are to be recognized for tax purposes before they are exercised. For these corporations, volatility can have a significant impact on an option's value—much more significant than the time value of money. There are two approaches that can be used in order to account for volatility for tax purposes. First, the corporation (upon which the administrative burden of valuing employee stock options for tax purposes would be placed, as discussed below) could be required to estimate the volatility using factors such as those suggested by the IASB.[24] Alternatively, the recognition and determination of the employment benefit could be deferred until the options are exercised, at which point volatility is an irrelevant consideration.[25] These alternatives are considered below in the context of the benchmark tax treatment.

Assuming that the proposals for reforming the accounting treatment of employee stock options are adopted, it is likely that their use will be curtailed significantly,[26] perhaps making much of the discussion of the appropriate tax treatment moot for practical purposes.

Taxation of Employee Stock Options

The Benchmark Tax Treatment

The tax treatment of employee stock options is distinct from the tax treatment of non-employee stock options. Consider first the general tax treatment of stock options. In both Canada and the United States, there are differences between the treatment of stock options granted by a corporation for its own shares and other options to acquire property. In Canada, the tax treatment is enshrined in section 49 of the Income Tax Act.[27] In the United States, the tax treatment is derived from case law, various statutory provisions, regulations, and Revenue rulings.[28] Unlike most other option writers, a corporation does not recognize any income at the time it grants options on its own shares (that is, if an amount is paid for the options).[29] The option holder is treated as having acquired an asset—the option—the cost of which is equal to the amount paid for the option (the option premium). When the option is exercised, the option holder does not recognize any gain or loss, but rather adds the option premium to the strike price to determine the cost of the optioned property acquired.[30] The corporate grantor does not recognize any gain or loss if the option is exercised.[31] From the option holder's perspective, the entire gain realized from the option (whether expected or unexpected) is therefore generally deferred until the disposition of the underlying property. If the stock option expires unexercised, the option holder recognizes a loss equal to the option premium previously paid;[32] in Canada, the corporate grantor recognizes a gain equal to the option premium,[33] while in the United States, the corporate grantor has no tax consequences if the option expires unexercised.[34]

An employee stock option is similar to other stock options (ignoring their tax treatment), although there are a number of important distinctions. The following example highlights many of the features of employee stock options (particularly those used in the high-tech sector).

Example 1

An employee, A, is hired by a high-tech company, X Co. As an incentive, X Co grants A options to acquire 46,000 shares of X Co at the price of $1 per share, which is the fair market value of the shares of X Co on the date that A is hired. The options may be exercised at any time over the following 10 years, subject to the following restrictions. A cannot exercise any of the options until the first anniversary after commencing employment with X Co, at which time, if A is still employed by X Co, A has the right to exercise 10,000 of the 46,000 options. In business parlance, 10,000 of the options "vest" after one year. Thereafter, 1,000 further options vest at the end of each subsequent month, provided that A is an employee of X Co at the time, so that the options will be fully vested after four years. In the event that A's employment with X Co is terminated at any time, all unvested options are immediately forfeited and any vested options automatically expire after three months. In effect, A is given three months after the termination of employment to exercise any vested options; otherwise, they expire. The options are non-transferable except in the event of A's death, in which case any vested options may be transferred in accordance with A's will or under the laws of intestacy, and A's estate or beneficiaries have one year to exercise any vested but unexpired options (any unvested options are forfeited as a consequence of A's death). Finally, any shares of X Co acquired by A under the options may be subject to trade restrictions under applicable corporate or securities laws and may be subject to certain buyback rights (at a price computed under a predetermined formula) in the even that A's employment is terminated at a time when the shares are not publicly traded.

This example highlights a number of the key distinctions between employee stock options and publicly traded stock options. First, an employee does not generally pay an option premium for the options; rather, the options are granted as part of the employee's compensation package. Second, employee stock options are often subject to a vesting period[35] during which they may be forfeited if certain conditions are not met.[36] Third, the term of employee stock options is generally much longer than that of publicly traded stock options, although the term may be shortened in certain circumstances, such as the loss of employment or death. Fourth, vested stock options are generally non-transferable (except to family members of the employee in certain circumstances). Finally, shares acquired under the options may be subject to trade restrictions or buyback rights in the event that employment is terminated.

There are two paramount considerations for both the appropriate accounting treatment and the appropriate income tax treatment of employee stock options (for both the employer and employee):

- When should the transaction be recognized?
- What value is placed on the transaction?

The appropriate accounting treatment is based on generally accepted accounting principles (such as the matching principle); the appropriate tax treatment is governed by legal principles and the statutory rules governing the deduction of business expenses and the recognition of employment income.

For income tax purposes (as for accounting purposes), the value of an employee stock option is to a large extent determined by the time at which the option should be recognized. The timing issue is particularly important for employees in countries such as the United States and Canada whose tax systems distinguish between ordinary income (including income from employment) and capital gains. Capital gains are generally recognized on a realization basis and are subject to a lower rate of tax than ordinary income. Thus, the answers to the timing and valuation questions not only affect the time at which income should be recognized in the hands of the employee but also the effective tax rate on the gain (or loss) ultimately derived from the option (or the shares acquired on its exercise). In essence, the earlier the value of the option is recognized, the earlier the employee switches from income treatment to capital gains treatment.

Since the timing of recognition of employee stock options largely dictates their value, the following discussion concentrates on timing. There are only three points in time that are worth considering in the benchmark tax treatment of employee stock options: the time that the option is granted; the time that the option vests (if it is different from the time of grant); and the time that the option is exercised. Delaying the taxable event until the underlying securities are sold—which is done in certain circumstances in both Canada and the United States—cannot be justified on normative grounds and can only be justified as a tax expenditure, and should be evaluated as such.

In theory, employees should be subject to tax on stock options at the same time and in the same manner as they are on any other income from employment. Similarly, employers should report a deduction on account of stock options granted in the same manner as they report any other compensation expense.

Employee stock options are a form of compensation, similar to other forms of non-cash compensation. They should be treated for tax purposes in the same manner as a payment of salary by the employer to the employee immediately followed by the acquisition by the employee of stock options from the employer. Thus, the employer would recognize a deduction and the employee would recognize an income inclusion equal to the amount of notional salary represented by the options (that is, the value of the stock options). The primary issue is when the deduction and inclusion should be recognized.

It is well established that business expenses (assuming that they are current expenses) are deductible when they are incurred: that is, when there is a legal and unconditional though not necessarily immediate obligation to pay a determined amount.[37] Consequently, no deduction is permitted for an expense that is a contingent liability.[38] The vesting restrictions imposed on stock options are conditions precedent that must be satisfied before the employer is obliged to honour the options. In the event that the conditions are not satisfied—for example, if employment is terminated before the options vest—the options are forfeited without compensation. In effect, an unvested stock option is no different from an employer's promise to pay a bonus to the employee in the future with payment subject to forfeiture if certain conditions are not met. Consider, for example, an employer who has promised to pay an employee $20,000 at a future date—say, in two years' time—provided that the employee is still employed at that time. For financial accounting purposes, the matching principle would require the employer to amortize the expense over the two-year period, perhaps discounting the amount claimed as an expense in the first year (assuming that the employee is employed at the end of the first year) to account for the possibility that the condition will not be met. If the condition is met and the $20,000 is paid (or becomes legally payable), the employer would recognize the balance of $20,000 in the second fiscal period. If the employee leaves in the second year, the employer would add back in that year any amount claimed on account of the promised payment in the previous year. For tax purposes, however, the employer cannot claim an expense until the expense has been incurred, when the condition precedent has been satisfied and the employer's legal obligation to pay becomes unconditional: at the end of the two-year period. Similarly, an employer could not claim any expense on account of employee stock options before the options vest.

Employees, the recipients of stock options, are taxed on a cash basis in both the United States and Canada. Thus, if there are vesting restrictions on an employee stock option, the benefit would not be taxed before the option vests (as opposed to when it is granted) because the employee has not received a benefit until that time. Consider the promise of the $20,000 bonus. Although the promise may have some value to the employee at the time the promise is made,[39] the employee would not be taxed on any part of the $20,000 until it is actually received. Similarly, the grant of unvested stock options may have some value to the employee at the time the options are granted, but the employee receives no benefit before the options vest.

Whether the recognition of an expense by the employer and an income inclusion by the employee should be delayed beyond the vesting date depends on whether the value of the employee stock options can be determined with sufficient certainty on the vesting date. If the value cannot reasonably be determined at that time, recognition should be delayed until the value can be determined (that is, when the options are exercised or sold). The general failure of income tax legislation to recognize employee stock options until they are exercised or sold (at the earliest) may be explained by the fact that such legislation predates the development of option-pricing models. However, option-pricing models such as the Black-Scholes model have been in existence for over 30 years. It has taken the accounting profession that long to accept that the value of employee stock options should be recognized for financial accounting purposes. The tax treatment should follow suit.

Although this treatment presents valuation difficulties in many cases—and reasonable assumptions will have to be made in determining the value of relevant factors to be taken into account in an option-pricing model, such as the expected life of the option and the expected volatility of the underlying stock—similar valuation issues exist in other circumstances. For example, the fair market value of shares of a private corporation must be determined in circumstances such as the death of a shareholder (at least in Canada) or on a non-arm's-length transfer of shares. Even the preferential treatment accorded to employee stock options in the United States and Canada may depend on the correct valuation of shares of a private corporation, because preferential treatment is usually contingent on the strike price under the options being equal to the fair market value of the shares on the date the options are granted. Valuing private corporation shares is as much an art as it is a science, and involves making assumptions about the future profitability of the corporation.[40]

The difficulties in valuing employee stock options could be alleviated considerably if recognition is deferred until the options are exercised.[41] If it is not possible to reasonably value employee stock options when they vest, then their recognition, as an expense to the employer and as income to the employee, should be deferred until their value becomes more certain (that is, until they are exercised or sold). In my view, option-pricing models are sufficiently well developed to permit a reasonable valuation at the time that options vest. If this benchmark treatment were adopted, the administrative burden of determining the value should be borne by the employer. If the Internal Revenue Service (IRS) or the Canada Revenue Agency (CRA) disputes the value, it would be left to a court to weigh competing experts' opinions in determining the correct value. Valuation disputes arise in many circumstances in both countries, including the provision of other forms of non-cash compensation to employees.[42] Employee stock options are not unique in this respect, although the valuation issues that they pose (in the case of options that are not publicly traded) are among the most challenging.

If the value of a stock option is recognized on the vesting date, then this amount (plus the amount, if any, that the employee paid for the option) would be considered the cost of the option to the employee. Going forward, the option would be treated in the same manner as any other option granted by a corporation for its own shares.[43]

The Tax Treatment of Employee Stock Options in the United States

In the United States, employee stock options are categorized as one of three types for tax purposes. The first two types, incentive stock options (ISOs)[44] and employee stock purchase plans (ESPPs),[45] are governed by the provisions in Code section 421 and are commonly referred to as statutory stock options. Stock options that do not meet the requirements of Code section 421, including failed ISOs and ESPPs, are referred to as non-statutory stock options (NSOs) and are governed by Code section 83, a general provision dealing with the transfer of property in connection with the performance of services.

The tax treatment of employee stock options has had a checkered history in the United States. As Boris Bittker and Martin McMahon comment, "[f]ew legal devices have been more buffeted about by turbulent administrative, judicial, and legislative currents than the employee stock option."[46] The tax history began in 1923 when the Treasury department ruled that the value of stock issued to an employee on the exercise of an option, less the option price, was income to the employee when the option was exercised.[47] Subsequently, courts debated whether stock options should be considered compensatory or whether they were awarded to employees in order to give them a "proprietary interest" in the employer corporation and were therefore not compensatory.[48] This threshold issue was finally settled by the US Supreme Court in 1956 in *Commissioner v. LoBue*,[49] where the court dismissed the "proprietary interest" argument as unfounded. The court relied on the broad wording of the former version of Code section 61(a), which included in gross income "gains, profits, and income derived from . . . compensation for personal service . . . of whatever kind and in whatever form paid." Only those gains specifically exempted, such as gifts, were not part of gross income, and the stock options granted to the taxpayer were certainly not gifts. As to the timing and value of the benefit, Black J adopted the Treasury practice adopted in 1923 because there was "no reason for departing from [it]."[50]

The major distinctions between NSOs and statutory stock options are the time the benefit is taxed, the characterization of the benefit as ordinary income or a capital gain, and whether the corporation that grants the options is entitled to a deduction. The tax treatment of NSOs is considered before the treatment of statutory stock options.

Non-Statutory Stock Options

Even after the *LoBue* decision, it remained unclear when the benefit derived from an NSO should be taxed. Courts generally held that the benefit was taxed at the time the option was exercised and the amount of the benefit was the difference between the fair market value of the stock at that time and the exercise price. A few taxpayers successfully argued, however, that the benefit arose at the time the option was granted, and was equal to the excess of the fair market value of the option over the cost of the option.[51] Further uncertainty as to timing (and valuation) arose if the stock acquired pursuant to the NSO was subject to significant transfer restrictions. If the employee was taxed at the time of exercise, then the restrictions could reduce the stock's fair market value and therefore the amount that the employee must recognize as ordinary income. If taxation was deferred until the restrictions lapsed, taxation was postponed but at the cost of potentially more tax payable based on the difference between the value of the stock when the restrictions lapsed and the exercise price for the stock.

Regulations published in 1959 contained a series of rules governing the taxation of NSOs.[52] If the option had a "readily ascertainable fair market value" at the time of grant (a rare occurrence), the employee was deemed to receive compensation income at that time equal to the difference between the fair market value of the option and the amount, if any, paid for the option. If the option did not have a readily ascertainable fair market value at the time of grant, the employee was deemed to receive compensation income equal to the difference between the amount paid for the stock and its fair market value at the time the employee received an unconditional right to the stock (usually at the time of exercise). If, when the employee received an unconditional right to the stock, there were restrictions that had a "significant effect" on its value, then taxation was delayed until the restrictions lapsed or the employee sold the stock in an arm's-length transaction. The amount of compensation income was equal to the difference between the exercise price and the lesser of the value of the stock when the option was exercised, ignoring the restrictions, and the value of the stock when the restriction lapsed or the employee sold the stock. In all of these cases, the corporate employer was entitled to a corresponding deduction at the same time that the compensation income was considered received by the employee.

In 1969, Code section 83 was enacted,[53] in part to accelerate the taxation of NSOs as provided under the 1959 regulations. Code section 83 is a general provision that governs the transfer of property in connection with the performance of services. It applies to all employee stock options that do not meet the requirements of Code section 421. Under Code section 83, NSOs always create compensation income and a corresponding deduction to the corporation, although whether this amount is recognized at the time of grant, exercise, or some future time depends on a number of factors.

Under Code section 83, compensation income is recognized at the time of grant if the NSO has a "readily ascertainable fair market value" at that time, a test adopted from the *LoBue* decision (although fleshed out in the regulations under the provision). If the option has a readily ascertainable fair market value, the difference between the option's value and the amount, if any, paid by the employee for the option is taxed as compensation income to the employee at the time the option is granted.[54] In most cases, employees pay nothing for the option, so the entire value of the option is treated as compensation income. If the employee is taxed at the time the option is granted, there are no tax consequences when the option is exercised; further taxation is deferred until the underlying shares are sold, and the gain realized at that time is taxed as a capital gain (either long-term or short-term depending on how long the shares were held before sale).[55]

To have a readily ascertainable value, either an option must be actively traded on an established stock exchange (such as the NYSE, ASE, or NASDAQ)[56] or its fair market value "can otherwise be measured with reasonable accuracy."[57] In order for the value of the option to be measured with reasonable accuracy, the option must meet four conditions: (1) it must be transferable; (2) it must be exercisable immediately in full; (3) neither the option nor the underlying property may be subject to any condition that has a significant effect on the fair market value of the option; and (4) the fair market value of the option privilege (that is, the right of the option holder to benefit from any appreciation in the underlying property's value during the life of the option without risking any capital) must be readily determinable.[58] In the case of most NSOs, it is unlikely that any of these conditions, let alone all of them, will be met.

If the fair market value of the option is not readily determinable at the time it is granted (even if it can be determined at some point prior to exercise), income is not recognized before the option is exercised. If the option is exercised, Code section 83 applies to the transfer of stock to the employee pursuant to the option.[59] Under Code section 83(a), subject to making an election under Code section 83(b), discussed below, the amount included in the employee's income is calculated and included when the stock received is transferable or is not subject to a substantial risk of forfeiture, whichever occurs earlier.[60] The amount included is the difference between the amount paid for the stock and its fair market value at that time, determined without regard to any restriction other than a restriction that will never lapse.[61] The employer is entitled to deduct the same amount as a compensation expense at that time.[62] The basis of the stock to the employee is increased by the amount included under Code section 83.[63]

Stock that is both non-transferable and subject to a substantial risk of forfeiture is generally referred to as "restricted stock." Where a taxpayer receives restricted stock on the exercise of an NSO option, Code section 83(b) permits the taxpayer to accelerate the determination of the amount included under section 83 to the year in which the restricted stock is acquired.[64] If the election is made, the taxpayer must include in income the difference between the fair market value of the restricted stock (determined as if the requirements of Code section 83(a) did not apply) and the amount paid for the restricted stock. Only non-lapse restrictions are taken into account in determining the fair market value. The employer corporation is entitled to a corresponding deduction at that time.[65] Thus, the election permits the taxpayer to convert any future appreciation in the stock's fair market value (until the stock is sold or the restrictions expire) from compensation income into a capital gain. However, the taxpayer must make the election within 30 days after acquiring the restricted stock, and the election, once made, cannot be revoked without the consent of the commissioner.[66]

If the taxpayer makes a Code section 83(b) election and the restricted stock is forfeited before it becomes substantially vested, no income deduction is allowed in respect of the forfeiture.[67] Rather, the forfeiture will be treated as a disposition of property and the taxpayer's capital loss will be the difference between the taxpayer's basis of the stock (including the amount included in income under Code section 83(b)) and any amount realized at the time of the forfeiture.[68]

In determining the amount to be included in income under Code section 83(a) or (b), a distinction is made between a restriction that will never lapse ("a non-lapse restriction") and a restriction that may lapse ("a lapse restriction"). A non-lapse restriction is a permanent limitation on the transferability of property that will require the transferee of the property to sell, or offer to sell, the property at a price determined under a formula, and that will continue to apply to and be enforced against the transferee or any subsequent holder (other than the transferor) of the property.[69] For property that is subject to a non-lapse restriction, the price determined under the formula is considered to be the fair market value of the property unless established to the contrary by the commissioner.[70] The effect of a non-lapse restriction is taken into account when determining the amount to be included in income under Code section 83(a) or (b).[71] However, the effect of a lapse restriction is not taken into account. Limitations imposed by registration requirements of state or federal security laws or similar laws imposed with respect to sales or other dispositions of stock or securities are not non-lapse restrictions,[72] and therefore are not taken into account in determining the amount included in income under Code section 83(a) or (b). An obligation to resell or to offer to sell property transferred in connection with the performance of services to a specific person or persons at the property's fair market value at the time of sale is also not a non-lapse restriction.[73]

The application of the NSO rules is illustrated in the following five examples.

Example 2

Z Co grants employee C options to purchase 10,000 shares of Z stock. The options do not satisfy the requirements of Code section 421. The options are not actively traded and do not have a readily ascertainable fair market value at the time of grant. The exercise price is $5 per share, which is equal to the fair market value of the shares at the time of the grant. C exercises all of the options in 10 months, when the shares are worth $8 per share. Apart from general provisions dealing with transfers under the appropriate corporate and securities legislation, there are no restrictions on C's ability to deal with the shares. C sells the shares 18 months later, when the shares are worth $15 per share.

In example 2, C must include in income $30,000 (10,000 × ($8 − $5)) and Z Co is entitled to deduct $30,000 when the options are exercised.[74] C's cost of the shares is increased by the same amount, to $80,000. When C sells the shares, the gain of $70,000 is taxed as a long-term capital gain.

Example 3

Assume the same facts as in example 2, except that C must sell any shares acquired on any exercise of the options to Z Co for $5 per share if C leaves the employ of Z Co within five years after the options are granted. During the five-year period, however, up to 2,000 shares per year (one-fifth of the total) acquired by C pursuant to the exercise of the options fully vest. C exercises all of the options in 10 months, when the shares are worth $8 per share. At the end of the first, second, third, fourth, and fifth years, the shares are worth $10, $15, $20, $30, and $50 per share, respectively. C remains employed by Z Co and sells the shares in the seventh year for $55 per share.

In example 3, at the time of exercise, the shares are both non-transferable and subject to a significant risk of forfeiture (a lapse restriction). The lapse restriction does not affect the value of the shares for the purpose of determining the amount included under Code section 83(a). However, no amount is included until the shares vest. Therefore, C is required to include an amount in income in each of the first five years equal to the difference between the fair market value of the vested shares at the end of each of those years (ignoring the effect of the lapse restriction) and the cost of the shares. Thus, C is required to include in income in each of years 1 through 5 the amounts of $10,000 (2,000 shares worth $10 per share, less the cost of the shares, $10,000), $20,000, $30,000, $50,000, and $90,000, respectively, and Z Co is entitled to corresponding deductions. C's basis in the shares ($50,000) is increased by these amounts to $250,000. Therefore, when C sells the shares for $550,000, C realizes a gain of $300,000.

Example 4

Assume the same facts as in example 3, except that C makes an election under Code section 83(b) within 30 days after acquiring the 10,000 shares.

Example 4 illustrates the benefits of a Code section 83(b) election in circumstances in which the shares continue to increase in value. As a result of this election, C is required to include in income, when the option is exercised, the amount of $30,000 (the difference between the exercise price and the shares' then fair market value, ignoring the effect of the lapse restriction). Z Co is entitled to deduct $30,000 at that time. C's basis in the shares is increased to $80,000. When C sells the shares in the seventh year, C realizes a gain of $470,000. In effect, $170,000 has been converted from compensation income to a long-term capital gain, which, rather than being taxed during the first five years, is deferred until the shares are sold in the seventh year.

Example 5

Assume the same facts as in example 3, except that C leaves the employ of Z Co during the fourth year and is therefore required to forfeit 4,000 of the shares at a price of $5 per share. C sells the remaining 6,000 shares in the seventh year for $55 per share.

In example 5, 6,000 shares vest by the end of the third year and C must include in income $10,000, $20,000, and $30,000 in the first, second, and third years, respectively, under Code section 83(a). Z Co is entitled to corresponding deductions in those years. These amounts are added to C's basis of the shares, increasing the basis to $110,000. When, in year 4, C forfeits 4,000 shares for $20,000, C realizes a capital loss of $24,000 (the difference between the basis of 4,000 shares ($110,000 × 0.4 or $44,000) and the proceeds on the disposition of the shares). When C sells the remaining 6,000 shares for $330,000, C realizes a long-term capital gain of $264,000.

Example 6

Assume the same facts as in example 5, except that C makes an election under Code section 83(b) within 30 days after acquiring the 10,000 shares.

In example 6, C is required to include in income, when the option is exercised, the amount of $30,000 (the difference between the exercise price and the shares' then fair market value). Z Co is entitled to deduct $30,000 at that time. C's basis is increased to $80,000. When C forfeits 4,000 shares for $20,000, C realizes a capital loss of $12,000 (the difference between the basis of 4,000 shares ($80,000 × 0.4 or $32,000) and the proceeds on the disposition of the shares). When C sells the remaining 6,000 shares for $330,000, C realizes a long-term capital gain of $282,000.

NSOs have many non-tax advantages over ISOs and ESPPs. In particular, the strike price of NSOs can be whatever amount the employer determines. It need not be equal to (as required for ISOs), or at least 85 percent of (as required for ESPPs), the fair market value of the shares when the options are granted (or exercised). In contrast to ISOs and ESPPs, there is no limit on the number of NSOs an employee can hold and no limit on the time in which the options must be exercised. These advantages obviously must be weighed against the tax treatment of NSOs as compared with ISOs and ESPPs.

Statutory Stock Options[75]

Historical Development

The Code has had special rules for statutory stock options since 1950. The first statutory options were known as restricted stock options (RSOs).[76] To qualify as an RSO, an option had to meet four conditions:

1) the recipient must have been an employee when the option was granted and must have exercised the option while an employee or within three months after employment terminated (except in the event of death, in which case the three-month requirement did not apply);
2) the option must have been non-transferable except at death;
3) the option period could not have exceeded 10 years from the date of grant, or 5 years if the employee owned more than 10 percent of the voting stock; and

4) the option price must have been at least 85 percent of the fair market value of the stock at the time of grant, or at least 110 percent of the stock's fair market value if the employee owned more than 10 percent of the voting stock.

If an option qualified as an RSO, the employee was not considered to have received taxable income at the time of grant or exercise. If the exercise price was at least 95 percent of the fair market value of the stock at the time of grant, any gain realized by the employee at the time the shares were sold was taxed as a long-term capital gain,[77] provided that the share sale occurred at least two years after the option was granted and at least six months after it was exercised. If the option price was between 85 percent and 95 percent of the market value at the time of grant, the difference between the market value of the share at the time of grant and the exercise price was taxed as ordinary income when the shares were sold. If, however, the actual gain (the difference between the sale proceeds and the strike price) was less than this spread, only the actual gain was taxed as ordinary income. If the gain exceeded this spread, the excess was taxed as a long-term capital gain, provided that the holding-period requirements applicable to 95 percent options were met. In no case was any amount deductible by the corporate employer.

If the employee sold the shares acquired under an RSO before the end of the required holding period (a "disqualifying disposition"), then the difference between the fair market value of the stock at the time of exercise and the exercise price was taxed as ordinary income when the shares were sold. The difference between the amount realized on the sale of the shares and this fair market value was taxed as a long- or short-term capital gain or loss, depending on how long the shares were held. On a disqualifying disposition, the employer was generally entitled to a deduction equal to the ordinary income taxable to the employee, assuming that the amount of compensation was considered reasonable.

In his 1963 *Tax Message to Congress*, President Kennedy strongly criticized RSOs for a number of reasons, all of which remain valid:

> 1. Stock options represent compensation for services. Taxpayers are generally required to pay ordinary income tax on their compensation. To the extent that the stock option provisions allow highly-paid executives to pay tax at capital gains tax rates or to escape all tax on part of their compensation, they are not consonant with accepted principles of tax fairness. . . .
>
> 3. Enactment of the present treatment of employee stock options was based on the belief that such options provide a unique incentive to recruit, to hold, and to stimulate business executives to greater effort. While management has increased its stock ownership through options, the advantages claimed do not appear to be substantiated by experience.
>
> a. Option benefits are haphazardously distributed. The rewards they confer on highly paid executives have been related not so much to their efforts in improving company profits as to changes in investor outlook and stock prices.

b. Sizable option grants to executives who are large stockholders and already have an important stake in company earnings cannot be justified on incentive grounds. . . .

c. The use of stock options frequently tends to impede rather than to improve executive mobility. The available evidence suggests that options are used almost entirely to reward present management rather than to attract new executives. The conditions of their exercise are usually calculated to tie executives to their present jobs.

4. Extensive selling of option stock is inconsistent with the objective of stock options to create proprietary interest in the business for executives. Treasury studies show that about two-thirds of the recipients dispose of all or part of their option stock within three years. . . .

6. Stockholders have become increasingly concerned over the dilution of their equity by the considerable amounts of stock reserved for option plans. The spread between option price and market price frequently involves a substantial cost which is not reflected on the corporation's books and is not fully disclosed in its financial report. In a significant proportion of cases in some years this cost has exceeded 10 percent of after-tax earnings.[78]

The president recommended that the RSO provisions be repealed and that, for stock options granted after January 24, 1963 (the date of the message), the difference between the exercise price and the fair market value of the stock on the date the options are exercised be taxed as ordinary income. Any resulting bunching of income would be relieved through proposed averaging provisions and a further proposed instalment payment privilege, under which tax attributable to the exercise of an option could be paid in equal instalments over five years.

Although Congress did not adopt the president's recommendations, it did seek to tighten the circumstances in which preferential tax treatment was accorded in the Revenue Act of 1964.[79] The Revenue Act of 1964 also introduced ESPPs, for different reasons. According to Stanley Rubenfeld and Peter Blessing:

Congress determined that corporations had issued restricted stock options for two entirely different purposes: to provide incentives to key employees and to raise capital by making discounted sales of their stock to their employees at eighty-five percent of market price. Congress sought to provide for two separate kinds of options with substantially different requirements to meet these two purposes.[80]

The Revenue Act of 1964 replaced RSOs (subject to certain grandfathering provisions for existing RSO plans) with qualified stock options (QSOs). As with RSOs, the employee was not subject to tax at the time of grant or exercise of the option. To qualify as a QSO, an option had to meet the following conditions:

1) the recipient must have been an employee when the option was granted and must have exercised the option while an employee or within three months after employment terminated (except in the event of death, in which case the three-month requirement did not apply);

2) the option must have been granted pursuant to a stock option plan that stipulated the total shares issuable under options and the employees eligible to receive options; the plan must have been approved by shareholders within 12 months before or after its adoption;
3) options must have been granted within 10 years after the earlier of shareholder approval and corporate adoption of the plan;
4) the option must have been non-transferable except at death;
5) the option period could not exceed five years;
6) the exercise price must have been at least equal to the fair market value of the stock when the option was granted;
7) the option could not be exercised while the employee held options granted at an earlier time with a higher option price; and
8) the employee could not be a "substantial" shareholder of the company (a person holding 5 percent or more of the voting stock of the corporation).

Provided that the taxpayer owned the stock for at least three years prior to sale, the gain realized at that time would be taxed as a long-term capital gain. The employer was not entitled to any deduction. If the stock was sold in less than three years, the employee recognized as ordinary income in the year of sale the lesser of (1) the difference between the fair market value of the stock on the date of exercise and the exercise price, and (2) the difference between the proceeds of disposition and the exercise price. If the proceeds of disposition exceeded the fair market value on the date of exercise, then the excess realized on the sale was taxed as a long- or short-term capital gain, depending on how long the shares were held. If the proceeds of disposition were less than the exercise price, the employee realized a long- or short-term capital loss at the time of sale. If the stock was sold in less than three years, the employer was generally entitled to a deduction equal to the ordinary income inclusion of the employee, provided that the amount was considered a reasonable amount of compensation.

The beneficial tax treatment of QSOs was reduced in 1969 with the introduction of a minimum "add-on tax," applicable to certain "items of tax preference."[81] Items of tax preference included both the excess of the fair market value of stock acquired at the time of exercise of a QSO (or grandfathered RSO) over the exercise price[82] and the deductible portion of the individual's long-term capital gain (including any gain realized on the sale of stock acquired under a QSO or grandfathered RSO).[83] In addition to the potential application of the minimum add-on tax, items of tax preference reduced the amount of the employee's personal service income otherwise eligible for the 50 percent maximum rate applicable to earned income.[84]

As a result of these changes, more corporations began to use NSOs to reward employees, particularly if the employer could fully use the deduction available (corresponding to the income inclusion to the employee). Since the employee's taxable amount under an NSO was generally eligible for the 50 percent maximum rate applicable to earned income, and the employer's matching deduction reduced corporate income otherwise taxable at a corporate rate of 46 to 48 percent, the net tax rate applicable to NSOs was 2 to 4 percent. Corporations could share the overall tax savings with their employees (for example, by reducing the option price payable under the NSO or increasing the number of NSOs granted).

QSOs were abolished in 1976,[85] although their use had diminished before then anyway. Three reasons were given for their abolition:

> First, Congress doubted that a qualified stock option gave key employees more incentive than any other form of compensation, particularly in light of the uncertainties of the stock market. Second, even to the extent a qualified stock option provided an incentive, it still represented compensation, and Congress believed that, as such, it should be subject to tax in a manner similar to other compensation. Finally, to the extent qualified stock options provided an incentive, they discriminated in favor of corporations . . . [over] all other forms of business organizations.[86]

Five years later, the Economic Recovery Tax Act of 1981[87] reintroduced the beneficial treatment of certain employee stock options with the current ISO regime, discussed below. The Joint Committee on Taxation provided the following policy rationale for the reintroduction of preferential tax treatment:

> The Congress believed that reinstitution of a stock option provision will provide an important incentive device for corporations to attract new management and to retain the service of executives who might otherwise leave, by providing an opportunity to acquire an interest in the business. Encouraging the management of a business to have a proprietary interest in its successful operation will provide an important incentive to expand and improve the profit position of the companies involved. The provision is designed to encourage the use of stock options for key employees without reinstituting the alleged abuses which arose with the restricted stock option provisions of prior law.[88]

Somewhat ironically, both the repeal of QSOs in 1976 and the introduction of ISOs in 1981 were projected to increase net tax revenues.[89]

The main benefit of a statutory stock option is that neither the grant, the vesting, nor the exercise of the option gives rise to a tax liability to the employee. Furthermore, if certain holding requirements are met, the gain derived on the sale of the shares is treated as a capital gain rather than as income from employment. The employer, however, is not entitled to any deduction for statutory stock options.[90] The main differences between ISOs and ESPPs are that the exercise price for an ESPP may be less than the fair market value of the corporation's stock when the option is granted (within limits) and that ESPPs *must* be offered to all employees (subject to certain exceptions), whereas ISOs can be limited to key employees.

Code section 421 contains rules applicable to both ISOs and ESPPs. In particular, if an employee receives stock pursuant to a qualifying ISO or ESPP, no income is recognized at the time the option is exercised, no deduction is permitted by the employer at that time, and no amount other than the price paid under the option is considered to have been received by the corporation for the shares acquired.[91]

Incentive Stock Options

The conditions that an option must meet in order to qualify as an ISO are set out in Code section 422. The main features of ISOs are as follows:[92]

1) Any stock received on the exercise of an ISO must be held for the longer of (a) two years from the grant date and (b) one year from the exercise date.[93]

2) The exercise price may not be less than the fair market value of the stock at the time the ISO is granted.[94]

3) ISOs may be granted only to employees of the granting corporation or a parent or subsidiary of the corporation. The recipient must remain an employee at all times, from the grant of the option to the day that is three months prior to the exercise of the option. In other words, if employment is terminated before the option is exercised, the employee has three months to exercise the ISO in order to remain eligible for ISO treatment.[95]

4) An ISO may only be granted pursuant to a written plan that has been approved by a majority of the employer's voting shareholders within 12 months after the plan is adopted by the employer's board of directors.[96] The plan must indicate the aggregate number of shares that may be issued under options and the employees (or class of employees) who are eligible to receive ISOs. Any ISOs must be granted within 10 years of the plan's adoption or approval by the shareholders, whichever is earlier.[97]

5) An ISO must, by its terms, be non-transferable except by will or the laws of descent and distribution, and an ISO may be exercisable only by the employee during the employee's lifetime.[98]

6) An ISO may not be exercisable more than 10 years after the date of grant, although a shorter period may be specified in the ISO plan.[99]

7) An ISO may not be granted to an employee who owns stock with more than 10 percent of the total combined voting power of all classes of employer's stock at the time of the grant, unless (a) the exercise price is at least 110 percent of the stock's fair market value at the time of the grant and (b) the option is not exercisable more than 5 years after the grant.[100]

8) An employee cannot have the right to exercise in any one year ISOs with a combined value, based on the fair market value of the underlying ISO stock at the time the ISOs were granted, of more than $100,000. To the extent that the value of the ISOs exceeds $100,000, the options are considered NSOs.[101]

The limitations in the ISO provisions, such as the monetary limitation and the holding-period requirements, are designed to prevent abuse, particularly in small closely held companies. The ISO plan may include other provisions not outlined in Code section 422—for example, ways in which the employee can finance the exercise price of the ISO.

Any disposition of stock acquired under an ISO prior to the expiration of the holding period set out in item (1) above is considered a "disqualifying disposition." On a disqualifying disposition, the employee must recognize as compensation income in the year of disposition the difference between the fair market value of the stock at the time the option is exercised and the exercise price of the option ("the bargain purchase element").[102] The employer is entitled to deduct the same amount in the same year as a business expense under Code section 162.[103] This amount is added to the basis of the employee's stock for the purpose of determining the employee's gain on the disposition of the shares. If these rules would cause the employee to recognize a loss on the sale of the shares (that is, the proceeds of disposition are less than the fair market value of the shares on the day the options were exercised), the employee's compensation income and the employer's corresponding deduction is limited to the difference between the sale proceeds and the basis of the shares.[104]

The application of the ISO rules is illustrated in the following examples. In all three situations, the grant and the exercise of the option do not give rise to any tax consequences to A or X Co. However, different results occur when the shares are sold.

Example 7

X Co grants to employee A options to purchase 10,000 shares of X Co pursuant to a qualified ISO plan. The exercise price is $10 per share, which is the fair market value of a share at the time the options are granted. The options are exercisable immediately. Eighteen months later, when the value of the shares is $16 per share, A exercises all 10,000 options by tendering $100,000 to X Co. A sells the stock to a third party 14 months later for $20 per share.

In example 7, A has met the holding-period requirements in Code section 422(a)(1), so the full amount of the gain ($100,000, which is the difference between the sale price of the shares and the strike price under the option) is considered a capital gain. Furthermore, since A held the shares for more than one year, the gain is considered a long-term capital gain and is taxed at the preferential rate of 15 percent.

Example 8

Assume the same facts as in example 7, except that after 18 months A exercises the options and sells the shares immediately for $16 per share.

In example 8, A does not meet the holding-period requirements because the shares are sold less than one year after the options are exercised. Therefore, the difference between the exercise price ($100,000) and the fair market value at the time the options are exercised ($160,000) is treated as income from employment in the year of disposition and is also added to the cost of the shares to A. In addition, X Co can deduct $60,000 in that year as a business expense.

No gain or loss is realized on the disposition of the shares because the proceeds equal the adjusted basis of the shares.

> *Example 9*
>
> Assume the same facts as in example 7, except that A exercises the options immediately and sells the shares 18 months later for $16 per share.

In example 9, the disposition is not a qualifying disposition because the shares are not held for at least two years after the options are granted. However, the amount of compensation income that A must realize when the shares are sold is nil because the value of the shares at the time the options are exercised does not exceed the exercise price. Accordingly, X Co is not entitled to any deduction. Finally, since A holds the shares for at least one year, the gain realized on the sale ($60,000) is a long-term capital gain.[105]

Employee Stock Purchase Plans

ESPPs have been in the Code since their introduction in 1964.[106] The requirements to qualify as an ESPP are set out in Code section 423, and in many ways are similar to the ISO requirements. The main requirements are as follows:[107]

1) Any stock received on the exercise of an ESPP must be held for the longer of (a) two years after the grant of the option and (b) one year from the date the option is exercised.[108] Any disposition of stock prior to the expiration of the holding period is considered a "disqualifying disposition,"[109] the consequences of which are similar to those applicable to a disqualifying disposition of stock acquired under an ISO, described above.

2) The exercise price of an ESPP cannot be less than the lesser of (a) 85 percent of the stock's fair market value at the time the ESPP is granted and (b) 85 percent of the stock's fair market value at the time the ESPP is exercised.[110]

3) An ESPP may be granted only to employees of the granting corporation or a parent or subsidiary of the corporation.[111] The recipient must remain an employee at all times, from the grant of the option to the day that is three months prior to the exercise of the option.[112] In other words, if an employee's employment ends before the option is exercised, the employee has three months to exercise the ESPP in order to remain eligible for ESPP treatment.

4) An ESPP must be offered to all employees. However, certain employees may be excluded from the ESPP plan, including:
   a) employees who have been employed less than two years;[113]
   b) part-time employees (employees whose customary employment is 20 hours or less per week);[114]
   c) seasonal employees (employees whose customary employment is for not more than five months in any calendar year);[115] and

d) "highly compensated employees," as defined in Code section 414(q).[116]

5) Under the terms of the plan, all employees who are granted ESPPs must have the same rights and privileges. However, the amount of stock that can be purchased by any employee may bear a uniform relationship to the total compensation of the employee. In addition, the plan may provide that no employee may purchase more than a maximum amount of stock fixed under the plan.[117]

6) An ESPP may only be granted pursuant to a written plan that has been approved by a majority of the employer's voting shareholders within 12 months after the plan is adopted by the employer's board of directors.[118]

7) An ESPP must, by its terms, be non-transferable except by will or the laws of descent and distribution, and an ESPP may be exercisable only by the employee during the employee's lifetime.[119]

8) An ESPP may not be exercisable more than (a) five years after the date of grant if the exercise price is at least 85 percent of the stock's fair market value at the time *of exercise*, or (b) 27 months after the date of the grant if (a) does not apply (for example, if the exercise price is determined by some other method, including a price based on the fair market value at the time of the grant).[120]

9) An ESPP may not be granted to an employee who, immediately after the option is granted, owns stock with more than 5 percent of the total combined voting power of all classes of employer's stock.[121]

10) Under the plan, no employee can accrue the right to purchase stock of the employer (or a parent or subsidiary of the employer) at a rate that exceeds $25,000 worth of ESPP stock (based on the stock's fair market value at the time of the grant) for any one calendar year in which the option is outstanding.[122]

In practice, ESPPs are rarely granted to all employees, though they are made available to all employees. As their name implies, most ESPPs are established as stock purchase plans, whereby all employees have the option to purchase the employer's stock, usually through payroll deductions. An ESPP might create a purchase window of, say, six months: on the first day of the period, the employee is "granted" an option to purchase a fixed number of shares (based on a certain percentage of the employee's salary at that time); over the course of the six-month period, regular payroll deductions are made; and on the last day of the period, the employee "exercises" the option to acquire the number of shares that the accumulated payroll deductions will purchase.[123] This system virtually ensures that the employees exercise their options.

ESPPs do not create compensation income (that is, income from employment) at the time the option is granted or exercised. They can, however, create compensation income when the stock is sold or the employee dies while owning the stock, regardless of the holding period, if the exercise price was less than 100 percent of the stock's fair market value at the time the option was granted. The amount of compensation income is equal to the lesser of (1) the amount by which the fair market value of the stock at the time of grant exceeded the exercise price and (2) the amount by which the fair market value of the stock at the time of disposition exceeded the exercise price.[124] However, the employer corporation is not entitled to any deduction at that time.[125] If the fair market value of the stock on the disposition date is less than the amount paid for the stock, the employee will not realize any compensation income, and the resulting loss is a capital loss.

The application of the ESPP rules is illustrated in the following three examples. In the third example, since the exercise price is at least 85 percent of the fair market value at the time of exercise, the option period must be no more than five years; in the first two examples, the option period can be no longer than 27 months. In all three examples, there are no tax consequences to B or Y Co when the options are granted or exercised because the requirements of Code section 423 have been met in all cases.[126]

Example 10

Y Co grants employee B options to purchase 1,000 shares of Y Co's stock pursuant to a qualified ESPP. The exercise price is $5 per share, which is equal to the fair market value of the shares at the time the options are granted. Eighteen months later, when the stock is worth $8 per share, B exercises all 1,000 options by tendering $5,000 to Y Co. Fifteen months following the exercise of the options, B sells the shares for $12 per share.

In example 10, the holding-period requirements have been met and the exercise price is equal to the fair market value of the shares at the time the options are granted. Therefore, B will not have to recognize any compensation income and Y Co cannot claim any compensation deduction when the shares are sold. At the time of sale, B recognizes a long-term capital gain of $7,000 (proceeds of $12,000 less basis of $5,000).

Example 11

Assume the same facts as in example 10, except that the exercise price is $4.25 per share, which is 85 percent of the fair market value of the shares at the time the options are granted.

In example 11, B must recognize compensation income when the shares are sold because the exercise price has a built-in bargain purchase element. B must recognize as compensation income $750, and the basis of the shares is increased by $750 to $5,000. B also recognizes a long-term capital gain of $7,000 at the time of sale. Y Co is not entitled to any deduction.

Example 12

Assume the same facts as in example 10, except that the exercise price is stipulated to be 85 percent of the fair market value of the shares when the options are exercised (that is, the exercise price is $6.80 per share when B exercises the options).

In example 12, B does not recognize compensation income when the shares are sold because the exercise price under the option ($6.80) exceeds the fair market value of the shares when the option was granted ($5.00). Therefore, the cost of the shares to B is $6,800, and at the time of sale B recognizes a long-term capital gain of $5,200.

The Tax Treatment of Employee Stock Options in Canada

There have been specific federal legislative provisions governing the tax treatment of stock options since 1953.[127] Before 1948, when the Income Tax Act of that year replaced the original Income War Tax Act, there had been no case involving the bargain purchase of stock by employees in their corporate employers, which suggests that until 1948 "profits from stock options were treated as capital gains."[128] From 1948 to 1953, stock option benefits were treated as income from employment under old paragraph 5(1)(a). The leading case on point was *No. 247 v. MNR*.[129] In that case, the taxpayer, the general manager of a corporation, was granted the option to acquire 45,000 shares of his employer pursuant to an agreement dated May 19, 1951. Under the terms of the agreement, the taxpayer could exercise up to 15,000 options between May 15, 1951 and May 15, 1952 (at $5.00 per share), up to 15,000 options between May 15, 1952 and May 15, 1953 (at $4.00 per share), and up to 15,000 options between May 15, 1953 and May 15, 1954 (at $3.50 per share). The agreement further provided that the options terminated in the event that the taxpayer's employment ceased. In modern parlance, of the 45,000 options granted, 15,000 vested immediately and had a one-year term; 15,000 vested in one year and had a two-year term (from the grant date); and 15,000 vested in two years and had a three-year term. The taxpayer exercised 15,000 options on May 2, 1952 (at $5.00 per share) and a further 15,000 options on June 11, 1952 (at $4.00 per share). The minister reassessed the taxpayer and added to the taxpayer's income in 1951 as an employee benefit an amount per share equal to the difference between the value of each share on May 19, 1951 (the date of the option agreement) and the strike price paid under the option. Mr. Fordham for the Tax Appeal Board dismissed the taxpayer's appeal. Interestingly, the grounds of the taxpayer's appeal were limited exclusively to factors affecting the value of the options in 1951. The taxpayer did not argue that the benefit should have been taxed in 1952 (when the first 15,000 options were exercised and the second 15,000 options vested and were exercised). Although Mr. Fordham was troubled by the fact that the options were acquired in one year and exercised in another, he concluded that "an examination of the authorities indicates that once such an option has been exercised, the advantage thereby gained is deemed to relate back to the time of receipt of the document granting the option."[130]

From 1953 to 1972, stock options were generally accorded favourable tax treatment from the employee's perspective. Options were not taxed prior to their exercise by employees. The amount of the benefit included in an employee's income was the difference between the fair market value of the shares at the time of exercise and the exercise price. Originally, this amount was subject to tax at a rate 20 percent below the taxpayer's average tax rate (excluding provincial, dividend, and foreign tax credits) in the previous three years.[131] In 1966, the tax savings from the 20 percent reduction was limited to a maximum of $200. However, even if this de maximis rule applied, the tax treatment remained favourable because the benefit was taxable at the employee's average effective tax rate rather than at his or her marginal rate.[132]

Tax reform in 1972 essentially eliminated the preferential tax treatment of stock options,[133] at least briefly. As originally conceived in the 1972 Act, the difference between the fair market value of the shares at the time of exercise and the strike price was included in income from employment in the year the option was exercised.[134] Given the difficulty in valuing the stock option at the time of grant,[135] deferral of recognition of the benefit until exercise, when the amount of the benefit could be easily quantified, was appropriate on the grounds of administrative efficiency. From the outset, however, employers have not been entitled to any deduction for the amount of the taxable benefit associated with employee stock options.

Preferential tax treatment of certain employee stock options was reintroduced in 1977, applicable to stock options granted by a Canadian-controlled private corporation (CCPC) to an arm's-length employee.[136] The stock option benefit—the difference between the fair market value of the shares at the time of exercise and the strike price—was ignored if the shares were held for at least two years after acquisition. The cost of the shares to the employee was the strike price under the option (plus any amount paid for the option). When the shares were sold, the difference between the proceeds of disposition and the acquisition cost of the shares was treated as a capital gain, and therefore only 50 percent of the gain was subject to tax. If the shares were held for less than two years after acquisition, the stock option benefit was subject to tax as employment income, but not until the year the shares were sold. Any excess was then taxed as a capital gain. According to the minister of finance, Donald S. Macdonald,

> [a] particular problem for small business is the difficulty of matching higher salaries offered by larger enterprises. I propose to introduce a special tax treatment for stock option plans established for employees of Canadian-controlled private corporations. The difference between the option price paid for the shares and their sale proceeds will be taxed as a capital gain and then only when the shares are disposed of. This will permit a company to reimburse its employees in a way that does not impair its working capital.[137]

Subsection 7(1.1), as introduced in 1977, provided that paragraph 7(1)(a) did not apply to stock options granted by a CCPC to its arm's-length employees.

Because paragraph 7(3)(a) provided that employee stock options were taxable only in accordance with section 7, the exclusion of CCPC employee stock options from paragraph 7(1)(a) left them to be dealt with under the general rules applicable to options in section 49. Under subsection 49(3), if a taxpayer exercised an option to acquire property, the adjusted cost base of the option (if any) was added to the cost of the property acquired. If the option had no cost (the usual case for employee stock options), the cost to the employee of the shares would simply be the exercise price. When an employee of the CCPC[138] sold the shares so acquired, the gain realized would generally be treated as a capital gain (unless the employee was considered a trader or dealer in securities). If the employee did not hold the shares for at least two years before their disposition, subsection 7(1.2) provided that paragraph 7(1)(a) applied, but at the time the shares were disposed of rather than at the time the option was exercised.

Preferential tax treatment was extended to other stock options in the 1984 federal budget with the introduction of paragraph 110(1)(d).[139] Under paragraph 110(1)(d), if a non-CCPC grants to an arm's-length employee options to acquire qualifying equity shares and the exercise price is at least equal to the fair market value of the shares when the options are granted, the employee is entitled to deduct an amount equal to 50 percent of the stock option benefit. In effect, the benefit is taxed at the same rate as a capital gain. According to the budget documents, the deduction was intended "[t]o encourage more widespread use of employee stock option plans which promote greater employee participation and increased productivity."[140]

In 1985, the $500,000 lifetime capital gains exemption was introduced.[141] As a result, certain amendments were made to the CCPC stock option rules so that the new lifetime capital gains exemption would not apply to the portion of the gain on the sale of the shares that reflected the stock option benefit (that is, the difference between the fair market value of the shares at the time of exercise and the exercise price). Subsection 7(1.1) was amended and new paragraph 110(1)(d.1) was introduced. The stock option benefit is still effectively taxed at capital gains tax rates, but cannot benefit from the lifetime capital gains exemption. Under amended subsection 7(1.1), through a cross-reference to paragraph 7(1)(a), the difference between the share value at the time of exercise and the strike price is treated as an employment benefit (rather than excluded from paragraph 7(1)(a)), but the inclusion of the benefit is deferred until the shares are sold. Under paragraph 110(1)(d.1), the employee is entitled to a deduction when the shares are sold equal to one-half of the employee benefit, provided that the shares are held for at least two years before their disposition. Thus, the remaining one-half of the employee benefit is taxed as ordinary income and does not benefit from the capital gains exemption.

The two-year holding period is the primary distinction between paragraphs 110(1)(d) and (d.1). It reflects the fact that CCPC stock options may be granted "in the money" and still benefit from a deduction equal to one-half of the benefit at the time of sale, provided that the shares are held for at least two years after acquisition.[142] The deduction under paragraph 110(1)(d) is available only if the option is not in the money at the time of grant. For CCPC stock options, if the employee does not own the shares for two years prior to their sale, the employee may still benefit from the deduction under paragraph 110(1)(d) in the year of sale, provided that the preconditions for that provision's application are met.[143]

With tax reform in 1988 and the increase in the capital gains inclusion rate to three-quarters (two-thirds for 1988 and 1989), the deduction under both paragraphs 110(1)(d) and (d.1) was reduced to one-quarter (one-third for 1988 and 1989).

The 2000 federal budget introduced a number of reforms to the treatment of employee stock options.[144] Most significantly, it extended the deferral of taxation from the time of exercise of the options to the time of sale of the underlying securities to $100,000 per year of public company stock options, measured by the value of the underlying shares at the time the options are granted. The corporation need not be a public company at the time the options are granted, but when the options are exercised, the shares acquired must be of a class listed on a prescribed stock exchange.[145] To benefit from the deferral, the employee must qualify for the deduction under paragraph 110(1)(d) (that is, the shares must be ordinary common shares and the strike price under the options must be at least equal to the value of the shares when the options are granted), and the employee cannot have owned more than 10 percent of the shares of the corporation at the time the options are granted. The new provisions apply to eligible options exercised after February 27, 2000, irrespective of when the options were granted or became vested.

Competition with the United States motivated the amendments introduced in the 2000 federal budget. According to the federal budget documents:

> To assist corporations in attracting and retaining high-calibre workers *and make our tax treatment of employee stock options more competitive with the United States*, the budget proposes to allow employees to defer the income inclusion from exercising employee stock options for publicly listed shares until the disposition of the shares, subject to an annual $100,000 limit. . . . Employees disposing of such shares will be eligible to claim the stock option deduction in the year the benefit is included in income. The new rules will also apply to employee options to acquire units of a mutual fund trust. The proposed rules are generally similar to those for Incentive Stock Options in the United States.[146]

In addition to this extension of the tax preference to certain public company employee stock options, the deduction permitted under paragraph 110(1)(d) or (d.1) was increased from one-quarter to one-third and then to one-half, corresponding to the changes in the capital gains inclusion rates in the February 2000 budget and October 2000 economic statement.

The Ontario 2000 budget introduced more far-reaching incentives for employees subject to tax in Ontario. The May 2, 2000 budget introduced a new Ontario research employee stock option deduction,[147] under which eligible employees[148] of an eligible corporation[149] are exempt from tax on the first $100,000 per year of employee benefits arising on the exercise of qualified stock options[150] or on eligible capital gains arising from the sale of shares acquired by the exercise of eligible stock options. The provisions apply to stock options granted, and sales of shares acquired under such options, after December 21, 2000 (the date the budget legislation received royal assent). According to former Ontario minister of finance Ernie Eves:

> New R&D-intensive companies are increasingly using stock options to attract and retain highly skilled workers. Our Government is committed to providing a competitive tax system to help these young Ontario companies find and keep bright, innovative minds.
>
> We will be introducing legislation so that the first $100,000 each year in taxable employment benefits arising from designated stock options and capital gains will not be taxed by the Province of Ontario.
>
> I encourage the federal government to join us and do the right thing for these innovative companies and their employees.[151]

Before turning to an evaluation of the favourable tax treatment of employee stock options, it is worth highlighting certain differences between the current US and Canadian tax treatment.

Five Key Differences and One Observation Concerning the Tax Treatment of Employee Stock Options in the United States and Canada

The tax treatment of stock options in Canada, even after the 2000 budget amendments, differs from that in the United States in a number of respects. Although the 2000 budget amendments have some similarities to the ISO rules in the United States, there are significant distinctions. The differences discussed here are limited to the regime in Canada, as amended by the 2000 budget, as compared with the treatment of ISOs and NSOs in the United States.

First and foremost, the proportion of employee stock option benefits that are taxed at capital gains tax rates is significantly higher in Canada than in the United States. There are two reasons for this: in Canada, there are no monetary limits on the options that qualify for capital gains tax rates, and there is no holding-period requirement to benefit from preferential treatment.[152] In the United States, in contrast, few employee stock options benefit from capital gains treatment for two reasons. First, ISOs and ESPPs are subject to monetary limits, so most employee stock options (in terms of quantum) are NSOs. Second, to get the benefit of capital gains treatment for ISOs or ESPPs, an employee must hold the shares acquired under an option for the longer of one year after the exercise of the option and two years from the date of grant. If the employee sells the shares early, the stock option benefit—the difference between the fair market value of the shares at the time of exercise and the strike price—is taxed as ordinary income at the time of sale, and the employer is entitled to a corresponding deduction. Despite the availability of capital gains tax rates if the holding-period requirements are met, the vast majority of employees in the United States with ISOs and ESPPs exercise and sell on the same day.[153] Accordingly, in the United States, almost all employees are subject to tax on their stock option benefits at full employment rates, and the employer is entitled to a corresponding deduction.[154] Assuming that Canadian employees behave like American employees and exercise and sell their options on the same day, the employee stock option rules in Canada are significantly more generous than those in the United States for the vast majority of employees. The imposition of a holding period between the date of grant of the options and the date of sale of the underlying securities follows logically from the stated rationale for stock options: to attract and retain employees. The one-year holding period following the date of exercise in the United States is not tied to continued employment and is therefore unlikely to create an incentive for employees to remain with the same employer. The post-exercise one-year holding period simply creates a lock-in effect that is likely tied to the one-year holding period for long-term capital gains.[155] The holding period does, however, have the practical effect of limiting the amount of employee stock options that benefit from capital gains tax rates. At the very least, Canada should introduce holding-period requirements similar to those in the United States before an employee can benefit from the deduction in paragraph 110(1)(d).

The second major difference between the Canadian and US treatment of employee stock options concerns the capital gains tax treatment of stock options in employees' hands and the deductibility of options by employers. In the United States, options that are taxed preferentially at capital gains rates in an employee's hands are not deductible by the employer. In Canada, this is not necessarily the case. First, there are circumstances in which the employee must recognize the stock option benefit at full tax rates,[156] and even in such circumstances the employer is not entitled to a corresponding deduction. Second, and more significantly, it is possible in Canada to structure employee stock option payments—specifically, a payment by the employer on the cancellation of an option—so that the employer is entitled to a full deduction while the employee benefits from effective capital gains tax treatment. To achieve this result, the employee must have the right, but not the obligation, to surrender the options to the corporate employer for cancellation (in lieu of exercising the option) for a cash payment equal to the economic value of the options (that is, the difference between the fair value of the underlying shares when the options are surrendered and the strike price under the options). The CRA has ruled that, in these circumstances, the employee can benefit from a deduction under paragraph 110(1)(d), provided that the preconditions for the deduction are met (that is, the employee is an arm's-length employee, the strike price under the options is at least equal to the fair market value of the shares on the grant date, and the underlying shares are ordinary common shares) and the employer is entitled to deduct the amount paid on the surrender of the options (unless the amount is considered unreasonable).[157] Because the corporate employer does not issue shares in these circumstances, the CRA has ruled that paragraph 7(3)(b) does not deny the deduction of the payment by the employer. This ability to reduce the tax rate on employment income by half *and* provide the employer with a full deduction is wholly inappropriate.

Third, ISO treatment in the United States is generally limited to employees who own less than 10 percent of the voting stock of the employer.[158] If the employee owns more than 10 percent, the strike price must be at least 110 percent of the fair market value of the shares on the date of grant and the exercise period cannot exceed five years. In Canada, the stock option benefit for public company shares is limited to employees who are not specified shareholders, regardless of the strike price. Accordingly, there is little room for abuse of these options in Canada. However, the CCPC stock option benefit is available to any employee who deals at arm's length with the employer. An "arm's-length" test is more difficult to apply and open to more abuse than a 10 percent test.[159]

Fourth, provided that ISO or ESPP requirements are met, the stock option benefit in the United States is taxed as a capital gain, whereas in Canada its treatment is similar to that of a capital gain. This distinction is important, particularly if the shares decline in value between the time the option is exercised and the ultimate sale of the shares. Consider, for example, options to acquire 1,000 ordinary common shares at a price of $10 per share (assumed to be the value of the shares at the time the options are granted). On the day the options are exercised, the shares have a fair market value of $40 per share; however, when they are sold, the value has declined to $15 per share. In the United States, if the sale of the shares is a disqualifying disposition (that is, the holding-period requirements have not been met), only $5,000 must be reported as compensation income, and no capital gain or loss arises. If the sale is a qualifying disposition, $5,000 will be reported as a long-term capital gain, which is taxed at the preferential rate of 15 percent. In Canada, the stock option benefit is considered to be $30 per share, based on the difference between the share value and the strike price on the day the options are exercised. If the options qualify under the CCPC rules or under the new public company rules, the employee must include $30,000 in income in the year the shares are sold as an employee benefit and is entitled to a deduction under paragraph 110(1)(d) or 110(1)(d.1) of $15,000 (one-half of the benefit).[160] The adjusted cost base of the shares is increased by $30,000 (to $40,000), giving rise to a capital loss of $25,000 when the shares are sold. This capital loss may be used by the employee only to reduce realized capital gains. If the employee has not realized any capital gains, the capital loss may be of little or no use.[161] Therefore, even though the employee's economic gain is only $5,000, the employee will have to pay tax on an additional $15,000 of income, and the capital loss realized may provide no relief from the tax payable.[162]

Fifth, the technical requirements for ISO or ESPP treatment in the United States are generally more stringent than the requirements for preferential treatment in Canada. Apart from the holding period and monetary limits discussed above, the requirements of prior shareholder approval and continual employment until exercise, the maximum option period, and the non-transferability of options—all conditions imposed under the Code—do not have counterparts under the Income Tax Act. In practice, however, similar requirements may be found in stock options granted by Canadian companies.

Before turning to an evaluation of the preferential tax treatment of employee stock options, one observation is worth noting, particularly in the context of stock options granted by venture-backed companies. In both countries, in order to benefit from capital gains treatment, the strike price under an option must equal or exceed the fair market value of the stock on the date the option is granted. For publicly traded shares, this requirement is easy to meet. For private companies, however, particularly startup companies, valuing the company can be a difficult exercise.[163] In the United States, this requirement is considered to be met as long as an attempt was made, *in good faith*, to ensure that the exercise price of the options was at least equal to the fair market value of the shares.[164] No similar provision exists in the Act.

In the United States, it is common practice for venture-backed firms to issue preference shares rather than common shares to venture capitalists,[165] primarily because the issuing of preference shares supposedly substantiates a significantly lower valuation of the common shares of the company and a significantly lower strike price for employee stock options.[166] For example, in first- and second-round financings, it is not uncommon for the common shares to be valued for employee stock options granted around the same time at one-tenth the value of the preference shares issued to venture capitalists.[167] Evidently, the lower valuation of the common shares is justified on the basis that the common shares do not have the same rights as the preference shares. As the company gets closer to an initial public offering, however, the valuation of common shares must converge with the issue price of preference shares.[168] It is surprising that the IRS has not challenged the early-round valuation practice. It is arguable that common shares have a fair market value substantially equal to the amount paid for preference shares in the early financing rounds.[169] The priority rights attaching to preference shares are relevant primarily in the event of bankruptcy, at which time neither the preference shares nor the common shares would likely realize anything.

One reason for the IRS's failure to challenge employees may be that if the challenge is successful and an employee is taxed on the benefit at the time of exercise at full employment rates, the employer is entitled to a corresponding deduction and therefore the Treasury would be no further ahead.[170] However, until the "tech bust" in mid-2000, when the number of initial public offerings of venture-backed Internet companies was significantly reduced, many new economy companies that went public on NASDAQ did not have positive earnings and did not forecast positive earnings for the foreseeable future.[171] If the IRS reassessed employees of these companies on their stock option benefits, a significant amount of which would likely have been realized as early as possible after the companies went public, there would be little downside risk of financial loss to the Treasury. Why the IRS has failed to do so is unclear.[172]

I am not aware of the extent to which a similar practice for setting the strike price exists in Canada. The Canadian venture capital industry is much smaller and less developed than the US industry and may not have developed any practice in this regard. The CRA has not published any administrative guidance on this point and the vigilance with which it will enforce the valuation requirement necessary to benefit from effective capital gains treatment of employee stock options is unclear.[173]

Evaluating the Favourable Tax Treatment of Employee Stock Options

Compared with other forms of employee compensation, stock options receive very favourable tax treatment. Their treatment in the United States and Canada is equivalent to an employee receiving additional tax-free employment income that is used to acquire stock options. If the business succeeds, the employee will exercise the option without tax consequences (assuming that certain conditions are met) and, if he or she ultimately sells the shares, will benefit from preferential capital gains tax treatment (or the equivalent of capital gains tax treatment in Canada). In contrast, an investor outside the company must invest after-tax earnings to buy shares. In effect, the employee is subject to one level of taxation on the human capital invested through stock options, while the outside investor is subject to two levels of taxation.[174] Furthermore, there is both a significant deferral element and absolute tax savings if the stock option benefit is taxed as a capital gain. Alan Auerbach suggests that, as far as founders and other employees who receive stock options as a key source of compensation are concerned, "this compensation is tax-favored by deferral relative to straight wage and salary income, [so that] even if capital gains are fully taxed, it is unclear that efficiency considerations would call for a widening of this difference associated with a reduction in the rate of capital gains taxation."[175]

Employee stock options are a form of compensation, similar to any other form of non-cash compensation. In my view, they should be treated for tax purposes in the same manner as a payment of salary by the employer to the employee immediately followed by the acquisition by the employee of stock options from the employer. Thus, the employer would recognize a deduction and the employee would recognize an income inclusion equal to the amount of notional salary represented by the options (that is, the full value of the stock options) on the date that the options vest.

Various rationales have been put forward in both Canada and the United States for the preferential tax treatment of employee stock options. One rationale common to both countries is that employee stock options increase employee productivity by aligning the interests of employees, both management and others, with shareholders. A second rationale that is relevant in both countries but that has only been espoused in Canada is that employee stock options, appropriately targeted, make small businesses more competitive with big businesses in attracting key employees. The US statutory stock option provisions have never been grounded on this rationale and their terms have never favoured small corporations over large. In contrast, Canada's CCPC stock option provisions were introduced in 1977 for this very reason, although their efficacy has since been undermined. A third rationale, unique to Canada, is suggested by the amendments made to the federal and Ontario employee stock option provisions in 2000: to stem the "brain drain" from Canada to the United States. These three rationales are considered in turn.

Increasing Productivity

In the United States, the favourable tax treatment of employee stock options has generally been based on the premise that they align the interests of senior executives (and employees generally) with the interests of shareholders.[176] When Canada extended the preferential tax treatment of employee stock options to certain options of non-CCPCs in 1984, the rationale given was that options increased worker participation and increased productivity because employees were given compensation that was "directly related to their ability to increase the productivity, competitiveness, and growth of their company."[177]

There are a number of problems with the suggestion that employee stock options increase productivity by aligning the interests of employees with shareholders. First, it is highly unlikely that the fluctuation in the value of the employer's stock reflects employees' actions. Most stock market volatility arises from "market-wide or industry conditions that cannot be correlated with the separate performance of the individual firm,"[178] let alone the employees of that firm. Calvin Johnson estimates that 80 percent of the variation in a company's stock price is correlated with overall market movements or industry-wide price changes and that only 20 percent has something to do specifically with the company.[179]

Second, the extent to which stock options provide an incentive to increase productivity is questionable.[180] According to Johnson, "[s]tock options . . . create truly bizarre incentives for management to squelch dividends and to seek out risk, even though it damages shareholder wealth."[181] The first point is obvious: stock options may induce management to retain earnings rather than pay out dividends, because stock options do not participate in dividends but do generally benefit from retained earnings through increased share value. The second point requires some explanation. Johnson argues that stock options actually induce management to undertake high-risk investments that may have a negative expected value, "because the holder of an option participates in the gains in value, but not the losses."[182] Employee stock options are, in essence, a one-sided bet: the options come at no cost to the employee because no tax is payable when the options are granted. If a high-risk decision proves successful, the value of the options will increase significantly. If the decision proves a failure, the employee will simply not exercise the option.

Third, even if one accepts the argument that employee stock options do lead to higher employee productivity, then granting employee stock options would be a sound business decision. No preferential tax treatment should be necessary in order to compel a corporation to do what is in its own best interests. In fact, Johnson suggests that options are not warranted even as a sound business decision. He argues, contrary to the general perception that stock options have no cost to the employer, that stock options are a "particularly expensive way for the issuer to pay employees" because stock is simply a proxy for the future cash needed to pay out on the stock, and the discount rate used to compute the present value of the future cash needed "is brutal for the issuer, far higher than it would be with other forms of compensation."[183]

Allowing Small Companies To Attract and Retain Employees

When Canada's CCPC stock option rules were introduced in 1977, it was suggested that stock options granted by smaller companies were a means by which such companies could increase the compensation paid to attract and retain employees without impairing their cash flow. This rationale is premised on the belief that small companies are an essential part of the Canadian economy and that the human capital that small companies attract in the absence of some form of tax preference for employees is suboptimal. There are two problems with this rationale.

First—a problem that is likely more theoretical than practical—the CCPC rules apply to all small businesses, not just "innovative" businesses. Technically, the preferential treatment applies to lifestyle businesses as well as rapid-growth small and medium-sized enterprises (SMEs). In practice, however, it is highly unlikely that lifestyle businesses would provide stock options to arm's-length employees, because most lifestyle-business owners are unwilling to give up share ownership and employees are probably not interested in receiving shares that are unlikely ever to be transferable and are unlikely to pay dividends.

Second, and more problematic, Canada's employee stock option provisions do not necessarily fulfill the policy objective of attracting and retaining employees in any event. In the United States, both ISOs and ESPPs require that the employee remain an employee at all times from the grant of the options until no more than three months prior to their exercise.[184] In contrast, there is no requirement in Canada that the employee remain an employee until the options are exercised in order to benefit from preferential treatment. On the contrary, subsection 7(4) of the Income Tax Act provides that the stock option rules continue to apply even if the employee ceases employment with the employer; furthermore, paragraph 110(1)(d.1) (and paragraph 110(1)(d) for that matter) does not include a continued-employment requirement—that is, until the options are exercised—in order to benefit from (effective) capital gains treatment. In practice, however, employee stock option plans will likely contain similar provisions, although there is no statutory requirement that they do so.

The extension of capital gains treatment (at exercise rather than at sale) to non-CCPC employee stock options in 1984 severely undermined the preference given to CCPC options; this preference was further undermined by the 2000 amendments that extended the deferral benefit that only CCPC stock options had enjoyed to options of publicly listed companies, subject to a fairly generous de maximis amount. Thus, the extent to which a CCPC can offer a preferential compensation package compared with a public company through the use of employee stock options has been significantly curtailed.

Stemming the Brain Drain

The amendments to Canada's employee stock option provisions in 2000, like virtually all of the recent amendments to the Income Tax Act targeting venture capital investment in Canada, focused on the differing tax treatment of this type of income in Canada and the United States. In particular, the amendments to the stock option provisions in Canada (and in Ontario) were intended to make the tax treatment of employee stock options more favourable in Canada than in the United States. In other words, the competitiveness issue has shifted from one concerning small companies versus big companies to one concerning Canadian companies versus US companies. The fact that the tax treatment of stock options was already more favourable in Canada than it was in the United States for the vast majority of employees has been conveniently lost in these debates.

The implied rationale for the changes introduced in the 2000 federal and Ontario provincial budgets was to stem the perceived "brain drain" to the United States of would-be entrepreneurs and employees, particularly in the high-tech sector. Certainly, the North American free trade agreement (NAFTA) and its predecessor, the Canada-US free trade agreement, have made the migration of workers in the high-tech sector remarkably easy. A TN-1 visa, applicable to "professionals" under NAFTA, is a one-year temporary visa that can be obtained with relative ease on entry into the United States and can be renewed an indefinite number of times.[185] Given the relatively free mobility of workers across the Canada-US border, it is useful to consider whether there is in fact a brain drain to the United States and, if so, the impact of the tax treatment of employee stock options (or capital gains or income tax generally) on the brain drain.

In the past few years, a number of studies have attempted to determine the existence of and to measure the size of the brain drain from Canada to the United States. Although all of the studies indicate that there is some annual net migration from Canada to the United States, the volume of this migration and its implications for Canada are hotly disputed. Studies by Human Resources Development Canada and Statistics Canada[186] and John and David Helliwell[187] suggest that the brain drain is not significant, even when the study is limited to post-secondary graduates. Others such as Mahmood Iqbal,[188] Daniel Schwanen,[189] and Don DeVoretz and Samuel Layrea[190] suggest that there is much greater cause for concern.[191]

The "brain drain" focuses on Canadian-educated individuals who migrate, either permanently or temporarily, to the United States. Overall, though, Canada is a net importer of highly educated individuals. According to a study by John Zhao, Doug Drew, and Scott Murray, despite the fact that Canadian migrants to the United States are more highly educated than recent Canadian immigrants, because of the much larger number of Canadian immigrants, university graduates migrating to Canada from all countries in the world outnumber graduates leaving for the United States (permanent and temporary) by a ratio of approximately 4 to 1. There are as many immigrants entering Canada with a master's or doctorate as the number of university graduates at all levels leaving for the United States.[192]

In addition, recent immigrants to Canada are twice as likely as the Canadian-born population to be employed in high-tech jobs. Throughout the 1990s, Canada has more than made up for any brain drain to the United States through a "brain gain" from recent immigrants. That is not necessarily a cause for celebration. In global terms, the brain gain that Canada and the United States benefit from is a brain drain from other countries, particularly developing countries. And recent studies made some disturbing findings. For example, Canada produces fewer graduates in the fields of mathematics, sciences, and engineering than other G7 countries with the exception of Italy.[193] More generally, the percentage of the population with a bachelor's degree or higher in urban centres, where high-tech firms tend to congregate,[194] is significantly higher in the United States than in Canada.[195] Furthermore, it has been suggested that Canada cannot continue to rely on immigration to fill high-tech jobs, and the loss of individuals educated in Canada in government-subsidized universities should be a cause for concern. These findings suggest that Canada should be devoting more resources to university institutions, particularly post-graduate programs, rather than continuing the current trend of cutting university budgets. These findings also suggest that taxes should be increased, if necessary, to support public spending on education. The introduction of the Canada research chairs program in 2000[196] is a welcome initiative in this respect, and similar initiatives should be encouraged.

Even if there is a brain drain from Canada to the United States, the question remains: Is reducing the tax payable on stock options (or on capital gains, or taxes generally) an appropriate response? To answer this question, it is necessary to evaluate the impact, if any, that tax has on a person's decision to migrate and the prospective destination. While a number of studies suggest that differing tax rates may be a primary reason for southern migration,[197] there has been little empirical study of the actual impact of tax rates on migration from Canada to the United States. Simply comparing migration in the 1990s with the different levels of tax in the two countries has about the same persuasive value as a study comparing migration with average annual temperatures.[198] Survey evidence suggests that job opportunities and higher salaries are cited most frequently as reasons for moving, while taxes rank much lower.[199] These findings are intuitively appealing, but, as John Helliwell points out, they are "impressions and . . . hard to convert into numerical estimates of what would happen if there were changes in the level or structure of Canadian tax rates."[200]

In an interesting study, Don Wagner attempted to model the effect of tax on migration from Canada to the United States, taking into account both economic and non-economic variables, and the impact that reductions in Canadian tax would have on such migration.[201] He concluded that both income and tax were positively correlated with the migration decision, both historically and for individuals migrating in the 1990s. Individuals with a university education had a greater propensity to move, even after controlling for income and tax differences.[202] However, his computation of the impact of reductions in Canadian tax and increases in Canadian income opportunities provides some food for thought in light of recent amendments to the tax system to make Canada more "competitive" with the United States. According to Wagner's calculations, if Canada adopted "the same tax rates, tax deductions and tax rules as the US . . . Canada's southward migration drain would have declined by only 10 per cent, though the true decline may be somewhat higher since . . . my measurements have a tendency towards underestimation."[203]

Wagner estimates that if both taxes *and* income opportunities had been equal in the two countries, migration to the United States in the 1990s would have been 41 percent lower. In effect, he suggests that even if all of the economic incentives in both countries were *identical*, 59 percent of university graduates who moved south would have moved south in any event.[204]

His calculations of the impact of other percentage reductions in Canadian taxes and emigration rates are worth reproducing:[205]

Taxes	Emigration of graduates
5	3
10	6
15	9
20	11
25	14

A number of conclusions may be drawn from these results. Most important, Wagner himself acknowledges that

> what is remarkable in this analysis is how few people move despite substantial economic incentives to do so. In the early 1990s, the average university-graduate household could earn 27 per cent more in the US and could pay 18 per cent less in taxes for a given income level. Yet, only 2.5 per cent of university-graduate households moved.[206]

There must be some reason why 97.5 percent of university-graduate households remain in Canada. Simply because some of those who chose to move took the tax differential into account does not justify wholesale changes to important components of the Canadian tax system. In particular, if one were to extrapolate from Wagner's estimated changes in migration caused by reductions in Canadian taxes, Canada would have to more than eliminate income tax altogether in order to stop the brain drain. Is a 25 percent reduction in Canadian taxes justified in order to stop 14 percent of the small number who actually moved? Hardly.

Helliwell concludes:

> at least for the personal income tax, Canadian policy should be focused on what is best for Canada and Canadians; presumably migration pressures should not force it to follow whatever the US Congress generates.[207]

Neil Brooks is more blunt:

> if some individuals move because they are unhappy with the net benefits they receive from government in Canada, it would be a terrible mistake to attempt to address that by making Canada more like the United States. The great majority of Canadians prefer the social and cultural life of Canada to that in the United States. It would be ironic if the government were to respond to the emigration of a few by attempting to make Canada more like the United States. At some point, the two countries would be so much alike that all mobile Canadians would move since they see little reason to put up with the cold weather. If rich Canadians prefer United States society, and do not wish to remain and attempt to democratically persuade other Canadians to adopt their view, then they should leave. It would be odd to allow their departure to cause Canadians to rethink their collective aspirations when the force of the emigrants' arguments could not.[208]

The wage and unemployment gaps between Canada and the United States grew significantly in the 1990s, and by all accounts higher salaries and greater job opportunities were the primary reasons for individuals moving to the United States. Furthermore, the general profile of recent migrants to the United States who work in the knowledge economy—predominantly university-educated, single, childless individuals—might also explain the decision to move. Such individuals are highly mobile with few significant ties to Canada. They will likely benefit from private health-care plans in the United States. They may have little appreciation for, or perceive little benefit from, the different social policy choices made in Canada as compared with the United States, which is an important factor in the differing levels of taxation in the two countries. As a result, they may tend to migrate, at least temporarily, simply to maximize their disposable income.[209]

Canada should not introduce tax cuts that have the effect of undermining its social policy foundations. The 2000 federal and Ontario budget amendments to the employee stock option provisions were wholly unwarranted and should be repealed.[210] They cannot be justified on any basis, let alone that of competitiveness with the United States. Indeed, the preferential tax treatment of any employee stock option is unwarranted in Canada and the United States. The professional accounting associations are finally recognizing the cost of employee stock options for financial statement purposes. Similar measures should be adopted for income tax purposes: the full value of employee stock options should be included in the employee's income when the options vest and a corresponding amount should be deducted by the employer as an expense at that time.

Notes

1 Justin Fox, "The Next Best Thing to Free Money," *Fortune*, July 7, 1997, 52.

2 With respect to the more technical detail of the tax treatment of employee stock options in Canada, see, for example, Donald A.C. Stewart, "Stock Option Plans: Bright Past, Dim Future" (1972) vol. 20, no. 4 *Canadian Tax Journal* 299-309; Robert E. Beam and Stanley N. Laiken, "An Employee Stock Option Update," Personal Tax Planning feature (1987) vol. 35, no. 5 *Canadian Tax Journal* 1275-91; Suzanne Michaelson, "Employee Stock Options Revisited" (1992) vol. 40, no. 1 *Canadian Tax Journal* 114-47; and Michael F.T. Addison and Gil J. Korn, "Employee Stock Options: An Update," Personal Tax Planning feature (2000) vol. 48, no. 3 *Canadian Tax Journal* 778-811.

    For the treatment of employee stock options in the United States, see, for example, Everett L. Jassy, "Incentive Stock Options: The Reincarnation of Statutory Stock Options Under the Economic Recovery Tax Act of 1981" (1982) vol. 37, no. 4 *Tax Law Review* 359-409; and Stanley I. Rubenfeld and Peter H. Blessing, "Taking Stock: Executive Stock Options After the Economic Recovery Tax Act of 1981" (1983) vol. 36, no. 2 *The Tax Lawyer* 347-419.

3 In the United States, it is common for the founding employees (the original entrepreneurs) of venture-backed companies to be granted unvested stock, rather than options, at a nominal price, with the stock vesting to the founder over a period of time (for example, four years). If the founder leaves the company before any of the stock vests, the company reserves the right to buy back unvested stock, usually at the original purchase price. The vesting rights applicable to founders, similar to the vesting rights typically attached to employee stock options, reflect the understanding that the founders are "earning" their shares over time; they also prevent an ex-founder from otherwise benefiting from a "free ride" on the backs of the remaining founders. If the company does not impose vesting restrictions on founders' stock when the stock is first issued (for example, because professional venture capitalists are not involved at the outset), it is quite common for venture capitalists to impose such restrictions as a condition of their investment. Founders' stock is not generally used in Canada because most Canadian corporate statutes provide that stock cannot be issued until it is fully paid for. For this reason, founders in Canada—at least once venture capitalists become involved in the corporation—are generally granted stock options similar to those granted to other employees. In this chapter, any consideration of founders' stock is subsumed in the discussion of employee stock options.

4 Amin Mawani, "Tax Deductibility of Employee Stock Options" (2003) vol. 51, no. 3 *Canadian Tax Journal* 1230-58, at 1244.

5 If the options are performance-related—that is, if the number of options that vest is contingent on certain performance thresholds being met—the expense (the intrinsic value of the options) is measured and recognized at the appropriate "measurement date," which is the date when both the number of options that the employee is entitled to receive and the exercise price are fixed.

6 Financial Accounting Standards Board, *Opinion* no. 25, "Accounting for Stock Issued to Employees," October 1972.

7 Fisher Black and Myron Scholes, "The Pricing of Options and Corporate Liabilities" (1973) vol. 81, no. 3 *Journal of Political Economy* 637-54. One of the more

accessible discussions of option-pricing theory is found in Charles T. Terry, "Option Pricing Theory and the Economic Incentive Analysis of Nonrecourse Acquisition Liabilities" (1995) vol. 12, no. 2 *The American Journal of Tax Policy* 273-397, at 327-43. For a more detailed discussion, see Charles W. Smithson, *Managing Financial Risk: A Guide to Derivative Products, Financial Engineering, and Value Maximization*, 3d ed. (New York: McGraw-Hill, 1998), chapters 10 and 11; and Robert A. Haugen, *Modern Investment Theory*, 4th ed. (Upper Saddle River, NJ: Prentice Hall, 1997), chapters 16 to 18.

The Black-Scholes model was originally developed for "European options"— options that are exercisable only on the strike date—rather than "American options"—options exercisable at any time on or before the strike date. Employee stock options are generally American options. An American option gives its holder all of the rights of a European option plus the additional right to exercise early. It follows that an American option will have a value at least equal to that of a European option. Whether or not an American option is worth more than a European option depends on the circumstances. According to the literature on this point, the value of an American option should equal that of a European option where the underlying security does not pay dividends, because it is never optimal to exercise an American option early in these circumstances. For a discussion of the rationale, see Smithson, supra, at 215. Thus, the Black-Scholes model can be used to value American options on stock that pays no dividends during the exercise period of the option. If the underlying stock does pay dividends, early exercise may be optimal if the dividend is sufficiently large. Early exercise will occur, if at all, immediately before the stock goes ex dividend. A model for the valuation of American options was developed by Richard Roll, "An Analytical Formula for Unprotected American Call Options on Stocks with Known Dividends" (1977) vol. 5, no. 2 *Journal of Financial Economics* 251-58; Robert Geske, "A Note on an Analytical Valuation Formula for Unprotected American Call Options on Stocks with Known Dividends" (1979) vol. 7, no. 4 *Journal of Financial Economics* 375-80; and Robert Whaley, "On the Valuation of American Call Options on Stock with Known Dividends" (1981) vol. 9, no. 2 *Journal of Financial Economics* 207-12.

Other option-pricing models have been developed since 1972, generally seeking to remove one or more of the assumptions on which the Black-Scholes model is based and which influence its general utility.

8   A good proxy for the riskless rate of interest is the interest rate on government debt with a term similar to the term of the option. Ten-year government of Canada benchmark bonds (that is, assuming that options granted currently have a 10-year option period or, more specifically, as discussed below, a 10-year expected life) currently bear a yield to maturity of approximately 5 percent. Therefore, a riskless rate of 5 percent is used for illustration purposes throughout this chapter.

9   Determined by the formula: $10,000 - [10,000 \times (1/1.05^{10})]$. For the sake of simplicity, it is assumed that the shares do not pay dividends and that A derives no benefit from the fact that the shares may be voting. The formula also ignores the probability of A leaving X Co's employ before the expiry date of the option (and thus reducing the term of the options to less than 10 years). In effect, the determination assumes that there is no justification for A exercising the options before they expire. For an explanation of the formula used, see Terry, supra note 7, at 333-34.

10   Financial Accounting Standards Board, *Proposed Statement of Financial Accounting Standards*, "Accounting for Stock-Based Compensation," June 1993.

11   Financial Accounting Standards Board, *Statement of Financial Accounting Standards* no. 123, "Accounting for Stock-Based Compensation," October 1995 (herein referred to as "SFAS no. 123"), paragraphs 61 and 62 state in part: "The Board continues to believe that financial statements would be more relevant and representationally faithful if the estimated fair value of employee stock options was included in determining an entity's net income, just as all other forms of compensation are included. To do so would be consistent with accounting for the cost of all other goods and services received as consideration for equity instruments. . . . [T]he Board . . . continues to believe that disclosure is not an adequate substitute for recognition of assets, liabilities, equity, revenues and expenses in financial statements. . . . The Board chose a disclosure-based solution for stock-based employee compensation to bring closure to the divisive debate on this issue not because it believes that solution is the best way to improve financial accounting and reporting."

12   International Accounting Standards Board, *International Financial Reporting Standard*, "Exposure Draft ED 2: Share-Based Payment," November 7, 2002 (herein referred to as "the draft IFRS"). The IASB released with the exposure draft a separate document that provides a comprehensive discussion of the rationale underlying various aspects of the draft IFRS: International Accounting Standards Board, *Basis for Conclusions on Exposure Draft ED 2: Share-Based Payment* (London: International Accounting Standards Board, November 7, 2002). Comments were invited on the exposure draft before March 7, 2003.

13   Canadian Institute of Chartered Accountants, *CICA Handbook* (Toronto: CICA) (looseleaf), section 3870, which governs stock-based compensation and other stock-based payments, was first released in December 2001. Stock options are covered in paragraphs 3870.24 through 3870.37 and 3870.44 through 3870.52. Section 3870 is accompanied by two appendixes that provide guidelines on applying the recommendations (appendix A) and examples that illustrate their application (appendix B). Section 3870 is based on SFAS no. 123 and, like the US standard, requires only that Canadian enterprises disclose (that is, in notes to the financial statements but not in the statements themselves) the impact of stock options on net income and, if also presented in the financial statements, earnings per share.

14   Financial Accounting Standards Board, "FASB Adds Project to Its Agenda on Employee Stock Options and Pensions," *News Release*, March 12, 2003 (available from the FASB Web site: http://www.fasb.org/). According to FASB chairman Robert Herz, quoted in the news release, "[i]n the wake of the market meltdown and corporate reporting scandals, the FASB has received numerous requests from individual and institutional investors, financial analysts and many others urging the Board to mandate the expensing of the compensation cost relating to employee stock options." In November 2003, the FASB indicated that it expected to issue the exposure draft in the first quarter of 2004 and issue a final statement in the second half of 2004. For the status of the FASB deliberations, see the FASB Web site.

15   In both cases, the "expected life" of an option rather than its term is used for nontransferable options: *CICA Handbook*, at paragraph 3870.33; and the draft IFRS, at paragraph 21 (see also *Basis for Conclusions*, supra note 12, at paragraphs

BC152 through BC165). The rationale for employing the expected life rather than the option's term is considered in notes 17-19 and accompanying text, infra.

16 The rationale for this factor in an option-pricing model for American options is explained in note 7, supra.

17 See, for example, Steven Huddart and Mark Lang, "Employee Stock Option Exercises: An Empirical Analysis" (1996) vol. 21, no. 1 *Journal of Accounting and Economics* 5-43; and Jennifer N. Carpenter, "The Exercise and Valuation of Executive Stock Options" (1998) vol. 48, no. 2 *Journal of Financial Economics* 127-58. Many factors influence an employee's decision to exercise a stock option. Huddart and Lang, supra, identify strong associations between the following factors and exercise: recent stock price movements, the spread between market price and exercise price, proximity to vesting dates, time to maturity, volatility, and the employee's level within the company. See also Chip Heath, Steven Huddart, and Mark Lang, "Psychological Factors and the Stock Option Exercise" (1999) vol. 114, no. 2 *Quarterly Journal of Economics* 601-27.

18 *CICA Handbook*, at paragraph 3870.33, note 7.

19 Ibid., at paragraph 3970.30.

20 *Basis for Conclusions*, supra note 12, at paragraph BC191.

21 Section 3870 of the *CICA Handbook* also permits the enterprise to revise its estimate of the number of options that will ultimately vest during the vesting period and make any consequential adjustments at that time (and at the end of the vesting period based on the number that actually vested). See *CICA Handbook*, at paragraph 3870.47 and appendix B, paragraphs B11 through B20 for examples.

22 *Basis for Conclusions*, supra note 12, at paragraphs BC137 through BC143. As noted previously, the Black-Scholes option-pricing model was developed for publicly traded European options. Obviously, future volatility of the underlying stock can only be estimated. The Black-Scholes model (and other option-pricing models) use past performance of stock as a basis for determining future volatility. Trading history is simply not available for shares of private corporations (although there may be some history of share issuances at different times). See infra note 24 for the IASB's proposals for determining private equity volatility in these circumstances.

23 Calvin H. Johnson, "Stock and Stock Option Compensation: A Bad Idea" (2003) vol. 51, no. 3 *Canadian Tax Journal* 1259-90, at 1264.

24 With regard to private corporations, the *Basis of Conclusions*, supra note 12, at paragraph BC139 states: "An unlisted entity that regularly issues options or shares to employees (or other parties) might have an internal market for its shares. The volatility of the internal market share prices provides a basis for estimating expected volatility. Alternatively, an entity could use the historical or implied volatility of similar entities that are listed, and for which share price or option price information is available, as the basis for an estimate of expected volatility. This would be appropriate if the entity has estimated the value of its shares based on the share prices of these similar listed entities. If the entity has instead used another methodology to value its shares, the entity could derive an estimate of expected volatility consistent with that methodology. For example, the entity might value its shares on the basis of net asset values or earnings, in which case it could use the expected volatility of those net asset values or earnings as a basis for

estimating expected share price volatility." The IASB acknowledges that these approaches are subjective and that in practice corporations would underestimate expected volatility out of caution. In any event, using some amount for expected volatility will produce a more reliable measure of the fair value of options than will ignoring volatility completely.

For newly listed entities, the IASB (ibid., at paragraph BC142) refers to commentary provided in SFAS no. 123 (at paragraph 285b): "For example, an entity that has been publicly traded for only one year that grants options with an average expected life of five years might consider the pattern and level of historical volatility of more mature entities in the same industry for the first six years the stock of those entities were publicly traded." *CICA Handbook*, at section 3870, appendix A, paragraph A5, provides similar guidance for enterprises in Canada whose common stock has only recently become publicly traded.

25 If the shares are not publicly listed, there will remain some difficulty in valuing the shares at that time.

26 Mawani, supra note 4, at 1258.

27 RSC 1985, c. 1 (5th Supp.), as amended (herein referred to as "the Act"). Unless otherwise stated, statutory references in this chapter are to the Act. Section 49 was introduced as part of the 1972 tax reform. Previously, there was no provision in the Act that governed the treatment of options. See, generally, John A. Zinn, "The Taxation of Capital Gains: Selected Topics," in Brian G. Hansen, Vern Krishna, and James A. Rendall, eds., *Canadian Taxation* (Toronto: De Boo, 1981), 363-441, at 382-88.

28 See, generally, Boris I. Bittker and Martin J. McMahon Jr., *Federal Income Taxation of Individuals*, 2d ed. (Boston: Warren, Gorham & Lamont, 1995), paragraphs 28.7[1] and 31.8; and James M. Lynch, "Treatment of Options and Warrants in Tax: Free and Taxable Transactions" (1999) vol. 77, no. 3 *Taxes: The Tax Magazine* 46-63, at 46-49.

29 In Canada, paragraph 49(1)(b) of the Act; in the United States, section 1032 of the Internal Revenue Code of 1986, as amended (herein referred to as "the Code"). In Canada, the grant of most other options is considered a disposition of property, the cost of which to the grantor is nil: see subsection 49(1). In the United States, the grant of virtually all options is considered an "open transaction," and no tax consequences are recognized until the options are exercised, are sold, or expire: see *Virginia Iron Coal & Coke Co.*, 37 BTA 195 (1938); aff'd. 99 F. 2d 919 (4th Cir. 1938); cert. denied 307 US 630 (1939).

30 In Canada, paragraph 49(3)(b) of the Act; in the United States, this position is derived from a series of General Counsel's Memoranda (GCMs) and rulings (Rev. rul. 78-182, 1978-1 CB 265; GCM 34507, May 1971; GCM 34595, September 1971; GCM 36041, October 1974; all cited in Lynch, supra note 28, at 61, note 19).

31 In Canada, the amount paid for the option is added to the paid-up capital of the shares: *Interpretation Bulletin* IT-96R6, "Options Granted by Corporations To Acquire Shares, Bonds, or Debentures and by Trusts To Acquire Trust Units," October 23, 1996, paragraph 6; and *Interpretation Bulletin* IT-463R2, "Paid-Up Capital," September 8, 1995, paragraph 10. In the United States, see Code section 1032(a).

32   In Canada, subparagraph (b)(iv) of the definition of "disposition" in subsection 248(1) includes the expiry of an option, and therefore the option holder is considered to dispose of the option for nil proceeds on its expiry. In the United States, see Code sections 1234(a)(1) and (2).

33   Subsection 49(2) of the Act.

34   Code section 1032(a).

35   In the example, no options vest until the first anniversary after commencing employment. This initial period in which no options vest is referred to as a "cliff." "Graded vesting" refers to the situation in which some of the options vest at successive time intervals, as is the case in years 2 through 4 in example 1.

36   Example 1 illustrates the most common vesting restriction: continued employment. Other possible vesting restrictions are performance conditions such as achieving a specified growth in sales, earnings, or share price.

37   The meaning of "incurred" is taken from *J.L. Guay Ltée v. MNR*, 71 DTC 5423; [1971] CTC 686 (FCTD); aff'd. 73 DTC 5373; [1973] CTC 506 (FCA); aff'd. 75 DTC 5094; [1975] CTC 97 (SCC). Paragraph 18(1)(a) denies the deduction of an expense "except to the extent that it was made or incurred" for the purpose of earning income from business.

38   Paragraph 18(1)(e).

39   Assuming that the employer is economically sound and there is no risk of defaulting on the payment, the value of the promise is the present value of $20,000, discounted by the probability that the employee will not be employed in two years' time. Assuming a riskless rate of interest of 5 percent and a 25 percent probability that the employee will not be employed at the end of the two-year period, the promise has a present value of $0.75 \times [20,000 \times (1/1.05^2)]$, or $13,605.44.

40   See, for example, the recent decision of *McClintock v. The Queen*, 2003 DTC 576 (TCC), in which the employee was denied the preferential treatment of employee stock options because the strike price was found to be less than the value of the underlying shares on the grant date.

41   Even so, if the shares are not publicly traded at the time of exercise, the value of the stock option benefit remains dependent on the valuation of shares of a private corporation.

42   In Canada, see, for example, *Mommersteeg et al. v. The Queen*, 96 DTC 1011; [1995] 2 CTC 2767 (TCC), concerning the value of frequent-flyer awards under paragraph 6(1)(a).

43   Supra notes 29 to 34 and accompanying text. A criticism of the general rules applicable to the tax treatment of non-employee stock options is beyond the scope of this study.

44   The requirements for ISOs are set out in Code section 422.

45   The requirements for ESPPs are set out in Code section 423.

46   Bittker and McMahon, supra note 28, at paragraph 40.4[1].

47   TD 3435, II-1 CB 50 (1923); Treas. reg. 86, article 22(a)-1 (1935).

48   This distinction was first raised by the Tax Court in *Delbert B. Geeseman*, 38 BTA 258 (1938).

49   351 US 243 (1956).

50   Ibid., at 249. In his judgment concurring in part and dissenting in part, Harlan J
     concluded (ibid., at 250-51) that the taxable event was the grant of the option:
     "When the respondent received an unconditional option to buy stock at less than
     the market price, he received an asset of substantial and immediately realizable
     value, at least equal to the then-existing spread between the option price and the
     market price. It was at that time that the corporation conferred a benefit upon
     him. At the exercise of the option, the corporation 'gave' the respondent nothing;
     it simply satisfied a previously-created legal obligation. . . . The option should be
     taxable as income when given, and any subsequent gain through appreciation of
     the stock, whether realized by sale of the option, if transferable, or by sale of the
     stock acquired by its exercise, is attributable to the sale of a capital asset and, if
     the other requirements are satisfied, should be taxed as a capital gain. Any other
     result makes the division of the total gains between ordinary income (compensa-
     tion) and capital gain (sale of an asset) dependent solely upon the fortuitous
     circumstance of when the employee exercises his option" (footnotes omitted).
     With respect to the final remark, Harlan J gave the example of two employees,
     both of whom are given unconditional options to buy stock at $5, the current fair
     market value. The first exercises the options immediately and sells the shares one
     year later for $15. The second holds the options for one year, exercises them
     when the shares are worth $15, and sells the shares immediately. The $10 gain
     realized by the first employee would be considered a capital gain whereas, on the
     basis of the majority judgment, the $10 realized by the second would be ordinary
     income because it is compensation for services.

51   See, for example, *McNamara v. Commissioner of Internal Revenue*, 210 F. 2d
     505 (7th Cir. 1954); and *Commissioner of Internal Revenue v. Stone's Estate*, 210
     F. 2d 33 (3d Cir. 1954). In both cases, there were no vesting restrictions on the
     options granted and they were freely assignable. In *McNamara*, the options
     granted were in the money, and the option agreement specifically provided that
     the options were granted as additional compensation for the current year. In
     Stone's Estate, the options granted were out of the money, although the taxpayer
     paid $1,000 for them and reported $5,000 as additional income in the year the
     options were granted. That case considered the tax treatment of an amount re-
     ceived on an assignment of some of the options. The court held that the options
     were additional compensation in the year they were acquired, and their subse-
     quent assignment was on capital account.

52   See Treas. reg. sections 1.421-6(c)(1), (d)(1), and (d)(2). The regulations are dis-
     cussed in Rubenfeld and Blessing, supra note 2, at 356-57, from which this
     discussion is derived.

53   Tax Reform Act of 1969, Pub. L. no. 91-172, enacted on December 30, 1969; 83
     Stat. 487, section 321 (1969).

54   Code sections 83(a) and (e)(3); Treas. reg. section 1.83-7(a).

55   The distinction between long-term and short-term capital gains is discussed in
     chapter 3, note 21. The time period distinguishing long-term from short-term capi-
     tal gains has been amended on numerous occasions. Currently, long-term capital
     gains arise on dispositions of capital property held for more than one year.

56   If an option is actively traded on an established stock exchange, the readily
     ascertainable value is equal to the price at which the option trades: Treas. reg.
     section 1.83-7(b)(1).

57   Treas. reg. section 1.83-7(b)(2).

58   Ibid.

59   Treas. reg. section 1.83-7(a).

60   Code section 83(a). In other words, the employee will be taxed at the time of exercise if the underlying stock is either transferable *or* not subject to substantial risk of forfeiture. If both of these restrictions apply at the time of exercise, then taxation is deferred until one of the restrictions disappears. Under Code section 83(c)(1), the rights of a person in property are subject to a substantial risk of forfeiture if the person's rights to full enjoyment of the property are conditional on the future performance of substantial services by any individual. If, for example, the stock received on the exercise of the options are non-transferable and must be forfeited if the employee leaves employment with the employer within three years, the stock will be considered subject to a substantial risk of forfeiture until the end of that three-year period and the benefit will not be computed and included in income until the end of the three years. At the end of the three years, the amount of compensation income will equal the difference between the fair market value of the shares at that time and the amount paid for the shares under the options.

61   Code section 83(a). The distinction between a "non-lapse" and a "lapse" restriction are considered in notes 69-73 and accompanying text, infra.

62   Code section 83(h).

63   Treas. reg. section 1.83-4(b)(1).

64   The manner in which the election is made, and the contents of the election, are set out in Treas. reg. sections 1.83-2(c) and (e). A corporation's founders who are subject to vesting restrictions on their stock (discussed supra note 3) can file a section 83(b) election when the stock is acquired in order to preserve capital gains treatment on any subsequent increases in the value of the stock.

65   Code section 83(h).

66   Under Treas. reg. section 1.83-2(f), the commissioner's consent will be granted only if the transferee has made a mistake of fact as to the underlying transaction and must be requested within 60 days of the date on which the mistake of fact first became known to the person who made the election. A mistake as to the value or a decline in the value of the property with respect to which a section 83(b) election was made is not considered a mistake of fact. The 30-day period in Code section 83(b) essentially requires the employee who makes the election to take certain investor-type risks with respect to the transaction. One of these risks is that the transferred property may decline in value.

67   Code section 83(b).

68   Treas. reg. section 1.83-2(a).

69   Treas. reg. section 1.83-3(h).

70   Code section 83(d)(1); Treas. reg. section 1.83-5(a).

71   See the words in parenthesis in Code sections 83(a)(1) and 83(b)(1)(A).

72   Treas. reg. section 1.83-3(h).

73   Ibid.

74   Since the restriction on share transfers is not a non-lapse restriction, it is not taken into account in determining the value of the shares at the time of exercise.

75   For a more detailed history of the statutory stock option provisions and the technical rules applicable to ISOs, see Rubenfeld and Blessing, supra note 2, and Jassy, supra note 2.

76   Introduced in the Revenue Act of 1950, Pub. L. no. 81-814, enacted on September 23, 1950; 64 Stat. 906, section 281 (1950).

77   At that time, one-half of a long-term capital gain was included in income.

78   *President's 1963 Tax Message to Congress*, HD no. 43, January 24, 1963, exhibit 16, at 455-56, reproduced in Douglas J. Sherbaniuk, *Specific Types of Personal Income*, Studies of the Royal Commission on Taxation no. 16 (Ottawa: Queen's Printer, 1967), 170-71.

79   Pub. L. no. 88-272, enacted on February 26, 1964; 78 Stat. 19, section 221(a) (1964). According to the Treasury Department, "The basic idea underlying the new provisions is that stock options are a privilege which should be accorded favorable tax treatment only when justified as an incentive technique. In this view, therefore, stock options may be desirable as a means of permitting key executives to acquire a proprietary interest in corporations, but should not be used merely as a means of providing additional compensation on which ordinary income taxes can be avoided" (United States, Treasury Department, *Summary of Provisions in the Revenue Act of 1964*, TP-26 (Washington, DC: Treasury Department, March 1964), quoted in Sherbaniuk, supra note 78, at 172).

80   Rubenfeld and Blessing, supra note 2, at 350, citing HR rep. no. 88-749, 88th Cong., 1st sess. (1963), 64, reprinted in 1964-1 (part 2) CB 125, at 188.

81   Tax Reform Act of 1969, supra note 53, section 301. See further chapter 3, at note 42 and accompanying text.

82   Code section 57(a)(6) (prior to amendment of section 57 by the Tax Equity and Fiscal Responsibility Act of 1982, Pub. L. no. 97-248, enacted on September 3, 1982; 96 Stat. 324, section 201(b)(1)(B) (1982)).

83   Code section 57(a)(9) (prior to amendment of section 57 by the Revenue Act of 1978, Pub. L. no. 95-600, enacted on November 6, 1978; 92 Stat. 2763, section 421 (1978)).

84   The 50 percent maximum rate applicable to earned income was also introduced in the Tax Reform Act of 1969, supra note 53, sections 301 and 804. At that time, the highest marginal rate was 70 percent.

85   Tax Reform Act of 1976, Pub. L. no. 94-455, enacted on October 4, 1976; 90 Stat. 1520, section 603(b) (1976).

86   Jassy, supra note 2, at 362, citing United States, Staff of the Joint Committee on Taxation, *General Explanation of the Tax Reform Act of 1976, 94th Cong., 2d sess.* (Washington, DC: US Government Printing Office, 1976), 152-53.

87   Pub. L. no. 97-34, enacted on August 13, 1981; 95 Stat. 172, section 251(a) (1981), introducing section 422A (now section 422) of the Code.

88   William A. Klein, Joseph Bankman, Boris I. Bittker, and Lawrence M. Stone, *Federal Income Taxation*, 8th ed. (Boston: Little, Brown and Company, 1990), 392, citing United States, Staff of the Joint Committee on Taxation, *General Explanation of the Economic Recovery Act of 1981*, JCS-71-81 (Washington, DC: US Government Printing Office, 1981), 157.

89   Jassy, supra note 2, at 363. The former was likely explained as a consequence of the removal of the beneficial treatment. The latter likely reflected "the widespread use of nonqualified stock options and other employee incentive awards that generated tax reductions for the employer-corporations": Jassy, ibid.

90   The employee will recognize ordinary income, although the corporation is not entitled to a corresponding deduction, in the case of ESPPs whose exercise price is less than the fair market value of the stock on the date the options are granted. The employee will recognize ordinary income *and* the corporation will be entitled to a corresponding deduction if the disposition of the stock acquired under the ISO or ESPP is a "disqualifying disposition," as discussed in notes 102, 103, and 109 and accompanying text, infra.

91   Code section 421(a).

92   There are a number of further restrictions that are not germane to this study.

93   Code section 422(a)(1).

94   Code section 422(b)(4). The employer must make a good-faith attempt to determine the fair market value of the underlying stock: Code section 422(c)(1).

95   Code section 422(a)(2). The three-month period is extended to one year in the case of an employee whose employment is terminated owing to disability: Code section 422(c)(6). The period is further relaxed for the estate of a deceased employee, as discussed in note 98, infra.

96   Code section 422(b)(1).

97   Code section 422(b)(2).

98   Code section 422(b)(5). Code section 421(c) contains rules governing the exercise of an ISO or ESPP by the estate of an employee or by a person who acquired the option by bequest or inheritance or by reason of the death of the employee. In general, both the holding period and the requirements of Code section 422(a) or 423(a) do not apply in these circumstances.

99   Code section 422(b)(3).

100   Code sections 422(b)(6) and (c)(5).

101   Code section 422(d). For the purpose of determining which excess ISOs are NSOs, the options shall be taken into account in the order in which they were granted. A plan can provide that more than $100,000 worth of optioned stock can be exercised in any given year if the plan specifically states which part of the option is an ISO and which is an NSO: Notice 87-49, 1987-2 CB 355. The company can also designate which stock is ISO stock by issuing separate certificates for such stock when the options are exercised.

102   Code section 421(b).

103   Ibid.

104   Code section 422(c)(2).

105   Harlan J, in *LoBue*, supra note 49, suggested that the results of examples 8 and 9 are inappropriate because the employee is in the same economic position, although in example 8 the employee's gain is taxed at full tax rates, whereas in example 9 the gain is taxed as a long-term capital gain. However, these results may be justified on the basis that the employee in example 9 has put money at risk,

in the same manner as any other investor, from the outset when the options were exercised, whereas the employee in example 8 did not put any capital at risk.

106 See the text accompanying notes 79-80, supra.

107 There are a number of further requirements that are not germane to this study.

108 Code section 423(a)(1).

109 Code section 421(b).

110 Code sections 423(b)(6)(A) and (B).

111 Code section 423(b)(1).

112 Code section 423(a)(2).

113 Code section 423(b)(4)(A).

114 Code section 423(b)(4)(B).

115 Code section 423(b)(4)(C).

116 Code section 423(b)(4)(D).

117 Code section 423(b)(5) and Treas. reg. section 1.423-2(f)(1). These limitations cannot be used to exclude certain employees from the plan. For example, the plan cannot restrict the number of options to a percentage of each employee's compensation above $50,000.

118 Code section 423(b)(2).

119 Code section 423(b)(9). For rules applicable in the event of the death of an employee, see supra note 98.

120 Code sections 423(b)(7)(A) and (B). The option may provide that the option price is the lesser of 85 percent of the fair market value of the stock on the date of exercise and 85 percent of the fair market value of the stock on the date of grant. In this case, the option period must not exceed 27 months.

121 Code section 423(b)(3).

122 Code section 423(b)(8). For the purposes of this rule, the right to purchase stock is considered to accrue when the option first becomes exercisable. Suppose, for example, that on June 1, 2003 an employee is granted options to buy 1,000 shares of A Co for $85 per share and at that time each share is worth $100. The option agreement must further provide that the employee cannot purchase more than 250 shares by the end of 2003, more than 500 shares (in the aggregate) by the end of 2004, and so on. So, if the employee exercises options to acquire 100 shares in 2003, a further 400 shares may be acquired in 2004.

123 For example, the ESPP may stipulate that each employee authorize his or her participation by electing to have payroll deductions of 1 percent to 10 percent of his or her base salary on the commencement date of the offering. The employee is deemed to acquire options to purchase that number of shares equal to the elected percentage multiplied by the base salary and divided by 85 percent of the market value of the corporation's stock on the commencement date. The ESPP may stipulate that the option price is equal to the lesser of 85 percent of the fair market value of the stock on the commencement date and 85 percent of the fair market value on the termination date of the offering (that is, six months after the commencement date). On the termination date, the employee is deemed to exercise the option to acquire that number of shares at the applicable option price that the accumulated payroll deductions can purchase.

124 Code section 423(c). If the employee dies while holding the stock, the amount of compensation income must be recognized on the employee's final return. If the option price is not fixed or determinable on the day the option is granted (that is, the option price is based on the fair market value of the stock when the option is exercised), then the option price is determined as if the option were exercised on the day of death.

125 Code section 421(a)(2).

126 Even in the second and third examples, where the exercise price has a "built-in bargain purchase element," no benefit or deduction is recognized at the time of grant or exercise.

127 A good history, up to the 1972 tax reform, can be found in Sherbaniuk, supra note 78.

128 G. McGregor, "Upset Apple Cart," Around the Courts feature (1960) vol. 8, no. 6 *Canadian Tax Journal* 391-92, at 391.

129 55 DTC 192; 12 Tax ABC 335.

130 Ibid., at 194; 338. Unfortunately, none of the authorities cited by Mr. Fordham in reaching this conclusion dealt with employee stock options. Furthermore, the result obviously poses administrative difficulties where the options are exercised beyond the assessment limitation period for the year in which the options are granted.

131 Subsection 75A(4) of the 1948 Income Tax Act, as added by SC 1952-53, c. 40, section 28. According to the minister of finance, D.C. Abbott, the section was designed to close a loophole through which Parliament thought that stock option benefits might go untaxed: "it was felt that it was necessary to prevent an abuse of these stock option devices through allowing employees, perhaps executives of a corporation, to get very large benefits which would not be taxable." Canada, House of Commons, *Debates*, April 10, 1953, 3721.

132 SC 1966-67, c. 47, section 9. The new provision applied to benefits received after March 29, 1966 unless the stock option agreement was in place before March 30, 1966, in which case the provision did not operate until January 1, 1968. In effect, for existing stock options, the option holder was given 21 months to exercise the options in order to take advantage of the earlier preferential rate.

133 Section 7 of the Income Tax Act, RSC 1952, c. 148, as amended by SC 190-71-72, c. 63, section 1.

134 The taxpayer could make use of the two averaging techniques then available, general averaging and income-averaging annuity contracts (a form of forward averaging through the purchase of annuity contracts). Both of these schemes were replaced with a form of forward-averaging in 1982, which was phased out under the 1988 tax reform.

135 In 1972, even the Black-Scholes model did not exist.

136 Subsections 7(1.1) and (1.2), added by SC 1977-78, c. 1, section 3(2), applicable to agreements entered into after March 31, 1977.

137 Canada, House of Commons, *Debates*, March 31, 1977, 4537.

138 To qualify for special treatment under subsection 7(1.1), the employer must have been a CCPC when the options were granted. The employer need not be a CCPC when the options are exercised or when the underlying shares are ultimately sold.

139   Enacted in SC 1984, c. 45, section 35(3).

140   Canada, Department of Finance, 1984 Budget, Budget Papers, February 15, 1984, 7. In the Budget Speech, at 9, the minister of finance, Marc Lalonde, justified the extended preferential treatment on the following basis: "Employee stock options are important in compensating dynamic and entrepreneurial employees. They provide such employees with incentives directly related to their ability to increase the productivity, competitiveness, and growth of their company."

141   Section 110.6, introduced in SC 1986, c. 6. See further chapter 3, at notes 187-189 and accompanying text.

142   The other major distinction between paragraphs 110(1)(d) and (d.1) is that the CCPC shares need not be "prescribed shares" in order to benefit from the deduction in paragraph 110(1)(d.1).

143   That is, the options are not in the money at the time of grant and the shares of the CCPC are prescribed shares.

144   Subsections 7(8) through 7(16) of the Income Tax Act, introduced in SC 2001, c. 17, section 2(9).

145   Subparagraph 7(9)(d)(i). Prescribed stock exchanges are listed in regulations 3200 and 3201.

146   Canada, Department of Finance, 2000 Budget, Budget Plan, Tax Measures: Supplementary Information and Notices of Ways and Means Motions, February 28, 2000, 230-31 (emphasis added).

147   Ontario, Ministry of Finance, 2000 Ontario Budget, Budget Paper C, May 2, 2000, 90-92. The exclusion (characterized in the legislation as a tax overpayment) is contained in section 8.7 of the Ontario Income Tax Act, RSO 1990, c. I.2, as amended by SO 2000, c. 42, which received royal assent on December 21, 2000. The complexity of this tax benefit is reflected in the 41 subsections that comprise section 8.7.

148   Eligible employees are full-time or permanent part-time employees who have been employed by the eligible corporation for at least six months and who

   1) spend at least 30 percent of their time undertaking directly, supervising, or supporting the performance of scientific research and experimental development in Ontario;
   2) are not specified shareholders of the eligible corporation;
   3) in respect of the stock option benefit, are resident in Ontario at the end of the year in which the options are granted and in which a deduction under paragraph 110(1)(d) or (d.1) of the federal Income Tax Act is claimed; and
   4) in respect of the capital gain deduction, are resident in Canada at the end of the year in which the options are granted and in which the underlying shares are sold.

149   An eligible corporation is a corporation that carries on business in Ontario and undertakes scientific research and development in Ontario (either directly or through a partnership) of an amount of at least $25 million or 10 percent of its aggregate total revenue in the year prior to the year in which the stock options are granted.

150   Options that qualify for deduction under paragraph 110(1)(d) or (d.1) of the federal Income Tax Act.

151 Ontario, Ministry of Finance, 2000 Ontario Budget, Budget Speech, May 2, 2000, 24.

152 The two-year holding period for CCPC options applies only to those options that are granted in the money or for shares that are not prescribed shares. The primary rationale for the holding period stems from deferral of taxation even on those options that are in the money at the time of grant.

153 A study of psychological factors affecting the exercise of employee stock options noted that over 90 percent of stock options exercised by over 50,000 employees at seven companies were "cashless exercises," through which the broker immediately sold the stock and issued a cheque to the employee for the difference between the proceeds and the exercise price: Heath, Huddart, and Lang, supra note 17, at 601, note 1.

154 This deduction has been criticized because it significantly reduces the tax liability of the corporate employer. In a report on corporate income taxes, McIntyre and Nguyen reviewed the tax paid in 1996-1998 by 250 major companies, of which 233 reduced their taxes by a total of $25.8 billion through employee stock option deductions. The top 10 beneficiaries of this deduction (including Microsoft, Cisco Systems, General Electric, IBM, and Intel) saved over $10 billion and had their effective tax rates cut by an average of 9.3 percent. See Robert S. McIntyre and T.D. Coo Nguyen, *Corporate Income Taxes in the 1990s* (Washington, DC: Institute on Taxation and Economic Policy, October 2000), 8-9.

155 Supra note 55.

156 The circumstances in which Canadian employees are taxed at full employment rates on their stock option benefits are limited in practice, certainly much more limited than those in the United States.

157 CRA document no. 9919173, 1999.

158 For ESPPs, the employee must own less than 5 percent, without exception.

159 Generally, an employee is at arm's length with the corporate employer if the employee is not "related" to the corporate employer. A person is related to a corporation if the person has voting control of the corporation or is related to a person who has voting control of the corporation. If the employee is not related to the employer, it is a question of fact whether the employee and the employer are at arm's length. Thus, employees in Canada may own substantially more stock in their corporate employer and still benefit from preferential tax treatment. Furthermore, a factual non-arm's-length test is more difficult to apply than a bright-line 10 percent test.

160 If the employee does not benefit from the CCPC or public company stock option rules, then the stock option benefit of $30,000 and offsetting deduction of $15,000 (under paragraph 110(1)(d)) would be recognized in the year the options are exercised rather than deferred until the year of sale. The capital loss arising in the year of sale is treated in the same manner as outlined in the text.

161 A capital loss may be carried back three years or forward indefinitely, but may only be applied against capital gains in those years.

162 In fact, the employee may realize an economic loss and still owe tax (that is, if, after the options are exercised, the value of the shares drops below the exercise price). Following numerous submissions made by employees (many of whom exercised stock options in Nortel Networks Corporation) who were adversely

affected by the inability to deduct capital losses on stock acquired from employee stock options following the stock market meltdown in 2000, the Department of Finance agreed to review this concern: see, for example, CRA document no. 2001-0081454, May 31, 2001; and CRA document no. 2001-0076195, May 31, 2001. The department decided (rightly, in my view) that no changes would be made to the legislation to provide for this relief. It concluded that "it is difficult to justify granting special retroactive tax relief to individuals who chose to accept the risk of the market after acquiring shares under their employer's share purchase plan" (CRA document no. 2003-0007795, April 15, 2003).

163 Valuation issues and techniques are considered briefly in Beam and Laiken, supra note 2, at 1284-86; Michaelson, supra note 2, at 132-35; and Michael J. Fremes, Perry Phillips, and Harvey Wortsman, "Employee Share Ownership Plans," in *R & D: Credits Today, Innovation Tomorrow*, 1999 Corporate Management Tax Conference (Toronto: Canadian Tax Foundation, 1999), 15:1-77, at 15:26-27, table 7. See also Line Racette, "Valuing Intellectual Properties and Technology Companies," ibid., 10:1-30, at 10:5-21.

164 Code section 422(c)(1). Accordingly, as long as the attempt was made in good faith, an undervaluation would convert a larger amount of income into a capital gain.

165 Venture capitalists typically subscribe for preference shares, in series, at each round of venture financing. These preference shares are convertible, at the option of the holder, into common shares on a one-for-one basis.

166 A low valuation for the common shares is important for employees who are compensated with stock (for example, founders' stock) or stock options. In the former case, the employee must include in income the value of the shares at the time they are received, unless the shares are "restricted stock" (that is, not transferable and subject to a substantial risk of forfeiture because, for example, they are subject to vesting restrictions). Even if the shares received are restricted stock, the employee will often file an election under Code section 83(b) to tax the value of the shares when received (disregarding the restrictions for this purpose) in order to ensure that subsequent growth in the value of the shares is taxed as a capital gain rather than as employment income: supra notes 59-66 and accompanying text.

For employees who receive stock options, the options can qualify only as ISOs if the strike price under the options is at least equal to the fair market value of the shares at the time of grant. Even for options that do not qualify as ISOs, a low valuation for common shares is beneficial because the employee must include in income the difference between the value of the shares and the strike price at the time the options are exercised (unless the shares are restricted stock, in which case taxation is deferred until the shares become transferable or are no longer subject to a substantial risk of forfeiture unless the taxpayer elects under Code section 83(b)). Thus, for NSOs, a low common share valuation reduces the amount of employment income that must be recognized when the options are exercised and the stock is held until a later date.

See, generally, Ronald J. Gilson and David M. Schizer, "Understanding Venture Capital Structure: A Tax Explanation for Convertible Preferred Stock" (2003) vol. 116, no. 3 *Harvard Law Review* 875-916, at 889-901. See also Jacqueline A. Daunt, *Venture Capital for High Technology Companies* (Palo Alto, CA: Fenwick & West, 2002) (available at the Fenwick & West LLP Web site:

http://www.fenwick.com/). Daunt indicates (at 14-15): "It is typical for early stage companies (though not approved by the IRS) to establish a fair market value for common stock for such employee plans within a range of 10 to 20 percent of the most recent value of the preferred stock. This price differential must disappear as you approach a public offering or acquisition of the company or the company may be required to take a 'cheap stock' charge to earnings by the SEC." The cheap stock charge is considered in note 168, infra. There are other reasons for issuing convertible preference shares to venture capitalists, particularly to separate the control rights attached to shares from their cash flow rights: see chapter 1, at note 34 and accompanying text.

167 For example, if, in the first round of financing, the series 1 preference shares are issued at $1.00 per share, the common shares may be valued at that time for employee stock option purposes at $0.10 per share. Similarly, if, in the second round, the series 2 preference shares are issued for $2.50 per share, the common shares may be valued at that time at $0.25 per share.

168 Apart from the tax issues, concerns also arise with the Securities and Exchange Commission (SEC) when the company plans to go public if employee stock options are granted deep in the money. Depending on the circumstances—for example, the number of options issued and the amount by which the strike price is below fair market value—the SEC may require the company to take a charge against earnings in its financial statements for prospectus purposes. Negotiation over this point can significantly delay the prospectus process. See, generally, Michael J. Halloran and David R. Lamarre, *Identifying and Avoiding "Cheap Stock" Problems* (San Francisco: Pillsbury Winthrop LLP, 1999) (available at the Pillsbury Winthrop LLP Web site: http://www.pillsburywinthrop.com/).

169 Daunt herself suggests (supra note 166, at 13) that "[a]fter venture funding, valuation is easy. Just multiply the fully diluted outstanding capital of your company by the price per share paid by the last round investors."

170 This was the response given by Daunt at the conference sponsored by the Canadian Consulate Trade Office San Francisco | Silicon Valley, The Next Level Conference—Round 1: The Mechanics Behind Structuring a Deal the Silicon Valley Way, Redwood City, CA, March 30, 2000.

171 The following extract (taken from the form S-1, Registration Statement of Nuance Communications, February 4, 2000, available from the Edgar database at http://www.sec.gov/) is typical of the "risk factors" included in the prospectuses of such companies:

> We have a history of losses. We expect to continue to incur losses and we may not achieve or maintain profitability. . . .
> We expect to have net losses and negative cash flow for at least the next 24 months. We expect to spend significant amounts to enhance our products and technologies, expand international sales and operations and fund research and development. As a result, we will need to generate significant additional revenue to achieve profitability. Even if we do achieve profitability, we may not be able to sustain or increase profitability on a quarterly or annual basis. If we do not achieve and maintain profitability, the market price for our common stock may decline, perhaps substantially.

See also chapter 1, at notes 27-28 and accompanying text.

172   It may be that most employees do not, in fact, realize a benefit because they generally exercise and sell on the same day so that the stock options are taxed as NSOs in any event. It may not be worth the administrative cost to pursue the assessment of those employees who actually hold their shares for the requisite period to benefit from capital gains treatment.

173   But see the recent decision in *McClintock*, supra note 40.

174   Leonard E. Burman, *The Labyrinth of Capital Gains Tax Policy: A Guide for the Perplexed* (Washington, DC: Brookings Institution, 1999), 76.

175   Alan J. Auerbach, "Capital Gains Taxation and Tax Reform" (1989) vol. 42, no. 3 *National Tax Journal* 391-401, at 396.

176   Supra note 78 and accompanying text (the rationale for RSOs criticized by President Kennedy in 1963); supra note 79 (the rationale for the QSO rules introduced in 1964); and supra note 88 and accompanying text (the rationale for the ISO rules introduced in 1981).

177   Budget Speech, supra note 140, at 9.

178   Calvin H. Johnson, "Stock Compensation: The Most Expensive Way To Pay Future Cash" (1999) vol. 52, no. 2 *SMU Law Review* 423-54, at 433.

179   Ibid., at 433.

180   Some of the economics literature considering this point is surveyed in Douglas Kruse, Joseph Blasi, James Sesil, and Maya Kroumova, *Public Companies with Broad-Based Stock Options: Corporate Performance from 1992-1997* (Oakland, CA: National Center for Employee Ownership, 2000) (available at the NCEO Web site: http://www.nceo.org/).

181   Johnson, supra note 178, at 442.

182   Ibid.

183   Ibid., at 424. See also Johnson, supra note 23.

184   Supra notes 95 and 112 and accompanying text.

185   For an overview of the TN-1 visa, including the categories of professionals who qualify and how to apply, see the US Department of State Bureau of Consular Affairs Web site: http://travel.state.gov/tn_visas.html.

186   See Jeff Frank and Éric Bélair, *South of the Border: Graduates from the Class of '95 Who Moved to the United States* (Ottawa: Human Resources Development Canada and Statistics Canada, 1999) (Statistics Canada catalogue no. 81-587-XIB) (available at the Human Resources Development Canada Web site: http://www.hrdc-drhc.gc.ca/sp-ps/arb-dgra/). For a summary of the report, see Jeffery Frank and Jim Seidle, "Pathways to the United States: Graduates from the Class of '95" (2000) vol. 6, no. 3 *Education Quarterly Review* 36-44. This survey indicated that only 1.5 percent of the individuals who graduated from Canadian post-secondary institutions in 1995 moved to the United States between graduation and the summer of 1997. However, master's and PhD graduates were overrepresented among migrating graduates; for example, 12 percent of PhD graduates (excluding US citizens who returned to the United States after completing their studies) migrated to the United States.

187   John F. Helliwell and David F. Helliwell, "Where Are They Now? Migration Patterns for Graduates of the University of British Columbia," paper prepared for the University of British Columbia, Centre for Research on Economic and Social

Policy, 2000 (available online at http://www.arts.ubc.ca/cresp/grads.pdf). See also John F. Helliwell and David F. Helliwell, "Tracking UBC Graduates: Trends and Explanations" (2000) vol. 1, no. 1 *Isuma* 101-10. John Helliwell examined the residence of all UBC alumni (for which information was available) since 1920, and concluded that the level of migration to the United States has declined since the 1940s and 1950s. Furthermore, the number of PhD and master's graduates remaining in Canada exceeded the number of Canadian citizens entering these programs, suggesting a net inflow of such individuals. However, only 7 percent of PhD entrants at UBC were US citizens, while more than 15 percent of 1990s PhD graduates reside in the United States. Helliwell provides a more general survey of migration trends in John F. Helliwell, *Checking the Brain Drain: Evidence and Implications*, Department of Economics Working Paper (Vancouver: University of British Columbia, Department of Economics, July 1999).

188   Mahmood Iqbal, "Brain Drain: Empirical Evidence of Emigration of Canadian Professionals to the United States" (2000) vol. 48, no. 3 *Canadian Tax Journal* 674-88. Iqbal disputes the Helliwell and Human Resources Development Canada/Statistics Canada studies, suggesting that they grossly underestimate southern migration because they consider only "permanent" emigration, and fail to take into account "non-permanent" immigrants who work in the United States under temporary visas, particularly TN-1 visas. According to Iqbal, on the basis of statistics prepared by the US Immigration and Naturalization Service (INS), the number of non-permanent and permanent emigrants (based on visas issued) increased from 17,000 in 1988 to 98,000 in 1997. Helliwell counters that the INS statistics include a significant amount of double counting because they include people who are renewing short-term visas. Iqbal acknowledges later in the article the problem of multiple counting and suggests that a more conservative estimate of Canadian professionals moving to the United States in 1997 would be 35,000, as opposed to the 98,000 figure he earlier suggested.

189   Daniel Schwanen, *Putting the Brain Drain in Context: Canada and the Global Competition for Scientists and Engineers*, C.D. Howe Institute Commentary no. 140 (Toronto: C.D. Howe Institute, April 2000). Schwanen acknowledges that the number of university-educated individuals immigrating to Canada exceeds the number emigrating from Canada to the United States by approximately four to one and the number emigrating worldwide by approximately two to one. However, he states (at 17) that those leaving Canada "include more than the expected share of the country's best and brightest." Schwanen also contrasts the makeup of the high-tech industry in Canada and the United States, suggesting (at 13) that "the United States seems to have the upper hand in deploying nonproduction resources (including scientists and engineers) in the most science- and engineering-intensive, productive, and fastest-growing sectors of its economy, while Canada has been specializing in production work in the same industries."

190   Don DeVoretz and Samuel A. Laryea, *Canadian Human Capital Transfers: The United States and Beyond*, C.D. Howe Institute Commentary no. 115 (Toronto: C.D. Howe Institute, October 1998). DeVoretz and Laryea suggest that the skills and wages of skilled immigrants to Canada are not as large, per person or in the aggregate, as those of migrants from Canada to the United States. For a critique of their study, see Helliwell, *Checking the Brain Drain*, supra note 187, at 7-8.

191   The major difference among the studies is the use made of the INS data on temporary visas. Even those who rely on these data, such as Iqbal, confirm that

they include an element of multiple counting. The problems with the INS data, as a gauge of the brain drain, are detailed in Zhao, Drew, and Murray, infra note 192, at 15-16. In addition to the problem of renewals mentioned above, supra note 189, the data include multiple entries by the same individual in a year (since individuals on a TN visa must fill out a new I-94 form—the basis of the INS data—any time they re-enter the United States after an absence of at least 30 consecutive days) as well as single or multiple entries involving very short stays.

192　John Zhao, Doug Drew, and T. Scott Murray, "Brain Drain and Brain Gain: The Migration of Knowledge Workers from and to Canada" (2000) vol. 6, no. 3 *Education Quarterly Review* 8-35, at 23.

193　In 1995, there were 741 university graduates in science-related fields per 100,000 people aged 25 to 34 in the labour market in Canada, compared with 938 in the United States and an average of 831 in all OECD countries: Organisation for Economic Co-operation and Development, *Education at a Glance: OECD Indicators* (Paris: OECD, 1998), 345, table G4.1, cited in Zhao, Drew, and Murray, supra note 192, at 19.

194　See chapter 1, at notes 44-45 and accompanying text.

195　That is, 18.5 percent compared with 13.8 percent: Meric S. Gertler, Richard Florida, Gary Gates, and Tara Vinodrai, "Competing on Creativity: Placing Ontario's Cities in North American Context," a report prepared for the Ontario Ministry of Enterprise, Opportunity and Innovation and the Institute for Competitiveness and Prosperity, November 2002, 16, table 2 (available from the Institute for Competitiveness and Prosperity Web site: http://www.competeprosper.ca/institute/). See further chapter 1, at note 45.

196　The program provides $900 million to support the establishment of 2,000 Canada research chairs at universities across the country by 2005, with approximately 400 new chairs to be named each year. The key objective of the program is "to enable Canadian universities, together with their affiliated research institutes and hospitals, to achieve the highest levels of research excellence to become world-class research centres in the global, knowledge-based economy." See the program's Web site: http://www.chairs.gc.ca/.

197　See, for example, Iqbal, supra note 188, at 683. See also Serge Nadeau, Lori Whewell, and Shane Williamson, "Beyond the Headlines on the 'Brain Drain'" (2000) vol. 1, no. 1 *Isuma* 154-57. This study compares the after-tax wage differentials of a hypothetical entry-level engineer and a hypothetical vice-president in the high-tech industry in Ontario and in North Carolina. After-tax wages are significantly higher for both in the United States. However, the source of the after-tax wage gap differs significantly. For the engineer, 92.3 percent of the difference is due to higher wages and only 7.7 percent is due to lower tax. For the vice-president, 60.3 percent is due to higher wages and 39.7 percent is due to lower tax (table 1 at 156). They conclude (at 157) that "[c]areer opportunities and higher salaries appear to be the main motivating factors, but taxes may also play a role for senior skilled workers."

198　In fact, it is arguable that temperature is more relevant to the migration decision than taxes. The point is that simply comparing migration and taxes does not prove any causal connection between them.

199　Frank and Bélair, supra note 186, and Helliwell and Helliwell, "Where Are They Now?" supra note 187. The limited mention of tax as a rationale for migrating has sometimes been attributed to the open-endedness of the questions such as those used in the Human Resources Development Canada/Statistics Canada study. The question asked of graduates was: "What aspects of the job or other work-related factors attracted you to the United States after graduation? Please be as specific as possible." Frank and Seidle, supra note 186, at 40, state: "Somewhat surprisingly, given the debate and media coverage of this issue, an insignificant proportion of graduates explicitly said that lower taxes in the United States were a factor that attracted them to work there. For some, however, lower taxes may have been implicit in mentioning higher salaries. Also, differences in Canadian and U.S. personal income tax rates tend to be smaller at lower income levels. At this early stage in their careers, many of these graduates may have been most concerned with finding an opportunity in their field."

200   John F. Helliwell, *Globalization: Myths, Facts and Consequences*, C.D. Howe Institute Benefactors Lecture (Toronto: C.D. Howe Institute, October 23, 2000), 23.

201   Don Wagner, "Do Tax Differences Contribute Toward the Brain Drain from Canada to the U.S.?" paper presented at the Annual Meeting of the Canadian Economics Association, Vancouver, June 2000. A shorter version of his findings is published in Don Wagner, "Do Tax Differences Cause the Brain Drain?" (2000) vol. 21, no. 10 *Policy Options* 33-41.

202   Interestingly, the addition of a post-graduate degree was not statistically significant.

203   Wagner, "Do Tax Differences Cause the Brain Drain?" supra note 201, at 40.

204   Perhaps it is my patriotic feeling for Canada, but it is difficult to believe that non-economic factors (for example, family or the weather) have a greater impact than economic factors on the decision to migrate south.

205   Wagner, "Do Tax Differences Cause the Brain Drain?" supra note 201, at 40, table 3.

206   Ibid., at 40-41.

207   Helliwell, supra note 200, at 43. Ross Finnie reaches a similar conclusion: Ross Finnie, *The Brain Drain: Myth and Reality—What It Is and What Should Be Done*, School of Policy Studies Working Paper 13 (Kingston, ON: Queen's University, School of Policy Studies, January 2001). He states (at 16-17) that "general tax cuts would comprise an extremely blunt instrument, since they would apply to all individuals, most of whom are not at the slightest risk of leaving the country, and would thus be very costly in terms of revenue losses and the required reductions in public spending. Even under the most optimistic assumptions, the cost per brain [not drained from Canada] would be high, on the order of half a million dollars, and might well be several times this amount, all on a perpetual basis." However, Finnie does believe (at 14) that recent tax amendments (including changes to the treatment of employee stock options, the reduction in the capital gains inclusion rate, the introduction of the angel capital rollover, and the reduction in general corporate tax rates), while not specifically targeting the high-tech or research and development sectors, have their greatest influence in these sectors and their effect should be "to direct investment funds to these sectors and make working in Canada more attractive for this very important and mobile group of workers."

208   Neil Brooks, "Flattening the Claims of the Flat Taxers" (1998) vol. 21, no. 2 *Dalhousie Law Journal* 287-369, at 366.

209   A recent study by Ross Finnie examines the incidences of leaving and returning to Canada taking into account individuals' characteristics: Ross Finnie, *Leaving and Coming Back to Canada: Evidence from Longitudinal Data*, School of Policy

Studies Working Paper 32 (Kingston, ON: Queen's University, School of Policy Studies, December 2002). The study uses data from the Statistics Canada Longitudinal Administrative Database (LAD), a 20 percent representative sample of all Canadian tax filers (and identified spouses) covering the period 1982 to 1999, which is constructed from the CRA's tax files. There are obvious challenges in defining who "leaves" and who "returns" for the purpose of the study. Finnie uses three different definitions of leaving: definition A includes individuals who have declared their departure on their tax form; definition B includes those in definition A plus those who are observed to have a declaration of non-residence in Canada; definition C includes those in definitions A and B plus those who are observed to have a foreign mailing address while still indicating residence in a particular province (as required on the tax return) but who have not declared a departure. His findings are similar across all three definitions. "Return" is defined in two ways: definition A includes those who have declared their return to Canada on their tax form; and definition B includes those in definition A plus those who had a Canadian address and were assigned a Canadian province of residence. Models of departure and return were run for all six combinations, although the discussion in the study focuses on the A-A and C-B combinations (that is, the narrowest and widest definitions in each case).

Personal characteristics examined in the study include age, family status, province/region, minority-language indicator, area size of residence, provincial unemployment rate, market income in last full year in Canada, and an indicator of receipt of unemployment insurance in that year. As Finnie indicates, there is no variable indicating level of educational achievement (since there is no such measure in LAD), although the income level is used as a rough proxy for focusing on the "brain drain." In the context of the brain drain, the study suggests a few interesting results. First, it is important to bear in mind that the number of people departing Canada in any given year is extremely small, representing approximately 1/100 of 1 percent of the adult population. Not surprisingly, individuals in the age group 25-34 and individuals in the highest income brackets ($60,000-$100,000 and $100,000+) are most likely to leave (the correlation between age and leaving is statistically significant at the 1 percent level for both males and females; interestingly, the correlation between income and leaving is statistically significant for females only). Somewhat surprising is the fact that couples with children are more likely to leave than singles without kids; however, singles with kids are the most likely to leave, which is difficult to explain. As a general trend, leaving tended to be inversely related to the country's economic performance.

The study found that only a small minority of those leaving tended to return: 14 to 15 percent of all leavers return within five years and about 19 percent return after 10 years. Leavers are most likely to return after two years, although the rate of return is low. Since 1997, however, the leaving rate has declined and at the same time the return rate has increased substantially from 1992 onward, with return rates doubling in recent years. Finally, and an important factor in the context of the brain drain, the likelihood of return is the highest for individuals in the highest income levels, which is, as Finnie suggests, a reflection of the mobility of individuals in this group. It also suggests that taxes are not what drive the best and brightest out of Canada.

210   In its May 2004 budget, Ontario repealed the research employee stock option tax preference: Ontario, Ministry of Finance, 2004 Budget, Budget Paper C, May 18, 2004, 135.

5

Tax Credits for Direct Investment in Small Businesses*

Three provinces[1] and a number of states have introduced or proposed tax credits for seed capital investment in small and medium-sized enterprises (SMEs).[2] These tax credits act as a front-end incentive targeting primarily angel capitalists. By reducing the after-tax cost of the investment, the government essentially assumes some of the risks associated with the SME investment. In this respect, the tax credits act like increased loss relief for venture capital investments. However, the credits are provided regardless of an investment's success, whereas loss relief is available only if the investment fails.

In general, state and provincial governments exercise more control over SME investments that qualify for the tax credits than the Canadian and US federal governments exercise in their targeted capital loss relief measures, considered in chapter 3.[3] The US and Canadian angel capital tax credit programs are better targeted toward investment in rapid-growth SMEs than the enhanced loss relief provided by the federal governments. As indicated in chapter 3, the loss relief measures for investment in SMEs in both countries should be more narrowly targeted; their application should be limited to (or should exclude) businesses similar to those that benefit from (or are excluded from) tax credit incentives such as those discussed in this chapter and in chapter 6. In my view, such amended loss relief measures better address the equity gap faced by SMEs than the direct investment tax credit measures considered in this chapter.

Salient Features of Direct Investment Tax Credit Programs

An angel tax credit may form part of a comprehensive program targeting venture capital in the particular province or state, as is the case in British Columbia, Nova Scotia, Missouri, and Iowa. The other tax incentives in these jurisdictions are considered further in chapter 6 because they target investment in venture capital funds (VCFs)—that is, they target taxpayers who make passive venture capital investments, leaving the investment decision making and monitoring to others. There is, however, some overlap between the tax credits for direct and indirect investment where both target individual investors who invest in small businesses.[4]

---

* Unless otherwise stated, US monetary amounts are in US dollars and Canadian monatary amounts are in Canadian dollars.

The legislative regimes in the three provinces that offer an angel tax credit and the regimes in four US states[5] are summarized in appendix 5A. Because these programs operate in both countries at a subnational level and vary both within and between countries while sharing many common elements, the salient features of the various programs are easiest to compare and contrast in tabular format. The following section evaluates the angel capital tax credit programs using the salient features of the programs as a guide.

Evaluation of Direct Investment Tax Credit Programs

Eligible Investors

Some of the state and provincial tax credit regimes are limited to investment by individuals while others apply to all taxpayers. Given that the intention is to attract seed capital funding, which is provided primarily by love and angel capitalists, it is perhaps understandable that such tax expenditure programs are limited to individuals. However, corporations and certain non-taxable entities such as universities often provide seed capital to businesses spawned within the corporate or university environment. If the intention of the program is to promote innovation through seed capital investment and the government is prepared to underwrite some of the cost, consideration could be given to expanding the list of eligible investors to include all taxpayers that provide seed capital as well as tax-exempt entities (for example, by making the tax credit either refundable or saleable or by providing a grant in such cases).[6] If such entities are likely to fund enough investments to diversify their risk, a tax credit may be unnecessary. In addition, it may well be that such entities would provide substantially the same amount of seed capital financing without a tax incentive, thereby making the tax credit (or grant) an unnecessary expenditure. Given the precarious nature of university budgets, however, particularly at government-funded institutions in the two countries, it is likely that many universities are extremely cautious in making venture capital investments, if they make them at all (other than by providing the research facilities in which ideas are originally formed). By extending a refundable tax credit to universities, the government may promote equity investment by the universities in the businesses that they nurture. Universities might also use the availability of tax credits to promote fundraising (for example, for a university-administered seed capital fund), which might free up more of the university's budget for general expenditures.

There are a number of considerations in the context of individual investment in the various programs that warrant comment. First, it is questionable whether tax credits should be extended to individuals who invest through retirement savings plans, as is the case in all three provinces with an angel tax credit program. British Columbia goes further, permitting investment through registered retirement income funds (RRIFs), thus extending its tax credit to investors who are past retirement age. The credit, which is provided directly to the individual investors, will likely be consumed rather than set aside for retirement. Thus, the government is actively encouraging the investment of retirement savings in extremely high-risk investments without reducing the risk of loss in the retirement savings account. A similar provision is made in virtually every provincial VCF program (discussed in chapter 6). However, a VCF diversifies the taxpayer's risk to some extent. The angel capital tax credit, in contrast, does not require any diversification (provided that the investment complies with relationship restrictions and de maximis provisions). Whether or not retirement savings are an appropriate target for venture capital investment is considered further in chapter 7. At this point, it suffices to say that targeting retirement savings, particularly when securities regulation governing disclosure by private corporations is being relaxed,[7] is problematic.

Second, none of the regimes requires the investor to have any investment knowledge or experience, although Iowa requires the business's operator to have a minimal level of education or business experience. This is perhaps the most problematic element of a tax credit program. To what extent should the government be encouraging unsophisticated investors to make venture capital investments, especially with their retirement savings? None of the jurisdictions imposes restrictions on which individuals (or other taxpayers, where permitted) can benefit from the credit (except in some cases, where the individual has close ties to the recipient business, discussed below), although applicable securities legislation may impose some restrictions. However, securities regulation in a number of jurisdictions has been relaxed in recent years, particularly in the context of private company share offerings.[8]

Unsophisticated investors are not necessarily capable of evaluating business plans or of managing their investment by monitoring the activities of the business's managers. In short, unsophisticated investors cannot reduce the information asymmetries or moral hazard associated with venture investing. Furthermore, from the business's perspective, not all angels are necessarily good angels. Sophisticated angels provide more than capital to a fledgling business; their expertise may assist the business in developing its products and perhaps in accessing additional capital. In contrast, unsophisticated angels can act as impediments when additional capital is sought.[9] It is difficult for a tax credit program to target only those angel investors who will add value (other than capital) to the qualified business, and it is perhaps inappropriate for governments to engage in such paternalistic behaviour. However, where the government introduces a tax credit (or other tax or financial incentives) to encourage investment in SMEs and, at the same time, provides little if any protection in the form of information disclosure requirements to investors in the securities legislation or the tax credit program, it opens up the potential for unscrupulous behaviour that can undermine investor confidence.

Restrictions on Relationship Between Eligible Investor and Eligible Business

Some regimes provide a tax credit only to individuals who deal at arm's length with the business in which they invest. There are a number of plausible rationales for extending the regime to love capitalists (as distinct from angel capitalists), who tend to be closely connected to the businesses in which they invest. First, the tax credit may induce a potential entrepreneur to leave a salaried position to start a business by reducing the upfront costs of such a career change. This rationale is similar to one of the arguments in favour of some form of capital gains tax preference. The distinction is that, in the absence of extended loss relief provisions, a capital gains tax preference rewards success only and therefore may not be sufficient inducement for prospective entrepreneurs to leave the greater security of employment. Second, for both the founder and other love capitalists, a tax credit reduces the investor's cost of investment, thus increasing (at least in theory) the amount that such individuals should be willing to put at risk. The tax credit thus acts like extended loss relief for venture capital investment.[10] Love capitalists are less likely than angels to have a diversified capital investment portfolio; like an extended loss relief provision, the tax credit compensates for undiversified risk.

However, it is arguable that love capitalists (as distinct from angel capitalists) should be excluded from a tax credit program altogether because they are likely to invest to the same extent in the particular business without government incentives. A tax credit would reward them for investments that they would make in any event. In addition, there is potential for abuse in a variety of forms. For example, the business's founders could multiply the credits available by providing funds to other family members for investment purposes. Anti-avoidance measures can limit such abuse, although they must be carefully drafted and appropriately monitored. For example, investors qualifying for the Maine tax credit must collectively own less than one-half of the business. In addition, principal owners (defined broadly[11]) and their spouses are not eligible for the tax credit, and immediate family members of principal owners are eligible only if they do not have an existing ownership interest in the business. However, it is relatively simple to circumvent this rule. Consider an existing small business that meets the qualified business test and is 100 percent owned by its principal owner. The owner is contemplating investing additional funds in the business. A direct investment by the owner or the owner's spouse would not benefit from the tax credit. However, the individual could provide funds to another family member, who invests the funds in the business and can thus benefit from the tax credit. Similarly, Iowa's tax credit is not available to any current or previous owner, member, or shareholder in the qualified business. However, nothing prevents close family members of a current or previous shareholder from claiming tax credits for investments (regardless of the actual source of the funds financing this investment). In contrast, Missouri's tax credit is not available to principal owners, their spouses, or any family member within the third degree of consanguinity. The planning opportunities for a principal owner to invest through another family member are therefore severely restricted.

In my view, making the tax credits available to non-arm's-length investors is, on the whole, open to too much abuse. To the extent that the credits for investment in SMEs are warranted at all—which I doubt—they should be limited to arm's-length investors. The two reasons suggested above for extending a program to non-arm's-length investors—to encourage would-be entrepreneurs to leave employment and to compensate for undiversified risk—can be better addressed through other means, such as increased (but better targeted) loss relief provisions, as suggested in chapter 3.

Nature of Investment

A number of the jurisdictions limit qualified investments to equity investments, and of these, Newfoundland and Labrador and Nova Scotia[12] permit only common share investments. Maine, Missouri, and Indiana also provide tax credits for certain types of debt. In the case of equity investment, particularly where the credits are available only to individuals, it is not necessary to limit qualified investments to common shares. It is unlikely that preference shares significantly reduce the risks associated with angel investment. In the formal venture capital industry, venture capitalists often subscribe for convertible preference shares, not to give the investor greater financial security, but to substantiate a reduced strike price for employee stock options, to provide for special rights, such as guaranteed representation on the board of directors, and to give at least some priority over the business's founders and employees in the event that the business fails (although it is unlikely that assets would be available to any shareholders in this case). There is no reason why an investment in preference shares should not be eligible for a tax credit. Even if the shares were redeemable at the option of the holder (which the legislation could preclude, if a right of redemption were considered inappropriate), most of the regimes have minimum holding-period requirements that investors must meet so as not to lose the benefit of the credits.

Whether a credit should be extended to debt is more problematic. If it is extended, it should be limited to debt that is unsecured—debt that is subject to similar risks as equity investment. The limitations imposed by Maine and Missouri are appropriate in this respect. The Indiana credit is not so limited, at least by the governing legislation; on its face, the legislation appears to provide a tax credit to a bank or other financial institution that makes a secured loan to a qualified business. No tax credit should be available in such circumstances because it does not address the funding gap faced by SMEs.[13]

Nature of Incentive

All of the jurisdictions offer a credit equal to a percentage of the eligible investment (generally ranging from 20 percent to 40 percent, although a larger credit is provided in Maine and Missouri for certain investments). In some cases the credits are limited to a maximum amount per individual or per qualified business and in some cases to an overall cap, thus imposing a ceiling on the potential expenditure of the province or state.

In most cases, the tax credits that can be used by an investor in a year are limited to the tax otherwise payable, with unused credits carried over to other years (the extent of the carryover varies). Only British Columbia provides a refundable tax credit, although the maximum tax credit that can be applied (whether to reduce taxes or as a refund) in any one year is $60,000. Because individuals can carry over credits exceeding $60,000 for a maximum of four years, British Columbia effectively allows an aggregate tax credit or refund of $300,000 over any five-year period (corresponding to a $1,000,000 investment over a five-year period).

In addition to permitting the carryover of tax credits, Missouri permits a taxpayer to sell its tax credit certificates. As far as the cost to the government is concerned, there is little distinction between a refundable tax credit and a freely transferable tax credit.[14] From the investor's perspective, however, a transferable tax credit entails higher transaction costs than a refundable credit. These costs include expenses incurred to locate a willing purchaser plus the inevitable discount necessary to induce a purchaser to buy the credits. Transferable tax credits are more pervasive in US VCF programs,[15] where they are used to attract investment by non-taxable entities such as pension plans. Given that non-taxable entities are not permitted investors under Missouri's angel capital tax credit program, it is unclear why a transferable credit is used rather than a refundable credit, or indeed why transfers are permitted at all.

Since the intention of the regime is to promote investment in SMEs, it is unclear why the Canadian programs impose an annual limit (other than the amount of tax otherwise payable if the credit is non-refundable) on the tax credits to which an individual is entitled. The approach of US states, in limiting the tax credits to which an individual is entitled for investment in a particular qualified business or a limit on the capital of a corporation that can benefit from a tax credit, is more appropriate than an overall cap on each investor. Even then, it may be sufficient to impose limits on the size of the business itself (for example, measured in terms of the value of its assets after the particular share issuance) rather than on the maximum amount of new capital that can benefit from tax credits.

Besides capping the amount of claimable credits or the number of credits available, the costs of a tax credit program can be managed in other ways, particularly when unused credits can be carried over. First, the credit could be limited to a percentage of the tax otherwise payable, as in Maine. Second, the credit could be spread out over a number of years, again as in Maine. Third, the ability to apply the credit can be deferred to a subsequent year, as in Iowa, where the credit cannot be claimed until the third year after the eligible investment is made. One rationale for postponing the use of the credit or spreading the credit over a number of years, apart from cost savings to the province or state, is to better match the cost of the program to its benefits (derived through the use of the funds by the qualified SME).

An annual maximum or aggregate maximum amount of tax credits that the government will issue is appropriate in virtually all government expenditure programs. It may also be appropriate to make the program subject to a sunset clause or to require that the program be reviewed after an appropriate time period (say, five years).

Eligible Businesses

All of the jurisdictions prescribe limits on eligible businesses that can benefit from the tax credits. These limits always include the geographic location of the business (that is, within the particular province or state or within a particular region of the province or state[16]) and the size of the business, measured in terms of total assets, sales, or number of employees.

All of the jurisdictions also limit the nature of the qualifying business, although the limitations vary depending on the aims of the tax credit program. Retail sales, restaurants, personal services businesses, and other lifestyle businesses generally do not qualify for the tax credit, and rightly so. Tax credits should not be granted for investment in so-called lifestyle businesses that are not innovative and do not have the potential to create significant jobs or add meaningfully to the economy of the province or state. Businesses that provide financial services or are involved in real estate development are also generally excluded from investment tax credit programs.[17] Other limitations depend, to a large extent, on the nature of the businesses that the government wishes to develop in the region. However, governments must be realistic about the limitations of this type of program (or any venture capital program, for that matter). For example, it is unlikely that tax credit programs can foster the development of a high-tech sector where one does not already exist. The geographic clustering of high-tech businesses occurs for reasons other than a local supply of venture investment. Clustering occurs because of the availability of specialized labour markets, knowledge spillovers, and the presence of critical suppliers to the industry.[18] Simply creating or expanding the potential supply of venture capital will not, in and of itself, attract high-tech businesses. Such companies have voracious appetites for capital, and companies that show promise at an early stage will quickly grow well beyond the financial means of angels. As discussed in chapter 6, VCFs, which are the predominant suppliers of capital to the high-tech sector in terms of the amount of capital invested, tend to be geographically clustered, and the bulk of investment is made in geographic proximity to fund managers. Thus, the development of a high-tech sector also depends on the existence of a local formal venture capital industry.

Given an appropriately targeted definition of qualified business, it is necessary to determine the extent, if any, to which government should have a role in deciding which qualified businesses benefit from the tax credits. In the formal venture capital industry, venture capital firms act as specialized financial intermediaries that reduce moral hazard and information asymmetries associated with small business investments for the passive investors in VCFs. Angel investors do not benefit from such financial intermediaries and are left on their own to deal with the problems of information asymmetries. Successful investment depends on the skill or luck of individual investors. If the government intends to provide tax credits for angel investment, one question is whether the government also plans to fill—indeed, is competent to fill—the role of the financial intermediary. Most jurisdictions with angel tax credit programs have detailed registration procedures that businesses must follow before they can issue equity capital (or debt, where permitted) that benefits from the tax credits. The procedures generally require, among other things, that an applicant submit a detailed business plan. However, government officials do not evaluate these plans beyond ensuring that they meet the basic legislative requirements (size, location, nature of business, intended use of funds, etc.). In this respect, there is a concern that registration provides the government's "stamp of approval" of the business, which may be misleading, especially for unsophisticated investors.[19]

Eligible Uses of Capital

It is somewhat surprising that two of the programs impose no limits on the use of the invested funds. For example, it is inappropriate to permit the capital that benefits from the tax credits to be invested in non-business activities such as portfolio investment. It is equally inappropriate for such capital to be used to replace other capital in the business, such as debt, particularly shareholder loans, or other equity. Both uses wholly undermine one of the main rationales for the tax credit program: to provide seed or startup capital in order for the business to expand. While a program should not be too rigid in describing permitted uses— excluding impermissible uses is perhaps the better approach, as in Nova Scotia—it is appropriate to impose some time limit in which the funds must be employed for business purposes.

Cost-Benefit Analyses of Direct Investment
Tax Credit Programs

It is difficult to assess the efficacy of existing angel capital tax credit programs or their feasibility in other jurisdictions because the programs in most jurisdictions are too new for any meaningful cost-benefit analysis. There are, however, two exceptions where further analysis is possible: Maine, whose angel capital tax credit program commenced in 1989, and Nova Scotia, whose program commenced in 1993. Both of these programs have been in existence long enough to allow meaningful cost-benefit analysis. Both jurisdictions have undertaken internal, rather rudimentary, cost-benefit analyses, considered here. Both jurisdictions warrant more detailed study.

The Finance Authority of Maine (FAME), which is responsible for administering Maine's angel capital tax credit program, has maintained statistics since the program's inception showing the cost of the program in terms of tax credits issued, and the amount of capital generated by the credits. Before July 1, 2002, however, it was not required to and did not gather or report on any other information, such as employment created, capital spent, or taxes paid by qualified businesses.[20]

In 2000-1, FAME conducted an informal survey of the 60 or so businesses that had until then benefited from about $5 million in tax credits. It received responses from 29 businesses, 27 of which were still operating. These 27 respondents had aggregate private capital of $42.6 million and had created over 300 jobs between 1996 and 2001. FAME estimated that the 27 businesses generated annual tax revenue to the state of about $750,000,[21] leading it to conclude that "the $5,000,000 in tax credits issued to 60 companies between 1989 and 2001 are already, or soon will be, completely offset just by the taxes generated from the 27 active respondents to the survey."[22]

There are a number of difficulties with this analysis. First, the analysis assumes that the tax credits are solely responsible for the tax revenue from the 27 businesses; in other words, were it not for the tax credits, the 27 businesses would not have generated any tax revenue. That assumption fails to consider the amount of private investment that did not benefit from tax credits ($25.9 million) or the amount of private investment that would have occurred in the absence of the credits. While it is fair to say that the tax credits generated $16.7 million in capital for the 27 businesses, it is not necessarily the case that the credits were responsible for the rest of the private capital invested in these businesses. Indeed, some portion of the $16.7 million that benefited from tax credits might have been invested even in the absence of tax credits. Second, the analysis assumes that the individuals employed by the 27 businesses (whose employment income gave rise to the state tax revenue) would not have found employment in the state in the absence of the incentive. Third, the costs of the program fail to take into account overhead costs incurred by FAME in administering the program.[23] Furthermore, no attempt was made to determine whether the businesses that did not respond to the survey were still in business; the survey assumes that all non-respondent businesses had failed.[24] The survey also excludes corporate taxes paid by the respondents[25] or any multiplier effects[26] generated by successful investments. However, given the small size of the businesses that benefited from the tax credit, it is likely that any multiplier effects would be small.

An internal cost-benefit analysis of Nova Scotia's tax credit incentive programs, including the angel tax credit, was begun in 1999. The *Phase I Report* was issued in April 2000 and the *Phase II Report* in March 2001.[27] The equity tax credit (as the angel capital tax credit is known) was evaluated in both reports (in the latter report with updated data). The *Phase II Report* indicated that from the inception of the tax credit in 1993 through February 2000, 277 companies and 2,985 investors participated in the program. Participants invested $31.5 million and have received $9 million in tax credits. As of November 1, 2000, 88 percent of the companies were still in business, compared with 72 percent of all companies incorporated in Nova Scotia during the same period.

The *Phase I Report* contained a detailed study of 31 corporations registered under the program between 1994 and 1997. On average, these companies increased revenues by 89 percent in the year following the receipt of capital under the program and a further 33 percent in the following year. Payroll expenditures doubled in the year after the receipt of capital and increased by a further

51 percent in the following year. The companies studied were not profitable, however, showing an average loss of $25,309 in the year that capital was received, increasing to $68,445 in the following year; they reported a modest average profit of $3,405 in the second year after the investment. These earnings figures are consistent with those of businesses in their startup phase.

The *Phase II Report* included an economic analysis of the equity tax credit. In determining the benefits of the program, the analysis used the Nova Scotia input/output model based on the assumption (similar to that in Maine) that the credit is "totally incremental." In effect, the analysis assumes that 100 percent of the economic benefits generated by an eligible business (for example, payroll and the tax revenue generated therefrom) stemmed from the tax credit.[28] On the basis of this assumption, the total expenditure over the period from 1994 to 1999 generated a positive cash flow to the provincial treasury in 2001 (which would continue to increase as long as the companies remained in business).

In the other jurisdictions, no economic analysis has been undertaken. In many cases, the government's statistical information comprises only the tax credits issued under the program, the corresponding amount of investment raised, and the number of businesses that benefited from the program.[29] Little if any analysis of the success of these businesses has been done.

It is perhaps cynical to suggest that it would be surprising if an internal cost-benefit analysis conducted by the government agency responsible for a tax credit program showed anything other than a positive result. However, it is difficult to assess the true impact of an angel capital tax credit: that is, the extent to which the tax credit generated seed capital, jobs, sales, tax revenue, or other measures *that would not have been generated in the absence of the tax credit.*[30]

On the whole, tax credits for direct angel investment are not appropriate for a variety of reasons. Unless the government is prepared to assume the role of financial intermediary—which is highly unlikely—government programs should target more sophisticated angel capitalists or specialized investment vehicles, such as professionally managed small business investment funds, that can better evaluate potential investments and nurture the businesses in which investments are made. With respect to direct angel investment, I submit that an angel capital rollover and greater loss relief for small business investments (as suggested in chapter 3) are more appropriate and better targeted incentives than an angel tax credit. At the very least, if a government introduces an angel tax credit, the program should be subject to a sunset clause and it should require the administering agency to collect sufficient data from businesses that benefit from the credit to enable the government to properly evaluate the program before deciding whether to renew it.

Appendix 5A: Summary of Angel Capital Tax Credit Programs, All Provinces and Four Select States

Contents

Governing Legislation 225
Eligible Investors 225
Nature of Investment 226
Nature of Incentive 226
Maximum Tax Credit/Maximum Investment 227
Eligible Businesses 228
Use of Proceeds 230
Application for Registration 231
Restrictions on Relationship Between Eligible Investor and Eligible Business ... 232
Holding Period 233
Limit on Amount Raised by Each Eligible Business for Which a Tax Credit
 Is Available 233
Government Expenditure Limits 233
Sunset 234

Governing Legislation

British Columbia	Part 2 of the Small Business Venture Capital Act, RSBC 1996, c. 429, as amended (effective March 28, 2003).
Nova Scotia	Equity Tax Credit Act, SNS 1993, c. 3, part I, as amended, and section 37 of the Income Tax Act, RSNS 1989, c. 217, as amended.
Newfoundland and Labrador	Income Tax Act, 2000, SNL 2000, c. I-1.1, as amended, section 46, and Direct Equity Tax Credit Regulations 26/01, OC 2001-255.
Maine	Maine Revised Statutes, title 10, section 1100-T (eligibility for tax credit certificates) and title 36, section 5216-B (tax credit). Title 5, section 13070-J requires that annual reports of various state incentive programs, including the seed capital tax credit, be submitted to the legislature.
Missouri	Missouri Revised Statutes, title X, sections 135.400-135.430.
Iowa	2002 Iowa Acts, c. 1006, effective February 28, 2002, and applying retroactively to tax years beginning on or after January 1, 2002, introducing Iowa Code chapter 15E.
Indiana	Indiana Code 6-3.1-24, enacted by PL 192-2002, effective January 1, 2003.

Eligible Investors

British Columbia	Individuals (including RRSPs and RRIFs) and corporations that maintain a permanent establishment in British Columbia at any time in the year.
Nova Scotia	Individuals (including RRSPs).

Newfoundland and Labrador	Individuals (including RRSPs) and corporations (added in the 2003 budget).
Maine	Individuals, partnerships, trusts, limited liability companies (LLCs), corporations or other legal business entities. In the case of flowthrough entities (e.g., partnerships, trusts, or LLCs that elect to be so treated), the individual shareholders, members, partners, or beneficiaries are considered the investors.
Missouri	Individuals, partnerships, financial institutions, trusts, or corporations.
Iowa	Individuals. Credits may not be claimed for investments made by flowthrough entities.
Indiana	Any taxpayer (individual or entity that has any state tax liability). In case of passthrough entities that do not have any state tax liability, the individual shareholders, members, or partners are entitled to a tax credit pro rata on the basis of distributive income.

Nature of Investment

British Columbia	One class of shares without par value and with no special rights or restrictions; may not carry 50% or more of the votes for election of the directors.
Nova Scotia	Voting common shares.
Newfoundland and Labrador	Common shares.
Maine	Any investment (debt or equity) that is at risk (i.e., whose repayment entirely depends on the success of business operations). Must be unsecured and not guaranteed.
Missouri	Unsecured debt, unsecured loan, or equity.
Iowa	Equity.
Indiana	Debt or equity capital (no restrictions) provided to a qualified Indiana business after December 31, 2003.

Nature of Incentive

British Columbia	30% tax credit for individuals and corporations.
	For individuals, credits are refundable. For corporations, unused credits may be carried forward 4 years.
	See further below, under the heading "Maximum Tax Credit/ Maximum Investment."
Nova Scotia	30% tax credit.
	Unused credits may be carried back 3 years and forward 7 years.

Newfoundland and Labrador	20% or 35% tax credit, depending on where the business spends the proceeds of investment. The lower credit applies to qualified business activity in North East Avalon.
	Unused credits may be carried back 3 years (though not prior to 2000) and forward 7 years.
Maine	40% tax credit (increased from 30% in 2000); between July 1, 2002 and June 30, 2003 and after June 30, 2005, 60% tax credit if the investment is made in a high unemployment area.
	Credits realized equally over 4 years; however, for credits issued between July 1, 2003 and June 30, 2005, credits realized over 7 years (15% in each of the first 6 years, 10% in the 7th year).
	In any one year, the credit cannot exceed 50% of state tax payable.
	Unused credits may be carried forward 15 years.
Missouri	40% tax credit; 60% tax credit if the investment is in a Missouri small business in a distressed community; 50% tax credit if the investment is in a community bank or community development corporation.
	Unused credits may be carried forward 10 years.
	Tax credit certificates may be transferred, sold, or assigned by notarized endorsement.
Iowa	20% tax credit.
	Credits cannot be claimed before the third year after the year in which the investment is made.
	Unused credits may be carried forward 5 years.
Indiana	20% tax credit.
	Unused credits may be carried forward indefinitely.

Maximum Tax Credit/Maximum Investment

British Columbia	An individual's maximum annual tax credit is $60,000; credits in excess of $60,000 may be carried forward up to 4 years; any credit unused after 4 years must be refunded, to a maximum of $60,000. The maximum credits apply to the total credit under this program and the BC VCF program (see appendix 6A). In effect, an individual can invest up to $1 million in a 5-year period under the two programs and claim $300,000 of tax credits over 5 years. In any year, if the tax otherwise owing is less than the credit available for the year, the excess credit is refundable.
	A corporation has no maximum credit, but cannot use a credit to create a loss; any unused tax credit may be carried forward 4 years, but unused credits are not refundable.
Nova Scotia	$15,000 (corresponding to maximum investment of $50,000).

Newfoundland and Labrador	$50,000 (corresponding to a maximum investment of $142,857 to $250,000, depending on where the business spends the proceeds of investment).
Maine	An investor cannot invest more than $500,000 ($200,000 for investments made between July 1, 2003 and June 30, 2005) in any one business in a 3-year period.
Missouri	In any one business, the tax credit issued to a single taxpayer may not be less than $1,500 nor more than $100,000 in the aggregate (corresponding to a maximum investment of $250,000).
	No maximum for investments in Missouri small businesses in distressed communities, community banks, or community development corporations.
Iowa	The maximum tax credit for investment in a qualifying business is $50,000 (corresponding to a maximum investment of $250,000). An investor and all affiliates (spouse, child, or sibling or a corporation, partnership, or trust in which the investor has a controlling equity interest or exercises management control) may claim tax credits for no more than five different investments in five different qualifying businesses (i.e., the maximum credit for an investor and all affiliates is $250,000 per year).
Indiana	None (although there is a maximum tax credit per qualified business: see below, under the heading "Limit on Amount Raised by Each Eligible Business for Which a Tax Credit Is Available").

Eligible Businesses

British Columbia	An eligible business corporation (EBC) is a corporation that has no more than 100 employees, pays 75% of its wages and salaries to employees regularly in the province, and has equity capital of at least $25,000. An EBC must be substantially engaged in prescribed business activities in British Columbia: manufacturing and processing; a destination tourist resort (if more than 50% of its gross revenue comes from tourists); research and development of proprietary technologies including services directly associated with the export of technology; an activity carried on outside Victoria or Vancouver that promotes community diversification; or development for commercial exploitation of interactive digital media products for various purposes. Certain activities are excluded: natural resource exploration or extraction; financial services; real estate development or management; agricultural activities; retail or commercial services other than those listed; restaurant or food services; and leasing property for personal use.
Nova Scotia	An eligible business is a corporation that has fewer than 500 employees, pays at least 25% of its salaries or wages in Nova Scotia, has assets of less than $25 million, and uses all or substantially all of its assets in an active business. The business cannot be the

professional practice of an accountant, dentist, lawyer, medical doctor, veterinarian, or chiropractor.

Newfoundland and Labrador	An eligible business is a corporation that is incorporated and controlled in Canada, that is not publicly traded, and that has a permanent establishment in Newfoundland, less than $10 million in assets, no more than 50 full-time employees, and at least $25,000 in capital.

The permitted uses of proceeds effectively limit the nature of eligible businesses. See below, under the heading "Use of Proceeds."

Maine	An eligible business must be located in Maine, have gross sales of $3 million or less, and be engaged in certain types of business: manufacturing, developing or applying advanced technologies, providing a product or service where at least 60% of customers are outside Maine and employment functions are predominantly inside Maine, or a business that brings capital into Maine on a permanent basis as determined by the Finance Authority of Maine (FAME). Factors include job creation or sales and/or income tax revenue and bringing new capital into Maine in an amount at least equal to the credit sought within 2 years. In addition, at least one principal owner's principal activity must be operating the business.

Missouri	An eligible business is an independently owned and operated business that is headquartered in Missouri, has annual revenues of $2 million or less, and employs a maximum of 100 employees, at least 80% of whom are in Missouri. The business must be engaged in certain types of activities: manufacturing, processing, or assembling products or conducting research and development. Explicitly excluded businesses are retail sales, real estate, insurance, and professional service organizations.

Iowa	A qualifying business must have its principal business operations in Iowa; have been in operation for 3 years or less; have a net worth not exceeding $3 million; not be engaged primarily in retail sales, real estate, or the provision of health care or other professional services; and secure equity or near equity financing of at least $250,000 within 24 months of the first tax-credit-qualifying investment. In addition, the owner of the qualifying business must have a certain amount of education or business experience.

Indiana	An eligible business is an independently owned and operated business that is a high-growth company entering a new product or process area, has a substantial number of employees in jobs that either require post-secondary education or its equivalent or are highly skilled (based on occupational codes used by the US Bureau of Labor Statistics). The business must be headquartered in Indiana and primarily focused on research and development, technology transfers, the application of new technology, or the development of commerce with the potential to bring substantial capital into Indiana, create jobs, or significantly promote the purpose of the program in some other way. The business must have average annual revenues

of less than $10 million in the 2 years before receiving a qualified investment credit. 50% of the business's employees must reside in, and 75% of its assets must be located in, Indiana. The business must not be engaged in certain prohibited businesses: real estate; real estate development; insurance; professional services of an accountant, lawyer, or doctor; retail sales other than the development or support of electronic commerce; and oil and gas exploration.

Use of Proceeds

British Columbia	Proceeds must not be used for a number of purposes, including: relending, investment outside the province, investment in land, purchasing goods and services from an eligible investor unless at fair market value and in the seller's ordinary course of business, and payment of a debt (except in an emergency).
Nova Scotia	Proceeds must not be used to make loans or acquire securities, except in limited circumstances; and must not be used to pay dividends, repay shareholder loans, or redeem shares.
Newfoundland and Labrador	Proceeds must be spent on a "qualifying business activity" within 2 years. Qualifying business activities include: technology, research and development, aquaculture, forestry and agrifoods, manufacturing, processing, export, import replacement, tourism, and cultural industries in the province. Qualifying business activities do not include: wholesale or retail trade; establishments holding a liquor licence; personal services, business services, or professional practices and trades unless related to tourism activities or export or import activities; real estate marketing and development; mineral resources production; financial services; fish harvesting; and any activity that, in the opinion of the minister, "is not in keeping with the spirit or intent of the program."
Maine	Investment must be used for acquisition, improvement, or maintenance of real property or fixed assets; research and development or working capital; or other uses permitted by the chief executive officer of FAME. Investment must not be used to repay equity investment.
Missouri	Investment must be used for capital improvements, plant, equipment, research and development, working capital for the business, or such other business activity as may be approved by the Department of Economic Development.
Iowa	None specified.
Indiana	None specified.

Application for Registration

British Columbia

The administrator may register a small business that is an "eligible business" as described above.

An EBC must apply for the tax credit within 60 days after the calendar year in which equity capital was raised.

Nova Scotia

A corporation that intends to issue eligible securities must apply for registration. The application must include: financial statements for the preceding year; the corporate constitution; a list of investors, including each investor's name, social insurance number, occupation, and, if applicable, relationship to any current shareholder of the corporation; a business plan indicating the amount of equity to be raised, proposed use of the funds, a summary of major business activities including major revenue sources, and a list of directors of the corporation.

Newfoundland and Labrador

A corporation that intends to issue eligible securities must apply for registration. The application must include: an investment plan containing a detailed description of the corporation's proposed business activities and the proposed use of the capital to be raised by the issue, and significant financial information about the applicant. The application must specify the amount of capital to be raised by the issue and the location of the proposed qualifying business activity.

A certificate of registration is valid for 3 months after it is issued, unless the minister grants an extension.

Maine

An eligible business and its investors must submit an application, which must include: a general description of the business; the amount, source and purpose of the investment; terms and conditions of the investment; and, if the business has more than 10 employees, an employment plan. The application must also contain "such provisions as the Chief Executive Officer may require releasing [FAME] from any suits or claims arising out of the investment."

Missouri

An eligible business must submit an application for conditional approval. The application must include: a general description of the business; the amount of proposed investment and the tax credits requested; the proposed use of funds and timing of the project; and the estimated economic impact of the project (number of jobs created, estimated wage scales, and major job classifications).

Tax credit certificates are issued at the request of the qualified investor. The request shall be acknowledged under oath by the investor making the request for a tax credit.

Iowa

A taxpayer making an equity investment must submit an application to the Iowa Capital Investment Board (ICIB) by March 31 of the year following the year of investment. The qualifying business must submit information to the ICIB within 120 days of the issuance of qualifying investments, including: a general description of the business; the location of principal business operations; a balance sheet as of the close of the most recent month or quarter; a list of all shareholders who initially qualify for the credit; and a "certificate of existence of a business plan for the qualifying business which details the business's growth strategy, management team, production/ management plan, marketing plan, financial plan and other standard elements of a business plan."

Indiana	A business must apply to be certified on a form prescribed by the Department of Commerce. The application must include: general information about the corporation; a brief narrative history of corporation including business operations and product market; employment information; a projection whether the workforce will increase; and a statement whether the business will make a capital investment in the state.

Restrictions on Relationship Between Eligible Investor and Eligible Business

British Columbia	An investor (together with certain specified persons) cannot have voting control of the EBC (except in limited circumstances, as authorized by the administrator, when the EBC is in financial difficulty).
Nova Scotia	None, but there must be a minimum of three investors.
Newfoundland and Labrador	None.
Maine	Principal owners (any person who controls the business or is involved in the day-to-day operation of the business as a full-time professional activity—businesses must designate shareholders owning more than 50% of the stock as principal owners) and spouses are not eligible for tax credits. Immediate family members (parents, siblings, children, and respective spouses) of principal owners are not eligible if they already have an ownership interest in the business.
	Investors applying for the tax credit must collectively own less than one-half of the business.
Missouri	Principal owners (one or more persons who own an aggregate of 50% or more of the Missouri small business and who are involved in the operation of the business as a full-time professional activity), their spouses, and relatives within the third degree of consanguinity or affinity) are not eligible.
	Investors applying for tax credits must collectively own less than 50% of the business (taking into account investments for which credits are claimed).
Iowa	A person who is the current or previous owner, member, or shareholder of a qualified business is not eligible.
Indiana	None.

Holding Period

British Columbia	5 years.
Nova Scotia	4 years.
Newfoundland and Labrador	5 years.
Maine	An investment must be at risk for a minimum of 5 years. An investor can sell within the 5-year period, but a purchaser is not entitled to a tax credit.
	During the 5-year period, the investor may receive "a reasonable return on the investment from the business in the form of royalties, stock, stock options or warrants, interest, dividends or other form of return not intended to be a repayment of principal."
Missouri	An investment must be at risk for a minimum of 5 years. An investor can sell within the 5-year period, but a purchaser is not entitled to a tax credit.
Iowa	None specified.
Indiana	None specified.

Limit on Amount Raised by Each Eligible Business for Which a Tax Credit Is Available

British Columbia	$5 million.
Nova Scotia	None.
Newfoundland and Labrador	$700,000.
Maine	$5 million ($1 million for investments between July 1, 2003 and June 30, 2005).
Missouri	Minimum $5,000, maximum $1 million.
Iowa	None.
Indiana	$2.5 million.

Government Expenditure Limits

British Columbia	Aggregate tax credits cannot exceed $12 million annually. The limit is increased by $3 million if venture capital corporations (VCCs) invest outside Vancouver or Victoria, and by $5 million if VCCs invest in the development of interactive digital media products in British Columbia.
	The limits are shared with the BC VCF program (see appendix 6A).
Nova Scotia	Although permitted by legislation, none prescribed.
Newfoundland and Labrador	$1 million annually (at which point the minister may suspend the issuance of certificates of registration).

Maine	Aggregate of $2 million up to and including 1996; $3 million up to and including 1997; $5 million up to and including 1998; $8 million up to and including 2001; $11 million up to and including 2004; $20 million up to and including 2005; $23 million up to and including 2006; $26 million up to and including 2007; maximum $30 million thereafter.
	The limits are shared with the Maine PVCF program (see appendix 6B).
Missouri	$13 million. At least $4 million must go to investments made in distressed communities.
	Maximum 20% of credits in any one year for investments in community banks or community development corporations.
Iowa	$10 million. Cannot exceed $3 million for the fiscal period beginning July 1, 2002; $3 million for the fiscal period beginning July 1, 2003; and $4 million for the fiscal period beginning July 1, 2004. If the annual maximum is exceeded, credits are granted on a first-come, first-served basis.
	The limits are shared with the Iowa VCF program (see appendix 6B).
Indiana	$10 million per year (if the maximum is exceeded, credits are granted on a first-come, first-served basis).

Sunset

British Columbia	None specified.
Nova Scotia	December 31, 2006.
Newfoundland and Labrador	None specified.
Maine	None specified (although subject to aggregate expenditure limit).
Missouri	None specified (although subject to aggregate expenditure limit). $13 million expended by 1999; no further funding has been provided.
Iowa	None specified (although subject to aggregate expenditure limit).
Indiana	December 31, 2008.

Notes

1   British Columbia, Nova Scotia, and Newfoundland and Labrador. New Brunswick introduced similar legislation in 1999, although it has not yet been proclaimed into force: Equity Tax Credit Act, c. E-9.4; royal assent March 12, 1999. The New Brunswick legislation was passed shortly before a provincial election in June 1999, at which time a Conservative government replaced the former Liberal government. The New Brunswick Ministry of Finance is currently evaluating the legislation, and no decision has been made whether to proclaim it in force. A number of key features of the legislation require implementation through regulations, none of which has been drafted. Quebec introduced an angel tax credit in 1992 effective January 1, 1993. Although the legislation governing the conditions of eligibility remain in force (An Act To Promote the Capitalization of Small and Medium-Sized Businesses, RSQ, c. A-33.01 (originally SQ 1992, c. 46)), the tax credit was repealed from the Taxation Act effective May 9, 1995 by SQ 1995, c. 63, section 177.

2   Quebec provides a tax credit for equity investment in qualifying public Canadian corporations (a public corporation whose central management is in Quebec or that pays more than half of its payroll to Quebec residents). The amount of the tax credit varies depending on the size of the corporation. However, because the corporation must be publicly listed, the tax credit is excluded from discussion in this study. For further information, see Lawrence Teltscher, "Small Business Financing," in *Income Tax and Goods and Services Tax Considerations in Corporate Financing*, 1992 Corporate Management Tax Conference (Toronto: Canadian Tax Foundation, 1993), 6:1-67, at 6:59-63.

3   See chapter 3, under the heading "Preferential Treatment of Capital Losses from Small Business Securities."

4   For example, the VCF tax credits in Nova Scotia and Iowa apply to individuals who invest in community-based VCFs. One important distinction between the angel capital tax credit and VCF tax credit programs in Canada is that a provincial tax credit or other form of assistance provided to an investor for direct investment in a business will reduce the investor's adjusted cost base of the investment for federal income tax purposes: subparagraph 53(2)(k)(i) of the Income Tax Act, RSC 1985, c. 1 (5th Supp.), as amended. However, specifically excluded from this cost base grind is prescribed assistance received for investment in a prescribed venture capital corporation or a prescribed labour-sponsored venture capital corporation (the primary venture capital fund regimes in Canada). The community-based VCFs in Nova Scotia are prescribed venture capital corporations: regulation 6700(a)(xiv) under the Income Tax Act.

5   As far as I am aware, few other states offer such incentives.

6   The difference between the three delivery mechanisms is considered in chapter 6, in the context of VCF tax credit programs, under the heading "Evaluation of VCF Tax Credit Programs: Eligible Investors and Nature of Investment."

7   See infra note 8.

8   A comprehensive review of the securities regulation governing private financings is beyond the scope of this study, although a few comments are warranted. Securities regulation is under provincial jurisdiction in Canada and both state and federal jurisdiction in the United States. In general, any issue of securities to the public

is subject to extensive (and costly) information disclosure requirements. However, most jurisdictions provide exemptions for private business financings if certain conditions are met. The scope of these exemptions has an effect on the cost of venture capital to private businesses as well as on the spectrum of potential love and angel investors whom these businesses can solicit for investment purposes. For an overview of the most relevant exemptions in the United States, see Louis Loss and Joel Seligman, *Fundamentals of Securities Regulation*, 3d ed., vol. 3, rev. (New York: Little Brown, 1995) and *2000 Supplement* (Gaithersberg, NY: Aspen Law and Business, 2000), 1326-1461.

Most jurisdictions exempt private companies from prospectus requirements. A private company, by definition, is a company that does not offer its securities to the public. However, "public" may not be defined for this purpose, leaving the scope of this general prospectus exemption uncertain. For example, under Ontario's Securities Act, RSO 1990, c. S.5, as amended, a private company is defined in section 1(1) as a company where the right to transfer shares is restricted, the number of shareholders cannot exceed 50, and any invitation to the public to subscribe for its securities is prohibited. "Invitation to the public" is not defined, and the Ontario Securities Commission (OSC) has interpreted the phrase broadly: see, for example, *Re Shelter Corporation of Canada Ltd.*, [1977] OSCB 6 (OSC). Not only must the potential investor be in no need of a prospectus, but there must be a common bond or pre-existing relationship with the issuer. In the United States at the federal level, section 4(2) of the Securities Act of 1933, Pub. L. no. 73-22, enacted on May 27, 1933, c. 38, title I; 48 Stat. 74, provides simply that the registration requirements do not apply to "transactions by an issuer not involving any public offering." The Securities and Exchange Commission (SEC) and the courts have interpreted this provision to require that the offering involve sophisticated offerees and purchasers (that is, knowledgeable investors) who have access to the same kind of information that a registered offering would provide, and the offering be conducted in a non-public manner: see, for example, *SEC v. Ralston Purina Co.*, 346 US 119 (1953).

Because of the broad wording of the "private company" exemption and the uncertainty of its application, many companies will rely on more specific exemptions and use the private company exemption as a backstop. Few venture investments could safely rely on a vague private company exemption: perhaps some love capital investments, but not most angel capital investments. Accordingly, such investments would generally have to rely on more specific exemptions contained in the legislation.

In determining the scope of the more specific exemptions to prospectus (or prospectus-like) requirements, the government must balance competing objectives: protecting investors by requiring full disclosure of information considered necessary to make informed investment decisions (the primary mandate of securities legislation), and promoting investment in small businesses without imposing significant financing costs for such businesses (considered desirable for economic growth, and the objective of tax incentives for angel capital investment). Securities issued to "sophisticated investors" are often exempted because these investors are considered to have sufficient knowledge and experience in financial and business matters to evaluate the merits and risks of a potential investment and will independently seek the information required to evaluate the investment. Financial institutions, governments, corporations with significant assets, and wealthy individuals are often included in the list of sophisticated investors. The asset base of the corporation or the wealth of the individual essentially acts as a proxy for knowledge and expertise. However, the minimum size of the asset base or wealth of the individual specified in securities regulations varies among jurisdictions. Even so, it is debatable whether a particular amount (or any amount) is an appropriate proxy for knowledge and expertise.

Asset-base and individual-wealth exemptions assume that certain investors do not need the protection generally offered by securities legislation. However, exemptions that focus solely on the size of the securities offering of a small business without regard to the personal characteristics of potential investors or the size of their investment are more problematic.

The history of recent amendments to Ontario's securities legislation highlights the difficulties in balancing the competing objectives of promoting full disclosure and promoting investment in SMEs. In 1994, the OSC established the Task Force on Small Business Financing "to review, and make recommendations in respect of, the Ontario legislative and regulatory framework governing the raising of equity capital by SMEs from sources other than governments and financial institutions." The task force published its final report in October 1996 (Ontario Securities Commission, Task Force on Small Business Financing, *Final Report* (Toronto: Queen's Printer for Ontario, October 1996)), and in 2001 the OSC implemented suggestions contained in the report in amending its rules governing exempt distributions: OSC Rule 45-501, "Exempt Distributions," November 23, 2001. The previous exemptions—the private company exemption, the private placement exemption, and the seed capital exemption—focused primarily on the financial wherewithal of investors as a proxy for their expertise. Even the seed capital exemption, under which no more than 50 prospective purchasers could be solicited and no more than 25 could purchase securities, imposed restrictions on advertising (since no more than 50 prospective purchasers could be solicited) and required that each purchaser have sufficient net worth and investment experience to be able to evaluate the information about the investment provided by the issuer. On the basis of the task force report, the previous exemptions were replaced by two new exemptions: the "closely-held business issuer" and the "accredited investor" exemptions.

The "accredited investor" exemption is an exemption for sophisticated investors. There are 27 classes of accredited investors, including financial institutions, governments, and pension funds. A company, limited partnership, or trust is also accredited if it shows net assets of at least $5 million on its most recent financial statements. An individual is accredited if he or she owns financial assets (cash and securities) with a realizable value net of liabilities (other than tax) exceeding $1 million or if the individual's net income before taxes in each of the preceding two years exceeded $200,000 ($300,000 if combined with the income of the individual's spouse).

The "closely-held issuer" exemption permits an issuer to raise a maximum of $3 million from not more than 35 persons, exclusive of accredited investors and employees, without regard to the sophistication or qualifications of the investors. The issuer is not permitted to incur selling or promotional expenses in connection with the issuance, except for services performed by a registered dealer. The only "protection" provided to unsophisticated investors is contained in an information statement, similar to form 45-501F3, that must be provided to investors at least four days before the trade. Form 45-501F3 spells out the risks of small business investments and provides some guidelines for evaluating such investments. It states in part (in bold capitalized letters): "Never make a small business investment that you cannot afford to lose in its entirety."

9   Joshua Lerner, "'Angel' Financing and Public Policy: An Overview" (1998) vol. 22, no. 6-8 *Journal of Banking & Finance* 773-83, at 780.

10 See chapter 3, at notes 263 through 268 and accompanying text.

11 See appendix 5A, the description of Maine under the heading "Restrictions on Relationship Between Eligible Investor and Eligible Business."

12 Nova Scotia's legislation appears to allow a corporation to register any class of shares for the credit, except in the case of a community economic development corporation or a corporation that intends to issue shares only to arm's-length employees (in which cases the shares must be common shares). However, according to the Nova Scotia Ministry of Finance, in practice the only type of shares that have been registered for the tax credit have been common shares.

13 See chapter 1, at note 29 and accompanying text.

14 Some administrative costs may be entailed in monitoring the transfer of tax credits and ensuring that they are claimed by the appropriate taxpayer. US states with VCF programs that offer transferable tax credits generally issue a tax credit certificate to each qualified investor who has provided the state with proof of investment. The certificate is then filed with the investor's tax return. When tax credits are assigned or sold, appropriate transfer forms must be filed with the government agency responsible for the program and a new tax credit certificate is issued to the transferee.

15 See chapter 6, at notes 147 and 148 and accompanying text.

16 The location may be based on the corporation's head office, location of employees, or location of assets.

17 In general, financial services and real estate development businesses have sufficient assets that can be pledged as collateral. In some cases, for social policy reasons, these businesses may be included if they provide financial services or low-cost housing in economically depressed areas—that is, where their business risks are greater and provide some social return to the state or province.

18 See, generally, AnnaLee Saxenian, *Regional Advantage: Culture and Competition in Silicon Valley and Route 128* (Cambridge, MA: Harvard University Press, 1994).

19 In Maine's seed capital tax credit program, the application for the tax credit, which must be submitted by the business seeking funding and the investors seeking the credit, "shall contain such provisions as the Chief Executive Officer [of the Finance Authority of Maine] may require releasing the Authority from any suits or claims arising out of the investment." (Finance Authority of Maine, 94-457, c. 307, rule 2.D.) Similarly, the tax certificate issued by the Iowa Capital Investment Board must contain the following statement: "The Iowa Capital Investment Board has not recommended or approved this investment or passed on the risks of such investment. Investors should rely on their own investigation and analysis and seek investment, financial, legal and tax advice before making their own decision regarding investment in this enterprise." (Iowa Capital Investment Board, rule 123-2.6(15E), adopted November 11, 2002, effective January 1, 2003.)

20 Maine Code, title 5, c. 383, section 13070-J requires the Department of Economic and Community Development to submit various annual reports to the legislature. Before July 1, 2002, there was no specific obligation to report on the seed capital tax credit program. In 2002, section 13070-J.4.D was added to the legislation (by PL 2002, c. 642, section 3):

> D. The department shall report by October 1st annually to the Legislature the following: . . .
>
> (2) The activities in the State, in the aggregate, of businesses receiving funds through the Maine Seed Capital Tax Credit program, including the following:
>
> (a) The total amount of tax credit certificates issued by the Finance Authority of Maine;
>
> (b) The total amount of private investment;
>
> (c) Total employment;
>
> (d) The total number of jobs created;
>
> (e) The total number of jobs retained;
>
> (f) Total payroll; and
>
> (g) Total annual sales.
>
> The Finance Authority of Maine shall provide the department with the information collected in accordance with Title 10, section 1100-T, subsection 6 and assist in the preparation of this report.

21 This figure is based on aggregate income tax revenue, based on the companies' payrolls, and sales tax revenue; it does not include sales tax revenue generated from one-time capital expenditures.

22 Finance Authority of Maine, "Maine Seed Capital Tax Credit Program: Results of FAME Survey Conducted During 2000/2001," issued January 31, 2002 (unpublished). I am grateful to the chief executive officer of FAME for providing me with a copy of the report.

23 During most of the program's existence, it seems that FAME was relatively inexpensive to run because the qualifications for the tax credit were straightforward and the qualified investment consisted almost exclusively of common stock. In many cases, applications could be turned around by FAME within 24 hours. Now, applications take longer to administer because the rules governing the program are more detailed and the investments have become more sophisticated. (Telephone conversation with the chief executive officer of FAME, September 30, 2002.)

24 Supra note 22.

25 The survey suggests that the amount of corporate taxes "could vary greatly based on historical profitability, but clearly also contributes to offsetting tax-credits."

26 The multiplier effects are indirect and induced effects of the direct expenditure, such as additional taxes generated through jobs created in other businesses and additional state sales taxes paid by other businesses as a result of expanded activity within the state's economy. See further chapter 6, at note 168 and accompanying text.

27 Nova Scotia, Department of Finance, *Nova Scotia Tax Credit Review: Phase I Report* (Halifax: Nova Scotia Department of Finance, April 2000) and *Nova Scotia Tax Credit Review: Phase II Report* (Halifax: Nova Scotia Department of Finance, March 2001) (both reports are available from the Nova Scotia Ministry

of Finance Web site: http://www.gov.ns.ca/finance/publish/taxcredit/index.htm). The cost-benefit analysis includes the amount invested in small businesses through community economic development corporations.

28   The report justifies the assumption on the basis that 75 percent of the respondents to the Ministry of Finance survey indicated that they would not have started a company or expanded operations without the credit. The survey, which was included in the *Phase I Report*, was sent to all companies certified from inception until 1998 (197 companies) and had a 25 percent response rate (49 companies).

29   For example, Missouri's angel capital tax credit had authorized funding from 1993 to 1998. Under the original program, investors benefited from a 30 percent tax credit for investment in qualified businesses. The original funding was capped at $5 million. The program was not particularly well used until the tax credit was increased to 40 percent effective January 1, 1997. More than half of the original $5 million was expended in the 1998 fiscal year (July 1, 1997 to June 30, 1998). During the 1998 legislative session, the Missouri Department of Economic Development requested additional funding for the program. Funding was renewed effective January 1, 1999 with an additional $8 million that could be allotted in tax credits. The renewed program provided an enhanced tax credit of 60 percent for investment in qualified small businesses located in "distressed communities" (the tax credit remained at 40 percent for investment outside distressed communities). From January 1, 1999 to July 31, 1999, 25 businesses, mostly located in distressed communities, were qualified to issue tax credit certificates. The full $8 million of additional funding was exhausted during this seven-month period.

       Since 1999, no further funding for the program has been appropriated. Although the cost of the program has been relatively low, it would be beneficial, particularly if additional funding is sought, to determine the extent to which the state has benefited from the program. Evidently, no cost-benefit analysis has been undertaken.

30   Similar concerns arise in any cost-benefit analysis of any venture capital program. See, for example, the discussion in chapter 6 of the cost-benefit analyses that have been undertaken of various labour-sponsored venture capital corporation (LSVCC) programs in Canada and certified capital company (CAPCO) programs in the United States.

6

Tax Incentives for Investment in Venture Capital Funds*

On the surface, the most significant distinction between the formal venture capital industries in Canada and the United States is the importance of tax incentives and government-controlled venture capital funds (VCFs) to the Canadian venture capital industry. Labour-sponsored venture capital corporations (LSVCCs), virtually all of whose capital is raised on the basis of federal and provincial tax credits, manage over 36 percent of all formal venture capital in Canada; government funds manage another 9 percent. In effect, government expenditure is responsible for almost half of all capital under management in the Canadian formal venture capital industry. In contrast, private VCFs manage over 80 percent of the capital in the US industry. Digging below the surface, though, government incentives play an important role in increasing the geographic diversity of the US venture capital industry. The US venture capital statistics do not include (or, in the case of investment in private VCFs by funds of funds, do not sufficiently distinguish) state-sponsored VCFs or other venture capital investment entities that benefit from state tax incentives. While these funds account for an insignificant amount of capital under management in terms of the overall size of the industry in the United States, they are very important to individual states given the geographic concentration of private VCFs along the Atlantic and Pacific coasts. Historically, the US small business investment company (SBIC) program, which was introduced in 1958 and is administered by the federal Small Business Administration (SBA), was the first government-sponsored VCF program in North America. It played an important role as a catalyst in the evolution of the fledgling US formal venture capital industry for over 20 years and remains important today as the primary venture capital investment vehicle for banks. The SBIC program is considered in more detail in chapter 8.

The US formal venture capital industry is large, by any standards. However, it is a mistake to generalize about a "US" venture capital industry because relatively little of the country, in terms of geographic area, benefits from that industry. Furthermore, the increasing size of private VCFs and their propensity for shorter-term commitments has prompted state governments to promote investment in VCFs that concentrate on seed capital investments with longer expected

---

* Unless otherwise stated, US monetary amounts are in US dollars and Canadian montary amounts are in Canadian dollars.

holding periods. In other words, the evolution of the US private venture capital industry has not eliminated all gaps in the financing of small and medium-sized enterprises (SMEs); it has reduced the gaps to particular geographic areas (that is, much of the country outside certain areas) and to particular stages of investment, particularly seed and startup capital.

As a result of the limited geographic scope of venture capital investing, many US states and Canadian provinces (with the financial support of the Canadian federal government in some instances) have adopted programs to increase venture capital investment as a means of creating quality jobs and new wealth and fostering economic development. Government programs aim to educate both entrepreneurs and potential investors about venture capital investing and to facilitate contact between entrepreneurs and investors (by supporting the development of angel capital networks or sponsoring venture capital fairs). These elements of government programs are considered in chapter 8. Beyond these elements, state and provincial governments have also become involved in creating a more localized venture capital industry focusing on earlier-stage, longer-term investment in the jurisdiction. Some programs are tailored to a particular industry or sector, perhaps one not generally attractive to private venture capitalists. Other programs have a wider scope, seeking to develop a venture capital industry where one has not previously existed. For some jurisdictions, the venture capital program is a key element of the government's efforts to diversify its economy. For example, the desire for diversification underlay the introduction of Louisiana's certified capital company program in 1983 (to reduce the state's economic reliance on the oil and gas industries), Michigan's Venture Capital Fund in 1983 (to counteract unemployment caused by the decline in the automotive industry), and Kansas's certified capital formation company regime in 2001 (to reduce the state's reliance on agriculture).[1]

The primary programs through which state or provincial governments can facilitate formal venture capital investment are:

- government-funded and -managed VCFs;
- government investment in private VCFs; and
- tax credits for private investment in VCFs.

A review of programs employed by US states and Canadian provinces demonstrates the variety of programs that have been used, are in use, or are proposed.[2] This chapter focuses on the third type of program, the use of tax credits to stimulate private investment in VCFs. There are a variety of VCF structures for which tax incentives are provided by Canadian provinces and US states. The predominant structure that benefits from tax incentives in Canada, at both the federal and provincial level, is the LSVCC. There is no structure in the United States that has comparable appeal. The most common structure, in terms of the number of states that have adopted a VCF tax credit program, is the certified capital company (CAPCO). This chapter examines the historical development of these two programs, including the motivations behind their introduction. The salient features of various VCF tax credit programs used in Canada and the

United States, including the LSVCC and CAPCO programs, are summarized in appendixes 6A through 6D. Because these programs operate in both countries at a subnational level and vary both within and between countries while sharing many common elements, the salient features of the various programs are easiest to compare and contrast in tabular format.

This chapter evaluates all of the VCF programs, including the LSVCC and CAPCO programs. There is certainly some merit to government programs that foster the development of VCFs, as opposed to tax credit programs for direct investment in small businesses (considered in chapter 5), because the venture capital firms that manage VCFs play an important role in alleviating the information asymmetries that cause the funding gap faced by small businesses. However, the design of VCF programs must ensure that the venture capital firms function efficiently—in other words, firms managing VCFs that benefit from tax incentives must be driven by the same business judgments and behaviours as those driving venture capital firms that manage VCFs which receive no benefit. If the primary factor motivating investment in a VCF is generous tax incentives—if the government is assuming a significant part of the risk of the investment—fund managers have little incentive to perform their role efficiently by evaluating potential investments in detail and closely monitoring investments in order to maximize fund performance. In my view, this is a notable deficiency of the LSVCC and CAPCO programs. Various studies of the LSVCC and CAPCO programs support this conclusion. Some of these studies are reviewed following the evaluation of VCF programs.

This chapter concludes with a novel approach in VCF programs adopted by a number of states: the use of tax credits to *guarantee* investment in a state-sponsored fund of funds that invests in private VCFs. This is commonly referred to as the Oklahoma program, after the state where it was introduced. Elements of these programs warrant careful consideration in Canada, particularly as a vehicle through which to attract pension fund investment.

Taxation of Limited Partnership Venture Capital Funds: A Primer

Before reviewing the various VCF programs, it is useful to have an understanding of the manner in which limited partnerships are taxed in Canada and the United States and of the problems associated with their taxation in the venture capital industry. The predominant organizational form of private VCFs in both countries is the limited partnership because it is treated as a flowthrough entity for tax purposes. In the United States, limited liability companies (LLCs) are also being used as an organizational form for private VCFs because they can be treated as flowthrough entities.[3] Both taxable and tax-exempt taxpayers can invest in the same flowthrough entity without effectively penalizing the tax-exempt investors. In contrast, a VCF structured as a corporation is subject to tax (unless the tax legislation specifically exempts the particular corporation from taxation),[4] thus creating a tax cost for tax-exempt shareholders and an element of double taxation for taxable shareholders.

This section considers the taxation of limited partnerships. For US tax purposes, LLCs and LLPs that elect to be treated as partnerships[5] are taxed in the same manner as limited partnerships. Accordingly, reference in this section to limited partnerships includes, for US tax purposes, LLCs and LLPs.

In both Canada and the United States, a partnership (including a limited partnership) is not subject to tax. Income (or loss) and capital gains (or capital losses) are computed as if the partnership is a separate entity with its own fiscal period, and each partner is subject to tax on the partner's respective share of the income or loss for the fiscal period.[6] The cost of the partner's interest in the partnership (sometimes referred to as the partner's "outside basis") is adjusted to reflect the income or loss allocated to the partner. There are two important considerations in the taxation of limited partnerships and their partners that are particularly relevant to VCFs: the characterization for tax purposes of the gains derived by the partnership on the disposition of shares of portfolio companies, and the consequences to the partnership and its partners when shares of portfolio companies are distributed to partners. Each of these issues is considered in turn.

Characterization of Gains on Disposition of Portfolio Company Shares

In general, income is characterized at the partnership level and this characterization applies to each partner.[7] Accordingly, if a limited partnership disposes of shares of a portfolio company, the characterization of the resultant gain or loss as business income or loss or a capital gain or capital loss must first be determined at the partnership level.

United States

In the United States, the characterization of income is relatively straightforward and is identical to that applicable for individuals discussed in chapter 3.[8] Provided that the partnership is not a dealer in securities, as that term is narrowly construed, all gains and losses arising from the disposition of securities of portfolio businesses are treated on capital account for both the partnership and its partners. The general partner's carried interest is therefore assured capital gains treatment. Limited partners are also assured capital gains treatment, and tax-exempt limited partners are generally not subject to unrelated-business-income tax.[9] Non-resident limited partners are not considered to have income effectively connected with the conduct of a trade or business in the United States, provided that the only interests of the partnership are in C corporations (and not S corporations, partnerships, or other passthrough entities).[10]

Canada

The characterization of the gain or loss on the disposition of portfolio company shares is not nearly as straightforward in Canada as it is in the United States. As discussed in chapter 3, the characterization of a gain to an individual, such as an angel investor, who disposes of shares of a portfolio company is not clear. Given the nature of the shares (that is, generally non-dividend-paying) and the involvement of the individual in the portfolio business, a strong argument can be made that the gain or loss is characterized as business profits or loss because the individual is a trader in securities, as that term is construed in Canadian tax law and jurisprudence. For partners in a venture capital limited partnership—both the general partner(s) and limited partners—the matter is complicated by the fact that the partnership, by its very nature, is a relationship among persons carrying on business in common with a view to profit. For limited partners, the matter is also complicated by the expertise and involvement of the venture capital firm acting as general partner.

The characterization issue has a number of repercussions for limited partners, depending on the nature of the limited partner. For limited partners that are Canadian taxpayers, only one-half of a capital gain is subject to tax, while only one-half of a capital loss is deductible, and only against taxable capital gains. Canadian individual taxpayers may benefit from the $500,000 capital gains exemption where the limited partnership disposes of qualified small business corporation shares and may benefit from the angel capital rollover if the venture capital limited partnership is an eligible pooling arrangement.[11] None of these tax preferences applies if the gains from the disposition of portfolio businesses are characterized as business income.

Particular problems arise for two groups of taxpayers that invest in venture capital limited partnerships: charities and public and private foundations; and non-residents. A charity or public foundation may have its registration revoked if it carries on a business that is not a related business of the charity or public foundation,[12] and a private foundation may have its registration revoked if it carries on any business.[13] Thus, a private foundation cannot be a limited partner in a limited partnership that is carrying on business (for tax purposes), regardless of the nature of the income earned by the limited partnership, because the private foundation would be considered to be carrying on business solely by virtue of the ownership of the limited partnership interest.[14] For charities and public foundations, it is doubtful whether an investment business, the management of which is undertaken by an arm's-length general partner, would constitute a related business of the charity.[15] Thus, for Canadian charitable institutions, whether public or private, it may prove impossible to invest in venture capital limited partnerships.

Non-residents face two problems associated with investment in Canadian venture capital limited partnerships: whether they are considered to be carrying on business through a permanent establishment in Canada; and, if so, the application of tax treaty provisions to the gains realized by the venture capital limited partnership on the disposition of portfolio investments.

Intuitively, one could argue that where the primary activity of a partnership is the investment of funds in various portfolio companies (or other business structures), then the "business" of the partnership is the investment of funds, and any gains generated by those investments would be characterized as business income. From a partnership law perspective, the fact that a partnership exists necessarily implies that the partnership is carrying on business with a view to profit. However, "business" for both partnership law and tax law purposes is not a defined term. Commentators have suggested that business has a narrower meaning for tax law purposes than it does for partnership law purposes.[16] *Lindley & Banks on Partnership* suggests (for partnership law purposes) that

> an activity which might not ordinarily be classed as a business, e.g. buying, selling and holding investments, may qualify if it is carried on as a commercial venture; *a fortiori* if a partnership is formed to carry on such an activity.[17]

Smith v. Anderson[18] is cited as authority for this proposition. There, Jessel MR suggested that such activities may qualify as a business if a syndicate is organized to carry on the activity. Even if a partnership is found to exist for common (or civil) law purposes, the characterization of the partnership's income—indeed, whether or not the partnership is carrying on business—for tax purposes is a separate issue. While the common law makes a distinction between business income and property income, the distinction is not nearly as important as it is for tax purposes. Furthermore, the common law notion of "profit" does not make a distinction between capital gains and other income. Arguably, any net income, regardless of its source, would be considered business income for partnership law purposes if the partnership involves some activity or venture of a commercial nature.[19]

Paragraph 96(1)(c) of the Income Tax Act recognizes that partnerships earn income from different sources and can realize capital gains or losses from dispositions of property. Despite this recognition, there is a dearth of case law on whether a partnership can have *no* business income for tax purposes. The determination of whether a business exists is most acute where almost all of the income of the partnership is derived from the disposition of portfolio company shares.[20] However, the investments of a venture capital limited partnership are not restricted to equity. The partnership may make loans to portfolio companies, which loans are often subordinated and often convertible into common shares. Depending on the nature of the businesses in which it invests, especially the amount of tangible assets that could secure a loan, the partnership may invest for convertible debt rather than straight equity, because convertible debt gives the partnership the best of both worlds: greater security if the venture sours, and the ability to participate in the upside if the venture proves lucrative. Arguably, the partnership would be in the business of lending money, even on the narrower tax law definition of business, and the interest income earned on the loan should be characterized as business income rather than income from property. The partnership (that is, the general partner) is not a passive investor in debt securities. Rather, it is more akin to a financial institution: the general partner actively negotiates the terms of the loan and in many cases takes an active position in the portfolio company. It is likely that the venture capital general partner will negotiate representation on the board of directors of the portfolio company and may be actively involved in the day-to-day operations of the company.

Thus, it is highly likely that the venture capital limited partnership is carrying on business for tax purposes. It does not necessarily follow that all of the income of the partnership, particularly the gains and losses realized on the disposition of shares of portfolio companies, is classified as business income. It is not my intention to rehash the tremendous volume of case law and tax literature that addresses the distinction between capital gains and income. Suffice it to say that where the primary—indeed, exclusive—activity of a partnership is the investment of funds in shares of portfolio companies that are highly unlikely to pay dividends, a good argument could be made that for Canadian tax purposes the gains realized on the disposition of the shares by the partnership are business income and not capital gains. This argument is more persuasive when a limited partnership carries on the investment activity, for two reasons. First, as discussed above, a partnership by its nature is considered to be carrying on business and may be so considered for tax purposes. Second, the character of the income to the general partner should be determinative of its character to the partnership as a whole, and hence to the limited partners. The general partner (or manager) of a venture capital limited partnership is generally a venture capital firm (or specific members of that firm) whose business entails managing such partnerships and actively seeking, reviewing, and monitoring investments on behalf of the partnership. It is therefore arguable that the partnership's gains from the disposition of portfolio investments should be recognized on income account for the partnership (and hence the general and limited partners).[21]

Perhaps as a result of this ambiguity, a number of legislative amendments have targeted the uncertain characterization of income earned by certain types of VCFs. Three in particular warrant consideration: amendments to subsection 39(5) to permit LSVCCs (and certain other VCFs) to make a subsection 39(4) election; the addition of section 115.2, applicable to non-resident limited partners of a venture capital limited partnership; and the addition of section 239.1, applicable to certain holding company investors in limited partnerships. Each of these is considered in turn.

Subsection 39(4): The Canadian Securities Election

Taxpayers are permitted to file an election under subsection 39(4) to treat all Canadian securities as capital property, and therefore gains or losses from their disposition on capital account. However, the election is not available to taxpayers listed in subsection 39(5), including non-residents and traders or dealers in securities. In a technical interpretation dated September 15, 1994, the Canada Revenue Agency (CRA) referred to an earlier letter in which it stated that "it is likely that we would consider a venture capital corporation to be a 'trader or dealer in securities,' within the meaning of paragraph 39(5)(a) of the Act, unless the facts clearly indicated that the securities were acquired, not as part of the venture capital corporation's business, but as an adventure in the nature of trade."[22] In a subsequent technical interpretation dated January 31, 1995, the CRA indicated that the same factual determination applied to LSVCCs.[23]

In response to concerns expressed by the venture capital industry about the CRA's published administrative practice, the Ministry of Finance asked the CRA in late 1996 to review its position with respect to the treatment of gains realized by venture capital corporations. In its response, the CRA accepted the position that "a true venture capitalist is not automatically to be considered a trader or dealer in securities as a result of its functions in and by themselves."[24] In a technical interpretation published in 1997, the CRA appeared to soften its position further, stating that "it is a question of fact whether or not an acquisition of securities has been made on income or capital basis and depending on the circumstances of a particular fact situation, an acquisition of certain securities by a [venture capital corporation] on a private placement basis would not, in and of itself, disqualify the venture capital corporation from the 39(4) election."[25]

Perhaps as a result of the ambiguity of these pronouncements, the minister of finance announced in the 1997 budget that subsection 39(5) would be amended to exclude from its application mutual fund trusts and mutual fund corporations, thus permitting such entities to make a subsection 39(4) election. According to the budget documents:

> certain categories of taxpayers (including a trader or dealer in securities) are not entitled to [the subsection 39(4) election]. To remove uncertainty in this regard, the budget also proposes that there be changes to ensure that LSVCCs and other mutual funds can elect to treat gains from the dispositions of Canadian securities as capital gains.[26]

While this amendment permits LSVCCs and other VCFs structured as mutual fund trusts or mutual fund corporations to use a subsection 39(4) election, VCFs that are not so structured—that is, the vast majority of private VCFs, including those structured as limited partnerships—are not covered by the amendments. The characterization of the gains realized by such funds remains an open question. Resident limited partners of a venture capital limited partnership can make an election under subsection 39(4), in which case, by virtue of subsection 39(4.1), each Canadian security owned by the partnership is treated (for the purposes of the election) as if it were owned by the limited partner, and when the security is disposed of by the partnership it is treated as if it were disposed of by the limited partner. In these circumstances, the character of the income to the general partner would not be determinative of its character to the limited partner. However, this election is not available to non-resident limited partners. Nor is it available with respect to foreign securities acquired by the limited partnership (for example, shares of a US SME).

A limited partner carries on the business of the limited partnership, and if the limited partnership has a permanent establishment in Canada, then each limited partner has a permanent establishment in Canada.[27] If a limited partnership is carrying on business for tax purposes, the business would generally be considered to be carried on at the location where the general partner carries on the partnership's business. If the general partner operates from a permanent establishment in Canada, non-resident limited partners would be considered to have a permanent establishment in Canada. Accordingly, a non-resident limited partner of a Canadian limited partnership would generally be considered to be carrying on business through a permanent establishment located in Canada. The limited partner's share of the business income of the limited partnership would be considered taxable income earned in Canada under part I of the Act and would remain subject to tax under Canada's tax treaties as income derived from a permanent establishment in Canada.[28]

Capital gains derived by the limited partnership from the disposition of property may also be subject to tax in Canada. Whether or not a non-resident limited partner's share of such gains is subject to tax under Canada's tax treaties (for example, the Canada-US treaty) depends on whether the property is taxable Canadian property (the threshold requirement for non-resident taxation in Canada)[29] and, if it is, the scope and application of treaty provisions based on article 13(2) of the Model Tax Convention on Income and on Capital developed by the Organisation for Economic Co-operation and Development (the OECD model treaty). Article 13(2) states:

> Gains from the alienation of movable property forming part of the business property of a permanent establishment which an enterprise of a Contracting State has in the other Contracting State, including such gains from the alienation of such a permanent establishment (alone or with the whole enterprise), may be taxed in that other State.

The primary assets of a venture capital limited partnership are the shares of its portfolio companies. The issue is whether the shares of portfolio companies would be considered "movable property forming part of the business property of a permanent establishment."[30] According to the commentary to the OECD model treaty, "movable property" for this purpose means any property other than immovable property and includes both tangible and intangible property.

Concerns about the taxation of US pension plans involved in Canadian venture capital limited partnerships were expressed by the Canadian Venture Capital Association (CVCA) in its submissions prior to the November 2001 federal budget. It is unclear from the submissions whether the concerns arose from the characterization of portfolio gains (income versus capital) or the application of article XIII(2) of the Canada-US treaty (that is, on the assumption that the gains are on capital account). In either case, Canada's jurisdiction to tax depends on the non-resident partner's having a permanent establishment in Canada.

Section 115.2: Non-Residents with Canadian Investment Service Providers

In the absence of a permanent establishment, the foreign partners of a Canadian venture capital limited partnership would not be subject to tax in Canada on gains realized from the disposition of shares of portfolio firms, whether the gains are characterized as business income or as capital gains. Section 115.2 was added to the Act in 2000 in an attempt to achieve this result. It originally provided that, if certain conditions were met, a "qualified non-resident" would not be considered to be carrying on business in Canada solely because it engaged a Canadian firm to provide certain investment management and administration services. However, a partnership was not considered a qualified non-resident unless no member of the partnership was resident in Canada. Section 115.2 was amended in 2002 to provide that a non-resident person will not be considered to be carrying on business in Canada "solely because of the provision to a person, or a partnership of which the person is a member, . . . of designated investment services by a Canadian service provider."[31] The amendment extends the benefit of the provision to partnerships with both resident and non-resident limited partners. However, the provision remains limited to circumstances in which the person or partnership uses the services of a Canadian investment manager. It does not speak to the situation in which the non-resident partner's ties to Canada may be greater—for example, because the general partner of the partnership is resident in Canada.

Even if section 115.2 were further amended to address this limitation, other tax complications cannot be as easily remedied. In particular, a partnership with both resident and non-resident partners is not a "Canadian partnership" under the Income Tax Act. This exclusion has three consequences: all interest and dividends paid to the partnership are subject to withholding tax;[32] a section 116 certificate is required on dispositions by the partnership of taxable Canadian property;[33] and it is not possible to dissolve the partnership on a rollover basis.[34]

Section 253.1: Certain Limited Partners Deemed Not To Carry On Business in Canada

Section 253.1 was added to the Act in 2001 to ensure that certain corporations and trusts, the undertaking of which is limited to investing funds, are not considered to be carrying on business solely because they acquire and hold a limited partnership interest.[35] The provision applies only to unit trusts, mortgage investment corporations, mutual fund corporations, mutual fund trusts, pension fund holding corporations exempt from tax under paragraph 149(1)(o.2), prescribed small-business investment corporations, and prescribed master trusts. It does not benefit non-resident limited partners of Canadian private VCFs structured as limited partnerships.

All three provisions—subsection 39(5), section 115.2, and section 253.1— have their shortcomings. For example, neither subsection 39(5) nor section 253.1 expressly permits Canadian charities (including university endowment funds) or public or private foundations to invest in venture capital limited partnerships (assuming that the partnerships are businesses for tax purposes). Similarly, neither provision applies to non-residents who invest in Canadian venture capital limited partnerships. In fact, the very presence of these provisions suggests that a venture capital limited partnership and its limited partners are carrying on business in connection with the acquisition and disposition of shares of portfolio companies. In the case of charities and public and private foundations, this problem could be amended simply by adding them to the list of entities that benefit from section 253.1.

As a result of the uncertainty surrounding the characterization of portfolio gains of a Canadian venture capital limited partnership and the uncertainty whether the partnership is carrying on business through a permanent establishment in Canada, and despite the amendments to subsection 39(5) and the addition of sections 115.2 and 253.1, it is common practice of Canadian venture capital promoters to establish a parallel limited partnership with a non-resident general partner for all non-resident investors. Although the place of business of the general partner of the parallel fund is not necessarily determinative in establishing that the partnership does not have a permanent establishment in Canada, section 115.2 should ensure that no permanent establishment is found to exist in Canada on the basis of the operations of the Canadian promoters of the structure (who are likely the general partner of the Canadian limited partnership). A parallel fund structure has three other benefits: it limits the withholding requirements on dividends and interest to such income received by the parallel foreign limited partnership; a section 116 certificate is required only for securities disposed of by the foreign parallel fund; and the parallel structure permits the Canadian partnership to wind up and distribute any portfolio company shares to the partners rather than sell the shares (if possible) and distribute the proceeds. More important, the parallel foreign limited partnership, if located in the United States with US limited partners, can transfer the shares of portfolio businesses to its partners at any time on a tax-deferred basis under US domestic law and avoid taxation in Canada. This last point is considered in more detail under the next heading. While the parallel structure thus alleviates the concerns of non-residents regarding their taxation in Canada, the structure creates additional complexities and higher administrative and accounting costs.[36] In addition, the unfamiliarity of the structure may deter US pension fund managers from investing in Canada.

In response to concerns about the taxation of non-resident partners investing in a Canadian limited partnership, the Department of Finance stated in a private letter:

> We have consulted with the [CRA], and can now confirm that its interpretation of the law accords with our understanding of the law: partnerships are not subject to a unique test to determine whether they are carrying on business. The fact that an income earning activity is carried on by a partnership does not, in and by itself, give rise to an assumption that the activity must be a business or that the partnership is carrying on a business. Whether any activity carried on by a partnership constitutes carrying on business is, as in the case of any other entity, always a question of fact. Furthermore, there is no unique test applied to partnerships to determine whether property is held or used in a business.[37]

This most recent statement suggests that, as a practical matter, the CRA has backed away from its earlier published position and accepts that gains derived by venture capital limited partnerships on the disposition of shares of portfolio firms are on capital account and that the partnership is not carrying on business for tax purposes. Unfortunately, the CRA will not give an advance income tax ruling on the characterization of gains (and losses) from the disposition of portfolio company securities or whether the venture capital limited partnership is carrying on business for tax purposes, because both issues involve questions of fact. Thus, while the venture capital industry can take some comfort from the most recent pronouncements of the Department of Finance, as a matter of law, the characterization of the gains realized on the disposition of portfolio securities as capital gains and the suggestion that a venture capital limited partnership is not carrying on business are both problematic and case law would tend to contradict both suggestions. Having said that, I am not aware of any situations in which the CRA has reassessed or threatened to reassess a venture capital limited partnership or its limited partner investors, whether resident or non-resident, on the characterization of its gains from the disposition of portfolio company securities, or, for non-resident limited partners, whether such gains are subject to tax in Canada, although such reassessments were threatened in the early 1980s.[38]

Distribution of Partnership Property to Partners

Both Canada and the United States treat a current distribution of money from a partnership in the same manner. Money distributed to a partner is treated as a return of the partner's investment in the partnership. Therefore, the distribution is tax-free to the partner to the extent that it does not exceed the partner's outside basis; the partner's outside basis is reduced by the amount of the money distributed. If the amount distributed exceeds a limited partner's outside basis, the excess is generally treated as a capital gain.

The manner in which the two countries treat a distribution of property other than money differs significantly.

United States

In the United States, if a partnership makes a current distribution of property (other than money or marketable securities),[39] the partnership is generally treated for tax purposes as a mere extension of its partners. A current distribution of property is not a taxable event to the partner or the partnership (it is a non-recognition transaction).[40] The partnership does not recognize any gain or loss even if the value of the property differs from its cost to the partnership (commonly referred to as the "inside basis"). The partner does not recognize a gain even if the value of the property exceeds the partner's outside basis and does not recognize a loss if the value is less than the partner's outside basis. Rather, the cost of the property to the recipient partner is the property's inside basis to the partnership (unless the inside basis exceeds the partner's outside basis) and the partner's outside basis is reduced by a corresponding amount. If the partnership's inside basis of the property exceeds the partner's outside basis, then the cost to the partner of the property is the partner's outside basis and the partner's outside basis is reduced to zero; no gain is recognized for tax purposes.

One exception to the general non-recognition rule applicable to distributions of property is a distribution of a marketable security.[41] Since 1995, a distribution of a marketable security has been treated in the same manner as a distribution of money. The partnership does not recognize any gain or loss on the distribution. However, the partner receiving the marketable security recognizes a gain to the extent that the value of the marketable security exceeds the partner's outside basis. There are, however, a number of exceptions to the general rule applicable to marketable securities. Two of these exceptions are germane to a VCF structured as a limited partnership. First, a marketable security is excluded (that is, it is treated in the same manner as a distribution of property other than money or marketable securities) if it was not a marketable security when the partnership acquired it and three further conditions are met: (1) the entity that issued the securities had no marketable securities at the time the partnership acquired them; (2) the security was held by the partnership for at least six months before it became marketable; and (3) the partnership distributed the security within five years of the date that it became marketable.[42] These conditions seem tailor-made for the typical VCF structure in the United States: VCFs acquire shares of SMEs that have no actively traded shares; they hold the shares for a relatively long time before they become marketable (that is, the SME makes an initial public offering [IPO] of its shares); and they generally distribute the shares to the limited partners within five years of the shares becoming marketable. The second exception to the general rule applies if the partnership is an investment partnership and the recipient partner is an eligible partner thereof.[43] An investment partnership is a partnership that has never been engaged in a trade or business and substantially all of its assets consist of investment-type assets (money, shares, notes, bonds, debentures, foreign currencies, derivative financial instruments, etc.).[44] An eligible partner is any partner who did not contribute any property to the partnership other than investment-type assets.[45] Thus, in most cases, a US venture capital limited partnership can distribute its assets (that is, shares of portfolio companies) to its limited partners on a tax-deferred basis.

Canada

In contrast to the treatment of partnerships in the United States, a Canadian partnership is treated as a separate entity for tax purposes not only in computing the income of its partners but also with respect to the ownership of partnership property. In most cases, a partnership that transfers property to a partner is deemed to dispose of the property for its fair market value and the partner is deemed to acquire it at its fair market value.[46] Accordingly, the transfer of property to any partner gives rise to income at the partnership level that is attributable to all of the partners. This is the case even if identical property (for example, shares of a portfolio company) is transferred to all partners pro rata on the basis of their profit shares. The only exception is that a partnership can distribute its assets to its partners on a tax-deferred basis when the partnership is dissolved; even then, however, each partner must receive an undivided interest in each property of the partnership.[47]

Although a limited partnership is the typical organizational form of a private sector VCF in both the United States and Canada, the limited partnership structure is much more versatile in the United States than it is in Canada. It is common practice for a US VCF that has successfully exited an investment by taking the portfolio company public through an IPO to distribute the newly listed shares of the company to partners rather than sell the shares and distribute the proceeds. Distributions in kind are preferable for a variety of reasons. One reason is the deferral of tax. If the VCF sells the shares, taxable limited partners as well as the VCF's fund managers (who are entitled to a carried interest) will be taxable in connection with the disposition. If a distribution in kind is made to the limited partners and in satisfaction of the fund managers' carried interest, these taxpayers defer the tax until they ultimately sell the shares. Tax-exempt investors would not be subject to tax if the VCF sold the shares, but a distribution in kind gives these investors flexibility in deciding when to sell their shares.

However, a Canadian limited partnership cannot transfer shares of one investment that it successfully exited through an IPO and continue to hold the shares of other portfolio companies that are not publicly traded. The Canadian venture capital industry has not yet lobbied the Canadian government about this distinction in the tax treatment of partnerships in Canada and the United States. This omission likely stems from the fact that the Canadian industry is still relatively young and is concerned more about raising capital than about dealing with the distribution of publicly traded shares acquired on a successful exit.

Historical Evolution of the LSVCC and CAPCO Programs

Two VCF programs—the LSVCC program in Canada and the CAPCO program in the United States—are given particular attention in this chapter. Although they are not the oldest VCF programs in existence, they have gained some notoriety in their respective countries. Both programs originated in 1983, when Quebec introduced the first LSVCC program and Louisiana introduced the first CAPCO program. The LSVCC program spread to most other provinces shortly after 1985, when the federal government endorsed the program by providing a matching federal tax credit for investors in qualifying provincial LSVCCs. LSVCC programs are now found in seven provinces, with an eighth (Newfoundland and Labrador) possibly following in the near future,[48] and in one of the three territories.

The US CAPCO program does not share the LSVCC's popularity and has not spread to the same degree as LSVCC programs have in Canada. Of the various VCF tax credit programs in existence in the United States, it is the most common, although it did not gain prominence until the late 1990s. Eight states have adopted CAPCO programs since 1997, and numerous other states have considered or are considering adopting similar programs.

This section provides an historical overview of the two programs.

LSVCCs[49]

In 1983, Quebec enacted legislation that established the first LSVCC, the Fonds de solidarité des travailleurs du Québec (FSTQ).[50] The purpose of the legislation was to establish a fund, directed by the Fédération du travailleurs du Québec (FTQ), Quebec's largest trade union, that would invest in Quebec SMEs in order to create, maintain, or preserve jobs and to facilitate the training of employees in economic and financial matters. The genesis of FSTQ was the economic recession of 1981-1983. In Quebec, the labour movement was alarmed by permanent employment losses, plant closures, and production and investment relocation[51] that followed the election of the Parti Québecois government in 1976. Labour leaders became convinced that labour should be more directly involved in the capital markets. In 1982, FTQ (particularly former president Louis Laberge) suggested the idea of a labour-sponsored investment fund as a vehicle for stimulating economic development in Quebec. The proposal received the backing of the Parti Québecois government and some high-profile business and financial leaders at the Sommet du Québec in 1982, and the fund was created by special legislation in 1983. Both the Quebec and federal governments provided seed money in the form of a loan to FSTQ. Each government provided $10 million (the Quebec government in 1984 and the federal government in 1987). These loans were later converted to class G shares, which are non-voting, non-transferable, non-redeemable, and without dividend rights.[52] Originally, individuals resident in Quebec who invested in FSTQ were entitled to a provincial tax credit of 35 percent on the first $3,500 invested in shares of the fund.[53]

In the 1985 federal budget, the minister of finance introduced a number of measures to stimulate venture capital investment, specifically that of registered pension and other retirement plans. The main venture capital incentives introduced in the budget were:

- a matching federal tax credit for individuals who invested in provincial LSVCCs;
- the extension of "qualified investments" for registered retirement savings plan (RRSP) purposes to private corporations engaged in active business and to prescribed venture capital corporations;
- small business investment corporation (CanSBIC) provisions;
- small business investment limited partnership (SBILP) provisions;
- small business investment trust (SBIT) provisions; and
- the three-to-one leveraging of "small business investments" for the purpose of the tax penalty applicable to a retirement fund whose foreign property exceeds 10 percent of the fund's total assets.

The first measure is the focus of this section. The remaining measures are considered in chapter 7.

The introduction of a federal tax credit for investment in LSVCCs[54] proved to be the catalyst that created the largest pool of venture capital in Canada. Given the significance of LSVCCs as a source of venture capital and the cost of the scheme to the federal government and many provincial governments, it is unfortunate that there was no debate surrounding the introduction of the federal tax credit in 1985 or the introduction of a federal LSVCC regime in 1988.

At the time of the 1985 federal budget, only one LSVCC existed in Canada, FSTQ. However, the federal government expected, indeed, "encouraged other provinces to come along with their regimes to encourage labour-sponsored venture capital funds."[55] Over the next 10 years, a number of provinces did so. Some provinces established their own legislative requirements for LSVCCs;[56] others extended a provincial credit to certain federally registered LSVCCs, introduced in the February 1988 federal budget.[57]

When the minister of finance announced the establishment of measures for national LSVCCs, he stated that the credit would be available for investment in LSVCCs "that meet criteria similar to existing criteria applying to [FSTQ]."[58] However, the draft legislation, introduced in a January 12, 1990 press release, included material differences from the Quebec scheme. Two differences are worth noting. First, the federal scheme originally required investors to hold the shares of the LSVCC for a minimum of five years in order to avoid the repayment of the tax credits granted at the time of investment; in contrast, shareholders of FSTQ are required to hold their shares until retirement age, with early redemption permitted only in limited circumstances. Second, the investment requirements imposed on national LSVCCs included a generous startup period of five years,[59] during which the LSVCC was required to invest at least 80 percent of its capital in eligible investments[60] or reserves.[61] This is not a very cumbersome requirement because the LSVCC's investment in reserves can account for most if not all of this 80 percent requirement. Following the startup period, the LSVCC was required to have invested at least 60 percent of its equity in eligible investments in order to avoid deficiency penalties.[62] The first national LSVCC, Working Ventures Canadian Fund Inc., sponsored by the Canadian Federation of Labour, first offered its shares to the public in February 1990. The federal government provided the fund with a total grant of $14.55 million in monthly instalments over the period from 1988 to 1995.[63]

Ontario introduced LSVCC legislation as a followup measure to the New Democratic Party's first budget in April 1991. Like Quebec in the early 1980s, Ontario in the early 1990s was experiencing a severe economic depression. The 1991 budget called for a "new economic strategy based on broad social partnerships" in which government, labour, business, and community groups would participate.[64] The Ontario LSVCC regime was introduced as part of Bill 150. Bill 150 also included legislation governing employee ownership labour-sponsored venture capital corporations (EOLSVCCs) (now contained in part II of the Community Small Business Investment Funds Act).[65] The Ontario LSVCC regime was modelled on the 1988 federal regime. Bill 150 was the subject of substantial debate in the Legislative Assembly, but that debate concentrated primarily on the EOLSVCC regime. Opposition members supported the promotion of venture capital investment generally, but expressed concerns about several features of the proposed LSVCC regime: that the LSVCC must be sponsored by a labour union to the exclusion of other groups of employees (or, indeed, by employees at all); that the government significantly underestimated the tax expenditure involved; that the tax benefit offered to investors was too generous; and that the general body of taxpayers was assuming most of the risk involved. In hindsight, most of the concerns were valid. In particular, the level of investment in LSVCCs and, hence, the government's cost were drastically underestimated.

In 1992, investment in an LSVCC was made much more attractive, from an investor's tax perspective, in two ways. First, effective for 1992 and subsequent years, the maximum federal credit was increased to $1,000, so that the credit was available for up to $5,000 invested in an LSVCC.[66] Second, the tax credit was available directly to the individual investor if the individual's RRSP acquired shares of the LSVCC.[67] Consider an individual in the highest marginal tax bracket (assumed to be about 50 percent, combined federal and provincial) who made a $5,000 contribution to an RRSP that was used to purchase shares of an LSVCC. The RRSP deduction has an after-tax value of $2,500, effectively reducing the cost of the LSVCC shares to $2,500. The individual also received a 20 percent federal tax credit of $1,000 and an equivalent provincial tax credit. Of the $5,000 investment, the individual investor paid, on an after-tax basis, only $500, or 10 percent of the cost, while the federal and provincial governments—that is, the collective body of taxpayers in the province and across Canada—effectively paid the remaining 90 percent.[68]

The impact of these amendments on investment in LSVCCs was significant. Investment in LSVCCs increased from about $70 million for the 1990 taxation year to over $1 billion in 1996. In 1992, investment in LSVCCs doubled from the 1991 levels, and from 1993 to 1995 the amount invested in LSVCCs almost doubled year over year. The success of LSVCCs, especially outside Quebec, was driven by two factors: the generous tax benefits to investors; and very effective marketing campaigns, especially by Working Ventures Canadian Fund. The success of LSVCCs was clearly evidenced by the unprecedented levels of investment during the 1995 and 1996 RRSP seasons.[69]

Following the 1996 RRSP season, it became obvious that the federal and provincial governments would have to cap the level of investment in LSVCCs.[70] It was not simply the amount invested in LSVCCs (and the corresponding cost to the governments) that concerned the governments when planning their 1996 budgets; there were other aspects of the LSVCC schemes that were considered problematic. A number of issues—including the holding-period requirements of investors, the pacing requirements of the LSVCCs, and the consequences to the LSVCC of a failure to meet the pacing requirements—were subject to review. In addition, the impact of the LSVCC regime on the private venture capital industry raised questions about the long-term efficacy of the tax incentives.

One of the primary objectives of the 1996 federal budget amendments was to reduce the amount invested in LSVCCs. Short of eliminating the tax credit completely, the federal government could reduce the amount invested in LSVCCs in four ways: reduce the rate of the tax credit; reduce the total value of the tax credit; lengthen the holding-period requirement; and introduce a "cooling-off period"[71] for taxpayers who redeem shares of LSVCCs. All four means were employed in the 1996 budget amendments. The tax credit was reduced to 15 percent, with a maximum credit of $525 (equivalent to a maximum investment of $3,500). The holding period was lengthened from 5 years to 8 years to bring the holding period more in line with that of a typical venture capital investment (although still less than the typical 10-year life of a US private venture capital limited partnership). Finally, a 3-year cooling-off period was introduced, under which individuals who redeemed their shares of an LSVCC would not be entitled to claim an LSVCC tax credit in the year of redemption or the following two years.

Ontario introduced a number of measures in its 1996 budget, in addition to reducing the rate and maximum amount of the credit. To parallel the federal changes, the Ontario budget extended the holding period from 5 years to 8 years and introduced a 3-year cooling-off period.[72] The province also introduced a provision whereby tax credits would be suspended if an LSVCC failed to meet its investment targets in the time required under the legislation. The province significantly reduced the period in which an Ontario LSVCC was required to meet its investment requirements, and introduced a refundable tax on an Ontario LSVCC that failed to meet or maintain its investment level requirements at the end of a particular taxation year. The tax is designed to recapture the provincial LSVCC tax credit on the amount of the investment shortfall, similar to the federal tax imposed on national LSVCCs.[73] All of the other provinces also reduced the rate and (apart from British Columbia) the amount of the provincial credit and (where applicable) increased the holding-period requirement to 8 years. A number of provinces also introduced a cooling-off period.

The federal government expected to save about $145 million over three years as a result of the 1996 budget amendments.[74] The amount raised by LSVCCs in 1996-97, following the 1996 RRSP season and including the 1997 RRSP season, was about half of the amount raised in 1995.[75] On the basis of this figure, the federal government's tax expenditure in 1996 was about $97.5 million, or $137 million less than its expenditure in 1995.[76] The most significant drop in investment was in Ontario. The two Quebec funds raised about 85 percent of the amounts raised in 1995, whereas the Ontario funds raised about 30 percent of the amounts raised in 1995.[77] The impact of the 1996 budget changes continued through 1997, including the 1998 RRSP season. The capital raised by LSVCCs during 1997-98 (March 1, 1997 to February 28, 1998) was about $504 million, compared with almost $650 million in the previous year and almost $1.2 billion in 1995-96. Both the federal and Ontario budgets in 1997 contained measures to enhance venture capital investment in smaller SMEs, with LSVCCs targeted as a major vehicle for this investment,[78] although the tax credit incentives for investment in LSVCCs remained unchanged.

In 1998, the federal government went back to tinkering with the LSVCC rules. Investment in LSVCCs was still significantly below 1995 levels and below the projections made when the 1996 budget amendments were introduced, and LSVCCs had invested significantly in SMEs in the intervening period. On August 31, the government announced a number of revisions, including an increase in the maximum federal tax credit back to $750 (corresponding to a $5,000 investment) and the elimination of the cooling-off period.[79] It also introduced a number of other minor amendments dealing with the pacing requirements. The backgrounder to the press release stated:

> The federal government introduced a number of changes in its budget of March 6, 1996 to limit tax assistance for individuals investing in LSVCCs. Most provinces adopted similar measures. At that time, LSVCCs had large amounts of capital still to be invested in small and medium-sized enterprises (SMEs) and LSVCCs were also experiencing high growth in the sale of new share capital. Since then, LSVCCs have injected capital into SMEs at an unprecedented pace. According to data provided by Macdonald & Associates Limited, LSVCCs were the most active investors in the Canadian venture capital market during 1996 and 1997, with disbursements totalling almost $1.1 billion. During the same period, amounts raised by many LSVCCs declined substantially, leading to a situation where some LSVCCs have little capital to invest in business in coming years.
>
> Proposals to assist LSVCCs in maintaining their important role of providing venture capital to SMEs, thereby allowing SMEs to continue to maintain and create jobs, are described below.

Most provinces with LSVCC schemes (other than Quebec, whose LSVCC scheme is significantly different from the federal and other provincial schemes) amended their programs accordingly.

The 1998 amendments reflect the continuing reliance on LSVCCs as the backbone of the Canadian venture capital industry. No significant amendments have been made to the various provincial and the federal LSVCC programs since 1998. The Northwest Territories introduced an LSVCC program in 2000.[80] The structure of the program is substantially similar to the structure of provincial programs, except that the tax credits available for investors in a Northwest Territories LSVCC are richer than those provided under the federal and other provincial schemes in two respects. First, individuals are entitled to a credit of 15 percent on the first $5,000 invested plus a 30 percent credit on investments between $5,000 and $100,000. Second, a 15 percent tax credit is available for investors other than individuals for investments of up to $200,000. In 1998, New Brunswick amended its legislation so that LSVCC tax credits are available only in prescribed years, although every year has been prescribed since then. Newfoundland and Labrador proposed an LSVCC program in its 2001 provincial budget, but its introduction was delayed. In its budget of March 29, 2003, Newfoundland and Labrador again announced its intention to create an LSVCC program and indicated that it would call for proposals to establish a provincial labour-sponsored fund within 60 days from the release of the budget.[81]

CAPCOs

Louisiana was the first state to introduce CAPCO legislation, in 1983.[82] Since its enactment, the legislation has contained a sunset clause, originally applicable to capital companies certified between July 1, 1984 and December 31, 1989. The legislation was amended and extended numerous times until December 31, 2000. It then fell into a two-year hiatus due to significant dissent in the state legislature about its cost effectiveness. It was significantly amended and re-enacted on June 25, 2002.[83]

The history of the Louisiana CAPCO program is similar to the history of LSVCCs in Canada: over the first few years, the program was continually expanded and liberalized but in recent years its scope has been curtailed significantly.[84] The program has been emulated by a number of other states in recent years (beginning in 1997), including New York,[85] Wisconsin,[86] Florida,[87] Missouri,[88] Colorado,[89] Texas,[90] Alabama,[91] and Georgia.[92] Three states introduced CAPCO legislation in 1997, one in 1998, and four in 2001 or 2002. Its adoption in nine states and consideration in a number of others reflect in some measure the lobbying efforts of a relatively concentrated industry.[93]

The Louisiana CAPCO program was introduced primarily in response to a decline in the oil and gas sector in the early 1980s. During the 1970s, the Louisiana economy benefited significantly from oil and gas expansion, with employment in the sector doubling from 50,000 in the early 1970s to over 100,000 in the early 1980s. During this period, the state's economy was dependent on the oil and gas industry and any venture capital activity in the state at the time focused on that industry. In 1982, world oil prices started to decline and with it employment in the oil and gas sector. Economic development experts retained by the state suggested that the state introduce legislation to develop venture capital pools for investment in other sectors of the economy. At the time, venture capital markets had developed extensively in California, Massachusetts, and New York. The new CAPCO program was intended to "provide assistance in the formation and expansion of new businesses which create jobs in the state by providing for the availability of venture capital financing to entrepreneurs, managers, inventors, and other individuals for the development and operation of qualified Louisiana businesses."[94]

In its original incarnation in 1983, the CAPCO program was, in fact, a general VCF program. Any person could invest in a certified Louisiana capital company[95] and was entitled to an income tax credit of 20 percent of the person's cash investment (if the CAPCO had an initial capitalization of between $3 million and $20 million) or 35 percent (if the initial capitalization exceeded $20 million). A minimum initial capitalization of $3 million was required for a CAPCO to be certified. The original legislation did not define the nature of the investment in the CAPCO, although the underlying assumption seemed to be that investors would acquire equity of the CAPCO. The credit was transferable or saleable but not refundable. To maintain its certification, a CAPCO was required to make equity investments in Louisiana and other businesses according to certain timelines: by the end of four years, 30 percent of the CAPCO's capitalization had to be so invested, increasing to 50 percent after seven years and 75 percent after nine years. In each case, 60 percent of the business investments had to be in qualified Louisiana businesses. Qualified investments specifically excluded investments in businesses predominantly engaged in oil and gas exploration and development, real estate development or appreciation, or banking or lending. CAPCOs could not invest more than 10 percent of their capital in any one company.

The CAPCO program was amended in 1984 to introduce a premium tax credit for insurance companies.[96] The original premium tax credit was extremely generous, equal to 200 percent of the amount invested in a CAPCO. The entire tax credit could be claimed immediately. Unlike the income tax credit, however, the premium tax credit could not be assigned or sold when it was originally introduced. The 1984 legislation did not specify the nature of an insurance company's investment in a CAPCO, although, as in the original legislation, the insurance company was assumed to acquire equity of the CAPCO.

Over the period from 1984 to 2000, the CAPCO sunset was continuously extended while numerous amendments were made to the program. Between 1984 and 1989, the amendments were primarily expansive, in an attempt to bring more capital into the program. The income tax credit was increased to 35 percent in 1984,[97] while in 1986 the initial capitalization requirement for a CAPCO to be certified was reduced to $200,000 and the amount that a CAPCO could invest in any one company was increased to 25 percent of the CAPCO's capitalization.[98] Later the same year, CAPCOs were exempted from corporation income tax and corporation franchise tax for five consecutive taxable periods.[99] In 1987, the voluntary decertification process was relaxed, allowing CAPCOs that maintained 10 years of continued certification to voluntarily decertify without repaying the tax credits claimed by investors under the program.[100]

Further amendments in 1989 were also expansive, although the definition of a qualified Louisiana business was made more explicit.[101] In order to qualify, a business must have operated primarily in Louisiana or undertaken substantially all of its production in Louisiana, and had to have fewer than 500 employees and annual business receipts not exceeding $7 million. A business that met these requirements when a CAPCO made its first investment remained qualified for follow-on investment by the same CAPCO even if it no longer met the requirements at that time. The nature of an investment in a CAPCO was expanded to include a security that had debt characteristics but that was convertible into equity at a future date or had "equity features" (defined in rules promulgated by the Department of Economic Development). The CAPCO's pacing requirements were relaxed,[102] and the voluntary decertification process was expanded to permit decertification (without repayment of tax credits) once a CAPCO had invested 60 percent of its certified capital in qualified Louisiana businesses.

Significant restrictions were introduced later in 1989 in a special session of the legislature.[103] The premium tax credit was reduced significantly, from 200 percent to 120 percent, with no more than 10 percent of the total credit claimable in any one year. The premium tax credit deductible was further limited to 40 percent of the premium tax otherwise payable by the insurance company for 1989, 30 percent for 1990, and 25 percent for each of 1991 and 1992.[104] However, the manner of investment by the insurance company in the CAPCO was expanded to permit the insurance company to make an investment in the form of debt obligations to the CAPCO converted into cash investments at a rate of not less than 10 percent per year; in other words, the insurance company would make a capital commitment to the CAPCO—evidenced by a debt obligation—of which at least 10 percent must have been advanced each year. The nature of the insurance company's investment in the CAPCO remained unspecified, although it was still assumed to be an equity investment.

In 1992, the CAPCO program was extended to December 31, 1993[105] and in 1993 was extended again until July 31, 1994.[106] The 1993 legislation provided that the premium tax credit was transferable and saleable and subject to the same forfeiture and repayment provisions as the income tax credits (that is, if the CAPCO was involuntarily decertified for failure to meet the requirements of continued certification or if the CAPCO voluntarily decertified without meeting the requirements to avoid repayment of the tax credits). Late in 1993, the program was extended to December 31, 1995[107] and in 1994 it was extended to December 31, 1997 for certification of new CAPCOs and for investments in CAPCOs for any taxation years beginning no later than June 30, 1997.[108]

In 1996, the program was further extended to December 31, 1998.[109] The 1996 amendments finally defined the nature of investment that an insurance company could acquire in a CAPCO. The legislation defined investment for the purposes of the premium tax credit to "include the investment of cash by an insurance company in exchange for equity in a certified Louisiana capital company or a loan receivable from a certified Louisiana capital company which has a stated final maturity date of not less than five years from the origination date of the loan."[110] It was this ability of insurance companies to *lend* money to a CAPCO (on a secured basis) that spurred a significant expansion of the CAPCO industry and the formulation of the typical structure by which insurance companies financed CAPCOs. From 1988 to 1991, CAPCOs raised on average about $4.5 million per year. This increased to $17.2 million for 1992 to 1993 and $34.5 million for 1994 to 1996, and then jumped to $131.8 million in 1997.[111]

Although an insurance company's investment in a CAPCO can take a variety of forms—including a limited partnership interest (that is, if the CAPCO is structured similar to most private VCFs), preferred stock, or convertible stock or debt—insurance company investors typically invest in exchange for secured notes of the CAPCO. These notes carry an attractive rate of interest (often 200 to 300 basis points above that payable by state treasury bills) and are often guaranteed by a related party to the CAPCO. The terms of the note typically provide that it is repaid, with interest, through a combination of repayments from the CAPCO and the application of the tax credits receivable by the investor. The CAPCO sets aside a portion of the capital invested by the insurance companies sufficient to pay the CAPCO's anticipated payment liabilities under the note. This amount is invested in US treasury bonds or other safe, interest-bearing securities, with maturity dates corresponding to the CAPCO's payment schedule under the notes. Thus, the insurance company acquires a low-risk, high-interest-rate note. The secured note structure evolved primarily to satisfy the conservative investment requirements or practices of the insurance industry. CAPCOs simply were not successful in attracting insurance company investment using the more traditional venture capital limited partnership structure in which the insurance company investor acquired a limited partnership interest.

New York, Wisconsin, and Missouri introduced their CAPCO programs in 1997 and Florida followed in 1998. In each case, the regimes provided only a premium tax credit (no income tax credit) and were otherwise substantially similar to that in effect in Louisiana at the time, although the premium tax credit was limited to 100 percent of the certified capital invested, with a maximum of 10 percent applicable per year. The same secured note structure underlies the CAPCO programs adopted in other states, thus accounting for the relatively low qualified investment threshold (typically 50 percent) that CAPCOs must meet to maintain certification.

In 1998, the Louisiana program was extended to December 31, 1999 for new CAPCO certifications and to December 31, 2000 for certification of capital entitled to tax credits, although the premium tax credit was reduced to 110 percent (still exceeding the premium tax credit in other state regimes then in effect). An annual cap of $8 million of premium tax credits (corresponding to $72,727,272 of additional investment per year) was introduced to limit the state's cost exposure,[112] although no limit was placed on the income tax credit program at that time.[113] Three important amendments applied to capital pools created after January 1, 1999. First, following the decertification of a capital pool, the state would receive 25 percent of a CAPCO's investment appreciation exceeding an internal rate of return of 15 percent (not taking into account management fees not exceeding 2½ percent of certified capital and tax distributions). Second, 100 percent of a CAPCO's certified capital must be invested in qualified investments before it can apply for voluntary decertification.[114] Third, CAPCOs with newly certified capital pools must enter into agreements with the state requiring the CAPCO to invest up to 5 percent of the newly certified capital either in capital management funds that invest in pre-seed, seed, or early-stage companies or in another CAPCO whose investment objectives include disadvantaged businesses or economically distressed areas.

The Louisiana CAPCO program was not extended beyond December 31, 2000 until new amendments were introduced in June 2002, extending the program to June 30, 2003 for the certification of new CAPCOs and December 31, 2003 for the certification of new capital. The hiatus stemmed from concerns raised in the state legislature over whether the CAPCO program was accomplishing its objectives. Many of these concerns were outlined in a report prepared for the

Louisiana Department of Economic Development by Postlewaite & Netterville at the end of 1999.[115] It is somewhat surprising that no cost-benefit analysis of the program had been undertaken in the previous 15 years, although the costs of the program to the state did not become significant until the latter half of the 1990s.[116]

The 2002 amendments to the CAPCO program addressed many of the shortcomings highlighted in the Postlewaite & Netterville report. The income tax credit remained at 35 percent, while the premium tax credit was reduced from 110 percent to 100 percent. For capital raised on or after January 1, 2001, the premium tax credit cannot be used for two years after the date of investment, and thereafter no more than 12½ percent of the credit can be used in any year. This amendment is designed to ensure that the CAPCO invests in qualified investments faster than the tax credits are used. The annual maximum amount of income tax credits was set (by statute) at $2 million (corresponding to $5,714,285 of certified capital investment per year) and for premium tax credits at $5 million (corresponding to about $40 million of certified capital investment per year[117]). In addition, no certified Louisiana CAPCO group[118] is eligible for additional credits if it has certified capital in excess of $15 million and has not met the investment thresholds for voluntary decertification (that is, 100 percent of certified capital invested in qualified Louisiana businesses and 25 percent in disadvantaged businesses). This rule has caused some controversy because some of the largest Louisiana CAPCO groups are not eligible for future credits until they find investments for the excess money that their CAPCOs are holding.

The 2002 amendments also imposed new stricter investment requirements. Within three years, a CAPCO must invest at least 50 percent of the investment pool with at least 30 percent in qualified investments. For investment pools certified after January 1, 2002, at least 50 percent of the amount that must be invested in qualified investments must be invested in qualified Louisiana technology-based businesses,[119] qualified Louisiana startup businesses[120] and/or qualified technology funds, with at least 50 percent of the latter amount invested in qualified Louisiana technology-based businesses. Within five years, at least 80 percent of the certified investment pool must be invested with at least 50 percent invested in qualified investments. For investment pools certified after January 1, 2002, the same additional investment requirements as above apply, and at least 10 percent of the investment pool must be placed in qualified technology funds, qualified investments in approved technology-based businesses, and/or qualified investments in research park early-stage businesses. The list of excluded investments was expanded to include professional services provided by accountants, lawyers, or physicians, a prohibition similar to that found in other states that had adopted CAPCO programs. The definition of a qualified Louisiana business was narrowed somewhat, requiring that at least 80 percent of the employees of the business be domiciled in Louisiana and at least 80 percent of the payroll be paid to such employees.

The provisions governing voluntary decertification and payments to the state following any decertification were also significantly amended in 2002. Capital pools certified after December 31, 2001 can voluntarily decertify only if 100 percent of certified capital has been invested in qualified businesses with a minimum of 25 percent invested in disadvantaged businesses.[121] If a capital pool that was certified on or after January 1, 1999 is subsequently voluntarily decertified,[122] the CAPCO may be required to make payments to the state (specifically, the Louisiana Economic Development Fund) in certain circumstances. For a capital pool certified between January 1, 1999 and December 31, 2001 for which premium tax credits were granted, if the equity holders of the CAPCO earned an internal rate of return (IRR) on distributions of at least 15 percent of certified capital (excluding tax distributions and management fees not exceeding 2½ percent of certified capital), the CAPCO must pay the Louisiana Economic Development Fund 25 percent of all distributions in excess of the amount required to earn an IRR of 15 percent until the tax credits have been repaid, and thereafter the CAPCO must pay 5 percent of all such excess distributions. For capital pools certified after December 31, 2001 for which income tax credits or premium tax credits were granted, if the equity holders of the CAPCO earned an IRR on distributions of at least 10 percent of certified capital (excluding tax distributions and management fees not exceeding 2½ percent of certified capital), the CAPCO must pay the Louisiana Economic Development Fund 25 percent of all distributions in excess of the amount required to earn an IRR of 10 percent. In addition, if a capital pool certified after December 31, 2001 voluntarily decertifies (that is, if it meets the 100 percent and 25 percent qualified investment requirements noted above) but has failed to meet certain qualified investment milestones—40 percent invested in qualified investments after three years, 60 percent after five years, and 100 percent after seven years—the CAPCO must pay 25 percent of its distributions to the Louisiana Economic Development Fund until the tax credits are recouped, and thereafter the CAPCO must pay 10 percent of distributions regardless of the IRR generated for equity holders.[123] Finally, if a capital pool certified after December 31, 2001 does not voluntarily decertify within 10 years, the CAPCO shall pay to the Louisiana Economic Development Fund 50 percent of all distributions until the tax credits granted for the pool are recouped and thereafter shall pay 20 percent of all distributions. These amendments essentially put a 10-year life on new capital pools and expedite the investment milestones to avoid having the state participate in distributions. If the various milestones are met and the CAPCO is successful (that is, if it generates an IRR of at least 10 percent), the state will still share in distributions. The overall intention of these amendments is to ensure that the investment activities of the CAPCO are better targeted and undertaken more quickly.

Finally, the 2002 amendments require the secretary of the Department of Economic Development to report to various committees of the government before September 1, 2003 and every quarter thereafter on activities under the CAPCO program.[124] This report must include new capital certified, capital invested in qualified businesses, and a highly detailed report about each qualified business in which a CAPCO has invested capital certified after July 1, 2002.[125]

The 2002 amendments to the Louisiana CAPCO program reflect a variety of policy objectives. The primary objectives were to reduce the amount of the tax credit; shorten the time frame in which CAPCOs must invest in qualified businesses, with more severe penalties for failure to meet the pacing requirements; and target CAPCO investment to various sectors of the state economy, including the high-tech sector as well as businesses controlled by minorities and women. The introduction of detailed reporting requirements will enable the state to better monitor the program and assess whether its objectives are being met. I suspect, however, that the more stringent pacing requirements will have a stifling effect on the Louisiana CAPCO program.

Salient Features of VCF Tax Credit Programs

In Canada, VCF tax credit programs—commonly referred to as venture capital corporation (VCC) programs—were introduced in 1976 with Quebec's SODEQ legislation.[126] Over the next 10 years, the nine other provinces introduced their own VCC programs to enhance the supply of venture capital for SMEs.[127] Many of these schemes have since been cancelled or replaced,[128] but a number of provinces that cancelled their VCF programs adopted LSVCC programs. Only two provinces, British Columbia and Quebec, currently have more general VCF programs. Ontario replaced its VCC program, which was introduced in 1979 and effectively terminated in 1993, with an LSVCC program in 1991 and a community-based fund program in 1997. Under the community-based fund program, Ontario offers tax and other incentives to a variety of investors (including labour-sponsored funds, the Ontario equivalent of LSVCCs) in community small business investment funds (CSBIFs). Nova Scotia introduced a community-based scheme in 1993 when it introduced comprehensive legislation that included an angel capital tax credit, an LSVCC tax credit, and the tax credit for investment in community economic development corporations (CEDCs).[129] CSBIFs and CEDCs are similar to VCCs, except that their investment mandates are restricted to eligible small businesses within defined provincial communities (which may not necessarily correspond with municipalities).

The federal Income Tax Act does not include specific tax incentives for investment in provincial VCCs, other than LSVCCs, or in community-sponsored funds. Prescribed assistance given by a provincial government to investors with respect to an investment in prescribed VCCs (which include community-sponsored funds) does not reduce the adjusted cost base of the investors' shares,[130] but it does reduce the capital loss that an investor would otherwise realize on a disposition of such shares.[131] The Income Tax Act effectively draws a distinction between pooled venture capital incentives, in which case the provincial tax credit does not affect an investor's cost base, and direct (love and angel) incentives, where the provincial assistance does reduce the cost base. In addition, dividends received by a prescribed VCC from a qualifying corporation in which it invests are exempt from part IV tax even if the VCC owns 10 percent or less of the shares of the qualifying corporation.[132]

The salient features of the various provincial VCF programs other than LSVCC programs are summarized in appendix 6A.[133]

A number of US states introduced VCF tax credit programs in the 1980s. In many respects, the general VCF programs in the United States are similar to those in Canada. Investors are entitled to a tax credit, ranging from 10 percent to 50 percent, for investment in a qualified VCF. Like some Canadian provinces, a number of US states have introduced community-based VCF programs. Appendix 6B summarizes the salient features of the VCF programs in six states: Oklahoma, Maine, West Virginia, Iowa, Missouri, and Kansas. Iowa has a community fund program, and the other five have general VCF programs.

The two programs highlighted in this chapter—the LSVCC program in Canada and the CAPCO program in the United States—are summarized in appendix 6C and appendix 6D, respectively.

Evaluation of VCF Tax Credit Programs

Organizational Form of VCF

Most US VCF programs give fairly wide latitude to the organizational form of VCFs, including whether they are for-profit or not-for-profit. As a result, most VCFs are structured as for-profit limited partnerships, where permitted, in a manner similar to private VCFs that do not benefit from government incentives.

In contrast, all of Canada's VCF programs require VCFs to be corporations. There does not appear to be any policy rationale for a limiting a VCF to corporate form. For LSVCCs, corporate form was probably chosen as a simple structure through which to guarantee the rights of the employee organization that sponsors the LSVCC. The employee organization, at least in theory, is responsible for nominating at least half of the board of directors of the LSVCC.[134] To secure this right, the sponsoring organization owns shares in the LSVCC that are different from the shares acquired by individuals (or their RRSPs) who benefit from the tax credit. Similar rights could have been secured in a limited partnership structure, although the structure would have been more complex and would have required more than one type of limited partnership unit.

In most cases, VCFs are privately managed, for-profit entities whose management is independent of government. In general, a fund will attract less private sector investment if it is government-managed. There is usually greater expertise (or the perception of greater expertise) in the private sector for making investment decisions. In addition, private sector management removes (or greatly diminishes) the possibility of political interference in investment decisions. Some of the US VCF programs, but none of the Canadian programs, require a VCF to demonstrate venture capital management expertise in the certification process. A similar requirement is found in the SBIC program, discussed in chapter 8.[135] For example, most of the CAPCO programs require that a CAPCO have at least two principals with a minimum number of years experience (ranging from two to five years) in venture investing. Investors in a VCF can take some comfort in such a requirement.

The decision to invest in a VCF ultimately rests with investors, who should conduct their own due diligence with regard to the qualifications of the fund managers. However, the government should also be considered a substantial "investor" in the program because it is underwriting some (or, in certain cases, all) of the risk of investment and expects to derive benefits from its investment. If certification of a VCF is automatic, provided that certain conditions are met, and the government has little or no discretion in refusing certification, then an expertise requirement can be seen as part of the government's due diligence in selecting funds that qualify for tax incentives. Viewed in this manner, the level of expertise required should relate to the size of the government "investment" in the VCF program. A 100 percent tax credit—the benefit provided under the various CAPCO programs—should require a high degree of expertise. However, the level of expertise required is tempered by other factors, such as the depth and breadth of the venture capital industry in the jurisdiction and the ability to attract expertise to the jurisdiction. One of the concerns with the CAPCO program is that it tends to be concentrated among a handful of venture capital firms that spend significant time and resources lobbying to maintain existing CAPCO programs and establishing new programs in other states. These firms may lobby for the expertise requirement to retain some degree of exclusivity in the program.[136]

The VCFs permitted under a government program—that is, whether for-profit or not-for-profit—depends in part on the government's objectives in establishing the program. If a significant component of the program is educational, as it is in Nova Scotia, then non-profit organizations may be appropriate. However, the nature of the organization must be made clear to private sector investors. In programs with a substantial educational component, private sector investment should be viewed in part as a donation, and the tax credit provided may be considered compensation for this element. Obviously, the tax credit is not equivalent to that provided for a charitable donation because investors acquire an interest in the VCF in consideration for their investment.

If one of the objectives of a venture capital program that targets investment in VCFs is the establishment of VCFs that can ultimately thrive without government incentives, then VCFs registered under the program should be structured in the same manner as private VCFs. For this reason, Canadian programs should be amended to permit organizational forms that are conducive to the type of investor that the program should be targeting. To date, Canadian VCF programs have not targeted tax-exempt entities in any meaningful way, so a corporate structure would not be inappropriate. In my view, however, increased pension fund investment is critical to the growth of Canada's formal venture capital industry. To promote pension fund involvement, VCF programs should be amended so that funds can better attract investment by both taxable and tax-exempt entities. For this reason, VCF payments should permit VCFs to be structured as limited partnerships or other flowthrough entities.

Eligible Investors and Nature of Investment

Apart from the LSVCC and CAPCO programs,[137] most provincial and state VCF programs target any taxpayer (that is, any person subject to provincial or state tax) who invests cash in a qualified VCF in exchange for an equity interest in the fund. The VCF programs in Quebec, Nova Scotia, Maine, and Iowa are limited to individual investors.

The primary goal of most VCF programs is to increase the size of the venture capital pool available for SMEs. In principle, there is little reason to limit the investment incentive to specific taxpayers, especially individuals, unless the government determines that the only significant funding gap in the formal venture capital industry is individual investors (which is highly unlikely).[138] Although a VCF can to some extent reduce the risk of venture investing through diversification (assuming that diversification is required in the VCF program), VCFs remain relatively high-risk investments. Thus, investment in a VCF should form a small part of any person's portfolio. Arguably, a VCF program should target investors with the financial wherewithal to make high-risk investments, such as financial institutions, insurance companies, and pension funds, particularly if there is evidence that such entities are making insufficient venture investments relative to their capacity to do so. These entities have significant investment portfolios in which venture capital could make up an appropriately small component.

Individuals, especially at lower income levels, may not have sufficient investment capital to create a diversified portfolio, and it is therefore questionable whether they should be targeted by a government venture capital program. Perhaps more troubling is that all of the LSVCC programs and three of the four provinces with general VCF tax credit programs (Ontario being the exception) provide a tax credit to an individual when an investment is made through the individual's retirement savings plan. In some jurisdictions, the applicable securities legislation may restrict investors to individuals of substantial means because the VCF is not a publicly listed entity and therefore investment is restricted to certain qualified investors.[139] Kansas's VCF program specifies that, in the case of an investor who is a natural person, the investor must have a net worth of at least $1 million and at least 10 times the amount invested in the VCF. This limitation is similar to the "sophisticated" individual investor exemption found in some securities legislation.[140] Similarly, West Virginia's more recent VCF program is limited to accredited investors, as defined in regulation D under the Securities Act of 1933.

Both the LSVCC program and the CAPCO program target specific investors, although the targeted investors are radically different. LSVCCs target individuals (primarily through their individual retirement savings plans) while CAPCOs target insurance companies.[141] The juxtaposition of the LSVCC and CAPCO programs highlights a number of incongruities. In targeting individuals, the LSVCC program is significantly less regressive than other tax incentives in Canada that target savings, such as the capital gains exemption and the dividend tax credit,[142] and can thus can claim "success" in reaching its targeted audience— individuals across all income levels. Furthermore, the investment in LSVCCs is limited to equity investment, and the risk profile of the investment therefore reflects the underlying investments of the LSVCC. In other words, a significant number of Canadian individuals with lower incomes have put predominantly retirement savings into high-risk investments. More problematic still is that for some of these individuals, particularly in Quebec, their shares of LSVCCs are their only retirement savings outside of company pension plans.[143] In contrast, insurance companies, which command significant investment portfolios and are better equipped to diversify their investments, do not typically put money at any risk in a CAPCO. The CAPCO structure is designed so that the insurance company's investment is in the form of a fully guaranteed bond, which is generally appropriate for the fixed-income portfolio of the insurance company.

All of the VCF programs considered in this chapter provide tax credits, and are (at least superficially) aimed at taxable entities. Many of the programs permit taxpayers to carry forward unused tax credits, although the carryforward periods vary. Only two programs—the British Columbia and Kansas VCF programs—provide refundable tax credits, which in both cases are limited to particular taxpayers.[144] In many VCF programs, only the investor in the VCF can use the tax credit. All of the CAPCO programs, other than New York's, provide that the tax credits can be assigned or sold. However, in all of the CAPCO programs except that in Louisiana, qualified investors are restricted to insurance companies. Thus, for example, a non-insurance company cannot invest in a CAPCO and then sell the premium tax credit to an insurance company. The VCF programs in Missouri and Kansas also permit the assignment or sale of tax credits, even by persons not subject to state tax, such as tax-exempt and out-of-state entities.

The lack of venture capital investment by many Canadian pension funds has long been viewed as a gap in the Canadian industry. In the United States, these institutions have already made significant venture capital investments through private funds. Since non-financial incentives[145] have so far proved ineffectual in increasing investment by pension funds in provincial programs, consideration could be given to providing a financial incentive. Depending on how the incentive is structured, it could also promote investment from outside a particular province or from outside Canada.

There are three ways in which a financial incentive for investment in a qualified VCF[146] could be extended to tax-exempt entities or other persons with no tax liability in the jurisdiction: a grant, a refundable tax credit, or a transferable tax credit. A grant gives the government the greatest control over monitoring the benefit because it can establish criteria for the grant application and, more important, it can review that criteria before taking the positive act of writing a cheque to the grant recipient. In addition, a grant program is more visible and would show up in government program spending reports—not necessarily a bad thing from a policy perspective—whereas a tax credit reduces government revenue and would be disclosed in a less visible tax expenditure report. However, a grant is not necessarily the most efficient method to provide the incentive, particularly where the incentive targets both taxable and tax-exempt entities.

A refundable tax credit available to all investors in qualified VCFs is functionally equivalent to a grant, so a tax-exempt entity or other entity that cannot use or fully use the credit can claim a tax refund by filing a tax return or other claim for the credit. Missouri's VCF program, which is intended to attract tax-exempt entities, makes its tax credits transferable; the list of investors of the one VCF that has been registered by the state includes a number of tax-exempt entities, attesting to the success of the measure. Kansas's VCF program is similarly designed to attract investment from tax-exempt and out-of-state entities. As far as the cost to the government is concerned, there is little distinction between a refundable tax credit and a freely transferable tax credit.[147] From the investor's perspective, however, a transferable tax credit entails higher transaction costs than a refundable credit. These costs include expenses incurred to locate a willing purchaser plus the inevitable discount necessary to induce a purchaser to buy the credits. According to sources at the Missouri Department of Economic Development, the sale of Missouri VCF tax credits generates $0.85 to $0.90 on the dollar, or a 10 to 15 percent transaction cost in addition to the costs of locating a purchaser. These transaction costs introduce inefficiencies not associated with a refundable tax credit and may reduce the willingness of tax-exempt investors to invest. From a policy perspective, there is no justification for the use of transferable tax credits rather than refundable tax credits. The distinction may be more pragmatic (that is, political): there is a perceived difference between the government writing a cheque to a person, particularly a non-resident of the state, and the government collecting less tax from another person. It may be that transferable tax credits have an aura of marketable commodities and thus have greater appeal in a laissez-faire market-oriented society.

In summary, it is arguable that few of the various VCF regimes that use tax credit incentives target appropriate investors. The LSVCC program is the least appropriate in this respect in that it targets individuals across all income levels and particularly targets their retirement savings. More generally, because many of the regimes offer non-assignable and non-refundable tax credits, they do not target tax-exempt entities such as pension funds. Especially in Canada, where there is a recognized dearth of investment by pension funds, the use of refundable (or perhaps transferable) tax credits should be considered.[148]

Minimum/Maximum Capitalization

As indicated in appendixes 6A to 6D, most VCF programs—with the notable exception of most LSVCC programs—impose minimum capitalization requirements on VCFs. Some impose maximum capitalization requirements as well. All but one of the CAPCO programs require CAPCOs to raise a minimum of $500,000 of private equity before they can apply for registration; Louisiana's minimum capitalization requirement is $200,000. None of the CAPCO programs imposes a maximum certified capital limit on CAPCOs (subject to the government's aggregate expenditure limits). Surprisingly, only three of the provinces stipulate minimum capitalization requirements for LSVCCs, and in all three cases the minimum amount, $25,000, is insignificant.

A minimum capital requirement is appropriate for a number of reasons. First, a VCF must have sufficient capital to be viable, especially to create a diversified portfolio of SME investments (assuming that diversification is a requirement) and to have sufficient capital to make appropriate follow-on investments in its portfolio companies. Second, in order to attract experienced venture capital fund managers, a fund would likely require a relatively substantial amount of capital under management. The minimum size restrictions imposed in the British Columbia and Quebec VCF programs, $50,000 in both cases, are simply too small to fulfill these objectives, although, as discussed below, the BC regime has no diversification requirements. A significantly higher minimum capitalization—at least $1 million—is more appropriate.

A maximum capitalization requirement may be justified for a few reasons. Evidence from the formal venture capital industry in both Canada and the United States shows that individual deal sizes (that is, the size of investments in initial rounds of financing) have been increasing, particularly in the latter half of the 1990s.[149] Although the size of initial round investments has declined somewhat since its peak in 2000, the figures remain considerably higher than the mid-1990s. In both countries, the increasing size of the funds under management has been driving the increase in deal sizes, and increasing fund sizes have likely been driven by annual management fees. Management fees—in the range of 2 to 3 percent of capital under management—are not generally related to increased management costs, because the number of individual portfolio managers in venture capital firms has remained relatively static regardless of the amount of capital raised in funds managed by the firm. Each portfolio investment requires a significant time commitment, and relatively few individuals are responsible for managing each fund, regardless of its size. In other words, the number of portfolio companies in which a particular fund can invest is relatively static (based on the number of fund managers), while the amount of capital under management has increased. There is thus an inverse correlation between the size of a venture fund and the amount of seed capital financing that it undertakes. If a government program is intended to target primarily seed financing, because that is where it is believed that the greatest social return is generated and where the largest funding gap exists, then the program should restrict the size of each fund, restrict the size of the investment that the fund can make in each portfolio company, or require the VCF to invest some portion of its capital in seed financing.

One drawback of setting a maximum fund size is that it may deter more experienced venture capital fund managers from establishing a qualified VCF. In Canada, it is often suggested that there is a shortage of experienced venture capital fund managers. It is arguable that a secondary objective of a government incentive program (apart from increasing the pool of venture capital) is to increase the number of experienced fund managers. By setting a maximum size for each fund, a greater number of funds may be created, thus increasing the number of investment managers in the field and increasing competition among VCFs. The obvious drawback is that some funds may be managed, at least initially, by individuals with limited venture capital investment experience, unless that experience is a requirement for registration of the VCF under the program.

The tax credit provided to investors may be viewed in part as an underwriting of the risks and costs associated with educating investment managers new to the field of venture capital. Whether that is an appropriate use of government money and an appropriate means of encouraging investment by private sector investors is questionable. If a program targets new investors to venture capital— for example, pension funds in Canada—it should not at the same time have the goal of educating unseasoned venture capital fund managers.

Nature of Incentive

The amount of the financial incentive provided by VCF tax credit programs varies enormously across jurisdictions, ranging from a low of 15 percent for individual and corporate (non-financial institution) investments in an Ontario CSBIF[150] to a high of 100 percent for investments in all of the CAPCO programs. Missouri's VCF program offers a 100 percent tax credit, although all investors must invest an equivalent amount in a parallel fund for which they do not obtain any tax credit; the effect is similar to a 50 percent tax credit.[151] The LSVCC tax credit at the federal and most provincial levels is limited to 15 percent; however, since virtually all investors benefit from the tax credit at both levels, an LSVCC investment effectively receives a 30 percent tax credit. Under the West Virginia Venture Capital Act, West Virginia's more recent VCF program, the tax credit is stipulated to be "no more than 50 percent" of the investment in the VCF. This provision is intended to allow the West Virginia Economic Development Authority to negotiate with investors for a lower tax credit if market conditions permit. Where a particular investor's investment in a VCF is substantial or there is sufficient demand for investment, there may be scope to negotiate a lower percentage.

In determining the amount of the tax credit, governments must consider the cost of the program, although the total cost can be managed more effectively through an overall annual (or total) expenditure limit (discussed below). More important, the government must set the credit at a level that induces investment that would not have been undertaken without the credit, without being so generous as to provide a windfall. Determining this level is more an art than a science, particularly when establishing the rate on the program's introduction. The rate can be varied in subsequent years with the benefit of hindsight to achieve a more cost-efficient result.

Some jurisdictions limit the amount of the tax credit that can be claimed in any one year. For example, most of the CAPCO programs limit the amount of the premium tax credit that can be claimed in a year to 10 percent. This limitation may be simply a cost-saving measure, given the generous 100 percent premium tax credit incentive offered under the programs. Arguably, though, the staged credit better matches the economic benefits that the program is designed to achieve with the costs of the program. Under some VCF programs, the credit claimed in a year cannot exceed a certain percentage of the investor's state or provincial tax otherwise payable in that year, with unused credits carried forward.

In a comparison of the general VCF programs in Canada and the United States, a few distinctions stand out. The first, discussed above in the context of eligible investors, is that a number of state VCF programs permit the transfer or sale of tax credits. A second distinction is that under some state VCF programs, the investor is not entitled to any tax credit until the VCF invests an equivalent amount in qualified SMEs in the state. This limitation is necessary in a VCF program that permits investment in out-of-state VCFs or permits the VCF to invest its capital in out-of-state businesses, so that the state tax credit is deferred until the VCF invests an equivalent amount in the state. Equally important, though, and in contrast to the approach taken in Canada, the deferral means that the government expenditure is matched to the provision of capital to qualified SMEs in the jurisdiction, rather than acting as an incentive simply for creating a pool of investment capital regardless of when that pool is invested in SMEs. If the tax credit is not matched to investment in qualifying SMEs, VCF legislation becomes more complex in two respects. First, as discussed below, the program must incorporate investment targets (often referred to as pacing requirements) for the VCF to invest the capital raised in eligible small businesses. Second, there must be monetary and/or other penalties imposed so that the government may recoup its costs if the VCF fails to meet the pacing requirements. While a requirement that the credit be deferred until the VCF has invested the amount of capital raised (or a substantial portion thereof) in qualified businesses in the jurisdiction does impose monitoring requirements, it is less onerous than that for monitoring the pacing requirements and corresponding penalties. The concern with imposing such a requirement in Canada, given the history of the Canadian VCF programs, is that it will be difficult to convince investors to invest when the tax credit to which they are entitled may be delayed well beyond the year in which the investment in the VCF is made. However, this sort of requirement would likely ensure that the VCFs behave like most private VCFs: that is, the funds may seek capital commitments from qualified investors but not actually draw down on that capital—at which point the credit would be made available—until suitable investments have been found.

Government Expenditure Limits
and Government Profit Share

One fundamental feature of most government expenditure programs is a spending limit, so that the government can properly budget for the program and not be taken by surprise when its costs are reviewed. All of the US state VCF programs surveyed, including the CAPCO programs, contain expenditure limits. In contrast, few of the LSVCC or other Canadian VCF programs contain such limits.

A few of the US VCF programs also require that the government participate in the profitability of the VCF. For example, the legislation governing Missouri's VCF program provides that the Missouri seed capital investment board "shall establish policies and procedures requiring each authorized qualified economic development organization to secure from each qualified fund and its investors the maximum fund equity interest possible, as dictated by market conditions, in exchange for the use of the tax credits."[152] In effect, the Missouri legislation requires that the government—through its four economic development organizations, which are, in essence, business incubators—obtain a carried interest in the qualified fund as consideration for the tax credits. The legislation further provides that a qualified economic development organization that receives any distributions of dividends, earnings, equity, or the like from the fund "shall use such payments solely for reinvestment in qualified funds in order to provide ongoing seed capital, start-up capital and follow-up capital for Missouri businesses."[153] According to sources at the Missouri Department of Economic Development, the four qualified economic development organizations collectively have a 20 percent carried interest (similar to the interest that a fund manager has in a VCF) in the only qualified fund under the program.

Some of the CAPCO programs as well as the Kansas VCF program provide for a similar carried interest for the government, in most cases as long as the fund achieves a stipulated level of profitability. In most of the CAPCO programs in which the government has a notional carried interest, the equity holders in the CAPCO are entitled to a return of their capital plus an appropriate rate of return based on certified capital before the government is entitled to its carried interest.[154] Under the Kansas VCF program, the government effectively has a 10 percent carried interest in the certified VCF once investors have received back their original capital.

Where the government provides a 100 percent tax credit—as it does in all of the CAPCO programs—and therefore underwrites the entire cost of investment in the CAPCO, it should be entitled to a carried interest.[155] Where the tax incentive provided is substantially less, the carried interest would be correspondingly smaller. Providing the government with a passive carried interest in the VCF serves as a public acknowledgment of the fact that the government is underwriting some of the risk of investment. In the same way that fund managers are entitled to a carried interest for providing their expertise in investing the capital, it is appropriate that the government receive a quid pro quo for its assumption of some of the investor's risk.

Eligible Investments of the VCF

The definition of an eligible investment of the VCF is relatively consistent across all programs, although it varies depending on the investment objectives of the program. Some programs may emphasize particular industries (such as high-tech industries) or de-emphasize others (such as the natural resource sector, professional service businesses, and real estate development). Certain programs may be restricted to seed financing (as opposed to all stages of venture capital financing), and therefore restrict investment to young companies or companies with a smaller asset or sales base or fewer employees than the "normal" size restrictions under the "standard" definition of SMEs. Whether the size of the business should be restricted depends on whether the program is intended to target seed capital investment or investment in SMEs generally, which in turn depends on whether there are specific gaps in SME funding that the government wants to fill.[156]

All VCF programs should target those small businesses that will most benefit the economy—rapid-growth SMEs. Most VCF programs are so targeted, with one significant exception. Most LSVCC programs do not put any limits on the types of businesses that are qualified investments, other than size and geographic restrictions. The remaining VCF programs use a white list of qualifying business activities, a black list of non-qualifying business activities, or a combination of the two. Thus, personal services businesses and other lifestyle businesses are excluded from most VCF programs, and financial services businesses and real estate development or leasing businesses are also generally excluded because there is no perceived equity gap affecting them.[157] The failure of LSVCC programs to include similar limitations further undermines the credibility of these programs. The CAPCO programs, which, like LSVCC programs, are subject to much criticism in this book, cannot be faulted on this particular point. The CAPCO legislation in all states contains detailed black lists and white lists to target investment under the program. Given that the state governments are wholly underwriting such investments, this level of regulation is appropriate.

Apart from the types of businesses in which VCFs can invest, two other issues should be considered in the design of a VCF program: whether VCFs must diversify their investments and whether VCFs should be permitted to make follow-on investments (that is, even after the portfolio business exceeds the size restrictions imposed by legislation). The failure to impose diversification requirements undermines the effectiveness of a VCF program, as evidenced by Ontario's former small business development corporation (SBDC) program and British Columbia's existing VCC program.[158] The SBDC program was introduced in 1979[159] and became the model for VCC programs in several other provinces, most of which have since been repealed. One of the major problems with the SBDC program was that there was no requirement for an SBDC to diversify its investments. As a result, most VCCs established under the SBDC and similar programs invested in only one SME, making them functionally equivalent to a direct investment tax credit program.[160] This program structure effectively permits investors to earn a tax credit for direct investment in an SME where no such credit is specifically available; it also circumvents the federal Income Tax Act provisions that would otherwise reduce the cost of a direct investment by the amount of the provincial tax credit, assuming that the provincial VCC is a prescribed venture capital corporation under the Act. Even if this is a desired consequence of the program, the two-tier corporate structure increases the financing costs for the underlying small business, an ironic result given that the programs are intended to reduce financing costs. For this reason, British Columbia introduced a tax credit for direct investment in small businesses in its 2003 budget. Its VCC program remains in effect, although in practice it should be limited to the few diversified VCCs in the province.[161]

If the purpose of a VCF program is to create pools of professionally managed venture capital, then the investment restrictions imposed on VCFs should mirror those imposed on private funds that do not benefit from government support. Most private funds restrict the amount that can be invested in each portfolio company. According to Paul Gompers and Josh Lerner, this restriction is meant to ensure that the fund managers "do not attempt to salvage an investment in a poorly performing firm by investing significant resources in follow-on financing."[162] A similar restriction on funds benefiting from the VCF program would serve a similar purpose; more important, though, the restriction would ensure that the VCF does not act as a single-investment vehicle to provide investors with a tax credit where none is provided for direct investment in SMEs.

Follow-on financing is not generally used to salvage poorly performing portfolio businesses. Rather, seed-stage VCFs generally retain the right of first refusal with respect to further financing rounds as an anti-dilution measure so that they continue to benefit in well-performing, growing businesses. It is questionable whether government-sponsored VCF programs should permit follow-on investment once a business expands beyond the eligible investment criteria under the legislation. In making this determination, various possible objectives for the VCF program must be weighed: the extent to which the program targets a new class of investors in venture capital, the extent to which it intends to attract high-quality fund managers to the jurisdiction, and the extent to which it targets the largest equity gaps affecting small businesses (that is, at the seed and early stages). The first two objectives favour follow-on financing. If the program encourages investors that might not otherwise invest in venture capital (for example, Canadian pension funds), then limiting a VCF's ability to make follow-on investments may undermine the profitability of the VCF and therefore undermine the program's ultimate goal: sustained venture capital investment from such investors without the need of government incentives. Similarly, if the objective is to attract high-quality fund managers to the jurisdiction (an underlying goal of a number of CAPCO programs), then follow-on investment should be permitted because it will likely increase the return on the fund manager's carried interest and will cause the fund manager to act like fund managers who administer purely private VCFs. If, however, the goal of the program is to address the most significant funding gaps affecting rapid-growth SMEs, which occur at the earliest stages of development, then follow-on investment is not appropriate because such investment will ultimately use a substantial portion of the fund's capital. Once the portfolio business has reached the point where it can attract subsequent larger rounds of financing on its own, the VCF program has achieved its objective and should not commit further capital to that particular business, even if failure to do so will significantly dilute the VCF's interest in the business.

Timing Issues Affecting VCFs

A number of VCF programs impose pacing requirements on VCFs. These requirements are necessary where the tax credit is granted to investors when they invest in the fund, regardless of when the fund makes investments in qualified businesses. Pacing requirements are found in all LSVCC and CAPCO programs as well as in most other VCF programs. The only exceptions are certain state

VCF programs that defer an investor's eligibility for the tax credit until the VCF makes eligible investments.

Ideally, the government program should defer the tax credit until the VCF makes eligible investments. In this way, the government expenditure is matched to the ultimate objective of the program. However, other aspects of the program's design affect the timing of the tax credit. In an evergreen program, in which tax-favoured investment in the VCF can be made at any time, it is difficult to match eligible investments by the VCF with previous capital contributions to the VCF.[163] Similarly, if the program requires each VCF to attract a large number of investors, each of whom contributes a relatively small amount of capital—for example, under the LSVCC programs—it is difficult to match eligible investments by the VCF with previous contributions. For these programs, perhaps, pacing requirements are an appropriate second-best solution. However, where the program targets relatively few investors, each of whom invests a significant amount, it is easier to match investment by the VCF with contributions to the VCF. The difficulty with deferring credits in this manner is that the VCF is placed under considerable pressure from its investors to invest the capital as soon as possible so that the investors can obtain and use the credits. Such pressure might lead to rash investment decisions. Where the tax credits are large, the deferral creates a conflict between the government, which wants to match the incentive to qualified investments that will benefit the economy, and the program's investors, who want the use of the credits as soon as possible. Perhaps the only way to reconcile these differences is to provide upfront tax credits but impose pacing requirements on the VCF. Ontario's CSBIF program occupies a middle ground: half of the incentive is provided when an investor invests in the CSBIF, and the other half is deferred until the CSBIF makes qualified investments.

There are significant variations in the pacing requirements in the programs that grant upfront tax credits. For example, none of the LSVCC regimes and only one of the CAPCO regimes requires that 100 percent of the capital raised be invested in eligible businesses, although all of the CAPCO programs require 100 percent investment before the CAPCO can voluntarily decertify and return capital to the equity investors. In part, the LSVCC pacing requirements[164] are necessary to ensure some liquidity because LSVCC investors are entitled to redeem their shares after a minimum holding period (in most cases, eight years). This redemption feature may have been considered necessary in order to attract individual investors to the federal program. However, it was not available in the original LSVCC program in Quebec, on which the federal program was supposedly based; the Quebec program has always required that LSVCC shares be held until retirement age. Of course, this particular feature begs the question whether the individuals should have been targeted as investors in the first place. A redemption feature is completely at odds with the nature of investments that LSVCCs are required to make—that is, illiquid investments, at least initially— and completely at odds with the structure of private VCFs. The pacing requirements for LSVCCs have been tightened up in recent years[165] and are now at least as stringent as those of various state and provincial VCF programs and more stringent than those of most CAPCO programs (other than Louisiana's). However, the pacing requirements and corresponding penalties may cause an LSVCC to make less prudent investments in the face of looming investment target deadlines.[166]

The CAPCO pacing requirements raise a different issue—namely, the benefits to the state of a program in which the state is underwriting the entire cost of venture capital investment but the instrument of that investment, the CAPCO, is only required to invest at most 50 percent of its certified capital in eligible investments and has four to five years to meet this threshold.[167] The pacing requirements permit the CAPCO to invest a significant portion of the capital raised in low-risk securities; these investments, together with the 100 percent premium tax credits, are used to guarantee the principal and interest payments owing to insurance companies that lend money to the CAPCO. The only incentive for the CAPCO to meet the 100 percent eligible investment threshold is that the equity owners (generally, the CAPCO's promoters) cannot receive any non-qualifying distributions until the 100 percent investment requirement is met. In the mean time, however, they are permitted to receive quite generous management fees (generally, 2½ percent of certified capital, which includes the capital investment in low-risk securities).

Pacing requirements are wholly at odds with the general structure of private VCFs. Private VCFs generally seek capital *commitments* from their investors and either defer capital calls until appropriate investments have been found or draw down capital according to a stipulated schedule. Thus, private VCFs generally hold excess cash for relatively short periods. Some US VCF programs achieve the same result—from the perspective of the government's investment in the program—by deferring eligibility for the tax credit until the VCF has invested its capital in eligible investments. Pacing requirements and corresponding penalties add complexity to VCF program legislation, although the complexity may be unavoidable in evergreen fund programs.

Cost-Benefit Analyses of VCF Tax Credit Programs

The amount that governments spend on VCF programs is relatively small compared with their total expenditures, but it is certainly not insignificant (as the various spending limits set out in appendixes 6A to 6D attest). When the costs of all such regimes in Canada or the United States are aggregated, they total billions of dollars of government expenditures in each country. Considering the cost, it is surprising how few cost-benefit analyses of the various programs have been undertaken, especially given the propensity of provinces or states to adopt programs almost wholesale from other jurisdictions or to cobble together features of programs from other jurisdictions without really analyzing their efficacy.

The lack of analysis may stem in part from the failure of the legislation in most jurisdictions, at least historically, to require the government agency administering the program to collect data other than the amount of tax credits granted. This failure has been rectified in a number of jurisdictions, although it remains to be seen how much analysis will be applied to the data. Many programs are too new to allow any meaningful cost-benefit analysis, although governments should be collecting as much data as possible so that the programs can be effectively monitored and evaluated after an appropriate amount of time. Given the nature of venture capital investing, a full evaluation of the program after 8 to 10 years would be appropriate, although continual monitoring of the program would help ensure that it is meeting its stated objectives.

The costs of a VCF tax credit program are relatively easy to calculate. The tax credits make up the bulk of the costs. Administrative costs and any other costs incurred in developing the program should also be taken into account. Computing the benefits of the program is much more difficult. Direct benefits, indirect benefits, and induced benefits should all be taken into account. The primary direct benefits are income tax revenues from salaries paid to employees of businesses in which the VCF invests. Other direct benefits include income taxes from portfolio businesses (assuming that they are profitable) and sales tax revenues generated by the purchase of goods and services by the portfolio businesses and their employees.[168] Indirect benefits include government revenues derived from suppliers of portfolio companies, including business tax revenues and revenues from increased payrolls resulting from the purchase of the suppliers' goods and services. Induced benefits include the increase in consumer spending derived from employees' salaries. All of these benefits, particularly indirect and induced benefits, are difficult to quantify and necessarily rely on a number of assumptions. In most cases, an input/output (I/O) model developed for a jurisdiction is used to compute the benefits of the program to the jurisdiction. But in applying an I/O model, appropriate "inputs" must be chosen and certain assumptions must be made in determining these inputs. For example, if salaries or sales of portfolio firms are used as inputs, how much of the salaries or sales are attributable to VCF funding and what growth rate should be used for determining future benefits? One possibility is to use the incremental portion of the salaries or sales directly attributed to VCF funding (that is, prorate salaries or sales based on the proportionate equity capital of the portfolio business provided by the VCF). Alternatively, all salaries (or sales) might be attributed to the VCF on the premise that in the absence of VCF funding, the business would not exist; in other words, the business would not have attracted any funding but for that provided through the VCF tax credit program. Or, if it can be demonstrated that the business would likely have obtained financing in any event, then none of projected government revenue should be attributed to the VCF program. Furthermore, where salaries are used as a base measurement, an attempt should be made to measure the alternative scenarios if the VCF funding had not been provided: for example, the employees may have found work elsewhere, either inside or outside the jurisdiction, or may have received unemployment insurance or social assistance (adding to the cost to the government), or may have become inactive. In raising these concerns, I am not trying to strip cost benefit-analyses of value; rather, I want to emphasize that any cost-benefit analysis depends significantly on the validity of its assumptions.

The two most contentious programs, the LSVCC and CAPCO programs, have been the subject of a few cost-benefit studies undertaken with varying degrees of rigour. Few other programs are old enough to properly evaluate, although rudimentary analysis of some programs has been undertaken. Certain studies of the LSVCC and CAPCO programs are considered here.

Cost-Benefit Analyses of LSVCC Programs

It is virtually impossible to undertake a cost-benefit analysis of the full range of LSVCC programs because most LSVCCs have not been in existence long enough. Only three LSVCCs are at least 10 years old, which in my view is the minimum appropriate age for considering the benefits of a VCF program. FSTQ, Working Ventures Canadian Fund, and British Columbia's Working Opportunity Fund (WOF) have each been the subject of at least one study. However, there is a key distinction between most LSVCCs, including these three, and most private VCFs. Most LSVCCs are evergreen funds: they are constantly receiving new capital and seeking new investments. Thus, at any given point in time, the average age of their portfolio investments may be relatively young. The return on venture capital tends to follow a "J curve"—that is, poor investments generally appear soon after initial investment, while successful investments take a longer time to mature. Accordingly, LSVCCs with young venture capital portfolios will likely show poor returns. For these reasons, the approach of a number of more recent LSVCCs—to establish closed-end funds—should allow for better cost-benefit analyses and, incidentally, better comparisons of fund performance with private VCFs.

A number of studies have attempted to perform a cost-benefit analysis of the LSVCC tax expenditure associated with FSTQ, the oldest LSVCC. Some of these studies were commissioned by FSTQ itself. Three such studies, undertaken in 1994,[169] 1996,[170] and 2002,[171] computed the net fiscal cost of the FSTQ program, the time it took for the federal and provincial governments to recover their costs of the program, and the impact of FSTQ's venture capital investments on the Quebec economy. Perhaps not surprisingly, all three studies showed favourable results. The 2002 study, examining the period 1984 to 2000, suggested that the fiscal cost per dollar of venture capital investment by FSTQ was $0.62 and that the government recovered its costs in 2.3 years or 0.8 years, depending on the method used to determine the recovery period.[172] The 2002 study computed the aggregate cost to the federal and Quebec governments of the LSVCC tax credit for FSTQ shareholders for 1984 to 2000 to be $1.749 billion, $918 million incurred by Quebec and $831 million incurred by the federal government. The study concluded that, as of December 31, 2000, FSTQ's investments (together with those of its investing partners) sustained a total of 86,126 jobs—50,517 direct jobs, 22,895 indirect jobs, and 12,714 induced jobs. As of June 30, 2001, it was estimated that this figure had grown to 93,000 jobs.

In 1995, the Canadian Labour Market and Productivity Centre (CLMPC) undertook a cost-benefit analysis of two LSVCCs.[173] The study examined 10 investee firms, 7 of FSTQ and 3 of WOF. The methodology used to determine the fiscal benefits of the two LSVCCs were similar to those in the 1994 FSTQ study. This study estimated that the payback period to the federal and provincial governments under the two programs was less than three years.[174]

WOF has commissioned its own studies, similar to those undertaken by FSTQ. The first study was completed in November 1998[175] and an update was prepared in January 2001.[176] Again, not surprisingly, both studies concluded that the benefits derived by the federal and provincial governments far exceeded their costs under the LSVCC program.[177] The second WOF study considered costs over the period 1992 to 1997 and benefits over the period 1992 to 1999.[178] The study estimated the aggregate provincial and federal costs of the program over the five-year period to be $29.0 million and $24.4 million, respectively; over the seven-year period in which benefits were computed, the study estimated that the provincial benefits ranged from $41.3 million to $49.0 million, while the federal benefits ranged from $51.2 million to $61.1 million. The study went on to project benefits to 2004 on the assumption that the costs were frozen at the 1999 level (that is, no new capital would be raised by WOF, although it would continue to make new investments and follow-on investments during this period with the capital raised to 1999). On this basis, the 2001 study estimated that the net combined federal-provincial benefit (after deducting the costs of the program to 1999) ranged from $314.6 million to $360.6 million. The 2001 study also credited WOF with attracting significant venture capital from outside the province in syndicated deals. According to the study, each $1 million of WOF investment resulted in roughly $4 million of leveraged capital; put another way, each $1 million of provincial tax credits resulted in $20 million of venture capital investment in the province.

Probably the greatest problem with the cost-benefit analyses of FSTQ and WOF is that they were undertaken in the mid- to late 1990s, during a period of record economic growth across Canada and significant expansion in the high-tech sector, where a large portion of venture capital dollars were invested. Accordingly, the economic modelling tended to use relatively high growth rates in determining the benefits generated by VCF investment. Given the extreme downturn in the economy, particularly in the high-tech sector since mid-2000, it is doubtful whether a current analysis would yield similarly favourable results.

The conclusions reached in these studies were also disputed by François Vaillancourt, on other grounds, in a paper prepared for a 1995 conference sponsored by Industry Canada.[179] Instead of considering the microeconomic data that formed the foundation of the FSTQ and WOF studies, Vaillancourt introduced a variable representing FSTQ into a conventional model for sector-specific employment in order to determine the effect of LSVCCs on employment. His study examined the effect of the FSTQ variable in six specific manufacturing sectors and in the manufacturing sector as a whole and concluded that the FSTQ variable had "no significant impact on employment in the sectors studied,"[180] thus questioning an assumption in the FSTQ studies: the extent to which FSTQ's investments had an incremental effect on investee firms.

Vaillancourt also questioned whether the supply of venture capital in Canada was inadequate prior to the introduction of LSVCCs. In his comment on

Vaillancourt's study, Brian Smith shared the concern.[181] Smith compared the 10-year compounded rate of return of FSTQ (to 1995) and the 5-year return for Working Ventures Canadian Fund and FSTQ (to 1995) with the rate of return over the same periods of three-month Canadian treasury bills. In both cases, the LSVCCs underperformed the treasury bills, although Smith acknowledged that the return to investors in the LSVCCs, on an after-tax basis, were considerably higher. Smith concluded that "[s]ince the realized rate of return of venture capital in Canada does not exceed the expected risk-adjusted rate, this would suggest that the supply of venture capital is adequate."[182]

Smith's analysis and conclusions are inappropriate for a variety of reasons. First, as noted previously, FSTQ and WOF are evergreen funds and the average age of their investment portfolio in 1995, when Vaillancourt and Smith examined them, hardly mirrored of the age of the funds themselves. Second, Smith should have compared the returns of FSTQ and WOF with equivalent non-tax-sheltered investments, such as privately managed VCFs. Third, the appropriate comparison of returns *is* on an after-tax basis (where Smith acknowledged that LSVCCs performed well).

Efficiency theory suggests that in a market-driven economy, the after-tax benefit of tax-sheltered behaviour should be approximately equal to the after-tax benefit of its unsheltered counterpart. That is, there would be an increase in tax-favoured behaviour (and therefore an increase in the cost of and/or a decrease in return from the tax-sheltered behaviour) until the after-tax benefits are equalized (that is, until the tax benefits are competed away).[183] With respect to the LSVCC tax expenditure, the overall effect should be that the benefit of the expenditure is transferred to the portfolio businesses (the intended benefactors of the scheme) through a reduction in their cost of capital. If the after-tax returns on comparable investments are similar, the appropriate focus should be on the positive externalities generated by the resulting growth of portfolio firms rather than on the rate of return to investors. However, a number of features of the LSVCC regimes make this efficiency theory difficult to apply (or test). First, there is no secondary market for LSVCC shares. Second, most LSVCCs are open-ended funds and the subscription/redemption price for LSVCC shares is based on the net asset value per share and this value does not necessarily reflect the true value of the underlying investments of the LSVCC.[184] Finally, it is difficult to compare LSVCCs against themselves, let alone against comparable non-tax-favoured investments, because of the difficulty of predicting the return on a fund's venture capital portfolio at any given time.[185]

Despite the obvious flaws in this analysis, it is worth comparing the after-tax rates of return on LSVCCs over the past 5 to 10 years with the rates of return on comparable non-tax-favoured investments.[186] Table 6.1 compares the rates of return on an investment in LSVCCs with the rate of return on small- to mid-cap equity funds as well as with other indices. The rate of return on an LSVCC investment, not incorporating the tax benefits, is extremely low in comparison to that on small-cap equity funds (except, somewhat surprisingly, in the 5-year rate of return). This difference can be accounted for in part by higher management-expense ratios for LSVCCs.[187] In addition, the results for many of the LSVCCs

Table 6.1   Rate of Return on Investments in LSVCCs Compared with Other Investment Vehicles and Indices (for the period ended October 31, 2002)[a]

Fund	1-year rate of return	3-year rate of return	5-year rate of return	10-year rate of return
Axis Investment Funds	—	—	—	—
The BEST Discoveries I	−9.9	3.1	0.0	—
The BEST Discoveries II	—	—	—	—
The BEST Discoveries III	—	—	—	—
Canadian Medical Discoveries	−17.0	−0.1	−3.8	—
Canadian Medical Discoveries II	—	—	—	—
Canadian Science and Tech Growth	−22.6	1.2	0.1	—
Capital Alliance Ventures	−29.5	4.4	1.7	—
Covington Fund I	−17.6	−9.2	−4.2	—
Covington Fund II	−13.8	—	—	—
Crocus Investment	−7.0	−4.5	−0.9	—
Crown Ventures Fund	−0.0	—	—	—
DGC Entertainment Ventures	−2.7	−0.3	0.3	—
Dynamic Venture Opportunity	−2.9	3.0	6.8	—
E2 Venture Fund	—	—	—	—
ENSIS Growth	−5.9	−2.4	—	—
First Ontario	−19.2	−7.8	−3.7	—
First Ontario Growth	−23.2	—	—	—
Fondaction[a]	−3.9	0.1	1.3	—
Front Street Energy Growth	—	—	—	—
Front Street Energy Growth II	—	—	—	—
Front Street Energy Growth III	—	—	—	—
FSTQ[a]	−11.4	−0.1	2.5	4.6
Golden Opportunities Fund	0.0	7.3	—	—
Retrocom Growth	2.3	−1.1	0.6	—
StrategicNova Venture Growth	−16.1	−2.0	−0.7	—
Triax Growth	−27.5	−19.1	−10.9	—
Triax New Generation Biotech Balanced	−4.1	—	—	—
Triax New Generation Biotech Equity	−13.4	—	—	—
Triax New Millennium Internet Balanced	−2.7	—	—	—
Triax New Millennium Internet Venture	−18.0	—	—	—
Trillium Growth Capital Inc.	−10.3	−3.8	—	—
VenGrowth Advanced Life Science	—	—	—	—
VenGrowth I Investment	−14.7	−2.5	2.6	—
VenGrowth II Investment	−4.7	—	—	—
VentureLink Brighter Future Balanced	—	—	—	—
VentureLink Brighter Future I	—	—	—	—
VentureLink Brighter Future II	—	—	—	—
VentureLink Financial Services Innovation I	—	—	—	—
VentureLink Financial Services Innovation II	—	—	—	—
VentureLink Series I	−19.0	—	—	—
VentureLink Series II	−22.0	—	—	—

(The table is concluded on the next page.)

Table 6.1 Concluded

Fund	1-year rate of return	3-year rate of return	5-year rate of return	10-year rate of return
Workers Investment Fund Inc.	0.0	0.0	0.0	—
Working Opportunity Fund Balanced ...	−16.6	−0.6	6.6	5.7
Working Opportunity Fund Growth	−22.4	—	—	—
Working Ventures Canadian	−14.6	−14.1	−8.2	−2.7
Working Ventures II Technology	−13.8	—	—	—
Average[b]	−12.6	−2.5	−0.8[b]	1.5[b]
Mutual fund benchmarks				
S & P 500 composite (Cdn$)	−17.8	−11.7	1.4	10.6
S & P/TSX total return	−7.7	−3.4	−0.3	8.5
Canadian small-cap equity funds[c]	5.4	3.4	−1.6	7.7
5-year average GIC rate	3.9	4.6	4.6	5.6
Canada savings bonds	1.1	2.8	2.9	4.0

[a] The Globefund report does not include statistics for the two Quebec LSVCCs (Fondaction and FSTQ). The figures for Fondaction are average annual returns for the period ending May 31, 2002 and are taken from its 2002 annual report, available online from the Fondaction Web site: http://www.fondsftq.com/. According to the report, Fondaction's return since inception was 4.02 percent. The figures for FSTQ are average annual returns for the period ending June 30, 2002 and are taken from FSTQ's 2002 annual report, available online from the FSTQ Web site, ibid.

[b] The LSVCC averages do not include FSTQ or Fondaction. If they were included (using their figures to June 30, 2002 and May 31, 2002, respectively), the 5-year and 10-year LSVCC averages would be −0.6 percent and 2.5 percent, respectively.

[c] A minimum of 50 percent of total assets and 70 percent of non-cash assets must be in Canadian stocks. The threshold level, the average market capitalization of the equity holding, is 0.1 percent of the total market capitalization of the S & P/TSX composite index (August 31, 2002 = Cdn$710 million).

Source: "Report of Mutual Funds for Period Ending October 31, 2002" (for all funds other than FSTQ and Fondaction) from the Globefund Web site at http://www.globefund.com/.

are premature in the context of venture investing. Table 6.1 reflects the significant growth in the LSVCC industry in the past few years.[188] Of the 47 funds listed in the table, only 18 have been in existence for at least 5 years and only 3 for at least 10 years. Few LSVCCs have investment portfolios mature enough to generate return figures that in any way reflect their relative success in venture capital investment.

Having said that, in theory, the after-tax rates of return on the more mature LSVCCs—FSTQ, WOF, and Working Ventures Canadian Fund—should be approximately equal to the rates of return on equivalent non-tax-sheltered investments. Unfortunately, there are no directly comparable statistics available in the public domain for the returns on investment of Canadian private VCFs, which are the closest equivalent non-tax-sheltered investments to LSVCCs.[189] For illustration purposes, Canadian small-cap equity funds are used as a proxy for non-tax-sheltered equivalent investments. Even without performing any calculations, it is obvious that LSVCCs compare favourably with Canadian small-cap equity funds based on their 5-year rates of return, where LSVCCs posted better returns even without taking into account the tax credit. However, a 5-year period is rather short, particularly for venture capital investments; a 10-year comparison is more appropriate. Consider two individuals, Ms. X and Ms. Y, each of whom invests $5,000 in 1992 in her self-directed RRSP. Ms. X invests in an average Canadian small-cap fund and Ms. Y invests in an average LSVCC.[190] Each can deduct her RRSP contribution for tax purposes, generating an after-tax saving of $2,500 in 1993 (assuming an effective tax rate of 50 percent). Each reinvests the tax savings. In addition, Ms. Y reinvests the combined federal-provincial LSVCC tax credits obtained in 1993 ($2,000) outside her RRSP, in all cases in a riskless investment (Canada savings bonds are used as a proxy for a riskless investment). It is assumed that over the 10-year period the effective tax rate of the individuals is 50 percent (used as a proxy for the highest marginal rate), so the return on the amounts invested outside the RRSP by both Ms. X and Ms. Y is one-half the 4 percent benchmark rate for Canada savings bonds. In 2002, each individual withdraws the value of the RRSP investment; each withdrawal is subject to an effective tax rate of 50 percent. Ms. X's small-cap fund is worth $10,498.50 in 2002, netting her $5,249.25 when withdrawn from her RRSP. The $2,500 invested outside the RRSP has grown to $2,987.73, giving her a total of $8,236.98. Ms. Y's LSVCC fund is worth $6,421.27, netting her $3,210.64 when withdrawn from her RRSP. Her $4,500 invested outside the RRSP has grown to $5,377.92, giving her a total of $8,588.56, or $351.58 more than Ms. X. In summary, Ms. X's annualized after-tax rate of return over the 10 years is 5.12 percent whereas Ms. Y's return is 5.56 percent, a difference of less than one-half of 1 percent. On the basis of this simplistic analysis, the return on LSVCC investments is comparable to the return on small-cap funds. However, there were only three LSVCCs with a 10-year investment history, and their individual returns varied significantly. Although a 2.53 percent average is used for the purpose of the example, the sample size is too small to be representative of the entire class of LSVCCs.[191] In addition, the historical sample is based on an LSVCC investment made when the federal and provincial tax credits were both 20 percent rather than the current 15 percent. Thus, although the analysis suggests that LSVCC investments have performed comparably to non-tax-favoured investments on an after-tax basis over the past 10 years, it is questionable whether they will continue to do so in the future.

In theory, after-tax benefits are equalized if all of the tax-sheltered behaviour is undertaken by individuals in the highest marginal tax bracket. However, a "trickle-up phenomenon" results if the yield from the tax-exempt activity is raised in order to attract investors in lower tax brackets. In these circumstances, taxpayers in higher tax brackets would enjoy a windfall. As Boris Bittker suggests, "[f]or the rich, therefore, the best tax shelters are those that are patronized by the poor; on the other hand, the more exclusive the club, the less reason to join."[192]

The LSVCC tax credit does not set out to target lower-income Canadians, but it ends up doing that. If the after-tax rate of return from LSVCCs for lower-income investors is equal to the rate of return on an equivalent non-tax-sheltered investment, there is an incentive for high-income earners to invest in LSVCCs. Alternatively, if the equalization of rates of return applies to high-income Canadians—which the example above tends to suggest—then it is not worthwhile for lower-income earners to participate.

In summary, from the limited data available for long-term returns of LSVCCs and the absence of data for Canadian private VCFs, LSVCCs have compared favourably with non-tax-sheltered equivalent investments on an after-tax basis over past 10 years. However, if Canadian private VCFs had performed even half as well as their US counterparts over that 10-year period, the foregoing analysis would have yielded radically different results.[193] Similarly, an analysis of RRSP investments made currently in an LSVCC compared with a small-cap fund to be held for 20 years suggests that the small-cap investment will significantly outperform the LSVCC investment, although much depends on the assumed performance of the non-RRSP investments.[194] Assuming that prospective LSVCC investors are rational investors who would perform a similar analysis, the prognosis for the continued attractiveness of LSVCCs as an appropriate RRSP investment for Canadian individuals is not good.[195]

A related issue is whether the tax incentives that have facilitated the entry of LSVCCs into the venture capital market have created inappropriate distortions in that market—that is, whether incentives have exacerbated rather than compensated for market failures. The relatively easy money assembled by LSVCCs may give them a competitive advantage over private VCFs competing in the same marketplace. Unlike investors in private VCFs, individual investors in LSVCCs are, at least subjectively, less sensitive to the rate of return generated by the fund because of the significant upfront tax incentive and because each investor's investment is relatively small. In contrast, private VCFs tend to raise their capital from institutional investors that are highly sensitive to rates of return and that have a significant amount of capital at stake.[196]

As a result, LSVCC fund managers arguably have less incentive than private VCF managers to generate high returns on their investment portfolios. This factor, coupled with the obligation of LSVCCs to invest a portion of their capital in qualified small businesses within specified time periods, has two potential consequences. First, LSVCCs may be willing to invest in portfolio firms that private VCFs have rejected. Second, and more problematic, LSVCCs may place a higher value on potential business investments than their private VCF counterparts do. They are thus willing to pay more for an equivalent equity investment. Put another way, if a desirable portfolio business is seeking a particular amount of money, an LSVCC would be willing to take a smaller equity participation than a private VCF for the same cost. In other words, by choosing the LSVCC, the cost of capital to the small business has been reduced, as efficiency theory would suggest.

The LSVCC tax credit may reduce the cost of capital to SMEs in the same way that tax-free municipal bonds reduce the borrowing costs of US cities. In the municipal bond context, reduced borrowing costs are good for the city because the city is seeking only money, not opinions from lenders on how to spend the money it raises. However, in the venture capital context, the concern is that portfolio firms, unlike cities, require more than money. They require assistance in developing a strong management team to assist in product development and marketing and in general business administration. Private VCFs tend to be active participants in the development of their portfolio firms. LSVCCs, in contrast, tend to be passive investors that do not necessarily add the same value to their portfolio firms.

Arguably, LSVCCs can be beneficial if all they do is increase the pool of venture capital available. However, if they displace private VCFs, they may be detrimental not only to the venture capital industry, but also to the development of growth-oriented small businesses and therefore to overall economic growth. Using econometric modelling, Douglas Cumming and Jeffrey MacIntosh estimated the impact of provincial and federal LSVCCs on the supply of venture capital in Canada over the period 1977 to 2001. Their analysis suggests "not merely that LSVCCs have crowded out other Canadian funds, but that they have led to a *reduction* in the overall size of the venture capital pool."[197] They modelled the impact of LSVCCs both geographically and by financing stage. Geographically, their analysis suggests that LSVCCs, at best, crowded out private VCFs. However, federally registered funds for which certain provinces also provide a tax credit may have decreased the overall supply of venture capital in the maritime provinces and possibly Ontario.[198] By stage of financing, crowding out was most significant at the startup and expansion stages, which accounted for over 90 percent of the aggregate venture capital pool in 2001.

The conclusions reached by Cumming and MacIntosh are a cause for concern: not only are private VCFs being crowded out of the market, but their replacement, LSVCCs, are not providing the same value-added services for small businesses. Furthermore, the LSVCC program does not necessarily provide an adequate training ground for venture capital fund managers to develop their skills because LSVCCs do not necessarily manage their small business investment portfolio in the same manner as private funds. In particular, they are not necessarily as vigilant in the due diligence performed before making investment decisions or in monitoring investments once they are made. In short, LSVCCs may be not only crippling the existing private VCF industry, but also poisoning the well from which its future expertise is drawn. These concerns certainly warrant greater investigation. When these concerns are aggregated with all of the other concerns raised about LSVCC programs, they should cause governments to re-evaluate the continued use and cost of the programs.

Cost-Benefit Analyses of CAPCO Programs

The only cost-benefit analysis of a CAPCO program of which I am aware was a study commissioned by the Louisiana Department of Economic Development in 1999.[199] Before considering this study, it is worth summarizing the manner in which CAPCOs are typically financed. In most cases, the promoters of the CAPCO are its only equity holders and are generally required to contribute a minimum of $500,000 under most state regimes ($200,000 in Louisiana). Insurance companies typically lend money to CAPCOs on a fully secured basis. To support the secured loan structure, most state regimes require only 50 percent of a CAPCO's certified capital (which includes the amount loaned by insurance companies) to be invested in qualified businesses, leaving the remainder for investment in low-risk, liquid securities to fund the cash flow requirements under the notes (and management and other administrative fees of the promoters). A CAPCO typically cannot voluntarily decertify and cannot make distributions (other than qualified distributions, which include management fees in the neighbourhood of 2½ percent of certified capital) to its equity holders unless it achieves a 100 percent qualified investment threshold. Therefore, the CAPCO must churn investments in order to reach the investment threshold for voluntary decertification. Consider the typical CAPCO structure, as outlined in simplified manner in the Postlethwaite & Netterville study.[200] The CAPCO owners put in $200,000 (although, as noted, the minimum in most states is now $500,000) to establish the CAPCO; the CAPCO issues $25 million in secured notes to insurance companies. These notes generate $27.5 million in premium tax credits to the insurance companies over a 10-year period (assuming a 110 percent premium tax credit, which was in effect in Louisiana at the time of the study[201]). These premium tax credits, together with $10 million of the capital set aside by the CAPCO, cover the obligations of the CAPCO to the insurance companies under the secured loans.[202] A further $1 million covers financing and related costs, leaving $14 million to be invested by the CAPCO owners.[203] For a Louisiana CAPCO, prior to the 2002 amendments, at least 30 percent of the certified capital of $25 million, or $7.5 million, must be invested in qualified Louisiana businesses within 3 years and 50 percent, or $12.5 million, within 5 years, in order for the CAPCO to avoid involuntary decertification. However, in order to voluntarily decertify and make equity distributions to the CAPCO equity holders, the CAPCO must invest at least $25 million (that is, 100 percent of certified capital) in qualified Louisiana businesses. Assuming that it invests the entire $14 million available in qualified investments, the CAPCO must eventually liquidate some of these investments and reinvest at least $11 million in other qualified investments in order to reach the investment threshold necessary for liquidating distributions to the equity holders. The CAPCO can lose a substantial amount of the $14 million invested and still be highly lucrative to the CAPCO owners. One report on CAPCOs summarizes the program as follows:

> The heart of the CAPCO model is the commitment by the state of dollar for dollar tax credits, the provisions that permit the set-aside of capital to guarantee lenders from loss of principal, and the willingness of the state to accept little or no financial compensation for its contribution. All CAPCOs have these core provisions. The net effect of these provisions enables CAPCO owners to profitably operate a CAPCO with nearly any set of other conditions they may negotiate with a state.[204]

In summary, insurance companies earn a favourable rate of return on a relatively low-risk investment: an investment appropriate for the fixed-income portfolio of insurance companies. The equity holders in the CAPCO (primarily the fund managers) are compensated handsomely in two respects. First, the management fees permitted by legislation—generally, 2½ percent of total certified capital—are based on both actively managed venture capital and the capital set aside in US treasury bonds or other securities to cover the payments on the loans from the insurance company investors. So, in the above example, management fees can be $625,000 per annum (that is, 2½ percent of $25 million), even though only $14 million is actively invested in qualified venture-capital-type investments. Second, the entire venture portfolio of the CAPCO essentially belongs to the equity owners. Even if the CAPCO manager is successful only in maintaining the $14 million originally invested—in fact, even if it loses a significant portion of this investment—the entire amount belongs to the CAPCO equity owners who only invested $200,000.

In their report on the Louisiana CAPCO program, Postlethwaite & Netterville acknowledged that the program created a robust venture capital industry in the state, although it criticized the program for not using state resources efficiently. The premium tax credit at the time was higher than the credit in all other states with CAPCO programs, while the qualified investment requirements were among the least restrictive. As the study noted, the greatest value to the state of the CAPCO program is the investment activity, and the greatest benefit to the CAPCO is generated at the outset by raising money.[205] The typical CAPCO capital structure requires a significant portion of the capital raised to be used as collateral for the loans, thus reducing the amount of capital available for investment in qualified businesses.

The Postlethwaite & Netterville study provided a cost-benefit analysis of the Louisiana CAPCO program for the period 1988 to 2007 (the earliest year in which premium tax credits granted in 1998 could be fully utilized).[206] The cost of the program to the state—the value of all tax credits in 1999 (that is, using the present value of credits that could be applied only after that date)—was determined to be $405.5 million. The value of the benefit to the state was estimated in a highly simplified manner. Although the study described many variances that could be used to differentiate portfolio businesses (industry type, gross receipts, payroll size, profitability) and the type of financing provided by CAPCOs (early development, expanding markets, buyouts, refinancing, and other), the study used only gross receipts and industry type as the bases for estimating the economic benefit of the program. CAPCO-financed companies were classified by industry type (using standard industrial classification [SIC] codes), and aggregate gross receipts for each industry were used to estimate overall business transactions, personal earnings, and new jobs associated with the activities of these companies.[207] In all cases, the 1999 value of the estimated benefits exceeded the costs of the program, assuming that 100 percent of the gross receipts (that is, the increase in business) was attributable to CAPCO financing.

The study recognized that the qualified businesses did not rely exclusively on CAPCO financing. A random sample of 20 companies indicated that 22 percent of their financing was CAPCO financing. As the study noted, however, it is difficult to determine whether the non-CAPCO financing would have been made in the absence of CAPCO financing. The value of the benefits generated by CAPCO financing was redetermined assuming, first, that only 22 percent of gross receipts related to CAPCO financing and, second, that 50 percent was so related. On the basis of these assumptions, the benefits of the program exceeded the costs only where it was assumed that there was a 29.1 percent growth rate and 50 percent of gross receipts related to CAPCO financing. On the whole, the study suggested a positive cost-benefit analysis only if highly favourable assumptions about the success of CAPCO investments were made.[208] Other studies suggest that a CAPCO program is one of the most expensive ways to create jobs or facilitate the formation of venture capital.[209]

The CAPCO program is costly to the state introducing the program (although the cost can be limited by placing an overall cap on the tax credits given under the program) and the aggregate cost to all nine states with CAPCO programs to date is well over $1 billion.[210] Whether this cost is justified or not depends on the effects of the program. If the benefits to the state—direct, indirect and induced—exceed the costs, the program may be justified on a continuing basis. If, however, the costs exceed the benefits, the program makes sense only as a limited-term catalyst to create a self-sustaining venture capital industry. If the venture capital industry cannot be self-sustaining, there is little point in establishing the program in the first place.

It is highly unlikely that the CAPCO program, in its current incarnation, can act as a catalyst in establishing a private venture capital industry. The investors in the program—almost exclusively insurance companies—do not put money at risk in venture capital investments. They are secured creditors of CAPCOs making a good rate of return on their investment. The government is completely underwriting the investment risks with a 100 percent tax credit. Were it not for the tax incentives and the ability of CAPCOs to fully guarantee loans, insurance companies would not make similar investments. Furthermore, CAPCOs themselves are not motivated to generate positive returns to the same extent as private VCFs. In fact, CAPCOs can produce high returns for equity investors (primarily the fund managers) while sustaining significant losses on their investments. Thus, the CAPCO program would create a self-sustaining venture capital industry only if CAPCOs (or their investments) attract other venture capitalists, and sources of venture capital, to the state. That may be possible if the investments made by CAPCOs attract a concentrated pool of motivated entrepreneurs in growth businesses, who in turn attract private venture capitalists. However, like the fund managers of LSVCCs in Canada, the fund managers of CAPCOs do not have the same motivation as private sector fund managers to generate returns. Although I am not aware of any study that has addressed this issue, I suspect that CAPCOs are even more likely than LSVCCs to crowd out private sector funds rather than enhance their number.

Despite the doubtful benefits of the CAPCO program, it has garnered support in a number of states. The CAPCO industry is highly concentrated and is a powerful lobby group. Four major CAPCO groups—Advantage Capital, Enhanced Capital, Stonehenge Capital, and Newtek—accounted for approximately 80 percent of the $1.65 billion of the total state tax credits granted between 1986 and 2001 across all US states.[211] CAPCOs evidently spend a significant amount of time and money lobbying to maintain existing CAPCO programs and establish new ones.[212] Given their experience with the program in existing states, these CAPCOs tend to have a competitive advantage when a CAPCO program is established in other states.

Using Tax Credits To Guarantee Investment in VCFs

An innovative use of tax credits to enhance investment in VCFs was developed in Oklahoma in the late 1980s and introduced in 1991 with the passage of legislation establishing the Oklahoma Capital Investment Board (OCIB), a public trust of the state.[213] The purpose of the legislation is "to increase the availability of equity and near-equity capital for emerging, expanding and restructuring enterprises in Oklahoma" in a manner that will "result in significant potential to create jobs and diversify and stabilize the economy of the State of Oklahoma."[214]

The OCIB established Oklahoma Capital Formation Corporation to act as a fund of funds. The OCIB—that is, the Oklahoma government—holds the only equity interest in the corporation; its capital is raised through loans from institutional investors, the principal and interest on which are guaranteed by the OCIB. The state of Oklahoma has granted OCIB an aggregate of $100 million in state tax credits that it can sell in order to finance its obligations in the event that it is called on its guarantees, provided that no more than $20 million of these tax credits can be applied to any one fiscal year.[215] The fund of funds invests, as a passive investor, in private VCFs. In choosing the VCFs in which it invests, the OCIB is obliged to ensure that at least $2 will be invested in Oklahoma businesses for every $1 of principal that it guarantees.[216] The OCIB thus acts as a leverage of private capital. The returns that Oklahoma Capital Formation Corporation receives from its venture fund investments are used to pay the principal and interest obligations under its loans. Any excess forms part of the general revenue of the state.

Ideally, the tax credits will never be used and, to date, none has been used. If the program is successful, as it has been so far, it will come at no cost to the state other than the $600,000 spent in 1987-1989 to design the program. Through 2001, Oklahoma Capital Formation Corporation has committed $25.9 million to eight funds, of which $22.9 million has been drawn down. These eight funds target various stages of investment in various industries and through June 2001 had invested over $84 million in Oklahoma businesses, far exceeding the two-for-one requirement imposed by legislation on OCIB in choosing the funds in which it invests. From its inception in 1991 to June 30, 2001, Oklahoma Capital Formation Corporation generated an internal rate of return of 17 percent per annum. OCIB has allocated $60 million to a new round of investments, which it expects to commit to funds within three years.[217]

A number of other states have sought to emulate the Oklahoma program. For example, in 2002, Iowa introduced legislation creating the Iowa Capital

Investment Board (ICIB) and Iowa Capital Investment Corporation (ICIC) to organize an "Iowa fund of funds" and select a venture capital investment fund allocation manager to select venture capital funds in which to invest.[218] The Iowa fund of funds, as established by ICIC, is a private, for-profit limited partnership or limited liability company that is to be liquidated after 50 years. Under the legislation, preference will be given to investment in VCFs with experienced management, a proven record of venture capital investing, and a commitment to seek out businesses located within Iowa. Unlike the Oklahoma program, where the OCIB is the only equity investor in the fund of funds, the Iowa fund of funds is capitalized by private investors who purchase equity interests in the fund. The equity interests must provide a designated scheduled rate of return and a scheduled redemption that cannot occur within five years following the issuance of the equity interest.[219] Any returns exceeding the scheduled rate must be reinvested in the fund of funds by ICIC. The scheduled rate of return and the redemption of equity interests are guaranteed by tax credits issued by the ICIB. The ICIB may issue a maximum of $100 million of tax credits, with a maximum of $20 million applicable in any one year.[220]

Similar programs have been introduced in Arkansas[221] and Ohio.[222] The legislation is similar in all of the states in many respects. The capital raised through the use of the guarantees is invested in private VCFs rather than directly in SMEs. In effect, the capital raised capitalizes a fund of funds. The fund of funds may be managed by the state (that is, the state chooses in which private VCFs to invest) or by an independent gatekeeper selected by the state. Private investors provide the capital for the fund of funds through debt (as in Oklahoma) or equity (as in Iowa) guaranteed through the use of state tax credits. Thus, the state does not initially put up any of its own capital, nor does it provide any tax credits for the capital invested. The program will cost the state only if it is called on its guarantees—if the fund of funds fails to provide the return necessary to cover the capital and rate of return guaranteed to the private investors who are providing either debt or equity used to capitalize the fund of funds.

The various programs are therefore similar in overall structure and purpose, but there are important differences among them. In all programs, the government fully guarantees the principal and stipulated return to the private sector investors providing capital to the fund of funds. In all cases, the state benefits from the program in the same manner as states that have a more typical VCF program—through direct, indirect, and induced benefits generated by SMEs financed under the program. However, the Oklahoma program gives the state a direct equity interest in the fund of funds—in fact, the only equity interest in the fund of funds. Unlike other VCF programs, in which the state has no carried interest in the VCF or only a small carried interest, Oklahoma obtains all of the rewards from investing in the fund of funds (in exchange for bearing all of the risk of the investment). Other states, such as Iowa, provide an equity guarantee for others investing in the fund of funds. However, Iowa does not benefit directly from the successful performance of the fund of funds.

Conclusion

Provincial and state government programs in the formal venture capital industry should focus on two areas: attracting investors that can and should include private equity in a diversified portfolio; and strengthening the pool of knowledgeable venture capital fund managers. Neither the LSVCC program in Canada nor the CAPCO program in the United States accomplishes these objectives. First, neither program targets the appropriate sources of venture capital. The LSVCC program targets individuals across the economic spectrum and has garnered considerable participation from individuals in lower and middle income tax brackets (as well as the highest tax bracket). While the CAPCO program may target an appropriate investor class, insurance companies, they are not investing in risk capital. Rather, the CAPCO program has been structured to encourage secured debt financing by insurance companies through the provision of an extremely lucrative tax incentive. Both programs also fail to strengthen the pool of private equity fund managers. Indeed, they may accomplish the opposite. The incentives offered under both programs are too rich and the program design does not promote the operation of VCFs in the same manner as in the private sector. Both programs require upfront investment by qualified investors in order to obtain the tax credit (although the CAPCO tax credit is paid out over time) and then impose pacing requirements on the LSVCC or CAPCO. The significant upfront incentive reduces the pressure on the fund manager to invest the capital in qualified investments, while the pacing requirements with corresponding penalties may lead to last-minute, hasty investment decisions. Under neither program is the fund manager subject to appropriate pressure from the fund's investors to undertake the degree of due diligence or the extent of monitoring expected in private sector VCFs. In both cases, in fact, there is a distinct possibility that LSVCCs or CAPCOs may crowd out private sector VCFs.

Most other state and provincial VCF programs are also not appropriately targeted. In many programs, the only eligible investors are individuals and there are no restrictions on eligibility (although securities legislation in certain jurisdictions may apply appropriate limitations).[223] In many programs, the only incentive is a non-transferable tax credit, so tax-exempt entities and non-residents of the province or state cannot benefit. In the various VCF programs examined, the only exceptions are the CAPCO programs (except that in New York) and the general VCF programs in British Columbia, Missouri, and Kansas. Under the CAPCO programs, the premium tax credits are transferable, but authorized investors remain limited to insurance companies. British Columbia provides refundable credits, but only to individual investors. Under the Missouri VCF program, unused tax credits may be transferred. In Kansas, unused tax credits are refundable unless the investor is a non-resident of the state. The Missouri and Kansas programs were intended to attract tax-exempt entities as investors. In contrast, none of Canada's provincial VCF programs targets tax-exempt entities.

In many respects, Canada as a whole and its various provinces are comparable to the interior states in the United States and can learn from the various programs in use there. Certain programs or features of programs are worth considering in Canada. In particular, the Oklahoma program (or a variation) warrants consideration. The Oklahoma program has been successful in attracting $4 of investment in the state for every $1 raised by the state to capitalize the fund of funds. Under the Oklahoma program and all programs based on it, the government's maximum costs are fixed and no costs are incurred unless the fund of funds fails to produce the guaranteed investment returns. In all cases, investment decisions are left in the private sector in VCFs in which the state fund of funds is but one of many investors. Thus, the state program increases the capital available for venture capital investment in SMEs located in the state, while minimizing the risks of political interference in the investment decision-making process.

The Oklahoma program thus serves the second objective of strengthening the pool of private sector VCF managers. The funds in which the state fund of funds invests are private sector VCFs, managed in the same way as private sector VCFs in which no government money is invested. The Oklahoma program does not directly serve the first objective of targeting appropriate sources of venture capital, although the program's success (appropriately advertised) can serve as a signal to these investors. However, a variation of the program, such as that employed in Iowa, could accomplish both objectives. An equity guarantee program that targets specific investors such as pension funds could serve the dual purpose of increasing the venture capital pool under private sector management and targeting the investor classes that are necessary to ensure the future viability of the private sector venture capital industry.

Appendix 6A: Summary of Provincial Venture Capital Fund Tax Credit Programs

Contents

Governing Legislation 296
Number of VCFs Permitted 296
Organizational Form of VCF 296
Minimum/Maximum Capitalization 297
Eligible Investors 297
Nature of Investment in VCF 297
Nature of Incentive 298
Holding Period 299
Government Expenditure Limits 300
Eligible Investments 300
Pacing Requirements 301
Consequences of Failure To Meet Investment Requirements 302

Governing Legislation

British Columbia	Part 1 of the Small Business Venture Capital Act, RSBC 1996, c. 429, as amended.
Ontario	Part III.1 of the Community Small Business Investment Funds Act, SO 1992, c. 18, as amended.
Quebec	An Act Respecting Québec Business Investment Companies, RSQ, c. S-29.1.
Nova Scotia	Part 1 of the Equity Tax Credit Act, SNS 1993, c. 3, sections 11-13A.

Number of VCFs Permitted

British Columbia	Unlimited.
Ontario	Unlimited, although a community sponsor (municipality, First Nation council, Ontario university or college, or research institute affiliated with an Ontario university or a public hospital) must apply for registration before December 31, 2004.
Quebec	Unlimited.
Nova Scotia	Unlimited.

Organizational Form of VCF

British Columbia	Corporation.
	Memorandum limits the business of the company to assisting the development of small businesses by making investments and by providing business and managerial expertise to those businesses in which it has made or proposes to make an eligible investment.

Ontario	Corporation.
	Articles limit the corporation to assisting the development of eligible businesses and to creating and maintaining jobs by providing financial and managerial advice and making eligible investments.
Quebec	Corporation (Quebec business investment company [QBIC]).
	May be controlled directly or indirectly by one or more venture capital legal persons that are public legal persons.
	Articles limit the activities of the QBIC primarily to acquiring and holding shares of other legal persons.
Nova Scotia	Community economic development corporation (CEDC): non-profit, charitable, or non-taxable corporation or association incorporated in Nova Scotia. At least 25% of the CEDC's payroll is paid in the province, and the CEDC must meet criteria regarding the use of capital, educating investors in the defined community about venture capital, etc.

Minimum/Maximum Capitalization

British Columbia	Minimum $50,000.
	All additional equity capital must be approved.
Ontario	Minimum $2 million at the time of registration; maximum $10 million.
	For each investor, minimum $25,000, maximum $5 million.
Quebec	Minimum $50,000 paid-up capital made up of voting common shares.
Nova Scotia	Assets or revenues of less than $25 million.

Eligible Investors

British Columbia	Individuals (including RRSPs), corporations, and certain tax exempt entities.
Ontario	Labour-sponsored investment funds (LSIFs), certain financial institutions including insurance companies, individuals, pension funds, and corporations.
Quebec	Individuals (including RRSPs).
Nova Scotia	Individuals (including RRSPs).
	No individual may control more than 20% of the shares of the CEDC.

Nature of Investment in VCF

British Columbia	One class of shares without par value and with no special rights or restrictions.
Ontario	Class A shares that entitle the shareholder to vote and receive dividends.

Quebec   Common shares with full voting rights. The shareholder is the actual owner of the shares.

Nova Scotia   Fully paid, newly issued voting common shares. The shares are non-convertible and are not restricted in profit sharing or participation upon dissolution.

Nature of Incentive

British Columbia   30% tax credit (for individuals and corporations).

An individual's maximum annual tax credit for VCC investments is $60,000; however, credits in excess of $60,000 may be carried forward up to 4 years and any credit remaining unused after 4 years must be refunded, up to a maximum of $60,000. The maximum credits apply to the total credit under this program and the BC angel capital tax credit program (see appendix 5A). In effect, the taxpayer can invest up to $1 million in any 5-year period and claim $300,000 of tax credits over 5 years. In any year, if the tax otherwise owing is less than the credit available for that year, the excess credit is refundable.

A corporation has no maximum credit, but cannot use a credit to create a loss; any unused tax credits may be carried forward 4 years, but unused credits are not refundable.

Ontario   For an LSIF, twice the amount invested in a community small business investment fund (CSBIF) counts toward the LSIF's investment requirements or can be credited against the penalty taxes for failure to meet investment requirements. When the CSBIF makes an eligible investment, the LSIF's proportionate interest in the eligible investment counts toward the LSIF's investment requirements. The LSIF may report its initial investment in the CSBIF toward its own pacing requirements. See appendix 6C, under the headings "Pacing Requirements" and "Consequences of Failure To Meet Investment Requirements."

For a qualifying financial institution, a tax credit equal to 30% of the amount invested in a CSBIF; when the CSBIF makes an eligible investment, the financial institution is entitled to a further 30% tax credit based on its proportionate interest in the eligible investment.

For a qualifying individual or corporation, an investment incentive (i.e., a payment) equal to the lesser of $37,500 and 7.5% of the amount invested in a CSBIF (proposed to be increased to the lesser of $75,000 and 15% for investments between January 1, 2003 and December 31, 2004). When the CSBIF makes an eligible investment, a further investment incentive of the lesser of $37,500 and 7.5% of the investor's proportionate interest in the eligible investment (proposed to be increased to the lesser of $75,000 and 15% for investments in a CSBIF made after December 31, 2002).

No incentive for pension funds.

Quebec

An individual may deduct from taxable income his or her "adjusted interest in a qualified investment" for the year, as well as any unused portion from previous taxation years. The deduction permitted in any one year is limited to 30% of the individual's total income for that year. Unused amounts may be carried forward 5 years.

A taxpayer's "adjusted interest in a qualified investment" made after March 29, 2001 is 150% of the aggregate of the taxpayer's proportionate interest in a qualified investment made by a QBIC whose assets are under $25 million, or 125% of the aggregate of the taxpayer's proportionate interest in a qualified investment made by a QBIC whose assets are at least $25 million, plus, in either case, the taxpayer's proportionate interest in certain share issue expenses renounced by the QBIC. However, the adjusted interest cannot exceed 150% or 125%, as the case may be, of the taxpayer's financial commitment to the QBIC.

Nova Scotia

Tax credit equal to 30% of the amount invested to acquire the specified shares, with a maximum annual investment of $50,000. Unused credits may be carried back 3 years and carried forward 7 years.

The province will guarantee 20% of the amount invested for up to 4 years, provided that the CEDC has filed annual reports, has met its pacing requirements, and is in compliance with the legislation. If the CEDC is wound up before 4 years, or if the 4-year anniversary of the specified issue is reached, and the value of the eligible shares is less than 20% of the initial value, the province will make up the difference (provided that the stipulated conditions are met).

Holding Period

British Columbia

Minimum 3 years. If the shares are redeemed within 3 years, the VCC is subject to 30% tax on the original consideration for the shares. If the shares are redeemed between 3 and 5 years after issuance, there is partial abatement of the 30% tax.

Ontario

The VCC cannot pay a dividend or return any capital to an eligible investor until 6 years after its investment period and at least 70% of its equity capital has been invested in eligible investments.

Quebec

60 months. The QBIC is subject to 40% tax if it returns any capital to a shareholder before 60 months.

Nova Scotia

4 years. If an eligible investor disposes of shares within 4 years, the tax credit may be repaid plus a prescribed rate of interest (certain dispositions excluded).

Government Expenditure Limits

British Columbia Aggregate tax credits cannot exceed $12 million annually; an additional $3 million if eligible investments are outside Vancouver or Victoria; an additional $5 million if eligible investments are substantially engaged in the development for commercial exploitation of interactive digital media products developed in British Columbia.

Ontario None specified.

Quebec None specified.

Nova Scotia None specified.

Eligible Investments

British Columbia Equity shares, or a warrant, option, or right convertible into a share, of a business with no more than 100 employees that pays at least 75% of salaries to employees regularly in the province.

The business must be substantially engaged in prescribed business activities in British Columbia: manufacturing and processing; a destination tourist resort (if more than 50% of its gross revenue is from tourists); research and development of proprietary technologies including services directly associated with the export of technology; an activity carried on outside Victoria or Vancouver that promotes community diversification; and the development for commercial exploitation of interactive digital media products for various purposes. Certain activities are specifically excluded: natural resource exploration or extraction, financial services, real estate development or management, agricultural activities, retail or commercial services other than those specifically listed, restaurant or food services, and the leasing of property for a person's personal use.

Aggregate investment in any one eligible business by all VCCs cannot exceed $5 million.

Non-arm's-length transactions prohibited.

VCCs cannot control eligible business.

Ontario The total of the following must exceed 1.5: the percentage of total wages paid to employees performing eligible business activities within the community and the percentage of the gross assets of the portfolio company used in eligible business activities in the community (business activities other than a business that are a personal services business or specified investment business, as those terms are defined in the federal Income Tax Act, subsection 125(7)).

The gross assets of the portfolio company cannot exceed $1 million at the time of initial investment.

Investments must be arm's length (except if they are made in an aboriginal community).

No more than 20% of a CSBIF's equity capital may be invested in any one portfolio company.

Quebec   A CCPC with assets of less than $50 million and its head office in Quebec.

12 months before and after investment, 50% of salaries must be paid in, and 50% of employees must be situated in Quebec.

The investee firm cannot be the beneficiary of more than $10 million of investment.

The investee firm must deal at arm's length with the QBIC at the time of investment and for the following 24 months.

All investments must be validated by Investissement Québec.

The QBIC must hold the investment for 24 months, and the investee firm must operate for 24 months in a qualifiying sector of activity: manufacturing, tourism, tertiary actuators, exports, aquaculture, industrial creator, and the environment.

Nova Scotia   The capital raised must be invested in eligible business entities located within the defined community for which the CEDC was created to serve.

An eligible business entity is a taxable Canadian corporation, whose value is largely attributable to an active business, which has total assets (with associated corporations) not exceeding $50 million and employees not exceeding 500, and which pays 25% of wages and salaries in Nova Scotia.

Pacing Requirements

British Columbia   Must invest at least 40% of equity in eligible investments by the end of the next fiscal year, and at least 80% by the end of the second following fiscal year. Investments must be maintained for at least 5 years.

Ontario   By the end of 30th month after the investment period (its first year), at least 35% of equity must be invested in eligible investments. By the end of the 72d month, at least 70% of equity must be invested in eligible investments.

Quebec   None. However, a significant portion of the taxpayer's deduction is deferred until the QBIC makes qualified investments.

Nova Scotia   40% of equity capital must be invested in an eligible business entity within 12 months of the specified issue; 60% within 24 months; and 80% within 36 months.

Consequences of Failure To Meet
Investment Requirements

British Columbia	Registration may be suspended or revoked. All or a portion of the credit or grant must be repaid (the amount depends on the purchase price/fair market value of shares at the time). However, after 3 years of investment in SMEs, the administrator may forgive a portion of the repayment.
Ontario	Refundable tax equal to eligible investment shortfall multiplied by the following percentages of pro rata investment in the CSBIF (by investor type): 15% for an LSVCC, 30% for a qualifying financial institution, or 15% for an individual or corporation.
Quebec	None, since no pacing requirements. However, Investissement Québec may revoke the registration of the QBIC in certain circumstances.
Nova Scotia	The certificate of registration of a CEDC may be revoked. The CEDC must pay the minister the amount of the tax credits issued in respect of the specified issue.

Appendix 6B: Summary of Selected State Venture Capital Fund Tax Credit Programs

Contents

Governing Legislation 303
Number of VCFs Permitted 303
Organizational Form of VCF 304
Minimum/Maximum Capitalization 305
Eligible Investors 306
Nature of Investment in VCF 306
Nature of Incentive 306
Holding Period 308
Government Expenditure Limits 308
Eligible Investments 309
Pacing Requirements 311
Consequences of Failure To Meet Investment Requirements 312

Governing Legislation

Oklahoma	Qualified small business capital company (QSBCC): Small Business Capital Formation Incentive Act, title 68, sections 2357.60 to 2357.65 of the Oklahoma Statutes.
	Qualified rural small business capital company (QRSBCC): Rural Venture Capital Formation Incentive Act, title 68, sections 2357.71 to 2357.76 of the Oklahoma Statutes.
Maine	Title 10, section 1100-T of the Maine Revised Statutes.
West Virginia	West Virginia Code.
	West Virginia venture capital companies (WVVCCs): Article 5E-1, Venture Capital Company Act.
	West Virginia Economic Development Authority (WVEDA) fund of funds: Article 5E-2, West Virginia Venture Capital Act.
Iowa	Sections 15E.41 to 15E.46 of the Iowa Code.
Missouri	Missouri Revised Statutes, title XL, sections 620.635 to 620.653.
Kansas	Kansas Statutes, articles 74-8221 to 8229.

Number of VCFs Permitted

Oklahoma	Unlimited.
	QSBCC: Investments must be made after December 31, 1997 and before January 1, 2005.
	QRSBCC: Investments must be made after December 31, 2000 and before January 1, 2008.
Maine	Unlimited.

A private venture capital fund (PVCF) may or may not be located in Maine.

West Virginia — WVVCCs: Unlimited. Effective March 9, 2002, all qualified WVVCCs other than small business investment companies (SBICs) were decertified. Only qualified WVVCCs that are SBICs (i.e., registered with the US Small Business Administration [SBA]) remain eligible for tax credits. SBICs must be certified after January 1, 1999, be licensed by the SBA, and invest the leverage available to them.

WVEDA fund of funds: Funds selected by WVEDA. To date, seven funds have been approved: four SBICs; one new market VCC (see chapter 8, note 10); one foundation specializing in pre-seed intellectual property investments; and one private VCF.

Iowa — Unlimited.

Investments must be made in a community-based seed capital fund on or after January 1, 2002.

Missouri — One to four qualified funds, as described in the Missouri seed capital and commercialization strategy developed by the four qualified economic development organizations and approved by the Missouri Seed Capital Investment Board.

Only one qualified fund has been approved—Prolog Ventures, LLC.

Kansas — Unlimited.

The secretary of commerce authorizes and certifies entities to become capital formation companies (certified CFCs). The secretary also ensures that any potential director, trustee, manager, general partner, beneficial owner of 10% of any class of shares, or any promoter is in good standing to make venture capital investments. Furthermore, the secretary determines whether the potential managers possess sufficient investment knowledge to effectively manage a CFC.

The secretary publishes a list of every certified CFC in order to inform Kansas companies of available sources of investment capital.

Organizational Form of VCF

Oklahoma — A QSBCC or QRSBCC may be an S or C corporation, LLC, or a registered partnership. The VCF must be organized to provide the direct investment of equity and near-equity funds to companies within Oklahoma.

Maine — Private, professionally managed VCF. Must satisfy criteria set out in section 1026-N. The fund must have a business plan to create and retain jobs, assist businesses, show competence to administer venture capital investments, and propose performance standards and goals.

West Virginia — WVVCCs: SBIC (corporation, limited partnership, or LLC) with full-time office in West Virginia.

WVEDA fund of funds: A fund of funds. Each authorized fund may be a corporation, partnership, LLC, trust, or other business organization.

Iowa — Limited partnership or LLC.

Missouri — A fund established by any corporation, partnership, joint venture, unincorporated association, trust, or other organization. The Missouri Seed Capital Investment Board or the Missouri Technology Corporation approves the professional managers employed by the qualified funds according to criteria similar to that used in the SBIC program (see chapter 8, at note 87 and accompanying text).

In exchange for the availability of tax credits for investment in the fund, the fund must negotiate the largest possible equity interest in the fund for the four state qualified economic development organizations. (The qualified economic development organizations must reinvest all distributions of dividends, earnings, equity, or the like in the fund for investment in Missouri businesses.)

Kansas — Certified CFC can be a partnership, corporation, trust, or LLC, organized for profit or not for profit.

Minimum/Maximum Capitalization

Oklahoma — QSBCC: not less than $1 million.

QRSBCC: not less than $500,000.

Maine — None specified.

West Virginia — WVVCCs: Rules established by the SBA. Minimum equity of $5 million or $10 million if the SBIC plans to issue participating securities (see chapter 8, at notes 89 and 94-101 and accompanying text).

WVEDA fund of funds: None specified.

Iowa — Minimum $500,000; maximum $3 million. At least 10 investors with no one investor owning more than 25% interest.

Missouri — None specified.

Kansas — The CFC must have $500,000 of private capital to apply for certification. It must raise not less than $5 million of certified capital within 365 days ($1 million minimum for certain CFCs). The maximum capital eligible for tax credits in one certified CFC is $10 million.

Eligible Investors

Oklahoma	Individuals, corporations, fiduciaries, non-resident aliens, and insurers.
Maine	Individuals.
West Virginia	WVVCCs: Individuals, partnerships, corporations, or other entities that make capital investments.
	WVEDA fund of funds: Accredited investors, as defined in regulation D under the Securities Act of 1933.
Iowa	Individuals.
Missouri	Individuals, corporations, partnerships, LLCs, or other entities.
Kansas	Any person or entity subject to state tax. If a natural person, the investor must have a net worth of at least $1 million and at least 10 times the amount invested in the certified CFC.

Nature of Investment in VCF

Oklahoma	Equity and near-equity (common or preferred shares, warrants, rights to subscribe to shares, interest in partnership) or subordinated debt.
Maine	Cash actually invested in or unconditionally committed to a PVCF.
West Virginia	WVVCCs: Capital investment in an SBIC.
	WVEDA fund of funds: Investment in a fund specified in the application. Must invest a minimum of $200,000.
Iowa	Equity.
Missouri	Cash contribution in a qualified fund (i.e., limited partnership interest in Prolog A and Prolog B: see below, under the heading "Nature of Incentive").
Kansas	A beneficial ownership interest in the certified CFC.
	Investment in a single CFC cannot be less than $25,000 or more than $2 million; aggregate investments in all CFCs cannot exceed $5 million.

Nature of Incentive

Oklahoma	QSBCC: Tax credit equal to 20% of the cash invested in the QSBCC. However, the credit is limited to the amount of funds invested by the QSBCC in a qualified Oklahoma small business venture (QOSBV). No credit is provided where funds are used by a QOSBV to acquire another legal entity. Unused credits may be carried forward 10 years.
	QRSBCC: Tax credit equal to 30% of the cash invested in the QRSBCC. However, the credit is limited to the amount of funds

invested by the QRSBCC in a qualified Oklahoma rural small business venture (QORSBV). No credit is provided where funds are used by a QORSBV to acquire another legal entity. Unused credits may be carried forward 10 years.

Maine	Tax credit equal to 40% of the investment in a PVCF (between July 1, 2002 and June 30, 2003 and after 2005, 60% if the fund invests in high-unemployment areas). A tax credit certificate is not granted until the PVCF's investments in eligible businesses are at least equal to the amount of investment for which the tax credit is claimed. However, if the PVCF is located in Maine, is owned and controlled by residents of Maine, and has the objective of investing in Maine, a certificate equal to a 20% tax credit is granted at the time that money is invested in or unconditionally committed to the PVCF; the remainder (20% or 40%) is granted when the PVCF makes sufficient investment in eligible investments.
	Credits realized equally over 4 years; however, for credits issued between July 1, 2003 and June 30, 2005, credits realized over 7 years (15% in each of first 6 years; 10% in 7th year).
West Virginia	WVVCCs: Tax credit equal to 50% of investment. Unused credits may be carried forward 15 years. The maximum tax credits for investors in one SBIC cannot exceed $2 million.
	WVEDA fund of funds: Tax credit up to 50% of investment. An applicant must specify the minimum percentage tax credit that the applicant agrees to receive (i.e., WVEDA can negotiate with a taxpayer for a tax credit lower than 50%). If the applicant is a qualified WVVCC under section 5E-1 (which has the previous consent of WVEDA to invest under section 5E-2), the maximum credit is 10% of investment. The maximum credit for a single investor cannot exceed $2 million per year. Unused credits may be carried forward 15 years.
Iowa	Tax credit equal to 20% of equity investment in a community-based seed capital fund or directly in a qualifying business. The maximum credit for investment in any one qualifying business is $50,000. Each year, the taxpayer and affiliates can claim tax credits for up to 5 different investments in 5 different eligible businesses (i.e., maximum credit of $250,000).
	Unused credits may be carried forward 5 years.
	Credits cannot be claimed before the third tax year following the tax year in which the investment is made and no credit can be claimed before January 1, 2005.
Missouri	Tax credit equal to 100% of investment in a qualified fund. However, investors must invest an equivalent amount in a non-qualified parallel fund. Prolog Ventures, LLC is divided into Prolog A (100% credit) and Prolog B (no credit).
	Unused credits may be carried forward 10 years.
	Credits may be assigned, transferred, or sold.

Kansas — Tax credit equal to 50% of investment. The maximum tax credit is limited to a percentage of the credit proportional to the amount invested by the CFC in an eligible Kansas business, not to exceed 10% per year, commencing on and after January 1, 2005.

Unused credits in any taxable year are refunded, unless the investor is not subject to Kansas state tax, in which case the credit is transferable but not refundable.

Credits may be sold or transferred.

Holding Period

Oklahoma — None specified.

Maine — None specified.

West Virginia — None specified.

Iowa — None specified.

Missouri — None specified.

Kansas — None specified.

Government Expenditure Limits

Oklahoma — None.

Maine — An aggregate of $2 million, up to and including 1996; $3 million, up to and including 1997; $5 million, up to and including 1998; $8 million, up to and including 2001; $11 million up to and including 2004; $20 million up to and including 2005; $23 million up to and including 2006; $26 million up to and including 2007; maximum $30 million thereafter.

The limits are shared with the Maine angel capital tax credit program (see appendix 5A).

West Virginia — WVVCCs: Maximum $10 million per year, subject to reduction. The amount has been reduced in fiscal years beginning July 1 as follows: 1999—$6 million; 2000—$4 million; 2001—$4 million; 2002—$3 million.

WVEDA fund of funds: Any credits not allocated to WVVCCs within the first 30 days of the fiscal year. In addition, the West Virginia Economic Development Office can make its own direct investments in the fund of funds; by the end of 2002, it had invested $24.25 million.

Iowa — $10 million. No more than $3 million in the fiscal year starting July 1, 2002; $3 million for the fiscal year starting July 1, 2003; and $4 million for the fiscal year starting July 1, 2004. If the annual maximum is exceeded, credits are granted on a first-come, first-served basis.

The limits are shared with the Iowa angel capital tax credit program (see appendix 5A).

Missouri $20 million in aggregate; maximum $5 million per year.

In its first round of capital raising, Prolog Ventures, LLC raised $33 million: $16.5 million in Prolog A and $16.5 million in Prolog B.

Kansas $20 million in aggregate; maximum $2 million per year.

Note: When a certified CFC makes a liquidating distribution, the government is entitled to 10% of the distribution in excess of certified capital.

Eligible Investments

Oklahoma QSBCC: A QOSBV must be an incorporated or unincorporated business that has 50% of its assets or employees located in the state, and needs financial assistance to commence or expand business. The QOSBV must not be involved in specified businesses (oil and gas exploration, real estate development, real estate sales or rentals, wholesale sales, retail sales, farming, ranching, banking, or lending or investing funds in other businesses), and must qualify as a small business as defined by the SBA. A QSBCC may not invest more than 20% of its funds in any one QOSBV.

QRSBCC: A QORSBV must be an incorporated or unincorporated business that has 50% of its assets or employees in the state, its principal place of business in a non-metropolitan area, and at least 75% of gross annual revenue from a non-metropolitan area. The QORSBV must be engaged in specified business activities (any major group number of divisions A, C, D, E, F, or I of the *Standard Industrial Classification Manual, 1987*, except major groups 1 and 2 of division A), and must qualify as a small business as defined by the SBA. A QRSBCC may not invest more than 25% of its funds in any one QORSBV.

Maine At-risk investment in eligible businesses. An eligible business manufactures, develops, or applies advanced technologies; provides services that are sold or rendered predominantly outside Maine; or brings capital into Maine. An eligible business must have annual gross sales of $3 million or less, and the operation of the business must be the full-time professional activity of the principal owner.

The funds may be used by the eligible business for plant maintenance or construction, equipment, or research and development, or as working capital for the business.

For each eligible business, no more than $5 million of investment ($1 million for tax credits issued between July 1, 2003 and June 30, 2005) by any one PVCF is eligible for tax credits.

For each investor in the PVCF, no more than $500,000 aggregate investment ($200,000 for investments made between July 1, 2003 and June 30, 2005) in any one business over a consecutive 3-year period is eligible for tax credits.

No credit if the PVCF controls over 50% of an eligible business.

West Virginia — WVVCCs: Debt or equity financing of a West Virginia business: more than 50% of its assets and operations are in West Virginia and more than 50% of its employees are West Virginia residents. No size restrictions are imposed in the legislation. However, because qualified WVVCCs are now limited to SBICs, the size restrictions imposed by the SBA apply. The West Virginia business must be engaged in certain activities including: manufacturing; agriculture; forestry; mineral production, except for conventional oil exploration; a service industry (e.g., barbershops, laundries, car repairs); transportation; research and development; tourism; computer software development; and wholesale or retail distribution activities in West Virginia.

WVEDA fund of funds: Debt or equity financing of a West Virginia business: more than 50% of its assets and operations are in West Virginia and more than 50% of employees are West Virginia residents. No size restrictions are imposed in the legislation. No specific businesses are included or excluded. Presumably, WVEDA will take these issues into account when approving particular funds for the fund of funds.

Iowa — Eligible business: located in Iowa and in operation for less than 3 years, with a net value of less than $3 million. The owner has a prescribed amount of business experience or education. The business must not be primarily engaged in retail sales, real estate, or professional services. The business must secure, within 24 months of receiving an investment, equity financing of at least $250,000.

Missouri — Capital benefiting from the tax credit (i.e., Prolog A) must be invested in seed, startup, or follow-on capital in qualified businesses, but no more than 10% of qualified contributions may be invested in any one business. A qualified business is a business headquartered and operating in Missouri and is engaged in manufacturing, processing, research and development, or providing interstate commerce. In the case of seed capital and startup capital, the business cannot have had a positive cash flow in a past fiscal year.

Follow-on investment cannot exceed 40% of the fund's qualified contributions.

Capital invested in parallel fund (i.e., Prolog B) need not be invested in Missouri businesses.

Kansas — Investment of cash for capital of a qualified Kansas business: independently owned with its principal business office in Kansas, in need of venture capital and unable to obtain conventional financing, and at least 50% of its employees are resident in Kansas. The business must be less than 5 years old and have gross sales of no more than $1 million. The business cannot be a passive business.

The business must be engaged in manufacturing, processing or assembling, or distributing products, conducting research and development, or providing services in interstate commerce (and more than 50% of its revenue comes from services provided outside the state). Excluded activities include retail sales, real estate, real estate development, banking or lending, insurance, and personal services provided to non-commercial customers.

If a Kansas business qualified at the time of first investment, it remains qualified for 5 years for the purposes of follow-on investment.

A certified CFC cannot invest more than 20% of its certified capital or its certified capital plus any amount of net gains and losses and income and expenses, whichever is greater, in any one business.

A certified CFC cannot invest in an affiliate of the CFC or an affiliate of an investor (an affiliate is any person who owns 10% or more of the voting shares of the CFC or the investor, or any person in which the CFC or investor owns 10% or more of the voting shares, or any person who controls or is controlled by the CFC or the investor or any partnership in which the CFC or the investor is a general partner).

Pacing Requirements

Oklahoma	QSBCC: None, but, as noted above, no tax credit is available until capital is invested in eligible investments.
	QRSBCC: Same.
Maine	None, since generally no credit is granted until the PVCF invests an equivalent amount in eligible investments. (In the case of a PVCF that is a Maine fund, 50% of the credit is deferred until eligible investments are made; see below, under the heading "Consequences of Failure To Meet Investment Requirements.")
West Virginia	WVVCCs: SBICs conform to rules set by the SBA (i.e., every 18 months it must invest at least 20% of its capital in eligible businesses until 80% is so invested).
	WVEDA fund of funds: The manager of the fund of funds must establish a pacing schedule in agreement with each fund.
Iowa	The community-based seed capital fund must invest at least 33% of invested capital in at least two qualifying businesses within 36 months of starting investing activities.
Missouri	The qualified fund (i.e., Prolog A) must invest 100% of qualified contributions in qualified investments within 10 years of receipt (no intermediate pacing requirements).
Kansas	A certified CFC cannot make liquidating distributions until 100% of certified capital is invested in qualified businesses or the fair value of the certified CFC's assets plus any prior qualified and liquidating distributions equals or exceeds 110% of certified capital.

Consequences of Failure To Meet
Investment Requirements

Oklahoma	QSBCC: None, since no credits are granted until qualified investments made.
	QRSBCC: Same.
Maine	Where a tax credit certificate is granted at the time of investment in the PVCF (i.e., the PVCF is a Maine fund), the credit may be revoked to the extent that the PVCF does not make eligible investments within 3 years after the date of the tax credit certificate.
West Virginia	WVVCCs: Penalty equal to tax credits allowed to all taxpayers in the SBIC plus interest of $1\frac{1}{2}\%$ per month from the date that the credits are certified. The tax commissioner can abate a penalty for reasonable cause. Also subject to any penalties imposed by federal legislation on SBICs.
	WVEDA fund of funds: None specified in the legislation.
Iowa	Tax credit certificates are rendered null and void.
Missouri	The qualified fund (i.e., Prolog A) is subject to an annual tax of 15% of capital not invested as a qualified investment within 10 years (excluding management fees not exceeding 3% per year of committed contributions and other expenses or fees authorized by the board).
Kansas	None, since no credits are granted until qualified investments are made.
	Involuntary decertification (in case of other breaches of legislation); unused tax credits are forfeited commencing with the taxable year of the investor or transferee in which the decertification arose.

Appendix 6C: Summary of Federal and Provincial LSVCC Programs*

Contents

Governing Legislation 313
Number of LSVCCs Permitted 314
Sponsoring Organization 314
Organizational Form of LSVCC 315
Board of Directors of LSVCC 315
Minimum/Maximum Capitalization 315
Eligible Investors 316
Nature of Incentive 316
Holding Period 317
Government Expenditure Limits 317
Eligible Investments 317
Pacing Requirements 319
Consequences of Failure To Meet Investment Requirements 320

Governing Legislation

Federal	Part X.3 of the Income Tax Act, RSC 1985, c. 1 (5th Supp.), as amended.
British Columbia	Part 2 of the Employee Investment Act, RSBC 1996, c. 112, as amended.
Saskatchewan	The Labour-Sponsored Venture Capital Corporations Act, SS c. L-0.2.
Manitoba	Crocus Investment Fund: The Crocus Investment Fund Act, CCSM, c. C308.
	Other Manitoba LSVCCs: The Labour-Sponsored Venture Capital Corporations Act, CCSM, c. L12.
Ontario	Part III of the Community Small Business Investment Funds Act, SO 1992, c. 18, as amended.
Quebec	FSTQ: Act To Establish the Fonds de solidarité des travailleurs du Québec (F.T.Q.), RSQ, c. F-3.2.1.
	Fondaction: Act To Establish Fondaction, le Fonds du développement de la Confédération des syndicats nationaux pour la coopération et l'emploi, RSQ, c. F-3.1.2.
New Brunswick	New Brunswick Income Tax Act, SNB 2000, c. N-6.001, section 50.
	Act Respecting the Workers Investment Fund Inc., SNB 1994, c. 111.

---

* The Northwest Territories introduced an LSVCC program in 2000. Newfoundland and Labrador announced its intention to introduce an LSVCC program in both its 2001 budget and 2003 provincial budgets. Neither program is described in this appendix. For more detail, see notes 80 and 81 and accompanying text.

Nova Scotia	Parts II and III of the Equity Tax Credit Act, SNS 1993, c. 3, as amended.

Number of LSVCCs Permitted

Federal	Unlimited.
British Columbia	Unlimited. Currently, two are registered: Working Opportunity Fund (WOF) and Altura Growth Fund. A third fund is proposed.
Saskatchewan	Unlimited. New registrations may be denied if the annual tax expenditure exceeds $5 million.
Manitoba	Crocus Investment Fund.
	Other Manitoba LSVCCs: Unlimited. Currently, one is registered.
Ontario	Unlimited.
Quebec	FSTQ.
	Fondaction.
New Brunswick	Unlimited. Six have been prescribed, including the Workers Investment Fund, although two previously prescribed federal funds are not prescribed for 2004.
Nova Scotia	Unlimited. Currently, 8 are registered.
	Effective January 1, 2005, in order to be registered, the LSVCC must have its head office in Nova Scotia, employ at least three full-time residents of Nova Scotia, pay at least 75% of its salaries and wages in Nova Scotia, and have the majority of its principal decision makers resident in Nova Scotia. None of the 8 currently registered LSVCCs meets these criteria and, unless they do so by January 1, 2005, will be deregistered.

Sponsoring Organization

Federal	Trade union that represents employees in more than one province.
British Columbia	Union, group, or federation of unions headquartered in province.
Saskatchewan	Trade union under the Trade Union Act.
Manitoba	Crocus Investment Fund: Manitoba Federation of Labour (MFL).
	Other Manitoba LSVCCs: An employee organization.
Ontario	Trade union, association, or federation of trade unions.
Quebec	FSTQ: Fédération du travailleurs du Québec (FTQ).
	Fondaction: Confédération des syndicats nationaux (CSN).
New Brunswick	Same as federal. The Workers Investment Fund is sponsored by the New Brunswick Federation of Labour (NBFL).
Nova Scotia	For provincially registered funds, a trade union as defined in the Nova Scotia Trade Union Act. Otherwise, same as federal.

Organizational Form of LSVCC

Federal	Corporation.
British Columbia	Corporation.
Saskatchewan	Corporation.
Manitoba	Crocus Investment Fund: Corporation.
	Other Manitoba LSVCCs: Corporation.
Ontario	Corporation.
Quebec	FSTQ: Corporation.
	Fondaction: Corporation.
New Brunswick	Corporation.
Nova Scotia	Corporation.

Board of Directors of LSVCC

Federal	At least half appointed by the sponsoring organization.
British Columbia	No specific provisions in legislation.
	The articles of the Working Opportunity Fund and Altura both provide that the majority of the board must be elected by the sponsoring organization.
Saskatchewan	At least half appointed by the sponsoring organization.
Manitoba	Crocus Investment Fund: Majority appointed by the MFL.
	Other Manitoba LSVCCs: At least half appointed by the sponsoring organization.
Ontario	Majority elected by the sponsoring organization.
Quebec	FSTQ: 10 of 16 appointed by the FTQ.
	Fondaction: 4 of 11 chosen by the sponsoring organization, 2 by another union.
New Brunswick	Workers Investment Fund: 13 directors, of which 7 are appointed by the NBFL. Otherwise, same as federal.
Nova Scotia	For provincially registered funds, at least half appointed by the sponsoring organization. Otherwise, same as federal.

Minimum/Maximum Capitalization

Federal	None specified.
British Columbia	Minimum $25,000; maximum $5 million if not a reporting issuer.
Saskatchewan	None specified.
Manitoba	Minimum $25,000.
Ontario	None specified.

Quebec	None specified.
New Brunswick	None specified.
Nova Scotia	Minimum $25,000.

Eligible Investors

Federal	Individuals (including RRSPs).
British Columbia	Same as federal.
Saskatchewan	Same as federal.
Manitoba	Same as federal.
Ontario	Same as federal.
Quebec	Same as federal.
New Brunswick	Same as federal.
Nova Scotia	Same as federal.

Nature of Incentive

Federal	15% tax credit; maximum annual credit of $750.
British Columbia	15% tax credit; maximum annual credit of $2,000 (corresponding to an investment of $13,333).
	The maximum credits apply to shares acquired in employee venture capital plans (LSVCCs) and employee share ownership plans.
Saskatchewan	20% of the cost of acquiring shares in the LSVCC, to a maximum of $750.
Manitoba	15% tax credit; maximum annual credit of $750.
Ontario	15% tax credit; maximum annual credit of $750.
	For a research-oriented investment fund (ROIF), 20% tax credit; maximum annual credit of $1,000.
Quebec	15% tax credit; maximum annual tax credit of $750.
New Brunswick	Same as federal.
Nova Scotia	15% tax credit; maximum annual credit of $525.
	Effective January 1, 2005, 20% tax credit; maximum annual credit $1,000.
	The tax credit was due to expire on December 31, 2004. In the 2004-5 budget, the tax credit was extended to December 31, 2009 (although note criteria for an LSVCC to be registered, above, under "Number of LSVCCs Permitted").

Holding Period

Federal	8 years.
British Columbia	5 years.
Saskatchewan	Same as federal.
Manitoba	Same as federal.
Ontario	Same as federal.
Quebec	Until retirement age (generally, 65).
New Brunswick	Same as federal.
Nova Scotia	Same as federal.

Government Expenditure Limits

Federal	None.
British Columbia	$16 million annually in tax credits. Allocated $8.25 million for corporations with assets greater than $200 million (WOF) and $7.75 million for corporations with less than $200 million in assets.
Saskatchewan	$5 million annually in tax credits.
Manitoba	Crocus Investment Fund: None.
	Other Manitoba LSVCCs: $60 million annually.
Ontario	None.
Quebec	None.
New Brunswick	None.
Nova Scotia	Aggregate credits cannot exceed $5 million.

Eligible Investments

Federal	An SME with no more than 500 employees and $50 million in assets; at least 50% of employees must be employed in Canada; and at least 50% of salaries must be attributed to services rendered in Canada. The total cost of investment is not to exceed the lesser of $15 million and 10% of shareholder equity.
British Columbia	An SME that pays at least 50% of salaries to employees who are regularly in the province, and that has less than $50 million in assets.
	An eligible business cannot receive more than $5 million from an LSVCC within a 2-year period, unless the LSVCC already meets minimum investment levels (see below, under the heading "Pacing Requirements").
	Some secondary-market purchases are permitted if the purchase will result in job preservation, assist the business in dealing with the departure of an employee investor or venture capital investor,

facilitate orderly succession, or achieve some other substantial economic benefit.

Ineligible business activities include: primary resource exploration or extraction, financial services, property management or rental or leasing of land, development of land, agricultural activities (with some exceptions), and retail services.

Saskatchewan
An SME with fewer than 500 employees in Saskatchewan.

No more than 60% of a fund's equity capital may be invested in any one eligible business.

Manitoba
Crocus Investment Fund: An SME that has no more than $50 million in assets and employs more than 50% of its employees in Manitoba.

Other Manitoba LSVCCs: An SME that has no more than $50 million in assets and employs at least 50% of its employees in Manitoba. At least 50% of salaries must be attributed to services rendered in Manitoba.

For both the Crocus Investment Fund and other Manitoba LSVCCs, the cost of an eligible investment cannot exceed 10% of the fund's investment assets.

Ineligible investments include: a debt obligation secured by certain types of real property; an equity interest in the business of a profession; mineral development and exploration; production of agricultural or horticultural crops; or the leasing, development, or sale of real property.

Ontario
An SME as defined in federal legislation. At least 50% of salaries and wages are paid to employees from a place of employment in Ontario. At least 50% of employees are engaged in eligible activities (activities other than a personal services business or specified investment business as defined in subsection 125(7) of the federal Income Tax Act) carried on in Ontario. Gross assets may not exceed $50 million. SME and related businesses have no more than 500 employees.

An eligible investment may not exceed the lesser of $15 million and 10% of LSVCC's equity capital. LSVCC may not own more than 50% of the shares of an entity.

For an ROIF, at least 50% of its equity capital must be invested in research businesses.

Investments cannot be used by an eligible business for: relending, investment in land (unless incidental to the eligible business activity), reinvestment outside Canada, non-arm's-length transactions, and carrying on business outside Canada.

Quebec
FSTQ: An SME with less than $50 million in assets or $20 million in net assets; the majority of employees must be resident in Quebec.

Fondaction: An SME with less than $100 million in assets or $40 million in net assets; the majority of employees must be resident in Quebec. Mainly worker-controlled enterprises, enterprises where workers have greater control over their work, and environmentally concerned enterprises.

For both FSTQ and Fondaction, some secondary-market purchases are permitted.

New Brunswick	Same as federal.

For the Workers Investment Fund, at least 80% of an SME's investments must be in New Brunswick SMEs.

For a federally registered fund to be prescribed, the fund must agree to invest at least 80% of the capital that it raises in New Brunswick in New Brunswick businesses within 5 years.

Nova Scotia	An SME with no more than 500 employees and $25 million in assets; at least 25% of salaries must be paid in the province.

Pacing Requirements**

Federal	60% of shareholder equity, subject to a number of adjustments, must be invested in eligible investments within 1 year. Investments in smaller businesses count for 150% or 200% of cost, depending on size (assets not exceeding $10 million or $2.5 million, respectively).
British Columbia	Must invest a percentage of equity capital raised in a calendar year in eligible businesses in accordance with the following schedule: at least 20% by the end of the following calendar year; at least 40% by the end of the second following calendar year; at least 60% by the end of the third following calendar year; at least 80% by the end of the fourth following calendar year.
Saskatchewan	During the 24-month period following the end of the year in which the equity capital was raised, 75% of equity capital must be invested in equity shares and debt obligations of eligible businesses; after that 24-month period, 60% must be invested in equity shares.
Manitoba	Three investment limits must be met by both Crocus Investment Fund and other Manitoba LSVCCs:

1) 60% of equity on hand must be invested in eligible investments;

2) 70% of equity raised after 2000 and at least two years before the particular year must be invested in eligible investments acquired after February 2001; and

3) 14% of equity raised after 2000 and at least two years before the particular year must be invested in small eligible investments (total cost to the LSVCC of no more than $2 million) acquired after February 2001.

** Some jurisdictions (for example, the federal, Manitoba, and Nova Scotia regimes) have relaxed investment requirements during an initial startup period of the fund. This appendix does not list these relaxed investment requirements.

Ontario	At the end of each calendar year, 70% of shareholder equity must be invested, subject to several adjustments, in eligible investments.
	At the end of each calendar year, 14% of shareholder equity, subject to a number of adjustments, must be invested in small businesses (eligible businesses whose gross assets do not exceed $5 million and have no more than 50 employees).
Quebec	FSTQ: 60% of the previous year's average net assets must be invested in eligible investments.
	Fondaction: Same as FSTQ; in addition, two-thirds must be invested in enterprises with less than $50 million in assets and less than $20 million in net assets.
	FSTQ and Fondaction: Up to 25% can be secondary-market purchases. No more than 20% of net assets at the end of the previous year may be invested in secondary-market purchases.
New Brunswick	Same as federal.
Nova Scotia	For the first 12 months after the end of the year in which the equity was raised, 80% of equity must be invested in eligible businesses or reserves; 60% of equity raised in the province must be invested in eligible businesses in the province within 2 years after the year in which equity was raised (reduced from 4 years in 2002).
	Effective January 1, 2005, 60% eligible business investment requirement increased to 70% within 2 years and to 80% within 3 years.

Consequences of Failure To Meet Investment Requirements

Federal	Monthly deficiency tax; mostly refundable annual tax and penalty if 12 consecutive months of deficiencies; registration may be revoked if deficiencies in 18 of 36 months.
British Columbia	Registration may be suspended or revoked.
Saskatchewan	Registration may be revoked; tax credits must be repaid.
Manitoba	Same as federal.
Ontario	15% deficiency tax (refundable). Registration may be revoked. Tax credits must be repaid.
Quebec	Restriction on subsequent capital raising.
New Brunswick	Same as federal.
Nova Scotia	20% deficiency tax. Certificate of eligibility may be revoked.

Appendix 6D: Summary of State CAPCO Programs

Contents

Governing Legislation 321
Organizational Form of CAPCO 321
Minimum/Maximum Capitalization 323
Eligible Investors 323
Nature of Investment in CAPCO 323
Nature of Incentive 324
Maximum Investment/Benefit for Any One Certified Investor 325
State Share in Distribution 326
Government Expenditure Limits 327
Eligible Investments 327
Pacing Requirements 331
Requirements for Voluntary Decertification or for Distributions Other
  Than Qualified Distributions 332
Consequences of Failure To Meet Investment Requirements 332

Governing Legislation

Louisiana	Louisiana Revised Statutes, title 22, section 1068(E) (premium tax credit) and title 51, section 1921 et seq., as amended (income tax credit and general rules) (originally introduced 1983).
New York	New York State Consolidated Laws, c. 60, article 1, section 11 (effective since 1997). Credit found at c. 60, article 33, section 1511(k).
Wisconsin	Wisconsin Statutes, c. 560, section 560.30 et seq. and Wisconsin Administrative Code, c. Comm. 111 (introduced in 1997).
Florida	Florida Statutes, title XIX, c. 288, part XI, section 288.99 (effective 1998; amended in 2002 to add program #2, although no funding has yet been provided for program #2).
Missouri	Missouri Revised Statutes, title X, sections 135.500 to 135.529 (introduced in 1997).
Colorado	Colorado Revised Statues, title 10, article 3.5 (introduced in 2001).
Texas	Insurance Code, title 1, c. 4, subchapter B (introduced in 2001).
Alabama	Code of Alabama 1975, title 40, c. 14B (enacted April 18, 2002 and effective immediately).
Georgia	Official Code of Georgia, c. 48-18 (effective March 1, 2003).

Organizational Form of CAPCO

Louisiana	Partnership, corporation, or other legal entity. Organized for profit or not for profit.
	The officers, board of directors, partners, managers, or members must be thoroughly acquainted with the requirements of the CAPCO program and the certification and decertification procedures.

New York	Partnership, corporation, trust, or LLC. Organized for profit.
	At least 2 principals or any manager of the CAPCO must each have at least 5 years of experience in the venture capital industry or venture-capital-related industry.
Wisconsin	Partnership, corporation, trust, or LLC. Organized for profit or not for profit.
	At least 2 officers, directors, general partners, trustees, managers, or members must each have at least 2 years of experience in the venture capital industry.
Florida	Corporation, partnership, or LLC.
	At least 2 principals must each have at least 5 years of experience making venture capital investments out of private equity funds. Not less than $20 million must be provided by third-party investors for investment in the early stage of operating businesses. One full-time manager or principal with such experience must be primarily located in an office in Florida.
Missouri	Partnership, corporation, trust, or LLC. Organized for profit or not for profit.
	Officers and the board of directors, trustees or managers must be thoroughly acquainted with the CAPCO legislation.
Colorado	Partnership, corporation, trust, or LLC. Organized for profit. The principal office must be located or headquartered in Colorado.
	At least 2 principals or people employed to manage the fund must each have at least 2 years of money management experience in the venture capital industry.
Texas	Partnership, corporation, trust, or LLC. Organized for profit or not for profit.
	At least 2 principals or people employed to manage the fund must each have at least 4 years of experience in the venture capital industry.
Alabama	Partnership, corporation, trust, or LLC. Organized for profit or not for profit.
	At least 2 principals or persons employed or engaged to manage the funds must each have at least 4 years of experience making venture capital investments in small businesses on behalf of or as an institutional or accredited investor.
Georgia	Partnership, corporation, trust, or LLC. Organized for profit or not for profit.
	At least 2 principals or people employed to manage the fund must each have at least 2 years of experience in the venture capital industry. At least one principal or manager must be primarily located in an office in the state.

Minimum/Maximum Capitalization

Louisiana	Minimum $200,000.
New York	Minimum $500,000.
Wisconsin	Minimum $500,000.
Florida	Minimum $500,000.
Missouri	Minimum $500,000.
Colorado	Minimum $500,000.
Texas	Minimum $500,000.
Alabama	Minimum $500,000.
Georgia	Minimum $500,000.

Eligible Investors

Louisiana	Insurance company CAPCOs: Insurance companies.
	General CAPCOs: Any person subject to state income tax.
New York	Insurance companies.
Wisconsin	Insurance companies.
Florida	Insurance companies.
Missouri	Insurance companies.
Colorado	Insurance companies.
Texas	Insurance companies (or others subject to state premium tax liability).
Alabama	Insurance companies (or others subject to state premium tax liability).
Georgia	Insurance companies.

Nature of Investment in CAPCO

Louisiana	Equity; or a loan receivable that has a stated final maturity date of not less than 5 years from the original date of the loan.
New York	Equity; or a debt instrument with at least 5 years to maturity and no interest, distribution, or payment features that are related to the profitability of the CAPCO or the performance of the CAPCO's investment portfolio.
Wisconsin	Equity; or a debt instrument with at least 5 years to maturity and no interest, distribution, or payment features that are related to the profitability of the CAPCO or the performance of the CAPCO's investment portfolio until the CAPCO can make distributions other than qualified distributions.

Florida	Equity; or a debt instrument with at least 5 years to maturity and no interest, distribution, or payment features that are related to the profitability of the CAPCO or the performance of the CAPCO's investment portfolio.
Missouri	Equity; or a debt instrument with at least 5 years to maturity and no interest, distribution, or payment features that are related to the profitability of the CAPCO or the performance of the CAPCO's investment portfolio.
Colorado	Equity; or a debt instrument with at least 5 years to maturity and no interest, distribution, or payment features that are related to the profitability of the CAPCO or the performance of the CAPCO's investment portfolio.
Texas	Equity; or a debt instrument with at least 5 years to maturity and no interest, distribution, or payment features that are related to the profitability of the CAPCO or the performance of the CAPCO's investment portfolio.
Alabama	Equity; or a debt instrument with at least 5 years to maturity and no interest, distribution, or payment features that are related to the profitability of the CAPCO or the performance of the CAPCO's investment portfolio.
Georgia	Equity; or a debt instrument with at least 5 years to maturity and no interest, distribution, or payment features that are related to the profitability of the CAPCO or the performance of the CAPCO's investment portfolio until the CAPCO can make distributions other than qualified distributions.

Nature of Incentive

Louisiana	Insurance company CAPCOs: 100% premium tax credit. The credit cannot be used for 2 years after the date of investment; maximum 12½% per year.
	General CAPCOs: 35% income tax credit. No annual restrictions on use of the credit.
	In both cases, unused credits may be carried forward indefinitely.
	In both cases, credits may be sold or transferred.
New York	100% premium tax credit; maximum 10% per year. For program #1, none of the first $50 million of tax credits can be used before 1999, and for the second $50 million, none can be used before 2000. For program #2, credits cannot be used before 2001. For program #3, credits cannot be used before 2002. For a description of the programs, see below, under the heading "Government Expenditure Limits."
	Unused credits may be carried forward indefinitely.
	Credits are not transferable.
Wisconsin	100% premium tax credit; maximum 10% per year.

Unused credits may be carried forward indefinitely.

Credits may be sold.

Florida   100% premium tax credit; maximum 10% per year.

Credits for program #1 may be taken starting in 2000.

Credits for program #2 (if they are authorized) may not be taken until 2004 at the earliest. Tax credits will not be available under program #2 until the first fiscal year in which the total insurance premium tax collections as determined by the Revenue Estimating Conference exceed collections for fiscal year 2000-1 by more than the total amount of tax credits issued under program #1 that were used by certified investors in that year. Procedures for issuing credits under program #2 must be established within 180 days from the date of determination by the Revenue Estimating Conference.

Unused credits may be carried forward indefinitely.

Credits may be transferred or sold.

Missouri   100% premium tax credit; maximum 10% per year.

Unused credits may be carried forward indefinitely.

Credits may be transferred or sold.

Colorado   100% premium tax credit; maximum 10% per year.

Unused credits may be carried forward 10 years.

Credits may be transferred or sold.

Texas   100% premium tax credit; maximum 10% per year.

Unused credits may be carried forward indefinitely.

Credits may be transferred or assigned.

Alabama   100% premium tax credit, beginning in second year after year of investment; maximum 12½% per year.

Unused credits may be carried forward indefinitely.

Credits may be transferred or assigned.

Georgia   100% premium tax credit; maximum 10% per year commencing after July 1, 2005.

Unused credits may be carried forward indefinitely.

Credits may be transferred or sold.

Maximum Investment/Benefit for Any One Certified Investor

Louisiana   None specified.

New York   In any year, certified capital investments may not exceed $10 million for each of programs #1 and #3 and $8 million for program #2.

Wisconsin   In any year, certified capital investments may not exceed $10 million.

Florida	In any year, certified capital investments may not exceed $15 million for each of programs #1 and #2.
Missouri	In any year, certified capital investments may not exceed $10 million.
Colorado	Premium tax credits may not exceed 15% of the maximum aggregate of credits available under the program.
Texas	Credits may not exceed the greater of $10 million and 15% of the maximum aggregate of credits available under the program.
Alabama	Credits may not exceed the greater of $10 million and 15% of the maximum aggregate of credits available under the program.
Georgia	Credits may not exceed the greater of $10 million and 15% of the maximum aggregate of credits available under the program.

State Share in Distribution

Louisiana	25% of distributions exceeding the amount required to give equity holders a 10% internal rate of return (IRR).
	If certain qualified investment milestones are not reached (40% invested in qualified investments after 3 years, 60% after 5 years, and 100% after 7 years), then 25% of distributions until the tax credits are recouped and thereafter 10% of distributions regardless of the IRR generated for equity holders.
	If a CAPCO fails to voluntarily decertify within 10 years, 50% of all distributions until the tax credits granted for the pool are recouped and thereafter 20% of all distributions.
New York	None.
Wisconsin	None.
Florida	10% of distributions in excess of certified capital.
Missouri	25% of distributions exceeding the amount required to give equity holders a 15% IRR.
Colorado	30% of distributions exceeding the amount required to give equity holders a 10% IRR. The government's share is allocated one-half to local housing authorities, public non-profit corporations, or private non-profit corporations for various specified purposes, and one-half to approved community mental health clinics or approved community mental health centres.
Texas	None.
Alabama	10% of distributions exceeding the amount required to give equity holders a 15% IRR.
Georgia	None.

Government Expenditure Limits

Louisiana	Insurance company CAPCOs: Aggregate premium tax credits cannot exceed $5 million per year.
	General CAPCOs: Aggregate income tax credits cannot exceed $2 million per year.
	No CAPCO group is eligible for additional credits if it has certified capital in excess of $15 million and has not met the investment thresholds for voluntary decertification.
New York	Program #1: $50 million in credits in 1999, for which investments may be made in CAPCOs beginning in 1998; $50 million in additional tax credits in 2000 and thereafter for which investments may be made in CAPCOs beginning in 1999. Thereafter, total certified capital of $100 million.
	Program #2: $30 million in credits in 2001 for which investments may be made in CAPCOs beginning in 2000.
	Program #3: $150 million in credits in 2002, for which investments may be made in CAPCOs beginning in 2000.
Wisconsin	$50 million aggregate.
Florida	Program #1: $150 million in premium tax credits issued in 1999.
	Program #2: $150 million (if spending for program #2 is approved; it had not been approved as of July 31, 2003).
Missouri	For 1997, $5 million; thereafter, aggregate credits not exceeding $10 million per year. An additional $4 million per year for CAPCOs that invest in qualified Missouri businesses in a distressed community (as defined in section 135.530).
Colorado	$100 million in aggregate credits for investments made between January 31, 2002 and January 31, 2004; a further $100 million for investments made after January 31, 2004.
Texas	$200 million in aggregate credits; no more than $20 million per year.
Alabama	$100 million in aggregate credits.
Georgia	$7.5 million per year for 10 years.

Eligible Investments

Louisiana	An investment that in substance and form furthers economic development within Louisiana, and is a debt or equity investment in a qualified Louisiana business, an approved venture fund, an approved technology fund or an approved Louisiana-based economic development infrastructure project. A qualified Louisiana business must operate primarily in Louisiana or perform substantially all of its production in Louisiana, or be headquartered in Louisiana with a substantial portion of its assets in Louisiana. The business must be in need of capital and be involved in

commerce for the purpose of retail; the manufacturing, processing, or assembling of products; conducting research and development; or providing services. Together with its affiliates, it must have a net worth not exceeding $18 million; an average income in the 2 preceding years not exceeding $6 million; no more than 500 employees, of which at least 80% are domiciled in Louisiana; and at least 80% of the payroll is paid to such employees. Excluded businesses include professional services, real estate, oil and gas, gaming, banking, and financing.

New York

Qualified New York business: independently owned, headquartered with its principal business operations in New York; no more than 100 employees, of which 80% are employed in New York, or no more than 200 employees, of which 80% are employed in New York and gross revenues of no more than $5 million (unless the company is in an empire zone under program #3, then gross revenues of no more than $8 million). The business must be involved in commerce for the purpose of developing and manufacturing products and systems, conducting research and development on all types of products, or providing services. Excluded businesses include real estate development, insurance, or professional services.

For program #3, one-third of investments must be in businesses in empire zones and one-third in businesses in underserved areas outside empire zones.

A CAPCO cannot invest more than 15% of its certified capital in any one business.

Follow-on investment is permitted if the business was an eligible business at the time of initial investment and is still New York-based and conducting permitted business activities.

Wisconsin

Qualified Wisconsin business: headquartered with its principal business in Wisconsin; fewer than 100 employees, of which 75% are employed in Wisconsin; and net worth of no more than $2 million.

Excluded businesses include developing real estate for resale, banking, lending, and making loans to or investments in CAPCOs.

A CAPCO cannot invest more than 15% of its certified capital in any one business.

Florida

A business with fewer than 200 employees, of which 75% are employed in Florida. The business must be unable to obtain conventional financing. The business must be engaged in manufacturing, processing, or assembling products; conducting research and development; or providing services. Excluded businesses include real estate, banking, insurance, lending, and professional services.

An early-stage technology business (for the purposes of program #2) is a qualified business that is: involved in developing initial product or service offerings, such as prototype development; less than 2 years old with less than $3 million in annual revenues; the Florida Black

Business Investment Board (FBBIB); a business majority-owned by the FBBIB; or a business in which the FBBIB holds a majority voting interest on the board of directors.

A CAPCO cannot invest more than 15% of its certified capital in any one business.

Follow-on investment is permitted.

Missouri	Qualified Missouri business: independently owned; headquartered and located in Missouri; in need of venture capital and unable to obtain conventional financing; with fewer than 200 employees, of which 80% are employed in Missouri. The business must be engaged in manufacturing, processing, or assembling products; conducting research and development; or providing services in interstate commerce. Excluded businesses include retail, real estate, real estate development, insurance, and professional services. If the business has been in existence 3 years or less, gross sales may not exceed $4 million; if longer than 3 years, gross sales may not exceed $3 million. If the business is located in a distressed community, gross sales may not exceed $5 million. If the business qualified at the time of its first investment, it remains qualified for 7 years for the purposes of follow-on financing.

A CAPCO cannot invest more than 15% of its certified capital in any one business.

Colorado	Qualified business or qualified rural business.

Qualified business: headquartered in Colorado, with its principal business operations located in Colorado; a small business concern as described in the small business size standards set by US Small Business Administration (SBA); not a business predominantly engaged in professional services provided by accountants or lawyers.

Qualified rural business: a qualified business that has its principal business operations in a designated rural county.

A CAPCO cannot invest more than 15% of its certified capital in any one business.

Follow-on investment is permitted.

During each calendar year from 2003 to 2010, a meeting must be held in each of five counties that have populations of no more than 150,000 at which a representative from each certified CAPCO must be present to review business plans from qualified businesses headquartered in those counties.

Texas	Qualified business: headquartered in Texas with its principal business operations in Texas; will use qualified investment to support business operations in Texas; has fewer than 100 employees, of which 80% are employed in Texas. The business must be engaged primarily in manufacturing, processing, or assembling products; conducting research and development; or providing services. Excluded businesses include retail sales, real estate development,

insurance, banking or lending, and professional services of accountants, attorneys, or physicians.

A strategic investment business is one that principally operates in one or more strategic investment areas and intends to maintain operations in the areas after receipt of the investment by the CAPCO. A strategic investment area is an area with below-average employment and low GDP, a federally designated urban enterprise community, or a defence readjustment zone.

A CAPCO cannot invest more than 15% of its certified capital in any one business.

Follow-on investment is permitted as long as the principal business operations of the qualified business remain in Texas.

Alabama

Qualified technology business: headquartered in Alabama with its principal business operations in Alabama; no more than 100 employees, of which 80% are employed in Alabama. The business must be primarily engaged in manufacturing, processing, or assembling products; conducting research and development; or providing services. Excluded businesses include retail sales, real estate development, insurance, banking or lending, and professional services of accountants, attorneys, or physicians.

A CAPCO cannot invest more than 15% of its certified capital in any one business.

Follow-on investment is permitted as long as the qualified technology business maintains its headquarters in Alabama.

Georgia

Qualified business: headquartered in Georgia with its principal business operations located in Georgia; a small business as described in the small business size standards set by the SBA; fewer than 200 employees, of which 75% are employed in Georgia. Excluded businesses include retail sales, the selling of real estate, and professional services provided by accountants or lawyers.

A qualified technology business is a qualified business that either is less than 2 years old or has less than $3 million in annual revenue. The business must be engaged in developing or offering products or services involving: biotechnology; industrial use of microorganisms or biological techniques; biomedical engineering and the use of engineering technology, instrumentation, and methods to solve medical problems; pharmacology; uses and manufacture of drugs; pharmaceutical research, development, and testing; or bioagriculture.

If the business qualified at the time of first investment, it remains qualified for the purposes of follow-on investment.

A CAPCO cannot invest more than 15% of its certified capital in any one business.

Pacing Requirements

Louisiana	Within 3 years, 50% must be invested, with at least 30% in qualified investments; of the 30%, at least 50% must be invested in qualified Louisiana technology-based businesses, qualified Louisiana startup businesses, and/or qualified technology funds, with at least 50% invested in qualified Louisiana technology-based businesses.
	Within 5 years, 80% must be invested, with at least 50% in qualified investments. Same additional requirements as above (i.e., at least 50% of 50% invested in particular types of businesses), plus at least 10% of the investment pool must be placed in qualified technology funds, qualified investments in approved technology-based businesses, and/or qualified investments in research park early-stage businesses.
New York	25% must be invested in eligible business investments within 2 years; 40% within 3 years; 50% within 4 years, of which 50% must be early-stage financing (except for program #3, where qualified investments are made in a business in an empire zone, the requirement for early-stage businesses does not apply).
Wisconsin	30% must be invested in eligible investments within 3 years; 50% within 5 years.
Florida	Program #1: 20% must be invested in eligible investments by December 31, 2000; 30% by December 31, 2001; 40% by December 31, 2002; 50% by December 31, 2003, of which 50% must be invested in early-stage technology businesses.
	Program #2: The same pacing requirements must be met by December 31 of the 2d, 3d, 4th, and 5th calendar year, respectively, after the date established by the department for applications of additional premium tax credits.
Missouri	25% must be invested in eligible investments within 2 years; 40% within 3 years; 50% within 4 years.
Colorado	30% must be invested in eligible investments within 3 years; 50% within 5 years.
	Investments in qualified rural businesses are leveraged 2:1 in determining whether requirements have been met.
Texas	30% must be invested in eligible investments within 3 years, of which 30% must be invested in strategic investment business; 50% within 5 years, of which 50% must be invested in early-stage financing and 30% in strategic investment businesses.
Alabama	35% must be invested in eligible investments within 3 years; 50% within 5 years.
Georgia	30% must be invested in eligible investments within 3 years; 50% within 5 years. Investments in businesses in certain regions are leveraged 1.5:1 or 2:1 (depending on location) in determining whether requirements have been met.

Requirements for Voluntary Decertification or for Distributions Other Than Qualified Distributions

Louisiana	100% of certified capital invested in qualified businesses, with a minimum of 25% invested in disadvantaged businesses. Investment in a qualified venture fund counts toward the 25% requirement.
New York	100% of certified capital invested in qualified businesses or written authorization from the superintendent of the Department of Insurance, but in no event can non-qualifying distributions be made unless at least 90% of certified capital is invested in companies that conduct their principal business operations in New York.
Wisconsin	1) 10 years since the last certified capital investment was made in the CAPCO, or
	2) the CAPCO has invested 100% of its certified capital in qualified investments.
Florida	100% of certified capital invested in qualified businesses.
Missouri	100% of certified capital invested in qualified businesses.
Colorado	100% of certified capital invested in qualified businesses (two-for-one leveraging of investments in qualified rural businesses is not applicable for this purpose).
Texas	100% of certified capital invested in qualified businesses.
Alabama	100% of certified capital invested in qualified businesses.
Georgia	100% of certified capital invested in qualified businesses and 35% of certified capital invested in qualified technology businesses.

Consequences of Failure To Meet Investment Requirements

Louisiana	Involuntary decertification, unused tax credits are forfeited, and all or a portion (depending on the circumstances) of tax credits used must be repaid.
New York	Involuntary decertification, unused tax credits are forfeited, and all or a portion (depending on the circumstances) of tax credits used must be repaid.
Wisconsin	Involuntary decertification, unused tax credits are forfeited, and all or a portion (depending on the circumstances) of tax credits used must be repaid.
Florida	Involuntary decertification, unused tax credits are forfeited, and all or a portion (depending on the circumstances) of tax credits used must be repaid.
Missouri	Involuntary decertification, unused tax credits are forfeited, and all or a portion (depending on the circumstances) of tax credits used must be repaid.

Colorado	Involuntary decertification, unused tax credits are forfeited, and all or a portion (depending on the circumstances) of tax credits used must be repaid.
Texas	Involuntary decertification, unused tax credits are forfeited, and all or a portion (depending on the circumstances) of tax credits used must be repaid.
Alabama	Involuntary decertification, unused tax credits are forfeited, and all or a portion (depending on the circumstances) of tax credits used must be repaid.
Georgia	Involuntary decertification, unused tax credits are forfeited, and all or a portion (depending on the circumstances) of tax credits used must be repaid.

Notes

1   The Louisiana and Kansas programs are considered in this chapter because both are venture capital fund programs. Michigan's Venture Capital Fund is discussed briefly in chapter 7, at notes 195-198 and accompanying text, because it is an element of the Michigan state public pension fund.

2   Surveys of state programs are available from a variety of sources. See, for example, David L. Barkley, Deborah M. Markley, and Julia Sass Rubin, *Public Involvement in Venture Capital Funds: Lessons from Three Program Alternatives*, RUPRI Policy Paper 99-9 (Columbia, MO: Rural Policy Research Institute, November 1999) (available online from the RUPRI Web site: http://www.rupri.org/). See also Robert G. Heard and John Sibert, *Growing New Businesses with Seed and Venture Capital: State Experiences and Options* (Washington, DC: National Governors' Association, 2000) (available online from the NGA Center for Best Practices Web site: http://www.nga.org/center/).

3   See infra note 5. No Canadian jurisdiction has legislation recognizing the concept of LLCs. However, the Canada Revenue Agency (CRA) considers a US LLC to be a corporation for Canadian tax purposes.

4   For example, Canada exempts from taxation prescribed small business investment corporations, an entity used exclusively by pension funds for venture capital investment: paragraph 149(1)(o.3) of the Income Tax Act, RSC 1985, c. 1 (5th Supp.), as amended (herein referred to as "ITA"). Small business investment corporations are considered further in chapter 7, at notes 249-256 and accompanying text.

5   For US tax purposes, a partnership is a business entity with at least two members that is not a corporation and that has not elected to be treated as a corporation. See, generally, Treas. reg. section 301.7701-2(c)(1) to the Internal Revenue Code of 1986, as amended (herein referred to as "IRC"). A corporation is defined in Treas. reg. section 301.7701-2(b). Treas. reg. section 301.7701-3 authorizes any business entity that does not have to be treated as a corporation ("an eligible entity") to choose its classification for federal tax purposes (commonly referred to as the "check-the-box" regulations). If an eligible entity has at least two members, it can elect to be classified as either a partnership or an association (which is taxed as a corporation). Unless it elects otherwise, a domestic eligible entity is a partnership if it has two or more members: Treas. reg. section 301.7701-3(b)(1)(i). A foreign eligible entity is a partnership if it has two or more members and at least one member does not have limited liability: Treas. reg. section 301.7701-3(b)(2)(i)(A). Thus, a limited partnership or an LLC (where permitted), whether located in Canada or the United States, will be treated as a partnership for US tax purposes unless it elects to be treated as an association (and therefore taxed as a corporation). However, under IRC section 7704, a publicly traded partnership must be treated as a corporation (except in certain limited circumstances).

6   ITA subsection 96(1); IRC section 702. The tax legislation in both countries includes loss limitation rules applicable to limited partners. The application of these rules is not germane to this study.

7   In the United States, income characterization at the partnership level is provided for in IRC section 702(b). In Canada, it is implied in ITA subsection 96(1), although the case law on this point is unsettled (see infra note 21).

8   See chapter 3, at notes 75-81 and accompanying text.

9   Unrelated-business-income tax is considered further in chapter 7, in the context of venture capital investment by US pension funds. See chapter 7, at notes 223-230 and accompanying text.

10   Before amendments made in 1997, concerns arose for non-resident investors in a US venture capital limited partnership that the profits of the partnership (including gains from the sale of stock of investee firms) constituted income effectively connected with the conduct of a trade or business in the United States, thus making the non-resident partners subject to US tax on that income (IRC sections 871(b) (individuals), 882 (corporations), and 875 (individuals or corporations that are partners in a partnership engaged in a US trade or business)). These concerns are discussed in Adele M. Karig, "Taxation of Tax-Exempt and Foreign Investors in U.S. Private Investment Funds," in *Tax Planning for Domestic & Foreign Partnerships, LLCs, Joint Ventures & Other Strategic Alliances* (New York: Practising Law Institute, 2001), 885-916. Dealing in stocks or securities for one's own account (that is, by a taxpayer that is not a dealer in securities) is not considered to be a trade or business in the United States for taxpayers other than a "dealer in stock or securities": IRC section 864(b)(2). Before amendments made by the Taxpayer Relief Act of 1997, the exception for trading for one's own account did not apply to a corporation the principal business of which was trading in stocks or securities for its own account if the principal office of the corporation was in the United States (IRC section 864(b)(2)(A)(ii), as it read before amendment). A similar exception to the exception applied to members of a partnership (whether domestic or foreign) the principal business of which was trading in stocks or securities for its own account if the principal office of the partnership was in the United States: Treas. reg. section 1.864-2(c)(2)(ii). The corporation or partnership was not considered to have its principal office in the United States if "all or a substantial portion" of 10 functions (listed in Treas. reg. section 1.864-2(c)(2)(iii), sometimes referred to as the "10 commandments") were carried on from offices outside the United States. The amendments in 1997 were designed to simplify the exception for trading in stocks or securities by partnerships and foreign corporations.

For the purposes of IRC section 864(b)(2), a dealer in stocks or securities is defined in Treas. reg. section 1.864-2(c)(2)(iv) as

> a merchant of stocks or securities, with an established place of business, regularly engaged as a merchant in purchasing stocks or securities and selling them to customers with a view to the gains and profits that may be derived therefrom. Persons who buy and sell, or hold, stocks or securities for investment or speculation, irrespective of whether such buying or selling constitutes the carrying on of a trade or business, and officers of corporations, members of partnerships, or fiduciaries, who in their individual capacities buy and sell, or hold, stocks or securities for investment or speculation are not dealers in stocks or securities within the meaning of this subparagraph solely by reason of that activity. In determining under this subdivision whether a person is a dealer in stocks or securities such person's transactions in stocks or securities effected both in and outside the United States shall be taken into account.

A US venture capital limited partnership, an LLC, or an LLP would not be considered a dealer in securities. Consequently, non-resident partners of a US venture capital limited partnership would not be considered to have income effectively connected with a trade or business in the United States where the US venture capital limited partnership invests in shares of US C corporations. However, where the US venture capital limited partnership invests in a US SME that is structured as a flowthrough entity (such as a partnership or LLC that is taxed as a partnership or an S corporation), the foreign partner's share of the SME's income would be considered income effectively connected with a US trade or business. The Internal Revenue Service (IRS) also takes the position that any gain realized by the US venture capital limited partnership on a disposition of the SME and a portion of the gain realized by the foreign partner on a disposition of its interest in the US venture capital limited partnership would be considered income effectively connected with a US trade or business: Rev. rul. 91-32, 1991-1 CB 107. As a result, US venture capital limited partnerships typically require their portfolio companies to be organized as C corporations before the partnership will consider financing them.

11   All three of these benefits are discussed in chapter 3.

12   ITA paragraphs 149.1(2)(a) and (3)(a), respectively.

13   ITA paragraph 149.1(4)(a).

14   In CRA document no. 2000-0005475, May 10, 2000, the CRA states that "[t]he fact that the principal activity of the partnership may be the investment of funds does not alter our view that the partnership would be carrying on business with a view to profit. Consequently, if a private foundation acquires an interest in a partnership it is our view that the private foundation as a limited partner would be carrying on business through the partnership such that its registration would be subject to revocation." The technical interpretation goes on to suggest that "the registration of a private foundation would be subject to revocation where its investment activities are so significant as to constitute the carrying on of a business."

15   "Related business" is only partially defined in ITA subsection 149.1(1) to *include* "a business that is unrelated to the objects of the charity if substantially all persons employed by the charity in the carrying on of that business are not remunerated for that employment." There is a dearth of case law on whether a business is related to the objects of a charity. In *Alberta Institute on Mental Retardation v. The Queen*, [1987] 2 CTC 70 (FCA) (leave to appeal denied, [1998] SCCA no. 32), the majority of the Federal Court of Appeal suggested that a business would be related if all of the income of the business is used for charitable purposes. Given this conclusion, it is difficult to imagine any business carried on by a charity that would not be a related business. One noted commentator suggests that the conclusion in the case should be treated with caution: Arthur B.C. Drache, *Canadian Taxation of Charities & Donations* (Toronto: Carswell) (looseleaf), 1-15.

16   See, for example, Howard J. Kellough, *The Business of Defining Partnership Under the Canadian Income Tax Act* (Don Mills, ON: CCH Canadian, 1974), 20-21.

17   R.C. I'Anson Banks, *Lindley & Banks on Partnership*, 17th ed. (London: Sweet & Maxwell, 1995), 8.

18   (1880), 15 Ch. D. 247, at 261 (CA).

19   *Lindley & Banks on Partnership*, supra note 17, at 8. "Business" was defined in the Partnership Act 1890 to include "every trade, occupation, or profession." The

primary difference between this definition and that in the Income Tax Act is that the latter includes an "adventure or concern in the nature of trade." Arguably, the income tax definition is broader than that under the early Partnership Act, although a partnership is limited to persons "carrying on" business in common, and it is questionable whether a person carries on an adventure. In *Tara Exploration and Development Co. Ltd. v. MNR*, 70 DTC 6370, at 6376 (Ex. Ct.), Jackett P concluded "[w]ith considerable hesitation . . . that the words 'carried on' are not words that can aptly be used with the word 'adventure.'"

20 In CRA document no. 9219352, October 19, 1992, the CRA responded to questions concerning the participation of a charity in a limited partnership that invested in securities. The CRA stated in part: "The Department does not rule out the possibility that a partnership can earn property income. However, in our opinion, where the only activity of the partnership is the investment in shares of various corporations, such activity will likely be considered a business activity."

21 However, there is some case law supporting the proposition that the gains realized by a partnership should be characterized at the partner level. See, for example, *Grouchy v. The Queen*, 90 DTC 6267 (FCTD); and *Hyman et al. v. MNR*, 88 DTC 1352 (TCC). In *Grouchy*, the taxpayer successfully argued that his share of a gain realized by a partnership was a capital gain, even though the other partner was an individual who was actively engaged in the real estate business. According to the court, the characterization of the gain to the other partner was irrelevant in determining its character to the taxpayer. In *Hyman* (also dealing with a real estate partnership), the court concluded that one partner's share of a gain was entirely on capital account, while her spouse's share (who was actively involved in the partnership decisions) was partially on income account (following a change in the use of the property).

Other cases suggest that the intention of the partnership as a whole subsumes the intentions of its individual members: see, for example, *Mohawk Horning Limited et al. v. The Queen*, 86 DTC 6297 (FCA). Furthermore, the intention of the partnership is determined by ascertaining the intention of the person or persons who in fact control its operations and decisions: *Rothenberg v. MNR*, 65 DTC 5001 (Ex. Ct.). Thus, in the context of a limited partnership, the characterization of the partnership's income to the general partner should be determinative of its character to the limited partners. This latter approach is more sound, given that the Income Tax Act mandates that the computation of income be determined at the partnership level and then allocated to the partners.

22 CRA document no. 9416055, September 15, 1994. A similar position is stated in CRA document no. 9418185, September 15, 1994.

23 CRA document no. 9425695, January 31, 1995.

24 CRA document no. 9634801, February 7, 1997.

25 CRA document no. 9727485, November 17, 1997.

26 Canada, Department of Finance, 1997 Budget, Budget Plan, February 18, 1997, 186.

27 See, for example, *G. Grocott v. The Queen*, [1996] 1 CTC 2311 (TCC), in which Bowman J concluded that a non-resident was carrying on business in Canada as a consequence of being a limited partner of an Ontario limited partnership, despite the limitation of liability and prohibition against any active part in the control of

the business by the limited partner. Bowman J's reasoning was adopted by the Federal Court of Appeal in *The Queen v. Robinson (Trustee of)*, [1998] 1 CTC 272 (FCA), in which the court considered the status of a limited partner in a Manitoba limited partnership. In the view of the court, all of the partners in a limited partnership, whether general or limited, carry on the business of the partnership. The CRA has adopted the same position: see, for example, CRA document no. 2000-0059145, December 7, 2000; CRA document no. 2000-0005475, May 10, 2000; and CRA document no. 9716735, October 30, 1997.

28   Article XXI(2) of the Convention Between Canada and the United States of America with Respect to Taxes on Income and on Capital, signed at Washington, DC on September 26, 1980, as amended by the protocols signed on June 14, 1983, March 28, 1984, March 17, 1995, and July 29, 1997 (herein referred to as "the Canada-US treaty"), exempts from tax in Canada dividend and interest income derived by a US pension plan. However, business income derived by a US pension plan remains subject to tax in Canada under article VII to the extent that the income is attributable to a permanent establishment in Canada, and capital gains of the pension plan remain subject to tax in accordance with article XIII.

29   A non-resident is subject to tax in Canada on capital gains only if the gain is from a disposition of taxable Canadian property, as defined in ITA subsection 248(1). Taxable Canadian property includes shares of resident corporations that are not listed on a prescribed stock exchange and shares that are listed on a prescribed stock exchange (which includes both Canadian and foreign exchanges) where the taxpayer (and non-arm's-length persons) owns at least 25 percent of the shares of any class at any time in the five-year period before the disposition. If the gain is subject to tax in Canada, a treaty may remove Canada's jurisdiction to tax the gain. If the gain is not covered by a provision based on article 13(2) of the OECD model treaty (quoted in the text), Canada's tax treaties generally exclude from taxation in Canada gains from the disposition of shares of corporations other than corporations whose value is derived principally from real property located in Canada. See Organisation for Economic Co-operation and Development, *Model Tax Convention on Income and on Capital: Condensed Version* (Paris: OECD, January 2003).

30   The Canada-US treaty substitutes the term "personal property" for "movable property," although there is probably no distinction between the two.

31   Interestingly, the 2001 budget documents, in which the change was introduced, point out that "this assurance extends only to the non-resident partners: a partner who is resident in Canada . . . cannot benefit from section 115.2." Canada, Department of Finance, 2001 Budget, Budget Plan, December 10, 2001, 227. Thus, for Canadian limited partners, the characterization of the gains derived by the venture capital limited partnership remains a potentially problematic issue, unless the partner can elect under ITA subsection 39(4).

32   ITA paragraph 212(13.1)(b).

33   ITA section 116 applies to dispositions by a non-resident person and, unless otherwise stipulated, a "person" does not include a partnership. The CRA takes the position that a disposition by a partnership is considered a disposition by each partner, and accordingly a section 116 certificate is required unless all of the partners are residents of Canada (that is, the partnership is a Canadian partnership). See *Information Circular* 72-17R4, April 24, 1992, paragraph 10.

34   ITA subsection 98(3). It is also not possible to transfer property to a partnership that is not a Canadian partnership on a rollover basis: ITA subsection 97(2).

35   ITA section 253.1 was added in 2001 to overrule *Robinson (Trustee of)*, supra note 27, although only in limited circumstances.

36   For a detailed review of the technical complexities involved in a parallel fund structure, see Yvette Morelli, "Structuring Venture Capital Funds" (2003) vol. 51, no. 2 *Canadian Tax Journal* 806-62.

37   Letter from the Department of Finance dated February 25, 2002. I am grateful to Yvette Morelli of Goodman and Carr LLP for providing me with a copy of the letter.

38   See chapter 2, at note 81 and accompanying text.

39   A distribution of marketable securities is treated similarly to a distribution of money. "Marketable securities" are defined in IRC section 731(c)(2)(A) as "financial instruments and foreign currencies which are, as of the date of the distribution, actively traded." See notes 41-45 and accompanying text, infra.

40   IRC sections 731(a) and (b).

41   IRC section 731(c). A second exception, not germane to this discussion, is IRC section 751. Under this provision, where a partner receives as a distribution from the partnership unrealized receivables or "inventory items" (defined in IRC section 751(d)), the transfer is considered a sale or exchange between the partnership and the partner.

42   IRC section 731(c)(3)(A)(ii) and Treas. reg. section 1.731-2(d)(iii).

43   IRC section 731(c)(3)(A)(iii).

44   IRC section 731(c)(3)(C)(i). IRC section 431(c)(3)(C)(ii) further provides that a partnership shall not be treated as engaged in a trade or business "by reason of . . . any activity undertaken as an investor, trader, or dealer in any asset described in clause (i)."

45   IRC section 731(c)(3)(C)(iii).

46   ITA subsection 98(2). The three exceptions to this rule apply only where the partnership is wound up soon after the transfer of property (see ITA subsections 98(3), 98(5), and 85(3)).

47   Each share of a corporation is considered a separate property for this purpose. However, it may be possible for the partners to partition their undivided interests in each share into divided interests on a tax-deferred basis in accordance with subsection 248(21), although the procedure is cumbersome. See, for example, CRA document no. 2001-0095503, 2002; CRA document no. 2002-0134785, October 28, 2002; and CRA document no. 2003-0033363, 2003.

48   The other two provinces, Prince Edward Island and Alberta, do not have LSVCC programs. Prince Edward Island introduced a provincial LSVCC tax credit for prescribed federally registered LSVCCs in 1992, but eliminated the credit in the province's 1997 budget, effective April 9, 1997. Alberta has never introduced an LSVCC program. The Alberta Tax Review Committee, established in February 1998 to review and make recommendations concerning the government's role in financing knowledge-based industries, specifically rejected the introduction of an LSVCC program in Alberta: Alberta Tax Review Committee, *Phase 1: Report and Recommendations on Knowledge-Based Industries* (Edmonton: Treasury Alberta, May 1998).

49   The material in this section is derived from Duncan Osborne and Daniel Sandler, "A Tax Expenditure Analysis of Labour-Sponsored Venture Capital Corporations" (1998) vol. 46, no. 3 *Canadian Tax Journal* 499-574.

50   Act To Establish the Fonds de solidarité des travailleurs du Québec (F.T.Q.), SQ 1983, c. 58 (now RSQ, c. F-3.2.1) (herein referred to as "FSTQ Act"). Quebec added a second LSVCC in 1995, Fondaction, created by the Act To Establish Fondaction, le Fonds de développement de la Confédération des syndicats nationaux pour la coopération et l'emploi, SQ 1995, c. 48 (now RSQ, c. F-3.1.2) (herein referred to as "Fondaction Act").

51   Canadian Labour Market and Productivity Centre, "The Role and Performance of Labour-Sponsored Investment Funds in the Canadian Economy: An Institutional Profile" (mimeograph, November 1995), 67.

52   The $20 million has been characterized as a grant by those who have done studies of FSTQ: see, for example, Jean Marc Suret, *The Fonds de Solidarité des Travailleurs du Québec: A Cost Benefit Analysis* (Sainte Foy, QC: Université Laval, December 1993); and Jean Marc Suret, "Le Gouvernement du Québec et le Financement des Enterprises: Les Mauvaise réponses à un Faux Problème," in Filip Palda, ed., *L'État Interventionniste* (Vancouver: Fraser Institute, 1994), 113-68.

53   The rate and maximum investment entitled to the provincial tax credit have varied over time in order to match the federal tax credit following its introduction in 1985. The 35 percent credit on a maximum investment of $3,500 applied for 1983 and 1984. In 1985, the credit was reduced to 20 percent on a maximum investment of $3,500. The maximum investment was increased to $5,000 in 1992. In 1996, the tax credit was reduced to 15 percent on a maximum investment of $3,500. In 1998, the maximum investment was increased back to $5,000, although the maximum credit remained the same (15 percent).

54   ITA section 127.4. As originally enacted, the credit applied as long as the provincial credit did not exceed 20 percent of the cost of the individual's shares of the LSVCC. The maximum federal credit was $700, so the credit applied only to the first $3,500 invested in a prescribed LSVCC. Quebec reduced its provincial credit to the same rate and maximum amount, effective May 23, 1985: SQ 1987, c. 67, section 153.

55   Canada, *Minutes of Proceedings and Evidence of the Standing Committee on Finance*, 34th Parl., 3d sess., 1991, issue no. 22, November 20, 1991, 29.

56   The following provinces have established their own schemes (year established in parenthesis): Quebec (1983); Saskatchewan (1986); British Columbia (1989); Manitoba (1991-92); Ontario (1992); Nova Scotia (1993); and New Brunswick (1994). The Northwest Territories established its own scheme in 1998 (see infra note 80 and accompanying text). Newfoundland and Labrador announced its intention to introduce an LSVCC in both its 2001 and 2003 provincial budgets (see infra note 81 and accompanying text).

57   In 1993, New Brunswick extended a provincial credit to prescribed federally registered LSVCCs (five have been prescribed, although only three are prescribed for 2004). In addition to its own regime (under which no LSVCC has yet been established), Nova Scotia extends a provincial credit to prescribed federally registered LSVCCs (currently, seven are prescribed). Prince Edward Island introduced a provincial LSVCC tax credit for prescribed federally registered LSVCCs

in 1992, but eliminated the credit in the province's 1997 budget, effective April 9, 1997.

58   Canada, Department of Finance, *1988 Budget, Budget Papers*, February 10, 1988, 8.

59   The startup period was reduced to two years in 1999.

60   "Eligible investments" are essentially shares or certain debt of SMEs.

61   "Reserves" include cash and bank deposits, government bonds, bonds of a public company, guaranteed investment certificates, and qualified investment contracts.

62   The deficiency penalty is a monthly tax equal to 1/60 of the prescribed rate of interest on the LSVCC's investment deficiency. On an annualized basis, the tax is equivalent to 20 percent of the investment deficiency multiplied by the prescribed rate of interest. If a deficiency continues for 12 consecutive months, an additional tax and penalty are imposed. The additional tax is equal to 20 percent of the average monthly investment shortfall in the 12-month period. The penalty is equal to the amount of the additional tax. The tax and penalty effectively claw back the federal tax credit to the extent of the investment deficiency. The additional tax and 80 percent of the penalty may be refunded if the LSVCC subsequently meets the investment requirements for 12 consecutive months.

　　　　Originally, the deficiency penalty applied only to federally registered LSVCCs. In its 1997 budget, the federal government introduced a federal tax equal to any provincial tax or penalty imposed on a provincial LSVCC for failure to meet applicable provincial investment requirements. This federal tax is refundable to the same extent that the provincial tax or penalty is refundable.

63   The grant was provided pursuant to an agreement dated May 6, 1988, pursuant to which the minister of regional industrial expansion (representing Canada) agreed to pay the sum of $15 million. The amount was later reduced due to federal cutbacks. The fund must use the grant "to assist in the establishment, development, promotion and operation of, and investment through," the fund. The grant is not repayable unless the fund "misappropriates the grant, or does not carry out in a satisfactory fashion the activities for which the grant was intended": see Working Ventures Canadian Fund Inc., *1994 Annual Report*, 23.

64   Ontario, Ministry of Treasury and Economics, *1991 Ontario Budget, Budget Paper E*, April 29, 1991, 101.

65   According to Paul Johnson, parliamentary assistant to the minister of revenue, who introduced Bill 150 on behalf of Shelley Wark-Martyn, minister of revenue, Bill 150 "puts into place a plan for business, labour and government to work as partners to help Ontario meet the challenges of the changing economic environment. The Ontario investment and worker ownership program is an example of the government's commitment to create and maintain jobs, improve labour-management relations, increase productivity and competitiveness and bring stability to Ontario's economy" (Ontario, *Debates*, December 16, 1991, 4322). It is not necessary to deal with the EOLSVCC regime in detail. In brief, it was intended as an incentive to employees to invest in shares of their employer businesses by offering a tax credit for the acquisition of the shares. See, generally, Robin MacKnight, "ESOP's Fable: Gargoyles, Tax Policy, and Employee Ownership in Ontario," in *Report of Proceedings of the Forty-Sixth Tax Conference*, 1994 Conference Report (Toronto: Canadian Tax Foundation, 1995), 22:1-36.

66   The provinces with LSVCC regimes introduced corresponding increases in the provincial credit in the same year.

67   See ITA subsection 127.4(3), as amended by SC 1994, c. 8, section 17(2) and the definition of "qualifying trust" added by SC 1994, c. 8, section 17(1). Previously, the individual could obtain the benefit of both the LSVCC tax credit and the RRSP deduction, but only in a cumbersome manner: by acquiring the shares personally and then transferring them to his or her RRSP as a contribution in kind. Shares of a prescribed venture capital corporation (VCC) have been qualified investments for RRSP purposes since October 31, 1985: see regulations 4900(6)(a) and 5100(1)(b). Under regulation 6700, a prescribed VCC includes all of the prescribed LSVCCs.

68   It may be inappropriate to include in the federal and provincial governments' costs the tax expenditure associated with RRSP contributions because the expenditure is incurred regardless of the nature of the RRSP investment.

69   A significant amount of investment in LSVCCs occurs during RRSP season, which is the first 60 days of the following taxation year (for example, a contribution to an RRSP in the first 60 days of 2003 can be used as a deduction for tax purposes in either 2002 or 2003).

70   Evidently, many investors, particularly in Ontario, purchased LSVCC shares in $10,000 blocks in the 1996 RRSP season in order to maximize their investment (and corresponding tax credits and RRSP deductions) for both the 1995 and 1996 taxation years.

71   A cooling-off period refers to a period following the redemption of LSVCC shares during which the individual is not entitled to a tax credit for purchasing shares of an LSVCC.

72   Both changes were announced in the 1996 budget, but were not introduced in the legislation incorporating the 1996 budget measures. These amendments were incorporated along with the 1997 budget measures in Bill 164, which received royal assent on December 18, 1997, SO 1997, c. 43. Evidently, the legislation was delayed so that the province could match the wording of the federal legislation on these matters. The extended holding period applies to shares issued after May 6, 1996 (see sections 14.1(1)(a)(vi) and 14.1(3) of the Community Small Business Investment Funds Act (as the Labour Sponsored Venture Capital Corporations Act was renamed by SO 1997, c. 43, schedule C)).

73   Supra note 62.

74   Canada, Department of Finance, 1996 Budget, Budget Plan, March 6, 1996, 143, table A5.1. The projections were broken down by year and by the reduction associated with the reduced tax credit and the reduced contribution limit.

75   According to figures supplied by Macdonald & Associates Limited, $647 million was raised by LSVCCs between March 1996 and February 1997, compared with $1,230 million invested between March 1995 and February 1996. The source of the remaining venture capital statistics in this section is Macdonald & Associates Limited, Toronto (March 1997, unpublished).

76   In other words, the government met 94.5 percent of its target reductions in one year.

77   The fact that Working Ventures Canadian Fund had halted share sales since June 1996 may have also affected the decline in Ontario. However, the decline likely

related to the federal and Ontario legislative amendments. Most LSVCC share sales in Ontario are made through professional brokers and many professional brokers stopped marketing LSVCC shares because of the decline in the rate and maximum amount of the tax credit. According to one LSVCC manager, brokers were not interested in selling the smaller amounts because of the decrease in commission: Catherine Mulroney, "Report on Venture Capital," *Globe and Mail*, April 22, 1997. Evidently, the doubling-up strategy employed in 1996 (supra note 69) was used again by investors in the 1998 RRSP season, perhaps at the suggestion of investment dealers, in order to increase commissions.

The effect in Ontario varied from fund to fund. For example, First Ontario's investment dropped by only 30 percent, probably because of the volume of shares sold through union-trained salespeople.

78   The federal incentives are summarized in appendix 6C, under the heading "Investment Requirements." The Ontario measures were included in part III.1 of the Community Small Business Investment Funds Act, supra note 72. The community small business investment fund (CSBIF) program has many similarities to Quebec's SOLIDE program, established in 1991 with the creation of SOLIDEQ, a limited partnership between FSTQ and the Union des municipalités régionales de comtés du Québec (UMRCQ). FSTQ made an initial $10 million investment in the limited partnership and in 1996 invested an additional $20 million. SOLIDEQ's purpose is to contribute to the development of employment in local regions of Quebec by financing local investment funds, called sociétés locales d'investissement pour le développement de l'emploi (local investment corporations for the development of employment) (SOLIDEs). Each SOLIDE manages an investment fund of $500,000, half of which is provided on a matching basis by SOLIDEQ; the other investors in a SOLIDE are community-level partners. Since 1994, regional municipalities (MRCs) have been permitted to invest directly in SOLIDEs. SOLIDEs make investments of between $5,000 and $50,000 in small businesses. As of June 30, 2002, there were 87 SOLIDEs in operation in Quebec with over $40 million in aggregate capital. In 1995, FSTQ established regional solidarity funds for each administrative region of Quebec. As of June 30, 2002, the 17 regional funds had over $260 million in aggregate capital. Information about the SOLIDEs and the regional funds can be obtained from the FSTQ Web site: http://www.fondsftq.com/. The CSBIF program is summarized in appendix 6A.

79   Canada, Department of Finance, *Release* no. 1998-086, August 31, 1998. The provisions were part of SC 1999, c. 22, sections 49(3) (repealing ITA subsections 127.4(3) and (4), the three-year cooling-off period) and 49(4) (amending ITA paragraph 127.4(5)(a), increasing the maximum credit to $750).

80   Risk Capital Investment Tax Credits Act, SNWT 1998, c. 22, as amended, part II.

81   On May 27, 2003, the minister of industry, trade, and rural development issued a request for proposals for the establishment of a privately managed pooled venture capital corporation. The proposal indicated that the government was prepared to consider various tax-incentive-based models, including a provincial LSVCC, a federal LSVCC, or a venture capital corporation outside the LSVCC model. Government of Newfoundland and Labrador, "Ministers Announce Call for Venture Capital Proposals," *News Release* NLIS5, May 27, 2003. Proposals had to be submitted by August 29, 2003. Evidently, a number of proposals were received. However, with the change in government in the province in October 2003 (a

Liberal government replaced the former Progressive Conservative government), it is unclear what shape the proposed VCF program will take, or indeed whether one will be introduced at all.

82 Act 642 of the 1983 Regular Session.

83 Act 84 of the 2002 Regular Session.

84 The legislative history of the Louisiana CAPCO legislation is taken primarily from Postlethwaite & Netterville, *CAPCO Study*, prepared for Louisiana Department of Economic Development (Baton Rouge: Louisiana Department of Economic Development, December 31, 1999) (available online from the LDED Web site: http://www.lded.state.la.us/). The report is discussed in greater detail below, under the heading "Cost-Benefit Analyses of CAPCO Programs."

85 Chapter 60 of the Consolidated Laws, article 1, section 11. Effective since 1997.

86 Wisconsin Statutes, c. 560, section 560.30 et seq. and Wisconsin Administrative Rules, c. Comm. 111. The legislation was introduced in 1997 as SB333.

87 Florida Statutes, c. 288, part XI (section 288.99), effective 1998.

88 Missouri Revised Statutes, c. 135, section 135, introduced in 1997 as HB 1237.

89 Colorado Revised Statues, title 10, article 3.5, introduced in 2001 as HB01-1097.

90 Insurance Code, chapter 4, subchapter B, introduced in 2001 as SB601, session 77(R).

91 Alabama Code 1975, title 40, c. 14B, enacted April 18, 2002 and effective immediately.

92 Official Code of Georgia, c. 48-18, enacted in HB 1441, effective March 1, 2003.

93 Governments in other states are considering or have considered CAPCO programs. They include Arizona, Arkansas, Connecticut, Hawaii, Kentucky, Illinois, Iowa, Indiana, Maryland, Michigan, Mississippi, North Carolina, Ohio, Oklahoma, Rhode Island, South Carolina, Utah, Vermont, and Virginia. All of these states have rejected the proposals: see Chip Cooper, David Barkley, and Mike Williams, *Understanding CAPCOs* (Oklahoma City: National Association of Seed and Venture Funds, 2001) (available online from the NASVF Web site: http://www.nasvf.org/). As of July 31, 2003, only Rhode Island was considering a CAPCO program.

94 Louisiana Revised Statutes, title 51 (Trade and Commerce), c. 26 (the Louisiana Capital Companies Tax Credit Program), section 1922 (RS 51:1922).

95 A Louisiana capital company includes any partnership, corporation, or other legal entity, whether organized for profit or not for profit.

96 Act 537 of the 1984 Regular Session. A premium tax is a tax imposed by the vast majority of US states and all Canadian provinces on insurance companies that are licensed to operate in the state or province. The tax is imposed on gross insurance premium income earned in the state or province. The rate may vary depending on the nature of the insurance policy (life insurance, fire insurance, etc.). In the United States, the rates range from 0 percent to 3.5 percent; in Canada, the rates range from 2 to 4 percent.

97 Act 891 of the 1984 Regular Session.

98 Act 695 of the 1986 Regular Session.

99 Act 915 of the 1986 Regular Session.

100 Act 703 of the 1987 Regular Session.

101 Act 496 of the 1989 Regular Session.

102 Under the new requirements, within three years, at least 50 percent of a CAPCO's certified capital must have been invested in businesses with at least 30 percent invested in qualified investments (that is, qualified Louisiana businesses); within five years, at least 80 percent of certified capital must have been invested in businesses with at least 50 percent in qualified investments.

103 Act 15 of the First Extra Session of 1989.

104 Thereafter, the tax credit was limited to the premium tax otherwise payable in the year; however, the 25 percent limit was later extended to 1994 and again to 1999. For investments made after December 31, 2000, no tax credit was allowed, although in 2002 the sunset clause was extended to December 31, 2003.

105 Act 849 of the 1992 Regular Session.

106 Act 724 of the 1993 Regular Session.

107 Act 279 of the 1993 Regular Session.

108 Act 9 of the Third Extra Session of 1994.

109 Act 21 of the 1996 Regular Session.

110 Ibid., section 1. Other amendments in 1996 extended the 25 percent annual premium tax limitation to a group of affiliates and modified the definition of a qualified Louisiana business. The amended definition provides that the business must operate primarily in Louisiana or perform substantially all of its production in Louisiana and, together with its affiliates, have a net worth not exceeding $18 million, average income in the two preceding years not exceeding $6 million, and no more than 500 employees.

111 See Postlethwaite & Netterville, supra note 84, at 27 and 29, table 3.

112 If requests from all CAPCOs exceed the limit, the amount was allocated equally to all CAPCOs that apply for premium tax credits. If any CAPCO did not use its allocated amount, the unused premium tax credit allocation was redistributed among the remaining CAPCOs in proportion to the amount of the original request.

113 In 1998, related parties to two CAPCOs invested about $300 million under the income tax credit provisions of the program. Concerned about the reduction in state income tax revenue that these investments created, state officials negotiated an agreement with the two CAPCOs that reduced the amount of qualified investment to $150 million and spread the resulting income tax credits over four years for one CAPCO and five years for the other. In 1999, amendments were made by regulation to the CAPCO income tax credit program to limit total annual income tax credits to $4 million (corresponding to $11,428,571 of certified capital investment per year).

114 The qualified investment thresholds for voluntary decertification—60 percent for funds certified before December 31, 1998 and 100 percent for funds certified after that date—must be met before any distributions can be made to the CAPCO equity owners (that is, partners in a CAPCO limited partnership), with the exception of qualified distributions. Such distributions are management fees (not exceeding 2½ percent of certified capital), tax payments, and debt service.

115 Supra note 84.

116   In fact, no certified capital was raised under the program before 1988: see State of Louisiana Legislative Auditor, Department of Economic Development, Office of Financial Institutions, *A Review of the Louisiana CAPCO Program: Performance Audit* (Baton Rouge: Louisiana Legislative Auditor, January 2001), 2 (available online from the Legislative Auditor's Web site: http://www.lla.state.la.us/).

117   The maximum certified capital ignores the two-year deferral before the tax credits can be applied and is based on a maximum of 12½ percent of the tax credits applied in a year.

118   A certified CAPCO group includes CAPCOs that share common management or are under common control, whether the management or control is direct or indirect. The 32 active Louisiana CAPCOs in 1999 represented 17 distinct capital management firms. In terms of money under management, the largest management firm was Advantage Capital, which managed 13 CAPCOs.

119   A qualified Louisiana technology-based business is defined in Louisiana Revised Statutes, title 51, c. 26, section 1923(15) as "any qualified Louisiana business that is in need of capital for pre-startup, startup, survival, expansion stage, new product development, or similar business purpose that is engaged in or intends to provide technology-based products or services in information technology, communications, medical, biomedical, advanced materials, food, environmental, micro-manufacturing technologies, or that is determined by the secretary [of the Department of Economic Development] as meeting the criteria of this Paragraph."

120   A qualified Louisiana startup business is defined ibid., section 1923(13) as "any qualified Louisiana business that is in development or has been operational for less than two years and is in need of capital for pre-startup, startup, survival, expansion, new product development, or similar business purpose or that is determined by the secretary [of the Department of Economic Development] as meeting the criteria of this Paragraph."

121   A disadvantaged business is defined ibid., section 1923(13) as any qualified Louisiana business that has its headquarters located, at the time of investment, in a low-income community, as that term is defined in IRC section 45(D)(e), as amended.

122   If the capital pool is involuntarily decertified, unused tax credits are forfeited and all or a portion (depending on the circumstances) of tax credits used must be repaid.

123   Incentives are provided for the CAPCO to invest in a "qualified venture fund" after August 1, 2002. First, for the purpose of voluntary decertification, the amount of the investment counts 150 percent toward meeting the 100 percent qualified investment threshold and counts 100 percent toward meeting the 25 percent disadvantaged business threshold. In addition, the investment counts 150 percent toward meeting the seven-year 100 percent qualified investment milestone to avoid payment to the state of a portion of all distributions to equity holders. A qualified venture fund, defined in Louisiana Revised Statutes, title 51, c. 26, section 1923(15), is a smaller CAPCO that is controlled by minorities or women or invests more than half of its qualified investments in businesses controlled by minorities or women and whose primary investment objectives include investing in Louisiana businesses in amounts not exceeding $1 million and that must invest all capital received from a CAPCO in qualified Louisiana businesses.

124   Louisiana Revised Statutes, title 51, c. 26, section 1927.2.

125 Ibid., section 1927.2(6). The information must include new investment in physical assets in the state, payroll information, tax revenues generated by the company, and "[a]n estimate of the total direct and indirect economic impact on Louisiana for each company receiving an investment based upon the data collected in this Section."

126 An Act Respecting Corporations for the Development of Québec Business Firms, SQ 1976, c. 33. SODEQ was the acronym for Sociétés de développement de l'enterprise du Québec. The legislation was repealed on November 1, 1985, SQ 1985, c. 36, section 2, and a new program was introduced that year: An Act Respecting Québec Business Investment Companies, SQ 1985, c. 9 (RSQ, c. S-29.1).

127 The various provincial incentives in effect in 1986 are discussed in Peter E. McQuillan, "An Analysis of Venture Capital Incentives," in *Income Tax Considerations in Corporate Financing*, 1986 Corporate Management Tax Conference (Toronto: Canadian Tax Foundation, 1986), 169-253. See also Lawrence Teltscher, "Small Business Financing," in *Income Tax and Goods and Services Tax Considerations in Corporate Financing*, 1992 Corporate Management Tax Conference (Toronto: Canadian Tax Foundation, 1993), 6:1-67, at 6:50-64.

128 In some cases where the VCC program has been cancelled, the legislation remains in place to facilitate the program's winding down or to allow the government to revitalize the program if it decides to do so.

129 Referred to in provincial publications as community economic development investment funds (CEDIFs), although the legislation refers to them as community economic development corporations. The three programs are described in appendixes 5A, 6C, and 6A, respectively.

130 ITA clause 53(2)(k)(i)(C) and regulation 6700. In contrast, provincial tax credits for direct investment in SMEs, such as those currently in place in British Columbia, Nova Scotia, and Newfoundland and Labrador, reduce the investor's adjusted cost base of the shares of the SME for federal income tax purposes. Thus, a portion of the provincial incentive is effectively clawed back by the federal government when the shares of the SME are ultimately sold.

131 ITA paragraph 40(2)(i). In effect, the amount of a provincial tax credit reduces the amount of any capital loss, whether the tax credit is for direct investment in an SME (by reducing the cost of the share) or for investment in a VCC or LSVCC (by reducing the amount of the loss).

132 ITA section 186.2.

133 Programs for which legislation is in force but that are not currently funded (such as Nova Scotia's equity loan program and Ontario's former VCC program) are not included.

134 The shortcomings of employee organization involvement in many LSVCC programs in Canada is discussed in Osborne and Sandler, supra note 49, at 558-59.

135 See chapter 8, under the heading "The SBIC Program and the Evolution of US Private Venture Capital Funds."

136 For this reason, and more generally, the expertise requirement should focus on the fund managers' knowledge of venture capital investment rather than their knowledge of the CAPCO legislation (one of the problems with the CAPCO programs in Louisiana and Missouri: see appendix 6D, under the heading "Organizational

Form of CAPCO"). See further the discussion below of CAPCO programs, under the heading "Cost-Benefit Analyses of CAPCO Programs."

137   The Louisiana CAPCO program applies to any state taxpayers, although the premium tax credit, available only to insurance companies, is significantly larger than the income (and other) tax credits available to other taxpayers. The Louisiana CAPCO program is really two programs: a CAPCO program for insurance companies and a general VCF program for other taxpayers.

138   When Nova Scotia introduced a tax credit for investment in CEDCs in 1993, one of its objectives was to attract broader support from individuals in the community for venture capital funds. In 1999, three CEDCs raised $1.13 million from 260 investors; in 2000, four CEDCs raised $1.38 million from 353 investors; and in 2001, eight CEDCs raised $2.62 million from 368 investors.

139   Securities legislation is discussed briefly in chapter 5, at note 8.

140   Ibid.

141   In both cases, the different targeting can be explained by the history of the programs. The LSVCC program was developed by the Quebec labour movement in 1983 and primarily targeted unionized employees. The matching federal tax credit introduced in 1985 was limited to investment by individuals—the only investors permitted under the only LSVCC regime then in existence—and encouraged other provinces to introduce programs similar to Quebec's. All provincial LSVCC programs were therefore limited to individuals so that qualifying provincial investors would obtain a matching federal tax credit. Perhaps investment was limited to individuals because LSVCCs had to be sponsored by an employee organization, although this feature does not necessarily preclude extending the tax credit to other taxpayers. The LSVCC program in the Northwest Territories is the only program that extends a tax credit to taxpayers other than individuals.

    The first CAPCO program, introduced in Louisiana in 1983, did not originally target insurance companies. Rather, it was structured as a general VCF program. A premium tax credit targeting insurance company investors was not introduced until 1984. Despite originally offering a 200 percent premium tax credit, the program had difficulty attracting insurance company investors until amendments were made to the legislation in 1996, which clarified that an insurance company's investment in a CAPCO could be either equity or debt with a final maturity of not less than five years. The ability of an insurance company to lend money to the CAPCO on a secured basis revolutionized the CAPCO program, exponentially increasing insurance company participation. However, the typical investment of an insurance company in a CAPCO can hardly be described as venture capital.

142   Osborne and Sandler, supra note 49, at 553-55. They found that the LSVCC tax credit was significantly less regressive than the dividend tax credit and the capital gains exemption. It was more regressive than the RRSP deduction over lower income brackets (to about $40,000), although less regressive over higher income brackets.

143   Ibid., at 559, note 216.

144   The refundable tax credit in British Columbia is limited to individual investors. In Kansas, the credit is refundable only for investors who are "subject to taxation under the provisions of the Kansas income, privilege or premium tax." Otherwise, the tax credit is freely transferable but not refundable. I have been told by

an official at the Kansas Department of Revenue that the department has not yet published its interpretation of the VCF tax credit provisions. Specifically, I was advised that the meaning of "subject to taxation" is open to some interpretation, although it is likely that tax-exempt entities would not be considered subject to taxation in Kansas and therefore would be entitled to a transferable but not a refundable tax credit.

145   I include as non-financial incentives the various income tax reforms introduced in 1985 (supra, the text following note 53), discussed in chapter 7. Similarly, pension funds are permitted investors in Ontario CSBIFs and British Columbia VCCs, but they are not entitled to any financial incentive for making the investment. Not surprisingly, no pension funds have invested in Ontario CSBIFs or BC VCCs to date.

146   A qualified VCF is a fund that meets the requirements under the program, including the investment of all or a substantial portion of its capital in small businesses in the jurisdiction that provides the incentive program.

147   Some administrative costs may be entailed in monitoring the transfer of tax credits and ensuring that they are claimed by the appropriate taxpayer. US states with VCF programs that offer transferable tax credits generally issue a tax credit certificate to each qualified investor who has provided the state with proof of investment. The tax credit certificate is then filed with the investor's tax return. When tax credits are assigned or sold, appropriate transfer forms must be filed with the government agency responsible for the program, and a new tax credit certificate is issued to the transferee. In contrast, a VCF program in which the tax credit cannot be assigned generally requires the VCF to issue a certificate to the investor (with a copy provided to the government) evidencing the qualified investment; the investor includes the certificate with the tax return when the tax credit is first claimed.

148   The Missouri and Kansas VCF programs provide models for consideration in this respect. Both programs are too young to undertake a cost-benefit analysis. In Missouri, the Prolog fund began raising capital in August 2000 and it took until December 2001 to raise $33 million, less than the $40 million target. It raised capital from over 70 limited partners, including a number of institutional investors, pension funds, non-profit organizations, and non-residents of the state. The statute enacting the Kansas VCF program became effective July 1, 2002, and various rules and procedures still need to be drafted. Evidently, the government plans to contract out the administration of the program and intends to select an administrator before the end of June 2003. While the legislation appropriated money to fund the tax credits, no money was appropriated for the program's administration, so the administrator will have to set fee structures (for example, to register VCFs) that will be sufficient to recoup its costs and provide a margin of profitability.

149   See table 1.2 in chapter 1.

150   The 2003 Ontario provincial budget proposed to increase the credit available to individual and corporate investors to 30 percent. This proposal (contained in Bill 41 of 2003) failed to become law before the September 2, 2003 Ontario election call.

151   The reason for the structure is that the fund (Prolog A) benefiting from the 100 percent tax credit must invest exclusively in qualified businesses (that is, small

businesses in Missouri), whereas the parallel fund (Prolog B) is not subject to similar restrictions. This structure permits Prolog to more easily syndicate with other VCFs in investments that are not qualifying businesses. The expectation is that such syndications will likewise attract out-of-state VCFs to syndicate with Prolog in Missouri business investments.

152   Missouri Revised Statutes, c. 620, section 620.647(1).

153   Ibid., section 620.647(3).

154   Whether or not the state will actually benefit from its carried interest depends on its terms under the enacting legislation. For example, under most CAPCO programs, the state's participation arises only after the equity holders realize a stipulated internal rate of return (IRR) based on the amount of certified capital. If, however, as is generally the case under CAPCO legislation, the certified capital is raised exclusively through debt while only a nominal amount is contributed as equity, it is unlikely that the state will ever share in the CAPCO's distributions because the certified capital includes the debt. So, for example, under the Louisiana legislation, the equity holders, who may contribute only $200,000, must achieve a 10 percent IRR based on the entire amount of certified capital, which likely includes millions of dollars of debt, before the state receives anything. Under the 2002 amendments, the state is entitled to its carried interest regardless of the IRR of the equity holders if the fund fails to meet certain pacing requirements.

155   The carried interest should be based on the IRR to the equity holders that excludes any certified capital in the form of debt.

156   West Virginia's original VCF program, introduced in 1986, permitted qualified VCFs to invest in any West Virginia business engaged in certain prescribed activities, regardless of the business's size. As a result, most investments made by VCFs were not "true" venture capital investments. For example, they invested in entities that could easily have arranged bank financing, including larger companies (or companies related thereto). In addition, VCFs could take fully collateralized debt as security for their investment. Rather than amend the legislation to restrict the nature of qualified investments by the VCFs, the program was simply restricted to VCFs that were SBICs (which are regulated by the US SBA as to the types of investment that they can make), and all VCFs other than SBICs were decertified effective March 9, 2002.

157   The one exception that I came across is West Virginia's original VCF program, which lists personal services businesses as qualified investments. In addition, VCF programs that target investment in economically distressed communities often relax the investment restrictions.

158   Small Business Venture Capital Act, RSBC 1996, c. 429, as amended. The Ministry of Competition, Science and Enterprise, which administers the program, maintains budgets for two types of VCCs, regular VCCs and community VCCs, which invest outside major urban centres. The programs operate in exactly the same manner. A third program, the green venture capital program, was cancelled shortly after its inception, following a change in provincial government.

159   The 1974 Ontario budget proposed tax incentives for venture investment corporations (VICs). However, references in both the 1974 and 1975 budgets suggested that a viable VIC scheme required cooperation from the federal government on

the tax treatment of VICs. The Venture Investment Corporations Registration Act was passed in 1977, and then repealed in 1979 when the Small Business Development Act, RSO 1990, c. S.12, as amended, was passed. The SBDC program was effectively terminated in 1993, as a cost-saving measure (Ontario Ministry of Finance, 1993 Budget, Budget Paper C, May 19, 1993, 89), and in 1997 the legislation was repealed, on a day to be proclaimed: SO 1997, c. 10, sections 49 and 50(3). The legislation remains in force while the government winds down the program; no date has been proclaimed for its repeal.

160   The statistics for British Columbia's VCC program illustrate this point. From its inception in 1985 to May 31, 2002, 498 VCCs were registered. In total, the VCCs invested in 578 small businesses, an average of 1.16 small businesses per VCC. The 498 VCCs raised an aggregate of almost $400 million while investing about $315 million in small businesses. Investors in the VCCs received over $116 million in tax credits. Statistics provided by the Ministry of Competition, Science and Enterprise, British Columbia.

161   The British Columbia Ministry of Small Business, Tourism and Culture commissioned a cost benefit analysis of the VCC program in 2001: Grant Thornton LLP, *Cost Benefit Evaluation of Venture Capital Programs* (Victoria: Ministry of Small Business, Tourism and Culture, March 2001). The report concludes that the fiscal benefits to the province well exceeded the program's costs. In reaching this conclusion, the report cautions (at 1) that it provides "a simplistic historical quantification of the net economic benefits of the [VCC program], and does not consider economic multiplier effects or future economic benefits." This caution implies that, if anything, the report underestimates the benefits of the program to the province. However, the methodology applied in the report is so simplistic and the assumptions are so problematic that the report's conclusion is difficult to accept. The report is based on a relatively small sample size: 33 businesses "judgmentally selected by Ministry staff with an emphasis on finding completeness of financial data, and effort to reflect the concentration of the types of businesses participating in the [VCC program]." The costs of the program were limited to the tax credits granted to investors in VCCs that invested in the 33 businesses. The benefits were determined by computing the direct impact on tax revenues to the province for a five-year period from the date of investment by each VCC in its portfolio business(es). According to the report, the estimated provincial tax revenue collected from the sample businesses was $24.54 million, compared with $18.88 million in tax credits provided for investment in the VCCs that invested in these businesses. The report suggests that the $24.54 million is, if anything, an understatement because most of the 33 businesses in the sample were still in business when the last financial information was examined. Two key problems with the analysis that undermine its validity are the small sample size and the selection process. The selection criteria—particularly completeness of financial information—likely biased the sample in favour of successful businesses. The report does not consider whether the success rate of the 33 businesses appropriately reflected the success rate of the more than 550 businesses that had benefited from the program by the end of 2000. In particular, the 33 businesses represent less than 6 percent of total businesses that received capital under the program, while the $18.88 million in tax credits (the cost to the province) represents more than 16 percent of the total tax credits issued under the program. Thus, the investments in the 33 businesses were

proportionately larger than the average business benefiting from the VCC program, and the 33 businesses were likely substantially larger than the average small business. The cumulative statistics for the VCC program (supra note 160) indicate that 79 percent of the total equity raised by VCCs had been invested in small businesses. Even if the minimum 80 percent investment requirement is applied, the 33 businesses benefited from over $50 million in investment, an average of $1.515 million per business. In contrast, all 578 businesses that received VCC funding received a total of almost $315 million in investment, an average of $0.545 million per business, or 36 percent of the amount invested in the 33 businesses. As a result, these businesses likely had a longer survival period than the average small business under the program and their direct benefit to the province was disproportionately larger than the average. Furthermore, in determining the benefit to the province, the analysis assumes that the VCC program was solely responsible for the full amount of tax revenue collected. That assumption overstates (perhaps significantly) the amount of tax revenue generated by the selected businesses compared to the tax revenue that the same businesses would have generated in the absence of the VCC program.

162   Paul Gompers and Josh Lerner, *The Venture Capital Cycle* (Cambridge, MA: MIT Press, 1999), 38.

163   For example, some form of accounting methodology such as first-in, first-out would have to be applied.

164   The requirements vary across the provinces. Most provinces and the federal government require that 60 percent of shareholders' equity be invested in eligible businesses, usually within one year of the raising of the capital. In some provinces, the requirement reaches 70 or 80 percent, although time periods vary.

165   For example, Nova Scotia reduced the time in which LSVCCs must reach a 60 percent qualified investment level from four years to two years in response to the Nova Scotia Department of Finance's review of the LSVCC tax credit in *Phase II* of its comprehensive review of tax credits: Nova Scotia Department of Finance, *Nova Scotia Tax Credit Review: Phase II Report* (Halifax: Nova Scotia Department of Finance, March 2001) (available online from the Nova Scotia Ministry of Finance Web site: http://www.gov.ns.ca/finance/publish/taxcredit/index.htm). According to the report, Nova Scotia registered LSVCCs raised about $38.6 million between 1994 and 1999 at a cost to the province of $7.5 million in tax credits. Because LSVCCs were required to invest at least 60 percent of the capital raised in the province in eligible businesses, the credit was considered to have created a venture capital pool of about $23.2 million as of December 31, 1999, although only $15.8 million had been invested in eligible businesses by that time. The report criticized the slow rate of investment by LSVCCs, attributing the problem in part to the pacing requirements in Nova Scotia's legislation, which at the time were among the most lenient in the country. According to the report, it took LSVCCs about 3½ years to meet the 60 percent eligible investment threshold (at that time Nova Scotia LSVCCs had four years to meet this threshold), and since it would take four to five years before an "investment begins to show significant returns in the form of corporate tax revenue and employment expenditures . . . it may be close to a decade before the government realizes any benefit from the tax expenditure" (ibid., at 27). As a result of the report, the time period to meet the 60 percent eligible investment threshold was reduced to two years, in line with

most other provinces' LSVCC programs. In its 2004-5 budget, Nova Scotia announced further tightening of its pacing requirements; effective January 1, 2005, the eligible investment threshold was increased to 70 percent within two years and to 80 percent within three years.

166 The difficulty faced by most LSVCCs is that, as evergreen funds, they are not necessarily able to predict the amount of capital they will raise and fundraising tends to be concentrated in a relatively short period (that is, "RRSP season," the first 60 days of the calendar year). Without knowledge about the amount of capital coming in, it is difficult to search for appropriate investments in advance.

167 Louisiana, which used to have among the most lax pacing requirements, is now the only state that requires CAPCOs to meet a 100 percent eligible investment level (although CAPCOs have 10 years to do so).

168 Some programs could include in direct benefits the avoided cost of social assistance that the government would have had to pay if the portfolio business had closed down. This element would be important particularly to programs in which the VCF targets "rescue operations," as is the case with Quebec's LSVCC program.

169 Pierre Lamonde, Yvon Martineau, and Don Allen, *Impact Économique et Fiscal des Investissements du Fonds de Solidarité des Travailleurs du Québec (FTQ), 1984-1993* (Montreal: INRS-Urbanisation, October 1994). An executive summary of the study, in English, was prepared by the Canadian Labour Market and Productivity Centre.

The 1994 study was commissioned in response to a study published the previous year by Jean Marc Suret, criticizing the FSTQ expenditure for its high cost and largely ineffectual investment in Quebec: Suret, *The Fonds de Solidarité des Travailleurs du Québec*, supra note 52. See also Suret, "Le Gouvernement du Québec et le Financement des Enterprises," supra note 52. Suret's study cannot properly be called a cost-benefit analysis of FSTQ from the governments' perspective. Rather, it was a calculation of the unit cost to the federal and Quebec governments of venture capital investments made by FSTQ, without taking into consideration the benefits generated by FSTQ's venture capital investments.

170 Pierre Lamonde, Daniel Denis, and Don Allen, "Retombées Économiques et Fiscales des Investissements du Fonds de Solidarité des Travailleurs du Québec (FTQ), 1984-1995" (December 1996, unpublished). A summary of the study, in English, was prepared by FSTQ.

171 SECOR and Regional Data Corporation, "Analyse de l'Impact Économique des Investissements du Fonds de Solidarité des Travailleurs du Québec" (April 2002, unpublished). This study was prepared by Don Allen and Daniel Denis, two of the authors of the 1996 FSTQ study.

172 The first method assumed that FSTQ investment had an incremental effect on investee firms in computing the benefits to government. The second method determined what would have happened to the investee firm if FSTQ had not invested. If the firm would not have existed without FSTQ's investment, 100 percent of the fiscal benefits generated by the investee firm were attributed to FSTQ; if the firm would have survived in any event, 0 percent was attributed to FSTQ.

173 Edward T. Jackson and François Lamontagne, *Adding Value: The Economic and Social Impacts of Labour-Sponsored Venture Capital Corporations on Their Investee Firms* (Ottawa: Canadian Labour Market and Productivity Centre, 1995).

174   The differences in methodology between the 1993 FSTQ study and the 1995 CLMPC study stemmed primarily from the use of different multipliers and assumptions in their modelling.

175   Regional Data Corporation and Perrin, Thorau & Associates Ltd., *Analysis of Fiscal Costs and Fiscal & Economic Benefits of the British Columbia Working Opportunity Fund 1992-1998* (Vancouver: Working Opportunity Fund, November 1998) (herein referred to as "the first WOF study").

176   Perrin, Thorau & Associates Ltd., *The Working Opportunity Fund: Venture Capital Growth and Success for BC*, 2d ed. (Vancouver: Working Opportunity Fund, January 2001) (herein referred to as "the second WOF study").

177   In both studies, the fiscal cost of WOF comprised three elements: the startup costs and annual administrative costs of the program; the tax cost, determined by simulating the tax collected assuming actual investment in WOF and comparing this with the simulated tax that would have been collected in the absence of investment in WOF; and an interest factor, associated with the lag between investments in WOF and investments by WOF. The benefits of the program were estimated using the British Columbia I/O model that simulated the increased expenditure resulting from WOF's investments. For each investee business, increased expenditure was adjusted to account for two things: the portion of activity from projects financed by WOF (referred to in the second WOF study as "the project factor"); and the incremental impact of WOF's investment (that is, determining the degree to which WOF's investment was truly incremental or simply replaced alternative funding, referred to in the second WOF study as "the investment factor"). The second WOF study suggested that the determination of the project factor is a matter of judgment. To provide some sensitivity analysis, two estimates of the project factor were determined: an upper estimate of 60 percent (which was used in the first WOF study) and a more conservative lower estimate of 42 percent. The investment factor was determined on the basis of a survey of 37 portfolio businesses of WOF conducted for the first WOF study. The survey suggested that 26.5 percent of WOF's investments were fully incremental, 48 percent were partially incremental, and 25.5 percent were not incremental. On the basis of the survey results, an investment factor of 40 percent was used for non-payroll expenditure and 50 percent for payroll expenditure. In computing the benefits of the program, both studies also included 80 percent of WOF's own payroll and expenditure (on the assumption that any alternative activity from other aspects of the financial sector would have occurred primarily outside British Columbia).

178   In determining the benefits to the federal and provincial governments, the study assumed a two-year time lag between investment in WOF and WOF's investment in qualifying small businesses—a reasonable assumption, given that WOF has continuously met its 80 percent qualified investment pacing requirement within the requisite two-year period.

179   François Vaillancourt, "Labour-Sponsored Venture Capital Funds in Canada: Institutional Aspects, Tax Expenditures and Employment Creation," in Paul J.N. Halpern, ed., *Financing Growth in Canada* (Calgary: University of Calgary Press, 1997), 571-92.

180   Ibid., at 587.

181   Brian F. Smith, "Comment," in *Financing Growth in Canada*, supra note 179, 674-77.

182   Ibid., at 675.

183   See, generally, Borris I. Bittker, "Equity, Efficiency, and Income Tax Theory: Do Misallocations Drive Out Inequities?" (1979) vol. 16, no. 4 *San Diego Law Review* 735-48.

184   The method by which SME investments are valued for financial statement purposes is highly conservative. Apart from the difficulty of valuing these investments, it is not likely that they would be written up substantially prior to their disposition, because their lack of liquidity obviously affects the value: Duff Young, "Now's the Time To Buy Labour Funds," *Globe and Mail*, January 31, 1998. Young states: "A typical move, for example, at many funds is to select the lowest of the valuator's range of price estimates for an illiquid holding. It has always been this way with venture capital because pricing didn't really matter when closed-end venture capital pools were the norm. Today's open-end mutual fund structure (where new people can come in, and old investors can redeem) is what makes the issue thorny." Young gives the example of CI Covington's investment in Playdium Entertainment Corp. CI Covington invested $2.5 million in debt convertible to common shares at the price of $0.925 per share. According to Young, "[r]ecent financings for the growing company (some of which the Covington fund has participated in) have taken place at a share value of $5.75. Covington has reflected just a small part of this increase on its books."

185   Bittker's analysis (supra note 183), in contrast, used US tax-exempt municipal bonds as an example. At any given point in time, the return on a tax-exempt bond could be easily compared with similarly rated taxable bonds with the same maturity.

186   The theory is not intended to apply in hindsight, but that is the only way in which it can be tested for equity investments. The theory holds true for bonds where the interest rate is established at the time the bond is issued so that the return on a tax-exempt bond can be compared with the return on a taxable bond, assuming that both have similar terms to maturity. In contrast, the return on equity can only be determined when the investment is actually disposed of.

187   The following table compares the management-expense ratios (MERs) of LSVCCs and various other mutual fund investments. The figures are as of October 31, 2002 from the Globefund Web site: http://www.globefund.com/.

Type of investment	MER (average in group)
LSVCC	4.60
Canadian equity funds	2.66
Canadian small-cap equity funds	2.70
International equity funds	2.56
US equity funds	2.58

The MERs for LSVCCs ranged from a low of 1.6 percent to a high of 7.0 percent.

A brief study comparing fund performance and management compensation of LSVCCs and alternative investments available to Canadian investors concluded that the management compensation of LSVCCs was the primary reason for their poor performance. The higher MERs of LSVCCs are not the only factor, however; the authors claim that the manner in which LSVCC managers are compensated causes a significant misalignment of their interests with investors' interests, leading to poor investment decisions by managers and therefore poor fund performance. See Scott Anderson and Yisong S. Tian, "Incentive Fees, Valuation and Performance of Labour Sponsored Investment Funds" (May 26, 2003; the full version of the article is not yet published, although a shorter version, under the same title, is published in (2003) vol. 16, no. 3 *Canadian Investment Review* 20-27). I am grateful to the authors for providing me with a copy of their article. Not surprisingly, their conclusions have drawn extensive criticism from the LSVCC industry: see, for example, Rudy Luukko, "Views Clash over Findings on Labour Fund Fees," June 9, 2003 (available online from the Morningstar Web site: http://www.morningstar.ca/).

188   Contrast the funds listed in table 6.1 with those listed in Osborne and Sandler, supra note 49, at 512, table 1.

189   In the United States, the National Venture Capital Association includes a chapter on performance in its annual yearbook. The 2003 yearbook included the following table summarizing the performance of private equity funds as of September 30, 2002 (Thomson Venture Economics, *2003 National Venture Capital Association Yearbook* (Arlington, VA and Newark, NJ: National Venture Capital Association and Thomson Venture Economics, 2003), 81, figure 7.01):

	Net IRR to investors for investment horizon ending 9/30/2002 for private equity funds				
Fund type	*1 year*	*3 year*	*5 year*	*10 year*	*20 year*
Seed/early focused	−28.0	18.4	42.5	32.9	19.8
Balanced focused	−19.0	19.9	22.2	22.0	14.6
Later-stage focused	−16.7	4.0	12.7	23.5	15.9
All venture	−22.1	15.0	26.7	26.0	16.5
Buyout funds	−8.2	−4.2	1.6	9.1	12.6
Mezzanine debt	−1.6	5.2	7.7	11.1	11.1
All private equity	−12.1	1.2	8.4	15.2	14.5

As the table indicates, the long-term returns of US private VCFs have been significantly higher than those of the public stock market fund indices listed in table 6.1 over virtually the same time periods.

The CVCA recently released performance statistics for the Canadian venture capital industry for periods ending December 31, 2001 and December 31, 2002. Unfortunately, these statistics do not differentiate between LSVCCs and private VCFs, show gross returns rather than net returns, and are not based on a standardized valuation methodology. See further chapter 7, notes 306-308 and accompanying text.

190   For these purposes, FSTQ is included in computing the 10-year return of an "average LSVCC." Accordingly, the average LSVCC generated an annual return of 2.53 percent over 10 years rather than the return of 1.5 percent shown in table 6.1.

191   Individual results vary greatly among Canadian small-cap funds. However, there are a significantly greater number to choose from, so the average return of the class of funds is more meaningful.

192   Bittker, supra note 183, at 744.

193   As indicated in the table, supra note 189, US private VCFs generated an average return to investors of 26.0 percent over the 10-year period ending September 30, 2002. If, instead of investing in a Canadian small-cap fund, Ms. X invested in a Canadian private VCF (assuming that she could) that generated only half of the return of US private VCFs (13.0 percent), her $5,000 RRSP investment in 1992 would have been worth $16,972.84 in 2002. This would give her, together with

her non-RRSP investment, a total of $11,474.15 after tax, or an annualized 8.67 percent after-tax return, which is significantly greater than the 5.87 percent return generated by Ms. Y's investment in an average LSVCC investment.

194   Suppose that Ms. X and Ms. Y made their respective investments in 2003 (assuming a constant 46 percent tax rate) and held them for 20 years, applying the 10-year returns for LSVCCs, small-cap funds, and Canada savings bonds (to October 31, 2002) as the expected return over the 20-year period. Ms. X would have $2,300 to invest outside her RRSP (for 19 years), while Ms. Y would have $3,800 to invest (since the federal and provincial tax credits for LSVCC investments are generally 15 percent each). Ms. X's small-cap investment in her RRSP would be worth $22,044, netting her $11,904, while her non-RRSP investments would be worth $3,452, for a total of $15,365. Ms. Y's LSVCC investment in her RRSP would be worth $8,247, netting her $4,453, while her non-RRSP investments would be worth $5,553, for a total of $10,006. In other words, Ms. Y would accumulate slightly less than two-thirds of what Ms. X would accumulate. If, however, both Ms. X and Ms. Y invested their non-RRSP investments in an S & P 500 index fund (with a 10.6 percent per annum return), their non-RRSP investments would be worth $6,623 and $10,941, respectively. Even with a more risky investment acquired outside the RRSP, Ms. Y's accumulated capital would be only 83 percent of Ms. X's.

195   The fact that LSVCCs continue to attract large amounts of capital each year suggests that the immediate tax savings may lead to irrational behaviour on the part of investors. For example, taxpayers may be motivated by some psychic satisfaction from the immediate tax savings or perhaps from the knowledge that they are contributing to undefined cutting-edge research and development that will be performed by portfolio firms.

196   The primary investors in LSVCCs are RRSPs, which are tax-exempt. The primary investors in private VCFs, at least in the United States, are pension plans, which are also tax-exempt. As noted in chapter 1, private VCFs are generally structured as limited partnerships because they are treated as passthrough entities. LSVCCs are taxed in accordance with the rules applicable to mutual fund corporations. Accordingly, dividends received from taxable Canadian corporations are exempt from tax; income taxes paid by the LSVCC on taxable capital gains are refundable when capital gains dividends are paid to shareholders; and a portion of an LSVCC's tax on other investment income is refundable when ordinary (that is, taxable) dividends are paid to shareholders. Provincial income taxes generally apply in a similar manner, although Quebec effectively exempts its LSVCCs from provincial income tax. An LSVCC may also be liable for federal large corporations tax and provincial capital taxes. Thus, where the income of an LSVCC consists of dividends and/or capital gains, its tax treatment is similar to the passthrough treatment of a limited partnership once the LSVCC distributes its income to its shareholders. Therefore, ignoring the return on investment, the only significant distinction between an RRSP acquiring (for the benefit of the RRSP's annuitant) an interest in an LSVCC and a pension plan acquiring (for the benefit of its individual plan members) an interest in a private venture capital limited partnership is that, in the former case, the individual is entitled to upfront tax credits.

197   Douglas J. Cumming and Jeffrey G. MacIntosh, "Crowding Out Private Equity: Canadian Evidence" (2004, draft paper), 3 (emphasis in original). A previous

(2002) draft of the paper is posted on the Social Science Research Network Web site: http://www.ssrn.com/. See also Douglas J. Cumming and Jeffrey G. MacIntosh, "Comparative Venture Capital Governance: Private Versus Labour Sponsored Venture Capital Funds," in Vesa Kanniainen and Christian Keuschnigg, eds., *Venture Capital, Entrepreneurship and Public Policy* (Cambridge, MA: MIT Press, forthcoming).

198   Federal funds are predominant in the Maritimes.

199   Postlethwaite & Netterville, supra note 84. The State of Louisiana Legislative Auditor prepared a report on the Louisiana CAPCO program in January 2001: see supra note 116. This report considered the number of jobs created by CAPCOs and the costs of the CAPCO program and made a number of recommendations for legislative reform.

200   Postlethwaite & Netterville, supra note 84, at 33, figure 3.

201   However, the analysis for a 100 percent premium tax credit would be substantially the same.

202   If a premium tax credit of 100 percent rather than 110 percent were provided, a larger amount would have to be set aside and invested in low-risk investments.

203   The Postlethwaite & Netterville study, supra note 84, suggests not only that the amount of capital invested in qualified businesses is reduced by this structure, but also that the investments are weighted toward debt, which may restrict the potential growth of the qualified businesses. From 1988 to 1998, the Louisiana CAPCO program generated $517 million in tax credits, of which $136.9 million had been taken. CAPCOs reported $804 million in assets at the end of 1998, of which $145.7 million was invested in qualified investments. At the same time, $246.6 million was invested in restricted US government securities (as collateral for notes). More than half of the investments in qualified businesses were debt. Ibid., at 37 and 39-40.

204   Chip Cooper, David Barkley, and Mike Williams, *Understanding CAPCOs* (Oklahoma City: National Association of Seed and Venture Funds, October 2001), 13 (available online from the NASVF Web site: http://www.nasvf.org/).

205   Postlethwaite & Netterville, supra note 84, at 38.

206   Ibid., at 41-61. The economic impact of CAPCO investments was derived using an I/O model maintained by the US Department of Commerce for the State of Louisiana. The model is designed to capture direct, indirect, and induced effects of the expenditure.

207   Estimates of gross receipts for 1999 through 2010 were based on three different growth scenarios: the first assumed growth of 29.1 percent, which was the average growth of actual gross receipts over the previous five years of all companies that received CAPCO financing; the second assumed growth of 15 percent, based on startup companies with an above-average growth potential; and the third assumed a more conservative 10 percent. State tax collections were estimated to be 8 percent of the personal earnings determined by applying the I/O model.

208   Even assuming the most favourable conditions, the study can be criticized for the simplicity of its calculations of program benefits. According to the study, supra note 84, at 53: "In the end for the company to succeed it must have a positive net income, but gross receipts are an important measure of the impact of the company

on the local economy because this determines how many persons will be required to work for it, how many materials will be purchased from other businesses in the local economy, and how the company will possibly develop in the long-run." Even so, it is unlikely that a 29.1 percent growth rate could be sustained over a significant period of time if companies generate gross receipts but fail to show profits. Furthermore, the study apparently failed to take into account other factors, such as business failures, which tend to be more prevalent among small businesses, and the fact that while the growth rate for SMEs may be high in their earliest years due to the significant infusion of capital, they are unlikely to be sustained at the same rate over the longer term.

209 For example, the Missouri CAPCO program was estimated to cost the state $48,780 per job created, compared with $4,105 spent per job attracting businesses to enterprise zones, or $6,500 per job encouraging businesses to invest in research and development: Matt Williams, "Business Program Costs Missouri Thousands," *Digital Missourian*, November 19, 2001 (available online from the NASVF Web site: http://www.nasvf.org/).

210 See appendix 6D, under the heading "Government Expenditure Limits." See also infra note 211.

211 Joe Guy Collier, "How Investors Could Get $100 Million from S.C.: Critics Say Plan To Finance High-Tech Firms Puts All the Risk on Taxpayers," *The State*, April 28, 2002 (available online from the NASVF Web site: http://www.nasvf.org/).

212 Barkley, Markley, and Sass Rubin made a number of observations about the Louisiana CAPCO program, including the following: "Three, during the certification process, the emphasis in the management review appears to be on familiarity with CAPCO regulations rather than on venture capital investment experience. As a result, the structure does not ensure that the most experienced venture managers will become certified as CAPCOs. Four, CAPCO investment decisions are relatively insulated from political pressures that are typical of state direct investment programs. However, the legislative process is not insulated from CAPCO and/or insurance company influence. There are strong lobbying efforts on the part of the CAPCOs in support of continued reauthorization of the CAPCO legislation. This process creates a situation where industry resources are devoted to lobbying activities rather than investment activities." Barkley, Markley, and Sass Rubin, supra note 2, at 27-28.

213 Oklahoma Capital Formation Act, enacted by Oklahoma Laws 1991, c. 188. The legislation is found at Oklahoma Statutes, title 74, chapter 70, sections 74-5085.1 to 74-5085.14.

214 Ibid., sections 74-5085.2 and 74-5085.3.

215 The total amount of the tax credits and the terms on which they can be sold are set out in section 74-5085.7, ibid. The OCIB must indicate on the certificate of the tax credit the year or years in which it may be claimed, and any sale must be by competitive bidding unless the sale is for full face value. No tax credit granted by the OCIB is exercisable before July 1, 1990 or after July 1, 2015. The tax credits sold by the OCIB are freely transferable.

216 Ibid., section 74-5085.8(B).

217 All figures are taken from Oklahoma Capital Investment Board, *Report for the Year Ending June 30, 2001* (Oklahoma City: Oklahoma Capital Investment Board, 2001).

218   Business Growth and Development Initiatives—Seed and Venture Capital Invest-
        ments—Small Business Income Allocation, 2002 Iowa Acts, c. 1005, HF 2078,
        introducing sections 15E.221 to 15E.229 to the Iowa Code. The purpose of the
        ICIB is to mobilize venture equity capital for investment in such a manner that
        will result in a significant potential to create jobs and to diversify and stabilize
        the economy of the state.

219   Iowa Code, section 15E.225.2.

220   The ICIB issues tax credit certificates to designated investors in the fund of
        funds. Each certificate specifies a calendar-year maturity date not less than five
        years after its date of issuance. The tax credit is thereafter redeemable on a
        schedule similar to the scheduled redemption of investor's interest in the fund of
        funds. The amount of the credit is limited to the difference between the scheduled
        aggregate return to the investor and the actual aggregate return received by the
        investor. Unused credits may be carried forward seven years.

221   Venture Capital Investment Act of 2001, Act 1791 of 2001, effective on April 19,
        2001 and codified in the Arkansas Code of 1987 annotated, sections 15-5-1401 to
        1409.

222   Ohio Revised Code, title I, chapter 150, effective April 9, 2003.

223   There are two exceptions. First, under the Kansas VCF program introduced in
        2002, natural persons, in order to qualify under the program, must have a net
        worth of at least $1 million and at least 10 times the amount invested in a
        certified capital formation company. Second, West Virginia's Venture Capital Act
        (the newer of the state's two VCF programs) is limited to accredited investors, as
        defined in regulation D under the Securities Act of 1933 (Pub. L. no. 73-22,
        enacted on May 27, 1933; 48 Stat. 74, as amended), each of whom must invest a
        minimum of $200,000.

7

Venture Capital Investment from Retirement Funds*

Retirement funds are the largest source of formal venture capital in both Canada and the United States. However, the funds invested in venture capital in the two countries are markedly different. In Canada, individual retirement funds, specifically registered retirement savings plans (RRSPs), as the predominant investors in labour-sponsored venture capital corporations (LSVCCs), are the single largest source of capital in the formal venture capital industry. In the United States, in contrast, employer-sponsored pension funds have been the largest single source of venture capital in every year but one since 1979, and in some years have accounted for more than half of all new formal venture capital.[1] Employer-sponsored pension plans have not played a significant role in Canada's venture capital industry, certainly not the role that many commentators believe that they should.[2] In both countries, employer-sponsored pension funds have been targeted as an appropriate source of capital in part because of the vast amount of capital that they manage. In the United States, in mid-2000, private sector trusteed pension funds controlled about $4.8 trillion in assets, and public sector pension funds controlled another $2.2 trillion.[3] In Canada, private sector trusteed pension funds represent one of the largest pools of capital in Canada,[4] second in size only to chartered banks. In 2000, they controlled about $524.6 billion in assets.

This chapter considers the role of retirement funds in venture capital investment, both formal and informal. The retirement income systems in Canada and the United States may be divided into three broad categories:

- individual retirement funds, such as RRSPs in Canada and individual retirement plans in the United States;
- employer-sponsored pension funds, in both the public and private sectors; and
- government-administered retirement funds—namely, the Canada Pension Plan (CPP), Quebec Pension Plan (QPP), and US Social Security.

The chapter begins with an overview of tax legislation and, where applicable, pension fund legislation governing individual retirement plans and employer-sponsored pension plans. The next two sections examine the roles of the three

---

* Unless otherwise stated, US monetary amounts are in US dollars and Canadian montary amounts are in Canadian dollars.

categories of retirement savings in the two countries in the context of venture capital formation. Individual retirement funds and employer-sponsored pension funds are considered together because they share a number of issues. Government-sponsored retirement funds are considered in the last section and, at least at this point in time, are relevant only to the Canadian venture capital industry.

In the United States, individual retirement funds serve no practical role in the formal or informal venture capital industries. This is explained in part by the fact that the United States places significantly greater emphasis on employer-sponsored pension funds. For example, the amounts that could be contributed to individual retirement funds have historically been a small fraction of the amounts that could be contributed to employer-sponsored plans. In contrast, individual retirement funds in Canada are not only the largest source of formal venture capital through their investment in LSVCCs, but are also an important source of informal venture capital—angel as opposed to love capital. In both countries, tax legislation and pension legislation limit an individual's ability to access tax-assisted retirement savings for love capital investments, whether from an employer-sponsored plan (for example, when the employee terminates employment or retires) or from an individual retirement plan. These limitations are considered in the context of venture fund investing by individual retirement funds and employer-sponsored pension funds.

In both countries, the ability of employer-sponsored pension funds to invest in venture capital has been inhibited by pension legislation. In Canada, such investment has also been inhibited by income tax provisions. Both countries introduced amendments to their pension legislation promoting venture capital investment—the United States in 1979 and Canada in 1985. Canada also amended its income tax provisions in 1985 in an effort to promote venture investment by pension funds. The pension fund industries in the two countries have responded to these amendments in markedly different ways. While pension funds have become by far the largest single source of formal venture capital in the United States, Canadian pension funds have generally contributed less than 10 percent of new venture capital each year.[5] This section considers the steps that could be taken to increase pension fund venture capital investment in Canada.

The final section of this chapter considers government-administered retirement funds. In both countries, these funds operate on a "pay-as-you-go" basis (that is, current contributors pay for current pensioners). With an aging population in both countries, these funds have faced financial crises and have had to consider reforms. While US reforms have not yet progressed beyond the proposal state, legislative amendments were made to the CPP in the second half of the 1990s to address the plan's sustainability. These reforms increased contribution levels and, pertinent to this study, significantly altered the investment policy of the CPP. As a result of these amendments, the CPP will become one of the largest private equity investors in Canada. This shift in the composition of the CPP's investments could also demonstrate the viability of venture investment as a small but important part of a diversified investment portfolio. Such a signal to the industry would be meaningful, particularly given the enormous funding gap that many employer-sponsored pension funds are experiencing as a result of the downturn in public equity markets since 2000.

It is not necessary here to provide a detailed account of the history of the tax incentives applicable to retirement savings. It is important to emphasize, however, that these rules are designed to increase the amount of income that individuals can enjoy in their retirement years—or to make up for the shortfall in benefits provided by government-administered retirement funds (the CPP or QPP and US Social Security)—and to supplement or replace employer-provided pension plans. Therefore, both the security and the liquidity of investments made through these retirement vehicles are important considerations.

Individual and Employer-Sponsored Retirement Funds: An Overview of Applicable Pension and Tax Legislation

Both Canada and the United States offer tax incentives for retirement savings, through individual retirement plans and employer-sponsored plans. The primary difference between the two countries is that the United States places much greater emphasis on employer-sponsored plans.

Individual retirement plans are creatures of statute in both countries. These special accounts—RRSPs and registered retirement income funds (RRIFs) in Canada and individual retirement accounts and individual retirement annuities (both generally referred to as IRAs) in the United States—would not exist except for the tax measures that created them. Most of these plans operate on an exempt/exempt/taxable basis; that is, the individual is entitled to a deduction for plan contributions, the income of the plan is exempt from tax, and withdrawals from the plan are taxable. The United States also provides a second type of IRA, referred to as a "Roth IRA," which operates on a taxable/exempt/exempt basis; that is, the contributions to the plan come from after-tax earnings while the income of the plan and withdrawals from the plan are tax-exempt.

In contrast, employer-sponsored plans may or may not benefit from tax incentives, and both countries distinguish plans that do benefit ("registered pension plans" in Canada and "qualified plans" in the United States[6]) from those that do not.[7] In general, the rules governing registered pension plans and qualified plans benefit both employers and employees. First, employees can defer taxation on employer contributions until the year in which distributions from the plan occur. Second, employers (and possibly employees) can deduct contributions to the plan in the year in which they are made. Third, the plan is exempt from tax on its income; the plan beneficiaries pay tax on the income when they receive distributions from the plan. Thus, registered pension and qualified plans generally operate on an exempt/exempt/taxable basis.

Pension plans in both countries may be broadly classified into two categories: defined benefit plans and defined contribution plans. Under a defined benefit plan, the employer promises to provide benefits to retired employees according to a specific formula, such as a percentage of the employee's best three years of earnings. Under a defined contribution plan, the employer promises only to make specific contributions to the plan, which are allocated to separate accounts established for each participating employee. The retirement benefit that accrues to the employee depends on the plan's performance. Defined contribution plans include both money purchase plans and profit-sharing plans. In broad terms, the distinction between defined benefit and defined contribution plans lies in the bearer of the investment risk. Under a defined benefit plan, the employer is responsible for ensuring that the plan's assets are adequate to satisfy present and future benefits, and therefore the employer bears the investment risk. Under a defined contribution plan, the benefit that an employee receives depends on the contributions and earnings that accumulate in that employee's account, and so the employee effectively bears the investment risk associated with the plan. For this reason, many defined contribution plans allow some degree of self-directed investment by each employee participant.

Pension plan assets are managed either internally or externally (or both). Some large pension plans retain their own full-time asset managers to invest all or a portion of their investment portfolios. Other plans place their funds with outside fund managers, sometimes in pooled funds. Where funds are managed externally, an issue arises whether the outside managers are plan fiduciaries and therefore potentially liable to plan members under applicable pension legislation or general trust law if they are negligent in their asset-management activities. This issue is considered in the context of pension regulatory legislation.

Beyond these broad similarities, the technical rules applicable to the various types of pension plans in both countries are vastly different, and for the most part have no bearing on this study. Both countries have pension standards legislation applicable to all private employer-sponsored pension plans. Pension plans for public sector employees may also (or instead) be governed by this legislation and/or by legislation specific to the plan.[8]

United States

The first reported pension plan in the United States was the Plymouth Colony settlers' military retirement program of 1636. In 1759, a pension plan was established for widows and children of Presbyterian ministers. The first employer-sponsored pension plan was established by the American Express Company in 1875. In the century that followed, about 400 plans were established, primarily by the railroad, banking, and public utility industries.[9] The benefits provided in early private sector pensions were regarded as gratuities in recognition of long and faithful service, and the payments as entirely discretionary, with the employer having no legal obligation to provide payment. The most significant growth of private pension plans occurred in the 1940s and 1950s, primarily as a result of pressure from organized labour[10] and from changes in social attitudes following the economic upheaval of the 1930s.[11]

Tax incentives of some sort for employer-sponsored pension plans have been in the Internal Revenue Code since 1921, although a comprehensive regime applicable to qualified pension plans was not introduced until 1942.[12] The 1942 provisions, which established non-discriminatory eligibility rules for pension coverage, contributions, and benefits, were incorporated in the Internal Revenue Code of 1954 and were amended substantially by the Employee Retirement Income Security Act of 1974 (ERISA).[13] Since then, a number of other types of employer-sponsored plans have been added to the Code.

Until 1962, the only retirement funds that benefited from favourable tax provisions were employer-sponsored pension funds. The Self-Employed Individuals Tax Return Act of 1962[14] introduced tax-favoured retirement plans—commonly referred to as "Keogh" plans or "HR 10" plans—for self-employed partners and sole proprietors.

The one remaining gap—tax-favoured retirement savings for employees who did not benefit from an employer-sponsored pension plan—was filled in 1974 when individual retirement plans were introduced as part of ERISA. Any employee, sole proprietor, or self-employed person can establish an individual retirement plan and contribute to it. An individual retirement plan is commonly referred to as an IRA regardless of which approach to funding is used.

Application of the Internal Revenue Code to Retirement Funds

There has developed in the US tax system a patchwork of employer-sponsored and personal retirement savings vehicles that benefit from favourable tax treatment. The tax system does not easily differentiate between employer-sponsored plans and individual retirement plans in the same way that the Canadian tax system does. The following discussion addresses three kinds of plans: employer-sponsored pension funds, both qualified and non-qualified; Keogh plans, applicable exclusively to self-employed individuals; and individual retirement plans, applicable to employees and self-employed individuals.

Employer-Sponsored Pension Funds

The Code distinguishes between qualified plans and non-qualified plans.[15] There are few rules applicable to non-qualified plans, which are generally designed to preclude the mismatching of the employer deduction and employee inclusion of deferred compensation. The provisions generally require the employer to report the deduction in the year that the employee recognizes the income. Since virtually all employees recognize income on a cash basis, the employer's deduction is deferred until the amount is received by the employee.[16] For these purposes, "receipt" includes constructive receipt.[17] If the employer funds the deferred payment by depositing amounts in an irrevocable trust (which the employee can access only after normal retirement age but which is not otherwise forfeitable), the tax treatment depends on whether the trust is a "secular trust" or a "rabbi trust." The assets of a secular trust are protected from creditors of the employer's business. However, the tax treatment of a non-qualified secular trust plan is the least favourable to employees: the employee is taxed when vesting occurs (likely long before retirement), the employer can deduct the contribution at that time, and income is taxed to the trust (usually at the highest marginal rate). In contrast, under a rabbi trust, the trust assets remain subject to claims of creditors of the employer, the employee is taxed at the earlier of actual and constructive receipt of benefits, the employer is entitled to a deduction at that time, and any income of the trust is taxed to the employer.[18]

The Code provides tax incentives for three types of qualified plans: pension plans, profit-sharing plans, and stock bonus plans. A qualified plan is one that meets the requirements of section 401(a) of the Code. Section 401(a) governs a trust that is created or organized in the United States for the exclusive benefit of employees or their beneficiaries. The trust must meet minimum participation standards, comply with rules prohibiting discrimination in favour of highly compensated employees, and meet other conditions that protect beneficiaries and ensure that funds will be used to provide retirement benefits. Assuming that these requirements are met, the employer is entitled to deduct (subject to maximum limits, discussed below) contributions to the plan,[19] employees can defer the recognition of income until distributions are made from the plan,[20] and the plan is generally exempt from tax on its income[21] (subject to the possible application of unrelated business income tax,[22] discussed below).

Qualified pension plans may be categorized as defined benefit plans or defined contribution plans (which include profit-sharing plans). Section 415 of the Code imposes limits on the quantum of the benefit that such plans can provide in order to be qualified plans. Under a defined benefit plan, the benefit may not exceed the lesser of $160,000 per year and the participant's average compensation for his or her "high 3 years."[23] The employer's annual contribution is based on actuarially determined costs of providing the benefits prescribed in the plan documents. Under a defined contribution plan, the maximum annual employer contribution cannot exceed the lesser of $40,000 and the participant's compensation for the year. In general, only the employer may deduct contributions made to a qualified plan, although employees may deduct contributions made to certain types of qualified plans, as described below.

The Revenue Act of 1978[24] introduced two new types of qualified pension plans. The first, known as a simplified employee pension (SEP), was intended to reduce the administrative complexity and costs associated with trusteed defined contribution plans. Rather than a tax-exempt trust, the SEP uses an IRA for each employee. Employers can use a simplified model form to adopt a model SEP, which avoids special document preparation.[25] In addition, the use of IRAs relieves the employer from certain fiduciary obligations under ERISA otherwise associated with plans involving trusts. The employer contribution is limited to the lesser of 15 percent of the employee's compensation and $40,000.[26] However, the anti-discrimination rules in Code section 408(k)(3) limit the maximum compensation for each employee who maintains a SEP to $200,000, which effectively limits the maximum contribution to $30,000. Under a SEP, the employer is not required to make contributions every year. When contributions are made, they must be made pursuant to a written allocation formula[27] and must include all employees aged 21 and over who performed services during at least three of the five preceding years and who received at least $300 in compensation in the current year.[28] Certain SEPs for small businesses may be structured in the same way as a 401(k) plan, discussed below. Employees may elect to receive cash compensation or to make contributions to the SEP. Such contributions are subject to the same limitations on employee contributions under a 401(k) plan. This elective regime is permissible only if the employer has 25 or fewer employees and at least 50 percent of the employees elect to make contributions rather than take cash compensation.[29] All SEP contributions vest immediately, and employees are entitled to make withdrawals from the SEP in accordance with the normal withdrawal rules applicable to IRAs.[30]

The second retirement vehicle introduced in 1978, which has become extremely popular, is the cash or deferred arrangement (CODA), also known as a 401(k) plan.[31] Under a 401(k) plan, employees have the option of receiving cash compensation or contributing to a qualified trust.[32] If an employee elects to receive compensation, it will form part of the employee's taxable income. However, if an employee elects to contribute to the plan, the amount contributed is deductible so that it is, in effect, made from pre-tax compensation. The employer may, but is not obliged to, match employee contributions, subject to certain limitations to avoid discrimination in favour of highly compensated employees.[33] An employee may contribute a maximum of $12,000 to a 401(k) account in 2003, $13,000 in 2004, $14,000 in 2005, and $15,000 (adjusted for inflation) for years after 2005.[34] Furthermore, if the employer elects to match an employee's contribution, the combined limit cannot exceed certain amounts. The Economic Growth and Tax Relief Reconciliation Act of 2001[35] increased the maximum combined contribution for 2002 and subsequent years to the lesser of 100 percent of an employee's compensation and $40,000, adjusted for inflation.[36] This maximum is identical to the contribution limit for 401(a) defined contribution plans.

A second type of employee-participation account, the savings incentive match plans for employees (SIMPLE) account, was introduced in the Small Business Job Protection Act of 1996.[37] SIMPLE accounts were intended to increase retirement savings by employees of small businesses. The employer must have no more than 100 employees who received at least $5,000 of compensation in the previous year, and cannot have another qualified plan in place.[38] A SIMPLE account may be structured as either an IRA or a 401(k) plan. The maximum employee contribution, subject to a stipulated percentage of compensation, cannot exceed $8,000 in 2003, $9,000 in 2004, $10,000 in 2005, and thereafter adjusted for inflation.[39] Under a SIMPLE account, the employer must make annual contributions consisting of either

- matching contributions equal to the employees' salary reduction contributions, not exceeding 3 percent of each employee's compensation;[40] or
- non-elective contributions of 2 percent of compensation for each eligible employee, regardless of whether the employee makes a contribution.[41]

In all of the various employer-sponsored pension plans, there are virtually no limitations on the types of investment that a plan can make,[42] except as precluded by the prohibited transaction rules in section 4975 of the Code. These transactions are essentially the same as those prohibited under section 406 of ERISA, discussed below.[43] Section 4975 imposes a penalty tax on the disqualified person who participates in the prohibited transaction equal to 15 percent of the amount involved in the transaction. The 15 percent tax is imposed for every year or part year in the "taxable period."[44] If the transaction is not corrected in the taxable period (that is, if it is not corrected before a notice of deficiency or an assessment is issued), a further tax of 100 percent of the amount involved is imposed. Apart from various closely connected investments, the prohibited transactions do not limit the types of equity investments a pension plan can make. In particular, there are no limitations on investment in small and medium-sized enterprises (SMEs), whether directly or indirectly, unless the SME is a disqualified person (for example, the employer-sponsor).[45]

Keogh Plans

In theory, a Keogh plan may take the form of any qualified employer-sponsored plan, including a 401(a), 401(k), SEP, or SIMPLE plan.[46] The deductions for contributions, the limits on contributions, and the benefits associated with a Keogh plan are the same as those applicable to the qualified plan whose form is adopted.[47] Keogh plans are also subject to the prohibited transaction rules in section 4975 of the Code.

Individual Retirement Plans

There are two primary types of IRAs[48] under the Code:

1) Individual retirement accounts, which are trusts created or organized in the United States for the exclusive benefit of an individual or his beneficiaries. The written instrument creating and governing the trust must meet a number of requirements set out in section 408(a) of the Code.[49] Only banks and other financial institutions that fall within the scope of applicable regulations may offer and operate such an account.
2) Individual retirement annuities, which are annuity contracts or endowment contracts issued by an insurance company. These contracts must meet the requirements set out in section 408(b) of the Code.[50]

In addition, an employer, an employee organization, or an association of self-employed persons (for example, a law society) can establish a trust for retirement savings of employees or members, provided that the trust meets all of the requirements for individual retirement accounts and there is a separate accounting of the interest for each employee or member.[51]

The contribution limits on IRAs are significantly lower than those available for various employer-sponsored retirement plans, including those essentially funded by employees (such as 401(k) plans), and are also significantly lower than the contribution limits in Canada for RRSPs. According to Boris Bittker and Lawrence Lokken,

> [t]he comparatively low ceiling on IRA deductions is probably intended to keep IRAs from becoming a serious alternative to qualified plans for highly compensated employees. With a higher ceiling, shareholder-employees and other highly compensated employees of closely held enterprises could arrange for higher salaries and establish their own retirement programs, thus reducing the company's incentive to create a nondiscriminatory qualified plan covering rank and file employees as well as insiders.[52]

IRAs were originally available only to individuals who were not active participants in employer-provided retirement plans. This restriction was removed in 1981 in an attempt to increase retirement savings, although it proved short-lived. In 1986, a restriction was reintroduced that limited access to deductible IRA contributions in a taxable year for an employee who was an active participant in a qualified plan unless the employee's income fell below certain thresholds, as discussed below.

Before December 31, 2001, the maximum annual contribution for one person to an IRA was the lesser of $2,000 and 100 percent of the individual's compensation.[53] The maximum permitted contribution was increased by the Economic Growth and Tax Relief Reconciliation Act of 2001,[54] applicable to taxable years beginning after December 31, 2001. Under this Act, the maximum annual contribution was increased to the lesser of the individual's compensation[55] and $3,000 for 2002 to 2004, $4,000 for 2005 to 2007, $5,000 for 2008, and thereafter adjusted for inflation.[56]

The deductible amount of an individual's contribution to an IRA is reduced if the individual or the individual's spouse is an "active participant" in certain employer-sponsored pension plans.[57] An individual is permitted to make non-deductible contributions to an IRA to the extent that the deductible ceiling is reduced by the rule applicable to active participants. For example, an unmarried individual in 2004 who is an active participant in a qualified plan and whose income exceeds $44,000 can make a non-deductible contribution to an IRA not exceeding $3,000 for that year. Although non-deductible contributions do not generate a current-year tax benefit, the income generated by the contributions is not taxed until it is distributed from the plan.[58] If the individual's contribution to an IRA exceeds the amount allowed under the Code, a non-deductible annual excise tax of 6 percent is imposed on the excess contribution for each year that the excess contribution remains in the plan.[59] To avoid continuing excise taxes, the individual must either withdraw the excess contribution or offset it against contributions that could otherwise be made in future years.

The investment earnings of an IRA are fully exempt from federal income tax while they are held in the plan.[60] Distributions from an IRA are taxed in accordance with the annuity rules in section 72 of the Code, which allows the tax-free return of the individual's investment (that is, total non-deductible contributions)

in the IRA and taxes the excess as ordinary income.[61] Under the minimum distribution requirements, distributions from an IRA must not be delayed beyond
April 1 following the calendar year in which the individual reaches age 70½ or
in which the individual retires (if later).[62] Most distributions from an IRA before
the individual is 59½ are subject to an additional 10 percent excise tax, as
discussed below.[63]

The Taxpayer Relief Act of 1997[64] introduced the Roth IRA.[65] Contributions to a Roth IRA are not deductible, earnings are exempt from tax,[66] and
qualified distributions are excluded from gross income.[67] A non-qualified distribution is excluded from gross income only to the extent of the taxpayer's
contributions to a Roth IRA, less all prior distributions, whether qualified or
unqualified. Unlike a traditional IRA, a Roth IRA does not require that distributions begin by a particular time, and so may be used to accumulate earnings
until the individual's death. The amount that an individual can contribute to a
Roth IRA is restricted to the amount of the deductible contribution to a traditional IRA, computed without reference to the limitation imposed for active
participation in a qualified plan, less the amount contributed by the individual
to IRAs other than Roth IRAs. The amount that can be contributed is reduced if
the individual's adjusted gross income exceeds certain thresholds.[68] The economic effects of a Roth IRA are equivalent to those of a traditional IRA (where
the contributions are deductible) if a constant rate of tax is assumed at the time
of contribution and distribution.

As with employer-sponsored plans, there are, in theory, virtually no limitations
on the types of investment that a traditional IRA or Roth IRA can make,[69] except
as precluded by the prohibited transaction rules in section 4975 of the Code.

Pension Legislation

ERISA is the primary pension standards legislation in the United States. ERISA
evolved from government studies of private pension plans beginning in 1962.
These studies concluded that private pension plans played a significant role in
the nation's retirement security program, but that the system was deficient in a
number of areas, particularly information dissemination and protection of employee rights. Title I of ERISA is concerned with the protection of employee
benefit rights. It is governed primarily by the Department of Labor[70] and deals
with four main areas: reporting and disclosure; participation and vesting; funding;
and fiduciary responsibilities. Title I is applicable to all employee benefit plans,
including welfare plans (medical, death, disability, etc.) and pension plans, whether
qualified or non-qualified, that are established or maintained by employers
engaged in interstate commerce or by employee organizations representing employees engaged in interstate commerce. The provisions of ERISA supersede
state laws applicable to such employee benefit plans other than laws that regulate insurance, banking, or securities.[71] With respect to pension plans, title I of
ERISA is applicable to the three types of qualified asset accumulation plans
recognized by the Code—pension plans, profit-sharing plans, and stock bonus

plans—as well as to non-qualified plans that provide retirement income or result in the deferral of income.[72]

The key components of ERISA that have an impact on the permitted investments of pension plans are the prohibited transaction rules and the fiduciary obligation rules. The prohibited transaction rules, in section 406 of ERISA, preclude a plan from engaging in various transactions with certain persons.[73] In addition, most pension plans are prohibited from holding more than 10 percent of the plan's assets in securities or real property of the employer.[74] The fiduciary obligation rules are considered in the next section of this chapter. Historically, these rules limited the ability of pension funds to invest in venture capital, and it was the amendment of these rules beginning in the late 1970s that made pension funds the largest venture capital investors in the United States.

An individual's ability to access funds held in a qualified pension plan before retirement is, in theory, greater in the United States than in Canada. In the United States, unlike in Canada, termination of employment is an acceptable occasion for distribution of vested benefits from a pension plan.[75]

Certain plans are excluded from the application of title I of ERISA, including government plans,[76] church plans, unfunded "top hat plans" (that is, plans that provide benefits in excess of those that can be paid by qualified plans to a select group of management or highly compensated employees), and plans maintained outside the United States primarily for the benefit of non-residents.[77] ERISA does not apply to Keogh plans unless employees other than a self-employed business owner participate in the plan.[78] In addition, ERISA does not apply to IRAs, including most IRAs established under employer or union plans.[79]

Canada

Pension funds have been in existence in Canada since the 19th century, although until the end of that century they were limited primarily to the federal public service, the railways, and certain commercial banks.[80] The federal government sought to encourage the creation of pension plans by enacting the Pension Funds Societies Act, 1887[81] and the Government Annuities Act, 1908.[82] When the Income War Tax Act (IWTA) was introduced in 1917, employer contributions to employer-sponsored pension funds were considered a deductible business expense, with no limit placed on the amount contributed.[83] In 1919, the IWTA was amended to permit the deduction of employee contributions to employer pension plans.[84] Again, no limit was placed on the amount contributed. Limits were introduced on employee contributions in 1936 and on employer contributions in 1941.[85] The number of employer pension plans grew rapidly between 1940 and 1959, beginning with the adoption of group contracts by the Canadian Government Annuities Branch, which became a major underwriter of pension plans in Canada.[86] In 1942, the IWTA was amended to provide that the minister of national revenue must approve a pension plan before contributions were tax-deductible, and in 1946, the department published guidelines for ministerial approval.

Tax incentives for individual retirement funds—RRSPs—were introduced in Canada in 1957 as savings vehicles primarily for self-employed individuals and employees without employer pension plans.[87] From inception, RRSPs have been subject to maximum annual contribution limits (the lesser of a percentage of earned income and a specified dollar amount). Major reforms of the RRSP rules, primarily dealing with the annual contribution limit and its relationship to employer-sponsored pension plans, were introduced in 1986, although actual implementation was delayed until 1992. The Income Tax Act now includes a uniform comprehensive limit on the aggregate amount that can be contributed to registered pension plans (RPPs), deferred profit-sharing plans (DPSPs), and RRSPs in a year.

Application of the Income Tax Act to Retirement Funds

Like the United States, Canada limits tax incentives to certain types of employer-sponsored pension plans and individual retirement benefit plans. Unlike the United States, Canada draws clear distinctions between employer-sponsored and individual retirement plans and applies a uniform comprehensive limit on the aggregate amount that can be contributed annually to these plans. This section provides an overview of the retirement funds that benefit from tax incentives for contributions, including the contribution limits of the various plans. It then reviews the provisions that affect the investments that such plans can make.

RPPs, DPSPs, and RRSPs: Contribution Limits

Two employer-sponsored pension plans enjoy favourable tax treatment: RPPs and DPSPs. Subject to certain limits, employers (and, where permitted, employees[88]) are entitled to deduct contributions to an RPP or DPSP in the year the contributions are made (or within 120 days after the end of that year);[89] the income of the RPP or DPSP is exempt from tax;[90] and employees include benefits from the plan in income only when the benefits are received.[91] RPPs are governed primarily by sections 147.1 to 147.3 of the Act and related regulations. DPSPs are governed primarily by section 147 and related regulations. Retirement plans that do not qualify as an RPP or DPSP may be an employee benefit plan, a salary deferral arrangement, or a retirement compensation arrangement (RCA).[92] Which rules apply depends on the characteristics of the particular plan. If the plan is a trust, the trust is taxed on any undistributed income; otherwise, the custodian (the employer) is taxed on any undistributed income. Under a salary deferral arrangement, the employee's tax liability is accelerated to the year in which he or she has a right to receive the amount, and the employer can deduct the amount in that year (provided that the amount is reasonable and relates to earning income). A key distinction[93] between an RCA and an RPP is that the former is subject to a refundable 50 percent tax on contributions to and income earned by the RCA, which removes any deferral benefit otherwise associated with RCAs.

The only individual retirement fund that benefits from favourable tax treatment is the RRSP. As with RPPs, amounts contributed to an RRSP, subject to certain limits, are deductible by the plan holder ("the annuitant"), the income of the RRSP is exempt from tax, and distributions from the RRSP are included in the income of the annuitant when they are received. RRSPs are governed primarily by section 147 and related regulations. An RRSP must mature before the end of the year in which the annuitant reaches the age of 69. After that age, the annuitant can no longer make tax-deductible contributions to a personal retirement plan. At maturity, the annuitant must convert the amount accumulated in the RRSP to an RRSP annuity or a RRIF in order to avoid immediate taxation of the total value of the RRSP. A RRIF acts as an extension of the RRSP and, like an RRSP, can be self-administered. RRIFs are governed primarily by section 146.3 and related regulations. The main differences between a RRIF and an RRSP annuity are: (1) the payout under an RRSP annuity is guaranteed, whereas the payout under a RRIF is not; (2) a RRIF provides greater tax deferral because the amounts paid out increase over time; and (3) a RRIF provides greater flexibility with regard to investments permitted and amounts paid out (since any amount in excess of the annual minimum amount can be withdrawn).[94]

There are no limits on an individual's ability to withdraw funds from his or her RRSP before the individual reaches the age of 69,[95] although any amount withdrawn must be included in the recipient's income. Unlike the United States, Canada does not impose any additional tax on withdrawals prior to a certain age. Despite the moniker "retirement" savings plan, RRSPs are nothing more than deferred savings accounts. If RRSPs were intended to promote *retirement* savings, there would be additional obstacles to early withdrawals—such as the 10 percent excise tax imposed in the United States on early withdrawals from IRAs—except in limited circumstances (for example, death or permanent disability of the annuitant).

The contribution limits in the Income Tax Act for RPPs and DPSPs are substantially less generous than those provided under the Internal Revenue Code for most qualified pension plans, while the contribution limit applicable to RRSPs (before reduction as a result of contributions to RPPs and DPSPs) is greater than that applicable to IRAs under the Code. In all three cases, contributions are subject to certain monetary limits and a uniform comprehensive limit. The uniform comprehensive limit is applied by limiting the maximum amount that might otherwise be contributed to a DPSP or an RRSP in order to take into account the taxpayer's pension adjustment (PA).[96]

The monetary limit applicable to DPSPs and RRSPs is based on the monetary limit applicable to defined contribution RPPs, referred to as the "money purchase limit."[97] The maximum defined benefit to which an employee is entitled under a defined benefit RPP is also related to the money purchase limit.[98] The 2003 federal budget increased the money purchase limit from $13,500 (the limit in effect since 1996) to $15,500 for 2003, $16,500 for 2004, $18,000 for 2005, and thereafter indexed for inflation.[99] The maximum amount that an employer can contribute to a defined contribution RRSP on account of an employee is the lesser of the money purchase limit and 18 percent of the employee's compensation from the employer.[100] An employee is entitled to contribute an amount not exceeding the difference between this maximum amount and the amount contributed by the employer.[101]

The maximum contribution that an employer can make to a defined benefit RPP is the amount necessary to fund the benefits under the plan as determined in accordance with the recommendations of an actuary and approved in writing by the Canada Revenue Agency (CRA), subject to the maximum defined benefit limit stipulated under the Act.[102] As a result of the amendments to the money purchase limit in the 2003 federal budget, the maximum defined benefit limit increases to $1,833 in 2004 and $2,000 in 2005, and is thereafter indexed for inflation. The maximum deductible amount that an employee can make to a defined benefit RPP for current service is the lesser of 9 percent of the employee's compensation and $1,000 plus 70 percent of the employee's PA.[103]

The contribution limit applicable to DPSPs is the lesser of 18 percent of the individual's compensation from the employer and one-half of the money purchase limit (for example, $8,250 in 2004), subject to the comprehensive limit in the event that the employee is also a member of an RPP.[104]

The maximum permitted tax-deductible RRSP contribution is the lesser of 18 percent of the taxpayer's earned income and the RRSP dollar limit for the year, reduced by the taxpayer's PA from the preceding year. In general, the RRSP dollar limit is equal to the money purchase limit from the preceding year, except that the RRSP dollar limit for 2003 was set at $14,500 under the 2003 budget.[105] The RRSP dollar limit is $15,500 in 2004, $16,500 in 2005, $18,000 in 2006, and thereafter indexed for inflation. Since 1991, the Act has permitted the indefinite carryforward of unused RRSP contribution room from a particular year.

Provisions Affecting Investments by RPPs, DPSPs, and RRSPs

There are a number of provisions of the Act that constrain the types of investments that RPPs, DPSPs, and RRSPs can make. Similar to the US Code, the Act precludes an RPP from acquiring a share or debt of certain persons closely connected with the RPP.[106] In addition, and unlike the United States, Canada had a number of secondary objectives in crafting the tax-assisted retirement plan rules, beyond promoting retirement savings by both employers and employees. Specifically, the various plans that benefit from tax incentives in Canada must invest a significant portion of their assets in Canada. In addition to the "invest in Canada" provisions, the government takes a somewhat paternalistic role in certain cases by limiting the types of investment that a tax-favoured plan can make. The impact of these limitations on the ability of an RPP, DPSP, or RRSP to make venture investments is considered below, under the heading "Venture Capital Investment Using Individual and Employer-Sponsored Retirement Funds." The three general limitations imposed on investments by these plans are described more generally here.

First, RRSPs may invest only in "qualified investments," as defined in subsection 146(1) and applicable regulations.[107] If an RRSP acquires a non-qualified investment in a taxation year, the fair market value of the investment at the time it was acquired is included in the income of the annuitant at the end of that taxation year.[108] In addition, the RRSP is subject to tax on the net income and net capital gains (at full inclusion rates) derived from non-qualified investments.[109] Under part XI.1 of the Act, an RRSP is subject to a monthly penalty tax equal to 1 percent of the fair market value of its non-qualified investments at the time the RRSP acquired the investments, other than investments previously included in the income of the annuitant.[110]

Second, part X of the Act imposes a refundable penalty tax equal to 100 percent of the fair market value of a non-qualified investment acquired by a DPSP.[111] The penalty tax must be paid within 10 days of a DPSP's acquiring a non-qualified investment,[112] and the trustees of the DPSP are personally liable if the DPSP fails to remit the tax.[113] The penalty tax is refundable when the DPSP disposes of the non-qualified investment, although the refund is limited to the lesser of the amount of tax imposed when the non-qualified asset was acquired and the proceeds of disposition of the asset. Part X of the Act effectively limits the types of investments that a DPSP can make to "qualified investments" as that term is defined in section 204 (which is narrower than the definition of "qualified investments" for an RRSP).[114]

Third, part XI of the Act imposes a monthly penalty tax on RPPs, DPSPs, and RRSPs (as well as RRIFs and certain tax-exempt corporations used by RPPs to make investments, as described in paragraphs 149(1)(o.1) and (o.2)) equal to 1 percent of the fund's excess foreign property. Foreign investment limitations applicable to RPPs have been in the Act since 1960. In its original form, the limitation required pension plan trustees qualifying for tax-exempt status to derive at least 90 percent of their investment income from Canadian sources. The 1971 tax reform, which extended the limitation to other tax-favoured retirement savings vehicles, redefined the foreign property limit as 10 percent of the plan's aggregate assets (based on cost). Since the 1971 tax reform, part XI of the Act has imposed a monthly penalty tax equal to 1 percent of the excess foreign investments of many deferred income plans and trusts, including those listed above. The foreign property limit was increased to 20 percent in 1990 (in 2 percent increments between 1990 and 1994) and to 30 percent in 2000 (in 5 percent increments in 2000 and 2001).

Pension Legislation

Between 1965 and 1983, the federal government and seven provinces introduced legislation regulating pension plans. Ontario was the first province to introduce legislation, effective January 1, 1965.[115] Federal legislation was introduced effective October 10, 1967.[116] All of the provinces have pension regulatory legislation.[117] The legislation applies to RPPs (as defined in the Income Tax Act) as well as to unregistered plans under the jurisdiction of the particular legislation, unless the plan is specifically excluded.[118] In most cases, the application of the legislation depends on whether there is a "plan," a term that is not defined in the legislation. Where applicable, pension regulatory legislation governs all aspects of the pension fund, including eligibility conditions, vesting and locking in of benefits, retirement ages, death/survivor benefits, and portability of benefits. In addition, and germane to this study, the legislation governs permitted investments of regulated plans. In contrast to ERISA, both the federal and Ontario pension statutes[119] exclude DPSPs from their application (although, as noted previously, the Income Tax Act limits the investments that DPSPs can make).

The federal and most provincial pension statutes generally restrict an individual's ability to access funds in a regulated pension plan before the individual attains normal retirement age[120] or at the time of early retirement as permitted by legislation.[121] Once an individual's benefits under the pension plan vest,[122] the employee is entitled to a deferred pension in the event that employment is terminated before normal retirement age.[123] This deferred pension cannot be withdrawn from the plan except as permitted by legislation.[124] Cash withdrawals are allowed only in limited circumstances,[125] and are included in the recipient's income for tax purposes.[126]

The federal and Ontario pension statutes provide three transfer options for a commuted pension (that is, the deferred pension generated by vested pension benefits):[127] (1) it may be transferred to another pension plan if the administrator of the recipient plan agrees; (2) it may be transferred to a prescribed retirement savings vehicle, on a locked-in basis; or (3) it may be used to purchase a life annuity from an insurance company to provide a periodic amount of retirement income (that is, annuity payments cannot commence until the retirement date under the plan). Each jurisdiction prescribes a number of types of retirement savings vehicles for the second option.[128] Common to all of these vehicles is that the funds are locked in so that, except in limited circumstances,[129] the owner cannot withdraw funds, even on a taxable basis, except to provide retirement income. To facilitate these transfers, the Income Tax Act provides rollovers for transfers between RPPs, for transfers from an RPP to an RRSP or RRIF, and for the acquisition of an annuity from the commuted rights under an RPP. In all cases, certain conditions must be met.[130]

Venture Capital Investment Using Individual and Employer-Sponsored Retirement Funds

This section considers the effect of retirement funds on the informal and formal venture capital industries. The use of retirement funds to make informal venture capital investments requires a consideration of three situations:

- the extent to which individual retirement funds can invest in SMEs (that is, the extent to which individual retirement funds can make angel or love capital investments);
- the ability of an individual to withdraw funds or borrow money from an individual retirement fund in order to make venture capital investments, and the ability of an individual to use the assets of an individual retirement

fund as security for a loan (the proceeds of which are used to make venture capital investments); and
- the ability of an individual to withdraw funds from an employer-sponsored pension fund (for example, on termination of employment) in order to undertake an entrepreneurial endeavour—which may affect an employee's decision to leave employment to start up a business.

These limitations may also have an impact on an individual's decision whether to participate in a tax-assisted retirement savings plan. In any case, they can limit sources of love capital. The first two situations are governed exclusively by tax legislation in Canada and the United States, since individual retirement funds are creatures of tax legislation and are not subject to pension legislation.[131] The third situation may be affected by both pension legislation and tax legislation. As indicated in the previous section, ERISA allows an employee to withdraw vested pension benefits if employment is terminated; however, as discussed further below, early withdrawals not only are included in the recipient's income for tax purposes but also may be subject to an additional 10 percent excise tax under the Code. In contrast, Canada's pension legislation generally does not permit early withdrawal of vested pension benefits in the event of termination of employment.

The use of retirement funds to make formal venture investments—investments in venture capital funds (VCFs)—requires a consideration of two situations:

- the extent to which individual retirement funds can invest in VCFs; and
- the extent to which employer-sponsored funds can invest in VCFs.

Since 1995, RRSPs have become the most significant vehicle for retirement savings for Canadians in terms of annual contributions.[132] The money that has been invested in RRSPs has grown significantly, particularly since the legislative reforms in 1992.[133] Coincidently (or perhaps not), the ability of an RRSP to invest in LSVCCs and afford the annuitant of the plan (as opposed to the plan itself) a federal and provincial tax credit has made LSVCCs the largest source of formal venture capital in Canada. In contrast, it was amendments to pension legislation in the late 1970s that revitalized the venture capital industry in the United States and led to its significant expansion through the 1990s. Although attempts were made to amend both pension legislation and tax legislation in Canada in the mid-1980s to promote venture capital investment by employer-sponsored pension plans, these efforts proved to be short-lived. In my view, the long-term health of the Canadian venture capital industry hinges on the ability to attract broad-based pension plan investment to Canadian VCFs and wean the industry from its costly and problematic dependence on LSVCCs.

Following a discussion of the five bulleted elements noted above, the rules affecting informal and formal venture capital investment using retirement funds are evaluated.

Informal Venture Capital Investment
by Individual Retirement Funds

United States

Despite the general lack of restrictions on IRAs in terms of qualified investments, as a practical matter the small size of most IRAs as well as limitations
imposed by the financial institutions or insurance companies offering IRAs
militate against certain types of investments, including private equity investments. Most IRA assets are invested in certificates of deposit or in passbook
savings accounts of commercial banks, mutual savings banks, and savings and
loan associations. A significant amount is invested in mutual fund shares, including those of growth stock funds, income stock funds, balanced funds, and
money market funds. Some individuals establish custodial accounts and direct
the investment of their own accounts within the usual range of marketable
securities. However, even in such circumstances, it is unlikely that IRAs can or
will make any private equity investments.

Keogh plans are not, as a practical matter, subject to the same restrictions
as IRAs. Since 1996, more money has been invested in Keogh plans than in
IRAs, and the investment per Keogh plan is significantly larger than the investment per IRA.[134] Even so, the average annual contribution to IRAs is less than
$10,000. Although IRAs are limited in their investments only by the prohibited
transaction rules in the Code, it is unlikely that Keogh plans make significant
venture capital investments.

Canada

In contrast to the United States, Canada imposes significant restrictions on
investments by RRSPs that, in turn, affect the ability of plans to make informal
venture capital investments. Essentially, the same investment restrictions imposed on RRSPs are imposed on RRIFs. Accordingly, the discussion in this
section is limited to RRSPs.[135]

RRSPs can invest only in "qualified investments," as defined in subsection
146(1) of the Income Tax Act. Before 1985, RRSPs could not invest in shares of
any small businesses because they were not qualified investments. Although
RRSPs could invest in corporate equity, the shares had to be listed on a prescribed stock exchange in order to be a qualified investment. The limitation was
likely intended to ensure the liquidity of the investments; it may also have
stemmed from a paternalistic concern that unlisted securities were substantially
more risky than listed securities. As a result of the significant increase in assets
accumulated by RRSPs and the perceived lack of equity available to small
businesses, it is not surprising that the federal government was lobbied to relax
the RRSP rules to permit investment in small businesses. In its 1985 budget, the
government introduced rules permitting small business investments, although
with significant restrictions, primarily to ensure that RRSPs could invest only in
arm's-length corporations. Obviously, there were concerns with an RRSP investing

in a corporation related to the plan's beneficiary. These policy concerns are addressed below.

The 1985 budget introduced provisions that expanded the investments permitted by RRSPs, including certain direct and indirect investments in small businesses. As a further incentive for small business investment, an RRSP could increase its foreign property investments by $3 for every $1 invested in small business properties.[136] Regulation 4900(6)(a), added as a result of the 1985 amendments, prescribes as a qualified investment for RRSP purposes shares of an "eligible corporation," provided that the annuitant under the RRSP is not a designated shareholder of the corporation[137] and provided that, immediately after the acquisition of the shares, the total assets of the eligible corporation do not exceed $50 million and the aggregate cost to the taxpayer of all securities (equity, debt, and options) of the eligible corporation and associated corporations does not exceed $10 million. An eligible corporation is defined in regulation 5100(1) and includes a taxable Canadian corporation that is not controlled by non-residents and all or substantially all of the property of which is used in a qualifying active business.[138] Corporations involved in certain businesses, including securities dealers and various financial services businesses, are specifically excluded.[139] The 1985 amendments also expanded an RRSP's ability to make formal venture capital investments through VCFs that met certain stringent conditions. These investments are discussed in more detail below.

A fundamental problem with the eligible corporation provisions is that both eligible corporation status and non-designated shareholder status has to be maintained at all times that the RRSP owns the shares. Accordingly, even if a corporation qualifies when the RRSP makes its investment, the corporation could become ineligible if, at any subsequent time, its non-active business assets exceed 10 percent of the value of the corporation's property (that is, if "all or substantially all" of the assets of the eligible corporation are no longer used in a qualifying active business). In addition, once the corporation becomes ineligible, it cannot regain eligible status even if it meets all of the requisite conditions. If the shares became a non-qualified investment, the RRSP may also be exposed to part XI tax because the shares no longer qualify for the three-to-one leveraging for foreign property purposes. The RRSP will also be exposed to a monthly tax under Part XI.1 of the Act for non-qualified investments and will be subject to tax on any income arising from those shares, including any gain realized on the disposition of the shares. Finally, given the restricted transferability of shares, the RRSP may not be able to reduce its part XI.1 tax exposure by selling the shares.

Primarily in response to these concerns, regulation 4900(12) was introduced in 1992. It prescribes as a qualified investment for RRSP purposes shares of "small business corporations,"[140] provided that the annuitant is not a "connected shareholder"[141] of the corporation immediately after the shares are acquired by the RRSP. The small business corporation test must be met either at the time the RRSP acquired the shares or at the end of the most recent taxation year of the corporation before that time. The corporation need not maintain that status throughout the period that the RRSP owns the shares. Unlike a corporation subject to the eligible corporation provisions, a small business corporation is not restricted in the types of businesses that it can carry on. However, shares of small business corporations are not considered "small business properties" for the purpose of the three-to-one leveraging of foreign property.

Although regulation 4900(12) alleviates some of the key concerns with the eligible corporation provisions, RRSPs are still prohibited from investing in corporations in which the plan's annuitant owns a substantial block of shares. More specifically, an annuitant under an RRSP cannot generally own 10 percent or more of the shares of any class of the corporation, although if the RRSP's investment in an eligible corporation or small business corporation is less than $25,000, the annuitant may own more than 10 percent of the shares but must still deal at arm's length with the corporation (that is, not control it or be related to a person who controls it). At its earliest stages, a corporation most often raises capital from its owner-managers and related individuals. Investment by such individuals will not qualify under either the eligible corporation provisions or the small business corporation provisions.

At the provincial level, RRSPs are targeted under all three provinces' angel capital tax credit programs (see appendix 5A) by extending the tax credit to an RRSP annuitant when his or her RRSP makes a qualified investment under the provincial scheme. The investment must qualify as an eligible investment for RRSP purposes in order to avoid tax under part XI.1 of the Act. Thus, the investee corporation must be an eligible corporation or small business corporation and the RRSP cannot be a designated shareholder or specified shareholder, as the case may be. In all three provinces, the restrictions on the relationship between an eligible investor and the eligible business are more liberal than those imposed under the income tax regulations; in order to avoid part XI.1 tax, the more stringent conditions imposed under the income tax regulations must be met. In addition to the provincial tax credit, the investment may qualify for the three-to-one leveraging for small business properties, but only if the eligible business under the provincial scheme is an eligible corporation as defined in the income tax regulations and maintains its status as such.

Accessing Individual Retirement Funds To Make Informal Venture Capital Investments

United States

IRAs

Although individuals may withdraw funds from their IRAs at any time, withdrawals are taxed in accordance with the annuity rules in section 72 of the Code.[142] In addition, withdrawals that are included in gross income are subject to the 10 percent excise tax in section 72(t), subject to certain modifications.[143] First, there is no exception for a withdrawal on separation from employment after the attainment of age 55 or for distributions to an alternate payee pursuant to a qualified domestic relations order.[144] Second, the exception for distributions pursuant to an annuity over the life of the individual (or joint lives of the individual and his or her spouse) is not contingent on a separation from employment.

There are three additional exceptions to the excise tax applicable to distributions from IRAs. Distributions to an unemployed individual to cover health insurance premiums are exempt in certain circumstances.[145] The other two exceptions were added by the Taxpayer Relief Act of 1997 and were intended to benefit first-time homebuyers and individuals seeking to upgrade their educational skills. First, section 72(t)(2)(F) of the Code excludes from the 10 percent excise tax distributions from an IRA for "qualified first-time homebuyer distributions" as defined in section 72(t)(8). The maximum amount that can be withdrawn under this exemption is $10,000. The amount must be used within 120 days of receipt to pay qualified acquisition costs (costs of acquisition, construction, or reconstruction) of a principal residence of a first-time homebuyer[146] who is the individual, the individual's spouse, or any child, grandchild, or ancestor of the individual or the individual's spouse. Second, section 72(t)(2)(E) excludes from the 10 percent excise tax distributions from an IRA to the extent that the distributions do not exceed "qualified higher education expenses," as defined in section 72(t)(7), of the plan holder for the year. Such expenses include tuition, fees, books, supplies and equipment, and, if certain conditions are met, room and board at a post-secondary educational institution.[147] The expense may relate to the education of the plan holder or his or her spouse, child, or grandchild. Unlike the exemption under Canada's lifelong learning plan, there is no limit on the amount that may be withdrawn (subject to the aggregate amount of qualified higher education expenses).

Similar provisions are available to annuitants under RRSPs in Canada. However, unlike their Canadian counterparts, the US qualified first-time homebuyer distribution and the qualified higher education expense distribution must be included in the income of the recipient. The only relief provided for such distributions is that they are not subject to the additional 10 percent excise tax.[148]

Any loan from an IRA or the use of IRA assets as security for a loan has significant adverse tax consequences. If an owner of an individual retirement annuity borrows money under or by use of the annuity, the contract ceases to be an individual retirement annuity as of the first day of the year and the owner must include in income the full fair market value of the contract as of the first day of the year.[149] Similarly, borrowing money from an individual retirement account is a prohibited transaction,[150] and the account ceases to qualify as an IRA as of the first day of the year in which the loan occurs and the full fair market value of the account is deemed to be distributed as of that day.[151] Finally, if the holder of an individual retirement account uses any portion of the assets of the account as security for a loan, the portion so used is treated as a distribution.[152] If the recipient of the deemed distribution from an individual retirement annuity or individual retirement account is under age 59½ and is not disabled at the time of the distribution, the additional 10 percent excise tax applies to the amount of the distribution included in income.

In summary, an individual cannot access funds held in an IRA for entrepreneurial purposes without significant tax consequences. Amounts withdrawn from an IRA must be included in the gross income of the recipient (in accordance with the rules in section 72) and in most cases are subject to an additional 10 percent excise tax. If a person borrows from an IRA, the full value of the IRA is treated as a distribution. If IRA assets are pledged as security for a loan, either the full value of the IRA is treated as a distribution (in the case of an individual retirement annuity) or the portion pledged as security (in the case of an individual retirement account) is treated as a distribution.

Keogh Plans

Keogh plans are not subject to ERISA (specifically, the prohibited transaction provisions in section 406) unless employees other than a self-employed business owner participate in the plan. However, Keogh plans are subject to the prohibited transaction provisions of the Code, which prohibit investments in businesses controlled by plan beneficiaries. Since a Keogh plan is regulated by the type of qualified plan whose form it takes, withdrawals from the plan are subject to the same restrictions.[153]

Although qualified plans (including Keogh plans) may make loans to plan beneficiaries if certain conditions are met, a Keogh plan cannot make a loan to a self-employed individual who is an owner-employee.[154] Furthermore, it is unlikely that a Keogh plan could, in practice, be used as security for a loan because, under federal law, a creditor cannot levy on the assets of a Keogh plan outside of bankruptcy and would therefore not likely accept a Keogh plan as security for a loan.[155]

Canada

Despite the relatively free access to funds in an RRSP, it is simplistic to suggest that there are no impediments to withdrawing funds from an RRSP to make a venture capital investment. Apart from the fact that all withdrawals from an RRSP are included in income, once funds are withdrawn they no longer benefit from tax deferral and the annuitant's RRSP contribution room is not increased as a result. In addition to the immediate imposition of tax on the amount withdrawn (thus limiting the amount available to make an investment), the taxpayer suffers a permanent loss of the deferral opportunity for the withdrawn funds. Given the relative importance of RRSPs to the retirement savings of Canadians compared with IRAs of Americans, this loss of deferral can have a significant impact on the funds available to the taxpayer at the time of retirement.

A simple example illustrates the impact on retirement savings. Consider a relatively young individual (Ms. A, 40 years old) who is contemplating a business venture. Over time, Ms. A has made contributions to her RRSP totalling $100,000 (all of which she has deducted in previous years) and the current value of her RRSP is $200,000. Ms. A wants to invest $100,000 in the new business venture and her RRSP is the only source of funds available. For simplicity, assume that Ms. A's effective tax rate is 50 percent and the rate of return on RRSP investments is 8 percent. To invest $100,000, Ms. A would have to withdraw the entire $200,000 from her RRSP, since the withdrawn amount would be subject to tax at the rate of 50 percent. Suppose that after five years the business venture is successful enough to allow Ms. A to return the entire $200,000 to her RRSP. Even with a contribution limit of $15,500 (and assuming that Ms. A's earned income is sufficient for her to make the maximum contribution each year), it would take Ms. A 9-10 years to build up $200,000 again in her RRSP.[156] Assuming that she contributed $15,500 for 10 years and thereafter made no further contributions, the value of her RRSP at age 65 would be $484,768.73.[157] If Ms. A never made the venture capital investment and simply left the $200,000 in her RRSP until age 65, it would be worth $1,369,695.04. By withdrawing the entire amount, then, her RRSP has been reduced to about 35 percent of what it otherwise would have been, even if she redeposited the entire amount withdrawn.

If Ms. A could borrow the funds from her RRSP without immediate tax consequences, she would need to borrow only $100,000 and may be able to repay it sooner than five years. However, she can only borrow funds from her RRSP if the loan is a qualified investment. The only circumstance in which a loan to an annuitant by an RRSP is a qualified investment is where the loan is secured by an insured mortgage that is administered by an approved lender under the National Housing Act.[158] If Ms. A does not own real property in Canada or does not have sufficient equity in real property to secure a loan of $100,000, she would have to withdraw the entire $200,000 in order to have $100,000 to invest. Thus, as a means of funding a venture investment, a loan from an RRSP is a rather limited option. Furthermore, if a taxpayer uses RRSP assets as security for a loan, the fair market value of the property so used is included in the taxpayer's income.[159] Unlike an individual's benefits under a pension plan, an individual's interest in an RRSP (unless it is a locked-in RRSP arising from the transfer of pension benefits to the RRSP) is generally subject to the claims of creditors in the event of the individual's bankruptcy.[160]

If the Canadian government believes that there is a deficiency in the amount of love capital available for venture investment, it could expand an individual's ability to access RRSP capital without triggering immediate tax consequences. It is certainly not unknown for the government to allow tax-free access to RRSP funds to promote particular initiatives. The homebuyers' plan in section 146.01 and the lifelong learning plan in section 146.02 are examples of extended uses of RRSP funds to achieve certain objectives. In both cases, there are maximum amounts that may be withdrawn in any year and in the aggregate and there are stipulated repayment periods. Failure to repay the amounts as required results in an income inclusion to the individual.

The homebuyers' plan was originally introduced in the 1992 budget primarily to "stimulate home construction and job creation,"[161] not exactly objectives ordinarily associated with retirement savings.[162] It was originally intended as a temporary measure, applicable to withdrawals from an RRSP between February 25, 1992 (the budget date) and March 1, 1993. As enacted, the plan allowed an annuitant to borrow from his or her RRSP up to $20,000 on an interest-free basis to finance the purchase of a home (not restricted to the first home). The loan was repayable in equal annual instalments over 15 years from 1994 to 2008. Any shortfall in an annual payment was treated as a taxable withdrawal from the RRSP and included in the taxpayer's income in the year the shortfall occurred. The plan was extended by the December 2, 1992 economic statement to March 1, 1994[163] and then continued indefinitely in the 1994 budget, although restricted to first-time homebuyers.[164]

The lifelong learning plan was introduced in the 1998 budget:

> Lifelong learning is a key factor in preserving future employment income. However, individuals may have limited access to financial resources when the need for training occurs. For many people, the most readily available source of funds is their registered retirement savings plans (RRSPs). Although saving for retirement is important, keeping or finding a job is crucial to preserving retirement income.
>
> The budget therefore proposes to allow RRSP withdrawals for skills enhancement. Eligible individuals will be able to make tax-free withdrawals from an RRSP (other than a locked-in RRSP) to finance full-time training or education for themselves or their spouses.[165]

The maximum amount that an individual can "withdraw" is $10,000 in any year and $20,000 in the aggregate over a period of up to four calendar years. Permitted withdrawals are treated as an interest-free loan that must be repaid in equal instalments over a 10-year period, beginning no later than 60 days following the fifth year after the year in which the individual first received the funds. The repayment period begins earlier if the designated student (the individual or the individual's spouse or common law partner) is not entitled to annual full-time education tax credits for at least three months in two consecutive years that end before the fifth year. For example, if an individual withdraws $10,000 under the plan and is a full-time student for at least four years, the minimum annual repayment is $1,000 per year ($10,000 divided by 10 years), for 10 years commencing in the fifth year after the year in which the funds are withdrawn. There are no restrictions on the number of times that an individual can participate in the plan, although an individual cannot participate in a new plan before the end of the year in which all repayments from any previous participation have been made.[166]

It is implicit in the stated objectives of the lifelong learning plan that the individual will generally require retraining after a loss of employment.[167] Given this retraining objective, it is surprising that withdrawals were not permitted from locked-in RRSPs.[168] Furthermore, there are no limitations on the nature of the educational program that the individual undertakes using funds obtained under the plan. Obviously, there are no guarantees that the individual's education financed in part through the plan will lead to gainful employment. If the individual fails to repay the portion of the loan due in a particular year, the individual is subject to an income inclusion equal to the amount of the shortfall. In effect, the individual is taxed as if he or she withdrew the shortfall from the RRSP in that year.

The lifelong learning plan allows an individual to access RRSP funds as an interest-free loan in order to invest in human capital. As the 1998 budget documents suggest, human capital is intrinsically tied to the achievement of retirement security through employment. In the evaluation of the rules that affect the use of retirement savings to make informal venture investments, below, consideration is given to whether either the permitted investments of RRSPs or the use of interest-free loans from RRSPs should be expanded to include love capital investments, which may also be important for achieving financial security at the time of retirement.

Accessing Employer-Sponsored Retirement Funds To Make Informal Venture Capital Investments

United States

An individual's ability to access assets held in a qualified pension plan before retirement is, in theory, greater in the United States than in Canada. In the United States, unlike in Canada, termination of employment is a permitted occasion for distribution from a pension plan of vested benefits.[169] Qualified pension plans must generally limit distributions to the following events: death, retirement, separation from service, or disability.[170] A pension plan that permits distributions at other times may lose qualified status.

A 401(k) plan may also permit the distribution of employee contributions (that is, employer contributions made pursuant to the employee's election to contribute the amount rather than receive it as compensation, but not the amount of any matching employer contributions) in the event of "hardship."[171] A distribution on account of hardship is defined narrowly in the regulations to be a distribution that is made "on account of an immediate and heavy financial need of the employee and is necessary to satisfy the financial need."[172]

When permitted, distribution from a qualified pension plan must be included in the recipient's gross income and may also be subject to an additional 10 percent excise tax.[173] The excise tax does not apply if the distribution is made:[174]

1) on or after the date on which the employee attains age 59½;
2) on account of the death or disability of the employee;
3) in a series of substantially equal periodic payments over the life (or life expectancy) of the employee or the joint lives (or joint life expectancies) of the employee and his or her designated beneficiary, provided that the payments commence after separation from employment;[175]
4) after separation from service after the employee attains age 55; or
5) in an amount not exceeding the employee's deductible medical expenses or pursuant to a qualified domestic relations order.

Thus, in general, an individual who receives a lump-sum payment of vested pension rights on the termination of employment (prior to normal retirement age) must include the amount in income *and* pay an additional 10 percent excise tax if the individual is younger than 55.[176]

Although distributions from a pension plan have significant tax consequences, it is possible for employees to borrow money from their pension plans in certain circumstances. As a general rule, a loan from a qualified pension plan to an employee is a prohibited transaction under ERISA and, depending on the level of the employee (that is, whether highly compensated or not), may be a prohibited transaction under the Code.[177] In addition to the excise taxes associated with prohibited transactions under the Code,[178] a loan from a qualified plan (including the pledge of assets of a qualified plan by a plan participant as security for a loan) is considered a distribution from the plan (regardless of the level of the employee).[179] However, both ERISA and the Code exclude loans to participants or beneficiaries from the prohibited transaction provisions if the loan

1) is available to all participants or beneficiaries on a reasonably equivalent basis;
2) is not made available to highly compensated employees (as defined in section 414(q) of the Code) in an amount greater than the amount made available to other employees;
3) is made in accordance with specific loan provisions in the plan;
4) bears a reasonable rate of interest; and
5) is adequately secured.[180]

A permitted loan must meet additional conditions in order to avoid being characterized as a distribution for tax purposes. The loan must not exceed the lesser of: $50,000, reduced by the excess (if any) of the highest outstanding balance of loans from the plan during the one-year period prior to the day the loan was made over the outstanding balance of plan loans on the day the loan was made; and the greater of one-half of the present value of the employee's non-forfeitable plan benefits and $10,000.[181] In addition, the loan must be repaid within five years (unless the loan is a housing loan, in which case a reasonable time for repayment is permitted) and must require substantially level amortization payments payable at least quarterly.[182]

Thus, a beneficiary under a qualified pension plan such as 401(a) plan may borrow up to $50,000 from the plan (assuming that the plan permits such loans), provided that various conditions are met. However, the utility of such a loan for venture investing may be limited by the repayment requirements.

Canada

Federal and most provincial pension statutes generally restrict an individual's ability to access funds in a regulated pension plan before the individual attains normal retirement age or at the time of early retirement as permitted by legislation.

Once an individual's benefits under the pension plan vest, the employee is entitled to a commuted pension in the event that employment is terminated before normal retirement age, and can only transfer the commuted pension to certain other retirement plans on a locked-in basis.

In addition to these limitations on access to funds in pension plans, federal and provincial pension benefits statutes as well as the Income Tax Act[183] prohibit a plan member from using pension benefits, including commuted benefits transferred to a prescribed retirement savings vehicle, to secure a loan. Both the federal and the Ontario pension benefits statutes provide that any agreement pursuant to which a pension benefit is provided as security is void.[184]

Finally, pension legislation does not generally permit a pension plan to loan money to a plan member. Under the investment rules of the federal legislation, which since January 1, 2001, also apply to Ontario and have also been adopted by a number of other provinces, loans to a related party, which includes a member of the plan, are prohibited.[185]

Profit-sharing plans, including DPSPs, are not governed by either federal or most provincial pension benefits legislation. Under the Income Tax Act, there is no requirement that a DPSP retain a member's share until the member reaches retirement age. Subsection 147(2) sets out the conditions that a plan must fulfill in order to be registered as a DPSP. To be registered, the DPSP must stipulate that the plan will not provide loans to employees or other beneficiaries under the plan.[186] An employee's benefits under the plan vest (in the case of amounts allocated to the beneficiary after 1990) not later than the later of the time of allocation and the day on which the beneficiary completes 24 consecutive months as a beneficiary under the plan.[187] Paragraph 147(2)(k) provides that all amounts vested become payable to the beneficiary not later than the earlier of the end of the year in which the beneficiary attains age 69 and 90 days after the earliest of the time of the termination of the beneficiary's employment by the employer, the death of the beneficiary, and the termination of the plan. Obviously, the plan can provide for earlier payments. Any amount paid to the beneficiary from a DPSP must be included in the beneficiary's income.[188]

Individual Retirement Fund Investment in VCFs

United States

An IRA is generally prohibited from making any form of venture capital investment, whether formal or informal, by the financial institution or insurance company that offers the IRA. Unless a VCF is publicly traded, which is rarely the case, it is highly unlikely that a VCF will be available as an investment, even to a self-directed IRA.

Canada

The situation is vastly different in Canada. Specific tax incentives have been and continue to be offered at both the federal and the provincial levels to attract

RRSP investment in particular types of VCFs. Amendments were introduced in the Income Tax Act in the 1985 budget, primarily to promote investment by pension funds in venture capital. However, it was the introduction of a matching federal tax credit for investment in LSVCCs that proved to be the most significant amendment in the 1985 budget. In its original form, the tax credit was available to individuals who directly invested in LSVCCs. After acquiring LSVCC shares, individuals could contribute the shares to their RRSPs as a contribution in kind. However, this was a cumbersome way of getting the benefit of both the LSVCC tax credit and the RRSP deduction and probably was not done much in practice. It was the increase in the amount of the tax credit and the extension of the tax credit to individuals who invested in LSVCCs through their RRSPs under the 1992 budget that rocketed LSVCCs to the top of the venture capital pool in Canada. Annual investment in LSVCCs increased from about $70 million in the 1990 taxation year to over $1 billion in 1996. In 1992, investment in LSVCCs doubled from 1991 levels, and in 1993 through 1995 the amount invested almost doubled year over year. LSVCCs became and continue to be the largest source of formal venture capital in Canada solely because of the federal and provincial tax credits that are provided to individual investors. In addition to the tax credits available to annuitants of RRSPs that invest in LSVCCs, an RRSP that invests in an LSVCC benefits from the three-to-one leveraging for small business properties.[189]

Besides LSVCCs, other venture capital investment vehicles introduced in the 1985 budget are qualified investments for RRSPs. These vehicles, including small business investment limited partnerships and small business investment trusts, target primarily RPPs and are discussed in that context below.

At the provincial level, three of the four provincial VCF programs (Ontario being the exception) have targeted RRSPs by extending the tax credit to the individual annuitant where his or her RRSP makes a qualified investment. These investments are encouraged at the federal level in that they also qualify for the three-to-one leveraging for small business properties.[190] These RRSP investments are more precarious than investments in LSVCCs, which provide shareholders with the right to redeem the shares after the requisite holding period.

Employer-Sponsored Retirement Fund Investment in VCFs

Both Canada and the United States share some common history in the evolution of employer-sponsored pension funds as venture capital investors. In both countries, pension legislation significantly restricted, or was perceived to significantly restrict, the ability of pension funds to make venture capital investments until specific amendments were made to promote such investments, in the United States in 1979 and in Canada in 1985. This six-year gap has had a profound effect on how the private venture capital fund industries have evolved in the two countries. It has been suggested that Canada's private venture capital industry now lags the US industry by a decade. In my view, this lag will continue until Canada successfully attracts more broad-based pension fund investment and loses its dependence on LSVCCs. What remains to be seen is whether recent initiatives—particularly changes to the Canada Pension Plan's investment regulations (considered in the last section of this chapter)—will accelerate the evolution of the Canadian venture capital industry while the US industry is still suffering from the meltdown following the dotcom craze at the end of the 20th century.

In the United States, tax legislation has not been a significant impediment to venture capital investment by pension funds. Its one potential area of impact is the imposition of an unrelated business income tax. In Canada, pension fund investment has been impeded not only by pension legislation but also by tax legislation. Although pension legislation has been amended to remove these impediments, a number of pension fund managers remain of the view that their fiduciary obligations prevent them from investing in venture capital. The Canadian discussion reviews the historic development of investment restrictions imposed under Canada's pension legislation. More important, though, are tax provisions that not only hinder Canadian pension funds from investing in venture capital but also impede investment in Canadian VCFs by foreign pension funds.

United States

The Impact of Pension Legislation on Venture Capital Investment

Pension legislation was the main impediment to venture investment by pension funds in the United States, and is considered before the Code provisions on unrelated business income tax. ERISA is the primary pension fund legislation in the United States. However, it does not apply to government pension funds, including state public sector pension funds. Before the impact of ERISA is addressed, state public sector pension plans are briefly considered.

Public Sector Pension Funds

Certain states have relied on public sector pension fund investment when formulating policies to increase venture capital investment in the state.[191] Three examples of state initiatives to promote such investment are provided here for illustrative purposes.

Michigan formed the Michigan Venture Capital Fund (MVCF) in 1982 to combat high unemployment rates in the state following significant layoffs in the steel and automotive industries. MVCF was authorized to invest up to 5 percent of the assets of the state pension fund (the 14th largest public pension fund in the country) in venture capital, either directly in small businesses or as an investor in private venture capital funds. The legislation instantly created a potential venture capital pool of nearly $800 million, making it one of the largest venture capital investors at the time.[192] Michigan has since altered its pension fund venture capital program. The program is currently administered by the Alternative Assets Division of the Michigan State Treasury and has significant investments in leveraged buyout funds and special-situation investments (as well as in venture capital).[193] According to Thomson Venture Economics statistics, as of September 30, 2000, the Michigan pension fund's private equity holdings (which include mezzanine and buyout funds) included investments in venture capital funds valued at $1,314 million and 8,189 direct investments in SMEs (including venture capital, mezzanine, and buyout financing) at a total cost of $507 million,[194] making it one of the top five US government pension fund venture capital investors at the time.

Other states have similarly authorized the use of public sector pension fund assets to enhance venture capital investment within the state. For example, Massachusetts established the Pension Reserves Investment Trust Fund (PRIT) in 1984[195] as a pooled investment fund to invest the assets of the Massachusetts State Teachers' and Employees' Retirement Systems and various other funds that choose to invest in the fund. The Pension Reserves Investment Management Board (PRIM) manages and provides general supervision of PRIT.[196] PRIM also acts as trustee for each retirement system investing in PRIT. One of PRIM's investment objectives is to allocate 10 percent of the fund's assets in alternative investments, including venture capital and buyout funds.[197] In mid-2002, PRIM managed assets of about $29 billion, down from a high of $32 billion in mid-2000.[198]

Maryland established the Maryland Venture Capital Trust Fund in 1990 to permit Maryland state and local public pension funds and the state of Maryland and its political subdivisions to invest a portion of their funds in venture capital investments.[199] Under the original proposal, public sector pension plans were encouraged to invest up to one-half of 1 percent of their assets, which would result in a fund size of $15 to $20 million. The trust was originally administered by the Maryland Department of Business and Economic Development; it is now administered by the Maryland pension system. By 2002, the trust had raised $19.1 million.[200]

ERISA

Prior to the enactment of ERISA, fiduciary standards applicable to trustees of pension plans were governed by trust law and the Internal Revenue Code. To be afforded favourable tax treatment under the Code, a trust created under an employer's stock bonus, pension, or profit-sharing plan had to be for the exclusive benefit of employees or their beneficiaries and it must have been impossible to divert corpus or income away from this purpose before all liabilities to employees and their beneficiaries had been met. Prior to the enactment of ERISA, the IRS developed guidelines for the investment of qualified plan assets based on its view of the factors a prudent man devoting himself exclusively to the benefit of plan participants and their beneficiaries should consider (that is, the standards imposed on the fiduciaries of a trust).

In enacting ERISA, Congress adopted these guidelines as the core of the new fiduciary standards applicable to all employee benefit plans. Section 404(a)(1) of ERISA provides:

a fiduciary shall discharge his duties with respect to a plan solely in the interests of the participants and their beneficiaries and—

    (A) for the exclusive purpose of:

        (i) providing benefits to participants and their beneficiaries; and

        (ii) defraying reasonable expenses of administering the plan;

    (B) with the care, skill, prudence, and diligence under the circumstances then prevailing that a prudent man acting in a like capacity and familiar with such matters would use in the conduct of an enterprise of a like character and with like aims;

    (C) by diversifying the investments of the plan so as to minimize the risk of large losses, unless under the circumstances it is clearly prudent not to do so; and

    (D) in accordance with the documents and instruments governing the plan insofar as such documents and instruments are consistent with the provisions of this subchapter and subchapter III of this chapter.[201]

One of the purposes of the statutory standard was to ensure that the overall investment performance of the plan portfolio, rather than individual portfolio holdings, is considered.

The fiduciary standards imposed under section 404(a) of ERISA are reduced in pension plans that provide individual accounts and allow participants to exercise control over the investment of their pension assets.[202] Thus, lower standards apply to defined contribution pension plans that give participants control over investment decisions. Even in these circumstances, fiduciary duties require that the fund provide an appropriate range of investment alternatives and appropriate information about those alternatives.[203] In addition, a fiduciary will be liable if it acquiesces in making an investment that is a prohibited transaction, such as a loan to the plan sponsor, the acquisition or sale of employer real property, or the acquisition or sale of employer securities, except certain publicly traded securities.[204] Defined contribution pension plans in which participants exercise control over investment decisions are unlikely to make venture capital investments because the range of investment alternatives available to plan participants is unlikely to include private equity.[205] The remaining discussion in this section is limited to pension plans in which investment decisions are controlled by plan fiduciaries.

Despite the flexibility in portfolio management intended by the standards established in ERISA, the uncertain interpretation of these standards originally discouraged pensions from making high-risk investments, such as in venture capital. This concern was alleviated to some extent by the promulgation of a final regulation by the Department of Labor in June 1979 expounding on the "prudent man" rule in section 404.[206] According to the department's discussion of the regulation,

[t]he Department is of the opinion that (1) generally, the relative riskiness of a specific investment or investment course of action does not render such investment or investment course of action either *per se* prudent or *per se* imprudent, and (2) the prudence of an investment decision should not be

judged without regard to the role that the proposed investment or investment course of action plays within the overall plan portfolio. Thus, although securities issued by a small or new company may be riskier than securities offered by a "blue chip" company, the investment in the former may be entirely proper under the Act's "prudence" rule.[207]

The regulation is couched in general terms that support modern portfolio theory, including diversification based on risk/return analysis. In particular, the regulation provides that the "appropriate consideration" to be applied by the plan's fiduciaries in choosing an investment or an investment course of action "shall include, but is not necessarily limited to,"

> (i) A determination by the fiduciary that the particular investment or investment course of action is reasonably designed, as part of the portfolio (or, where applicable, that portion of the plan portfolio with respect to which the fiduciary has investment duties), to further the purposes of the plan, taking into consideration the risk of loss and the opportunity for gain (or other return) associated with the investment or investment course of action, and
> (ii) Consideration of the following factors as they relate to such portion of the portfolio:
>> (A) The composition of the portfolio with regard to diversification;
>> (B) The liquidity and current return of the portfolio relative to the anticipated cash flow requirements of the plan; and
>> (C) The projected return of the portfolio relative to the funding objectives of the plan.[208]

A "fiduciary" of a plan is defined in section 3(21)(A) of ERISA as any person who exercises any discretionary authority or control over the management of the plan or its assets.[209] Exactly who owes fiduciary duties to the plan and the scope of the duties owed are tied in part to the identification of "plan assets," a term that is not defined in ERISA. The question arises particularly in the context of investment by the plan in managed investment funds such as VCFs. If the interest in the other fund is the plan asset, then the fiduciary responsibilities do not extend to the managers of the other fund. If, however, the assets of the other fund are considered plan assets (that is, if a lookthrough approach is adopted), then the managers of that other fund are considered fiduciaries of the pension plan for the purposes of ERISA. ERISA specifically provides that the underlying assets of a mutual fund or other investment company registered with the Securities and Exchange Commission (SEC) under the Investment Company Act of 1940 are not considered plan assets.[210]

The regulations under ERISA extend this relief to investments in certain other entities. In August 1979, the Department of Labor published a proposed regulation describing property interests that would be regarded as plan assets under ERISA.[211] The proposed regulation provided that any property in which a plan had a beneficial ownership interest was a plan asset. In addition, the assets of any entity in which the plan had an equity investment would also be plan assets, unless

- the entity was an operating company (a company primarily in the business of providing goods or services, but not the investment of capital); or
- the securities were widely held (according to the Department of Labor, at least 100 security holders), freely transferable (no restrictions on transfer), and either registered under section 12 of the Securities Exchange Act of 1934 or registered under the Securities Act of 1933 when sold to the pension plan and were thereafter registered under section 12 of the Securities Exchange Act of 1934.

These proposals were criticized by a number of interest groups, including venture capitalists, because they would adversely affect the amount of capital available to small businesses. A privately managed VCF would not meet these requirements and would not be a plan asset. Because the lookthrough rules would therefore apply, a pension plan would not likely invest in VCFs for a number of reasons. First, the plan's fiduciaries would not be willing to assume the risk of personal liability for investment decisions of the manager of the VCF. Second, the manager of the VCF would not likely accept a pension plan as an investor because the manager would not want to be considered a fiduciary of the pension plan. Third (related to the second), the compensation scheme for the manager (which generally involves some form of carried interest in the portfolio investments of the VCF) could be considered "self-dealing" by a fiduciary and therefore a prohibited transaction under ERISA.

In response to written representations and public hearings, the department published a revised draft regulation in June 1980.[212] Among the criticisms of the original proposal that the revised draft sought to address was a concern that the regulation would discourage pension funds from investing in certain small business investment vehicles, commonly referred to as "venture capital companies" (VCCs).[213] VCCs posed a problem for the Department of Labor because an investment in a VCC "appears to possess characteristics of a delegation of investment management authority."[214] However, the Department of Labor considered VCCs unique in that they generally take an active role in the management of their portfolio companies. In the June 1980 proposals, the Department of Labor decided that if certain conditions were met, an investment in a VCC by a pension plan would not result in, or be deemed to be, a delegation of investment management authority. These conditions included:[215]

- the VCC is primarily engaged in the business of investing capital in enterprises "as to which it has or obtains the right to substantially participate or influence the conduct of the management of such enterprise";
- the securities of the VCC are issued to the pension plan in a non-public offering in compliance with section 4(2) of the Securities Act of 1933 and rule 146 of the SEC adopted thereunder;

- the VCC receives or has committed to it an aggregate of at least $5 million of investment capital from at least 10 non-affiliated persons; and
- various conditions with respect to the management of the VCC, including information disclosure, prohibitions on certain types of transactions by the managers of the VCC, and a requirement that the "persons responsible for investment decisions of the issuer [the VCC] will cause the issuer to conduct its activities with the care, skill, prudence and diligence under the circumstances then prevailing that a prudent manager of such an issuer would cause such issuer to use in the conduct of an enterprise of like character and with like aims."

If adopted, the proposed regulation would apply to investments of a pension plan acquired 30 days after the regulation was promulated.

The 1980 proposals prompted further submissions, some of which were addressed relatively quickly. For example, a final regulation dealing with the relatively narrow asset class of governmental mortgage pools was published in May 1982.[216] When these final regulations were released, the department indicated that it "intends to address the other issues that have been raised with respect to the proposed plan assets regulation in the near future." However, it was not until November 1986 that a comprehensive final regulation dealing with plan assets was promulgated.[217]

Under the final regulation, all publicly offered securities that are freely transferable, widely held, and registered under federal securities laws are considered plan assets and not subject to lookthrough treatment.[218] Beyond publicly offered securities, the department maintained the position that an investment in an entity includes an undivided interest in the underlying assets of the entity unless the entity is an operating company or the equity participation in the entity by pension or benefit plan investors is not significant.[219] However, in keeping with the June 1980 proposed regulation, the final regulation defined an operating company to include a "venture capital operating company" (VCOC), thus removing such entities from lookthrough treatment. Under the final regulation, a VCOC must

1) have at least 50 percent of its assets (other than short-term investments pending long-term commitment or distribution to investors), valued at cost, invested in operating companies in which the VCOC has bargained for direct contractual rights to "substantially participate in, or substantially influence the conduct of, the management of" the operating companies; and
2) in the ordinary course of its business, actually exercise those management rights with respect to one or more of the operating companies in which it invests.[220]

One key distinction between the 1980 proposed regulation and the 1986 final regulation is that the final regulation requires that the VCOC "actually exercise" its management rights with respect to one or more of the operating companies in which it invests.[221]

An entity cannot qualify as a VCOC before the date on which it makes its first venture capital investment. Accordingly, pension plans will not fund capital commitments to an entity intending to qualify as a VCOC until the date the entity makes its first venture investment.[222] The entity must meet the VCOC requirements at least annually.

These two Department of Labor regulations—the 1979 "prudent man" regulation and the 1980 proposed plan asset regulation (as adopted in the final regulation in 1986)—had profound effects on venture capital investment by pension funds in the United States. Since 1979, pension funds have been the largest source of venture capital in the formal venture capital industry in every year except 1981; since 1984 they have contributed at least 38 percent of all capital raised, and in some years have contributed as much as 60 percent. In contrast, Canadian pension funds have, with few exceptions, avoided venture capital investment completely in the past decade.

Impact of Tax Legislation on Pension Fund Venture Capital Investment

The US Code has had only limited impact on formal venture capital investment by pension funds. As noted previously, apart from the prohibited transactions rule in section 4975 of the Code, there are virtually no constraints on the types of investments that a pension fund can make. The one possible constraint is the imposition of the unrelated business income tax (UBIT).

UBIT was added to the Code in 1950 (although it was not extended to 401(a) pension funds until 1969) and was intended to remove a perceived unfair advantage (the exemption from tax) available to tax-exempt entities that operated businesses in competition with taxpaying businesses. The UBIT provisions may be sufficiently broad to include certain venture capital investments by tax-exempt entities such as pension plans, university endowment plans, and charities. In particular, portfolio investments structured as partnerships or other passthrough entities may pose problems for pension fund (and other non-taxable) investors. UBIT is imposed on a tax-exempt entity's unrelated business taxable income (UBTI).[223] UBTI is defined generally as the gross income derived from any "unrelated trade or business" less certain allowable deductions. An unrelated trade or business is defined in section 513(a) of the Code as a trade or business that is not substantially related to the performance by the entity of its exempt function. For qualified pension plans under section 401(a) of the Code, "any trade or business regularly carried on by such trust or by a partnership of which it is a member" is an unrelated trade or business.[224] If a partnership regularly carries on a trade or business that would be an unrelated trade or business if carried on directly by a partner that is a tax-exempt entity, the tax-exempt entity must include in UBTI its share of the gross income of the partnership from that business (and can deduct its share of partnership-level deductions related to that business).[225] In this respect, no distinction is made between limited and general partners. Thus, if a pension fund is a limited partner in a partnership that earns UBTI, the pension fund must include in its UBTI its share of the income of the limited partnership even though, as a limited partner, the pension fund was not actively engaged in partnership activities.[226]

Section 512(b) of the Code excludes from UBTI several categories of income, including various forms of passive investment income, even if they might be derived from the conduct of a trade or business by the tax-exempt entity. In addition to interest, dividends, real property rents, and royalties, section 512(b) excludes from UBTI

> (5) . . . all gains or losses from the sale, exchange, or other disposition of property other than—
>> (A) stock in trade or other property of a kind which would properly be includible in inventory if on hand at the close of the taxable year, or
>> (B) property held primarily for sale to customers in the ordinary course of the trade or business.
> There shall also be excluded all gains or losses recognized, in connection with the organization's investment activities, from the lapse or termination of options to buy or sell securities (as defined in section 1236(c)) or real property and all gains or losses from the forfeiture of good-faith deposits.

In the context of venture capital, if a pension fund acquires a limited partnership interest in a venture capital limited partnership that invests in SMEs, gains derived by the limited partnership from the disposition of corporate stock would be excluded from UBTI of the pension fund.[227] However, where the SME is structured as a partnership or other flowthrough entity, a pension fund's direct or indirect investment in the entity may give rise to UBTI to the pension fund.[228]

The rules are harsher for investment in S corporations. An investment by a 401(a) pension fund in an S corporation is considered an investment in an unrelated trade or business. All income of the S corporation allocated to the pension fund, including passive income, as well as any gain or loss realized on the disposition of S corporation stock is UBTI of the pension fund.[229]

The likely consequence of UBIT is that both pension funds and VCFs require the businesses in which they plan to invest to organize themselves as C corporations rather than as a partnership, S corporation, or other entity taxed as a partnership (for example, a limited liability company [LLC]).[230] Provided that the businesses are structured as C corporations, the UBIT rules would not apply to pension funds, whether they invest directly in the corporation or indirectly in a VCF that invests in the corporation.

Canada

The Impact of Pension Legislation on Venture Capital Investment

Originally, federal and provincial legislation imposed both quantitative and qualitative tests on pension fund investments. For example, under the Pension Benefits Standards Act (PBSA), there were two types of investments permitted by pension funds: "eligible" investments that met the criteria set out in the PBSA,[231] and "basket clause" investments that were not subject to any tests. However, basket clause investments were limited to 7 percent of a plan's portfolio.[232] This regulatory framework hindered investment in venture capital because "eligible" investments were perceived to be better quality investments by investment managers and few venture capital investments could meet the criteria for eligible investments.[233] Furthermore, the high risk associated with venture capital investment was perceived to be in conflict with the fiduciary duties of the plan trustees.[234]

Beginning in 1985, and purposely coinciding with various incentives introduced in the Income Tax Act (discussed below), the federal regulatory framework governing pension investment was revised to define the decision-making process of fiduciaries more broadly. The qualitative and quantitative standards were largely replaced by the requirement of "prudence" in investment and by the prudent portfolio concept. Both the PBSA and the Pension Benefits Act (PBA) have codified the common law prudence requirements and fiduciary principles governing the investment of pension trust funds.[235] At the federal level, the prudence requirement was clarified to include a prudent portfolio concept with the addition of subsection 8(4.1) in 1988:

> The administrator shall invest the assets of a pension fund in accordance with the regulations and in a manner that a reasonable and prudent person would apply in respect of a portfolio of investments of a pension fund.

This clarification was not intended to amend the prudence standard. Indeed, the 1985 amendments were meant to increase venture investing by pension plans.

Along with the prudent person rule, the regulations under the PBSA now provide certain quantitative, but no longer qualitative, requirements for pension plan investments.[236] These regulations provide that no more than 10 percent of a fund may be at risk in the assets of any one company or person, and that a pension fund may not own more than 30 percent of the voting shares of any one corporate entity.[237] Other restrictions apply to various other asset classes, such as real property and Canadian resource properties. Finally, the regulations prohibit a plan from engaging in various transactions with a related party, including lending money to or acquiring securities of a related party.[238] In addition to these general rules, the regulations provide that specific investments made by a pension fund are to be governed by the written statement of the investment policies established by the plan administrator.[239] These policies are intended to ensure that the assets of the fund are invested in compliance with the statutory requirements and in a manner consistent with the financial return, diversification, and risk objectives of the fund.

Unlike their US counterparts, Canadian pension funds did not have strong ties to the venture capital industry and their investment in SMEs had been relatively limited.[240] These amendments to the pension legislation, together with the 1985 federal budget amendments to the Income Tax Act (discussed below), were intended to promote greater venture capital investment by pension funds.

Impact of Tax Legislation on Pension Fund Venture Capital Investment

Parts X and XI of the Act contain measures that have restricted pension fund investment in venture capital. Part X limits the types of investments that a DPSP can make to "qualified investments," as that term is defined in section 204. Although a share of a public corporation is a qualified investment, a direct investment in a share of a corporation that is not listed on a prescribed stock exchange in Canada is a qualified investment only if the share is an "equity share" that meets certain historical dividend and earnings tests.[241] Shares of corporations seeking venture capital would not ordinarily meet the historical earnings and dividend tests, and therefore a DPSP could not invest in such shares. Since October 31, 1985, DPSPs have been able to make indirect venture capital investments through small business investment limited partnerships and small business investment trusts[242] (discussed below), but direct investments remain non-qualified investments.

The harshest limitation on venture capital investment by pension funds has been the part XI penalty tax on excess foreign property.[243] This tax is applicable to RPPs, DPSPs, RRSPs, and RRIFs, as well as certain investment vehicles that may be employed by RPPs.[244] The definition of "foreign property" in part XI includes not only interests in real property, tangible property, and intangible property outside Canada, but also any interest in a partnership, even if all of the partners are resident in Canada, except as prescribed by regulation.[245] Thus, the most common vehicle for pension venture capital investment in the United States, the limited partnership, is generally considered foreign property for the purposes of part XI, even if all of the partners are resident in Canada and even if all of the investments made by the partnership are in Canadian corporations.

It is no surprise that the tax legislation was amended in 1985 in conjunction with amendments to the federal pension legislation in order to promote venture capital investment by pension funds. Three new investment vehicles for pension funds were introduced in the 1985 budget:

- small business investment corporations (CanSBICs);[246]
- small business investment limited partnerships (SBILPs); and
- small business investment trusts (SBITs).

A fourth investment vehicle, the qualified limited partnership (QLP), was also introduced as an exception to the foreign property rules. Although it does not target venture capital investment by pension funds, the QLP has had the most significant impact on such investment because the three more specialized vehicles have not, in practice, been employed by pension funds or venture capital firms structuring VCFs.

CanSBICs were a new tax-exempt vehicle through which RPPs could invest in small businesses. The other three vehicles were introduced as exceptions to the "foreign property" rules in part XI.[247] In particular, SBILPs and QLPs were prescribed partnerships that would not be considered foreign property, and SBITs were prescribed trusts that would not be considered foreign property.

As a further incentive to promote venture capital investment, a pension fund could increase its foreign property holdings by $3 for every $1 invested either directly in qualifying SMEs or indirectly in CanSBICs, SBILPs, or SBITs, up to an additional 20 percent.[248] At the time of the 1985 amendments, the foreign property limit was 10 percent. Thus, an RPP could increase its foreign property holdings to 30 percent if at least 6.67 percent of its total assets were small business properties. The maximum additional foreign property that an RPP can obtain through leveraging has remained 20 percent, while the general foreign property limit has increased over time to 30 percent. Accordingly, an RPP can now increase its foreign property holdings to 50 percent if at least 6.67 percent of its total assets are small business properties. As discussed below, however, the leveraging rules are effectively limited to direct or indirect investments in SMEs that maintain their status as "eligible corporations" throughout the period that they are directly or indirectly owned. Failure to meet this requirement can expose the RPP to part XI tax.

Small Business Investment Corporations

Prescribed CanSBICs are exempt from part I income tax under paragraph 149(1)(o.3),[249] but they are subject to part XI tax.[250] Prescribed CanSBICs are defined in regulation 5101 and must meet a number of requirements. First, the only shareholders of the CanSBIC are RPPs or certain other registered pension fund entities.[251] Second, the only undertaking of the CanSBIC is the investment of its funds in certain specified assets.[252] Third, more than 75 percent of its assets (based on cost) must comprise small business securities,[253] interests of a limited partner in SBILPs, and interests in SBITs.[254] The CanSBIC must be the first person to own such securities, other than a broker or dealer, and must own the securities continuously from the time of acquisition. Fourth, except in limited circumstances, the CanSBIC cannot hold more than 30 percent of the outstanding shares of any class of voting shares of a portfolio company.[255] Fifth, the CanSBIC cannot borrow money, except from its shareholders, and cannot accept deposits.[256]

Small Business Investment Limited Partnerships and Small Business Investment Trusts

SBILPs and SBITs are other vehicles through which registered pension plans, as well as RRSPs and certain other specified plans, can invest in small businesses. In the absence of special rules permitting such plans to invest in SBILPs and SBITs, they would be considered foreign property for the purposes of part XI tax.[257]

SBILPs and SBITs must meet the conditions set out in regulations 5102 and 5103, respectively. Interests of limited partners of an SBILP or beneficiaries of an SBIT must be described by reference to units in the partnership or trust, as the case may be, that are identical in all respects. No limited partner or beneficiary or non-arm's-length group may hold more than a 30 percent interest in an SBILP or SBIT.[258]

Like the investments of a CanSBIC, the investments of an SBILP and SBIT are limited to certain types of assets, of which small business securities must make up a prescribed percentage.[259] The SBILP or SBIT must be the first person (other than a broker or dealer in securities) to acquire the small business securities and must continuously own the securities from the time of acquisition.[260] Essentially, the SBILP or SBIT has 12 months to invest at least 25 percent of the amount received for the issue of units in small business securities; 50 percent must be so invested within 24 months and 75 percent within 36 months.[261] These time periods are much longer than the period in which CanSBICs are required to meet their small business holding thresholds. Furthermore, SBILPs and SBITs can leverage their capital for investment purposes by borrowing amounts not exceeding in the aggregate 20 percent of the partnership or trust capital.[262] Finally, like CanSBICs, SBILPs, and SBITs cannot accept deposits.[263]

There are three main difficulties with CanSBICs, SBILPs, and SBITs as venture capital investment vehicles. First, to qualify as a CanSBIC, SBILP, or SBIT, an entity must meet the investment requirements at all times, from the time it was formed until the particular time. Specifically, the small business investments of the entity are limited to "small business securities," which require direct or indirect investment in eligible corporations. As discussed above in the context of RRSP investment in small businesses, an eligible corporation must maintain its eligible status at all times that the CanSBIC, SBILP, or SBIT owns its securities. Accordingly, even if a small business qualifies at the time that the CanSBIC, SBILP, or SBIT made its investment, it could become ineligible if at any subsequent time its non-active business assets exceed 10 percent of the value of the corporation's property. If the corporation fails to maintain eligible corporation status, the CanSBIC, SBILP, or SBIT may become non-qualifying then and forever after, exposing its RPP investors to part XI tax (in the case of an interest in an SBILP or SBIT, because the interest becomes foreign property, and in any case because the interest in the CanSBIC, SBILP, or SBIT no longer qualifies for the three-to-one leveraging for foreign property purposes).[264] Furthermore, it may be difficult for the RPP to minimize its part XI tax exposure because it cannot dispose of its interest in the CanSBIC, SBILP, or SBIT or cause the CanSBIC, SBILP, or SBIT to dispose of the now non-qualified investment.

Second, the maximum investment that an RPP can hold in a CanSBIC, SBILP, or SBIT is 30 percent. Therefore, at least four RPPs would be required in order to form one of these investment vehicles, assuming that RPPs are the only investors. Although this requirement was alleviated for QLPs in 2001 (discussed below), it remains applicable to CanSBICs, SBILPs, and SBITs. It is unclear why similar amendments were not made to these investment entities in 2001, apart from the fact that the National Venture Capital Association, in its pre-budget submissions, referred only to QLPs (further evidence of the fact that the venture capital industry does not consider CanSBICs, SBILPs, and SBITs to be practically useful venture capital investment vehicles).

Third, CanSBICs, SBILPs, and SBITs need not be registered with the CRA. Rather, enforcement of the requirements imposed by the regulations governing these investment vehicles is within the realm of the normal self-assessment system in Canada. If the taxpayer is challenged in an audit, it must satisfy the CRA that the particular provisions have been complied with. For a pension plan that is considering acquiring an interest in one of these entities but will not control the entity, the risk of non-compliance may cause the pension plan to avoid the investment.

Qualified Limited Partnerships

The QLP provisions were not intended to promote investment in small businesses. Rather, they were designed as a flowthrough vehicle for RPPs and other entities to invest in corporate debt and equity without falling offside the foreign property rules in part XI.[265] However, a QLP can be used as a vehicle to invest in venture capital without a number of the restrictions attached to the three targeted venture investment vehicles. The one drawback with QLPs, which has diminished over time as the foreign property limit has increased, is that an interest in a QLP does not qualify for the three-to-one leveraging of foreign property.

A QLP is defined in regulation 5000(7). There are relatively few restrictions on its investments compared with those on the investments of CanSBICs, SBILPs, and SBITs. A QLP itself is subject to the same foreign property limitations as specified in part XI. In other words, when the provisions were introduced, no more than 10 percent of the QLP's assets could be foreign property. The foreign property limit has since been raised to 30 percent. Apart from the foreign property limitation, a QLP can invest in equity (including rights, warrants, and put and call options) and debt of corporations as well as various liquid assets, such as bank deposits and guaranteed investment certificates.[266] A QLP is generally prohibited from investing in partnerships or trusts, although the 2003 federal budget relaxed this rule to allow a QLP to invest as a limited partner in another QLP.[267]

When the QLP rules were introduced, they limited the investment of any one limited partner (or group of non-arm's-length limited partners) to 30 percent of the units of the partnership. This limitation was removed in the 2001 federal budget, primarily in response to representations from the Canadian venture capital industry. The budget further proposed that any limited partner or group that holds more than 30 percent of the units in a QLP would be treated as owning a proportionate interest in each property owned by the QLP, including foreign property. However, this proposal was revised in the draft regulations released on February 5, 2002. Rather than a lookthrough rule, the draft regulations propose that for limited partners that own more than 30 percent of the units of a QLP, a specified portion of each unit will be prescribed not to be foreign property (based on the proportionate cost to the QLP of its non-foreign property).[268] Many Canadian private venture capital funds are structured as QLPs in order to permit Canadian pension fund investment.[269]

Evaluation of Venture Capital Investment by Individual and Employer-Sponsored Retirement Funds

The material presented in the previous section described five ways in which legislation affecting retirement savings can have an impact on venture investment. The following evaluation of these provisions is grouped by the type of venture investment—formal or informal—made using retirement savings.

Evaluating the Use of Retirement Funds for Informal Venture Capital Investment

The regulation of retirement savings plans, both individual and employer-sponsored pension plans, may inhibit would-be entrepreneurs from leaving employment to start a business. For would-be entrepreneurs, there is a distinction between the manner in which employer-sponsored retirement plans are regulated in Canada and the United States. In Canada, an individual's interest in an RPP is effectively locked in until the individual reaches retirement age. If an individual's employment is terminated before normal retirement age, the individual's ability to access vested pension benefits is extremely limited. In the United States, in contrast, termination of employment is generally considered an acceptable occasion for the distribution of vested pension benefits, although any amount withdrawn must be included in the recipient's gross income and may be subject to an additional 10 percent excise tax if the individual is not yet 55 years old. Therefore, in theory an individual in the United States has greater access to vested rights in an employer pension plan in order to start a business, but in practice the tax consequences may either restrict that behaviour or inhibit individuals from joining employer pension plans (if they can opt out of such plans). In both countries, great emphasis is placed on securing such funds for retirement purposes only, and it is doubtful whether that motivation should be undermined in order to promote entrepreneurial activity.

With regard to individual retirement plans, Canada is somewhat more generous than the United States. Pre-retirement withdrawals from such plans are included in income in both countries, but in the United States they are subject to a further 10 percent excise tax if the individual has not reached the age of 59½ when the funds are withdrawn. Thus, individuals in both countries can simply withdraw funds from individual retirement accounts for venture investment purposes, although the tax consequences of doing so may be prohibitive. In the United States, any loan from an IRA or pledge of IRA assets as security for a loan is treated as a distribution. In Canada, loans from an RRSP are permitted only if they are secured by an insured mortgage, while pledging RRSP assets as security for a loan is treated as a withdrawal. The economic penalties associated with early withdrawal—not only the immediate tax consequences but also the effect of early withdrawal on the value of the plan at the time of retirement—inhibit individuals from withdrawing funds for love capital investments or entrepreneurial activity. Given that the primary rationale for IRAs and RRSPs is to promote retirement savings, I do not propose that these economic penalties be relaxed. However, consideration could be given to expanding the ability of individuals to access plan assets for love capital investments.

In both countries, the retirement focus of such plans has been undermined to some extent by permitting access to plan assets to qualified first-time homebuyers or for qualified higher education expenses. In the United States, a plan beneficiary is relieved of the additional 10 percent excise tax; in Canada, a plan beneficiary is permitted to borrow certain amounts from the plan on an interest-free basis without incurring any tax liability, provided that the amount is repaid as required by the legislation. In each case, liberalized access is rationalized on the basis that a home or enhanced human capital, as the case may be, is an asset that can increase the value of an individual's savings at the time of retirement.

There are strong arguments that similarly favour access to individual retirement funds for love capital investments. A successful entrepreneurial endeavour is arguably as important for achieving retirement security as investing in one's human capital through education. The fundamental policy question is whether the restrictions on investments of individual retirement funds in a plan holder's business or restrictions on the ability of individual retirement funds to make a loan to a plan holder should be relaxed to permit such investments or loans and, if so, on what conditions. The first part of this question is a threshold issue: should individuals be permitted to use *retirement* savings to invest in high-risk, illiquid investments? In other words, do such investments undermine certain fundamental tenets of the RRSP provisions—security and liquidity?

The extension of permitted investments of RRSPs to certain private equity in 1985, as well as the direct targeting of RRSPs under the provincial angel capital tax credit programs, have undermined these tenets to some degree. First, there are no monetary limits on the amount that individuals can invest through their RRSPs in arm's-length private companies, provided that the RRSP does not acquire more than 10 percent of the shares of any one company (or does not invest more than $25,000 in any company and does not control the company). It may be that the Department of Finance assumed that only sophisticated investors would take advantage of these provisions, and Canadian securities laws supported this assumption to some extent.[270] Sophisticated investors would not be inclined to invest too much of their wealth in a single investment, whereas less sophisticated investors, if investments in non-arm's-length corporations were allowed, could lose their retirement savings altogether by investing in a pipe dream. That concern can be addressed by imposing some limitations on the amount that can be invested in non-arm's-length corporations. Besides, there is no guarantee that investment in publicly traded corporations brings any greater security for retirement savings, as public equity market performances since mid-2000 have so ably demonstrated, and there are no diversification requirements for RRSP investment in publicly traded securities.

In the United States, a number of "super IRA" proposals preceded the enactment of the Taxpayer Relief Act of 1997, which introduced the incentives for qualified first-time homebuyers and qualified higher education expenses. One of these proposals, the American Family Tax Relief Act,[271] contained a generous scheme allowing access to IRA funds for business startups. The proposal would have excluded certain distributions used for business startup costs from both the 10 percent excise tax on distributions and income inclusion generally.[272]

It is inappropriate to allow the tax-free withdrawal of funds from an IRA where the contributions to the IRA and the income generated by the IRA are both tax-exempt.[273] The IRA system is subsidized by the government (that is, taxpayers) and it makes little sense to allow its objectives to be undermined with few safeguards. Nothing can guarantee the success of the business venture being financed. However, the success of a venture should result in the return of funds to the IRA and its failure should not wholly deplete the IRA of funds set aside for retirement. The technical details of the proposal were also problematic. The one-year limitation on startup expenses was arbitrary and could lead to inappropriate business decisions.[274] There was no requirement that plan assets be used as a last resort.[275] The viability of the business venture was not scrutinized.[276] Finally, there was no limitation on the amount that could be withdrawn from the IRA other than the startup expenses.[277] With all of these flaws, the proposal was rightly dropped.

Following their evaluation of this proposal, Edward Gac and Wayne Gazur suggested that IRAs should be permitted to loan an amount to the IRA owner to cover startup costs of a new business, subject to a number of requirements. They suggested amending the loan rules rather than the distribution rules to better ensure that the funds used were returned to the IRA for retirement purposes. A cap would be placed on the amount of the loan to ensure that sufficient funds remain in the individual's various retirement accounts to ensure a certain income level at the time of retirement. The loan would include "hardship" rules similar to the section 401(k) hardship rules[278] to ensure that retirement funds are used as a last resort.[279] Finally, the repayment provisions would reflect the startup phase of a business: they suggested no payments for the first two years, followed by a five-year repayment term with interest.

The Gac and Gazur proposal has some attractions that could be incorporated in the Canadian context, although some elements of their proposal are problematic. In particular, the loan cap that they propose, which has intuitive appeal in theory, may prove unworkable in practice. It would require actuarial calculations based on the current age and health of the individual retirement plan holder, as well as projected assumptions about retirement income levels, other sources of retirement income, and so on. The required computations would be complex and costly to undertake and administer.

Legislative amendments should be considered in order to permit an RRSP to invest in a business venture of the RRSP annuitant. Since individuals are permitted to invest RRSP funds in their intellectual or human capital through the lifelong learning plan, there is little justification for limiting the ability to invest RRSP funds in an annuitant's (qualifying) business enterprise. It is questionable whether the risks of replacement of the RRSP funds used for venture capital are any greater than the risks associated with funds used to improve one's human capital.

There are two ways in which the RRSP rules can be amended to permit the use of RRSP funds for love capital. The first, similar to the homebuyers' plan and the lifelong learning plan, would be to permit an individual to borrow funds from an RRSP on an interest-free basis if the funds are invested in a "qualifying small business corporation share" (defined below) and the loan is repaid within a certain time. Consider the earlier example of Ms. A with $200,000 in her RRSP who wishes to invest $100,000 in a business venture.[280] As previously indicated, if Ms. A withdrew the entire $200,000 from her RRSP at age 40 and she were in a position to reinvest the entire amount in her RRSP five years later, the inability to invest more than $15,500 per year, combined with the loss of deferral on the original $200,000, would reduce the value of her RRSP at age 65 to $484,786.73, compared with $1,369,695.04 if she left the $200,000 in her RRSP and made no further contributions. If, however, Ms. A were permitted to borrow $100,000 from her RRSP on an interest-free basis with no immediate tax consequences for the purposes of making the venture investment, and if she repaid the entire $100,000 to her RRSP after five years, the value of her RRSP at age 65 would be $1,150,943.23.[281] That is, her RRSP at age 65 would be worth $666,174.50 more with an interest-free loan than it would be if she withdrew the entire $200,000 (as required under the current rules). The aggregate loss to her RRSP at age 65 if she were entitled to borrow $100,000 on an interest-free basis in order to make the investment is only $218,751.81, less than a third of the loss if the loan were not permitted. Of course, this example assumes that Ms. A's venture investment is successful. If Ms. A had to withdraw the entire $200,000 from her RRSP and the venture is a complete failure, Ms. A may not be able to replace the $200,000 in her RRSP for a significantly longer period of time, if ever. However, if Ms. A were permitted to borrow $100,000 from her RRSP, she would still have the remaining $100,000 in her RRSP for retirement.[282] Assuming that she made no further contributions to her RRSP, the remaining $100,000 would be worth $684,847.52 at age 65, or $200,000 more than her RRSP would be worth if the venture investment were successful and the funds were reinvested as early as possible (subject to the annual limits) but the initial withdrawal were subject to tax.

If the RRSP rules were amended to permit loans from an RRSP in order to acquire qualifying small business corporation shares, the definitions of "eligible small business corporation share" and "eligible small business corporation" in subsection 44.1(1)[283] should be adopted for these purposes, subject to three modifications. First, the types of shares that qualify should not be restricted to common shares. Second, the definition of "qualifying small business corporation" should restrict the types of business activities that the corporation can carry on (similar to the restrictions imposed under various provincial and state angel capital tax credit programs).[284] Third, the total carrying value of the assets of the qualifying small business corporation before and after the shares are issued should be an amount significantly less than $50,000,000—perhaps $10,000,000—reflecting the love capital nature of the investment.

As in the case of the two existing RRSP-loan plans (homebuyers' plan and lifelong learning plan), there should be a limit on the amount that can be withdrawn for this use and a stipulated period over which the amount must be repaid to the RRSP. The maximum amount that can be withdrawn could be limited to a fixed dollar amount or a fraction of the value of the RRSP at the time the investment is made, or a combination of the two. For example, the loan could be limited to an amount not exceeding the greater of $25,000 and 50 percent of the fair market value of the RRSP's investments. If the individual holds more than one RRSP, the maximum permitted loan would be based on aggregate RRSP assets. The repayment period must take into account the holding period normally associated with venture investing, particularly seed financing. For example, I would suggest that repayment could be deferred until the seventh year after the loan is made, and thereafter at least one-fifth of the loan must be repaid in each of the following five years. The plan annuitant would be required to recognize income to the extent that there is a shortfall in repayments. Furthermore, repayment would be accelerated to the extent that the annuitant disposed of the qualifying small business corporation shares.

Alternatively, the RRSP rules could be amended to permit the direct investment by the RRSP in "certified small business corporation shares." A "certified small business corporation" would be the same as a "qualifying small business corporation," but in this case the shares would have to be fixed-value preference shares that cannot be converted into common shares. This limitation would ensure that the tax-free return generated to the RRSP (assuming that the venture is successful) is restricted, to avoid excessive tax deferral through this mechanism. For this purpose, the definition of "specified class" of shares in subsection 256(1.1) of the Income Tax Act could be adopted.[285] While this restriction would preclude growth from accruing to the RRSP's shares, it would not prohibit the annuitant from owning growth shares (that is, common shares) outside the RRSP. In essence, the RRSP would provide love capital without permitting an excessive tax-free return to accrue to the RRSP. If the investment were successful, the RRSP's capital could be returned through a share redemption, while any growth in the love capital investment would accrue and would remain taxable to the individual outside the RRSP through ownership of the common shares. As in the case of the interest-free loan, the amount of the RRSP that can be invested in certified small business corporation shares should be restricted to avoid excessive risk exposure. The same limits noted above for RRSP loans (that is, the greater of $25,000 and 50 percent of the value of the assets of the RRSP) are recommended for this purpose.

Evaluating the Use of Retirement Funds for Formal Venture Capital Investment

It should come as no surprise that I think Canada needs to make radical reforms to promote venture investment by employer-sponsored pension funds (both public sector and private sector plans) and at the same time eliminate the generous tax incentives provided for LSVCCs.

The combined effect of the 1985 amendments to pension standards legislation and the Income Tax Act initially had a positive impact on Canadian pension fund investment in venture capital; however, it was relatively short-lived. In 1985, Canadian pension funds committed $20 million to venture capital. Commitments increased to $125 million in 1986, $185 million in 1987, and $176 million in 1988. In 1990 and 1991, venture capital investment by both US and Canadian pension funds dropped considerably, primarily because of the poor performance of investments as a result of the recession. Although venture capital investment by US pension funds recovered in 1992, investment by Canadian pension funds did not.[286] The continued impact of the 1985 budget proposals targeting pension fund investment in venture capital has to date proven to be insignificant. In fact, it is arguable that the 1985 amendments caused an overall decline in venture capital investment by Canadian pension funds. The late 1980s marked the end of an economic cycle and, in retrospect, the federal tax incentives may have prompted venture capital investment by pension funds at the worst possible time. The returns experienced by the pension funds were much lower than expected and may have poisoned the well, leading many pension funds to avoid venture capital investment completely.

The limitations imposed in Canada on venture capital investment (or any investment, for that matter) by pension funds are significantly greater than those imposed in the United States. The problems in Canada stem primarily from the "made in Canada" investment policy in the Income Tax Act that limits foreign property investment to 30 percent of fund assets and defines foreign property so broadly. Foreign property includes all interests in partnerships or trusts (unless prescribed), regardless of the residence of the partners or beneficiaries or the situs of the assets of the partnership or trust. Thus, an interest in a partnership all of the partners of which are resident in Canada and all of the assets of which are located in Canada is considered foreign property unless the partnership is either a QLP or an SBILP. Limited partnerships have been the investment vehicle of choice in the US venture capital industry. Particularly for tax-exempt entities such as pension plans (as well as registered charities and university endowment funds), a flowthrough vehicle is desirable to avoid taxation on gains arising from equity investments and at the same time permit the commingling of pension fund investments with investments by taxable entities. For the same reasons, and in order to attract US pension investment in Canada, limited partnerships would be the most appropriate investment vehicle for Canadian pension funds to make passive venture capital investments.

The foreign property limitation creates significant and unnecessary complexity in Canada's tax legislation applicable to RPPs. In fact, the limitation can be circumvented in many ways, such as through the use of derivatives, which make the rules extremely porous.[287] The most appropriate solution would be to eliminate the foreign property rules completely. As in the United States, pension fund investment would be limited only by the fiduciary obligations and prohibited transactions rules imposed in the pension legislation. However, it may be feared that the immediate elimination of the foreign property limitation would result in a flood of capital out of the country and cause Canadian equity markets to wither. Perhaps that accounts for the gradual rise in the foreign property limit since 1990 and the possibility that it will continue to increase until such time as it can be removed without a significant loss of capital investment in Canada.[288] In 1998, the Standing Committee on Banking Trade and Commerce recommended its gradual removal.[289]

Assuming that the foreign property limitation remains in effect, the inclusion of partnerships and trusts as foreign property is overly broad. With regard to venture investing, legislative amendments could be limited to the partnership provisions. In its submissions to the government prior to the 2001 federal budget, the Canadian Venture Capital Association (CVCA) suggested that the SBILP definition was too restrictive and that the 30 percent limit on QLP units was problematic in light of the few institutions that regularly invest in venture capital.[290] The CVCA suggested that the Act be amended to introduce a special rule for limited partnerships similar to the rule in section 259 applicable to qualified trusts and qualified corporations. Under section 259, a qualified trust or qualified corporation may elect to have its beneficiaries or shareholders treated, for the purposes of part XI, as though the beneficiary or shareholder directly held its proportionate share of each asset held by the trust or corporation.[291] Absent this election, an RPP's investment in a trust or corporation, in its entirety, would either constitute foreign property or not. A similar rule applicable to limited partnerships (perhaps applying automatically rather than on election by the general partner) could eliminate the need for the QLP and SBILP provisions. In fact, the requirements that qualified trusts must meet in order to make an election under section 259 are similar to the requirements that a QLP must meet in any event.[292] In addition, if such a provision were introduced, the three-to-one leveraging of foreign investments based on small business investments by the RPP would more accurately reflect the actual small business investments made, directly or indirectly, by each RPP.

There are a number of provisions in the Income Tax Act that affect the use of limited partnerships as venture investment vehicles in Canada, particularly for non-resident investors, including foreign pension funds. Pension funds in the United States are tax-exempt entities.[293] Subjecting foreign pension funds to tax on venture capital investments made in Canada, especially on investments in Canadian VCFs, would obviously deter such funds from investing in Canada. Limited partnerships are the venture capital investment vehicle of choice in the United States (particularly for tax-exempt investors such as pension funds) and are therefore commonly used in Canada. While a number of recent amendments to the Act have addressed concerns raised by the venture capital industry about the taxation of non-resident pension funds investing in Canadian venture capital limited partnerships, the law remains unclear. As a result, rather convoluted parallel fund structures are often used when a Canadian venture capital firm seeks to raise capital from both resident and non-resident investors.[294] The unfamiliarity of these fund structures to US pension fund managers may inhibit investment.

Many US pension funds that have been active venture capital investors may not be investing in private venture capital limited partnerships, whether in Canada or the United States, in the near future because the value of their existing venture capital investments exceeds the asset allocation permitted for this class of investment. Evidently, US venture capital fund managers have turned their sights to foreign pension funds, particularly in the United Kingdom and Japan, as the new untapped source of venture capital. US tax laws applicable to US limited partnerships are conducive to non-resident limited partners. Even if Canadian venture capital fund managers could encourage such pension funds to consider investment in Canada in addition to (or as opposed to) investment in the United States, the same structuring difficulties that have deterred US pension fund investment in Canada apply to any foreign pension fund. For example, all of the complexities and consequent costs and administrative problems of a parallel fund structure apply to any foreign pension fund, and are compounded by the lack of geographic proximity to the non-resident investors (and the non-resident parallel fund).

Other than income tax issues, there are a number of factors that influence venture capital investment by pension funds. For example, the type of plan—defined contribution or defined benefit—may affect the plan's ability to invest in venture capital. Many defined contribution plans, especially ones in which the employee-participant controls his or her plan investments, do not generally include VCFs (or any private equity funds) among the investments permitted by their investment guidelines. Therefore, in determining the total amount of pension fund capital that is potentially available for venture capital investment, defined contribution plans must be excluded. Although the number of defined contribution plans has been consistently higher than the number of defined benefit plans, the total assets that they represent (and the number of employees that they cover) are significantly less. According to recent statistics (for 2000), Canadian trusteed pension funds held assets worth just under $600 billion, of which defined benefit plans constituted over $553 billion, or 92.5 percent.[295] In contrast, in the United States, defined contribution plans control a significantly larger portion of pension plan assets—over 50 percent of the $4.8 trillion in private trusteed pension plans. Even if all of the public sector retirement plans (controlling a further $2.2 trillion in assets) are defined benefit plans, defined contribution plans still control over 40 percent of pension fund assets. Yet there is little if any concern in the United States that pension funds are not investing sufficiently in venture capital. Particularly for Canada, the fact that pension fund venture capital investment is more likely to come from defined benefit plans should not have an adverse impact on overall pension fund investment. If anything, the opposite is the case.

So what is deterring most Canadian pension funds from investing in venture capital? In his 1999 study of pension fund investment,[296] Kirk Falconer identified 14 barriers to pension fund investment in private equity. The Canadian Labour Market and Productivity Centre (CLMPC), for whom the study was conducted, sent a questionnaire to all members of the Pension Investment Association of

Canada (PIAC)[297] asking them to weigh the importance of the identified barriers. The results of the CLMPC-PIAC survey are worth noting in some detail. Many of the barriers considered to be the most important are interrelated and generally concern the perceived cost of investment, in terms of management time spent selecting and monitoring private equity investments, compared with the risk-adjusted return that can be derived therefrom.[298]

The most significant barrier, according to survey results, was a concern that private equity investment is management-intensive, resulting in unacceptably high pension operating costs. Most of the respondents had an external asset-management style (that is, they invested funds in various external pooling vehicles). Thus, the operating costs are not the costs of selecting specific SME investments, which is highly labour-intensive. Rather, the costs included management fees charged for investment in the external vehicle (such as a limited partnership) plus the internal costs of selecting, monitoring, and evaluating the external vehicle. US pension funds have similar concerns, and have used their investment clout to negotiate acceptable terms governing the management of VCFs in which they invest and the compensation of the funds' managers. In 1996, nine public sector plans in the United States commissioned William M. Mercer to prepare a report on private equity funds.[299] According to Falconer, the Mercer report "is considered to be a statement of 'best practices' by its pension sponsors for market-wide recommendation."[300] This report was commissioned at a time when private equity pools in the United States were a seller's market, with many large US pension funds vying to invest in a relatively small number of funds run by experienced venture capitalists. The report was critical of certain practices in the private equity industry and included a number of recommendations for reform. Given the fact that the situation in Canada is quite the reverse—pension fund investment in venture capital pools is relatively low—there is no reason why many of the best practices suggested in the Mercer report cannot be negotiated by Canadian pension funds, perhaps collectively under the auspices of PIAC. A second development in the US industry that may alleviate this concern is the use of gatekeepers, who can assume many of the management-intensive costs through a "fund of funds" or a separately managed account for the pension fund. Whether a gatekeeper subindustry develops in Canada will depend on perceived demand.[301]

The second highest barrier identified in the CLMPC-PIAC survey was a concern that there are too few knowledgeable, qualified, and/or experienced investment specialists to effectively manage pension assets internally or as part of an external pooling arrangement. A related barrier, the 11th, was a concern that managers of external private capital pools had insufficient familiarity with the needs and constraints of pension funds, particularly the fiduciary responsibilities of pension fund trustees and managers, accountability to plan members, and the need for low operating costs. Interestingly, a significant amount of pension fund venture capital investment in Canada in recent years (in terms of dollars invested) has been internally managed, as evidenced by the $1.9 billion that the Caisse de dépôt et placement du Québec ("the Caisse") contributed to its technology venture capital subsidiary in 2001. The Ontario Municipal Employees Retirement System (OMERS) and the Ontario Teachers' Pension Plan similarly manage internally over half of their venture capital investment portfolios. Thus, among the largest pension fund venture capital investors in Canada, there do not appear to be problems attracting specialists for internal investment management. Interestingly, it was the largest pension funds—funds with the greatest scope for internal asset management—that gave both of these barriers the greatest emphasis in the survey. Smaller pension funds do not have the option of internal management, particularly of such a small aspect of their portfolio, and have little choice but to consider external managers. One possible solution is the creation of larger pension fund pools, modelled on the Caisse (but without the social investment mandate). For example, the federal Public Sector Pension Investment Board manages most federal public sector pension funds. The development of a gatekeeping industry, similar to that in the United States, may also be helpful in this respect. However, it too is dependent on there being a critical mass of experienced venture capital asset managers. In this respect, government policy should not be aimed solely at creating a sufficient pool of venture capital dollars; it must also contribute to the development of sufficient numbers of qualified venture capital specialists. Unfortunately, in my view the current structure of the LSVCC regime—the primary tax expenditure in Canada in terms of cost—fails in this respect.[302]

A number of barriers identified in the CLMPC-PIAC survey dealt with the lack of information to adequately evaluate the private equity market, particularly as compared with the public equity market. The third barrier was a lack of information about private capital markets with which pension managers can make investment decisions and monitor their performance over time. This information barrier refers not to the lack of data to evaluate particular SME investments, but to the lack of long-term risk-adjusted returns data for the private capital industry as a whole, or particular sectors within it. The fourth barrier, a perception that risk-adjusted returns from such investments are inadequate or unreliable, stems primarily from the lack of information to evaluate the industry. Collecting this sort of data (which must be obtained from the SMEs themselves) must be done up front and is costly. In addition, at the time of the survey, in 1998, "returns from liquid, publicly-traded securities [had] been good enough in recent years to postpone entry into the private capital markets"[303] that were perceived to be too volatile by comparison. However, the more recent volatility in public equity markets—particularly the meltdown of tech stocks—coupled with concerns about the quality of information in the public markets may be a blessing in disguise for private equity. Public stock markets have demonstrated that they too can be extremely volatile, with the potential for high-profile bankruptcies. Perhaps public equity market volatility will cause pension funds to re-evaluate the relative risk profiles of the private and public equity capital markets—or it may cause them to re-evaluate their overall commitment to equity investment, whether public or private. The sixth barrier noted was the conflict between the traditional methods for measuring pension asset

performance and the longer-term performance of illiquid private capital investments. Pension asset management traditionally relies on stock market indices
and other market benchmarks to evaluate and monitor investments. Such data
(available quarterly, monthly, weekly, or daily) are used to determine whether
particular investments should be maintained and whether liquid asset classes
should be rebalanced. In addition, and perhaps underlying this set of concerns,
although not stated explicitly, is a concern that pension fund investing could
adversely affect the compensation of pension fund managers (the primary respondents to the survey). To the extent that their compensation is performance-driven
based on quarterly investment performance, realized cash-on-cash distributions,
and year-end returns—which is common practice in the pension industry—
pension fund managers may be loath to invest in venture capital, particularly
seed and early-stage funds, because these investments represent longer-term
holds that lack liquidity.[304] Fund managers that make venture capital investments may not be around long enough to reap the benefits of what they sow,
while their replacements may receive a windfall. In addition, there are currently
in Canada no available benchmarks against which to measure performance,
whether quarterly or annually. Venture capital investment is long term (most
venture capital limited partnerships have a 10-year life, which can be extended)
and performance can only be truly measured on liquidation. As a result, the
evaluation of private equity performance is a complex exercise. Reliable data
on the private equity market may be provided by gatekeepers, if there is sufficient demand for the development of a gatekeeper industry in Canada, and by
private capital market analysts. For example, Thomson Venture Economics in
the United States includes a discussion of venture capital fund performance in the
annual National Venture Capital Association *Yearbook*[305] and fund-specific (and
fund manager) performance information is available to subscribers of its
VentureXpert™ database. The CVCA, working in conjunction with Macdonald &
Associates Limited, Venture Economics, Inc., and Réseau Capital, released performance statistics for the Canadian venture capital industry for periods ended
December 31, 2001 and December 31, 2002. Unfortunately, the "data collected
to date [are] not based on a standardized approach to the valuation of unrealized
investments, and as a result, there is no consistency in valuation methodology."[306] In addition, the published investment returns are provided on a gross
return basis because the different entities that comprise the Canadian formal
venture capital industry (including LSVCCs, private VCFs, pension funds, and
captive corporate venture capital subsidiaries) "have differing objectives, sources
of funds, management compensation approaches and regulatory constraints
which significantly impact their management and operating cost structures."[307]
However, in order to be meaningful to investors, particularly in order to attract
new pension fund investors to venture capital, it is necessary to develop comparable data on a net return basis. Evidently, the CVCA is working with other
organizations to address this issue.[308] In addition, formal benchmarks can be
developed by the pension funds themselves to evaluate and monitor private
equity investments.[309]

The fifth barrier identified in the CLMPC-PIAC survey was a concern that private equity investment activity may result in high profile failures and/or severe cost liabilities. Many pension funds avoid any form of publicity and, unfortunately, failures tend to be much more widely reported than successes in business news. A related concern of pension funds is that they have little recourse in the event of failure, particularly against external managers of private equity pools. Falconer suggests that the "best practices" developed in the Mercer report, including provision for adequate protection of limited partners through the use of advisory boards, the ability to replace managing partners, and provision for termination/liquidation of the partnership, can be useful in this respect.

Five related barriers (the 7th, 9th, 10th, 12th, and 14th) focused on the mindset of the pension fund fiduciaries: insufficient familiarity with the private capital industry among pension plan fiduciaries and asset managers; a reluctance to invest based on past experience; a perception that high-risk investment activity is inconsistent with fiduciary responsibility to pension plan members; a perception that there are not enough high-quality small business investment opportunities to warrant pension fund investment; and a concern that high-risk investment activity may violate the letter or spirit of legislative fiduciary standards. According to respondents to the CLMPC-PIAC survey, weak support for private equity investment from the board of trustees or managing fiduciaries of pension funds was frequently based on gaps in knowledge about private equity. For some pension fund fiduciaries, their only knowledge of the sector is their bad investment experience (or the "horror stories" of others) in the late 1980s and early 1990s—investments that may have been encouraged by the incentives introduced in the 1985 federal budget. Some fund managers attribute the scarcity of quality investments to limited public awareness of private equity opportunities. In contrast, the public domain is inundated with information about securities listed in public equity markets, and as a result pension funds have few concerns with public equity investment or, indeed, retaining others to manage their public equity portfolios. As noted above, recent concerns with the quality of information disclosed in public equity markets may cause funds to re-evaluate this perception (at least of public equity markets). In any event, identifying appropriate venture capital investments is the responsibility of the venture capital professional (whether the external venture fund manager or the pension fund's internal private equity asset manager), not the pension fund's trustees. All of these concerns relate to the legitimacy of private equity (and specifically venture capital) as an appropriate asset allocation for a pension fund. According to Falconer, "[t]here is a widely-held view among Canadian pension fiduciaries, their agents and advisors that fiduciary obligations to plan participants and beneficiaries, by definition, preclude involvement in most private capital markets."[310] Similarly, there remains a perception that pension standards legislation, particularly the prudent person rule, prohibits high-risk investment activity. According to Falconer, this perception also exists in the United States despite published clarifications from regulatory officials about the prudent man rule. In Canada, section 8(4.1) was added to the PBSA in 1998 to clarify that the prudent person

standard applied to the entire portfolio rather than on an investment by investment basis; this clarification was added even though amendments to the PBSA
in 1985 were intended to increase private equity investment. Lack of knowledge, past knowledge, or misconceptions (about the fiduciary's role under the
plan and under the law) can be redressed through the education of pension
fiduciaries about venture capital and the role of venture capitalists. The CVCA
should approach PIAC to offer educational seminars in this respect. In addition,
representatives of the few pension funds that are making venture capital investments (for example, the Caisse, OMERS, and Ontario Teachers' Pension Plan)
could discuss their experiences in a seminar or conference for pension fund
fiduciaries and pension fund asset managers.

A barrier (the eighth in the survey) specific to small and medium-sized
pension funds ($1 billion in assets or less) is the concern that insufficient size
may prohibit diversification into private equity investment. The costs associated
with such investment, particularly the initial costs of selecting the appropriate
investment vehicle, as well as ongoing monitoring costs, are proportionately
higher for smaller pension funds and may act as impediments to private equity
investment. Smaller pension funds may benefit from a fund of funds model
(controlled by a gatekeeper) that reduces the cost of private equity investment
as well as deals with some of the other barriers to investment. The emergence
of money management institutions, particularly for public sector pension funds,
such as the Caisse in Quebec or the British Columbia Investment Management
Corporation, that manage multiple pension funds can generate the critical mass
that is perceived to be needed for private equity investment.[311] Such pooled
management can be especially important for public sector funds in the smaller
provinces in order to benefit from the increased diversification that a larger
asset pool can enjoy, and thus make private equity, including venture capital, an
appropriate asset allocation.

Impediments to pension investment may be caused inadvertently by public
policies, such as taxation (the 13th barrier identified in the CLMPC-PIAC survey).
The tax treatment of limited partnerships was mentioned by some respondents
as a barrier to investment, although they ranked it relatively low (33 percent
rated it as important or very important). In particular, PIAC has called for the
removal of the foreign property limitation (at a time when it was 20 percent),
alleging that it has cost pension funds billions of dollars in lost revenues. The
removal of the foreign property limitation would also remove any concern about
the tax treatment of Canadian pension fund investment in limited partnerships.

It is only this last barrier that is created by government policy. The remaining barriers primarily reflect the lack of confidence that pension fund trustees
and managers have in venture capital as an appropriate part of a pension fund
investment portfolio. Because the vast majority of pension funds are passive
investors, they must have confidence in the venture capital industry and managers
of venture capital pools in Canada before they will commit capital to this sector.
Pension standards legislation is no longer a barrier to pension fund investment
in venture capital. Although federal and provincial legislation imposes fiduciary

standards on pension fund asset managers, the move from quantitative and qualitative tests to a prudence test, based on the entire investment portfolio, clearly endorsed modern portfolio management theory and the acceptance of high-risk venture capital investments as an appropriate asset class for pension funds. While there is no doubt that private equity investment, particularly venture capital, is more costly to evaluate as an investment and bears significantly greater risk, it can be a small but important part of a broadly diversified portfolio with rewards commensurate with the risk. Despite the fact that venture capital investment is permitted under pension standards legislation, it is evident from the CLMPC-PIAC survey that there are pension fund trustees and asset managers that question whether such investment is compatible with their fiduciary obligations.

Overall, the results of the CLMPC-PIAC survey and the venture capital statistics in Canada and the United States clearly suggest that the market failure affecting investment in small businesses is much greater in Canada than in the United States as far as investment by pension funds is concerned. This market failure can be addressed on a number of fronts. Groups such as PIAC should be educating its members about the scope of fiduciary standards and the nature of investments that are permitted under such standards. A greater amount of information dissemination, either in the public media or in industry-specific media, about available forms of venture capital investment and their use in developing a diversified portfolio would also be useful. In this respect, the media attention that the CPP has received about its venture capital investments, all of which are passive in nature, may convince other pension funds to follow suit.

For Canadian governments at both the federal and the provincial levels, these survey results suggest that government intervention is appropriate to address the market failure and should specifically encourage venture investment by pension funds. Although the 1985 amendments to the Income Tax Act and to the federal pension legislation had these goals in mind, neither set of amendments provides an *incentive* for pension funds to invest in venture capital.[312] Furthermore, as discussed in more detail in chapter 6, none of the tax incentives currently offered at the federal or provincial level targets pension fund investment. None offers refundable tax credits or marketable credits to tax-exempt entities. In this respect, Canada and the provinces should carefully consider various VCF programs used in the United States—such as those in Missouri and Kansas—in which refundable or transferable tax credits are used to attract pension fund investors.[313] In addition, a variation of the "Oklahoma program," such as that used in Iowa, which provides an equity guarantee to investors in a VCF (but limits the guarantee to certain investors such as pension funds) should be considered for adoption in Canada.[314] Finally, the federal and provincial governments could consider mandating that public sector pension funds invest a stipulated (albeit small) percentage of their assets in private equity, as has been done in Michigan, Massachusetts, and Maryland. Smaller provinces, such as the maritime provinces, could consider pooling their resources through a fund of funds in order to establish a larger venture capital pool.

Venture Capital Investment by Government-Administered Pension Plans

US Social Security

US Social Security was established under the Social Security Act of 1935.[315] The objective of Social Security was to provide retired workers with a continuing stream of income. The program was extended to dependants in 1939, making Social Security a family-based economic security program. Further amendments in 1950 extended the program to disabled persons and introduced cost-of-living adjustments. Over the years, Social Security has assumed a prominent role in the United States. One in six Americans receives a Social Security benefit and about 95 percent of all workers are employed in jobs covered by Social Security. Also, Social Security benefits comprise about 5 percent of US total economic output.

Social Security operates as a pay-as-you-go system, funded by payroll taxes collected under the authority of the Federal Insurance Contributions Act (FICA).[316] For accounting purposes, the money collected goes into one of two trust funds maintained by the Department of the Treasury: Old-Age and Survivors Insurance (OASI) and the Disability Insurance (DI) trust funds. Any funds not required to pay immediate benefits or administrative expenses are invested. Currently, Social Security trust fund reserves exceed $1 trillion.[317] Although the DI trust fund holds a very small amount of publicly traded securities, the two trust funds hold almost exclusively interest-bearing "special obligation" securities issued by the Treasury, with both principal and interest guaranteed by the US government. Thus, the trust funds serve primarily as an accounting function and not a financial function. For this reason, critics of the Social Security program claim the system is based on an "IOU."[318]

Reform of US Social Security has been a contentious issue since the early 1980s. The first major report, by the Greenspan commission of the early 1980s, resulted in changes in 1983 to the manner in which funds were handled and counted; no changes were made to the core of the program.[319] However, a trustees' report in 2000[320] concluded that Social Security could only pay full benefits until about 2037 and that the standard 75-year test of actuarial balance was not met. Because of the aging US population, the system cannot continue to function on a pay-as-you-go basis without radical changes.[321]

In May 2001, President George W. Bush, after winning the election in which reforming Social Security was a major issue, announced the establishment of a 16-member bipartisan commission to make recommendations for the reform of Social Security based on six guiding principles stipulated by the president. Four of the more significant guiding principles were that the entire Social Security surplus must be dedicated to Social Security only; payroll taxes must not be increased; the government must *not* invest Social Security funds in the stock market; and modernization must include individually controlled, voluntary personal retirement accounts, which will augment Social Security. The final report of the bipartisan committee[322] suggested three alternative models, with personal accounts being the central component of each model.[323] A system of voluntary personal accounts would give individuals the freedom to pursue higher rates of return on their Social Security contributions. The assets obtained would be owned by the individual and could be inherited. The amount eligible for personal accounts would depend on which of the three alternative models was selected. None of the suggested reforms has yet been implemented.

Canada Pension Plan: Leading by Example

The CPP was created in 1965 in order to supplement the existing old age security benefit. In order to induce provinces to participate in a national plan rather than create their own plans, the CPP was originally structured to allow each provincial government to borrow from the CPP at interest rates at least equal to the rate on long-term federal securities—which was significantly below the rate available to smaller provinces borrowing funds on the open market. All of the provinces except Quebec became a party to the CPP. Quebec established its own scheme, the QPP. The two plans are not integrated and transfers between them are not possible, but the plans are substantially similar apart from their respective investment policies. Until changes in the late 1990s, CPP funds were invested exclusively in provincial government bonds (that is, each province, other than Quebec, borrowed from the plan as originally proposed). QPP funds have always been managed by the Caisse, which was established by the Quebec government in 1965 specifically to manage QPP funds. Its investment mandate has included a requirement that it invest the funds in secure and high-yield investments that would contribute to the development of the provincial economy. Until recently, the QPP consistently enjoyed a higher rate of return on its investments than the CPP.

Both the CPP and QPP operate as pay-as-you-go schemes. Contributions are compulsory for almost all employed and self-employed persons between the ages of 18 and 69. Both are financed by a proportional payroll tax, with a minimum exemption level and an upper contribution limit. Employers and employees contribute equal amounts while self-employed persons contribute both the employer and the employee portions. Although the CPP generated surpluses during its early years, it has never operated as a fully funded program. Contributions form part of the consolidated revenue fund (accounted for in the Canada Pension Plan Account). As a result of the original agreement creating the CPP, changes to the plan require the support of the federal government and two-thirds of the participating provinces representing two-thirds of the population of Canada.

In the 1990s, it became necessary to make significant changes to contribution levels and investment practices of the CPP to address the plan's sustainability, due primarily to the aging of the workforce.[324] According to the chief actuary of the plan in 1996, without changes, the CPP would run out of money in less than 20 years.[325] On the basis of public consultations in the spring of 1996, the federal and provincial governments agreed to preserve the CPP but to strengthen its financing by moving it from pay-as-you-go to fuller financing, improve its investment practices, and reduce its costs.[326] Unlike the reforms proposed to US Social Security, a key element of the proposed reforms to the CPP was the extension of qualified investments by the plan to higher-risk, potentially higher-return investments, including public and private equities.

Legislation to implement these changes was introduced in 1997. The most significant changes included an increase in contribution rates and the establishment of the Canada Pension Plan Investment Board (CPPIB) as an independent investment corporation to invest excess contributions to the CPP and the proceeds from maturing bonds.[327] Under the legislation, contribution rates were increased from 5.6 percent in 1996 to 9.9 percent in 2003 and thereafter.[328] The CPPIB was established as an independent agency in order to ensure that investment decisions were made independent of political intervention. These changes were designed to increase the reserve fund of the CPP to five years (from the current two years and declining). In addition, the 1997 amendments reduced the federal-provincial review period of the CPP from five years to three years.[329]

The primary objective of the CPPIB is to manage the assets under its control "in the best interests of the contributors and beneficiaries under [the CPP]" and to "invest its assets with a view to achieving a maximum rate of return, without undue risk of loss, having regard to the factors that may affect the funding of the Canada Pension Plan and the ability of the Canada Pension Plan to meet its financial obligations."[330] The CPPIB is subject to the same foreign property limitations imposed on RPPs and RRSPs.[331] Accordingly, no more than 30 percent of the CPPIB's investments can be invested in foreign property. Unlike the mandate of the Caisse, the CPPIB has no "social investment" objectives in its mandate, apart from the foreign property limitation to which all RPPs are subject. This distinction is considered further below.

The 1997 legislation included a number of transitional measures. First, with respect to maturing provincial government bonds, the provincial governments have the option of compelling the CPP to acquire a replacement provincial bond of the same principal amount for a term not exceeding 20 years at open market rates.[332] Second, for the first three years, provinces will have access to 50 percent of new CPP funds that the CPPIB chooses to invest in bonds. After this three-year period, new CPP funds invested in provincial securities will be limited to the proportion of provincial bonds held by pension funds in general. Third, to ensure the smooth entry of CPP funds into the equity markets, all domestic equity investments would be selected passively, mirroring broad market indices, until the CPP was subject to its next evaluation.

Directors were appointed to the CPPIB in October 1998 and it held its first meeting in November 1998. It began receiving funds from the CPP in March 1999. As originally proposed, the first funds were invested in broad market indices. However, in December 1999, the federal and provincial finance ministers agreed to relax the domestic equity investment restriction from 100 percent passive to up to 50 percent active.[333] The regulations under the CPPIB Act contain a number of other investment restrictions that are in many respects similar to those imposed on employer-sponsored pension plans. For example:

- no more than 10 percent of the CPPIB's assets can be invested in one person;
- an investment in one parcel of real property cannot exceed 5 percent of the CPPIB's assets;
- aggregate investments in Canadian resource properties and real properties cannot exceed 25 percent of the CPPIB's assets; and
- the CPPIB cannot directly or indirectly hold more than 30 percent of the votes of a corporation.

The regulations also require the CPPIB to establish investment policies, to be reviewed at least once a year. According to its published guidelines, in establishing these investment policies, the CPPIB will take into account the makeup of the CPP assets still administered by the minister of finance. Since at that time the CPPIB was investing only the excess funds of the CPP (and any matured provincial government bonds that were not renewed), the original investment policy was to invest 100 percent in equities, with up to 30 percent in a broad range of foreign equities. Over time, as the CPPIB has built its management team, the investment policies have become more sophisticated. According to the guidelines dated April 10, 2002,[334] the permitted investment activities of the CPPIB include venture capital investment, with an allocation of up to 7 percent of the CPPIB's funds.[335]

As of March 31, 2002, the CPPIB controlled $14.3 billion of the CPP's $53.6 billion in assets. In 2003, legislation was passed to consolidate the asset management of all CPP assets in the CPPIB over a three-year period, to commence on a date to be fixed by the governor in council.[336] It is anticipated that the CPPIB will control assets of $125 to $130 billion by 2012, making it one of the largest pension asset investment managers in Canada.

The CPPIB announced its first commitments to private equity (including buyout funds and venture capital funds) in August 2001. At that time, it expected that its private equity commitments would grow to 10 percent of its total assets. By June 2002, $905 million had been committed to six Canadian private equity fund managers, of which $497 million was targeted at venture capital opportunities. In addition, $2 billion had been committed to US private equity fund managers, of which $375 million was targeted at venture capital opportunities.[337] These commitments will be drawn down over several years. As of March 31, 2002, $458 million, or 3.2 percent of the CPPIB's total assets, were invested in venture capital.

It is worth highlighting one significant distinction between the CPP, as reconstituted, and the QPP. As noted above, the CPPIB's sole criteria in choosing investments is to maximize the return to its members without substantial risk of loss. In contrast, the statutory investment mandate of the Caisse includes a social investment policy: investment that benefits the economic development of Quebec.[338] As Quebec premier Jean Lesage commented in 1965:

> The interests of Quebeckers go beyond the security of the money they set aside for their retirement. Such considerable assets should be used to stimulate

the development of the public and private sectors, so that Quebec's social
and economic objectives can be achieved quickly and effectively.

Briefly, the Caisse should not be considered only as an investment fund
like any other, like RRSP's, for instance, but as an instrument of growth, a
lever that is more powerful than anything we have had in this province
until now.[339]

The Caisse's investments have had a significant impact on the economy of
Quebec. It is an important investor in Quebec SMEs as well as real estate, and
in its early years it helped reduce the interest rate spread between Quebec and
Ontario debt. Lesage commented in a 1970 interview that Caisse "literally
saved the province from bankruptcy."[340] The Caisse is now one of the largest
asset managers in North America, with offices worldwide. It manages not only
pension funds from the Quebec public sector, but also pension funds outside
Quebec (and Canada) as well as mutual funds. Its total assets under management
at the end of its 2001 year were over $133 billion (of which the QPP represented
approximately $15 billion). While its overall return between 1995 and 2000
exceeded that of the CPP, it has underperformed Canada's large pension funds.[341]

The QPP has been the subject of intense criticism in recent years for
putting politics ahead of the interests of its investors—for example, in its underwriting of high-cost takeovers to prevent the loss of Quebec ownership of
businesses.[342] Many have also questioned the amount invested in Quebec SMEs,
particularly in the retail and fashion trade and in telecom companies, as well as
the significant cost overruns in the construction of its new head office premises
in Montreal. On December 2, 2002, Henri-Paul Rousseau, the recently appointed
chief executive officer of the Caisse, announced sweeping changes, including
widespread layoffs, office closures, and a consolidation of its private equity
division, reducing the number of subsidiaries from six to three.[343] Rousseau
commented that the Caisse must focus on the needs of its depositors rather than
on the economic development of Quebec.[344]

Whether or not the CPPIB should include the economic development of
Canada in its investment mandate was raised in the House of Commons when
the CPPIB Act was introduced.[345] In the end, no economic or social mandate was
imposed on the CPPIB. That is the appropriate result for a number of reasons.
First and most important, the change in investment policy of the CPP was
prompted by the financial problems that it faced: it is inappropriate to impose on
the next generation of the Canadian workforce not only the full cost of insuring
their own retirement, but also the retirement of their predecessors. Without
question, the sole mandate for the CPPIB should be to maximize the return of
the beneficiaries of the CPP in a prudent manner while keeping the contribution
limits as low as possible. Second, the CPPIB must avoid political interference in
its investment decisions. Third, the provinces, which also have a significant say
in the CPP, would likely demand that investment be made in each province
proportionate (at least) to the contributions to the plan raised from that province,
a requirement that would be extremely unwieldy to manage. Finally, although

not one of the goals when the CPPIB was established, if the CPP's venture investing is to act as a signal for employer-sponsored pension plans, then the assets of the CPP should be managed in the same way as the assets of an employer-sponsored pension plan, which is essentially what the CPPIB Act and regulations provide. The foreign property limitation imposed on the CPPIB is the only economic constraint imposed on the board, similar to that imposed on all RPPs (as well as RRSPs). The foreign property limitation may be considered a loose proxy for an "invest in Canada" mandate, although it is highly porous.[346] It is also a rule that has attracted criticism from pension funds generally and, recently, by the CPP.[347]

Although investment in Canadian SMEs is not a specific mandate of the CPPIB, it has made significant private equity investments (in terms of dollars committed) as part of its diversified portfolio. The CPP's venture capital investments are similar to US pension fund venture capital commitments. It is not actively managing its venture capital portfolio; rather, it is investing in and through various private VCFs. The fact that it is not required to invest in venture capital may signal to other pension funds that venture capital is an appropriate investment. So far, few Canadian pension funds consider venture capital to be an appropriate investment. Compelling the CPP to invest in SMEs, or indeed in Canada, would distort the signal sent to other pension funds to follow suit.

If the signalling provided by the CPP does not result in an increase in venture capital investment by pension funds in Canada, the federal and provincial governments should consider changes to the VCF programs discussed in chapter 6 so that they target pension fund investment—for example, through the use of refundable tax credits or equity guarantees. In effect, the government should be prepared to underwrite some of the risk of pension investment in venture capital in the short term in order to attract pension funds as long-term investors. Underwriting pension fund risk would certainly be more appropriate to the long-term health of the venture capital fund industry than the continued reliance on LSVCCs.

There is one caveat that I must acknowledge. There is a concern that pension funds are not appropriate venture capital fund investors because they are the primary driving force behind the increased size of VCFs and the consequent larger investments per portfolio company. In addition, pension fund managers exert pressure for earlier cash distributions, which perhaps increase the speed at which VCFs drive portfolio companies to market (through initial public offerings). That is, institutional investors have exacerbated the funding gap applicable to smaller businesses and, to some extent, have added an "im" to patient capital. These factors were certainly all present during the growth of the US formal venture capital industry through the 1980s and 1990s, although it is not clear whether pension fund investment was causal or coincidental. Further research is essential in this respect.

Notes

1   See chapter 2, table 2.3. In 1981, individuals and families accounted for slightly more than 1 percent more capital than pension funds.

2   See Mary Macdonald and John Perry, *Pension Funds and Venture Capital: The Critical Links Between Savings, Investment, Technology, and Jobs* (Ottawa: Science Council of Canada, 1985). See also Kirk Falconer, *Prudence, Patience and Jobs: Pension Investment in a Changing Canadian Economy—Technical Report* (Ottawa: Canadian Labour Market and Productivity Centre, 1999). The lack of pension fund investment in Canada was also commented on by Paul Martin, then minister of finance, in a speech to members of the Canadian Venture Capital Association and the Toronto Stock Exchange in May 2002: Canada, Department of Finance, *Release* no. 2002-040, May 21, 2002.

3   Private sector statistics are prepared by the Employee Benefit Research Institute and are available from the EBRI Web site: http://www.ebri.org/. Statistics on public sector pension plans are prepared by the US Census Bureau and are available from the Bureau's Web site: http://www.census.gov/govs/www/retire.html.

4   A trusteed pension fund is a fund established according to the terms of a trust agreement between the employer (or plan sponsor) and an individual or corporate trustee. The trustee is responsible for the administration of the fund and/or the investment of the monies. The employer is responsible for the adequacy of the fund to pay the promised benefits. Trusteed pension funds make up over 68 percent of registered pension plans (RPPs). The remaining RPPs come from government consolidated revenue funds (covering federal public servants, the RCMP, the military, and certain provincial plans) (24 percent), pension funds deposited in total with insurance companies (7 percent), and government of Canada annuities (0.05 percent).

5   Pension fund investment in venture capital increased significantly between 2000 and 2002, comprising 29 percent, 44 percent, and 16 percent of Canadian venture capital investment in 2000, 2001, and 2002, respectively. However, these figures mask the limited number of pension funds actually making such investments. For example, one pension fund accounted for over 92 percent of pension fund investment in 2001. See chapter 2, text accompanying note 84. In 2003, pension fund investment dropped to less than 9 percent of new venture capital investments in Canada.

6   In the United States, qualified plans include three types of qualified asset accumulation plans: pension plans, profit-sharing plans, and stock bonus plans. In Canada, RPPs and deferred profit-sharing plans are governed by separate provisions in the Income Tax Act, RSC 1985, c. 1 (5th Supp.), as amended (herein referred to as "ITA" or "the Act"). There is no specific regime applicable to stock bonus plans, although the rules in ITA section 7 (also applicable to employee stock options) and ITA paragraphs 110(1)(d) and (d.1) apply to stock acquired pursuant to a stock bonus plan. Employee stock option plans are considered separately in chapter 4.

7   In both countries, the tax legislation contains myriad provisions that deal with non-registered or non-qualified plans. As discussed below, these rules are designed to remove the tax advantages otherwise enjoyed by registered or qualified plans.

8   For example, in the United States, state public sector pension plans are not governed by the primary pension fund legislation, the federal Employee Retirement Income Security Act of 1974, infra note 13. In Canada, a number of federal and provincial public sector pension plans are governed by legislation specific to the plan, in addition to the more general federal or provincial pension legislation: see infra notes 115, 116, and 118.

9   Employee Benefit Research Institute, *Fundamentals of Employee Benefit Programs*, 4th ed. (Washington, DC: Employee Benefit Research Institute, 1990), 39.

10   In the early 20th century, certain groups sought to impose a moral obligation on employers to provide pensions: "From the standpoint of the whole system of social economy, no employer has a right to engage men in an occupation that exhausts the individual's industrial life in ten, twenty, or forty years, and then leave the remnant floating on society at large as a derelict at sea": Lee Welling Squier, *Old Age Dependency in the United States: A Complete Survey of the Pension Movement* (New York: Macmillan, 1912), 272. This concept of compensation for depreciated human capital was adopted particularly by labour groups in the coal and steel industries. Until the late 1940s, however, labour unions were indifferent to the pension movement and at times hostile to it, viewing pensions as an anti-union paternalistic device used by employers to suppress wages. Then, in 1948, in the midst of labour negotiations in which it was difficult to justify wage increases, the National Labor Relations Board ruled that pension benefits were a bargainable issue under the Labor-Management Relations Act of 1947. This decision was upheld by the Seventh Circuit Court of Appeals in 1949: *Inland Steel Co. v. National Labor Relations Board*, 170 F. 2d 247 (1948); certiorari denied, 336 US 960 (1949). Since then, labour unions have been strong proponents of the private pension movement.

11   The Depression wiped out many people's life savings and created significant insecurity across the country. The resultant economic reforms included the introduction of the federal Old-Age, Survivors, and Disability Insurance (OASDI) program in the Social Security Act of 1935, infra note 312. The increase in employer-sponsored pension plans was to some extent driven by a societal expectation that employers would share the burden of ensuring that individuals have sufficient income for their retirement years.

12   Revenue Act of 1942, Pub. L. no. 77-753, enacted on October 21, 1942; 56 Stat. 798. The Revenue Act of 1921 exempted interest income of stock bonus and profit-sharing plans from current taxation. The Revenue Act of 1928 permitted employers to deduct a reasonable amount in excess of the amount necessary to fund current pension liabilities.

13   Pub. L. no. 93-406, enacted on August 31, 1974; 88 Stat. 829 (herein referred to as "ERISA"). ERISA gives jurisdiction over private pension plans to both the Department of Labor and Treasury (whose jurisdiction is assumed by the Internal Revenue Service [IRS]). Title I of ERISA, discussed in greater detail below, is applicable to all employee benefit plans, including welfare plans (medical, death, disability, etc.) and pension plans (unless prescribed to be excluded), but excluding government plans and church plans. Title II (which amended the Revenue Code of 1954) deals with tax matters and pertains primarily to qualified plans; it contains similar provisions to title I with respect to participation, vesting, and

funding. Thus, the term "pension plan" has different meanings in the context of titles I and II. In title II, it is limited to the three types of qualified asset accumulation plans recognized by the Internal Revenue Code of 1986, as amended (herein referred to as "IRC" or "the Code"): pension plans, profit-sharing plans, and stock bonus plans. Title I includes these plans as well as unqualified plans that provide retirement income or result in the deferral of income. Title III of ERISA deals with jurisdiction, administration, and enforcement. Title IV introduced a program of pension plan benefits insurance, administered through the Pension Benefit Guaranty Corporation at the Department of Labor.

14   Pub. L. no. 87-792, enacted on October 10, 1962; 76 Stat. 809.

15   Both qualified and non-qualified plans are considered in detail in Boris I. Bittker and Lawrence Lokken, *Federal Taxation of Income, Estates and Gifts*, 3d ed., vol. 3 (Valhalla, NY: Warren, Gorham & Lamont, 2001), part 8, at chapters 60 and 61.

16   IRC section 457, enacted in 1978, applies to plans of state and local governments and tax-exempt organizations. For such employers, the deferral of the deduction is irrelevant since their income is tax-exempt. Under IRC section 457, if the plan of such an employer does not meet the qualification requirements of an eligible deferred compensation plan (or a qualified plan), compensation deferred under the plan is taxed when the employee's rights vest, even if actual payment is deferred until retirement. Thus, IRC section 457 plans fit somewhere between non-qualified plans and qualified plans. See, generally, Bittker and Lokken, supra note 15, at paragraph 60.2.3.

17   See, generally, Boris I. Bittker and Martin J. McMahon Jr., *Federal Income Taxation of Individuals*, 2d ed. (Boston: Warren, Gorham & Lamont, 1995), paragraph 40.2.

18   See, generally, Ridgeley A. Scott, "Rabbis and Other Top Hats: The Great Escape" (1993) vol. 43, no. 1 *Catholic University Law Review* 1-58. As Bittker and Lokken suggest, rabbi trusts and secular trusts "distinguish between employees in a paradoxical way: Those with the least need for security, employees of employers solid as the Rock of Gibraltar, can rely on the employer's unsecured promise to pay deferred compensation and postpone its recognition. Employees working for a shaky employer, however, can protect their financial interest only by escrow or similar arrangements that are fatal for tax deferral." Bittker and Lokken, supra note 15, at 60-12.

19   IRC section 404(a)(1).

20   IRC section 402(a).

21   IRC section 501(a).

22   IRC section 512.

23   IRC section 415(b). The $160,000 limit is decreased where the benefit begins before age 62 and is increased where the benefit begins after age 65.

24   Pub. L. no. 95-600, enacted on November 6, 1978; 92 Stat. 2763.

25   Form 5305-SEP.

26   IRC section 402(h)(2).

27   IRC section 408(k)(5). Proposed regulations suggest that the formula can be amended each year: prop. Treas. reg. section 1.408-7(e)(2).

28   IRC section 408(k)(2).

29 IRC section 408(k)(6).

30 IRC section 408(k)(4). The withdrawal is subject to income taxes and potentially penalty taxes. See infra notes 142-144 and accompanying text.

31 From 1980 to 1994, 401(k) plans accounted for about 77 percent of the net increase in all private pension plans.

32 IRC section 401(k)(2).

33 IRC section 401(m).

34 IRC section 402(g)(1).

35 Pub. L. no. 107-16, enacted on June 7, 2001; 115 Stat. 38.

36 IRC sections 415(c) and (d).

37 Pub. L. no. 104-188, enacted on August 20, 1996; 110 Stat. 1755, sections 1421-1422. See, generally, IRC section 408(p).

38 IRC sections 408(p)(2)(C)(i) and (D).

39 IRC section 408(p)(2)(E).

40 IRC section 408(p)(2)(A)(iii). The employer can reduce the 3 percent limit only under certain conditions: IRC section 408(p)(2)(C)(ii).

41 IRC section 408(p)(2)(B). The non-elective contribution is limited to 2 percent of the maximum compensation limit in IRC section 407(a)(17), being $200,000 (as adjusted for inflation). The non-elective limit therefore cannot exceed $4,000.

42 The one limitation is that qualified plans cannot invest in collectibles: IRC section 408(m). A "collectible" is defined as any work of art, any rug or antique, any metal or gem (other than gold, silver, platinum, or palladium bullion), any stamp or coin (other than specified coins), any alcoholic beverage, or any other tangible personal property prescribed by regulation. Prescribed tangible personal property (see prop. Treas. reg. section 1.408-10) includes musical instruments, historical objects (documents, clothes, etc.), and any other tangible personal property that the commissioner determines is a "collectible."

43 Infra note 73. IRC section 4975 uses the term "disqualified person" rather than "party in interest" to describe the person with which the plan enters into a prohibited transaction. The definitions are substantially similar although there are some important differences. For example, whereas every employee of an employer-sponsor is a party in interest under ERISA, only a "highly compensated employee (earning 10 percent or more of the yearly wages of an employer)" is a disqualified person under IRC section 4975.

44 The taxable period begins on the day that the prohibited transaction occurs and ends at the earliest of the mailing of a notice of deficiency for the tax, assessment of the tax, and correction of the transaction.

45 Investment in employer-sponsor securities is permitted in the same circumstances as is permitted under ERISA: IRC section 4975(d)(14), referring to ERISA section 408(e). Thus, a qualified plan is generally permitted to invest not more than 10 percent of the plan assets in employer securities.

46 See the definitions of "employee" and "employer" in IRC section 401(c), applicable for 401(a) and 401(k) plans. The extended definition of employee (to include self-employed persons) is adopted for the purpose of SEPs (see IRC section 408(k)(7)) and SIMPLEs (see IRC section 408(p)(6)(B)).

47	For many years, Keogh plans had lower contribution limits than employer-sponsored plans. The disparity between the two was eliminated by the Tax Equity and Fiscal Responsibility Act of 1982, Pub. L. no. 97-248, enacted on September 3, 1982; 96 Stat. 324. Under this act, the contribution limit for Keogh plans was raised while that of various employer-sponsored plans was reduced.

48	For a more detailed discussion of the technical aspects of IRAs, see Bittker and Lokken, supra note 15, at paragraphs 62.3 and 62.4.

49	These requirements include limitations on the amount that can be contributed in any given year and how the trustee can administer the fund. The limitations include: funds cannot be invested in life insurance contracts; the interest of the individual in the balance of the account is non-forfeitable; and the assets of the trust cannot be commingled with other property except in a common trust fund or common investment fund.

50	These requirements include: the contract is not transferable by the owner; the premiums cannot be fixed or exceed the maximum dollar amount specified; and the entire interest of the owner is non-forfeitable.

51	IRC section 408(c).

52	Bittker and Lokken, supra note 15, at 62-49.

53	IRC sections 219(b)(1) and 408(o).

54	Supra note 35.

55	Compensation is essentially the earned income of an employed or self-employed person. There are special rules in IRC section 219(c) for spouses who file a joint return and the compensation (if any) of one spouse is less than the compensation of the other spouse. In these circumstances, the spouse with the lower compensation (or no compensation) is entitled to make a deductible IRA contribution equal to the lower of the dollar limit for the year (for example, $3,000 for 2004) and the combined compensation of the two spouses less any deductible IRA contributions and Roth IRA contributions (infra notes 64-68) made by the other spouse.

56	For years after 2002, the maximum contribution is increased by $500 ($1,000 for years after 2005) for individuals who are at least 50 years old at the end of the year.

57	IRC section 219(g). "Active participant" is defined in IRC section 219(g)(5). An individual is an active participant in a qualified plan only if benefits accrue to the individual during the taxable year. Benefits accrue under a defined benefit plan if the individual "is not excluded under the eligibility provisions of the plan for the plan year ending within the individual's taxable year." Benefits accrue under a defined contribution plan if the "employer or employee contributions or forfeitures are allocated to such individual's account" for the plan year ending within the individual's taxable year. See Bittker and Lokken, supra note 15, at 62-55 to 62-56 and references therein.

    The reduction is determined by a formula in IRC section 219(g)(2). If an individual's "adjusted gross income" exceeds an "applicable dollar amount," the contribution limit is reduced by the same proportion of the contribution limit that the excess is of $10,000 ($20,000 for a joint return where both spouses are active participants for 2007 and thereafter). The applicable dollar amount depends on the marital status of the individual and, if married, whether the individual files a joint or separate return. For an unmarried individual, the applicable dollar amount is $34,000 for 2002 (increasing to $50,000 in 2005 and thereafter). For a married individual filing a joint return, the applicable dollar amount is $54,000 for 2002 (increasing to $80,000 in 2005 and thereafter). For a married individual filing a separate return, the applicable dollar amount is zero (unless the individuals are living separate and apart in the year). Finally, for an individual who is not an active participant but files a joint return with someone who is, the applicable dollar amount is $150,000. Prior to 1997, active participant status was attributed from one spouse to the other, thus limiting the deductible contribution of both spouses.

The formula in IRC section 219(g)(2) applies as follows (in 2004). An unmarried individual who is an active participant in a qualified pension plan and has an adjusted gross income in excess of $44,000 cannot make a deductible contribution to an IRA in 2002 and the deductible amount is reduced for adjusted gross income between $34,000 and $44,000. A married individual who is an active participant in a qualified plan and who files a joint return cannot make a deductible contribution if the individual's adjusted gross income (including that of the spouse) exceeds $64,000 and the deductible amount is reduced for adjusted gross income between $54,000 and $64,000. A married individual who is not an active participant in a qualified plan but files a joint return with a spouse who is an active participant cannot make a deductible contribution if the individual's adjusted gross income (including that of the spouse) exceeds $160,000 and the deductible amount is reduced for adjusted gross income between $150,000 and $160,000.

58   It is unlikely that this deferral is sufficient to attract many non-deductible IRA contributions because the same advantage can be created through other investment vehicles: see Bittker and Lokken, supra note 15, at 62-58, note 57. In situations in which an individual is prohibited from making a deductible IRA contribution, the individual can make the equivalent contribution to a Roth IRA (assuming that the individual's adjusted gross income is less than the thresholds applicable for contributions to a Roth IRA), in which case income generated in the Roth IRA is also generally excluded from tax on distribution. See the discussion of Roth IRAs, infra notes 64-68 and accompanying text.

59   IRC section 4973.

60   IRC section 408(e).

61   IRC section 408(d)(1).

62   IRC section 401(a)(9). The annuitant is subject to a 50 percent excise tax if distributions from an IRA are less than the minimum required distribution for the year: IRC section 4974.

63   IRC section 72(t). See infra notes 143-144 and accompanying text.

64   Pub. L. no. 105-34, enacted on August 5, 1997; 111 Stat. 788.

65   The rules governing Roth IRAs are found in IRC section 408A.

66   IRC section 408A(a) provides that a Roth IRA is treated in the same manner as an individual retirement plan except as provided in section 408A. Thus, the earnings of a Roth IRA are also exempt from tax.

67   IRC section 408A(d). A qualified distribution is a distribution that is made not earlier than the fifth taxable year following the year in which a Roth IRA contribution was first made by the individual and is made: (1) on or after the date the

individual reaches age 59½; (2) on or after the death of the individual; (3) on account of the individual's disability; or (4) as a qualified first-time homebuyer distribution.

68   The contribution limit (for example, $3,000 for 2004) is reduced by 1 percent for every $150 ($100 for a joint return or a married individual filing a separate return) of adjusted gross income in excess of $95,000 ($150,000 for a joint return and zero for a married individual filing a separate return). The contribution limit disappears when adjusted gross income reaches $110,000 ($160,000 for a joint return).

69   Like employer-sponsored plans, IRAs cannot invest in collectibles: see IRC section 408(m) and supra note 42. An investment in collectibles is considered to be a distribution from the IRA.

70   The Treasury department enforces compliance for qualified plans through disqualification and excise taxes.

71   ERISA section 514.

72   ERISA section 3(2).

73   A fiduciary cannot allow the plan to engage in various activities, including sales, loans, the provision of goods or services, or the transfer of any assets of the plan, with a "party in interest." A "party in interest" is defined broadly in ERISA section 3(14) and includes: the plan's fiduciaries; persons providing services to the plan; the employer of any employees covered by the plan; a person who controls or is controlled by the employer; and an employee, officer, director, or 10 percent shareholder of the employer.

74   ERISA section 407. Certain qualified pension plans (for example, an individual account plan that is an employee stock ownership plan) may invest more than 10 percent.

75   However, the vesting requirements under ERISA are not as beneficial to employees as those in Canada: see infra note 122. Under ERISA, employee contributions vest in full immediately. However, the vesting of employer contributions must meet one of two standards (ERISA section 203(a)): either full vesting of accrued benefits after the employee has accumulated five years of recognized service; or at least 20 percent vested after three years with an additional 20 percent vesting in each of the following four years (the "three-to-seven" standard).
      Under the Internal Revenue Code, qualified plans must generally limit distributions to the following events: death, retirement, separation from service, or disability: Treas. reg. section 1.401-1(b)(1)(i). A pension plan that permits distributions at other times may lose qualified status.

76   State public sector pension plans are regulated by state legislation. For example, the California Public Employees' Retirement System (CalPERS), one of the largest employer pension plans in the United States, is governed by the California Government Code, title 2, division 5, part 3. The fiduciary obligations of its board members are set out in the Government Code, section 20151. It provides in part that "the board and its officers and employees shall discharge their duties with respect to this system solely in the interest of the participants and beneficiaries ... (c) [b]y investing with the care, skill, prudence, and diligence under the circumstances then prevailing that a prudent person acting in a like capacity and familiar with those matters would use in the conduct of an enterprise of a like

character and with like aims." Section 20190 provides that "[t]he board has exclusive control of the investment of the retirement fund. Except as otherwise restricted by the California Constitution and by law, the board may, in its discretion, invest the assets of the fund through the purchase, holding, or sale thereof of any investment, financial instrument, or financial transaction when the investment, financial instrument, or financial transaction is prudent in the informed opinion of the board." In 2001, CalPERS was the top-ranked government pension fund by market venture capital investments, totalling over $2 billion. Its total private equity investments were over $7.1 billion out of total pension plan assets of $172.5 billion: Thomson Financial Venture Economics, *2001 Investment Benchmark Reports: LP Analytics* (New York: Thomson Financial Securities Data Publishing, 2001), 21.

77   ERISA section 4.

78   29 Code of Federal Regulations (herein referred to as "CFR"), section 2510.3-3(b).

79   An employer-provided IRA is exempt from ERISA provided that employee participation is voluntary, the employer makes no contributions, and various other administrative conditions are met: see 29 CFR section 2510.3-2(d).

80   The first retirement plan for federal civil servants was introduced in 1870. The first industrial plan, for the Grand Trunk Railway, was introduced in 1874.

81   SC 1887, c. 21. Under this act, employees of federally chartered organizations could establish pension plans to which the employer could contribute.

82   SC 1908, c. 5. This act created a program under which individuals could provide for their old age through the purchase of government annuities.

83   The Income War Tax Act, SC 1917, c. 28, section 3, included in income the "profits from a trade or commercial or financial or other business." "Profits" was not (and has never been) a defined term in the tax legislation but has always been understood to be a net concept, permitting the deduction of expenses reasonably incurred for the purpose of earning income from business. In *British Insulated and Helsby Cables v. Atherton*, [1926] AC 205, the House of Lords denied the deduction of a lump-sum payment to establish a pension fund for employees. In his judgment (agreeing with this conclusion), Lord Carson stated (at 225): "It is not disputed that an annual sum contributed to the pension fund on an actuarial basis for the purposes of making the fund solvent for paying the pensions of the older members of the staff would be a proper deduction in arriving at the balance of profits and gains, it would be an ordinary business expense. Nor, I think, can it be disputed that if at any time the fund threatened to become insolvent after it was started a sum paid to prevent such insolvency would be a proper disbursement."

84   SC 1919, c. 55, section 2.

85   The maximum annual limit for employees was set at $300 (SC 1936, c. 38, section 5) and for employers was set at $300 per employee, with the total not to exceed 5 percent of payroll (SC 1940-41-42, c. 18, section 6). These limits have been amended on numerous occasions. In 1938, the Income War Tax Act was also amended to permit the deduction of employer contributions recognizing the past service of employees.

86   Although the cost of annuities increased dramatically in 1948 and sales were discontinued in 1975: Statistics Canada, *Canada's Retirement Income Program:*

A Statistical Overview, 1990-2000, catalogue no. 74-507-XIE, 48. In 1999, government of Canada annuities had a value of $330 million, or 0.05 percent of the total value of RPPs: Statistics Canada, Pension Plans in Canada, January 1, 2000, catalogue no. 74-401-XPB, 15, table 2.

87　Such individuals were at a distinct disadvantage compared with employees with employer pension plans. The latter benefited from a deduction for contributions (as did their employers) and the income in the plan accumulated tax-free. The former had to save for retirement out of after-tax earnings and the income earned on their savings was also subject to tax.

88　Since 1990, DPSPs have not been permitted to accept contributions from employees.

89　ITA subsections 147.2(1) and 147(8), respectively.

90　ITA paragraphs 149(1)(o) and (s).

91　Employer contributions to RPPs and DPSPs are not considered taxable benefits (ITA subparagraph 6(1)(a)(i)) at the time contributions are made. Benefits received from an RPP are included in income under ITA subparagraph 56(1)(a)(i); amounts received from a DPSP are included in income under ITA subsection 147(10).

92　For an overview of the Canadian tax rules applicable to these non-registered plans, see Rob Weil, "Deferred Income Arrangements—A Decade of Change," in Deferred Income Arrangements: A Practitioner's Guide to Proper Tax Planning (Toronto: Canadian Tax Foundation, 1997), tab 2; and William Johnston, "Taxation of Non-Registered Pension Plans," in Income Tax and Goods and Services Tax Planning for Executive and Employee Compensation and Retirement, 1991 Corporate Management Tax Conference (Toronto: Canadian Tax Foundation, 1992), 9:1-17.

　　ITA section 144 contains rules applicable to an "employees profit sharing plan." Unlike a DPSP, an employees' profit-sharing plan is not a method to defer tax. Section 144 is intended to provide certainty regarding the income tax consequences of contributions to such a plan, allocations to employees, income earned on trust assets, and distributions from the plan. Although the plan itself is exempt from tax, all amounts (including both employer contributions and plan income) allocated to an employee absolutely or contingently are included in the employee's income.

93　There are other important distinctions between the two. For example, RPPs are restricted as to the types of assets in which they can invest by "qualified investment" provisions and foreign property limitations, discussed below.

94　See Peter W. Hogg, Joanne E. Magee, and Jinyan Li, Principles of Canadian Income Tax Law, 4th ed. (Toronto: Carswell, 1999), 372.

95　Except to the extent that the funds are locked in because they were transferred from an RPP, as discussed below.

96　ITA regulation 8301(1) defines an individual's PA in terms of the individual's "pension credits" under DPSPs and under the benefit provisions of RPPs. Essentially, the pension credit under a DPSP or defined contribution RPP is the amount contributed in the year to the plan—in the former case, by the employer (since employees cannot contribute to a DPSP) and in the latter case by both the employer and employee. The pension credit under a defined contribution RPP is the assumed cost of providing pension benefits accrued to the individual in the year under the plan. The assumed cost of providing benefits is determined by a formula: 9 times the defined benefit earned in the year (in accordance with the RPP's formula) less $600 (ITA regulation 8301(6)). The "factor of 9" is arbitrary and intended to equate the value of a pension benefit earned today with the pension that is ultimately payable (see infra note 98). The $600 deduction is also arbitrary, and is designed to give members of a defined benefit RPP that has a generous formula at least some RRSP contribution room. The PA is subtracted from a member's comprehensive contribution limit to determine his or her maximum RRSP contribution for the following year. The manner in which an individual's PA is calculated is beyond the scope of this study. See, generally, Canada Revenue Agency, Guide T4084, "Employers Pension Adjustment Guide."

97 ITA subsection 147.1(1), definition of "money purchase limit."

98 The money purchase limit for defined contribution RPPs and the defined benefit limit for defined benefit RPPs were originally based on a number of premises: first, that the maximum tax-assisted pension benefit should be limited to 2 percent per year of the individual's average earnings from his or her best three years multiplied by the number of years of service, to a maximum of 35 years; second, that the maximum defined benefit after 35 years should be restricted to $60,278, being 2.5 times the average wage (defined in ITA subsection 147.1(1)) in 1976, when these amounts were originally determined; and third, that it takes $9 currently to buy $1 of pension benefit per year at age 65. Thus, to fund $60,278, the maximum benefit under a defined benefit plan that can be accrued each year is $1,722.22 ($60,278/35) and the maximum amount contributed annually to fund this benefit is $15,500 ($1,722.22 × 9). Accordingly, the maximum annual contribution to a defined contribution RPP should be $15,500. In both cases, however, since the benefit is capped at 2 percent of earnings, the annual contribution is limited to 18 percent (9 × 2 percent) of earnings.

Measures to reform tax-assisted retirement savings were proposed in the mid-1980s and were set out in draft legislation released on March 28, 1988, to take effect commencing in 1989. The figures for maximum contribution levels and maximum benefit levels were fixed at that time, subject to a phase-in period. The implementation date was deferred two years so that the reforms first became effective January 1, 1991, with the phase-in period running from 1991 to 1994 (when the $15,500 limit was to be reached) and thereafter the amount would increase based on increases in the average wage. The defined benefit limit of $1,722.22 was effectively frozen until 1995, when it would increase with the average wage in the same manner as the annual limit.

Since 1991, the rules have been amended a number of times. In 1992, the maximum limit of $15,500 was delayed until 1995. In 1995, the maximum limit was reduced to $13,500 for 1996, increased back to $15,500 over the following two years, and thereafter indexed. In 1996, the $13,500 limit was frozen until 2002, increased over the following two years to $15,500, and thereafter indexed. Throughout this entire period, the defined benefit limit for defined contribution plans has remained $1,722.22 (since it was based on a $15,500 per annum defined contribution limit in any event). It was then increased in the 2003 federal budget, as discussed in the text.

99 SC 2003, c. 15, section 84(1).

100 ITA paragraphs 147.1(8)(a) and 147.2(1)(a).

101   ITA paragraph 147.2(4)(a).

102   ITA subsection 147.2(2).

103   ITA paragraph 147.2(4)(a) and regulations 8501(1)(b) and 8503(4)(a).

104   ITA subsection 147(5.1).

105   ITA subsection 146(1), definition of "RRSP dollar limit."

106   An RPP may lose its registered status in certain circumstances, including where it becomes a revocable plan (ITA paragraph 147.1(11)(c)). A plan becomes a revocable plan if, among other things, it acquires a prohibited investment as defined in regulation 8514(1), or an investment prohibited under the pension legislation (federal or provincial) governing the plan (ITA regulations 8501(2)(a) and 8502(h)(i) and (ii)). Under regulation 8514(1), a prohibited investment includes a share or debt of: an employer who participates in the plan, a person connected with the employer, a member of the plan, or a person who does not deal at arm's length with any such person. Publicly listed shares and certain debt instruments are not prohibited investments, as set out in regulation 8514(2). The prohibited investment restrictions in the Income Tax Act are similar to the related-party transaction limitations in ERISA (supra note 73).

107   ITA subsection 146(1), definition of "qualified investment," paragraph (d) includes prescribed investments. Prescribed investments are set out in regulation 4900 et seq.

108   ITA subsection 146(10). Where the RRSP subsequently disposes of the non-qualifying asset, the annuitant is entitled to deduct the lesser of the amount previously included in the taxpayer's income under subsection 146(10) and the proceeds of disposition of the non-qualifying asset: ITA subsection 146(6).

109   ITA subsection 146(10.1).

110   In effect, the part XI.1 tax is limited to investments that became non-qualifying at some point after the RRSP acquired them. Because these investments were qualifying when they were acquired, ITA subsection 146(10) does not apply.

111   ITA subsection 198(1).

112   ITA subsection 198(2).

113   ITA subsection 198(3).

114   Infra notes 241-242 and accompanying text.

115   The Pension Benefits Act, 1965, SO 1965, c. 96. The current legislation is the Pension Benefits Act, RSO 1990, c. P.8, as amended (herein referred to as "PBA"). The PBA applies to every pension plan (whether or not an RPP) that is provided for persons employed in Ontario (PBA section 3), unless specifically excluded by regulation: see infra note 118.

116   Pension Benefits Standards Act, SC 1966-67, c. 92. The current legislation is the Pension Benefits Standards Act, 1985, RSC 1985, c. 32 (2d Supp.), as amended (herein referred to as "PBSA"). The PBSA applies to pension plans of employees employed in connection with the operation of any work, undertaking, or business that is within the legislative authority of the Parliament of Canada, other than plans for employees of Her Majesty in right of Canada and certain other excluded plans (see infra note 118). Effectively excluded from the PBSA are employees with any board, commission, corporation, or other body forming part of the federal public

service, whose pension is governed by the Public Service Superannuation Act, RSC 1985, c. P-36, as amended. Management of federal public sector pension funds is undertaken primarily by the Public Sector Pension Investment Board, which is governed by the Public Sector Pension Investment Act, SC 1999, c. 34. Section 8 of the Public Sector Pension Investment Board Regulations, SOR/2000-77, as amended, provides that in selecting investments, "the Board shall evaluate them having regard to the overall rate of return and risk of loss of the entire portfolio of investments held by the Board." This policy is consistent with the investment policies governing pension funds under the PBA and PBSA described herein.

117   The legislation in Prince Edward Island has never been proclaimed in force.

118   Both the PBA and the PBSA (or regulations thereunder) exclude certain plans from their application. For example, section 47(3) of the general regulations under the PBA (RRO 1990, reg. 909, as amended (herein referred to as "PBA reg.")) lists eight exemptions to the PBA and regulations, including: retirement compensation arrangements, supplemental pension plans (that is, plans that provide only benefits that exceed the maximum benefit limits specified in the Income Tax Act for RPPs), and specific plans such as the Legislative Assembly Retirement Allowances Act, the MPPs Pension Act, 1996, and the pension for provincial judges. Section 4(2) of the PBSA excludes from its application profit-sharing plans under ITA sections 144 and 147, arrangements that provide a "retiring allowance" as defined in the Income Tax Act, and prescribed arrangements.

119   The discussion in this section is limited to the PBSA and the PBA. A good summary of provisions in other provinces as well as the federal and provincial legislation and regulations can be found in William M. Mercer Limited, *The Mercer Pension Manual* (Toronto: Carswell) (looseleaf).

120   Under the PBSA, "pensionable age" is defined as the earliest age at which a pension benefit (other than a benefit in respect of a disability) is payable under the terms of the pension plan without consent of the plan's administrator and without reduction by reason of early retirement (PBSA section 2(1), definition of "pensionable age"). In Ontario, the normal retirement age must be specified in the plan submitted for registration and cannot be later than one year after the attainment of age 65 (PBA section 35(1)).

121   Under both the federal and the Ontario regimes, members are entitled to immediate pension benefits if they retire within 10 years of the normal retirement age: PBSA section 16(2); PBA section 41.

122   Under both the PBSA and the PBA, an employee's benefits vest once the employee has been a member of the plan for two years. Vesting requirements were more stringent before January 1, 1987.

123   PBSA section 17; PBA section 37.

124   PBSA section 18(1)(c); PBA section 63(1).

125   For example, a cash withdrawal may be permitted if a mental or physical disability is likely to considerably shorten the employee's life expectancy. In some jurisdictions, including Ontario but not Canada, excess employee contributions may be returned as a lump sum.

126   ITA subparagraph 56(1)(a)(i).

127   PBSA section 26(1); PBA section 42(1).

128   The federal legislation permits transfers to a locked-in RRSP or a life income fund (LIF) (a non-commutable RRIF): PBSA section 26(1)(b); reg. sections 19.1 to 20.1 of the Pension Benefit Standards Regulations, 1985, SOR/87-19, as amended (herein referred to as "PBSA reg."). Ontario permits transfers to a locked-in retirement account (similar to a locked-in RRSP), locked-in retirement income fund, or LIF: PBA section 42(1)(b); PBA reg. section 21.

129   Circumstances that may permit early withdrawal vary among jurisdictions. Examples include shortened life expectancy, financial hardship, non-residency, and small amounts.

130   For transfers from an RPP to another RPP or from an RPP to an RRSP or RRIF, see ITA section 147.3. The acquisition of an annuity from an RPP is governed by section 147.4.

131   The one exception is a US Keogh plan in which employees other than the self-employed business owner(s) participate.

132   An analysis of the growth of RRSP accounts and the changing composition of their assets was undertaken by Thomas A. Wilson and Steve Murphy, *Tax-Exempts and Corporate Capital Structure: An Empirical Analysis*, Working Paper 97-5 prepared for the Technical Committee on Business Taxation (Ottawa: Department of Finance, 1997). Their study indicated that from 1983 to 1996, assets held in RRSP accounts grew at an annual rate of 15.9 percent, higher than the rate of trusteed pension funds. In 1995, RRSP contributions surpassed those of RPPs, although RPPs still have significantly more assets under management. In 1999, RPPs had accumulated assets (reported at book value) of $684.114 billion, compared with $259.673 billion for RRSPs. However, the rate of growth of assets in RRSPs over the period 1989 to 1999 was 172 percent, compared with 126 percent for RPPs: see *Pension Plans in Canada*, supra note 86, at 15, table 2.

133   RRSP contributions increased from $15.033 billion in 1991 to $19.177 billion in 1993, $22.997 billion in 1995, $27.445 billion in 1997, and $27.789 billion in 1999. Over the period 1993 to 1999, contributions to RPPs (by both employees and employers) decreased each year, from a high of $20.197 billion in 1993 to $19.219 billion in 1999: *Pension Plans in Canada*, supra note 86.

134   The following table contrasts aggregate and average contributions to IRAs and Keogh plans in the period 1996 to 2000.

	IRAs			Keogh plans		
Year	Number of plans	Aggregate investment ($000s)	Investment per plan ($)	Number of plans	Aggregate investment ($000)	Investment per plan ($)
1996 ...	4,374,281	7,189,612	1,644	1,079,413	9,979,382	9,245
1997 ...	4,068,958	7,054,311	1,734	1,189,981	10,237,623	8,603
1998 ...	3,868,017	6,529,866	1,688	1,177,487	11,039,683	9,376
1999 ...	3,678,149	6,183,089	1,681	1,264,007	11,928,242	9,437
2000 ...	3,505,032	5,673,046	1,619	1,287,706	12,475,398	9,688

Source: United States, Internal Revenue Service, "Statistics of Income: Individual Income Tax Returns," table A, available at the IRS Web site: http://www.irs.gov/taxstats/.

135   See the definition of "qualified investment" in ITA subsection 146.3(1) and the list of taxpayers to which ITA part XI is applicable in section 205.

136   The three-to-one leveraging is found in ITA subsection 206(2) and is based on the taxpayer's "small business investment amount," defined in subsection 206(1) as the total cost amounts of the taxpayer's small business properties. A "small business property" is defined in ITA subsection 206(1) and, with respect to investments by an RRSP, includes a prescribed small business security, an interest in a small business investment limited partnership (SBILP), or an interest in a small business investment trust (SBIT) (with respect to SBILPs and SBITs, see infra notes 257-263 and accompanying text). A prescribed small business security is defined in ITA regulation 5100(2) as shares, subordinated debt (which may be secured by a floating charge), or certain options or rights to acquire shares of an "eligible corporation" (described infra notes 139-141 and accompanying text). As discussed below, maintaining eligible corporation status can be problematic. At the time of the 1985 amendments, the foreign property limit was 10 percent. The three-to-one leveraging allowed RRSPs to increase this limit by a maximum of 20 percent. Accordingly, an RRSP could increase its foreign property limit to 30 percent if at least 6.67 percent of its total assets were small business properties. The maximum increase to the foreign property limit for small business properties, still at a three-to-one leveraging, has remained 20 percent. With the increase in the foreign property limit to 30 percent, an RRSP can now increase its foreign property investments to 50 percent of plan assets if at least 6.67 percent of its total assets are small business properties.

137   "Designated shareholder" is defined in ITA regulation 4901(2) as a person who owns, or is related to a person who owns, directly or indirectly, at least 10 percent of the shares of any class of the corporation. For the purposes of applying the 10 percent test, a person is deemed to own any shares owned by a non-arm's-length person. However, a person will not be a designated shareholder if the person deals at arm's length with the corporation and owns shares with an aggregate cost of less than $25,000. Special rules apply where shares are owned by a trust or partnership.

138   Qualifying assets also include shares or debt of related eligible corporations. An eligible corporation also includes a prescribed venture capital corporation (which includes various venture capital corporations established under provincial tax incentives programs as well as federal and provincial LSVCCs).

139   Paragraph (c) of the definition of "eligible corporation" in ITA regulation 5100(1).

140   The definition of "small business corporation" in ITA subsection 248(1) was adopted for these purposes, except that the corporation must be a Canadian corporation that is not controlled by non-residents (rather than a Canadian-controlled private corporation).

141   "Connected shareholder" is defined in ITA regulation 4901(2) and is substantially similar to a "designated shareholder," supra note 137.

142   Supra note 61 and accompanying text. A qualified distribution from a Roth IRA is excluded from gross income (supra note 67). However, a non-qualified distribution is excluded only to the extent of the taxpayer's contributions to a Roth IRA, less all prior distributions, whether qualified or non-qualified.

143   For the complete list of exceptions to the excise tax, see infra notes 174-175 and accompanying text. All qualified distributions from a Roth IRA (supra note 67) are, by definition, excluded from the 10 percent excise tax. A non-qualified distribution is subject to the 10 percent excise tax to the extent that it is included in gross income.

144 IRC section 72(t)(3). However, an individual's transfer of an interest in an IRA to a spouse or former spouse under a divorce decree or separation instrument incident thereto is not considered a distribution: IRC section 408(d)(6). The transferred interest is considered to be an IRA of the transferee.

145 IRC section 72(t)(2)(D).

146 A first-time homebuyer is defined as an individual who has no ownership interest in a principal residence during the two-year period ending on the date of acquisition of the principal residence that is the subject of the distribution from the IRA.

147 IRC section 529(e)(3).

148 In effect, the US IRA legislation is geared much more toward savings for retirement than Canada's RRSP legislation, which permits withdrawals without penalty. The US excise tax is intended to remove the benefit derived from the deferral on withdrawals from an IRA prior to retirement age. It is a loose proxy in the sense that it can overpenalize withdrawals made within a few years of the deductible contributions to the IRA. For withdrawals made long after the original contributions were made, the 10 percent excise tax may not be considered a significant disincentive.

149 IRC section 408(e)(3).

150 IRC section 4975(c)(1)(B). The excise taxes usually applicable to prohibited transactions are not applicable because, as a result of the prohibited transaction, the account ceases to qualify as an individual retirement account: IRC section 4975(c)(3).

151 IRC section 408(e)(2).

152 IRC section 408(e)(4).

153 See below, under the heading "Accessing Employer-Sponsored Retirement Funds To Make Informal Venture Capital Investments."

154 IRC section 4975(f)(6).

155 Douglas G. Baird, *The Elements of Bankruptcy*, rev. ed. (Westbury, NY: Foundation Press, 1993), 46. In a bankruptcy, however, the bankrupt's interest in a Keogh plan may be available to creditors, depending on the state of residence of the debtor: see ibid., at 46-47.

156 The future value of an annuity is determined by the following formula: annuity × $\{[(1 + \text{interest rate})^{\text{time period}} - 1]/\text{interest rate}\}$. Thus, after 9 years of investing $15,500 annually and earning an 8 percent return, the value of Ms. A's RRSP would be $193,557.15. After 10 years, the value would be $224,541.72. This example ignores the increase in RRSP contribution limits announced in the 2003 federal budget. Even with a maximum contribution limit of $18,500, it would take just over eight years to replace the $200,000 withdrawn from the RRSP.

157 $224,541.72 × 1.08^{10}. Since Ms. A did not start recontributing to her RRSP until she was 45 and needed 10 years to accumulate $224,541.72, she had only 10 years remaining before reaching age 65. Even if Ms. A contributed $15,500 each year for the remaining 20 years, the RRSP would be worth only $709,310.44 at age 65.

158 ITA regulation 4900(1)(j).

159 ITA subsection 146(10). If in a year the loan ceases to be extant, the taxpayer is entitled to deduct the amount previously included under subsection 146(10) less

any net loss (other than interest paid by the RRSP on the loan) sustained by the RRSP in connection with the use of the property as security for the loan (not including any loss as a result of a change in the fair market value of the property used as security): subsection 146(7). In other words, if the loan ceases to exist and there was no loss as a result of using the property as security (that is, the property was not seized by the creditor), the total amount previously included in income under subsection 146(10) can be deducted under subsection 146(7).

160   Section 67(1)(b) of the Bankruptcy and Insolvency Act, RSC 1985, c. B-3, as amended, provides that the property of a bankrupt divisible among creditors does not include property that is exempt from execution or seizure under the laws applicable in the province in which the property is situated and within which the bankrupt resides. As noted infra note 184 and accompanying text, both the PBSA and the PBA contain provisions that exclude an individual's pension benefits from execution. Some provincial legislation may exclude certain RRSP assets from execution. For example, section 196(2) of the Insurance Act, RSO 1990, c. I.8, as amended, provides that "[w]hile a designation in favour of a spouse, same-sex partner, child, grandchild or parent of a person whose life is insured, or any of them, is in effect, the rights and interests of the insured in the insurance money and in the contract are exempt from execution or seizure." Life insurance is defined in section 1 and includes "an undertaking entered into by an insurer to provide an annuity." Thus, if an RRSP is in the form of a contract between the bankrupt and a life insurance company and the contract provides for the payment of an annuity and under the insurance contract a designation is made in favour of one of the individuals listed in section 196(2), the RRSP is exempt from execution: *Re Larocque* (1982), 38 OR (2d) 385 (HCJ). Discussions are underway at both the federal and the provincial levels over whether RRSPs should be excluded from seizure in a broader range of circumstances. See Canada, Office of the Superintendent of Bankruptcy, Personal Insolvency Task Force, *Final Report* (Ottawa: Office of the Superintendent of Bankruptcy, August 2002), 17-24. The report is available from Industry Canada's business and consumer Web site: http://www.strategis.ic.gc.ca/.

161   Canada, Department of Finance, 1992 Budget, Budget Papers, February 25, 1992, 142.

162   It may be argued, however, that home ownership is a means of forced retirement savings.

163   The December 2, 1992 economic statement also extended the first repayment date to December 31, 1995.

164   The homebuyers' plan was enacted in SC 1993, c. 24 and re-enacted in RSC 1985 (5th Supp.) format as SC 1994, c. 7, schedule VIII. The December 1992 economic statement amendment was enacted in SC 1994, c. 8. The 1994 budget amendments were enacted in SC 1995, c. 3. For withdrawals after March 1, 1994, the 15-year repayment period begins in the second calendar year following the calendar year in which the withdrawal is made, and the qualified home must be acquired before October 1 of the calendar year following the calendar year in which the withdrawal is made. An individual is considered a first-time homebuyer if neither the individual nor the individual's spouse owned a home and lived in it as a principal residence in any of the five calendar years beginning before the time of withdrawal. The 1994 budget amendments also restricted participation in the homebuyers' plan to one time per individual.

165   Canada, Department of Finance, 1998 Budget, Budget Plan, February 24, 1998, 179.
      The legislation incorporating the lifelong learning plan was included in SC 1999,
      c. 22, section 61, applicable after 1998.

166   Similarly, to limit administrative complexity, the recipient is not permitted to
      withdraw amounts from an RRSP for the education of the recipient's spouse
      while the recipient has an outstanding balance under the plan.

167   Generally, an individual must have had earned income in the past in order to have
      an RRSP.

168   As noted above, the lock-in requirements are not imposed by the Income Tax
      Act; they are imposed by federal and provincial pension legislation. However,
      many employees who have been made redundant may not have an RRSP or may
      have little contributed to an RRSP outside their pension plan. Access to locked-in
      RRSP funds for retraining of these individuals is certainly within the rationale for
      the lifelong learning plan.

169   However, the vesting requirements under ERISA are not as beneficial to employ-
      ees as those in Canada under the PBSA or the PBA: supra notes 75 (vesting
      under ERISA) and 122 (vesting under the PBSA and PBA).

170   Treas. reg. section 1.401-1(b)(1)(i).

171   IRC section 401(k)(2)(B).

172   Treas. reg. section 1.401(k)-1(d)(2)(i). The regulations provide a number of ex-
      amples of "immediate and heavy financial need," including expenses for medical
      care, costs incurred to purchase a principal residence or in preventing eviction
      from the principal residence, and certain post-secondary education expenses. The
      taxpayer must also demonstrate that the expenses cannot be satisfied from other
      resources available.

173   IRC section 72(t).

174   IRC section 72(t)(2). Even a distribution by a 401(k) plan permitted because of
      hardship is subject to the 10 percent excise tax, unless the hardship falls within
      one of the permitted exceptions (for example, the payment covers deductible
      medical expenses).

175   The proviso, found in IRC section 72(t)(3)(B), is applicable to payments from a
      trust described in IRC section 401(a) (including a 401(k) plan trust), which is
      exempt from tax under IRC section 501(a).

176   Like the ITA, the Code contains a number of provisions allowing the rollover of
      a lump-sum distribution from a qualified pension plan to another qualified plan
      or an IRA: IRC section 402(c).

177   ERISA section 406(a)(1)(B); IRC section 4975(c)(1)(B). Under ERISA, all em-
      ployees of the employer are parties in interest, and therefore a loan from a pension
      plan to any employee is a prohibited transaction. Under the Code, only officers,
      directors, and highly compensated employees (each employee earning more than
      10 percent of the yearly wages of the employer) are disqualified persons and
      therefore loans to such employees are prohibited transactions for the purposes of
      the excise tax in IRC section 4975. IRC section 401(a)(13) provides that a plan
      shall not be a qualified plan unless the plan provides that the benefits provided
      under the plan may not be assigned or alienated. However, a loan to a participant

or beneficiary shall not be treated as an assignment or alienation if the loan is secured by the participant's accrued non-forfeitable benefit and is exempt from the tax imposed by IRC section 4975.

178 Supra notes 43-45 and accompanying text.

179 IRC section 72(p)(1).

180 ERISA section 408(b)(1); IRC section 4975(d)(1). However, as discussed in notes 150-151 and 154 and accompanying text, supra, such loans are not permitted from an IRA or from a Keogh plan if the loan is made to the owner-employee:

181 IRC section 79(p)(2)(A).

182 IRC sections 79(p)(2)(B) and (C).

183 ITA regulation 8502(f) provides that every RPP must stipulate that no right of a person under the plan is capable of being "assigned, charged, anticipated, given as security or surrendered."

184 PBSA section 36(2); PBA section 65(1).

185 PBSA reg. section 16(1)(a). Previously, the Ontario legislation permitted a loan to an employee (or employee's spouse or child) if it was secured by a residential mortgage that was guaranteed or insured by a government in Canada or an insurance company: PBA reg. section 73(2), revoked by O. reg. 144/00.

186 ITA paragraph 147(2)(b).

187 ITA paragraph 147(2)(i).

188 ITA paragraph 56(1)(i) and ITA subsection 147(10).

189 Supra note 136 and accompanying text. An LSVCC is an "eligible corporation," as defined in ITA regulation 5100(1)(b), since all LSVCCs are prescribed venture capital corporations described in regulation 6700. Therefore, the investment in the LSVCC is a prescribed small business security (supra note 136). For these purposes, the total assets of an LSVCC are deemed not to exceed $50 million and the total cost to the taxpayer of all interests in LSVCCs is deemed not to exceed $10 million (see ITA regulation 5100(2.1)).

190 Supra note 136 and accompanying text. A VCF under any of the British Columbia, Quebec, and Nova Scotia VCF programs is an "eligible corporation," as defined in ITA regulation 5100(1)(b), because VCFs incorporated under the applicable provincial statutes are prescribed venture capital corporations. Therefore, the investment in the VCF is a prescribed small business security (supra note 136). For these purposes, the total assets of a prescribed venture capital corporation are deemed not to exceed $50 million and the total cost to the taxpayer of all interests in VCFs is deemed not to exceed $10 million (see ITA regulation 5100(2.1)).

191 See, generally, Mariana McNeill and Richard Fullenbaum, *Pension Funds and Small Firm Financing*, Small Business Research Summary no. 153 (Washington, DC: Small Business Administration Office of Advocacy, 1995). The report is available (in hard copy) from the National Technical Information Service (NTIS), Springfield, VA. This report considered economically targeted investments (ETIs), defined (at 7) as "investment programs designed to produce a competitive rate of return as well as create collateral economic benefits for a targeted geographic area, group of people, or sector of the economy." ETIs included, among other things, residential housing development, small business loans, and venture

capital. Venture capital was the most common form of ETI investment (at 45). As the report indicates, not all ETI programs were required by legislative mandate.

192   Terrance P. McGuire, "A Blueprint for Growth or a Recipe for Disaster? State Sponsored Venture Capital Funds for High Technology Ventures" (1994) vol. 7, no 2 *Harvard Journal of Law & Technology* 419-48, at 430.

193   McGuire, ibid., reports that at the end of 1993, the Alternative Assets Division was involved in 37 venture capital limited partnerships with a total net investment of $147 million and had invested an aggregate of $82.5 million directly in 30 companies. Its aggregate investment in private equity limited partnerships at that time was $708 million.

194   Thomson Financial Venture Economics, supra note 76, at 4 and 21.

195   Chapter 661 of the Massachusetts Acts of 1983. See part I, title IV, c. 32, section 22(8) of the General Laws of Massachusetts.

196   See part I, title IV, c. 32, section 23 of the General Laws of Massachusetts.

197   Edward Mason, "State Pension Eyes More Equity Plays," *Boston Business Journal*, June 7, 2002 (available online at http://boston.bizjournals.com/boston/stories/2002/06/10/story2.html).

198   Yvonne Abraham, "State Pension Fund Lost $1.89 Billion This Year, Plunged in US Ranks," *Boston Globe*, August 9, 2002. The article also reports that PRIM, since its inception, has yielded a 10.74 percent rate of return. According to the Thomson Financial Venture Economics 2001 statistics, supra note 76, at 8, as of June 30, 2000, PRIM had aggregate plan assets of $32.3 billion, including $1,968 million of alternative assets (6.1 percent of aggregate assets). Of that amount, $609 million represented investments in venture capital funds.

199   The governor of Maryland proposed the establishment of the Maryland Venture Capital Trust Fund in 1989.

200   Of the $19.1 million raised, $15 million was raised from the State Retirement and Pension System, $2.1 million from the Fire and Police Employees' Retirement System of the City of Baltimore and the Employees' Retirement System of the City of Baltimore, and $2 million from the state of Maryland.

201   29 USCA section 1104.

202   ERISA section 404(c)(2) provides in the case of such plans that "no person who is otherwise a fiduciary shall be liable under this part for any loss, or by reason of any breach, which results from such participant's, or beneficiary's exercise of control."

203   29 CFR section 2550.404c-1(b).

204   29 CFR section 2550.404c-1(d)(ii)(E).

205   There are exceptions to the general rule. The Thomson Financial Venture Economics 2001 statistics, supra note 76, list a few defined contribution plans that have made venture capital investments, including Arthur D. Little, Inc. Employees MDT Retirement Plan (venture capital investments worth $81 million, or 68 percent of the plan's private equity investments) and University of California Defined Contribution Plans (venture capital investments worth $234 million, or 50 percent of the plan's private equity investments).

206   29 CFR section 2550.404a-1; 44 Fed. Reg. 37,225 (1979).

207   44 Fed. Reg. 37,222 (1979).

208   Ibid., paragraph (b)(2).

209   The written instrument establishing the employee benefit plan must name the fiduciaries responsible for the control and management of the plan. The fiduciaries appoint the trustees who have exclusive authority and discretion to manage the assets of the plan. The trustees can either manage the assets themselves or delegate their authority to investment managers (if delegation is permitted by the plan document). The named fiduciaries, trustees, and investment managers are all considered fiduciaries of the plan.

210   ERISA section 401(b).

211   44 Fed. Reg. 50,363 (1979). The proposed regulation replaced a proposal that the Department of Labor made in December 1974 but never finalized: 29 CFR section 2552.1.

212   45 Fed. Reg. 38,084 (1980).

213   Public hearings on the 1979 proposal were held in February 1980, at which more than 30 commentators made oral submissions. The record was kept open until March 28, 1980 to permit additional representations, more than 200 of which were received. When the June 1980 proposals were released, the Department of Labor commented that the "testimony and comments have given the Department reason to believe that one part of the [August 1979] proposals, however, may be having a present, adverse impact on the operations of certain money managing entities commonly known as 'venture capital companies' in attracting funds for management from employee benefit plans." Venture capital companies, for this purpose, meant "limited partnerships or corporations that reinvest funds invested in them in selected securities issued by small businesses (portfolio companies). As part of the investment arrangements with portfolio companies, the managers of VCC's may participate in or obtain the right to participate in the management of the portfolio companies. Investments in portfolio companies, and in VCC's, generally are illiquid and long-term." 45 Fed. Reg. 38,085 (1980), note 8.

214   45 Fed. Reg. 38,085 (1980).

215   Proposed regulation 2550.401b-1(e)(ii).

216   47 Fed. Reg. 21,241 (1982).

217   29 CFR section 2510.3-101; 51 Fed. Reg. 41,280 (1986), as amended.

218   51 Fed. Reg. 41,280 (1986); 20 CFR sections 2510.3-101(a) and (b).

219   29 CFR section 2510.3-101(a)(2) provides in part:

> Generally, when a plan invests in another entity, the plan's assets include its investment, but do not, solely by reason of such investment, include any of the underlying assets of the entity. However, in the case of a plan's investment in an equity interest of an entity that is neither a publicly-offered security nor a security issued by an investment company registered under the Investment Company Act of 1940 its assets include both the equity interest and an undivided interest in each of the underlying assets of the entity, unless it is established that—
>
> (i) The entity is an operating company, or
> (ii) Equity participation in the entity by benefit plan investors is not significant.

> Therefore, any person who exercises authority or control respecting the management or disposition of such underlying assets, and any person who provides investment advice with respect to such assets for a fee (direct or indirect), is a fiduciary of the investing plan.

Under paragraph (f) of the regulation, "benefit plan investors" include any employee benefit plan, whether or not subject to title I of ERISA. Equity participation is considered "significant" if benefit plan investors own more than 25 percent of the value of any class of equity interest in the entity.

220　29 CFR section 2510.3-101(d).

221　For a discussion of this requirement, see Joseph W. Bartlett, "ERISA and Venture Capital Investing—Who Is a 'Fiduciary'?" (1989) vol. 93, no. 3 *Dickinson Law Review* 573-78.

222　If an entity does not qualify as a VCOC on the date that it makes its first venture capital investment, it may be precluded from ever qualifying.

223　IRC section 512. The tax is imposed under IRC section 511 at the rate applicable to corporations or trusts (depending on the nature of the tax-exempt entity).

224　IRC section 513(b)(2).

225　IRC section 512(c).

226　*Service Bolt & Nut Co. v. CIR*, 724 F. 2d 519 (6th Cir. 1983). The same position would hold true if the pension fund invests in an entity, such as a limited liability company (LLC) that elects to be taxed as a partnership.

227　The same exclusion would apply if the VCF was an LLC that elected to be taxed as a partnership. In the absence of IRC section 512(b)(5), there is some concern that the gains realized by the venture capital limited partnership may be considered business income (and therefore UBTI to a tax-exempt limited partner) rather than capital gains, on the basis that the activities of the fund manager (that is, the general partner or its designate) are unrelated business activities, particularly given the professional qualifications of the fund manager and its involvement in the management of portfolio businesses.

228　For a detailed discussion of UBIT concerns arising from pension fund investment in flowthrough operating companies, see Robert A. Rizzi, "Tax Exempts' Investments in Pass-Through Entities," in *Tax Strategies for Corporate Acquisitions, Dispositions, Spin-Offs, Joint Ventures, Financings, Reorganizations and Restructurings* (New York: Practising Law Institute, 2000), 905-69.

229　IRC section 512(e).

230　The same requirements are necessary in order for non-resident investors in a VCF to avoid taxation in the United States: see chapter 6, at note 10.

231　See the original regulations to the PBSA, SOR/67-328, schedule C, sections 1(a) to (r). A good summary of these standards can be found in Macdonald and Perry, supra note 2, at 41.

232　SOR/67-328, schedule C, section 4.

233　For common shares to qualify as eligible investments, in at least four of the last five years, the company must have paid dividends or had earned an amount available for dividend payment on its common shares of at least 4 percent of the average value for which common shares were carried in the company's stated capital account: SOR/67-328, schedule C, section 1(n).

234 Macdonald and Perry, supra note 2, at 47 and 56.

235 For example, section 8(4) of the PBSA now provides that, in administering a pension fund, the administrator "shall exercise the degree of care that a person of ordinary prudence would exercise in dealing with the property of another person." PBA section 22(1) is similar. Both statutes impose enhanced standards of care on plan administrators who possess greater plan administration skills: PBSA section 8(5); PBA section 22(2).

236 See PBSA reg. section 6 and schedule III (introduced in SOR/93-299). These provisions apply to pensions under both the PBSA and, since January 1, 2001, the PBA (PBA reg. section 79, as amended by O. reg. 144/00, section 31). British Columbia, Alberta, Saskatchewan, Manitoba, and Newfoundland and Labrador have also adopted the PBSA investment provisions, and the provisions in Nova Scotia conform to these provisions.

237 Exceptions apply with respect to investments in real estate corporations, resource corporations, or investment corporations, as those terms are defined in the investment regulations. The Income Tax Act contains corresponding provisions exempting such corporations from tax: see ITA subparagraphs 149(1)(o.2)(ii), (ii.1), and (iii). Numerous conditions apply if the pension fund invests in securities that represent more than 30 percent of the votes of such entities: see PBSA reg. schedule III, sections 12-14. See also infra note 244.

238 PBSA reg. schedule III, sections 15-18. For the purpose of these provisions, a "related party" is defined broadly in section 1, and includes the administrator of the plan (and its officers and directors), an employer who participates in the plan (as well as its employees, officers and directors, corporate affiliates, shareholders that hold more than 10 percent of the voting stock of the employer, and subsidiaries of the employer), members of the plan, and the spouse, common law partner, or child of any of the aforementioned individuals. Section 17 permits certain transactions with related parties. For example, a plan may acquire securities of a related party if the securities are acquired over a public exchange (defined in section 1 to include a number of Canadian, American, French, and British stock exchanges). In addition, a plan may enter into a transaction with a related party "if the value of the transaction is nominal or the transaction is immaterial to the plan" (section 17(3)) or if the transaction is required for the operation or administration of the plan and the terms and conditions of the transaction are not less favourable than market conditions (section 17(1)).

239 PBSA reg. section 7.1(1).

240 By the end of 1983, trusteed pension assets were worth an estimated $84 billion and total pension-related assets (including CPP, QPP, federal superannuation accounts, and trusteed pensions) were worth an estimated $196 billion: Macdonald and Perry, supra note 2, at 15. Macdonald and Perry estimated that only $72 million, or 0.3 percent of the assets of Canada's largest pension funds, and $25 million, or 1 percent of the assets of small and medium funds, were invested in venture capital: ibid., at 45, table 4.

241 Paragraph (e) of the definition of "qualified investment" in ITA section 204. "Equity share" is also defined in ITA section 204. The definition is complex, but for the vast majority of companies it means ordinary common shares.

242 Paragraph (i) of the definition of "qualified investment" in ITA section 204 and ITA regulation 4900(7). Regulation 4900(11) provides that where the SBILP or

SBIT acquires a small business security (as defined in regulation 5100(2)) of a corporation and the corporation has made payments to the DPSP, the interest in the SBILP or SBIT will not be a qualified investment unless the small business security is an equity share (as defined in section 204)).

243 Note also that an RPP may lose its registered status if it becomes a revocable plan, which occurs if it acquires a prohibited investment: supra note 106.

244 For example, an RPP may incorporate an investment corporation as a wholly owned subsidiary to undertake its venture capital investments. The investment corporation must comply with the provisions in ITA subparagraph 149(1)(o.2)(iii) in order to be exempt from tax (see also subsection 227(14)), although the corporation is independently subject to ITA part XI tax (since the shares of the investment corporation would not constitute foreign property to the RPP). The requirements of subparagraph 149(1)(o.2)(iii) are fourfold: first, the corporation's investments must be permitted by applicable pension legislation (for example, the PBSA); second, the assets of the corporation must be at least 98 percent cash and investments; third, the corporation must not have issued debt obligations or accepted deposits; and fourth, the corporation must derive at least 98 percent of its income from, or from the disposition of, investments. This last requirement has posed some concerns where the investment corporation invests in a venture capital limited partnership, for reasons similar to those affecting non-resident pension funds investing in Canadian venture capital limited partnerships (see chapter 6, at notes 27-28 and accompanying text). ITA section 253.1 now provides that, for certain limited purposes including paragraph 149(1)(o.2), a corporation that holds an interest in a limited partnership "shall not, solely because of its acquisition and holding of that interest, be considered to carry on any business or other activity of the partnership." Section 253.1 was added to the ITA by SC 2001, c. 17, section 193, applicable after 1992; a transitional measure to similar effect applies to taxation years that end after December 16, 1999 and before 2003.

245 Paragraph (i) of the definition of "foreign property" in ITA subsection 206(1). Any interest in a trust is also considered foreign property unless prescribed.

246 The acronym "CanSBIC" is used in order to avoid confusion with the US SBIC regime, considered in detail in chapter 8.

247 The investment vehicles discussed herein are not the only types of partnerships and trusts that are prescribed not to be foreign property. Other investment vehicles, such as "pooled fund trusts," "master trusts," and "quasi mutual fund trusts," are also prescribed not to be foreign property, subject to certain conditions. For a discussion of these and certain other investment vehicles, see Eva M. Krasa, "Income Tax Implications of Joint Investment by Pension Plans Through a Private Pooled Fund Vehicle" (1997) vol. 45, no. 1 *Canadian Tax Journal* 1-24.

248 ITA subsection 206(1), definition of "small business property."

249 ITA paragraph 149(1)(o.3) is limited to part I tax. Prescribed CanSBICs are also exempt from part I.3 tax (large corporations tax) (ITA paragraph 181.1(3)(c)) and taxes under parts IV, IV.1, VI, and VI.1 (ITA subsection 227(14)).

250 ITA paragraph 205(g), which subjects to part XI tax "any other person, other than a prescribed person, exempt from tax under Part I."

251 ITA regulation 5101(1)(a).

252 ITA regulation 5101(1)(b).

253 "Small business security" is defined in ITA regulation 5100(2) as property of a person that is a share of the capital stock of an eligible corporation or a debt obligation of an eligible corporation that is unrestricted and either unsecured or secured only by a subordinate floating charge on assets of the eligible corporation. Options and rights granted by an eligible corporation as part of an issue of a share or debt obligation that qualifies as a small business security are also considered small business securities, as are options and rights granted to a shareholder of a small business security without consideration. In order to be a small business security, the aggregate costs to the shareholder of all shares, options, rights, and debt obligations of the eligible corporation and associated corporations cannot exceed $10 million and the total assets of the eligible corporation and associated corporations cannot exceed $50 million. The $10 million and $50 million limits do not apply if the eligible corporation is a prescribed venture capital corporation. "Eligible corporation" is defined in ITA regulation 5100(1): supra notes 139-140 and accompanying text.

254 ITA regulation 5101(2). The CanSBIC has 90 days after receiving additional debt or equity capital to invest at least 75 percent in these small business investments. Furthermore, proceeds from the disposition of a small business investment must be reinvested in other small business investments or distributed to the CanSBIC's shareholders within 90 days of the disposition.

255 ITA regulation 5101(1)(d). A CanSBIC can hold more than 30 percent of the shares of a portfolio company in certain situations in which the portfolio corporation is in financial difficulty, as set out in regulation 5104(2), or if the portfolio company is a prescribed venture capital corporation.

256 ITA regulations 5101(1)(e) and (f).

257 ITA regulations 5000(1.1)(a) and (b) deem a limited partnership interest in an SBILP and an interest in an SBIT, respectively, not to be foreign property for the purposes of part XI.

258 ITA regulations 5102(1)(e) and 5103(1)(c), respectively.

259 ITA regulations 5102(1)(f) and 5103(1)(d), respectively, list permitted investments. Regulations 5102(2) and 5103(2), respectively, stipulate the minimum amount of assets that must comprise small business securities. Apart from small business securities, SBILPs and SBITs can invest in "specified property" (defined in ITA regulation 5100(1)), which comprises various types of corporate debt and equity (including rights, warrants, and options), as well as a number of liquid assets (bank deposits, bonds, guaranteed investment certificates, etc.).

260 ITA regulations 5102(1)(f)(i) and 5103(d)(i), respectively. In both cases, an exception set out in regulation 5104(1) allows the SBILP or SBIT to acquire small business securities that another person had previously acquired if the securities are the capital stock of an eligible corporation with full voting rights and are acquired in specified circumstances described in regulation 5104(2).

261 ITA regulations 5102(2) and 5103(2), respectively. Similar to CanSBICs, SBILPs and SBITs have 90 days after the disposition of a small business security to reinvest the proceeds in other small business securities or distribute the proceeds to its partners or beneficiaries, as the case may be: regulations 5102(3) and 5103(3), respectively.

262 ITA regulations 5102(1)(h) and 5103(1)(f), respectively.

263 ITA regulation 5102(1)(i) and 5103(1)(g), respectively.

264 For CanSBICs, SBILPs, and SBITs, a property that was not foreign property when first acquired is not considered foreign property for part XI tax purposes until 24 months after it becomes foreign property. In effect, the entity is given a 24-month grace period in which to dispose of property that becomes non-qualifying. See ITA subparagraph 206(2)(a)(iii).

265 An interest in a QLP is prescribed not to be foreign property: ITA regulation 5000(1.1)(c). The draft regulations released on February 5, 2002 repealed this provision and replaced it with regulations 5000(1.3)-(1.5), discussed in note 268 and accompanying text, infra. See Canada, Department of Finance, "Draft Income Tax Regulations and Explanatory Notes," in *Explanatory Notes Relating to the Air Travellers Security Charge and to Income Tax* (Ottawa: Department of Finance, February 2002), appendix C.

266 Paragraph (f) of the definition of "qualified limited partnership" in ITA regulation 5000(7).

267 Canada, Department of Finance, 2003 Budget, Budget Plan, February 18, 2003, 331. The units of the other QLP are treated as foreign property of the investing QLP in the same proportion as the foreign property owned by the other QLP.

268 Proposed regulations 5000(1.3)-(1.5), supra note 265, applicable after 2001. For a limited partner that holds less than 30 percent of the units of the QLP, each entire unit is prescribed not to be foreign property.

269 See, generally, Yvette Morelli, "Structuring Venture Capital Funds" (2003) vol. 51, no. 2 *Canadian Tax Journal* 806-62.

270 But see chapter 5, at note 8, which outlines recent changes to Ontario's securities legislation that potentially erode the protection given to investors in the case of seed capital investment in closely held companies.

271 S 2, 105th Cong., 1st sess. (introduced on January 21, 1997).

272 Ibid., section 404 proposed the addition of new section 408(d)(8) to the Code, which would have excluded from taxation distributions "from an individual retirement plan . . . to the extent the aggregate amount of such payments and distributions does not exceed the business start-up costs of the taxpayer for the taxable year." Business startup costs were defined as "any amount which is paid or incurred . . . in connection with a trade or business with respect to which the taxpayer is a 50-percent owner, and . . . on or before the date which is one year after the date on which the active conduct of such trade or business began (as determined under section 195(c))."

273 In effect, the proposal would have converted the treatment of such amounts to an expenditure tax rather than an income tax. The taxpayer is effectively getting the benefit of a deduction for amounts invested in the startup.

274 The one-year cutoff would likely lead entrepreneurs to increase the incidence of expenses that do not make business sense. It was also unclear whether any amount invested in the stock or debt of a corporation (the corporation being the business) qualifies irrespective of what the corporation does with the money. In addition, the proposals would have created questions as to whether the taxpayer has a single business (close to the end of its first year) or whether a new and separate business (for example, at a new location or with a new piece of machinery) has commenced. See Edward J. Gac and Wayne M. Gazur, "Tapping 'Rainy Day'

Funds for the Reluctant Entrepreneur: Downsizing, Paternalism, and the Internal Revenue Code" (1997) vol. 86, no. 1 *Kentucky Law Journal* 127-61, at 157-58.

275 As Gac and Gazur note, the proposal "does not require disposal of the vacation home, the boat, the recreational vehicle, non-retirement stock market speculations, and so forth. There is no need to miss a vacation. Instead, the taxpayer is permitted to deplete his or her retirement assets with impunity. One could speculate that without the discomfort imposed by a last-resort rule, there is less planning and thought in connection with the viability of the proposed venture—an easy money, credit card mentality extended to retirement assets." Ibid., at 156.

276 However, imposing any form of scrutiny would be difficult. Even if the applicant had to include a business plan or description of the proposal, the IRS would not likely have the capacity or skills to evaluate it.

277 Although normal contribution limits to IRAs are relatively small, the proposals did not appear to prohibit access to IRA amounts received on a rollover from a qualified pension plan: Gac and Gazur, supra note 274, at 159.

278 Supra notes 171-172 and accompanying text.

279 The authors acknowledge that the hardship rules combined with the base retirement asset level "may create a 'Catch-22' for many. Wealthier participants with other assets and investments would be ineligible for a loan under the exhaustion test. In contrast, . . . [for] less wealthy participants, the lack of other assets could reflect fewer years of employment at a substantial salary, which in turn would cause the base retirement asset level to not be met. In this regard, our proposal is admittedly conservative—though hopefully not irrelevant." Supra note 274, at 161.

280 Supra notes 156-157 and accompanying text.

281 Since Ms. A needs to withdraw only $100,000 from the RRSP, the remaining $100,000 would remain invested and would be worth $146,932.81 after five years. With the repayment of the $100,000 after five years, $246,932.81 would be invested for another 20 years and would be worth $1,150,943.23 when Ms. A reaches age 65.

282 If Ms. A failed to repay the $100,000 to her RRSP, she should have to recognize the amount as income. However, she should be entitled to an offsetting deduction because the failure of her investment should give rise to a business investment loss. Since the deduction for business investment losses is currently limited to one-half of the losses, there would be net tax payable. However, if as proposed in chapter 3 the entire amount of a business investment loss is deductible, the net effect would be a wash. If, on the other hand, Ms. A withdrew the entire $200,000, the government would have an additional $100,000 in taxes in the year it was withdrawn, some of which may be needed to provide future welfare payments to Ms. A.

283 See chapter 3, under the heading "Angel Capital Rollover: Canada."

284 See chapter 5, under the heading "Evaluation of Direct Investment Tax Credit Programs: Eligible Businesses."

285 Under that provision, the shares must be non-convertible, non-voting, and subject to a fixed dividend rate not exceeding the prescribed rate of interest at the time the shares are issued, and the amount that the shareholder is entitled to receive on redemption or cancellation of the shares must not exceed the amount for which the shares are issued plus any unpaid dividends.

286   Between 1989 and 1996, venture capital commitments of Canadian pension funds never exceeded $100 million annually. Canadian pension fund investment increased in 1997 to $233 million, although it declined in 1998 and 1999 to $126 million and $134 million, respectively. In 2000, it increased to $1.1 billion and in 2001 to over $2 billion, before receding to $510 million in 2002 and to $175 million in 2003. Moreover, recent venture capital investment has been concentrated in a handful of pension funds. Canadian pension fund investment in venture capital (contrasted with US pension fund investment) is shown in chapter 2, figure 2.7. Statistics for Canadian pension fund investment in venture capital are taken from Falconer, supra note 2, at 28, figure 7 (whose source was Macdonald & Associates Limited) (for years preceding 1995); and Macdonald & Associates Limited (unpublished) (for 1995 and following years).

287   For a discussion of some techniques, see David Burgess and Joel Fried, "Canadian Retirement Savings Plans and the Foreign Property Rule" (1999) vol. 25, no. 3 *Canadian Public Policy* 395-416. According to the authors, these techniques require some level of sophistication and sufficient capital in the fund; they also restrict portfolio strategy and are limited to particular sectors of world markets.

288   According to Burgess and Fried, even if the foreign property restriction were eliminated, it is unlikely that more than 32 percent of retirement savings would be invested in foreign property: ibid., at 411. Keith Ambachtsheer similarly concluded that with the removal of the ceiling, Canadian institutional investment would probably settle naturally at a level of around 30 percent: Keith Ambachtsheer, "Canada's 20% Foreign Property Rule: Why and How It Should Be Eliminated," a paper commissioned by PIAC and the Investment Funds Institute of Canada, 1995, cited in Falconer, supra note 2, at 83. Both studies were written at a time when the foreign property limit was 20 percent. On the basis of data available at that time, Canadian pension funds maintained a foreign content exposure slightly under 20 percent. Burgess and Fried further suggest that the removal of the foreign property limit would not lead to a significant outflow of capital. In fact, its removal may lead to an inflow of capital because "the removal acts as a signal about future government policies of taxation of capital, with the liberalization acting as a favourable signal." Burgess and Fried, supra note 287, at 405, relying on Leonardo Bartolini and Allan Drazen, "Capital-Account Liberalization as a Signal" (1997) vol. 87, no. 1 *The American Economic Review* 138-54.

289   Canada, Standing Committee on Banking, Trade and Commerce, *The Governance Practices of Institutional Investors*, 36th Parl., 1st sess., November 1998.

290   Canadian Venture Capital Association, "Submission to the Senate Standing Committee on Banking, Trade and Commerce on Equity Financing" and "Pre-Budget Submission to the House of Commons Standing Committee on Finance," both dated October 24, 2001 and available through the CVCA Web site: http://www.cvca.ca/.

291   A qualified trust is defined in ITA subsection 259(5) as a trust where: the trustee is appropriately licensed; the interests of all beneficiaries are described by reference to the number of units held and the units have identical terms; the trust has never borrowed money for a term exceeding 90 days; and the trust has never accepted deposits. A qualified corporation is a corporation described in paragraph 149(1)(o.2) in which all of the shares are identical or all of the shares are held by one person.

292   For example, all of the limited partners of a QLP must have interests described as units that are identical in all respects (see paragraph (d) of the definition of

"qualified partnership" in ITA regulation 5000(7)). In the 2003 federal budget, it was announced that the identical unit requirement would be relaxed "to accommodate differences in units that do not impact on the share or nature of the partnership's income or loss allocated among limited partners. With this change, matters such as variations in voting rights, the right to participate in investment advisory committees, and co-investment rights will not be taken into account in determining whether the units of a QLP are identical" (2003 Budget, supra note 267, at 331). The only distinctions between QLPs and qualified trusts (other than the more stringent requirements germane to qualification as a QLP) are that QLPs have somewhat broader borrowing powers and QLPs can accept deposits. Neither of these distinctions nor the amendment announced in the 2003 budget appears particularly relevant to the rationale underlying the election in section 259.

293 Subject to the possible application of the unrelated business income tax in IRC sections 511 et seq.

294 See chapter 6, at note 36 and accompanying text.

295 *Pension Plans in Canada*, supra note 86, at 78, table 3B-10.

296 Falconer, supra note 2.

297 At that time, PIAC represented 127 pension organizations that collectively managed almost 350 pension funds with about $400 billion in assets. The members of PIAC thus controlled almost 80 percent of pension fund assets. Slightly more than half (53 percent) of the members responded to the survey. The respondents reflected a wide representation of funds according to size.

298 In its review of the Canadian private equity market in 2002, Macdonald & Associates Limited indicated that many of these barriers continue to inhibit pension fund investment in Canada. Macdonald & Associates Limited, "Canada's Private Equity Market in 2002," May 2003, 14 (available from the Macdonald & Associates Web site: http://www.canadavc.com/).

299 William M. Mercer Limited, "Key Terms and Conditions for Private Equity Investing," 1996, referred to in Falconer, supra note 2, at 71.

300 Falconer, supra note 2, at 71.

301 Macdonald & Associates Limited reported the creation of the first three funds of funds in 2002 with a fourth anticipated in 2003, marking a "milestone event in the history of the Canadian private equity market." Macdonald & Associates Limited, supra note 298, at 15. The report indicated that 120 funds of funds are currently in operation in the US private equity market with assets in excess of $60 billion, and that these funds of funds have been responsible for about 15 percent of new private equity market resources in recent years.

302 See the discussion of LSVCCs throughout chapter 6.

303 Falconer, supra note 2, at 73.

304 In William D. Bygrave and Jeffry A. Timmons, *Venture Capital at the Crossroads* (Boston: Harvard Business School Press, 1992), the authors note (at 317): "The current compensation practices in the pension industry are diametrically at odds with the longer holding periods, illiquidity, higher risk, more difficult and complex valuation requirements, deal flow sources and deal sizes, potential rates of return, and value-added investing strategies of classic venture capital. Such a mismatch can only lead to disappointment and failure."

305   Thomson Venture Economics, *2003 National Venture Capital Association Year-book* (Arlington, VA and Newark, NJ: National Venture Capital Association and Thomson Venture Economics, 2003), 81, figure 7.01. See also chapter 6, at note 189.

306   See the CVCA Web site: http://www.cvca.ca/. The December 31, 2001 performance statistics are available from http://www.cvca.ca/downloads/index.html. Perform-ance statistics for periods ending December 31, 2002 are available from the Macdonald & Associates Limited Web site: http://www.canadavc.com/files/public/2002ReturnsLtrCVCAMembership.pdf.

307   Note 9 of the explanatory notes to the December 31, 2002 performance data, ibid. In contrast, US data included in the annual National Venture Capital Asso-ciation *Yearbook* are calculated on a net basis: supra note 305.

308   In July 2003, the CVCA proposed to its members that the valuation principles and guidelines of the European Venture Capital Association be adopted for use, subject to certain CVCA modifications. For these proposals and the responses received from CVCA members, see the CVCA Web site: http://www.cvca.ca/.

309   Falconer, supra note 2, gives the example of PERA of Colorado, which measures private equity returns against a benchmark of the 10-year Standard & Poor's 500 Index plus 500 basis points. CalPERS uses a similar measure in combination with other tools.

310   Falconer, supra note 2, at 80.

311   The Caisse managed about $130 billion in assets as of the end of 2001. British Columbia Investment Management Corporation (bcIMC) had about $60 billion under management as of March 31, 2002. A similar consolidation of public sector funds is found in Alberta (through Alberta Treasury's Investment Management Division) and New Brunswick (through the New Brunswick Investment Management Corpora-tion) and at the federal level (through the Public Sector Pension Investment Board).

312   Although described as an incentive, the three-to-one leveraging of small business investments for the purpose of the foreign property limitations simply provides a means of redressing an unnecessary impediment.

313   See chapter 6, under the heading "Evaluation of VCF Tax Credit Programs: Eligible Investors and Nature of Investment."

314   See chapter 6, under the heading "Using Tax Credits To Guarantee Investment in VCFs."

315   Pub. L. no. 74-271, enacted on August 14, 1935; 74 Stat. 620.

316   Originally title VII of the Social Security Act of 1935; in 1939, title VII was removed from the Social Security Act and included in the Internal Revenue Code.

317   It is anticipated that Social Security will be in a yearly surplus position until about 2012: infra note 318.

318   Matt Moore and John C. Goodman, "Straight Talk About the Social Security Trust Fund," National Center for Policy Analysis, *Brief Analysis* no. 366, August 10, 2001.

319   National Commission on Social Security Reform, *Report of the National Commis-sion on Social Security Reform* (Washington, DC: Social Security Administration, 1982). The 1983 legislation was enacted in the Social Security Amendments Act of 1983, Pub. L. no. 98-21, enacted on April 20, 1983; 97 Stat. 65.

320   United States, Social Security Administration, *Annual Report of the Board of Trustees of the Federal Old Age and Survivors Insurance and Disability Trust Funds* (Washington, DC: Social Security Administration, 2000).

321   See, generally, Daniel N. Shaviro, *Making Sense of Social Security Reform* (Chicago: University of Chicago Press, 2000).

322   President's Commission To Strengthen Social Security, *Strengthening Social Security and Creating Personal Wealth for All Americans* (Washington, DC: President's Commission To Strengthen Social Security, December 2001) (herein referred to as "the Social Security report") (available online at http://www.csss.gov/reports/ Final_report.pdf).

323   Ibid., at 11.

324   Other factors contributed to the financial problems of the CPP, including slower economic growth rates than predicted when the plan was established in the 1960s, enriched CPP benefits (such as indexing), and increased disability payments. In fact, higher contribution limits were introduced in 1987. According to changes made at that time, a 25-year schedule of contribution rates was introduced, to be reviewed by the federal and provincial governments as joint stewards of the plan on a rolling basis every 5 years. A revised 25-year schedule was introduced in 1992. The actuarial report for the year ended December 31, 1993 prompted the consultation process, leading to significant changes in 1997.

325   See Canada, Department of Finance, *An Information Paper for Consultations on the Canada Pension Plan: Released by the Federal, Provincial and Territorial Governments* (Ottawa: Department of Finance, 1996), appendix A. The chief actuary of the plan estimated that the CPP's unfunded liability (the present value of future benefits to be paid out under the plan less the value of the plan's reserve plus the present value of future contributions to the fund when the contribution rate is set at the full cost rate for new entrants) at its 1995 year-end to be $556 billion. In order to preserve the fund without making changes in its investment policy, the contribution rate would have to be increased to 14.2 percent by 2030 despite a full-cost rate of 7 percent. In effect, an 18-year-old entering the plan would have to pay twice his or her fully funded contribution in order to satisfy the liability of the fund to both the new member and existing and retired members. To put this in perspective, the contribution rate (combined employer and employee rate) was 3.6 percent from 1966 to 1986. Between 1987 and 1996, it increased 0.2 percent per year to 5.8 percent. The original architects of the CPP projected the contribution rate to be 5.5 percent in 2030.

326   The proposals were outlined in September 1997 in Canada, Department of Finance, *Securing the Canada Pension Plan: Agreement on Proposed Changes to the Canada Pension Plan* (Ottawa: Department of Finance, 1997).

327   Canada Pension Plan Investment Board Act, SC 1997, c. 40 (herein referred to as "CPPIB Act"). The increased contribution rates came into force on January 1, 1998. The provisions creating the CPPIB and changes to the investment provisions of the CPP came into force on April 1, 1998.

328   According to the 25-year schedule then in effect, rates were scheduled to increase from 5.6 percent in 1996 to 10.1 percent in 2016.

329   Canada Pension Plan, RSC 1985, c. C-8, as amended, section 113.1(1).

330   CPPIB Act section 5.

331   CPPIB Act section 37.

332   Canada Pension Plan sections 110(4), (5), and (6).

333   Canada Pension Plan Investment Board Regulations, PC 1999-731, SOR/99-190, as amended, section 10 (amended by SOR/2000-333, section 1). Section 10 provides

that at least 50 percent of the book value of securities of Canadian corporations "substantially replicates the composition of one or more widely recognized broad market indexes of securities traded on a public exchange located in Canada."

334   CPP Investment Board, "Investment Statement," April 10, 2002, available from the CPPIB's Web site: http://www.cppib.ca/.

335   Ibid., at paragraph 3.2.2.

336   SC 2003, c. 5, section 19.

337   "CPP Investment Board Commits Half-Billion Dollars to Canadian Venture Capital," *News Release*, June 19, 2002, available from the CPPIB's Web Site: http://www.cppib.ca/.

338   An Act Respecting the Caisse de dépôt et placement du Québec, RSQ, c. C-2, section 36.2 provides:

> The Fund [the Caisse] shall, annually, adopt an investment policy under which the distribution of assets among shares and titles of indebtedness of legal persons is in keeping with the practices of major North American pension funds.
>
> The policy must also take into account the financing needs of the public sector and economic development of Québec.

339   As quoted by Francine Lalonde in Canada, House of Commons, *Debates*, October 6, 1997, 544.

340   Jean Lesage, interview on Channel 4, Quebec City, January 27, 1970.

341   Its 10-year return ending December 31, 2001 was 9.3 percent, compared with the 10.6 percent median return for large Canadian pensions: Diane Francis, "Caisse Crisis Hits 'Quebec Inc.' Concept," *Financial Post*, December 3, 2002.

342   For example, the Caisse wrote down by $2.9 billion its investment in Quebecor Media Inc. in 2002, resulting in part from the high price Quebecor Inc. paid to prevent Groupe Vidéotron Ltée from being bought by Rogers Media Inc. in 2001.

343   Of the 138 layoffs announced on December 2, 2002, over half were in the private equity division. The Caisse also announced the closure of 8 of its 11 international offices. It will retain international offices only in Paris, Los Angeles, and Hong Kong.

344   Sean Silcoff, "Sweeping Shakeup at the Caisse," *Financial Post*, December 3, 2002. See also Bertrand Marotte, "New CEO Shifts Direction at Caisse," *Globe and Mail*, December 9, 2002.

345   See, for example, the comments of various members of Parliament, Canada, House of Commons, *Debates*, October 6, 1997, 506-10, 541, 544, 551, and 619.

346   Supra note 287 and accompanying text.

347   Derek DeCloet, "Foreign Content Limit Must Rise, Says CPP," *National Post*, June 28, 2002. The article notes that the foreign content rules were criticized in February 2002 by Tom Gunn, senior vice-president of investments at OMERS, not only because they were inappropriate for investors but also because, in his view, they failed in their purpose to create jobs and economic growth in Canada. Similar comments followed from the Caisse and Ontario Teachers' Pension Plan.

8

Selected Non-Tax Government
Venture Capital Programs*

Non-tax government expenditures, particularly direct government expenditures on infrastructure, research and development, and higher education, continue to have a much more significant impact on technological development than tax expenditure programs targeting rapid-growth small and medium-sized enterprises (SMEs). While the emphasis in this book is on tax incentive programs, it would be remiss to ignore various other government programs that target the market failures associated with financing high-growth SMEs.

The tax incentives discussed in the previous chapters do not specifically target the market failures associated with financing SMEs; rather, they seek to compensate for failures by expanding the pool of venture capital available. However, there are problems with expanding the pool too quickly. The US formal venture capital industry was inundated with funding in the late 1990s (although not directly as a result of government expenditure programs), which significantly increased fund sizes and deal sizes. The exponential increase in funding was not matched, however, by a similar increase in viable business investment opportunities. One consequence of this mismatch between funding and opportunity was that a substantial amount of capital invested in or committed to US venture capital funds was still uninvested in mid-2003. Another consequence, certainly apparent in hindsight, was that some venture capital funds invested in precarious ventures without subjecting them to the same rigorous analysis that was applied in earlier, leaner times. An oversupply of venture capital can lead to an incredibly wasteful misallocation of resources. As one of the reviewers of an earlier draft of this book put it, "an economy that had an apparently unlimited amount of venture capital available for such projects as selling pet food over the Internet should probably not be imitated," particularly where the government is underwriting a substantial portion of the risk of the investments. In other words, governments should take care in designing their spending programs to address the fundamental reason for the shortage in venture capital: the market failures that create the equity gap faced by SMEs.

To the extent possible, government expenditure programs should target the causes of these market failures rather than alleviate their symptoms. One obvious way in which to eliminate government-subsidized funding for Internet pet food

---

* Unless otherwise stated, US monetary amounts are in US dollars and Canadian monetary amounts are in Canadian dollars.

vendors (and businesses of a similar ilk) is for the government to make the investment decisions rather than underwrite the investments of others. Alternatively, government expenditure can directly attack the market failures that lead to the misallocation of resources. The direct government spending programs that are considered in this chapter include examples of both types of programs.

Probably the most visible federal agencies involved in funding small businesses in the United States and Canada are the US Small Business Administration (SBA) and the Business Development Bank of Canada (BDC). These agencies are considered first. Direct government expenditure on research and development (R & D) is obviously important to innovation. One way in which to marry this expenditure with the provision of financial assistance to rapid-growth SMEs is to require government agencies to spend a portion of their research budget on research undertaken by SMEs. Two such programs used in the United States, the small business innovative research (SBIR) program and the small business technology transfer (STTR) program, are administered by the SBA and are reviewed in that context.

One of the key US federal government programs that was an important catalyst in the early development of a formal venture capital industry in the United States was the small business investment company (SBIC) program, created in 1958 in the wake of the *Sputnik* crisis. Although the program had obvious failings, as described in more detail below, it played a key role in fostering the development of venture capital specialists who went on to start private venture capital firms. The SBIC program was also important as an investment vehicle through which banks could invest in venture capital. SBICs remain an important venture capital investment vehicle for banks to this day, although recent amendments to banking regulations have reduced their importance in this respect.[1] The SBIC regime does not have any counterpart in Canada, but the federal regulation of banks has had a similar impact on their ability to make venture capital investments.[2] The lack of a similar program in Canada that fostered the early development of a private sector venture capital firms, prior to the targeting of pension funds for venture capital investment, accounts in part for the overall failure of the 1985 pension fund initiatives to sustain investment through the recession of the early 1990s. This was not the only cause of this failure; timing, in this as in so many things, turned out to be crucial. Government initiatives targeting pension funds were introduced in the United States in 1979, six years before similar initiatives were undertaken in Canada. Thus, when the recession hit in 1990, US pension funds had been involved in venture capital investments for over a decade, had developed relationships with venture capital fund managers, and were prepared to weather the storm. Most Canadian pension funds, in contrast, had just begun venture investing in the latter half of the 1980s at the end of the economic cycle, and lost substantial amounts in the recession. Many were so discouraged by their first foray into venture capital investing that they have yet to reconsider venture capital as an appropriate asset allocation.

A second response to the *Sputnik* crisis in the United States was the creation of the Advanced Research Projects Agency (ARPA) as an agency to fund cutting-edge technological research with advanced military capabilities. ARPA and its successor, the Defense Advanced Research Projects Agency (DARPA), are considered in this chapter in order to highlight the importance of military spending on innovation in the United States. Like the SBIC program, the staggering amount of US military spending is not mirrored in Canada. This spending has an important impact on innovation (both for military and commercial purposes) and on financing SMEs, which benefit from DARPA (and other Department of Defense) R & D spending through the SBIR and STTR programs as well as through the significant amount of commercial spillovers that such R & D spending generates.

Two other more recent government programs that have an impact on early-stage financing are briefly considered in this chapter: angel capital networks and business incubators. Angel capital networks facilitate the provision of capital to businesses at their earliest stages of development by reducing the financing costs associated with locating possible sources of capital. Business incubator programs, as the name implies, also foster the earliest stages of a business's development, not through the provision of capital, but through the provision of basic services, including secretarial assistance, research labs, and sometimes research assistance.

The government expenditure programs discussed in this chapter are not intended to be an exhaustive list of the ways in which governments in Canada and the United States can and do assist in capitalizing small businesses. Rather, they illustrate other targeted means through which assistance can be provided. In reviewing these programs, it is important to consider how they compare with, coordinate with, and complement the tax expenditure programs considered in the previous chapters.

Primary Federal Small Business Development Agencies

US Small Business Administration

The SBA was established by the Small Business Act of 1953,[3] as the successor to several agencies created during the Great Depression and the Second World War.[4] The SBA was originally intended as a temporary measure to address several perceived problems facing small businesses. The enabling legislation declared it to be the policy of Congress that the federal government should "aid, counsel, assist, and protect insofar as is possible the interests of small-business concerns in order to preserve free competitive enterprise, to insure that a fair proportion of the total purchases and contracts for supplies and services for Government be placed with small business enterprises, and to maintain and strengthen the over-all economy to the Nation."[5] Since its inception, the SBA's mission has been to promote and assist the development of SMEs through two primary methods: "[c]hampioning small business interests" and "[e]mpowering entrepreneurs."[6] The first method includes minimizing the regulatory burden faced by small businesses, providing easy access to information, and ensuring that small businesses are treated fairly in the regulatory process. The SBA's efforts to reduce legal and regulatory burdens on SMEs are directed through a variety of programs, two of the more important of which are the Office of Advocacy and the National Ombudsman. Through its lobbying efforts and reports to Congress, in fiscal year 2002, the SBA claimed to have saved small business $21.1 billion in regulatory costs.[7] Concurrently, the ombudsman tries to create a more "friendly" environment between federal regulatory agencies and small businesses. The ombudsman receives and substantiates complaints from the small business community and reports to Congress on how to redress any problems that may exist in the regulatory environment.[8]

The second role that the SBA plays is that of empowering entrepreneurs. Within this role, there are two broad categories: financing SMEs and providing counselling and technical assistance to SMEs. The financing category involves equity financing and debt financing. I also include in the financing function the SBA's administration of federal government programs through which R & D financing is provided to SMEs.

Unlike the BDC in Canada, the SBA does not make direct equity investments in or loans to SMEs.[9] In terms of equity financing, the SBA administers the SBIC, specialized SBIC (SSBIC), and New Markets Venture Capital Company (NMVCC) programs.[10] The SBIC program, which played an instrumental role in the evolution of the private venture capital industry in the United States and remains important to this day, is considered separately below.

The vast majority of SBA financing of SMEs is provided through loan guarantees. The SBA has numerous loan guarantee programs. The primary lending program—the "7(a) loan guaranty"—is typical of the SBA's loan guarantee programs and is used to illustrate the various programs available. The 7(a) loan guaranty program operates through private sector lenders. The loan guaranty is available to a small business that meets certain SBA requirements, such as firm size, type of business, and appropriate use of funds and that has been rejected for a loan under normal circumstances. When a private sector loan has been rejected, the business can request that the private lender reconsider the loan under the conditions established by the SBA for a 7(a) loan guaranty. If both the lender and the SBA accept the loan, the SBA will guarantee part of the loan: up to 85 percent of loans not exceeding $150,000 are guaranteed, and up to 75 percent of loans exceeding $150,000 are guaranteed.[11] The interest rate, not exceeding the maximum rate established by the SBA, is determined by the lender and the entrepreneur. In fiscal year 2002, there were 51,666 approved 7(a) loans with a net dollar amount of $9.4 billion.[12] These loans were credited with creating 370,000 jobs.[13] Other SBA loan guarantee programs target special-need areas; for example, the 8(a) program is available to small businesses owned and controlled by socially and economically disadvantaged individuals.[14]

The SBA is also responsible for administering a number of federal government programs through which R & D funding is provided to SMEs. One of the earliest examples of such programs was a small business military procurement set-aside program organized by the SBA and the Department of Defense in

1953. In the small business financing hearings leading up to the development of the SBIC program, SBA officials reported that the US military's Quartermaster Research and Development Command at Natick, Massachusetts set aside one-quarter of its procurements for small businesses during the last half of 1956 and that small businesses received 6 percent of R & D prime defence contracts in fiscal 1956.[15] On average, about 4 percent of federal R & D funds went to small businesses during the late 1950s, and as much as 8.5 percent in April 1958.

A more formalized federal set-aside program, the small business innovative research program, was established in 1982.[16] The SBIR program requires any federal government agency that spends more than $100 million annually on external research to set aside a fixed percentage of these funds for awards to small businesses.[17] Recipients of SBIR awards must be independent, for-profit, US firms with fewer than 500 employees. The SBA administers the federal agencies' implementation of the program, reviews their progress, and reports annually to Congress on the program's operation. There are three phases to the SBIR program, although funding is only provided for the first two: phase I awards, for periods of up to six months in amounts up to $100,000, help winners determine a project's feasibility; and phase II awards, for periods of up to two years in amounts up to $750,000, support the development of phase I ideas. Phase III is for the commercialization of the results in phase II and requires private sector or non-SBIR funding. About half of phase I winners go on to receive phase II awards. Awards are made to companies as contracts or grants. The government does not receive any equity participation in the businesses in which awards are granted. The size of the SBIR program is significant. In 2001, the SBIR program provided 3,215 phase I awards and 1,533 phase II awards totalling about $1.5 billion.[18]

A similar set-aside program administered by the SBA, although operating on a much smaller scale, is the small business technology transfer program, which began making awards in 1994.[19] The STTR program requires any federal government agency that spends more than $1 billion annually on external research to set aside a fixed percentage of these funds for awards to small businesses.[20] The STTR program is designed to foster joint venture opportunities between small businesses and research centres. Eligible small businesses are essentially the same as those under the SBIR program (independent, for-profit, US firms with fewer than 500 employees).[21] The research centre must be located in the United States and be a non-profit college or university, a domestic non-profit research organization, or a federally funded R & D centre. The STTR program involves three phases similar to those under the SBIR program. Phase I is the startup phase, involving awards of up to $100,000 for about one year to fund the exploration of scientific, technical, and commercial feasibility of an idea or technology. Phase II awards are up to $750,000[22] for up to two years to expand on phase I ideas and explore commercial potential. Phase III involves commercialization, for which private sector or non-STTR federal funding must be sought. The aggregate size of the STTR program is significantly smaller than the SBIR program: in 2001, 224 phase I and 113 phase II awards were made, totalling about $78 million.[23]

The SBA has extensive programs that provide counselling and technical assistance to small businesses. These programs have the common goal of providing small businesses with a business plan and other counselling services so that the entrepreneur will have the knowledge to be successful and be able to better attract venture capital funding. Arguably the most important counselling program is the Small Business Development Center (SBDC), a corroborative program with the private sector and various levels of government that is administered by the SBA.[24] There is at least one lead SBDC in every state and SBDC services are available in more than 1,100 locations. Funding for each SBDC is a joint effort: the SBA will provide a maximum of 50 percent, and the rest will come from other sources such as state legislatures, private sector foundations, state and local chambers of commerce, state-chartered economic development corporations, public and private universities, vocational and technical schools, and community colleges. SBDCs deliver counselling and training in all aspects of small business management. In fiscal year 2002, over 650,000 clients utilized SBDCs.[25] Another popular and related program is SCORE—Service Corps of Retired Executives. SCORE is a non-profit association of retired persons experienced in business who counsel and mentor small business entrepreneurs for free.[26] In fiscal year 2002, SCORE provided 440,293 services to SMEs.[27]

Business Development Bank of Canada

The Canadian federal government has a long history of providing alternative financing to Canadian small businesses, although it has never sought to create a separate agency that advocates on behalf of SMEs. In terms of financing SMEs, though, the Canadian government has been active since the end of the Second World War. Unlike the SBA, the BDC, through which the Canadian government provides financial support to SMEs, makes direct equity investments in and loans to SMEs.

The Industrial Development Bank (IDB) was created in 1944[28] primarily "to help wartime manufacturers convert their facilities for peacetime operations."[29] The IDB had an initial capitalization of $25 million, which consisted of par value shares held by the Bank of Canada.[30] The role of the IDB was that of a "lender of last resort": the IDB had the power to lend or guarantee loans to industrial enterprises that could not obtain other financing on reasonable terms and conditions.[31] As a result, its lending activities were limited primarily to small businesses. In 1971, the IDB began to provide small businesses with advice on how to operate successfully.

In 1974, the IDB was replaced by the Federal Business Development Bank (FBDB).[32] The FBDB was to continue to act as a "lender of last resort" and to provide counselling services to small businesses. The counselling program became known as CASE—Counseling Assistance for Small Enterprises—and was funded by the government in collaboration with the private sector. The only significant difference between the IDB and the FBDB was that the FBDB could provide equity financing to SMEs. The IDB was permitted to hold stock of a corporation but only with a view to resale; the FBDB was not subject to a similar condition.[33]

By the mid-1990s, significant changes to the FBDB were considered necessary. Not only had the FBDB nearly reached its lending ceiling of $3.2 billion,[34] various problems with the FBDB had to be addressed. Most notable was the perception that Canadians had of the FBDB, as remarked by John Manley, former minister of industry and in charge of the FBDB: "[the FBDB] was not exactly well respected by its customers, by the professions that dealt with it or by government. It was seen as a political bank which had done a lot of stupid stuff over the years."[35] A more substantive concern was that the FBDB was not meeting the changing needs of the Canadian economy. As small businesses moved away from traditional business sectors into the "new economy"—businesses dependent on knowledge and technology—private financial institutions, as well as the FBDB, were not keeping pace. The government believed that it had to demonstrate to private sector banks that investment in these new types of small businesses could be commercially successful. The FBDB's mandate of being a "lender of last resort" would no longer suffice to meet this objective. To change the behaviour of chartered banks, the "new" FBDB would be aggressive and signal to chartered banks the types of investments that could be made if the banks chose to do so;[36] in addition, the new FBDB would maintain the role of a complementary lender.

The Business Development Bank of Canada was created in 1995[37] as a continuation of the FBDB.[38] The BDC assumed the property, obligations, and liabilities of the FDBD and continued supporting Canadian entrepreneurship by providing financial and management services. However, the BDC was given a "refocused" mandate, no longer confined to the role as "lender of last resort." The BDC was given the flexibility to achieve its new mandate: providing complementary services to Canadian SMEs[39] while operating on a commercial basis so that it earns a rate of return at least equal to the government's cost of funds and recovers its costs for its consulting services.[40] The capital available to the BDC was increased significantly because the FBDB had reached its lending ceiling of $3.2 billion in 1995. The BDC is authorized to have capital not exceeding $1.5 billion and is permitted borrowings and contingent liabilities of 12 times equity.[41] In other words, the BDC has potentially $19.5 billion available for financing SMEs, an increase of $16.3 billion over the previous limit.

The new operating mandate of the BDC identified four "gaps" in the marketplace that were considered to limit the proliferation and growth of SMEs and technology-based companies and therefore to have a detrimental impact on the future of Canada's economy: the risk gap, the size gap, the flexibility gap, and the knowledge gap.[42] The knowledge gap is considered particularly important as the Canadian economy shifts to new economy businesses competing in a global economy. Consequently, 50 percent of all BDC new financings over the long term are to be in knowledge-based industries (KBIs) and exporters.[43] The gaps approach seeks to address fears that the BDC will crowd out private sector investment that would have occurred in any event. By focusing on the gaps and other areas that private sector financial institutions are perceived to have ignored, such as women, aboriginal, and youth entrepreneurs, BDC investing will ideally result in minimal crowding out, so that the BDC complements rather than competes with private sector investment.[44]

In seeking to fulfill this complementary mandate, the BDC maintains three operating groups: the loans group, the investment group, and the consulting group.[45] The loans group is the largest of the three groups and continues the mandate of the FBDB to act as a lender of last resort. The nature and quality of the loans are designed to suit the needs of SMEs that are unable to acquire sufficient funding from private institutions. For example, the BDC will take less security for a loan and invest at the early stages of a business's development. As a result, the BDC's loan loss experience "is at least double that of its industry peers, and can even be three times higher in riskier product categories."[46] The BDC maintains 80 branches nationwide and 95 percent of all credit decisions are made at the local level to take account of regional economic conditions.[47] The investment group is responsible for venture capital and subordinated financing. The main focus of the BDC's venture capital investing is to act as a "path breaker" by supporting high-growth SMEs that do not have the tangible assets generally considered necessary to obtain funding from private sector financial institutions. The intention of this "path breaking" is to demonstrate to the private sector the commercial viability of investing in KBIs. For subordinated financing, a hybrid of debt financing and venture capital, the BDC "accounts for three of every four dollars of SME subordinated financing in Canada for amounts under $1 million."[48] The role of the third group, the consulting group, is considered essential to the development of Canadian SMEs; according to the BDC, "[t]he main detriment of success for Canada's one million SMEs is management capability."[49] The consulting group consists of a national network of partnerships with small and mid-sized consulting firms.

The venture capital group at the BDC—the group most germane to the programs considered in this book—includes about 40 professionals in six locations across Canada: Vancouver, Calgary, Toronto, Ottawa, Montreal, and Halifax, with larger concentrations in the three largest cities. The group operates in a manner similar to private sector venture capital firms. Its venture capital professionals are divided by expertise into four groups within the KBI industry: telecommunications; information technology; advanced technologies; and biotechnology and life sciences. The professionals' compensation includes a performance-related element as a long-term incentive. This portion of the compensation is a multiple of salary, subject to a cap, based on the performance of the investment portfolio. In addition to direct investment in SMEs, the BDC invests in private venture capital funds that it sees as complementary to its investment activities. The private funds have been predominantly seed capital funds because the BDC did not have the in-house expertise to invest at this stage. However, in May 2002 the BDC commenced its own seed capital initiative and since then has hired a number of seed capital specialists. Other than seed capital financing—which the BDC only started in early 2003—all of the venture capital investments undertaken by the BDC have been syndicated deals; it is not the sole investor in a portfolio company, and in the majority of cases it is not the lead investor. The BDC estimates that it accounts for about one-fifth of the venture capital raised by the portfolio companies in which it invests (that is, for every $1 of BDC venture capital, the company raises $4 of private sector venture capital).

BDC loan and investment commitments have reached a record high of about $7.2 billion.[50] Of this total, $6.8 billion consists of loans and $374 million of venture capital. Of the $1.7 billion of lending authorized in fiscal 2002, $855 million was provided to KBIs and exporters. Furthermore, over half of these loans were for amounts under $100,000, and 73 percent were for amounts under $250,000.[51] The BDC earned $80 million on its loans operations in 2002.[52] These statistics suggest that the BDC is adhering to its lending mandate. Of the $374 million in venture capital, 99 percent was committed to KBIs.[53] In fiscal year 2002, 72 percent of venture capital was invested in seed, startup, or development stages.[54] The venture capital portfolio suffered an income loss of almost $21 million in 2002, after earning over $56 million in 2001 and over $80 million in 2000.[55] The consulting group participated in 5,000 projects in fiscal 2002 and suffered operating losses of $5.7 million.[56] The consulting group has yet to meet its mandate of recovering its costs.

Since its inception in 1995, the BDC has met many of its goals. It has provided financial and consulting services for many SMEs across Canada in ways that the private sector may not have. The BDC has made a profit in each year of operation, and 2002 was the sixth consecutive year that a dividend was paid to the government of Canada.[57] But this success must be seen in the light of the phenomenal growth that the Canadian economy has experienced since the BDC's inception in 1995. The BDC's success may be correlational rather than causal. The true value of the BDC will be seen in the next few years, in the wake of the tech bust and with significantly lower forecasts for economic growth.

A comparison of the BDC and the SBA illustrates a key philosophical difference between the Canadian and US federal government expenditure programs that target SME financing. Through the BDC, the Canadian federal government makes available debt and equity financing directly to SMEs.[58] The SBA, in contrast, facilitates private sector investment through loan guarantees and through the SBIC, SSBIC, and NMVCC programs. These three equity-financing programs, considered in the next section, exemplify the aversion in the United States to any form of government equity participation in private enterprises.[59] Unlike the BDC, the SBA does not make direct loans or grants to SMEs. As a guarantor of loans or as a passive investor or guarantor of investors in privately managed SBICs, SSBICs, and NMVCCs, the SBA allows small businesses to develop relationships with private sector financial institutions and investors. The BDC, in contrast, endeavours to "complement" the private sector by investing where "gaps" are believed to exist in the economy that inhibit a vibrant small business community.

Direct investment by the BDC gives the federal government greater power in deciding which SMEs and which sectors of the economy to support, thus adding a degree of political accountability for the investment decisions. It also exposes the BDC to allegations of political manipulation in those decisions.[60]

The US approach, in contrast, leaves the investment decisions in the private sector, thus reducing the potential for political interference in the investment decision-making process (although not eliminating it entirely).

The R & D spending programs administered by the SBA have also acted as an important signal for private sector venture capital investment. In his examination of the SBIR program, Josh Lerner found that, over the long run, SBIR awardees had substantially greater employment and sales growth than similar non-awardees, although this growth was confined to firms in geographic areas with substantial venture capital activity.[61] Lerner also found that awardees were significantly more likely to obtain venture capital funding in years after receiving an award, whereas in previous years the likelihood did not differ significantly. Lerner concluded that the SBIR awards provide an important certification function or signal for the formal venture capital industry. He suggested that

> it might be possible that a program that offered much more modest subsidies could also be effective in certifying the quality—and spurring the growth— of small high-technology firms. Two crucial assumptions, however, are that such recognition would be sufficient to motivate firms to seek awards and that the integrity of the selection process could be insured.[62]

It would be useful to know whether BDC funding provides the same sort of signalling to private sector venture capital firms. I am not aware of any studies similar to Lerner's that examine businesses that have received BDC funding in Canada, although a study like Lerner's is certainly warranted for rapid-growth SMEs that have received financing.

Lerner's finding that there is a geographic concentration of successful SBIR awards—which is consistent with the geographic concentration of high-tech firms[63]—calls into question congressional efforts to promote greater geographic dispersion of SBIR awards. This concern can bear on any federal government direct spending program where Congress members or members of Parliament believe that businesses in their constituencies deserve a "fair share" of federal government spending. I suspect that the BDC must be under the same sort of political pressure to ensure that small businesses across Canada benefit from its loan and equity investments.[64] The possibility of such pressure highlights one of the potential advantages of a tax expenditure program, such as a tax credit program, in which private sector investors (including venture capital funds) determine which businesses to support and the geographic location of the tax credits falls out accordingly.

The Sputnik Crisis, Military R & D, and Venture Capital Funds

In retrospect, the *Sputnik* crisis in 1958 may have been one of the best things to happen for innovative small businesses and the venture capital industry in the United States. The vulnerability felt by the United States when the Soviet Union appeared to be winning the space race sparked two key government responses, one a new military research and development program and the other a federally sponsored national small business venture capital investment fund program.

DARPA and Innovative Research

The first response of the United States to the *Sputnik* crisis was to establish the Advanced Research Projects Agency, in February 1958, in order to ensure that the United States would never again be technologically surprised by its adversaries.[65] ARPA (later DARPA)[66] was designed to operate in conjunction with but independent of the conventional military R & D establishment. It has no laboratories or facilities. Rather, it hires expert program managers to take fundamental research and accelerate its development for current military use. Only about 5 percent of DARPA's research is basic research. About 90 percent of DARPA's budget—which, over its 45-year history, has exceeded $50 billion, and is currently about $2 billion per year—is spent through organizations outside the federal government, including universities and private industry. DARPA essentially underwrites part of the risk of developing new technologies, thus encouraging applied research in the private sector. DARPA's current mission is

> to maintain the technological superiority of the U.S. military and prevent technological surprise from harming our national security by sponsoring revolutionary, high-payoff research that bridges the gap between fundamental discoveries and their military use.[67]

Although DARPA's mandate is the military use of technology, it is often the case that the technologies developed under DARPA projects have commercial, non-military potential. The dual use of technology has been a specific mandate of DARPA in the past (for example, in the changes initiated in 1993 under the Clinton administration) and remains important today. Probably the most famous spinoff from a DARPA project is the Internet, which began in the 1960s-1970s with the development of ARPANet and its associated TCP/IP network architecture.

DARPA has four basic funding mechanisms for research and development:[68]

- procurement contracts, which are available to any organization, typically on a cost-plus-fixed-fee basis;
- grants, which are awarded to universities and other non-profit organizations, usually for a fixed sum;
- cooperative agreements, which are similar to grants except that substantial involvement is expected between DARPA and the funding recipient, and the recipient can be a non-profit or for-profit organization; and
- "other" transactions, which usually involve consortiums and commercial firms and typically use a milestone payment method.

A particular type of "other" transaction, a section 845 prototype agreement, focuses on the development of prototypes for weapons or weapons systems.

Section 845 prototype agreements typically apply to a consortium or defence contractor and use milestone, cost-plus-fixed-fee, or cost-plus-incentive-fee payment methods.

DARPA has had the authority to enter into "other" transactions since 1989. This contractual method has become increasingly popular because it gives DARPA authority to waive most traditional rules and regulations in order to tailor the specific needs of the program.[69] An "other" transaction cannot be used where the principal purpose is to acquire goods and services for the direct benefit of the acquiring agency or for research that duplicates work under any existing Department of Defense program. "Other" transactions are used as the funding mechanism "when the use of a standard contract, grant, or cooperative agreement for such project is not feasible or appropriate."[70] Where cost sharing is practicable under a cooperation agreement or "other" transaction (other than a section 845 prototype agreement), government funds must be matched by an equal amount of funds from the other participants.[71]

Military R & D spending remains one of the most important sources of innovation in the US economy, generating significant spillovers that have commercial application and that benefit rapid-growth SMEs. Canada simply does not undertake the same amount of government R & D that is undertaken in the United States. Thus, Canadian government R & D spending does not provide the same degree of spillovers nor the same opportunity for financing rapid-growth SMEs as that provided in the United States.

The SBIC Program and the Evolution of US Private Venture Capital Funds

The second response of the US government to the *Sputnik* crisis was the creation of a national program to finance small businesses, although without any direct federal government investment in these businesses. The Small Business Investment Act of 1958[72] established a new division of the SBA to administer a new venture capital investment vehicle, small business investment corporations. Congress appropriated a $250 million revolving fund to start the SBIC program. It was, in effect, the first government-sponsored venture capital fund program in North America.

Originally, SBICs needed $300,000 of capital to be licensed, of which at least one-half had to be raised by private investors. The SBA was authorized to match private investors' funds, to a maximum of $150,000, by purchasing subordinated debentures of the SBIC. In addition to matching the private sector investment, the SBA could lend additional funds to an SBIC, not exceeding one-half of its paid-in capital and surplus (including, for this purpose, the amount of any subordinated debentures acquired by the SBA). As a result, if private investors raised $150,000 of capital for an SBIC, the SBA could leverage it with an additional $300,000. SBIC investors also benefited from tax incentives, in the form of additional loss relief.[73] The federal government could not own stock in SBICs, and, as originally conceived, SBICs could not make equity investments: they could make loans and purchase debentures convertible into common stock, but could not make initial investments in common stock. The availability of cheap government money induced many, perhaps ill-qualified, people to form SBICs.[74]

Between 1958 and 1971, a number of amendments were made to the SBIC program, increasing the amount of leverage that could be provided by the SBA. In 1967,[75] SBA leverage was increased with a distinction made between "regular" SBICs that provided both debt and equity capital and SBICs that invested at least 65 percent of their funds in "venture capital."[76] For the former, private equity could be leveraged 200 percent with SBA debentures, to a maximum of $7.5 million of leverage. For the latter, private equity could be leveraged 300 percent, to a maximum of $10 million of leverage. In 1971, the SBA was authorized to guarantee (as an alternative to purchase) debentures of SBICs.[77] In 1972, the amount of leverage that could be provided by the SBA was doubled ($15 million for "regular" SBICs and $20 million for SBICs making sufficient venture capital investments),[78] and in 1976, the amount of leverage was further increased to 300 percent for regular SBICs and 400 percent for venture capital SBICs, in both cases with a ceiling of $35 million.[79]

Despite the significant increases in SBA leverage, the SBIC program as originally conceived was doomed to failure primarily because the government (or government-guaranteed) leverage was provided to SBICs as debt even though they were intended to make long-term, primarily equity, investments in small businesses. This mismatching of debt obligations to equity investments inevitably led to cash flow problems and brought about the demise of many SBICs. Those that survived often provided primarily or exclusively debt financing rather than equity financing to small businesses, which stifled their ability to expand. In addition, SBICs did not invest in high-technology ventures. In 1966, only 3.5 percent of SBIC investments were in high-technology firms, and many SBICs turned from financing new ventures to other pursuits such as real estate development.[80] Successful SBICs, in terms of fulfilling the objective of providing equity financing to small businesses, were limited primarily to bank-owned SBICs, which did not rely on government (or government-guaranteed) loans to leverage their capital. Private venture capital firms proliferated as the SBIC movement waned. By 1989, only about 200 SBICs were active, compared with about 370 active private independent firms at the time.

When the SBIA was enacted in 1958, it permitted national banks and other member banks of the Federal Reserve System and non-member insured banks to the extent permitted under applicable state law to invest in SBICs, "except that in no event [could] any such bank hold shares in [SBICs] in an amount aggregating more than 1 percent of [the bank's] capital and surplus."[81] In 1961, this limit was increased to 2 percent.[82] Bank of America organized the first bank-owned SBIC in 1959 (the Small Business Enterprises Corporation). Between 1958 and 1965, 14 banks began venture investing, all through SBICs. Between 1966 and 1970, 11 more banks began venture investing, 8 through SBICs and 3 through other types of venture capital affiliates. These bank-related SBICs also served as training grounds for future private venture capital fund managers. By 1968, there were 30 SBICs wholly owned by banks and another 80 with substantial investments from banks. The 1967 amendments to the SBIA increased permitted SBIC investment by banks to 5 percent of their capital, but precluded a bank from owning 50 percent or more of an SBIC's stock.[83] In the three-month window before the amendments took effect, four major banks organized SBICs and added more than $15 million in private capital. In 1976, the 50 percent ceiling on SBIC stock ownership by banks was removed.[84] The 5 percent limitation has remained in place since 1967.

Significant changes were made to the SBIC regime in 1992 in an effort to rejuvenate the program (apart from its application to banks).[85] The amendments were designed to remove the cash flow problems associated with leverage provided by government or government-guaranteed debt. There were three primary changes: a new form of government leverage provided through "participating securities" was introduced; private capital requirements (as a means of reducing government risk) were increased; and the regulation of SBICs that did not rely on SBA-leveraged financing (primarily bank-owned SBICs) was reduced. In addition to describing these amendments, the remainder of this section summarizes the salient features of the current SBIC regime.

An SBIC may be organized as a corporation, a limited partnership, or a limited liability company.[86] To be licensed by the SBA, an SBIC must demonstrate that its proposed management has the knowledge, experience, and capability necessary to comply with the objectives and obligations of the SBIA, regulations, and the business plan of the proposed SBIC,[87] and that it has sufficient private capital. Well-qualified managers must have experience in dealing with small businesses and also have an interest in serving small business concerns. However, the management and ownership of the SBIC must be sufficiently diverse to ensure independence and objectivity in the investment decisions and operations of the SBIC.[88] An SBIC must have a minimum capitalization of $5 million, or $10 million if the SBIC intends to seek authority to issue participating securities to be purchased or guaranteed by the SBA.[89] In addition, at least 30 percent of the capital must be provided by sources that are not affiliated with the management of the SBIC.[90] The minimum capitalization requirements do not include borrowed funds or SBA-backed leverage.[91]

An SBIC is authorized to borrow money and to issue securities, promissory notes, or other obligations.[92] The SBA can guarantee debentures of an SBIC, subject to certain limits discussed below. As noted above, the 1992 amendments also introduced a new form of SBA leverage, participating securities. The SBA can guarantee the redemption price and prioritized payments[93] of participating securities, and a trust or a pool acting on behalf of the SBA is authorized to purchase such securities. Participating securities are defined to include "preferred stock, a preferred limited partnership interest or a similar instrument, including debentures under the terms of which interest is payable only to the extent of earnings."[94] Participating securities are also subject to a number of restrictions and limitations:[95]

- they must be redeemed no later than 15 years after the date of issuance for an amount equal to the issue price plus any accrued prioritized payments;[96]

- prioritized payments are preferred and cumulative, with a rate based on US government marketable obligations with a similar maturity[97] plus, for securities obligated after September 30, 2001, an additional charge payable to the SBA, not to exceed 1.38 percent, intended to cover the SBA's cost of purchasing and guaranteeing participating securities;[98]
- an SBIC that issues participating securities must invest an amount equal to the outstanding face value of the securities solely in equity capital;[99] and
- where the SBA guarantees the participating securities of the SBIC, the SBA is entitled to a participating share in the SBIC's profits based on a formula that takes into account the amount of leverage provided by participating securities.[100]

Section 303(g) of the SBIA further provides that "this paragraph shall not be construed to create any ownership interest of the [SBA] in the [SBIC]."[101]

In addition to its profit allocation for participating securities—whether through prioritized payments as the holder of the participating securities, or through its (non-cumulative) profit share as the guarantor of participating securities— the SBA is entitled to a leverage fee (for both debt and participating security leverage) equal to 3 percent of the face amount of leverage granted to the SBIC.[102]

The 1992 amendments created a new schedule of the maximum leverage available to SBICs. After March 31, 1993, the following limits were introduced:[103]

- for SBICs with private capital of not more than $15 million, up to 300 percent of private capital;
- for SBICs with private capital between $15 million and $30 million, up to $45 million plus 200 percent of the amount of private capital over $15 million; and
- for SBICs with private capital exceeding $30 million, up to $75 million plus 100 percent of the amount of private capital over $30 million, but not to exceed an additional $15 million (that is, the maximum leverage for such companies cannot exceed $90 million).

However, in no event can participating securities exceed 200 percent of private capital.[104]

An SBIC can provide financing to small businesses in the form of equity or debt,[105] although the SBIC must provide equity financing at least equal to the outstanding amount of any participating securities.[106] The Small Business Act defines a small business as a business that has net assets not exceeding $18 million and average after-tax income for the prior two years not exceeding $6 million.[107] If these limits are exceeded, the business may still qualify if it meets certain size standards for its industry group.[108] An SBIC is specifically precluded from investing in certain businesses, including finance and investment companies, unimproved real estate, companies with less than one-half of their assets and operations in the United States, and passive or casual businesses.[109] An SBIC can acquire shares of an incorporated business or a limited partnership interest, but it may not become a general partner or jointly or severally liable for any obligations of an unincorporated business. Loans from an SBIC must have terms of at least 5 years[110] and must not mature beyond 20 years, although under certain conditions repayment may be extended for another 10 years. SBIC loans can have equity features, such as an option to convert or any other right to acquire equity shares. There are two limitations on the overall financing provided by an SBIC. First, the SBIC is not permitted to control, directly or indirectly, any small business,[111] although temporary control is permitted in order to protect its investment. Second, the SIBC may not invest more than 20 percent of its capital in any one small business.[112] Non-leveraged SBICs are exempt from this portfolio diversification requirement.[113]

To maintain its licence, an SBIC must "conduct active operations," which means that it must not have idle funds in excess of 20 percent of its total assets (at cost) or that it must have made financings totalling at least 20 percent of its regulatory capital in the 18 months preceding its fiscal year-end.[114] In effect, every 18 months, an SBIC must invest 20 percent of its regulatory capital in small businesses until at least 80 percent of its total capital has been so invested. Furthermore, at least 20 percent of all financings must be invested in "smaller enterprises."[115]

Where an SBIC fails to comply with any provision of the SBIA or regulations, all of its rights, privileges, and franchises may be forfeited.[116] However, before the SBIC can be dissolved or have its rights forfeited, the non-compliance or violation must be determined and adjudged in court. If an SBIC fails to comply with the terms of a leveraging agreement, the entire indebtedness may immediately become due and payable.[117] Where the leverage is in the form of participating securities, the sanction will depend on the nature of the non-compliance.[118] If the non-compliance is severe, such as insolvency or wilfully violating the SBIA or regulations, the SBA may, among other things, replace the majority of the board of directors of the SBIC with approved individuals, or appoint a receiver for the purpose of continuing the SBIC's operations. For a violation of any of the substantive provisions of the SBIA or regulations, such as not maintaining sufficient regulatory capital, the SBA may, among other things, prohibit additional investments from being made or not permit distributions by the SBIC until all leverage is redeemed and amounts owing are paid.

The 1992 amendments have had a profound impact on the amount of capital raised by SBICs. Between 1976 and 1988, the total capital under management by SBICs grew from about $1 billion to a little over $3 billion. It remained at this level until 1993, when it started to increase quite dramatically, to over $20 billion in the fiscal year ending September 30, 2002.[119] Of this amount, $11.7 billion represented private capital, and the rest consisted of either outstanding or committed leverage from the SBA. More than one-quarter of all SBIC capital—$5.4 billion of $20 billion—was controlled by 87 bank-owned SBICs. In addition, only 0.6 percent of bank-owned SBIC capital was provided through leverage from the SBA. Participating security SBICs accounted for $10.5 billion, of which over $6.1 billion was leverage or committed leverage from (or guaranteed by) the SBA. Debenture SBICs accounted for the remaining $3.9 billion.[120] The most significant changes between 2001 and 2002 were the continued decline in the number of bank-owned SBICs and the continued increase in participating security SBICs. The decline in bank-owned SBICs probably stems from the liberalization of bank regulation in 1999,[121] when the number of bank-owned SBICs peaked at 101 and bank-owned SBICs controlled over 45 percent of all SBIC capital.[122]

The nature of investments by SBICs also changed dramatically in the past decade. In 1992, the majority (in number) of SBIC financings were straight debt, accounting in monetary terms for 28.4 percent of financings; equity-only financings accounted for 45 percent; and debt with equity financings accounted for the rest. Equity-only financings made up half of all financings by 1995 and almost 74 percent by 2002, while straight debt declined to 7 percent. In 2002, straight equity financings made up 62 percent of all financings, while straight debt made up 12 percent.[123]

In summary, the 1992 amendments succeeded in rejuvenating the SBIC program, both in the overall capital raised through SBICs and in the nature of SBIC investment in small businesses. Although the SBIC program from 1958 to 1992 may be viewed as having failed to create adequate pools of venture capital, it was instrumental in the evolution of the private US venture capital industry in two respects. First, it served as a training ground for venture capital fund managers, a number of whom went on to establish private venture capital funds. Second, it helped bring banks into the venture capital industry.

Government Leveraging Versus Tax Credits

The SBIC program—through which the government leverages private sector investment through government (or government-guaranteed) investment—may be contrasted with the various venture capital fund (VCF) tax credit programs discussed in chapter 6. In Canada, VCF tax credit programs made their debut in the mid-1970s in Quebec. The federal government has provided a tax credit for investment in labour-sponsored venture capital corporations (LSVCCs) since 1985, although it does not provide a tax credit for investment in other types of VCFs. Most provinces currently have some form of VCF tax credit program, whether an LSVCC program, a community-based VCF program, or a general VCF program. In the United States, state-level VCF programs were introduced in the early 1980s, and a variety of VCF programs are currently in force. The US federal government does not offer tax incentives for investment in VCFs. However, the federal SBIC program, which may be considered the first government VCF program in North America, has the same objective as the various VCF programs: alleviating the equity gap faced by small businesses by leveraging private sector investment in VCFs.

There are many similarities between the SBIC program and VCF tax credit programs. The investment criteria that govern both SBICs and many VCFs are similar in terms of the types of businesses that they finance and the investment pacing requirements that they must meet. In many VCF programs—certainly in the more appropriately targeted ones—business types are restricted through either a "black list" of excluded businesses or a "white list" of included businesses.[124] The SBIC program applies a black list. In terms of pacing requirements, most VCF programs require a substantial portion of capital that VCFs raise in a year to be invested in qualified businesses within two to three years. The SBIC program is more generous in this respect; it requires 80 percent of the capital to be invested within 72 months (at the rate of 20 percent every 18 months), with at least 20 percent invested in smaller SMEs. Under the program, SBIC managers must demonstrate knowledge, experience, and capability of venture capital investing; this requirement, which is appropriate to any government-subsidized VCF plan, is found in relatively few VCF programs.

There are, however, important distinctions between the SBIC program and the various VCF programs, particularly the manner in which risks and returns are shared by the government and private sector investors. Consider the following simple example, in which a 50 percent tax credit is contrasted with 100 percent government leveraging through its investment in preferred shares with a fixed cumulative dividend (similar to participating securities that may be issued by SBICs). Investor group A invests $1,000,000 in fund A for common shares of fund A, and derives tax credits of $500,000. The after-tax cost to the investors is thus $500,000. Investor group B invests $500,000 (of after-tax dollars) in fund B for common shares of fund B, which the government matches with an investment of $500,000 for preferred shares of fund B (with a cumulative dividend of 4 percent per annum). Both funds therefore have $1,000,000 to invest, in amounts provided equally by the government (or through government guarantees[125]) and private sector investors. In both cases the funds have a life of 10 years. It is assumed that no dividends are paid during this period by fund B (dividends accumulate until the fund disposes of its investments when it is wound up).

In the first scenario, suppose that both funds do well and at the end of 10 years have assets (cash from realized investments as well as shares of portfolio companies) worth $2,000,000, double the initial capital invested. In fund A, investor group A is entitled to the entire amount as the only shareholders of the fund. Investor group A's return on their initial investment over the 10 years, based on its after-tax cost and ignoring taxes on realization, is 300 percent. In fund B, before investor group B can be paid out, the government is entitled to a return of its capital ($500,000) plus its cumulative dividends ($20,000 per year × 10 years), or $700,000. Investor group B receives the balance or $1,300,000, for a return on its (after-tax) investment of 160 percent.

In the second scenario, each fund's assets are worth $1,000,000 after 10 years; there is no return over the period. However, investor group A receives the entire $1,000,000, thus realizing a 100 percent return on its initial investment. In fund B, the first $700,000 of assets (original capital plus cumulative dividends) goes to the government, leaving investor group B with only $300,000, for a loss of 40 percent.

In the third scenario, each fund's assets are worth only $700,000 after 10 years. Investor group A receives the entire amount and realizes a 40 percent return on its initial investment. Investor group B receives nothing, because the government has the preferred position, and thus loses its entire investment.

In highly simplified terms, fund A does not have to do very well in order for investor group A to come out ahead on an after-tax basis. In fact, the fund can lose money over its 10-year existence and still generate a positive return for investor group A on its investment. Fund B, in contrast, must generate an annual return of at least 4 percent (the return necessary to cover the cumulative dividend on the government's preferred shares, ignoring the effects of compounding) simply to preserve investor group B's original capital.

A tax credit program thus provides a much greater incentive than a leveraging program does to potential investors—and so also provides a reduced incentive for the venture capital firm to manage the fund efficiently—because the government assumes a much larger share of the risk for no direct return from the investment. The government's return is derived only from the spinoff effects of its investment: the direct, indirect, and induced benefits generated by the fund's investment in portfolio companies.[126] In the leveraging program, the spinoff effects are the same—arguably better because the fund will be run more efficiently—but the government also shares in the actual return of the VCF in return for its share of the risk.

The spinoff effects must therefore be greater under the tax credit program in order to generate the same return to the government as the leveraging program. Put another way, in order for the government's return in fund A to be comparable to that in fund B, fund A must invest in more high-growth companies (that employ more people and/or have greater profits over the long term) than fund B does. In effect, the investment managers of fund A must invest in higher-risk businesses that have the potential to generate greater returns. At the same time, the investment managers of fund A are under less pressure from its investors to make high-risk investments because its investors have obtained an upfront, visible, and easily quantifiable incentive to invest. The tax credit program is thus less likely to create a thriving venture capital industry that can eventually survive in the absence of government incentives. However, the availability of government leverage may not be sufficient to attract the necessary investors in the first place. The choice between the two programs, or variations thereof, thus depends to a large extent on the perceived risk aversion of the targeted investors in the venture capital fund.

It is often said that Canadian investors and entrepreneurs are more conservative than their US counterparts—that US culture fosters individualism and daring, whereas Canadian culture encourages aversion to risk. These differences, or perceived differences,[127] may have had some influence on the venture capital programs adopted at the national level in both countries. The US SBIC program, which depended on government-guaranteed leveraging rather than tax credits, had many failings in the years before 1992, when it was amended to remove the cash flow problems associated with government-provided leverage. The program had some success, though, in fostering the development of the US private sector venture capital industry, particularly leading up to the late 1970s, when pension fund money came flooding into the industry. In Canada, no similar preparation underlay the relaxation of investment restrictions on—really, the introduction of positive incentives for—pension fund investment in 1985. This lack of ground-work may have led most Canadian pension funds to abandon venture capital investments in the recession of the early 1990s, in many cases not to return.

Innovation in the Venture Capital Industry: Angel Capital Networks and Incubators

A variety of innovative features have been developed in the formal and infor-mal venture capital industries to address the equity gap affecting SMEs. Two are considered here: angel capital networks and incubator programs. They both address the common problems of information asymmetries in the financing of SMEs. Angel capital networks are intended to reduce the transaction costs asso-ciated with matching entrepreneurs with seed capital investors, thus reducing pre-investment information asymmetries, or adverse selection. Incubator pro-grams provide services (such as research labs, bookkeeping, and secretarial assistance) rather than capital to innovative small businesses. Incubators are a method of controlling post-investment information asymmetries, or moral hazard.

Angel Capital Networks

Information about government sources of capital[128] and private venture capital funds[129] is available to SMEs, but there are no directories of angel investors for entrepreneurs, nor are there lists of investment opportunities available to angel investors. Entrepreneurs seeking capital are matched to business angels prima-rily by word of mouth. This is highly inefficient. Both public sector economic development organizations and private sector companies have responded by creating business introduction services, commonly referred to as "angel capital networks." These services are intended to make the informal venture capital market more efficient by reducing the costs associated with venture investing. As discussed below, however, such networks, even if they are successful, will only reduce the costs of introducing the entrepreneur to the potential investor. The more significant costs—the costs of evaluating potential investments and monitoring investments made—are not affected by the manner in which most angel capital networks operate.

Business introduction services in North America generally operate as com-puter matching services. The first such service, the Venture Capital Network (VCN), was established at the University of New Hampshire in 1984 by William Wetzel Jr. and has been copied in many places throughout the United States, as well as in Canada, with varying degrees of success.[130] Given the nature of the potential investors involved and their propensity to invest close to home, business introduction services usually operate on a regional basis. They tend to be managed by not-for-profit organizations such as universities, chambers of commerce, or economic development agencies. They are funded by a variety of sources including subscriptions (by entrepreneurs, investors, or both), national and subnational governments, and charitable foundations, as well as sponsorship from service providers such as banks, utility companies, accounting and law firms, and other firms that have an interest in the local economy and that advertise on the network.

Under most computer matching services, investors complete a short questionnaire outlining the investment opportunities that interest them. Entrepreneurs also complete a short questionnaire providing information about the business venture that they want financed, including highlights of their business plan. The databases of investors and entrepreneurs are compared to determine whether an angel's investment preferences match the characteristics of a business seeking finance. If they do, the entrepreneur's application (excluding personal identification) is sent to the angel, who, if interested, can request a more detailed business plan. Until this point, the review is undertaken on an anonymous basis. If the investor wishes to pursue the opportunity, contact details are provided to both parties. At this point, the involvement of the matching service ends. It is up to the investor and the entrepreneur to meet and evaluate the business opportunity. The matching service does not vet the information provided to it by either entrepreneurs or investors. In both Canada and the United States, this limitation is generally considered necessary in order to avoid registering the network under applicable securities regulation.

Studies of US matching services suggest a variety of factors that contribute to the success of the services, although the studies are inconclusive. For example, a 1991 study of 17 venture capital networks concluded that a well-organized, well-funded network with an aggressive marketing program would help ensure the success of obtaining a critical mass of entrepreneurs and potential investors.[131] Five years later, when the authors of the study found that only 8 of the 17 networks remained operational, they concluded that other factors were at least as important as money.[132] In particular, success was dependent on the network's location in a heavily populated area close to areas with a high formal venture capital density. In other words, they appear to function well in areas where there is a developed high-tech sector that spins off both new venture opportunities and successful entrepreneurs who often become angel investors themselves. Unfortunately, these findings do not bode well for the successful development of a matching service outside such areas.[133]

The failure to successfully replicate VCN on a national basis in Canada is equally indicative of the problems in creating a viable informal investment network beyond certain relatively small geographic regions. In 1986, the Ontario Chamber of Commerce advanced the idea of an Ontario version of VCN. The 1986 Ontario government speech from the throne announced the Computerized Ontario Investment Network (COIN), initially funded by the provincial government. Like VCN, COIN did not screen applications by either entrepreneurs or investors and could not provide investment advice. COIN was launched in November

1986 and later expanded its operations to a national basis as the Canada Opportunities Investment Network (and kept the same acronym). On its national launch, it undertook a significant media campaign and "road show" with the goal of enlisting 1,000 users. According to its first financial statements, in the four months ending in April 1987, COIN had attracted 60 to 75 investors and 75 to 125 entrepreneurs. Three years later, its financial statements suggested that it had managed to attract only 200 to 400 entrepreneurs and 80 to 100 investors.[134] COIN no longer operates.

An empirical study of the impact of COIN published in 1996[135] suggested that the network failed primarily because it did not reflect the nature of the informal venture capital marketplace. As all studies of informal venture capital suggest, the informal venture capital market is highly localized and personal: angels tend to co-invest with acquaintances whose opinions they trust. "Establishing a *national* and *impersonal* referral service is fundamentally at odds with the nature of the market."[136] The study concluded that a matching service, to be successful, must be local in scope and must create a client base of quality entrepreneurs and investors. The creation of such a base requires knowledgeable individuals working for the matching service who can effectively screen both entrepreneur and investor applications. However, a service that performs these functions requires significantly greater personnel and financial support, and may have greater compliance requirements under applicable securities legislation, than a service that does not vet applications.

In 1995-96, Industry Canada developed the Canada Community Investment Plan (CCIP), a seven-year pilot project to establish investment facilitation services in a number of communities across Canada. The CCIP chose 22 communities to receive startup funding to establish such services. The CCIP created a "best practices" report, based on the experiences of these communities.[137] According to the report, the successful establishment of an investment facilitation service requires a community with certain characteristics, including a minimum population of 75,000; a diverse industry base; a critical mass of growth-oriented entrepreneurs (at least 15); a critical mass of private investors (at least 10); available accounting, legal, and financial services; and an entrepreneurial spirit. The report suggests that an investment facilitation service must provide five core activities, well beyond those provided by a simple matching program. The service must assess the level of knowledge of venture capital in the community; provide educational workshops to entrepreneurs on venture capital and accessing investors; provide coaching and mentoring services and review investment proposals; identify sources of equity financing, particularly local angels (actual or potential); and introduce SMEs and investors through activities such as investors' forums. The report acknowledges that, due to securities regulations in most provinces, the investment facilitation service cannot include direct negotiation on behalf of investors or entrepreneurs.

At the formal venture capital level, "venture capital fairs" are organized by both public sector and private sector organizations with the goal of matching entrepreneurs to potential investors, primarily venture capital funds.[138] At these fairs, selected entrepreneurs are given the opportunity to present their ideas to an audience of potential investors. In many cases, the financial needs of entrepreneurs have grown beyond the means of angel capital investors. The venture capital fair provides an alternative to entrepreneurs making "cold calls" to venture capital firms.

These various matching services all seek to directly redress one pre-investment information asymmetry—the cost of locating potential investors. Unless a matching service is prepared to vet both investment proposals and potential entrepreneurs, in the manner suggested by CCIP's statement of best practices, the small business financing costs that such programs can save are relatively insignificant. Even if a matching service provided the "core activities" suggested by the CCIP, it would likely need a great deal of time and highly publicized success stories before it could attain credibility among a wide array of angel capitalists. "Informal" venture capital is just that: informal. Investors rely primarily on word of mouth in making investment decisions because they trust their friends and business associates more than they do third-party matching services, and they will continue to do so until such services are proven to be trustworthy.

Community small business investment funds, for which tax incentives are provided, may have greater success in closing the equity gap faced by smaller businesses, and at earlier stages of development, than angel capital networks. The stage of investment and deal size that are targeted by such funds usually fall in the grey area between angel investment and formal venture capital fund investment. With the increasing size of venture capital funds and deal sizes in which formal venture capital funds participate, the equity gap that angel investors are expected to fill has widened. Community small business funds tend to provide the five core activities that the CCIP expects of a good investment facilitation service. To be successful, such funds require the financial support of local angels.[139]

Business Incubators

A business incubator is intended to nurture the development of small businesses at their embryonic stage. An incubator reduces overhead costs to small businesses by providing premises, including research facilities, and general secretarial and administrative support. Incubators may also assist business development in other ways, by providing technical support through databases and researchers, by assisting in the development of business plans, and perhaps by introducing potential venture capitalists. There are a variety of ways in which incubators operate. Under a typical "commercial" model, incubators essentially provide "seed financing" in the form of goods and services in exchange for an equity position in the company.

Most incubator programs in the United States and Canada operate at the local level. However, state or provincial governments may finance the establishment of incubators—for example, by providing grants to organizations such as universities or municipalities.[140] Alternatively, governments may provide tax credits to persons who contribute to the development of incubators.[141] The most important assets of successful incubator programs are state-of-the-art research facilities. Consequently, research-focused universities may be the most appropriate sites for incubators, at least those sponsored with government funding. Universities often generate the basic research that has commercialization potential.

Business incubators effectively reduce the moral hazard associated with venture capital investment. By providing the services (instead of the capital) needed to promote the development of startup businesses, incubators reduce the potential for wasteful expenditures by the businesses' founders and managers. Like angel capital networks, incubator programs seek to directly redress, rather than simply compensate for, the market failures that cause the inefficient allocation of capital. Incubator programs may thus be considered a more appropriate use of government funding than programs that seek simply to increase the amount of venture capital financing available in order to compensate for market failures.

Notes

1 Before the SBIC program, commercial banks that were part of the Federal Reserve System were effectively precluded from making venture capital equity investments. Historically, regulation of the financial services sector sought to completely separate the three key pillars of the sector: banking, insurance, and securities underwriting and dealing. The impact of the SBIC program on bank investment in venture capital is considered in notes 82-84 and accompanying text, infra. Significant reforms to US banking legislation were passed in 1999 in the Gramm-Leach-Bliley Act, Pub. L. no. 106-102, enacted on November 12, 1999; 113 Stat. 1338 (herein referred to as "GLBA"). Its primary purpose is to improve competition among financial institutions and give US institutions the ability to compete internationally. The GLBA is designed to allow financial institutions from all three sectors—banks, insurance companies, and securities firms—to compete with each other by offering a full range of products and services and to affiliate freely with one other. The legislation permits indirect, but not direct, combining of commercial and investment banking. There are two primary means through which commercial and investment banking services can now be indirectly combined. Under the first, a bank holding company can elect to become a financial holding company and engage in an expanded list of financial activities, including merchant banking activities, which encompass investments in venture capital as well as mezzanine capital and leveraged buyouts. The second alternative for affiliation permits a national bank to form a "financial subsidiary," which is also permitted to engage in activities that are financial in nature. Generally, the same list of financial activities is adopted for the purpose of this provision, although notably excepted are merchant banking activities. However, GLBA section 122 provides that five years after its date of the enactment, the board of governors of the Federal Reserve System and the secretary of the treasury may jointly adopt rules that permit financial subsidiaries to engage in merchant banking activities. At this point, it is unclear what affect the GLBA will have on venture investment by banks in the United States, particularly whether they will continue to use SBICs as a venture capital investment vehicle or take advantage of the alternatives permitted under the GLBA.

2 In Canada, the ability of banks to make venture capital investments was extremely limited before 1980. Under the 1967 Bank Act (SC 1966-67, c. 87), a bank could own shares of a corporation, but it would not own more than 50 percent of the voting rights of a Canadian corporation if the bank paid or agreed to pay $5 million or less for voting shares or, in any other case (that is, if it paid more than $5 million), more than 10 percent of the voting rights. Despite these limitations, a few banks used creative means to establish venture capital operations in the late 1960s. The 1980 Bank Act (SC 1980-81-82-83, c. 40) included comprehensive changes to the previous legislation, including, for the first time, a separate subdivision under the business and powers division governing investments of a bank. The 1980 act permitted a bank to own shares in a venture capital corporation (as defined and subject to various investment guidelines) that was a subsidiary of the bank— similar to the role of SBICs as venture capital investment vehicles for banks in the United States. The investment activities permitted to banks, as well as those permitted to trust companies and insurance companies, were significantly expanded in legislation introduced in 1991. The 1991 Bank Act (SC 1991, c. 46),

the 1991 Trust and Loan Companies Act (SC 1991, c. 45), and the 1991 Insurance Companies Act (SC 1991, c. 47) greatly increased the types of services and investment activities that banks, trust and loan companies, and insurance companies could provide or undertake. These institutions were permitted to acquire or increase a substantial investment in a number of types of corporations, including specialized financing corporations (SFCs). SFCs were corporations primarily engaged, under prescribed conditions, in providing specialized business management, in making investments, or in providing financing or advisory services. Since 1991, most venture capital investment undertaken by institutions in the financial services sector has been through wholly owned SFCs.

The legislation affecting banks, trust companies, and insurance companies was further integrated in 2001. Under the Financial Consumer Agency of Canada Act (SC 2001, c. 9), the SFC provisions in all three 1991 acts were replaced with specialized financing regulations, which permit banks, trust companies, and life insurance companies to make both direct and indirect (through "specialized financing entities") investments in other entities. Most of the schedule I banks in Canada now have venture capital entities that undertake venture capital investment at home and abroad.

A detailed consideration of the regulation of the banking industry in Canada and the United States is beyond the scope of this book.

3   Small Business Act of 1953, title II, Pub. L. no. 83-163, enacted on July 30, 1953; 67 Stat. 232, made a separate act by Pub. L. no. 85-536, enacted on July 18, 1958; 72 Stat. 384, as amended (herein referred to as "the Small Business Act").

4   For a brief history of the evolution of the SBA, see the SBA's Web site: http://www.sba.gov/.

5   Small Business Act of 1953, section 202.

6   Small Business Administration, *SBA Budget Request & Performance Plan: FY 2004 Congressional Submission* (Washington, DC: Small Business Administration, February 10, 2003), 1. The report is available from the SBA Web site: http://www.sba.gov/aboutsba/.

7   Ibid., at 3. The SBA's goal in this respect for 2002 was $3.5 billion, which is more in keeping with its actual and projected savings in other years.

8   Small Business Act section 30(b). The ombudsman's responsibilities are described on the SBA Web site: http://www.sba.gov/ombudsman/index.html.

9   The Microloan program is close to a direct lending program. Under the program, the SBA loans up to $750,000 to non-profit community-based lenders that make the appropriate credit decisions and loan the money to small businesses. The loans under this program are small—$35,000 and under—and the SBA does not guarantee them. For more detail about the program, see the SBA Web site: http://www.sba.gov/financing/frmicro.html. In the 2002 fiscal period, the Microloan program had advanced about $36.7 million. Supra note 6, at 25.

10 The SSBIC program was created in 1972 to promote investment in small business concerns in such a way as to facilitate ownership by "persons whose participation in the free enterprise system is hampered by social or economic disadvantages": section 301(d) of the Small Business Investment Act of 1958, infra note 72, added by the Small Business Investment Act Amendments of 1972, Pub. L. no. 92-595, enacted on October 27, 1972; 86 Stat. 1314. Since 1969, the SBA had licensed a special class of SBICs, known as "minority enterprise small business investment

companies" (MESBICs). The primary purpose of the 1972 amendments was to codify this practice, although the reference to MESBICs was dropped to remove the impression that only members of minority groups were eligible for the incentives. Section 301(d) was ultimately repealed in 1996, although licences issued to SSBICs prior to the date of repeal remained in effect: Small Business Programs Improvement Act of 1996, Pub. L. no. 104-208, division D, title II, section 208(b)(3)(A), enacted on September 30, 1996; 110 Stat. 3009-724.

A program similar to the SSBIC program, the New Markets Venture Capital Company (NMVCC) program, was added to the SBIA in 2000: New Markets Venture Capital Program Act of 2000, Pub. L. no. 106-554, enacted on December 21, 2000; 114 Stat. 2763A-653, introducing sections 351-368 to the SBIA. The NMVCC program is geographically focused rather than racially focused, although there is likely significant overlap between businesses that are qualified investments of an SSBIC and an NMVCC. The purpose of the new program (set out in section 352) is to "promote economic development and the creation of wealth and job opportunities in low-income geographic areas and among individuals living in such areas by encouraging developmental venture capital investments in smaller enterprises located in such areas." The term "low-income geographic areas" is defined in section 351(3). Under the program, the SBA will guarantee the timely payment of principal and interest on debentures issued by an NMVCC. The face amount of outstanding guaranteed debentures cannot exceed 150 percent of the private equity of the NMVCC. The SBA is also authorized to provide grants to NMVCCs as well as to SSBICs to provide operational assistance to smaller enterprises financed, or expected to be financed, by such companies.

An analysis of the SSBIC and NMVCC programs is beyond the scope of this study. For a discussion of these types of programs, see Timothy Bates, "Financing the Development of Urban Minority Communities: Lessons from History" (2000) vol. 14, no. 3 *Economic Development Quarterly* 227-41; and Timothy Bates, "Government as Venture Capital Catalyst: Pitfalls and Promising Approaches" (2002) vol. 16, no. 1 *Economic Development Quarterly* 49-59.

11   For a discussion on the requirements for a 7(a) loan guaranty, see the SBA Web site: http://www.sba.gov/financing/fr7aloan.html.

12   Supra note 6, at 22.

13   Ibid.

14   For an overview of the 8(a) program, see the SBA Web site: http://www.sba.gov/8abd/.

15   From the prepared statement of Wendell B. Barnes, SBA administrator, in United States, Senate Committee on Banking and Currency, Subcommittee on Small Business, *Credit Needs of Small Business*, 85th Cong., 1st sess., 340-404, at 343-44 and 373 (1957).

16   Small Business Innovation Development Act of 1982, Pub. L. no. 97-219, enacted on July 22, 1982; 96 Stat. 217. See now 15 USC chapter 14A, section 638. Further information about the SBIR program can be obtained from the SBA Web site: http://www.sba.gov/sbir/.

17   The program originally required the agencies to set aside 1.25 percent of these funds. When the program was renewed in 1992, the set-aside was increased to 2.5 percent: Small Business Innovation Research Program Reauthorization Act of 1992, Pub. L. no. 102-564, title I, enacted on October 28, 1992; 106 Stat. 4250. There

are 10 federal departments and agencies that meet the minimum R & D spending requirements under the SBIR program: Department of Agriculture, Department of Commerce, Department of Defense, Department of Education, Department of Energy, Department of Health and Human Services, Department of Transportation, Environmental Protection Agency, National Aeronautics and Space Administration, and National Science Foundation.

18 Statistics on the SBIR program are available at the SBA Web site: http://www.sba.gov/sbir/.

19 Small Business Technology Transfer Act of 1992, Pub. L. no. 102-564, title II, enacted on October 28, 1992; 106 Stat. 4249. See now 15 USC chapter 14A, section 638(n). Further information about the STTR program can be obtained from the SBA Web site: http://www.sba.gov/sbir/.

20 The program originally required the agencies to set aside not less than 0.15 percent of these funds. When the program was renewed in 2001, the set-aside was increased to 0.3 percent, beginning in 2004: Small Business Technology Transfer Program Reauthorization Act of 2001, Pub. L. no. 107-50, enacted on October 15, 2001; 115 Stat. 263. There are five federal departments and agencies that meet the minimum R & D spending requirements under the STTR program: Department of Defense, Department of Energy, Department of Health and Human Services, National Aeronautics and Space Administration, and National Science Foundation.

21 The only distinction is that under the SBIR program, the principal researcher must be an employee of the business, whereas under the STTR program, the principal researcher need not be employed by the business.

22 When the program was renewed in 2001, phase II awards were increased from $500,000 to $750,000, beginning in 2004.

23 Statistics on the STTR program are available at the SBA Web site: http://www.sba.gov/sbir/.

24 For further information, see the SBA Web site: http://www.sba.gov/sbdc/mission.html.

25 Supra note 6, at 56.

26 For general information, see the SCORE Web site: http://www.score.org/.

27 Supra note 6, at 54.

28 Industrial Development Bank Act, SC 1944-45, c. 44 (herein referred to as "the IDB Act").

29 Canada, House of Commons, *Debates*, May 29, 1995, 12880.

30 IDB Act section 12.

31 IDB Act section 15.

32 Federal Business Development Bank Act, SC 1974-74-76, c. 14 (herein referred to as "the FBDB Act"). The IDB Act was repealed by section 50 of the FBDB Act.

33 IDB Act section 15(1)(c); FBDB Act section 20(2).

34 FBDB Act section 31(3).

35 Canada, *Proceedings of the Standing Senate Committee on Banking, Trade and Commerce*, 35th Parl., 2d sess., issue no. 7, July 3, 1996.

36 Canada, House of Commons, *Debates*, May 29, 1995, 12879.

37   Business Development Bank of Canada Act, SC 1995, c. 28 (herein referred to as "the BDC Act").

38   The FBDB Act was repealed by section 41 of the BDC Act. Section 42 of the BDC Act states that the BDC continues the existence of the Federal Business Development Bank.

39   See section 14 of the BDC Act. The BDC is to complement, not compete with, private financial institutions.

40   Industry Canada, *Supporting Small Business Innovation: Review of the Business Development Bank of Canada* (Ottawa: Industry Canada, June 2001), 25. The report is available from the Industry Canada Web site: http://www.ic.gc.ca/.

41   Sections 23(1) and 30(1) of the BDC Act, respectively.

42   Supra note 40, at 14. The report describes the four gaps as follows:
   • risk gap: an aversion to riskier loans despite higher interest rates;
   • size gap: the high costs of dealing with small loans;
   • flexibility gap: rigid financing schemes despite the unique needs of SMEs;
   • knowledge gap: for knowledge-based industries, SMEs' lack of tangible assets and lenders' lack of industry knowledge.

43   Ibid., at 38.

44   Unfortunately, a similar concern with crowding out caused by labour-sponsored venture capital corporations (LSVCCs) has not been addressed by the federal or provincial governments. See chapter 6, at notes 197-198 and accompanying text.

45   Supra note 40, at section 7.0.

46   Ibid., at 36.

47   Business Development Bank of Canada, *2002 Annual Report: What Innovation Means to Entrepreneurs*, financial year ending March 31, 2002 (Ottawa: Business Development Bank of Canada, 2002), 16.

48   Supra note 40, at 51.

49   Business Development Bank of Canada, *Summary of Corporate Plan, Fiscal 2002-2006: Supporting Small Business Productivity and Innovation* (Ottawa: Business Development Bank of Canada, 2002), 19.

50   Supra note 47, at 11.

51   Ibid., at 22.

52   Ibid., at 85.

53   Ibid., at 25.

54   Ibid., at 26.

55   Ibid., at 83.

56   Ibid., at 85.

57   Supra note 40, at 29.

58   The Canadian federal government also has a loan guarantee program, governed by the Canada Small Business Financing Act, SC 1998, c. 36 and regulations, although its scope is rather limited. The program applies to loans to purchase or improve real property, leasehold improvements, or equipment necessary to the operation of the borrower's small business.

59   This difference between the two countries is also reflected in the recent reforms in Canada and proposed reforms in the United States to government-administered pension schemes, discussed in chapter 7 under the heading "Venture Capital Investment by Government-Administered Pension Plans." The assets of the Canada Pension Plan (CPP) are now managed by the CPP Investment Board (CPPIB), which is intended to act independently of government interference and can make equity investments, including private equity investments, in order to achieve the maximum rate of return, without undue risk of loss. The CPP's structure as a "pay-as-you-go" defined benefit plan remained unchanged. In contrast, when President Bush appointed a bipartisan committee to consider proposals for social security reform, one of the president's guiding principles for the commission was that the government must not invest social security funds in the stock market. All the recommendations made by the commission focus on providing some element of investment control to the beneficiaries of the plan. An element of the plan is thus effectively converted from a defined benefit plan to a defined contribution plan, which shifts the risk of that element of the plan's performance to individual beneficiaries.

60   Consider the "Shawinigate" affair, which occupied media attention for almost two years, between May 1999 and March 2001, and which still appears sporadically in newspaper stories. Shawinigate involved a loan from the BDC to Auberge Grand-Mère, a hotel in Shawinigan, Quebec in former prime minister Chrétien's home riding. Before he became prime minister, Chrétien had business interests in the hotel and an abutting golf course. He sold his interest in the hotel a few months before becoming prime minister in October 1993, and sold his shares in the golf course shortly thereafter. In January 1996, Chrétien learned that he had not yet been paid for his interest in the golf course. In April 1996, the prime minister spoke with François Beaudoin, then president of the BDC, about a loan sought by Auberge Grand-Mère to finance expansion plans. The loan was ultimately rejected, in September 1996, as being too risky. In February 1997, Chrétien spoke with Beaudoin about a scaled-back loan, which was ultimately approved. Opposition MP allegations of impropriety (that is, that Chrétien put pressure on the BDC to make the loan in order to better secure the payment of the amount owing from his sale of the golf course) were first raised in May 1999 and continued to be made through the election campaign in the fall of 2000. (Chrétien was re-elected for a third term as prime minister in November.) In February 2001, the Royal Canadian Mounted Police indicated that there was no basis for a criminal investigation in the case, and in March 2001 Chrétien was cleared (for the second time) by the ethics counsellor of any wrongdoing. At the end of March 2001, Chrétien agreed to release all documents involved in the affair. A timeline of the Shawinigate affair is available from the Canadian Broadcasting Corporation Web site: http://cbc.ca/news/indepth/background/shawinigan.html.

61   Josh Lerner, "The Government as Venture Capitalist: The Long-Run Impact of the SBIR Program" (1999) vol. 72, no. 3 *The Journal of Business* 285-318.

62   Ibid., at 317.

63   See chapter 1, at notes 44-45 and accompanying text.

64   However, at least the BDC venture capital group invests exclusively in syndicated deals and compensates its employees on the basis of performance (in the same manner as private sector venture capitalists), and so preserves a degree of independence from political manipulation.

65   United States, Department of Defense, directive no. 5105.17, February 7, 1958 and Pub. L. no. 85-325, February 12, 1958; 72 Stat. 111.

66   The name has flip-flopped between ARPA and DARPA. In 1972, the agency was renamed DARPA. In 1993, as part of President Clinton's economic initiatives to promote technological advancement, the agency was renamed ARPA with its program "expanded in ways that increase the likelihood that defense research can lead to civilian product opportunities": W.J. Clinton and A. Gore Jr., *Technology for America's Economic Growth: A New Direction To Build Economic Strength* (Washington, DC: Office of the President, 1993), under the heading "Technology Development, Commercialization and Use." In 1996, the name was changed back to DARPA under title IX of the National Defense Authorization Act for Fiscal Year 1996, Pub. L. no. 104-106, enacted on February 10, 1996; 110 Stat. 186.

67   Defense Advanced Research Projects Agency, *Strategic Plan* (Washington, DC: DARPA, February 2003), 1. The *Strategic Plan* is available from the DARPA Web site: http://www.darpa.mil/. For a review of some of the technological advances funded by DARPA, see Defense Advanced Research Projects Agency, *Technology Transition* (Washington, DC: DARPA, 1997), also available from the DARPA Web site.

68   The contract award types are described at the DARPA Web site: http://www.darpa.mil/cmo/pages/QA.htm. The statutory authority for the various types of contracts are found in 10 USC chapter 139, specifically sections 2304 (contracts), 2358 (grants and cooperative agreements), and 2371 ("other" transactions).

69   See Michael S. Nash, William E. Atkin, Richard E. Entlich, and R.N.C. Lightfoot, *Participant Views of Advanced Research Projects Agency "Other Transactions,"* Institute for Defense Analyses Document D-1793 (Washington, DC: DARPA, November 1995), available from the DARPA Web site: http://www.darpa.mil/body/d1793/.

70   10 USC section 2371(e)(2).

71   10 USC section 2371(e)(1)(B). Cost sharing is permitted, though not required, under any contract, grant, cooperation agreement, or "other" transaction.

72   Pub. L. no. 85-699, enacted on August 21, 1958; 72 Stat. 689, as amended (herein referred to as "SBIA").

73   See chapter 3, at notes 249-250 and accompanying text.

74   Many SBICs were formed within a few years of the program's introduction: 113 in 1960, 273 in 1961, and 216 in 1962. Then, fewer and fewer were formed: 65 in 1963, 49 in 1964, 8 in 1965, and 8 in 1966. The SBA maintains comprehensive statistics on various elements of the SBIC program. These figures are taken from table 43 of the SBIC "Program Statistical Package February 2003," available at the SBA's Web site: http://www.sba.gov/INV/stat/2003.html. By 1967, 791 SBICs were licensed and had invested more than $1 billion in small businesses: Martha Louise Reiner, "The Transformation of Venture Capital: A History of Venture Capital Organizations in the United States" (PhD thesis, UC Berkeley, 1989), 281.

75   Small Business Investment Act Amendments of 1967, Pub. L. no. 90-104, title II, enacted on October 11, 1967; 81 Stat. 268.

76   The term "venture capital" was defined in section 205 to include "such common stock, preferred stock, or other financing with subordination or nonamortization

characteristics as the [SBA] determines to be substantially similar to equity financing."

77   Pub. L. no. 92-213, enacted on December 22, 1971; 85 Stat. 775.

78   Pub. L. no. 92-595, enacted on October 27, 1972; 86 Stat. 1314.

79   Pub. L. no. 94-305, enacted on June 4, 1976; 90 Stat. 663.

80   Reiner, supra note 74, at 282. In early 1966, one-third of SBIC investments were in real estate and related activities.

81   SBIA section 302(b) (as originally enacted).

82   Pub. L. no. 87-341, section 3, enacted on October 3, 1961; 75 Stat. 752.

83   Supra note 75, at section 204.

84   Pub. L. no. 94-305, title I, section 107, enacted no June 4, 1976; 90 Stat. 666.

85   Small Business Equity Enhancement Act of 1992, Pub. L. no. 102-366, title IV, enacted on September 4, 1992; 106 Stat. 986.

86   SBIA section 301(a).

87   13 Code of Federal Regulations (herein referred to as "CFR") section 107.130.

88   SBIA section 302(c).

89   SBIA section 302(a)(1). The SBA has the discretion to reduce the $10 million threshold to an amount not less than $5 million if the reduction would not create an unreasonable risk of default: SBIA section 302(a)(2).

90   SBIA section 302(a)(2).

91   Ibid.

92   SBIA section 303(a).

93   "Prioritized payments," defined in the opening words of SBIA section 303(g), include "dividends on stock, interest on qualifying debentures, or priority returns on preferred limited partnership interests which are paid only to the extent of earnings."

94   SBIA section 303(g).

95   Set out in SBIA section 303(g).

96   SBIA section 303(g)(1).

97   Prioritized payments must be paid only if the SBIC has profits, as computed under the SBIC regulations. If SBIC does not have profits, the prioritized payments are accumulated until it does. See 13 CFR section 107.1520.

98   SBIA section 303(g)(2).

99   SBIA section 303(g)(4). "Equity capital" is defined as "common or preferred stock or a similar instrument, including subordinated debt with equity features which is not amortized and which provides for interest payments contingent upon and limited to the extent of earnings."

100 SBIA section 303(g)(11). In essence, if the SBA guarantees rather than acquires the participating securities, it is entitled to a non-cumulative profit participation rather than a cumulative prioritized payment. The SBA's profit share is up to 12 percent, depending on the amount of leverage provided by participating securities, and assuming that the interest rate on 10-year treasury bonds issued on the day that the participating securities are marketed is 8 percent. For leverage up to 100 percent,

the SBA's profit share is that proportion of 9 percent that the leverage is of private capital. For leverage between 100 and 200 percent, up to an additional 3 percent is added to the SBA's profit share. For example, if the leverage is 50 percent of private capital, the SBA's profit share is 4.5 percent; if 100 percent, 9 percent; if 150 percent, 10.5 percent; if 200 percent, 12 percent. If the 10-year treasury bond rate is other than 8 percent, the SBA's profit share is increased or decreased by the same percentage increase or decrease in the bond rate.

101   SBIA section 303(g)(11)(B)(iii).

102   SBIA section 303(i).

103   SBIA section 303(b)(2)(A). The dollar amounts are adjusted annually to reflect increases in the consumer price index since March 31, 1993. For example, the maximum leverage currently authorized is $108.8 million (the inflation-adjusted equivalent of $90 million).

104   SBIA section 303(b)(3).

105   13 CFR section 107.800-825.

106   See supra note 99.

107   Small Business Act, supra note 3, at section 3. See also infra note 115.

108   13 CFR section 121.201, which lists industry size standards by number of employees or by annual receipts, depending on the nature of the business.

109   13 CFR section 107.720.

110   13 CFR section 107.830(a).

111   13 CFR section 107.865.

112   13 CFR section 107.740.

113   13 CFR section 107.1000(a)(1). This exception for non-leveraged SBICs was the third significant change introduced in 1992, intended to reduce the regulation of non-SBA financed SBICs.

114   13 CFR section 107.590. "Financings" and "regulatory capital" are defined in 13 CFR section 107.050. Regulatory capital is essentially private capital (that is, excluding leverage obtained through the SBA).

115   A smaller enterprise has net assets not exceeding $6 million and average after-tax income for the prior two years not exceeding $2 million: 13 CFR section 107.710.

116   SBIA section 308(d).

117   13 CFR section 107.1810(h).

118   13 CFR section 107.1820.

119   Table 38 of the SBIC "Program Statistical Package February 2003," supra note 74. The SBA statistics break down SBICs into four types: bank-owned SBICs (regular SBICs more than 70 percent owned by a single bank or a bank holding company); participating security SBICs (regular SBICs that are eligible to issue participating securities); debenture SBICs (all regular SBICs that are not bank-owned or not eligible to issue participating securities); and SSBICs. For the purposes of statistical reporting, a bank-owned SBIC that is eligible to issue participating securities is considered to be a participating security SBIC. A bank-owned SSBIC is considered to be an SSBIC.

120 Ibid., table 39.

121 Supra note 1.

122 Table 39 of the SBIC "Program Statistical Package February 2003," supra note 74.

123 Derived from ibid., table 2.

124 See chapter 6, at appendixes 6A to 6D, in each case under the heading "Eligible Investments."

125 As described above, under the SBIC program, the SBA may itself invest in participating securities or guarantee participating securities acquired by others. If the government guarantees someone else's preferred share investment rather than making the investment itself, the government's position is somewhat different. The government's costs are reduced, in the sense that it does not use any capital unless it is called on the guarantee. The government is not entitled to the prioritized payments (essentially, a cumulative dividend), but it is entitled to a (non-cumulative) profit participation payment plus a guarantee fee.

In the example described, the matching capital could be provided to fund B by outside investors (that is, other than investor group B) other than the SBA, whose investment in preferred shares is guaranteed by the SBA. The government would be entitled to a fee for its guarantee plus a share of the fund's profits (if it is profitable), but would not be entitled to a cumulative return (that is, if the fund is not profitable). The government's guarantee fee, participating payment (if any), and the cumulative dividends to which the preferred shareholder is entitled would reduce the gain or increase the loss ultimately realized by investor group B.

126 See chapter 6, at the text accompanying note 168.

127 A study sponsored by the Canadian Federation of Independent Business, Canadian Manufacturers and Exporters, and RBC Financial Group, *The Path to Prosperity: Canada's Small- and Medium-Sized Enterprises* (Ottawa and Toronto: Canadian Federation of Independent Businesses, Canadian Manufacturers and Exporters, and RBC Financial Group, October 2002), suggests (at 2) that SMEs in Canada are "just as entrepreneurially inclined and growth oriented [as their US counterparts]." The report is available from the Web sites of each of the three survey sponsors: http://www.cfib.ca/; http://www.cme-mec.ca/; and http://www.rbc.com/newsroom/index.html.

128 For Canada, see, for example, *Canadian Subsidy Directory, 2002* (St. Andrews West, ON: MG Publishing, 2002) (published annually). For the United States, see, for example, *American Grants and Loans Directory, 2002* (St. Andrews West, ON: MG Publishing, 2002) (published annually). Information is also available from federal, provincial, and state government Web sites.

129 For example, the Web sites of the NVCA (http://www.nvca.org/) in the United States and the CVCA (http://www.cvca.ca/) in Canada provide contact details of their member organizations.

130 For an older list of such services, see Richard T. Harrison and Colin M. Mason, "Informal Venture Capital," in Richard T. Harrison and Colin M. Mason, eds., *Informal Venture Capital: Evaluating the Impact of Business Introduction Services* (London: Prentice Hall, 1996), 3-26, at 16, table 1.7.

131 Donald J. Brown and Charles R.B. Stowe, "A Note on Venture Capital Networks: Promise and Performance" (1991) vol. 1, no. 1 *Journal of Small Business Finance*

75-87, discussed in Donald J. Brown and Charles R.B. Stowe, "Private Venture Capital Networks in the United States," in *Informal Venture Capital*, supra note 130, 101-15, at 108.

132   Brown and Stowe, "Private Venture Capital Networks," supra note 131, at 109-10.

133   Wetzel and Freear's review of VCN is equally bleak in terms of duplicating the success of such a network outside areas with an established high-tech sector: William E. Wetzel Jr. and John Freear, "Promoting Informal Venture Capital in the United States: Reflections on the History of the Venture Capital Network," in *Informal Venture Capital*, supra note 130, 61-74. Although the VCN did enjoy some initial success in New Hampshire, at its peak client fees paid for only about 60 percent of its operating budget, and the University of New Hampshire provided free office and utilities (other than phone) as well as $15,000 for operational support. Other sponsorship funding was essential to maintain a sufficient operating budget. However, after an unsuccessful attempt to raise $300,000 in late 1988 and early 1989, VCN moved to the Massachusetts Institute of Technology (MIT) in 1990 as a not-for-profit affiliate of the MIT Enterprise Forum and was renamed Technology Capital Network Inc. From 1984 to 1990, VCN had about 1,200 entrepreneurs and 800 investors registered. Approximately 35,000 computer matches generated 3,500 investor requests for additional information, and more than 1,000 introductions for over 200 entrepreneurs from 30 states and over 300 entrepreneurs from 33 states. As a result of VCN introductions, 31 ventures raised about $12 million from 50 investors. Roughly 80 percent of the ventures were technology-based.

134   Rena Blatt and Allan Riding, "'. . . Where Angels Fear To Tread': Some Lessons from the Canada Opportunities Investment Network Experience," in *Informal Venture Capital*, supra note 130, 75-88.

135   Ibid.

136   Ibid., at 85.

137   Industry Canada, *The Winning Formula: Facilitating Investment in Small Business Growth, Lessons from 22 Pilot Projects Under the Canada Community Investment Plan* (Ottawa: Industry Canada, 2003), available from the CCIP Web site: http://ccip.ic.gc.ca/.

138   For example, the Canadian IT Financing Forum has been hosting such events since 1995, generally twice a year, once in Toronto and once in Vancouver. For further information, see its Web site: http://www.financingforum.com/. The Banff Venture Forum began similar events in 2001. See http://www.banffventureforum.org/. The Ottawa Centre for Research and Innovation (OCRI), a non-profit organization, established the Ottawa Capital Network (OCN) in 1992 and has hosted an annual Ottawa Venture Capital Fair since 1996. See the OCN Web site: http://www.ottawacapitalnetwork.com/. In the United States, there are numerous similar events hosted by a variety of organizations. For example, the National Venture Capital Association and American Entrepreneurs for Economic Growth (AEEG) cosponsor a number of networking lunches across the country. See the NVCA Web site: http://www.nvca.org/. There are also a variety of industry-specific venture capital fairs, such as the Semiconductor Venture Fair, started in 2002 (see http://www.semiconductorventurefair.com/) and the Energy Venture Fair, started in 2001 (see http://www.energyventurefair.com/).

139   The results of the CCIP program suggest that such support is not necessarily forthcoming. Seven of the 22 communities that received funding under the program were in Ontario. Of these, only one, the regional municipality of Niagara, has sponsored a community small business investment fund (see appendix 6A), Niagara Growth Fund Inc. It is surprising that none of the other seven Ontario communities has sponsored a CSBIF, although universities in two of these communities (The University of Western Ontario in London, and the University of Waterloo, Wilfrid Laurier University, and Conestoga College, all in Kitchener-Waterloo) have sponsored CSBIFs.

140   A good overview of various incubator programs is found in Organisation for Economic Co-operation and Development, *Technology Incubators: Nurturing Small Firms* (Paris: OECD, 1997). This OECD report discusses the rationale underlying incubator programs, considers various "best practices," and summarizes programs available in Australia, France, United Kingdom, Austria, Germany, United States, Israel, Russia, and Eastern European countries.

141   Missouri offers such a tax credit program: see Missouri Revised Statutes, c. 620, section 620.495. Information about the program can be obtained from the Missouri Department of Economic Development (DED) Web site: http://www.ded.state.mo.us/. The program was established in 1990. The legislation authorizes the DED to provide loans, loan guarantees, and grants for the establishment, operation, and administration of incubators. However, no government money has ever been appropriated to carry out this element of the program. Since 1990, the DED has also been authorized to grant tax credits, equal to 50 percent of the amount a taxpayer contributes to the Missouri small business incubators fund (a state fund used to provide loans, loan guarantees or grants for establishing incubators) or to specific incubator projects. The minimum contribution is $5,000; the maximum contribution is $100,000 if it is made to a specific incubator project, or $200,000 if it is made to a local sponsor with multiple locations of incubator projects. The aggregate amount of tax credits that may be granted in any year is $500,000. The program has not been popular. Between 1990 and September 2002, only $1.3 million in tax credits were granted under the program, and in no year has the aggregate amount of tax credits granted exceeded $160,000.

9

The Way Forward

In recent years, federal, state, and provincial governments in the United States and Canada have focused their attention on small and medium-sized enterprises (SMEs) as important engines of economic growth, and have introduced a plethora of measures to address the market failures that affect the supply of capital to SMEs. There is little doubt that these market failures exist. The inefficient functioning of the financial markets, which creates an "equity gap" for small businesses, as well as the positive externalities or spillovers that are not captured by small business investors, are well documented. These market failures are inherent in a free market economy and justify government action. The question is what government action can best address these market failures. This concluding chapter, rather than summarizing the discussion of the various programs in the preceding chapters, highlights a few key areas where governments, particularly those in Canada, should consider reforms to their incentive programs targeting informal and formal venture capital investment.

Today's innovative small businesses—the focus of venture capitalists, both private and public—are concentrated in the high-tech sector. Employees in this sector are highly educated and highly mobile and their businesses, which depend more on human capital than on infrastructure, particularly at the early stages of development, are equally mobile. The close geographic proximity of Canada to the United States, the openness of the border between the two countries, especially for individuals involved in the high-tech sector, and the fact that the countries share a common language make competitiveness with the United States a key criterion in the evaluation of the Canadian tax system. Indeed, competitiveness with the United States is often viewed as a rationale unto itself for tax reforms that target venture capital investors, high-tech companies, and their employees.

Informal Venture Capital and "Sweat Equity"

The extent to which Canada has followed the US lead in its measures targeting informal venture capital is illustrated by three reforms undertaken in 2000: the general reduction in capital gains tax rates; the introduction of an angel capital rollover (and its subsequent liberalization in 2003); and the addition of incentive stock option (ISO)-type measures for employee stock options of publicly listed companies. Competitiveness with the United States was cited as one of the reasons for the capital gains tax cuts and the employee stock option amendments and, while not specifically noted when the angel capital rollover was introduced, the source of the idea was obvious. However, Canada lost the competitive edge in capital gains tax rates in 2003 when the United States reduced its long-term capital gains tax rate to 15 percent. A "tit-for-tat" reduction in Canadian capital gains tax rates, as some commentators have advocated, will not improve SME investment in Canada. In fact, in my view, it will do quite the reverse. As capital gains tax rates fall in Canada, so too does the relief provided for capital losses. And enhanced relief for capital losses from dispositions of venture capital investments will have a greater impact on informal venture capital investment than the preferential treatment of capital gains.

Preferential Tax Treatment of Capital Gains

It is unfortunate that both Canada and the United States have focused on the preferential tax treatment of capital gains as an appropriate vehicle for increasing informal venture capital investment. The measure is poorly targeted and, indeed, undercuts more appropriately targeted incentives. Although I would recommend that both countries repeal the tax preference generally accorded to capital gains, I acknowledge that the likelihood of either country doing so is virtually non-existent. Certainly, Canada will not act unilaterally in this respect. As long as there are tax preferences that require a distinction between capital gains and ordinary income,[1] the income tax legislation should clearly distinguish between dispositions of venture capital investments that give rise to capital gains and those that do not. Under the US Internal Revenue Code ("the Code"), the distinction is clear; under the Canadian Income Tax Act ("the Act"), it is not. Under the Code, only dealers in securities—those who acquire securities for sale to customers—are taxed on income account, and even they can clearly segregate securities held for investment purposes (which are subject to capital gains treatment) from those held primarily for sale to customers (which are subject to mark-to-market treatment). The distinction between dealers and others applies regardless of the nature of the investor, whether it is an individual, partnership, trust, or corporation. Traders in securities and other investors who do not achieve even trader status are subject to capital gains treatment and will benefit from a capital gains tax preference if the securities are held for more than one year. In Canada, in contrast, gains derived from a business or "an adventure or concern in the nature of trade" are taxed as ordinary income. Thus, Canadian dealers, traders, and adventurers in securities do not benefit from a capital gains tax preference. For angel investors who actively manage their investment portfolios as well as for both general and limited partners in venture capital limited partnerships, there is a risk that the tax authorities can (legitimately) treat the gains realized from their SME investments as being on income account, because the angel investor or the partnership (through the activities of its general partner) is in the business of buying and selling securities, or is at least involved in an adventure or concern in the nature of trade. Given the apparent assessing policy of the Canada Revenue Agency (CRA), the characterization issue may exist more in theory than in practice, but any uncertainty may have a chilling effect on angel capitalists as well as on certain formal venture capital investors.

For these reasons, the Act should distinguish between traders and dealers in the same manner as in the United States, at least with respect to securities transactions. Preferably, the Act should be amended to eliminate the trading of securities (or perhaps any property) from the definition of business, unless the trading is with customers. If the government considers that some securities trading (as opposed to dealing) should be taxed on income account, then it should adopt a statutory bright-line holding-period test, such as that applied in the United States, that distinguishes between short- and long-term capital gains.

Preferential Treatment of Gains from Small Business Securities

Provided that the threshold characterization issue is dealt with, Canada's $500,000 capital gains exemption for qualified small business corporation (QSBC) shares compares favourably to the reduced capital gains tax rate applicable to qualified small business stock (QSBS) in the United States, at least from the investor's perspective. However, as an instrument to enhance innovation by promoting investment in rapid-growth SMEs, the QSBC share preference is, in my view, a failure. First, it is available to secondary-market acquisitions of QSBC shares, whereas the QSBS preference is not. More important, the QSBS measures incorporate a statutory "black list" of excluded business activities that includes many (but not all) types of lifestyle businesses. The QSBC share preference contains no such limitations. It simply does not target the right SMEs. While the QSBC share preference could be amended to make it better targeted, I recommend that it be abolished completely in order to partially fund the costs of an enhanced, but better focused, loss-relief mechanism, described below.

Angel Capital Rollover

The angel capital rollover is a better targeted preference than either the general capital gains tax preference or the tax preference for capital gains from small business securities. It targets repeat investors who have successfully exited an SME investment; repeat angels can apply what they have learned from previous investments in order to reduce the information asymmetries in subsequent ones. In addition, from a fiscal cost perspective, a rollover provides a tax deferral rather than an outright tax saving.

Various reforms of the angel capital rollover should be considered in both countries. Both countries currently limit the rollover to individuals. In the United States, this limitation mirrors that imposed on the tax preference for capital gains (and that for QSBS). Canada may have simply copied this limitation (or may have taken it from its QSBC share preference). However, corporations also make venture capital investments, often at the seed or startup stage—perhaps as a key supplier to or customer of a startup company, or perhaps in an employee venture as an incentive to retain key employees. A rollover would provide an incentive to corporate investors to reinvest proceeds in other venture investments. A further reform to consider is an extension of the rollover to gains realized from dispositions of any capital property where the proceeds are reinvested in SMEs. This amendment could expand the availability of the rollover to first-time angel investors, although it would likely exacerbate the information asymmetries associated with small business investment and therefore undermine one of the virtues of the existing rollover. For this reason, I recommend maintaining the current limitation on the angel capital rollover to repeat angel investors, although it should be expanded to include corporate investors.

Canada's angel capital rollover suffers from two problems that should be addressed. The first stems from the characterization issue discussed above. Experienced angel investors, who devote significant time and attention to their venture investments, may be considered "traders" in securities as that term is understood for Canadian tax purposes, and therefore the gains from their angel investments would be considered income gains rather than capital gains. Because the rollover is restricted to capital gains, the very people the rollover is intended to benefit may be denied access to the provision. Again, given CRA assessing policy, this is a concern that exists more in theory than in practice. Elimination of the characterization issue eliminates this problem as well. The second problem is that the rollover is limited to common shares. Preference shares are often acquired by venture capital investors; although these shares may be convertible into common shares, the common shares acquired on conversion may not qualify for the rollover (for example, because the shares are then publicly traded or the SME no longer meets the size restrictions). Furthermore, a successful entrepreneur in Canada who has undertaken an estate freeze usually owns non-convertible common shares, and could not benefit from the rollover if the business is subsequently sold. Accordingly, the rollover should be expanded to include any shares of a qualifying SME, so that it is similar in application to the US angel capital rollover.

Preferential Treatment of Capital Losses from Small Business Securities

In my view, the most important reforms that Canada must consider in the context of informal venture capital relate to its small business investment loss (the allowable business investment loss [ABIL]) provisions. Both Canada and the United States recognize the importance of preferential relief for capital losses from SME investments as a means of promoting venture capital investment. However, neither country's regime is appropriately targeted because neither country imposes any restrictions on the nature of the business carried on by SMEs whose securities qualify for preferential loss relief. The vast majority of SMEs are lifestyle businesses, so the vast majority of losses that qualify for preferential loss relief are from investments in lifestyle businesses. These losses do not warrant preferential treatment. Both countries can better target this tax preference by limiting it to rapid-growth SMEs. The simplest approach, which is consistent with better targeted small business investment tax preferences, would be to incorporate a "black list" of non-qualifying businesses including typical lifestyle businesses (for example, professional services businesses, restaurant or food services, and retail sales) as well as other businesses, such as financial services and real estate leasing and development, that should not benefit from the tax preference.

In Canada, the tax preference for ABILs has been diluted as a consequence of the reduction in the capital gains inclusion rate in 2000. Now, only one-half of business investment losses are deductible (rather than the previous three-quarters). In my view, Canada should amend its business investment loss provisions to allow the full deduction of business investment losses, subject to four modifications. First, the deductible loss should be limited to a maximum amount for each small business in which the taxpayer invests, sufficient to account for most love and angel investments (for example, Cdn $100,000). Second, the taxpayer should be required to recognize accrued but unrealized gains on other capital property before any excess business investment loss is deductible. Third, a size restriction should be imposed on each SME in which an investment qualifying for loss relief is made, determined at the time of the investment (for example, similar to the limitation used in the United States for section 1244 stock). Fourth, as noted above, the tax preference should be limited to investment in rapid-growth SMEs.

Employee Stock Options: "Sweat Equity" Venture Capital

Both Canada and the United States offer generous tax incentives for certain employee stock options: the recognition of the option benefit is deferred, in many cases until the optioned shares are sold, at which time the benefit is taxed as (or equivalent to) a capital gain. In my view, there is no justification for the preferential tax treatment enjoyed by employee stock options in either country. The imminent changes in the accounting treatment of employee stock options— specifically, the requirement that employers expense their value on income statements—may lead to a significant decline in their use, at least for publicly listed companies.[2] However, their use by rapid-growth SMEs will likely continue, particularly prior to an initial public offering of shares.

Despite the lack of justification for the preferential tax treatment of employee stock options, the US and Canadian federal governments have increased the tax preference in recent years. The United States has reduced the long-term capital gains tax rate, while Canada has introduced ISO-type measures for publicly listed shares and reduced capital gains tax rates (which has correspondingly reduced the amount of the taxable benefit for qualifying stock options). The recent Canadian amendments have been justified as an alignment of Canada's tax treatment of employee stock options with the treatment of ISOs in the United States. In reality, however, the Canadian income tax treatment has been much more generous than the US treatment (from the employee's perspective) for many years. Canadian employees can benefit from effective capital gains tax treatment even on a "cashless" exercise of stock options (that is, the exercise of options and the simultaneous sale of the optioned shares), whereas US employees must hold the optioned shares for at least one year after the options are exercised in order for the gain to be taxed as a long-term capital gain. On a cashless exercise, US employees must recognize the full value of the options as employment income (and the corporate employer is entitled to a corresponding deduction).

The Canadian tax treatment of employee stock options is made even more perverse by the fact that appropriately structured employee stock options can give employees effective capital gains tax treatment, and at the same time allow the employer to deduct the full value of the stock option benefit.[3] At the very least, this planning opportunity must be closed.

In my view, employee stock options should be taxed in the same manner as any other non-cash compensation. The full value of the options should be included in the employee's income when the options are unconditionally received (that is, when they vest), provided that the options can be valued with a reasonable degree of certainty at that time. The employer should recognize a corresponding deduction.[4] The onus would be on the employer to value the options on a reasonable basis using an appropriate option-pricing methodology.

Tax Credits for Direct Investment in SMEs

A number of provinces and states offer tax credits for seed capital investment in SMEs. These angel capital tax credits are, in my view, a poor response to the market failures affecting SME investment. They do not adequately address the information asymmetries associated with investment in small businesses. In fact, it is arguable that they exacerbate the market failures because the credits attract individual investors who are ill-suited for venture capital investment.

Angel capitalists must rely on their own ability to choose appropriate investments; there is no professional intermediary that assists in this function in the informal venture capital market. An angel capital tax credit does not distinguish between sophisticated and unsophisticated angels. Securities legislation has acted as a safeguard in this respect; however, some jurisdictions have relaxed their securities regulations affecting private placements in order to promote SME investment, to the point where this safety feature has been eliminated.[5] Unsophisticated angels are more likely than sophisticated ones to make poor investment choices, and even where they do make good choices, they will likely add less value to the businesses in which they invest. Unsophisticated angels may also be inclined to view provincial or state certification of an SME for tax credit purposes as a "stamp of approval," despite express statements by the government to the contrary. Unless the government is prepared to assume the role of financial intermediary and undertake a full evaluation of the SMEs applying for the tax credits in an attempt to select "winners"—a role for which the government is ill-equipped—government programs should target more seasoned angel capitalists or specialized investment vehicles, such as professionally managed small business investment funds, that can better evaluate potential investments and nurture the businesses in which they invest. The various angel capital tax credit programs in Canada and the United States do none of these things. Generally speaking, there are minimal requirements that SMEs must meet before receiving government certification for the credits. An angel capital tax credit combined with the recent tendency to relax securities regulation affecting private financings is a recipe for disaster.

Informal venture capital investment is best served by an expanded angel capital rollover and greater loss relief for appropriately targeted small business investments.

Accessing Retirement Savings for Informal Venture Capital Investment

The regulation of retirement savings plans, both individual and employer-sponsored pension plans, may inhibit would-be entrepreneurs from leaving employment to start a business. Both countries impose severe restrictions on an employee's ability to access employer-sponsored pension plan assets prior to retirement. In Canada, pension plan assets are generally locked in until retirement age, even if employment is terminated. In the United States, termination of employment is considered an acceptable occasion for the distribution of vested pension benefits, although the tax consequences of doing so are harsh. Not only is the amount withdrawn included in income, but it also is subject to an additional 10 percent excise tax if the individual is younger than 55. In both countries, great emphasis is placed on securing pension funds for retirement purposes only, and I would not recommend that this security be undermined in order to promote entrepreneurial activity.

However, there is some scope for amending Canada's registered retirement savings plan (RRSP) provisions in order to promote investment by entrepreneurs or would-be entrepreneurs in their own businesses (that is, love capital). Even though an individual can freely withdraw capital from an RRSP (other than a locked-in RRSP) at any time, the withdrawal must be included in income. This requirement reduces the amount available for investment purposes and inhibits the individual's ability to accumulate retirement savings in an RRSP in the future, even if the venture investment proves successful. Accordingly, I recommend the introduction of an interest-free "venture capital loan" program, along the lines of the existing homebuyers' plan and lifelong learning plan. In my view, entrepreneurial endeavour is as important for achieving retirement security as investing in one's human capital through education. The proposed venture capital loan program has the same objectives as the lifelong learning program. Under my proposal, an RRSP annuitant would be entitled to borrow the greater of Cdn $25,000 and 50 percent of the fair market value of the RRSP's assets in order to make an eligible investment in an eligible SME, including an SME related to the annuitant.[6] As an alternative to the loan program, the qualified investments of an RRSP could be expanded to include investment in an eligible

SME related to the annuitant (an investment that is currently prohibited), subject to monetary limits similar to the proposed loan program. However, in order to avoid excessive tax deferral through this mechanism, the SME investment should be restricted to either non-convertible debt or non-participating, non-voting, non-convertible shares with a fixed (low-rate) dividend.

Pension Funds and the Formal
Venture Capital Industry

Tax incentive programs targeting the formal venture capital industry in Canada and in certain US states require a significant overhaul. The federal and provincial labour-sponsored venture capital corporation (LSVCC) programs—which have created the largest pool of venture capital in the country—target the wrong investors for investment in a poorly designed investment vehicle. The makeup of investors in the formal venture capital industries in Canada and the United States highlights one of the main problems with Canada's principal program. Individuals—and not just high-net-worth individuals, but individuals from across the economic spectrum—have been the largest venture capital investors in Canada since the early 1990s, following the proliferation of LSVCC programs across the country. Employer-sponsored pension funds, which have been the largest venture capital investors in the United States since the late 1970s, remain reluctant investors in Canada. To ensure the long-term viability of a venture capital industry that is not dependent on government handouts, the Canadian federal and provincial governments must restructure their incentive programs.

Government incentive programs for formal venture capital investment must have two primary objectives: attracting investors that can and should include private equity within a diversified portfolio; and strengthening the pool of private venture capital fund (VCF) managers. The LSVCC programs in Canada accomplish neither objective. First, the LSVCC program targets individuals across the economic spectrum and has garnered considerable participation from individuals in lower and middle income tax brackets. A comparable US program, the certified capital company (CAPCO) program used by a number of US states, targets an appropriate investor class: insurance companies. However, insurance companies investing in CAPCOs are not investing in risk capital. Rather, the CAPCO program has been structured to permit (indeed, encourage) secured debt financing by insurance companies through the provision of an extremely lucrative tax incentive. Second, LSVCCs (as well as CAPCOs) fail to strengthen the pool of private equity fund managers. In fact, they may accomplish the opposite. Both programs offer overly rich incentives and are poorly designed to promote the operation of LSVCCs and CAPCOs in the same manner as private sector funds. In particular, the LSVCC and CAPCO programs require upfront investment (as opposed to upfront commitment) by qualified investors in order to obtain the full tax credit (although the CAPCO tax credit is paid out over time). Because the tax credit is provided up front, the legislation imposes investment pacing requirements on the LSVCC or CAPCO in order to ensure that the tax credit promotes venture capital investment. However, the significant upfront incentive reduces the pressure on fund managers to invest capital in qualified investments, while the pacing requirements (and accompanying penalties) may lead to last-minute, hasty investment decisions. Under neither program are fund managers subject to appropriate pressure from investors to undertake the due diligence or monitoring expected of private sector VCFs. In both cases, in fact, there is a distinct possibility that LSVCCs or CAPCOs may overvalue potential investments and therefore crowd out private sector funds.

Many of the other state and provincial VCF programs discussed in chapter 6 are also not appropriately targeted. In many programs, the only eligible investors are individuals and there are no explicit restrictions on which individuals are eligible (although securities legislation in some jurisdictions may appropriately limit investment to high-net-worth individuals). In many programs, the only incentive is a non-transferable tax credit, so tax-exempt entities and non-residents of the province or state cannot benefit. None of Canada's provincial VCF programs (including the LSVCC programs) targets tax-exempt entities, particularly pension funds. This is their greatest failing.

The incentives targeting pension funds for venture capital investment that were introduced by the Canadian federal government in 1985 have not proved successful over the long term. Though they had some success in the late 1980s, most Canadian pension funds that invested in venture capital abandoned this asset class following the dismal returns posted during the recession in the early 1990s. According to survey data, their failure to return is due to a number of related factors. Underlying many of these factors is a lack of faith in the performance of venture capital and VCF managers. If pension fund managers are to increase their venture capital investments, they must become more comfortable with the venture capital industry and more inclined to treat venture capital (and private equity generally) as an appropriate asset allocation. The only "incentive" currently offered to pension funds for venture capital investment is the three-to-one leveraging of small business investments for the purposes of the foreign investment restrictions imposed under the Act. However, the increase in the foreign investment limit from 10 percent in 1985 to the current 30 percent has reduced the potential impact of this incentive.[7]

The recent changes to the Canada Pension Plan (CPP), though not motivated by a specific desire to increase the pool of venture capital in Canada, may provide appropriate signalling to pension funds in the public and private sectors. The assets of the CPP are now managed by the CPP Investment Board (CPPIB) as an independent investment manager. The CPPIB manages the CPP's venture capital portfolio in a manner similar to that of large US pension funds. The board invests funds in private, independently managed VCFs. It has no "social mandate" in its investment objectives, unlike the Caisse de dépôt et placement in Quebec. In fact, the CPP's investment limitations are similar to those applicable to any pension fund in Canada, including the foreign investment restrictions imposed under the Act. Over the next few years, the CPPIB will become one of the largest venture capital investors in Canada. Its success (or failure) in these investments can have an important influence on the decision of other pension funds to make venture capital investments.

In the meantime, Canadian federal and provincial VCF programs should be revamped to target pension fund investment in privately managed VCFs. This could be accomplished by introducing a refundable (or perhaps transferable) tax credit for such investment. A direct monetary incentive may prove to be a better catalyst for pension fund venture capital investment than an "incentive" that permits only an increase in foreign investment. Alternatively, an equity guarantee program similar to that used in Iowa but restricted to pension funds should be given serious consideration.[8] Certain provinces could also consider the approach used by some US states of requiring public sector pension funds to invest a certain (relatively small) percentage of their capital in private VCFs. Smaller provinces, such as the maritime provinces, could consider pooling their resources or using a gatekeeper in order to establish a larger capital pool for venture capital investment purposes. In any event, the venture capital raised should be invested in privately managed VCFs whose other investors have not benefited from any form of incentive. This will better ensure the independence of fund managers and their motivation to vet and closely monitor their SME investments.

Perhaps one of the most startling observations from the review of the government incentive programs used in Canada and the United States to enhance the supply of venture capital is the similarity among many of the programs' features. Unfortunately, many of the programs are also similar in their failure to properly target the measures to those few SMEs that are the real engines of economic growth, and Canada and the United States are similar in their failure to coordinate the incentive programs at play. A primary objective of this book has been to gather sufficient information to allow those who have a stake in the venture capital marketplace—entrepreneurs, venture capitalists (both formal and informal), and governments—to properly evaluate the various programs that are used to address the market failures affecting SME investment, with the goal of determining the best options for the future. In designing its venture capital programs, Canada has much to learn from its southern neighbour. Although I do not advocate the wholesale adoption of US policy or programs, a number of US initiatives warrant serious consideration in Canada.

Notes

1   In fact, the distinction is applicable in all four tax expenditures affecting capital gains—the general preferential tax treatment of capital gains, the specific preference for capital gains from small business investments, the angel capital rollover, and the preferential relief for losses resulting from small business investments—and is crucial to the first three.

2   For example, Microsoft Corporation announced on July 8, 2003 that it would replace its employee stock option plan with a stock awards plan starting September 2003: Microsoft Corporation, "Microsoft Reshapes Compensation for Continued Success," *Press Release*, July 8, 2003 (available from the Microsoft Web site at http://www.microsoft.com/).

3   See chapter 4, at note 157 and accompanying text.

4   If the options cannot be valued with a reasonable degree of certainty when they vest, the employee's income inclusion and corresponding employer deduction could be deferred until the options are exercised.

5   See chapter 5, at note 8.

6   As with the proposals for greater loss relief for SME investment, eligible SMEs could be limited to rapid-growth SMEs; a "black list" of non-qualifying businesses could also be used. However, since this proposal targets an individual's own entrepreneurial endeavours, as opposed to angel capital or formal venture capital investment, lifestyle businesses need not be excluded.

7   In addition, as discussed in chapter 7, there are a number of deficiencies with the leveraging mechanism itself, including the limited types of investment vehicles that can be used for SME investment by pension funds.

8   See chapter 6, at notes 218-220 and accompanying text.

Selected Bibliography

Amit, Raphael, James Brander, and Christoph Zott. "Why Do Venture Capital Firms Exist? Theory and Canadian Evidence." (1998) vol. 13, no. 6 *Journal of Business Venturing* 441-66.

Anand, Bharat Narendra. "Survivors, Angels, and Taxes: Essays in the Economics of Entrepreneurship." PhD thesis, Princeton University, 1994.

Auerbach, Alan J. "Capital Gains Taxation and Tax Reform." (1989) vol. 42, no. 3 *National Tax Journal* 391-401.

———. "Capital Gains Taxation in the United States: Realizations, Revenue, and Rhetoric." [1988] no. 2 *Brookings Papers on Economic Activity* 595-637.

———. "The Effects of Reducing the Capital Gains Tax." (1989) vol. 43, no. 8a *Tax Notes* 1009-12.

———. "On the Design and Reform of Capital-Gains Taxation." (1992) vol. 82, no. 2 *The American Economic Review* 263-67.

———. "Retrospective Capital Gains Taxation." (1991) vol. 81, no. 1 *The American Economic Review* 167-78.

Auerbach, Alan J., Leonard E. Burman, and Jonathan M. Siegel. *Capital Gains Taxation and Tax Avoidance: New Evidence from Panel Data.* NBER Working Paper 6399. Cambridge, MA: National Bureau of Economic Research, February 1998.

Bankman, Joseph. "The Structure of Silicon Valley Start-Ups." (1994) vol. 41, no. 7 *UCLA Law Review* 1737-68.

Barker, Michael. "Must We Burn Gilder? Or, Taxes and the Entrepreneur." (1985) vol. 27, no. 5 *Tax Notes* 541-47.

———. "Quoth the Maven: Venture Capital and Tax Reform." (1986) vol. 32, no. 11 *Tax Notes* 1087-89.

Barkley, David L., Deborah M. Markley, and Julia Sass Rubin. "Certified Capital Companies (CAPCOs): Strengths and Shortcomings of the Latest Wave in State-Assisted Venture Capital Programs." (2001) vol. 15, no. 4 *Economic Development Quarterly* 350-66.

———. *Public Involvement in Venture Capital Funds: Lessons from Three Program Alternatives.* RUPRI Policy Paper 99-9. Columbia, MO: Rural Policy Research Institute, November 1999.

Beltz, Cynthia, ed. *Financing Entrepreneurs.* Washington, DC: AEI Press, 1994.

Birch, David L. *Choosing a Place To Grow: Business Location Decisions in the 1970's.* Cambridge, MA: MIT Program on Neighborhood and Regional Change, 1981.

———. *The Job Generation Process.* Cambridge, MA: MIT Program on Neighborhood and Regional Change, 1979.

———. *Regional Differences in Factor Costs: Land, Labor, Capital, and Transportation.* Cambridge, MA: MIT Program on Neighborhood and Regional Change, 1978.

Bittker, Boris I. and Lawrence Lokken. *Federal Taxation of Income, Estates and Gifts,* 3d ed. Valhalla, NY: Warren, Gorham & Lamont, 2001.

Bittker, Boris I. and Martin J. McMahon Jr. *Federal Income Taxation of Individuals*, 2d ed. Boston: Warren, Gorham & Lamont, 1995.

Black, Bernard S. and Ronald J. Gilson. "Venture Capital and the Structure of Capital Markets: Banks Versus Stock Markets." (1998) vol. 47, no. 3 *Journal of Financial Economics* 243-77.

Blum, Walter J. "A Handy Summary of the Capital Gains Arguments." (1957) vol. 35, no. 4 *Taxes: The Tax Magazine* 247-66.

Brooks, Neil. "Flattening the Claims of the Flat Taxers." (1998) vol. 21, no. 2 *Dalhousie Law Journal* 287-369.

———. "Taxation of Closely-Held Corporations: The Partnership Option and the Lower Rate of Tax." (1986) vol. 3, no. 4 *Australian Tax Forum* 381-509.

Burgess, David and Joel Fried. "Canadian Retirement Savings Plans and the Foreign Property Rule." (1999) vol. 25, no. 3 *Canadian Public Policy* 395-416.

Burman, Leonard E. *The Labyrinth of Capital Gains Tax Policy: A Guide for the Perplexed*. Washington, DC: Brookings Institution Press, 1999.

Business Development Bank of Canada. *2002 Annual Report: What Innovation Means to Entrepreneurs*. Financial year ending March 31, 2002. Ottawa: Business Development Bank of Canada, 2002.

———. *Summary of Corporate Plan, Fiscal 2002-2006: Supporting Small Business Productivity and Innovation*. Ottawa: Business Development Bank of Canada, 2002.

Bygrave, William D. and Jeffry A. Timmons. *Venture Capital at the Crossroads*. Boston: Harvard Business School Press, 1992.

Carpenter, Jennifer N. "The Exercise and Valuation of Executive Stock Options." (1998) vol. 48, no. 2 *Journal of Financial Economics* 127-58.

Carragher, Andrew and Darren Kelly. "An Evaluative Comparison of the Canadian and American Private Equity Markets." (1998) vol. 1, no. 3 *The Journal of Private Equity* 23-39.

Cooper, Chip, David Barkley, and Mike Williams. *Understanding CAPCOs*. Oklahoma City: National Association of Seed and Venture Funds, 2001.

Cumming, Douglas J. and Jeffrey G. MacIntosh. "Comparative Venture Capital Governance: Private Versus Labour Sponsored Venture Capital Funds." In Vesa Kanniainen and Christian Keuschnigg, eds., *Venture Capital, Entrepreneurship and Public Policy*. Cambridge, MA: MIT Press, forthcoming.

———. "Crowding Out Private Equity: Canadian Evidence." Draft paper, 2004.

Cunningham, Noël B. and Deborah H. Schenk. "The Case for a Capital Gains Preference." (1993) vol. 48, no. 3 *Tax Law Review* 319-80.

Dal Cin, Patrizia E. "Canadian Informal Investors: Towards a Framework for Policy Initiatives." MMS thesis, Carleton University, School of Business, 1993.

Defense Advanced Research Projects Agency. *Strategic Plan*. Washington, DC: DARPA, February 2003.

———. *Technology Transition*. Washington, DC: DARPA, 1997.

DeVoretz, Don and Samuel A. Laryea. *Canadian Human Capital Transfers: The United States and Beyond*. C.D. Howe Institute Commentary no. 115. Toronto: C.D. Howe Institute, October 1998.

Eisenstein, Louis. *The Ideologies of Taxation*. New York: Ronald Press, 1961.

Eisinger, Peter K. *The Rise of the Entrepreneurial State: State and Local Development Policy in the United States*. Madison, WI: University of Wisconsin Press, 1988.

Elango, B., Vance H. Fried, Robert D. Hisrich, and Amy Polonchek. "How Venture Capital Firms Differ." (1995) vol. 10, no. 2 *Journal of Business Venturing* 157-79.

Esenwein, Gregg A. *Individual Capital Gains Income: Legislative History*. CRS Report for Congress. Report no. 98-473 E. Updated June 29, 1998.

Falconer, Kirk. *Prudence, Patience and Jobs: Pension Investment in a Changing Canadian Economy—Technical Report*. Ottawa: Canadian Labour Market and Productivity Centre, 1999.

Finnie, Ross. *The Brain Drain: Myth and Reality—What It Is and What Should Be Done*. School of Policy Studies Working Paper 13. Kingston, ON: Queen's University, School of Policy Studies, January 2001.

Frank, Jeff and Éric Bélair. *South of the Border: Graduates from the Class of '95 Who Moved to the United States*. Ottawa: Human Resources Development Canada and Statistics Canada, 1999. Statistics Canada catalogue no. 81-587-XPB.

Frank, Jeffrey and Jim Seidle. "Pathways to the United States: Graduates from the Class of '95." (2000) vol. 6, no. 3 *Education Quarterly Review* 36-44.

Freear, John, Jeffrey E. Sohl, and William E. Wetzel Jr. "Angels and Non-Angels: Are There Differences?" (1994) vol. 9, no. 2 *Journal of Business Venturing* 109-23.

Freear, John and William E. Wetzel Jr. "Who Bankrolls High-Tech Entrepreneurs?" (1990) vol. 5, no. 2 *Journal of Business Venturing* 77-89.

Gac, Edward J. and Wayne M. Gazur. "Tapping 'Rainy Day' Funds for the Reluctant Entrepreneur: Downsizing, Paternalism, and the Internal Revenue Code." (1997) vol. 86, no. 1 *Kentucky Law Journal* 127-61.

Gertler, Meric S., Richard Florida, Gary Gates, and Tara Vinodrai. "Competing on Creativity: Placing Ontario's Cities in North American Context." Report prepared for the Ontario Ministry of Enterprise, Opportunity and Innovation and the Institute for Competitiveness and Prosperity. November 2002.

Gilson, Ronald J. "Engineering a Venture Capital Market: Lessons from the American Experience." (2003) vol. 55, no. 4 *Stanford Law Review* 1067-1103.

Gilson, Ronald J. and David M. Schizer. "Understanding Venture Capital Structure: A Tax Explanation for Convertible Preferred Stock." (2003) vol. 116, no. 3 *Harvard Law Review* 875-916.

Gompers, Paul A. and Josh Lerner. *The Venture Capital Cycle*. Cambridge, MA: MIT Press, 1999.

Gordon, Roger H. "Can High Personal Tax Rates Encourage Entrepreneurial Activity?" (1998) vol. 45, no. 1 *International Monetary Fund Staff Papers* 49-80.

Green, Milford B., ed. *Venture Capital: International Comparisons*. London: Routledge, 1991.

Guenther, David A. and Michael Willenborg. "Capital Gains Tax Rates and the Cost of Capital for Small Business: Evidence from the IPO Market." (1999) vol. 53, no. 3 *Journal of Financial Economics* 385-408.

Gupta, Anil K. and Harry J. Sapienza. "Determinants of Venture Capital Firms' Preferences Regarding the Industry Diversity and Geographic Scope of Their Investments." (1992) vol. 7, no. 5 *Journal of Business Venturing* 347-62.

Haar, Nancy E., Jennifer Starr, and Ian C. MacMillan. "Informal Risk Capital Investors: Investment Patterns on the East Coast of the U.S.A." (1988) vol. 3, no. 1 *Journal of Business Venturing* 11-29.

Haliassos, Michael and Andrew B. Lyon. "Progressivity of Capital Gains Taxation with Optimal Portfolio Selection." In Joel Slemrod, ed., *Tax Progressivity and Income Inequality*, 275-308. Cambridge, UK: Cambridge University Press, 1994.

Halpern, Paul J.N., ed. *Financing Growth in Canada*. Calgary: University of Calgary Press, 1997.

Harrison, Richard T. and Colin M. Mason, eds. *Informal Venture Capital: Evaluating the Impact of Business Introduction Services*. London: Prentice Hall, 1996.

Harroch, Richard D., ed. *Start-Up and Emerging Companies: Planning, Financing, and Operating the Successful Business*. New York: Law Journal Press, looseleaf.

Heard, Robert G. and John S. Silbert. *Growing New Businesses with Seed and Venture Capital: State Experiences and Options*. Washington, DC: National Governors' Association, 2000.

Heath, Chip, Steven Huddart, and Mark Lang. "Psychological Factors and the Stock Option Exercise." (1999) vol. 114, no. 2 *Quarterly Journal of Economics* 601-27.

Heilbroner, Robert and Lester Thurow. *Economics Explained: Everything You Need To Know About How the Economy Works and Where It's Going*, rev. ed. New York: Touchstone, 1998.

Helliwell, John F. *Checking the Brain Drain: Evidence and Implications*. Department of Economics Working Paper. Vancouver: University of British Columbia, Department of Economics, July 1999.

―――. *Globalization: Myths, Facts and Consequences*. C.D. Howe Institute Benefactors Lecture. Toronto: C.D. Howe Institute, October 23, 2000.

Helliwell, John F. and David F. Helliwell. "Tracking UBC Graduates: Trends and Explanations." (2000) vol. 1, no. 1 *Isuma* 101-10.

―――. "Where Are They Now? Migration Patterns for Graduates of the University of British Columbia." Paper prepared for the University of British Columbia, Centre for Research on Economic and Social Policy, 2000.

Henderson, James W. *Obtaining Venture Financing: Principles and Practices*. Lexington, MA: Lexington Books, 1988.

Holtz-Eakin, Douglas. "Should Small Business Be Tax-Favored?" (1995) vol. 48, no. 3 *National Tax Journal* 387-95.

Huddart, Steven and Mark Lang. "Employee Stock Option Exercises: An Empirical Analysis." (1996) vol. 21, no. 1 *Journal of Accounting and Economics* 5-43.

Industry Canada. *Supporting Small Business Innovation: Review of the Business Development Bank of Canada*. Ottawa: Industry Canada, June 2001.

―――. *The Winning Formula: Facilitating Investment in Small Business Growth, Lessons from 22 Pilot Projects Under the Canada Community Investment Plan*. Ottawa: Industry Canada, 2003.

Iqbal, Mahmood. "Brain Drain: Empirical Evidence of Emigration of Canadian Professionals to the United States." (2000) vol. 48, no. 3 *Canadian Tax Journal* 674-88.

Jackson, Edward T. and François Lamontagne. *Adding Value: The Economic and Social Impacts of Labour-Sponsored Venture Capital Corporations on Their Investee Firms*. Ottawa: Canadian Labour Market and Productivity Centre, 1995.

Jensen, Michael C. and W.H. Meckling. "Theory of the Firm: Managerial Behavior, Agency Costs and Ownership Structure." (1976) vol. 3, no. 4 *Journal of Financial Economics* 305-60.

Jog, Vijay M. "The Lifetime Capital Gains Exemption: Corporate Financing, Risk-Taking and Allocation Efficiency." (1995) vol. 21, supplement *Canadian Public Policy* S116-35.

Johnson, Calvin H. "Stock Compensation: The Most Expensive Way To Pay Future Cash." (1999) vol. 52, no. 2 *SMU Law Review* 423-54.

Johnson, Calvin H. "Stock and Stock Option Compensation: A Bad Idea." (2003) vol. 51, no. 3 *Canadian Tax Journal* 1259-90.

Karig, Adele M. "Taxation of Tax-Exempt and Foreign Investors in U.S. Private Investment Funds." In *Tax Planning for Domestic & Foreign Partnerships, LLCs, Joint Ventures & Other Strategic Alliances*, 885-916. New York: Practising Law Institute, 2001.

Kleiman, Robert T. and Joel M. Shulman. "The Risk-Return Attributes of Publicly Traded Venture Capital: Implications for Investors and Public Policy." (1992) vol. 7, no. 3 *Journal of Business Venturing* 195-208.

Kozmetsky, George, Michael D. Gill Jr., and Raymond W. Smilor. *Financing and Managing Fast-Growth Companies: The Venture Capital Process*. Lexington, MA: Lexington Books, 1985.

Krasa, Eva M. "Income Tax Implications of Joint Investment by Pension Plans Through a Private Pooled Fund Vehicle." (1997) vol. 45, no. 1 *Canadian Tax Journal* 1-24.

Krever, Rick and Neil Brooks. *A Capital Gains Tax for New Zealand*. Wellington, NZ: Victoria University Press for the Institute for Policy Studies, 1990.

Kuttner, Robert. *Everything for Sale: The Virtues and Limits of Markets*. New York: Knopf, 1997.

Lavery, J. Michael. "A Review of Developments in the Venture Capital Field." In *Report of Proceedings of the Thirty-First Tax Conference*, 1979 Conference Report, 508-23. Toronto: Canadian Tax Foundation, 1980.

Lee, John W. "Critique of Current Congressional Capital Gains Contentions." (1995) vol. 15, no. 1 *Virginia Tax Review* 1-88.

Lerner, Joshua. "'Angel' Financing and Public Policy: An Overview." (1998) vol. 22, no. 6-8 *Journal of Banking & Finance* 773-83.

———. "The Government as Venture Capitalist: The Long-Run Impact of the SBIR Program." (1999) vol. 72, no. 3 *Journal of Business* 285-318.

Lewis, Michael. *The New New Thing: A Silicon Valley Story*. New York: Norton, 2000.

Livingston, Michael. "Risky Business: Economics, Culture and the Taxation of High-Risk Activities." (1993) vol. 48, no. 2 *Tax Law Review* 163-232.

Lodge, Arthur. "Whence Will Come Venture Capital?" (1987) vol. 164, no. 5 *Journal of Accountancy* 168.

Loss, Louis and Joel Seligman. *Fundamentals of Securities Regulation*, 3d ed. New York: Little Brown, 1995.

————. *Fundamentals of Securities Regulation*, 3d ed., *2000 Supplement*. Gaithersberg, NY: Aspen Law and Business, 2000.

Macdonald, Mary and John Perry. *Pension Funds and Venture Capital: The Critical Links Between Savings, Investment, Technology, and Jobs*. Ottawa: Science Council of Canada, 1985.

MacKnight, Robin. "ESOP's Fable: Gargoyles, Tax Policy, and Employee Ownership in Ontario." In *Report of Proceedings of the Forty-Sixth Tax Conference*, 1994 Conference Report, 22:1-36. Toronto: Canadian Tax Foundation, 1995.

Mawani, Amin. "Tax Deductibility of Employee Stock Options." (2003) vol. 51, no. 3 *Canadian Tax Journal* 1230-58.

McGee, M. Kevin. "Capital Gains Taxation and New Firm Investment." (1998) vol. 51, no. 4 *National Tax Journal* 653-73.

McGill, Dan M., Kyle N. Brown, John J. Haley, and Sylvester J. Schieber. *Fundamentals of Private Pensions*, 7th ed. Philadelphia: University of Pennsylvania Press, 1996.

McGuire, Terrance P. "A Blueprint for Growth or a Recipe for Disaster? State Sponsored Venture Capital Funds for High Technology Ventures." (1994) vol. 7, no. 2 *Harvard Journal of Law & Technology* 419-48.

McNeill, Mariana and Richard Fullenbaum. *Pension Funds and Small Firm Financing*. Small Business Research Summary no. 153. Washington, DC: Small Business Administration Office of Advocacy, 1995.

McQuillan, Peter E. "An Analysis of Venture Capital Incentives." In *Income Tax Considerations in Corporate Financing*, 1986 Corporate Management Tax Conference, 169-253. Toronto: Canadian Tax Foundation, 1986.

————. "Tax Incentives for Venture Capital in Canada: The SODEQ, the VIC and the IIC." In *Report of Proceedings of the Twenty-Eighth Tax Conference*, 1976 Conference Report, 35-61. Toronto: Canadian Tax Foundation, 1977.

Mintz, Jack M. and Stephen R. Richardson. "The Lifetime Capital Gains Exemption: An Evaluation." (1995) vol. 21, supplement *Canadian Public Policy* S1-12.

Morelli, Yvette. "Structuring Venture Capital Funds." (2003) vol. 51, no. 2 *Canadian Tax Journal* 806-62.

Morse, Edward A. "Travails of the Entrepreneurial Ant: Reforming Tax-Favored Retirement Saving for Small Business Owners." (2000) vol. 50, no. 1 *DePaul Law Review* 49-110.

Nash, Michael S., William E. Atkin, Richard E. Entlich, and R.N.C. Lightfoot. *Participant Views of Advanced Research Projects Agency "Other Transactions."* Institute for Defense Analyses Document D-1793. Washington, DC: DARPA, November 1995.

Needham, M.J. "Venture Capital in Canada." In *Report of Proceedings of the Twenty-Eighth Tax Conference*, 1976 Conference Report, 28-35. Toronto: Canadian Tax Foundation, 1977.

Norton, Edgar and Bernard H. Tenenbaum. "Specialization Versus Diversification as a Venture Capital Investment Strategy." (1993) vol. 8, no. 5 *Journal of Business Venturing* 431-42.

Organisation for Economic Co-operation and Development. *Government Venture Capital for Technology-Based Firms*. Paris: OECD, 1997.

————. *Technology Incubators: Nurturing Small Firms*. Paris: OECD, 1997.

————. *Venture Capital and Innovation*. Paris: OECD, 1996.

————. *Venture Capital: Context, Development and Policies*. Paris: OECD, 1986.

Osborne, Duncan and Daniel Sandler. "A Tax Expenditure Analysis of Labour-Sponsored Venture Capital Corporations." (1998) vol. 46, no. 3 *Canadian Tax Journal* 499-574.

Postlethwaite & Netterville. *CAPCO Study*. Prepared for the Louisiana Department of Economic Development. Baton Rouge: Louisiana Department of Economic Development, December 31, 1999.

Poterba, James M. "Capital Gains Tax Policy Toward Entrepreneurship." (1989) vol. 42, no. 3 *National Tax Journal* 375-89.

————. "Venture Capital and Capital Gains Taxation." In Lawrence H. Summers, ed., *Tax Policy and the Economy*, vol. 3, 47-67. Cambridge, MA: MIT Press, 1989.

Reiner, Martha Louise. "The Transformation of Venture Capital: A History of Venture Capital Organizations in the United States." PhD thesis, UC Berkeley, 1989.

Reynolds, Paul D., William D. Bygrave, Erkko Autio, Larry W. Cox, and Michael Hay. *Global Entrepreneurship Monitor: 2002 Executive Report*. Wellesley, MA: Babson College, 2002.

Reynolds, Paul D., S. Michael Camp, William D. Bygrave, Erkko Autio, and Michael Hay. *Global Entrepreneurship Monitor: 2001 Executive Report*. Wellesley, MA: Babson College, 2001.

Reynolds, Paul D., Michael Hay, William D. Bygrave, S. Michael Camp, and Erkko Autio. *Global Entrepreneurship Monitor: 2000 Executive Report*. Wellesley, MA: Babson College, 2000.

Richardson, Stephen R. and Kathryn E. Moore. "Canadian Experience with the Taxation of Capital Gains." (1995) vol. 21, supplement *Canadian Public Policy* S77-99.

Riding, Allan L. *Financing Entrepreneurial Firms: Legal and Regulatory Issues*. Research paper prepared for the Task Force on the Future of the Canadian Financial Services Sector. Ottawa: Department of Finance, 1998.

Riding, Allan A., P. Dal Cin, L. Duxbury, G. Haines, and R. Safrata. *Informal Investors in Canada: The Identification of Salient Characteristics: A Report Submitted to the Federal Department of Industry, Science, and Technology Canada and to the Ministry of Economic Development and Trade of the Province of Ontario*. Ottawa: Department of Industry, Science and Technology, 1993.

Riding, Allan and Barbara Orser. *Beyond the Banks: Creative Financing for Canadian Entrepreneurs*. Etobicoke, ON: Wiley, 1997.

Rizzi, Robert A. "Tax Exempts' Investments in Pass-Through Entities." In *Tax Strategies for Corporate Acquisitions, Dispositions, Spin-Offs, Joint Ventures, Financings, Reorganizations and Restructurings*, 905-69. New York: Practising Law Institute, 2000.

Sahlman, W. "The Structure and Governance of Venture-Capital Corporations." (1990) vol. 27, no. 2 *Journal of Financial Economics* 473-521.

Sandler, Daniel. "The Benchmark Income Tax Treatment of Employee Stock Options: A Basis for Comparison." (2003) vol. 51, no. 3 *Canadian Tax Journal* 1204-29.

————. "The Tax Treatment of Employee Stock Options: Generous to a Fault." (2001) vol. 49, no. 2 *Canadian Tax Journal* 259-319.

Saxenian, AnnaLee. *Regional Advantage: Culture and Competition in Silicon Valley and Route 128*. Cambridge, MA: Harvard University Press, 1994.

Schilit, W. Keith. *Dream Makers and Deal Breakers: Inside the Venture Capital Industry*. Englewood Cliffs, NJ: Prentice Hall, 1991.

Schwanen, Daniel. *Putting the Brain Drain in Context: Canada and Global Competition for Scientists and Engineers*. C.D. Howe Institute Commentary no. 140. Toronto: C.D. Howe Institute, April 2000.

Small Business Administration. *SBA Budget Request & Performance Plan: FY 2004 Congressional Submission*. Washington, DC: Small Business Administration, February 10, 2003.

Stanford, Jim. *Paper Boom: Why Real Prosperity Requires a New Approach to Canada's Economy*. Ottawa: Canadian Centre for Policy Alternatives and Lorimer, 1999.

Statistics Canada. *Canada's Retirement Income Program: A Statistical Overview, 1999-2000*. Statistics Canada catalogue no. 74-507-XIE.

―――. *Pension Plans in Canada*. January 1, 2000. Statistics Canada catalogue no. 74-401-XPB.

Suret, Jean Marc. *The Fonds de Solidarité des Travailleurs du Québec: A Cost Benefit Analysis*. Sainte Foy, QC: Université Laval, December 1993.

Surrey, Stanley S. and Paul R. McDaniel. *Tax Expenditures*. Cambridge, MA: Harvard University Press, 1985.

Teltscher, Lawrence. "Small Business Financing." In *Income Tax and Goods and Services Tax Considerations in Corporate Financing*, 1992 Corporate Management Tax Conference, 6:1-67. Toronto: Canadian Tax Foundation, 1993.

Terry, Charles T. "Option Pricing Theory and the Economic Incentive Analysis of Nonrecourse Acquisition Liabilities." (1995) vol. 12, no. 2 *The American Journal of Tax Policy* 273-397.

Thomas, Joseph. "Ten Investment Trusts in America—A Three-Year Record." (1930) vol. 9 *Harvard Business Review* 79-88.

Thomson Financial Venture Economics. *2001 Investment Benchmark Reports: LP Analytics 2001*. New York: Thomson Financial/Securities Data Publishing, 2001.

Thomson Venture Economics. *2003 National Venture Capital Association Yearbook*. Arlington, VA and Newark, NJ: National Venture Capital Association and Thomson Venture Economics, 2003.

Timmons, Jeffry A. *New Venture Creation: Entrepreneurship for the 21st Century*, 5th ed. Boston: Irwin McGraw-Hill, 1999.

United States, Department of the Treasury, Office of Tax Analysis. *Report to Congress on the Capital Gains Tax Reductions of 1978*. Washington, DC: US Government Printing Office, 1985.

United States, Treasury Department, Tax Advisory Staff. *Federal Income Tax Treatment of Capital Gains and Losses*. Washington, DC: United States Treasury Department, 1951.

Van Osnabrugge, Mark and Robert J. Robinson. *Angel Investing: Matching Start-Up Funds with Start-Up Companies—The Guide for Entrepreneurs, Individual Investors, and Venture Capitalists*. San Francisco: Jossey-Bass, 2000.

Viard, Alan D. "Taxation and Venture Capital." (1985) vol. 28, no. 8 *Tax Notes* 915-19.

Vonk, Gerro. *Venture Capital Beyond Boundaries: International Cooperation Between Venture Capital Funds in Europe, America, and Japan*. Utrecht, the Netherlands: Driestar, 1988.

Wagner, Don. "Do Tax Differences Cause the Brain Drain?" (2000) vol. 21, no. 10 *Policy Options* 33-41.

Weil, Rob. "Deferred Income Arrangements—A Decade of Change." In *Deferred Income Arrangements: A Practitioner's Guide to Proper Tax Planning*, tab 2. Toronto: Canadian Tax Foundation, 1997.

Wetzl, William E., Jr. "The Informal Venture Capital Market: Aspects of Scale and Market Efficiency." (1987) vol. 2, no. 4 *Journal of Business Venturing* 299-313.

Wilson, Thomas A. and Steve Murphy. *Tax-Exempts and Corporate Capital Structure: An Empirical Analysis*. Working Paper 97-5 prepared for the Technical Committee on Business Taxation. Ottawa: Department of Finance, 1997.

Zhao, John, Doug Drew, and T. Scott Murray. "Brain Drain and Brain Gain: The Migration of Knowledge Workers from and to Canada." (2000) vol. 6, no. 3 *Education Quarterly Review* 8-35.

Zodrow, George R. "Economic Analyses of Capital Gains Taxation: Realizations, Revenues, Efficiency and Equity." (1993) vol. 48, no. 3 *Tax Law Review* 419-527.

Index

ABIL, *see* allowable business investment loss (ABIL)

AMT, *see* alternative minimum tax (AMT)

AMTI, *see* alternative minimum taxable income (AMTI)

ARD, *see* American Research and Development Corp. (ARD)

ARPA, *see* Advanced Research Projects Agency (ARPA)

Advanced Research Projects Agency (ARPA), 454, 455, 463

adverse selection, 14

Alabama, CAPCO program
  eligible investments, 330
  eligible investors, 323
  failure to meet investment requirements, consequences, 333
  governing legislation, 321
  government expenditure limits, 327
  incentive, nature of, 325
  introduction of, 260
  investment, nature of, 324
  maximum investment/benefit per investor, 326
  minimum/maximum capitalization, 323
  organizational form, 322
  pacing requirements, 331
  state share in distribution, 326
  voluntary decertification requirements, 332

allowable business investment loss (ABIL)
  angel capital investment, effect on, 77
  compared with section 1244 stock relief, 112

alternative minimum tax (AMT)
  Canada, introduction of, 92-93
  Canadian QSBC, and, 103
  United States, introduction of, 82-83
  US QSBS, and, 102

alternative minimum taxable income (AMTI), 82-83

American Research and Development Corp. (ARD), 45

angel capital investors
  capital gains taxation, preferential treatment of
    Canada, 95-96, 102-3, 107-9
    United States, 87, 100-2, 106-7
  capital losses, preferential treatment of
    Canada, 114-15
    United States, 112-14
  defined, 4, 5-6
  factors influencing decision to invest, 36
  tax credits, influence on, 215-24
  traits, 36

angel capital networks, 20, 242, 455, 472-75

angel capital rollover
  as distinct from other capital gains tax preferences, 105
  Canada, evolution of, 107-9
  evaluation as mechanism to encourage investment, 109-12, 491-92
  United States, evolution of, 106-7

angel tax credit programs
  application for registration, 231
  cost-benefit analyses, 222-24
  eligible businesses, 221-22, 228-29
  eligible investors, 216-17, 225-26
  eligible uses of capital, 222
  evaluation as mechanism to encourage investment, 494-95
  governing legislation, 225-26
  government expenditure limits, 233-34
  holding period, 233
  limit on amount raised per business, 233
  limitations, nature of incentive, 219-21, 226-27
  limitations, nature of investment, 219, 226
  maximum tax credit/maximum investment, 227-28
  relationship between investor and business, restrictions on, 217-19, 232
  sunset provisions, 234
  use of proceeds, 230
  use of retirement savings, 216-17

Auerbach, Alan, 187

BDC, *see* Business Development Bank of
Canada (BDC)
Beauvais, Emile, 88
Bittker, Boris, 164, 369
Black, Fisher, 154
Black-Scholes model, 154-55, 163
Blessing, Peter, 171
brain drain, significance of, 190-93
brain gain, significance of, 191
bridge financing, 8
British Columbia
    angel tax credit program
        application for registration, 231
        eligible businesses, 228
        eligible investors, 216, 225
        governing legislation, 225
        government expenditure limits, 233
        holding period, 233
        limit on amount raised per business,
            233
        limitations, nature of incentive, 220,
            226
        limitations, nature of investment, 226
        maximum tax credit/maximum
            investment, 227
        relationship between investor and
            business, restrictions on, 232
        sunset provisions, 234
        use of proceeds, 230
    LSVCC program
        board of directors requirements, 315
        eligible investments, 317-18
        eligible investors, 316
        failure to meet investment
            requirements, consequences, 320
        governing legislation, 313
        government expenditure limits, 317
        holding period, 317
        incentive, nature of, 316
        minimum/maximum capitalization, 316
        number of LSVCCs permitted, 314
        organizational form, 315
        pacing requirements, 319
        sponsoring organization, 314
    VCF program
        eligible investments, 276, 300
        eligible investors, 297
        failure to meet investment
            requirements, consequences, 302
        governing legislation, 296
        government expenditure limit, 300
        holding period, 299
        incentive, nature of, 298
        investment, nature of, 297
        minimum capitalization requirement,
            272, 297
        number of VCFs permitted, 296
        organizational form, 296
        pacing requirements, 301
        refundable tax credits, 270
Brooks, Neil, 15, 193
Bush, George W., 416
Bush, Vannevar, 44
business angels, *see* angel capital investors
Business Development Bank of Canada
    (BDC)
        as distinct from SBA, 461-62
        counselling programs, 460
        debt and equity financing, 461
        historical development, 458-59
        mandate, 56, 459
        operating groups, 460
business incubators, 455, 475-76

CAPCO, *see* certified capital company
    (CAPCO)
CASE, *see* Counseling Assistance for Small
    Enterprises (CASE)
CCIP, *see* Canada Community Investment
    Plan (CCIP)
CDC, *see* Canadian Development
    Corporation (CDC)
CED, *see* Canadian Enterprise Development
    Corporation Limited (CED)
CEDC, *see* community economic
    development corporation (CEDC)
CICA, *see* Canadian Institute of Chartered
    Accountants (CICA)
CLMPC, *see* Canadian Labour Market and
    Productivity Centre (CLMPC)
CODA, *see* cash or deferred arrangement
    (CODA)
COIN, *see* Canada Opportunities Investment
    Network (COIN); Computerized Ontario
    Investment Network (COIN)
CPP, *see* Canada Pension Plan (CPP)

CPPIB, *see* Canada Pension Plan Investment Board (CPPIB)

CSBIF, *see* community small business investment fund (CSBIF)

CVCA, *see* Canadian Venture Capital Association (CVCA)

Caisse de dépôt et placement du Québec, 58, 60, 61, 410, 411, 414, 417, 419-20

Canada
  angel capital rollover provisions, 107-9
  capital gains taxation, preferential treatment of, 87-96
  capital losses, preferential treatment of, 114-15
  employee stock options, taxation of, 179-83
  lifetime capital gains exemption, 102-3
  limited partnership income, taxation of, 244-52
    characterization of income, 245-47
    qualified non-residents, 249-50
    subsection 39(4) election, 247-49
  limited partnership property, distribution to partners, 253-54
  LSVCC program
    board of directors requirements, 315
    eligible investments, 317
    eligible investors, 316
    failure to meet investment requirements, consequences, 320
    governing legislation, 313
    government expenditure limits, 317
    holding period, 317
    incentive, nature of, 316
    minimum/maximum capitalization, 316
    number of LSVCCs permitted, 314
    organizational form, 315
    pacing requirements, 319
    sponsoring organization, 314
  pension fund venture capital investment, 57-61
  pension plans
    CPP, 417-21
    governing legislation, 375-76
    historical development, 371-72
    taxation of employer-sponsored plans, 372-75
    taxation of individual plans, 372-75

  venture capital investment, history of, 55-63

Canada Community Investment Plan (CCIP), 474

Canada Opportunities Investment Network (COIN), 474

Canada Pension Plan (CPP)
  as distinct from QPP, 419-20
  establishment, 59
  importance of, formal venture capital industry, 62, 421, 497-98

Canada Pension Plan Investment Board (CPPIB)
  establishment, 59, 418
  foreign property limitations, 418
  investment restrictions, 418-19, 497

Canadian Development Corporation (CDC), 55

Canadian Enterprise Development Corporation Limited (CED), 55

Canadian Institute of Chartered Accountants (CICA), 156

Canadian Labour Market and Productivity Centre (CLMPC), 281, 409

Canadian small business investment corporation (CanSBIC), 57, 398-401

Canadian Venture Capital Association (CVCA), 249, 408

CanSBIC, *see* Canadian small business investment corporation (CanSBIC)

capital asset, defined, US Internal Revenue Code, 78, 79, 86

capital gains exemption, angel capital formation, effect on, 37

capital gains taxation
  Canada, evolution of
    1969 white paper proposals on, 90
    1971 tax reform changes, 91
    1987 tax reform changes, 93
    academic perspective pre-1969 white paper, 89
    AMT, introduction of, 92-93
    Carter report recommendations, 88-90
    characterization of gain on disposition of investment, 94
    inclusion as ordinary income, 87-88
    inclusion rate, 91, 93, 94
    lifetime capital gains exemption, 92, 93, 102-5

capital gains taxation (cont.)
   Canada, evolution of (cont.)
      loss utilization amendments, 91
      practitioner perspective pre-1969
         white paper, 89-90
      Senate committee response to 1969
         white paper, 90-91
     employee stock options, 183-85, 489,
       493-94
     investment, effect on, 37
     preferential treatment of
      angel capital rollover, 105-12, 489,
       491-92
      Canada, 87-96
      Canada and United States compared,
       76-77, 490-91
      capital losses, 112-18, 492-93
      evaluation as risk-taking incentive,
       96-100
      QSBC, 102-5, 491
      QSBS, 100-2, 103-5
      United States, 77-87
    United States, evolution of
      add-on tax, 81, 82, 83
      AMT, introduction of, 82-83
      capital asset defined, 78, 79, 86
      capital gain and capital loss defined, 78
      characterization of gain on
       disposition of investment, 86
      holding-period requirement, 79-81, 85
      interest expense deduction limitation,
       81
      key features, 79
      long-term capital gains, legislative
       changes, 82, 83, 84,85
      loss utilization, and, 78, 80, 81, 83,
       112-18
      personal service income, tax rate cap,
       81
      rate reduction, 84-85
      stepped rate, introduction of, 79
      tax reform of 1986, 83
capital losses, preferential treatment of
   angel capital investment, effect on, 37
   Canada, 114-15
   Canada and United States, compared, 112
   evaluation as mechanism to encourage
    investment, 115-18, 492-93
   United States, 112-14

cash or deferred arrangement (CODA), 367
certified capital company (CAPCO), *see
also* labour-sponsored venture capital
corporation (LSVCC); venture capital fund
(VCF)
   cost-benefit analysis, 288-92
   eligible investments, 261, 270, 276, 327-30
   eligible investors, 270, 323
   evaluation as mechanism to encourage
    investment, 496
   failure to meet investment requirements,
    consequences, 332-33
   governing legislation, 321
   government expenditure limits, 274-75,
    327
   government profit share, 274-75
   historical development, 260-66
   incentive, nature of, 273, 324-25
   investment, nature of, 323-24
   minimum/maximum capitalization
    requirement, 271, 323
   maximum investment/benefit per
    investor, 325-26
   objectives, 260
   organizational form, 267-68, 321-22
   pacing requirements, 279, 331
   premium tax credit, 261, 262, 264
   state share in distribution, 326
   timing issues, 277-79
   voluntary decertification requirements,
    332
Chant, John F., 89
Charterhouse Canada Limited, 55
Chrétien, Jean, 91
Clark, Jim, 10
Colorado, CAPCO program
   eligible investments, 329
   eligible investors, 323
   failure to meet investment requirements,
    consequences, 333
   governing legislation, 321
   government expenditure limits, 327
   incentive, nature of, 325
   introduction of, 260
   investment, nature of, 324
   maximum investment/benefit per
    investor, 326
   minimum/maximum capitalization, 323
   organizational form, 322

pacing requirements, 331
state share in distribution, 326
voluntary decertification requirements, 332
community economic development
corporation (CEDC), 266
community small business investment fund
(CSBIF), 266, 273
Computerized Ontario Investment Network
(COIN), 473-74
convertible preferred stock, use as
investment vehicle, 14-15
Conway, Geoffrey, 88-89
Counseling Assistance for Small Enterprises
(CASE), 458
Cumming, Douglas, 288
Cunningham, Noël, 116

DARPA, *see* Defense Advanced Research
Projects Agency (DARPA)
DPSP, *see* deferred profit-sharing plan (DPSP)
Dal Cin, Patrizia, 37-40, 105
dealer
Canadian tax administration position,
subsection 39(4) election, 94-95
defined, US capital gain characterization,
86-87
Defense Advanced Research Projects
Agency (DARPA), 455, 463-64
deferred profit-sharing plan (DPSP)
contribution limits, 372-74
foreign property tax, and, 398
qualified investments, defined, 398
tax provisions affecting, 374-75
DeVoretz, Don, 190
Digital Equipment Corporation, 45
Drew, Doug, 190

EOLSVCC, *see* employee ownership labour-
sponsored venture capital corporation
(EOLSVCC)
ERISA, *see* Employee Retirement Income
Security Act of 1974 (ERISA)
ESBC, *see* eligible small business
corporation (ESBC)
ESPP, *see* employee stock purchase plan
(ESPP)
Eisinger, Peter, 16, 17
eligible small business corporation (ESBC),
107-8

employee ownership labour-sponsored
venture capital corporation (EOLSVCC),
256
Employee Retirement Income Security Act
of 1974 (ERISA), 98, 365, 370, 389-93
employee stock options
benchmark tax treatment, 159-64
Black-Scholes option-pricing model, 154,
156, 163
Canadian and US tax treatment
compared, 183-87, 493-94
Canadian tax treatment, 179-83
current accounting treatment, 154-56
employee and publicly traded stock
options, distinction, 160
evaluation as mechanism to encourage
investment
brain drain, effect on, 190-93
productivity increases, 188-89
rationales for preferential tax
treatment, 187
small company employee attraction
and retention, 189-90
proposed accounting treatment
fair value, factors affecting, 154
IASB and CICA compared, 157-59
US tax treatment
categorization of options, 164
ESPPs, 176-79
incentive stock options, 173, 174-76
non-statutory stock options, 164-69
statutory stock options, 169-79
employee stock purchase plan (ESPP)
as informal financing source, 6
compensation income calculation, 177-79
introduction, 171
requirements to qualify as, 176-77
employer-sponsored pension funds, *see also*
pension plans; registered retirement plan
(RPP)
as Canadian venture capital source, 57-60
as US venture capital source, 47-52, 361,
362, 495
investments in VCFs
Canada, 396-401
United States, 389-96
taxation, Canada, 372-75
taxation, United States, 365-68, 395-96
Eves, Ernie, 183

FAME, *see* Finance Authority of Maine
  (FAME)
FBDB, *see* Federal Business Development
  Bank (FBDB)
FICA, *see* Federal Insurance Contributions
  Act (FICA)
FSTQ, *see* Fonds de solidarité des
  travailleurs du Québec (FSTQ)
Falconer, Kirk, 409-15
Federal Business Development Bank
  (FBDB), 56, 458
Federal Insurance Contributions Act (FICA),
  416
Finance Authority of Maine (FAME), 222-23
first-stage financing, 7
Florida, CAPCO program
  eligible investments, 328
  eligible investors, 323
  failure to meet investment requirements,
    consequences, 332
  governing legislation, 321
  government expenditure limits, 327
  incentive, nature of, 325
  introduction of, 260
  investment, nature of, 324
  maximum investment/benefit per
    investor, 326
  minimum/maximum capitalization, 323
  organizational form, 322
  pacing requirements, 331
  state share in distribution, 326
  voluntary decertification requirements, 332
Fonds de solidarité des travailleurs du
  Québec (FSTQ)
  cost-benefit analysis, 281-83
  introduction, 61, 255
foreign property defined, RPP investment, 398
Freear, John, 36, 38
fund of funds, 9, 292, 293, 410

Gac, Edward, 404
gatekeeper investor, 9, 410
Gazur, Wayne, 404
Gompers, Paul, 277
Georgia, CAPCO program
  eligible investments, 330
  eligible investors, 323
  failure to meet investment requirements,
    consequences, 333

governing legislation, 321
government expenditure limits, 327
incentive, nature of, 325
introduction of, 260
investment, nature of, 324
maximum investment/benefit per
  investor, 326
minimum/maximum capitalization, 323
organizational form, 322
pacing requirements, 331
state share in distribution, 326
voluntary decertification requirements, 332
government-administered pension plans
  CPP, 417-21
  US Social Security, 416-17
government tax incentives
  first-round investment, concern with, 18
  market failures, response to, 13-16
  support of rapid-growth SMEs, 15-16
Grant, Donald, 88
Greenspan commission, 416

HOOPP, *see* Hospitals of Ontario Pension
  Plan (HOOPP)
Heilbroner, Robert, 3
Helliwell, David, 190
Helliwell, John, 190, 191, 192
Hewlett, William, 44
Hewlett-Packard, 2, 5, 44
Hospitals of Ontario Pension Plan
  (HOOPP), 60, 61

IASB, *see* International Accounting
  Standards Board (IASB)
IBA, *see* Investment Bankers Association of
  America (IBA)
ICIB, *see* Iowa Capital Investment Board
  (ICIB)
ICIC, *see* Iowa Capital Investment
  Corporation (ICIC)
IDB, *see* Industrial Development Bank (IDB)
IPO, *see* initial public offering (IPO)
IRA, *see* individual retirement account
  (IRA); individual retirement annuity (IRA)
ISO, *see* incentive stock option (ISO)
incentive stock option (ISO)
  compensation income calculation, 175-76
  disqualifying disposition, 175
  qualifying conditions, 174

Indiana, angel tax credit program
  application for registration, 232
  eligible businesses, 229
  eligible investors, 226
  governing legislation, 225
  government expenditure limits, 234
  holding period, 233
  limit on amount raised per business, 233
  limitations, nature of incentive, 227
  limitations, nature of investment, 219, 226
  maximum tax credit/maximum
    investment, 228
  relationship between investor and
    business, restrictions on, 232
  sunset provisions, 234
  use of proceeds, 230
individual retirement account (IRA), 368-70,
  380-82
individual retirement annuity (IRA), 368-70,
  380-82
Industrial Development Bank (IDB), 56, 458
information asymmetries
  defined, 13
  post-investment, 14, 472, 475-76
  pre-investment, 14, 472-75
initial public offering (IPO)
  impact on venture capital, 10-11, 21,
    253, 254
  statistics, 11, 12
International Accounting Standards Board
  (IASB), 156
Investment Bankers Association of America
  (IBA), 45
Investment Company Act (US), 45
investor distinguished from dealer, United
  States, 86-87
Iowa
  angel tax credit program
    application for registration, 231-32
    eligible businesses, 229
    eligible investors, 226
    governing legislation, 225
    government expenditure limits, 234
    holding period, 233
    limit on amount raised per business,
      233
    limitations, nature of investment, 226
    maximum tax credit/maximum
      investment, 228

  ownership restrictions, 218
  relationship between investor and
    business, restrictions on, 232
  sunset provisions, 234
  use of proceeds, 230
  VCF program
    eligible investments, 310
    eligible investors, 269, 306
    failure to meet investment
      requirements, consequences, 312
    governing legislation, 303
    government expenditure limits, 308
    holding period, 308
    incentive, nature of, 307
    investment, nature of, 306
    minimum/maximum capitalization, 305
    number of VCFs permitted, 304
    organizational form, 305
    pacing requirements, 311
Iowa Capital Investment Board (ICIB), 292-93
Iowa Capital Investment Corporation
  (ICIC), 293
Iqbal, Mahmood, 190

Jog, Vijay, 104
Johnson, Calvin, 159, 188

Kansas, VCF program
  eligible investments, 310-11
  eligible investors, 269, 306
  failure to meet investment requirements,
    consequences, 312
  governing legislation, 303
  government expenditure limits, 275, 309
  holding period, 308
  incentive, nature of, 308
  investment, nature of, 306
  minimum/maximum capitalization, 305
  number of VCFs permitted, 304
  organizational form, 305
  pacing requirements, 311
  refundable tax credits, 270
  transferable tax credits, 270, 271
Kennedy, John F., 170-71
Keogh plans, 365, 368, 382
Kuttner, Robert, 15

LBO, *see* leveraged buyout (LBO)
LLC, *see* limited liability company (LLC)

LSVCC, *see* labour-sponsored venture capital corporation (LSVCC)

Laberge, Louis, 255

labour-sponsored venture capital corporation (LSVCC), *see also* certified capital company (CAPCO); venture capital fund (VCF)
board of directors requirements, 315
cooling-off period, 258-59
cost-benefit analysis, 281-88
eligible investments, 276, 317-19
eligible investors, 269, 316
establishment of, 255
evaluation as mechanism to encourage investment, 496
failure to meet investment requirements, consequences, 320
federal government matching tax credit, 255-56
federal-provincial caps on levels of investment, 257, 258
governing legislation, 313-14
government expenditure limits, 274, 317
government profit share, 274
historical development, 255-59
holding period, 256, 258, 317
importance of, formal venture capital industry, 62
incentive, nature of, 273, 316
introduction of, 56, 61
minimum capitalization requirements, 271, 315-16
number of LSVCCs permitted, 314
organizational form, 267, 315
pacing requirements, 278-79, 319-20
RRSP investment in, 361, 388
sponsoring organization, 314
timing issues, 277-78

later-stage financing, 8

Layrea, Samuel, 190

Lerner, Josh, 277, 462

Lesage, Jean, 419, 420

leveraged buyout (LBO), 8, 60

Lewis, Michael, 10, 11

limited liability company (LLC), 243, 244

limited partnership
distribution of partnership property re partners
Canada, 253-54
United States, 252-53

formation of, 56
income characterization for tax purposes
Canada, 244-52
United States, 244
venture capital funds, use of 243-44

Livingston, Michael, 99

loan guarantees, 456

Lokken, Lawrence, 369

Louisiana, CAPCO program
eligible investments, 330, 270, 327
eligible investors, 323
failure to meet investment requirements, consequences, 332
governing legislation, 321
government expenditure limits, 327
incentive, nature of, 324
introduction of, 260-66
investment, nature of, 323
maximum investment/benefit per investor, 325
minimum/maximum capitalization, 323
organizational form, 321
pacing requirements, 331
state share in distribution, 326
voluntary decertification requirements, 332

Louisiana Economic Development Fund, 265

love capital
investors, 4, 5
RRSP funds, and, 385, 405-6

MIT, *see* Massachusetts Institute of Technology (MIT)

MVCF, *see* Michigan Venture Capital Fund (MVCF)

Macdonald, Donald S., 180

MacEachen, Allan, 92

MacIntosh, Jeffrey, 288

Maine
angel tax credit program
application for registration, 231
cost-benefit analysis, 222-23
eligible businesses, 229
eligible investors, 226
governing legislation, 225
government expenditure limits, 234
holding period, 233
limit on amount raised per business, 233

limitations, nature of incentive, 219, 220, 227

limitations, nature of investment, 219, 226

maximum tax credit/maximum investment, 228

ownership restrictions, 218

relationship between investor and business, restrictions on, 232

sunset provisions, 234

use of proceeds, 230

VCF program

eligible investments, 309

eligible investors, 269, 306

failure to meet investment requirements, consequences, 312

governing legislation, 303

government expenditure limits, 308

holding period, 308

incentive, nature of, 307

investment, nature of, 306

minimum/maximum capitalization, 305

number of VCFs permitted, 303

organizational form, 304

pacing requirements, 311

Manitoba, LSVCC programs

board of directors requirements, 315

eligible investments, 318

eligible investors, 316

failure to meet investment requirements, consequences, 320

governing legislation, 313

government expenditure limits, 317

holding period, 317

incentive, nature of, 316

minimum/maximum capitalization, 316

number of LSVCCs permitted, 314

organizational form, 315

pacing requirements, 319

sponsoring organization, 314

Manley, John, 459

Massachusetts Institute of Technology (MIT), 43

McMahon, Martin, 164

mezzanine financing, 8, 57, 60

Michigan Venture Capital Fund (MVCF), 389

Missouri

angel tax credit program

application for registration, 231

eligible businesses, 229

eligible investors, 226

governing legislation, 225

government expenditure limits, 234

holding period, 233

limit on amount raised per business, 233

limitations, nature of incentive, 219, 220, 227

limitations, nature of investment, 219

maximum tax credit/maximum investment, 228

ownership restrictions, 218

relationship between investor and business, restrictions on, 232

sunset provisions, 234

use of proceeds, 230

CAPCO program

eligible investments, 329

eligible investors, 323

failure to meet investment requirements, consequences, 332

governing legislation, 321

government expenditure limits, 327

incentive, nature of, 325

introduction of, 260

investment, nature of, 324

maximum investment/benefit per investor, 326

minimum/maximum capitalization, 323

organizational form, 322

pacing requirements, 331

state share in distribution, 326

voluntary decertification requirements, 332

VCF program

eligible investments, 310

eligible investors, 306

failure to meet investment requirements, consequences, 312

governing legislation, 303

government expenditure limits, 274-75, 309

holding period, 308

incentive, nature of, 307

introduction of, 260

investment, nature of, 306

minimum/maximum capitalization, 305

Missouri (cont.)
    VCF program (cont.)
        number of VCFs permitted, 304
        organizational form, 305
        pacing requirements, 311
        transferable tax credits, 270, 271
moral hazard, 14, 472, 476
Murray, Scott, 190

NAFTA, *see* North American free trade
    agreement (NAFTA)
NMVCC, *see* New Markets Venture Capital
    Company (NMVCC)
NSO, *see* non-statutory stock option (NSO)
NVCA, *see* National Venture Capital
    Association (NVCA)
National Venture Capital Association
    (NVCA), 400, 412
Netscape, 2, 10-11
New Brunswick, LSVCC program
    board of directors requirements, 315
    eligible investments, 319
    eligible investors, 316
    failure to meet investment requirements,
        consequences, 320
    governing legislation, 313
    government expenditure limits, 317
    holding period, 317
    incentive, nature of, 316
    minimum/maximum capitalization, 316
    number of LSVCCs permitted, 314
    organizational form, 315
    pacing requirements, 320
    sponsoring organization, 314
New Markets Venture Capital Company
    (NMVCC), 456
New York, CAPCO program
    eligible investments, 328
    eligible investors, 323
    failure to meet investment requirements,
        consequences, 332
    governing legislation, 321
    government expenditure limits, 327
    incentive, nature of, 324
    introduction of, 260
    investment, nature of, 324
    maximum investment/benefit per
        investor, 326
    minimum/maximum capitalization, 323

organizational form, 321
    pacing requirements, 331
    state share in distribution, 326
    voluntary decertification requirements, 332
Newfoundland and Labrador
    angel tax credit program
        application for registration, 231
        eligible businesses, 229
        eligible investors, 226
        governing legislation, 225
        government expenditure limits, 233
        holding period, 233
        limit on amount raised per business,
            233
        limitations, nature of incentive, 227
        limitations, nature of investment,
            219, 226
        maximum tax credit/maximum
            investment, 228
        relationship between investor and
            business, restrictions on, 232
        sunset provisions, 234
        use of proceeds, 230
    LSVCC program, introduction of, 259-60
non-statutory stock option (NSO), 164-69
North American free trade agreement
    (NAFTA), 190
Northwest Territories, LSVCC program, 259
Nova Scotia
    angel tax credit program
        application for registration, 231
        cost-benefit analysis, 223-24
        eligible businesses, 228-29
        eligible investors, 225
        governing legislation, 225
        government expenditure limits, 233
        holding period, 233
        limitations, nature of incentive, 226
        limitations, nature of investment,
            219, 226
        maximum tax credit/maximum
            investment, 227
        relationship between investor and
            business, restrictions on, 232
        use of proceeds, 230
    LSVCC program
        board of directors requirements, 315
        eligible investments, 319
        eligible investors, 269, 316

failure to meet investment
requirements, consequences, 320
governing legislation, 314
government expenditure limits, 317
holding period, 317
incentive, nature of, 316
minimum/maximum capitalization,
316
number of LSVCCs permitted, 314
organizational form, 315
pacing requirements, 319
sponsoring organization, 314
VCF program
eligible investments, 301
eligible investors, 297
failure to meet investment
requirements, consequences, 302
governing legislation, 296
government expenditure limit, 300
holding period, 299
incentive, nature of, 299
investment, nature of, 298
minimum capitalization, 297
number of VCFs permitted, 296
organizational form, 297
pacing requirements, 301

OCIB, *see* Oklahoma Capital Investment
Board (OCIB)
OECD, *see* Organisation for Economic Co-
operation and Development (OECD)
OMERS, *see* Ontario Municipal Employees
Retirement System (OMERS)
OSRD, *see* Office of Scientific Research
and Development (OSRD)
Office of Scientific Research and
Development (OSRD), 43
Oklahoma, VCF programs
eligible investments, 309
eligible investors, 306
failure to meet investment requirements,
consequences, 312
governing legislation, 303
government expenditure limits, 308
holding period, 308
incentive, nature of, 306
investment, nature of, 306
minimum/maximum capitalization, 305
number of VCFs permitted, 303

organizational form, 304
pacing requirements, 311
Oklahoma Capital Formation Corporation, 292
Oklahoma Capital Investment Board
(OCIB), 292
Ontario
LSVCC program
board of directors requirements, 315
eligible investments, 318
eligible investors, 316
failure to meet investment
requirements, consequences, 320
governing legislation, 313
government expenditure limits, 317
holding period, 317
incentive, nature of, 316
introduction of, 256-57
minimum/maximum capitalization,
316
number of LSVCCs permitted, 314
organizational form, 315
pacing requirements, 320
sponsoring organization, 314
VCF program
eligible investments, 276, 300
eligible investors, 297
failure to meet investment
requirements, consequences, 302
governing legislation, 296
government expenditure limit, 300
holding period, 299
incentive, nature of, 298
introduction of, 256, 266
investment, nature of, 297
minimum/maximum capitalization,
297
number of VCFs permitted, 296
organizational form, 297
pacing requirements, 301
Ontario Municipal Employees Retirement
System (OMERS), 60, 61, 411, 414
Ontario Teachers' Pension Plan, 60, 61, 411,
414
Organisation for Economic Co-operation
and Development (OECD)
1996 study, venture capital availability
(US), 35
model convention, taxation of capital
gains of limited partnership, 249

PA, *see* pension adjustment (PA)
PBA, *see* Pension Benefits Act (PBA)
PBSA, see Pension Benefits Standards Act (PBSA)
PIAC, *see* Pension Investment Association of Canada (PIAC)
PRIM, *see* Pension Reserves Investment Management Board (PRIM)
PRIT, *see* Pension Reserves Investment Trust Fund (PRIT)
Packard, David, 44
pension adjustment (PA), 373-74
Pension Benefits Act (PBA), 397
Pension Benefits Standards Act (PBSA), 396-97, 414
Pension Investment Association of Canada (PIAC), 409-15
pension legislation
  Canada
    overview, 375-76
    prudence requirement, 397
    venture capital investment, impact on, 396-97
  United States
    ERISA fiduciary standard rules, 390-92
    overview, 370-71
    public sector pension funds, 389-90
    venture capital investment, impact on, 389
pension plans
  Canada
    CPP, 417-21
    deterrence, venture capital investment, 409-15
    historical development of, 371-72
    pension legislation, 375-76
    taxation of employer-sponsored pension funds, 372-75
    taxation of individual retirement plans, 372-75
  defined benefit plans, 363, 364
  defined contribution plans, 364
  governing legislation, *see* pension legislation
  government-administered, *see* government-administered pension plans
  United States
    historical development of, 364-65

pension legislation, 370-71
Social Security, 416-17
taxation of employer-sponsored pension funds, 365-68
taxation of individual retirement plans, 368-70
taxation of Keogh plans, 368
Pension Reserves Investment Management Board (PRIM), 390
Pension Reserves Investment Trust Fund (PRIT), 390
Perry, Harvey, 87
Public Sector Pension Investment Board, 411

QLP, *see* qualified limited partnership (QLP)
QPP, *see* Quebec Pension Plan (QPP)
QSBC, *see* qualified small business corporation (QSBC)
QSBS, *see* qualified small business stock (QSBS)
QSO, *see* qualified stock option (QSO)
qualified farm property, 102, 103
qualified investments, RRSPs, 378-80
qualified limited partnership (QLP)
  introduction, 57
  pension fund investments in, 401, 407-8
qualified small business corporation (QSBC)
  angel capital investment, effect on, 37, 105
  as distinct from general capital gains tax preference, 77
  asset test, enhanced capital gain exemption, 103
  evaluation as mechanism to encourage investment, 103-5, 491
  introduction, 93, 102
  United States and Canada compared, 103
qualified small business stock (QSBS)
  angel capital investment, effect on, 105
  as distinct from general capital gains tax preference, 77
  evaluation as mechanism to encourage investment, 103-5
  reinvestment of shares, 106
  United States and Canada compared, 103
  United States, evolution of, 100-1
qualified stock option (QSO), 171-73
Quebec
  LSVCC programs
    board of directors requirements, 315

eligible investments, 318-19
eligible investors, 316
failure to meet investment
    requirements, consequences, 320
governing legislation, 313
government expenditure limits, 317
holding period, 317
incentive, nature of, 316
introduction of, 255
minimum/maximum capitalization, 316
number of LSVCCs permitted, 314
organizational form, 315
pacing requirements, 319
sponsoring organization, 314
VCF program
    eligible investments, 301
    eligible investors, 269, 270, 297
    failure to meet investment
        requirements, consequences, 302
    governing legislation, 296
    government expenditure limit, 300
    holding period, 299
    incentive, nature of, 298
    introduction of, 255
    investment, nature of, 298
    minimum capitalization, 272, 297
    number of VCFs permitted, 296
    organizational form, 297
    pacing requirements, 301
Quebec Pension Plan (QPP)
    as distinct from CPP, 419-20
    establishment, 59, 417

RCA, *see* retirement compensation
    arrangement (RCA)
RPP, *see* registered pension plan (RPP)
RRIF, *see* registered retirement income fund
    (RRIF)
RRSP, *see* registered retirement savings plan
    (RRSP)
RSO, *see* restricted stock option (RSO)
rapid-growth SMEs
    government support of, 15-16
    job creation and, 3
    location, factors determining, 16-18
registered pension plan (RPP)
    contribution limits, 372-74
    foreign property tax, and, 398

pension legislation applicable to, 375-76
tax provisions affecting, 374-75
venture capital investment, 398-401
registered retirement income fund (RRIF)
    distinguished from RRSP annuity, 373
    foreign property tax, and, 398
    qualified investments, defined, 378-80
    tax provisions affecting, 375
registered retirement savings plan (RRSP)
    access to funds for investment, 382-85
    contribution limits, 372-74
    foreign property tax, and, 398
    love capital, interest-free loans for, 385,
        405-6, 495
    LSVCCs, investment in, 388
    qualified investments, defined, 378-80
    tax provisions affecting, 374-75
    transfer options, 376
    venture capital investment, and, 57
restricted stock option (RSO), 169-71
retirement compensation arrangement
    (RCA), 371
retirement plans
    employer-sponsored plans, *see* deferred
        profit-sharing plan (DPSP); employer-
        sponsored pension funds
    individual, *see* individual retirement
        account (IRA); individual retirement
        annuity (IRA); registered retirement
        income fund (RRIF); registered
        retirement savings plan (RRSP)
Rousseau, Henri Paul, 420
Rubenfeld, Stanley, 171

SBA, *see* Small Business Administration
    (SBA)
SBDC, *see* Small Business Development
    Center (SBDC); small business
    development corporation (SBDC)
SBIA, see Small Business Investment Act
    (SBIA)
SBIC, *see* small business investment
    company (SBIC)
SBILP, *see* small business investment
    limited partnership (SBILP)
SBIR, *see* small business innovative
    research (SBIR)
SBIT, *see* small business investment trust
    (SBIT)

SCORE, *see* Service Corps of Retired
   Executives (SCORE)
SEC, *see* Securities and Exchange
   Commission (SEC)
SEP, *see* simplified employee pension (SEP)
SIMPLE, *see* savings incentive match plans
   for employees (SIMPLE)
SMEs, *see* small and medium-sized
   enterprises (SMEs)
SRI, *see* Stanford Research Institute (SRI)
SSBIC, *see* specialized small business
   investment company (SSBIC)
STTR, *see* small business technology
   transfer (STTR)
Saskatchewan, LSVCC program
   board of directors requirements, 315
   eligible investments, 318
   eligible investors, 316
   failure to meet investment requirements,
      consequences, 320
   governing legislation, 313
   government expenditure limits, 317
   holding period, 317
   incentive, nature of, 316
   minimum/maximum capitalization, 316
   number of LSVCCs permitted, 314
   organizational form, 315
   pacing requirements, 319
   sponsoring organization, 314
savings incentive match plans for employees
   (SIMPLE), 367
Schenk, Deborah, 116
Scholes, Myron, 154, 156
Schwanen, Daniel, 190
second-stage financing, 8
section 1244 stock, defined 113-14
Securities and Exchange Commission
   (SEC), 45
seed stage, business development, 5
Service Corps of Retired Executives
   (SCORE), 458
Shoup, Carl S., 89
Silicon Valley, 1, 3, 17, 43-44, 54, 63, 153
simplified employee pension (SEP), 366, 367
Slichter, Sumner, 44
small and medium-sized enterprises (SMEs)
   importance of, 2
   rapid-growth, *see* rapid-growth SMEs
   stages of business development, 5-13

Small Business Administration (SBA)
   as distinct from BDC, 461-62
   counselling programs, 458
   debt and equity financing, 456
   mandate, 455, 456
   research and development spending
      programs, 456-57, 462
Small Business Development Center
   (SBDC), 458
small business development corporation
   (SBDC), 276
Small Business Enterprises Corporation, 465
small business innovative research (SBIR),
   454, 457, 462
Small Business Investment Act (SBIA), 45,
   46, 47, 465-68
small business investment company (SBIC)
   active operations, requirement to
      conduct, 468
   as distinct from VCF programs, 470-72
   authorized activities, 466
   creation, 464
   historical development, 46-47, 454,
      464-66
   loss relief available, 113, 464
   maximum leverage available, 467
   minimum capitalization requirements, 466
   organizational form, 466
   pacing requirements, 470
   participating securities, limitations on,
      466-67
   pension fund investments in, 399-401
   SBA, and, 46, 241, 464-69
small business investment limited
partnership (SBILP)
   introduction, 57
   pension fund investments in, 399-401,
      407-8
small business investment trust (SBIT)
   introduction, 57
   pension fund investments in, 399-401
small business technology transfer (STTR),
   454, 457
Smith, Dan Throop, 89
Social Security, 416-17
Sohl, Jeffrey, 36, 38
specialized small business investment
   company (SSBIC), 106, 456
Sputnik I, 46, 54, 454, 462, 463, 464

Stanford Industrial Park, 44
Stanford Research Institute (SRI), 43-44
startup stage, business development, 5
statutory stock options
    employee stock purchase plans, 176-79
    historical development, 169-73
    incentive stock options, 173-76
sweat equity, 5, 153, 493-94

tax credit programs, *see* angel tax credit
    programs; venture capital fund (VCF)
Terman, Fred, 43, 44
Texas, CAPCO program
    eligible investments, 329-30
    eligible investors, 323
    failure to meet investment requirements,
        consequences, 333
    governing legislation, 321
    government expenditure limits, 327
    incentive, nature of, 325
    introduction of, 260
    investment, nature of, 324
    maximum investment/benefit per
        investor, 326
    minimum/maximum capitalization, 323
    organizational form, 322
    pacing requirements, 331
    state share in distribution, 326
    voluntary decertification requirements, 332
third-stage financing, 8
Thorsteinsson, P.N., 89
Thurow, Lester, 3
trader distinguished from dealer, United
    States, 86-87
trader in securities, Canadian tax treatment,
    95-96
trickle-down economics, 85
trickle-up phenomenon, 286

UBIT, *see* unrelated business income tax
    (UBIT)
UBTI, *see* unrelated business taxable
    income (UBTI)
United States
    angel capital rollover provisions, 106-7
    average first-round investment, 1980-2002,
        19
    capital commitment, limited partner
        type, 1979-2002, 49, 50

capital gains, preferential treatment of,
    77-87
capital losses, preferential treatment of,
    112-14
employee stock options, taxation of,
    164-79
government involvement in venture
    capital investment, importance of, 54
government ownership, mistrust of, 18
growth of venture capital industry,
    1980-2002, 48
limited partnership income, taxation of
    characterization of income, 244
    distribution of partnership property to
        partners, 252-53
pension fund venture capital investment,
    47-54, 58
pension plans
    governing legislation, 370-71
    historical development, 364-65
    Social Security, 416-17
    taxation of employer-sponsored
        plans, 365-68
    taxation of individual plans, 368-70
QSBS, disposition of, 100-2
venture capital investment, history of,
    43-54, 63
unrelated business income tax (UBIT), 395-96
unrelated business taxable income (UBTI),
    396

VCC, *see* venture capital corporation (VCC)
VCF, *see* venture capital fund (VCF)
VCN, *see* Venture Capital Network (VCN)
VCOC, *see* venture capital operating
    company (VCOC)
VEIC, *see* venture enterprise investment
    company (VEIC)
venture capital corporation (VCC), 56
    introduction of, 56
    pension plan investment in, 393-95
    programs, salient features, 266-67
venture capital fairs, 242, 474
venture capital fund (VCF), *see also*
    certified capital company (CAPCO);
    labour-sponsored venture capital
    corporation (LSVCC)
    as distinct from government-guaranteed
        investment, 470-72

INDEX

venture capital fund (VCF) (cont.)
 formation of, 4
 fund of funds, 9, 292, 293, 410
 limited partnership taxation
  distribution of partnership property to
   partners, 252-54
  gains on disposition of portfolio
   company shares, 244-52
 tax credit programs
  cost-benefit analysis, 279-92
  eligible investments, 275-77, 300-1,
   309-11
  eligible investors, 268-71, 297, 306
  failure to meet investment
   requirements, consequences, 302,
   312
  governing legislation, 296
  government expenditure limits, 274-75,
   300, 303, 308-9
  government profit share, 274-75
  holding period, 299, 308
  incentive, nature of, 273-74, 298-99,
   306-8
  individual retirement fund investment
   in, 387-88
  investment, nature of, 268-71, 297-98,
   306
  minimum/maximum capitalization
   requirements, 271-73, 297, 305
  number of VCFs permitted, 296, 303-4
  organizational form, 267, 296-97,
   304-5
  pacing requirements, 277-79, 301, 311
  salient features, 266-67
  timing issues, 277-79
venture capital investment
 classic, defined, 8
 exit strategies, 10-13
 formal
  annual capital commitments, Canada
   and United States, 39
  Canadian history, 55-63
  defined, 6-10
  employer-sponsored pension funds,
   evaluation of, 406-15
  fund types, Canada and United
   States, 40, 41, 242
  government-administered pension
   plans, 416-21

 individual retirement funds,
  evaluation of, 269-70
 investor types, 41-42
 managed, Canada and United States, 40
 US history, 43-54
 informal
  as a complement to formal industry,
   35-36
  business angels, and, 36-38
  Canadian tax legislation, effect on,
   398-401
  defined, 4, 5-6
  employer-sponsored pension funds,
   importance of, 385-87
  individual retirement funds,
   importance of, 378-85, 402-6
  pension legislation, effect on, 389,
   396-97
  relative importance compared with
   formal industry, 35
  US tax legislation, effect on, 395-96
 sources, *see* venture capital sources
venture capital limited partnerships
 distribution of partnership property to
  partners
  Canada, 253-54
  United States, 252-53
 income characterization
  Canada, 244-52
  United States, 244
Venture Capital Network (VCN), 472
venture capital operating company (VCOC),
 394
venture capital sources
 formal, 4, 6-10
 informal, 4, 5-6
venture capitalism, defined, 2
venture enterprise investment company
 (VEIC), 56

WOF, *see* Working Opportunity Fund (WOF)
Wagner, Don, 191-92
West Virginia, VCF programs
 eligible investments, 310
 eligible investors, 269, 306
 failure to meet investment requirements,
  consequences, 312
 governing legislation, 303
 government expenditure limits, 308

holding period, 308
incentive, nature of, 273, 307
investment, nature of, 306
minimum/maximum capitalization, 305
number of VCFs permitted, 304
organizational form, 305
pacing requirements, 311
Wetzel, William, 36, 38, 472
Wilson, Michael, 92
Wisconsin, CAPCO program
  eligible investments, 328
  eligible investors, 323
  failure to meet investment requirements, consequences, 332
  governing legislation, 321
  government expenditure limits, 327
  incentive, nature of, 325
  introduction of, 260
  investment, nature of, 324
  maximum investment/benefit per investor, 325
  minimum/maximum capitalization, 323
  organizational form, 322
  pacing requirements, 331
  state share in distribution, 326
  voluntary decertification requirements, 332
Working Opportunity Fund (WOF), 281, 282, 285

Zhao, John, 190